Vocational Behavior: Readings in Theory and Research

DONALD G. ZYTOWSKI
Iowa State University

Holt, Rinehart and Winston, Inc.

New York   Chicago   San Francisco   Atlanta   Dallas
Montreal   Toronto   London

Woodcut illustrations are from E. Hazen,
The Panorama of Professions and Trades.
Philadelphia: Uriah Hunt, Publisher, 1836.

Preface

To say that work is a vital part of human existence may be the most gross understatement. Almost everyone works at something: most persons spend more hours at work than in any other single activity, except perhaps sleep. We know that work is *important*. Freud believed that work, paired with love, were two necessities of man's life, while Karl Marx, predictably, thought that work alone would suffice. More pedestrian thinkers might say work provides the major source of satisfaction in adult life, or that it is the way in which man knows he *is*, or that it is his link to reality. The answer to the question "Who is he?" is frequently given in terms of that person's occupation. More than half of those who have not achieved a permanent work role will say that the purpose of their education is to prepare for work.

And yet what do we know about it? Vocational behavior is a minor topic in psychology compared, say, to the psychology of learning, or the psychology of abnormal behavior.

Counseling psychology, with its interest in the functioning of persons as they attend to the necessary and usual activities of life, embraces concern for persons and their work; how they attain it, how they survive in it, what it contributes to their life. Brayfield calls for a "solid foundation of occupational psychology under the practice of counseling," saying, "that the most significant contribution . . . to professional practice will be made by those who nourish us with testable hypotheses and empirical data . . . ." And so each issue of the journals relevant to counseling practice adds another article proffering an idea, a point of view, or contributing some data to an already jumbled accumulation. It has been ten years since two books, Donald Super's and Anne Roe's, appeared, bringing order to the confusion. Material which has been published since that time has not been assembled to make observable the progress which has occurred, to permit systematic and thoughtful examination, or to unify and integrate the advances beyond 1957. Thus, the present collection of readings is intended to bring the reader through the contributions of the last ten years; fully 85 percent of the articles have appeared since 1957.

The essences of the book are two: theory and research. Theoretical and heuristic propositions are matched at every possible opportunity with evidence which reflects on their validity. The collection begins with material on the nature and meaning of work and progresses through consideration of the structure and perceptual qualities of work. This is the foreground to material examining the work span, focussing successively on maturation, choice, satisfaction, and adjustment. Statements of the ways in which occupations and careers may be determined, a lateral expansion of the concept of vocational choice, comprise the core of the collection. Here especially, the editor's remarks are hoped to link the selections fore and aft, by means of the several threads which have run through theorizing in this field: psychoanalysis, individual differences, probability and utility theory, determinants of job satisfaction, and the like.

Sixteen different journals and other sources have contributed to this collection, including several ordinarily identified with industrial or personnel psychology, and several from sociology and social psychology. Additional coverage is offered via the annotated and other bibliography following each chapter.

Finally, it is hoped that the broad sampling exercised in collecting the articles will bring not only counseling and guidance workers, but also sociologists, industrial psychologists, labor economists, personnel workers, and the like to look outside the confines of their disciplines and perhaps discover that they share interests and concerns and could learn from each other.

Donald G. Zytowski

Ames, Iowa
June 1968

Contents

PART I

The Meaning of Work

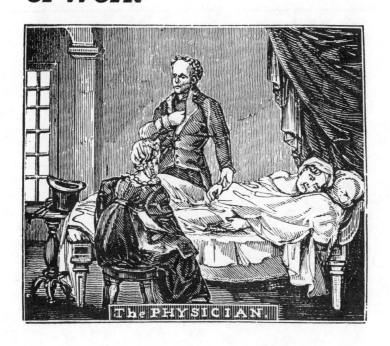

The PHYSICIAN

The Meaning of Work

1

Work!
Nearly everyone does it.
What is it?
What happens if you haven't any?
Why?

These questions may stand as the outline of Chapter 1. The first selection, by Paul Schrecker, is his definition of work, which he considers the elemental force in the flow of history. This proposition is outside our pale, but his consideration of what is generally understood by the word "work" is a profound and excellent way to delineate the subject of this book.

Primitive man was required to work in order to survive. But has man come to depend upon work for more than survival? Observations of men in retirement, of men out of work because of economic adjustments of great depressions or technological obsolescence, of men deprived of work by illness, suggest that work has more use to man than simply earning a living. Morse and Weiss discover that men would work if they could be financially independent of work. And though the respondent's subjective guess as to what would happen to them if they did not work might not be utterly reliable, it is hardly possible to deliberately deprive men of work in order to see whether the reasons they advance are valid.

The final selection on the meaning of work consults the psychoanalytic point of view. The followers of Freud's thinking have always been concerned about motivational matters, though not so much with motivation to engage in the ordinary activities of life, such as work and play. Readers of this book will find in it a thread of psychoanalytic conceptions, of which Neff's article is the first. Whether their conception of the basic spring to action, to participation in the world, in the form of libidinal force transformed and modified through infantile stages, is shared by the reader, the psychoanalytic view is bold enough to make explicit the *mechanism*, the *why*, of man's relationship to work.

3

The Definition of Work

PAUL SCHRECKER

Work, it has often been stated, is different from mere play. It is different also from passive receptivity, different again from mere automatic reaction, and from purposeless though voluntary movement. These are negative determinations; but what positive element is common to the activities of statesmen and woodcutters, teachers and students, surgeons and sculptors, composers and business executives, priests in the pulpit and professional boxers in the ring, fighting soldiers and praying believers who "work" at their salvation, toiling farmers and orating senators? The identical structure of such widely disparate performances does not show on the surface and is not easily grasped by a logical definition. In physics, the term "work" has been used since the time of Poncelet to express a definite meaning: the product of force and displacement, and Helmholtz rightly pointed out that this concept of dynamics most likely originated in the experience of human working. It may therefore be assumed that in human work there is some analogy to physical work, namely, that it involves force in action. But this analogy only yields a preliminary element of definition: that inherently in all human work, an expenditure of energy is required to overcome some resistance with which the object worked on opposes change; just as force is required in displacing a weight from one point to another.

That this element of definition alone is not sufficient appears when it is observed

Reprinted with the permission of the publisher from pages 13–18 of *Work and History: An Essay on the Structure of Civilization*, Princeton, N.J.: Princeton University Press, 1948.

that there are changes in objects brought about through human action and requiring expenditure of force which yet are not work, such as chewing one's food, walking up and down a platform waiting for a train, or any sort of gymnastic exercise. In order to discern other elements of definition, it must, firstly, be emphasized that all acts called work operate some change in the province of civilization in which they pretend to be considered as work. A man walking up and down aimlessly just to pass the time changes nature: namely, the distribution of matter and energy in the universe; he thereby also changes his own body, but he does not effect any change in any province of civilization. Mere transformation of potential energy into movement by human action, and vice versa, is therefore not a sufficient criterion for work. Every action, on the contrary, rightly called work actually changes, be it but infinitesimally, one or several fields of civilization. In most of the examples of work mentioned above, this effect is obvious. In other cases it needs some clarification. Commonplace experience provides many instances of activity which under certain conditions may be called work, but under others would be called play or sport or pastime. The professional chess-player, boxer, violinist, or hairdresser is certainly working while playing chess, boxing, performing a concerto, or dressing hair. The amateur player, boxer, musician, or hairdresser is just as certainly considered not to be working. What is the difference between the two groups? It is evidently the implication that by the professional activity at least one or even two or more provinces of civilization undergo change — namely, at least the economic and, in most cases, the juridical. The professional acquires by his activity the right to a fee, which changes the distribution of money or other goods in the world; and normally by his activity he fulfills certain stipulated obligations. The amateur, on the contrary, changes nothing by his act except the state of his own body, or mind, or both. The relevance of this second element of a definition of work — that it effects some change, however slight, in some province of civilization — will become clearer in the course of this analysis. It may be added that this change need not necessarily produce itself in fact, though it must be designed to be brought about by the relevant action. The professional boxer may not get his fee, because his manager goes bankrupt; he may not even acquire any legal claim, because his contract for some reason or other is null; yet he worked in the ring because his action was designed to fulfill his contract.

It may sometimes happen that a change actually resulting from work does not coincide with its intentional purpose. Saul went out to seek his father's asses, and found a kingdom; Columbus set about to explore a new route to India, and discovered a continent; but at any rate some change in a province of civilization was designed, and some change indeed resulted from the energy expended in overcoming resistance.

Yet this definition of work is still far from complete. Was Penelope actually working while weaving and unravelling her garment in order to postpone her choice of a suitor? Do we consider as work the activity of a schizophrenic who invents a new language of his own, or of a convict who toils to file through the iron bars of his cell window in order to escape? We would not, however, hesitate to call this latter activity work when performed by a prisoner of war attempting to escape in order to join his army. We must not allow ourselves to be taken in by the conspicuous similarities of these two activities. Were we to call the convict's toil work, we would have no reason not to use the same term for the doings of a burglar

or a counterfeiter. It cannot be denied, though, that the very notion of work involves an element of usefulness and respectability. ἔργον δὲ οὐδέποτε οὐδὲν ὄνειδος τὰ γὰρ καλῶς τε καὶ ὠφελίμως ποιούμενα ἔργα ἐκάλει. (Work is in no wise anything disgraceful; for he [Hesiod] called work what is done well and usefully. Plato, *Charmides*, 163.) Work, in other words, is something that ought to be done, not only in the interests of him who does it, but in more general and objective interests. We may therefore add as a third element to the definition of work the postulate that the expenditure of energy designed to overcome the resistance with which the object worked on opposes change, and actually effecting change in some province of civilization must, at least implicitly, be required by a norm of some province of civilization. The bearing of this element will become clearer once the norm structure of civilization has been discussed. Some examples may, however, serve to illustrate the idea that every act of work, in so far as it is an element of history — and every act of work will prove to be potentially such an element — complies implicitly with some claim objectively raised in an integrating sector of civilized life, and that this is precisely the criterion which allows the exclusion of senseless acts and, with certain reservations, crimes from the field covered by the term work.

Of course, it must not be surmised that the norm obeyed by work is always or most frequently given in a written or in some other equally explicit form. Usually it does not exist independently from its execution through the act of working. It is precisely its embodiment in this act which endows the latter with the character of something that ought to be performed. Later it will appear that the form under which the norms of civilization approach the working individual is a pattern conveyed by a prevailing tradition or convention. A scientist who today carried out experiments in the manner of a thirteenth century alchemist would not be considered to be doing scientific work, precisely because his experiments would not be obeying the norms of present-day scientific tradition. Nor would a painter be considered as doing other than commercial work — namely, the production of goods for a market — if he spent his time and energy in painting Byzantine icons. A writer who today expressed his ideas in the language of *Beowulf* would be satisfying a whim, not doing work in the field of language. And we would certainly not consider a civilized contemporary to be performing religious work, if he sacrificed to Moloch or Odin.

It was claimed above that in order for an act to pass as work an expenditure of human energy must be required by some norm of civilization. Hence this qualification was denied to such actions as are not only not required but forbidden, an exclusion which appears also to be sanctioned by linguistic usage: such actions are called crimes in the legal field, sins in the religious sphere, and though they have no particular name in the other provinces of civilization, they are obviously familiar and recurrent phenomena in each. Yet evidently not every action punishable or actually punished under the rule of positive law can thereby alone be disqualified as work. For the inference would otherwise have to be drawn that Socrates' teaching was not work and hence not an element or event of history, and that, in general, revolutions (being, as will appear later, essentially unlawful actions) could not be typical processes to be recorded in the histories of every province of civilization.

The absurdity of this conclusion originates in the tacit assumption that an action, by reason of being forbidden by a positive norm of one sector of civilization, cannot possibly be required by another or even by a higher norm of the same sector. To be acceptable, this assumption would have to presuppose a pre-established harmony among all the norm systems simultaneously actualized in a civilization, with no possibility of conflicts breaking out among them. Not only is such a consonance of norms (which, if extant, would manifest the perfect co-operation of all human incentives) contrary to historical experience; a closer structural analysis will show that civilization essentially involves the antagonism of simultaneously valid norms, and that therefore an action forbidden in one sector may well be demanded by a norm of different origin.

Socrates' teaching may have been a criminal offense against the Athenian Republic; it was, however, at the same time, in his own words, imposed upon him by God (*Apology*, 33) and thus genuine work. His judges on the contrary, acted as required by the law and their action was, therefore, legal work; but they sinned at the same time against the ethical religion proclaimed and obeyed by its doomed apostle.

This one instance may suffice to show that crime is not work if it is nothing but an infraction of some valid norm, without being required by others. As a mere misdeed, it would, indeed, not manifest an intestine conflict within the civilization in which it is committed, but only prove that, in this concrete instance, civilization has been overpowered by undisciplined human nature. From this angle, a nothing-but-crime is an event of nature, not a potential element of history.

This consideration leads to the last element in the concept of work. Why do men work? Is it not because they expect that something, perhaps only their own condition, but mostly also some objective sphere, will be improved by their activity? To work would be foolish if nothing were thereby changed; it would be insane to spend part of the limited energy of which man disposes, if this change were purposely a deterioration and not an amelioration. Whether an alteration of the existing state of things proves to be the one or the other depends, of course, upon the province of civilization in which the standpoint is chosen. The invention of a new machine may be an improvement from an economic, and a deterioration from a political or religious or hygienic point of view. Yet a change ensuing from an act of human work must essentially be intended as an improvement. We may formulate this condition, inherent in all activities usually called work, contending that all work implies the perfectibility of the object worked on, or, more generally, the perfectibility of our civilization, through work. This thesis manifests neither optimism nor pessimism: it implies neither that all work actualizes progress, nor that the perfectibility of civilization tacitly presupposed in every work is an illusion. It merely states that the very idea of work as appearing to a phenomenological analysis involves the perfectibility by work of the object worked on. . . .

The necessary and sufficient criteria of human work may thus be condensed as follows:

1. Work is an expenditure of energy, designed to overcome the resistance the object offers to change. Whether this resistance is physical inertia, gravity, cohesion, or impenetrability of matter, or human inertia acquired through habit and operating as an obstacle to innovation of whatever kind, is immaterial in this respect; it is therefore immaterial, too, whether the energy spent to overcome the particular resistance represents physical, mental, or moral exertion, or all of these together.

2. Work is designed to operate a change, which, to be sure, may be infinitesimal,

within the province of civilization where it claims to be work. If the relevant province remains *in statu quo ante* after work is done, the expenditure of energy simply means a change in nature; it is not an element of history.

3. All work is required by one or several provinces of civilization. There is no occult background associated with this condition. It merely asserts that work is not arbitrary or gratuitous action, but something which from some viewpoint within civilization ought to be done. And here again it makes no difference whether the purposed effect of the action is achieved or not; nor does the nature of the human need to be satisfied by the expenditure of human energy matter.

4. All work implies that the object is in some way perfectible through expenditure of energy in fulfillment of a norm. Neither a perfect nor an irreclaimable thing are objects for human work; perfect objects may be deteriorated or destroyed or used by human activity, and irreclaimable objects may be employed as instruments; but neither the one nor the other may be changed in a way which qualifies the human action effecting this change as work spent on it. The Danaïdes toiled, they did not work.

The Function and Meaning
of Work and the Job

NANCY C. MORSE

ROBERT S. WEISS, *VA Hospital, Palo Alto, California*

With the increasing complexity and industrialization of society, work for many people has become more and more simply

Reprinted by permission of the authors and publisher from the article of the same title in *The American Sociological Review*, 1955, 20, 191–198.

a means toward the end of earning a living. However, we are in danger of over-generalizing this trend and pushing it to its logical conclusion, expecting that working serves *only* a means function.[1] The present study of the meaning of work among a national sample of employed men indicates that for most men, having a job serves other functions than the one of earning a living. In fact, even if they had enough money to support themselves, they would still want to work. Working gives them a feeling of being tied into the larger society, of having something to do, of having a purpose in life. These other functions which working serves are evidently not seen as avilable in non-work activities.

This finding that work has other meanings is consistent with observations of the effect of retirement and the effect of unemployment on men. If men work only for money, there is no way of explaining the degree of dislocation and deprivation which retirement, even on an adequate salary, appears to bring to the formerly employed. The particularly interesting results of this national sample study on the meaning of working are: (1) that working is more than a means to an end for the vast majority of employed men; (2) that a man does not have to be at the age of retirement or be immediately threatened by unemployment to be able to imagine what not working would mean to him; and (3) that working serves other functions than an economic one for men in both middle class and working class occupations, but that the non-monetary functions served by working are somewhat different in these two broad classifications of occupations.

The method used to explore the function and meaning of work for employed men was a short "fixed question-free answer" interview of a random sample of employed men in the United States.[2] We shall report some of the results of the analysis of these interviews with the 401 men studied in the sample.[3]

GENERAL RESULTS

The conclusion that working is more than a means for economic support comes primarily from a question in the interview which was designed to remove hypothetically the economic function of working. The question asked the respondents was:

"If by some chance you inherited enough money to live comfortably without working, do you think that you would work anyway or not:"

TABLE 1

Percentage of Individuals for Whom Working Serves Non-Monetary Function

Question: "If by some chance you inherited enough money to live comfortably without working, do you think you would work anyway or not?"

	N	Per cent
Would keep working	314	80
Would not keep working	79	20
Total responding	393	100
Not ascertained	8	
Total sample	401	

The interviewer then followed this question with the probe:

"Why do you feel that you would work (not work)?"

Table 1 indicates that eighty per cent of the employed men answered that they would want to keep on working. It might have been expected that such a question would be considered quite unreal to the respondents. The quality of the responses, however, suggested that, while the question was not one for which they had a ready answer, it was one which they took seriously and could consider personally. Furthermore, the vividness and emotionality of their responses to this question indicated that we were tapping an area which was real and meaningful to them. It was almost as if they had never consciously thought about what working meant to them but now that they were presented with the imaginary removal of it, they could see for themselves and verbalize to another person the feelings which had really been there implicitly all the time.

When those who have stated that they would work anyway are asked for their reasons for feeling this way, they give quite a wide variety of answers. Approximately two-thirds of them give what we called positive reasons, that is, they talked of something positive about working (Table 2). The most common types of positive reasons were: working keeps one occupied, gives one an interest; working keeps an individual healthy, is good for a person; and the kind of work is enjoyable. A little more than a third of those who felt that they would want to continue working gave only what we called negative reasons, that is, they

TABLE 2

Reasons for Continuing Working

Question: "Why do you feel that you would work?"

	Number	Per cent
Positive reasons		
Enjoy the kind of work	27	9
To be associated with people	4	1
To keep occupied (interested)	93	32
Justifies my existence	14	5
Gives feeling of self-respect	13	5
Keeps individual healthy, good for person	30	10
Other	4	1
Total positive reasons	185	63
Negative reasons		
Without work, would:		
Feel lost, go crazy	42	14
Feel useless	5	2
Feel bored	11	4
Not know what to do with my time, can't be idle	29	10
Habit, inertia	17	6
To keep out of trouble	3	1
Other	2	0
Total negative reasons	109	37
Total responding	294	100
Not ascertained	20	
Total would work	314	
Total would not work	79	
Not ascertained	8	
Total sample	401	

talked of some negative consequences of not working. Frequent negative reasons for continuing working were: "would feel lost if didn't work, would go crazy" and "wouldn't know what to do with my time, can't be idle." The fact that thirty-six per cent of the men who want to continue working give only negative reasons for working (Table 2) indicates that for many men working serves as a means of warding off the dangers of loneliness and isolation. The finding that as many as fourteen per cent of the total sample express fears of being lost or going crazy if they did not work lends support to the consideration of work as an important positive element in the emotional economy of many individuals because it serves to anchor the individual into the society.

We should, however, be cautious about inferring too much from the answers to this one question and probe. It does not mean that people cannot readjust to not working; rather it means that not working requires considerable readjustment. The typical employed man does not *at present* have alternative ways of directing his energy and internal resources and does not *at present* have alternative ways of gaining a sense of relationship to his society which are sufficiently important to take the place of working.

The relationship of age to desire to keep working suggests that the nearer the individual is to retirement age (65), the more likely that he will say that he would not work if he did not need to for economic reasons. However, as we can see from Table 3, even in the age group of fifty-five years through sixty-four years almost two-thirds of the men would want to keep working.[4] The change with age in feelings about working indicates that some of the older men are becoming adjusted to the idea of not working. The high percentage of men over 65 who say they would continue to work even if they did not have to should be discounted. Individuals over 65 frequently have an option regarding whether they continue to work, and our sample is one of employed

TABLE 3

The Relationship between Desire to Keep Working and Age

Age Category	N	Percentage Who Would Want to Work	Percentage Who Would Not Want to Work	Total Percentage
21–34	106	90	10	100
35–44	123	83	17	100
45–54	79	72	28	100
55–64	46	61	39	100
65 or over	38	82	18	100
Total responding	392			
Not ascertained	9			
Total sample	401			

men, only. It does not include those who stop work.

The kind of job which the individual now has does not influence strongly his feeling that he would want to keep working at *some* job even if he inherited enough money to live comfortably without working. While the men in the working class occupations are slightly less likely to want to keep working, over three-quarters of those who are foremen, in the crafts and trades, or who are factory operatives and semi-skilled, would keep on working. The only occupational group which deviates from this overall pattern is the unskilled. Only slightly over fifty per cent of them would want to continue working.

The degree to which working becomes woven into the pattern of life of the employed man is also attested to by the results on job satisfaction. When asked the question: "Taking into consideration all the things about your job (work), how satisfied or dissatisfied are you with it?" eighty per cent of the employed men said they were either very satisfied or satisfied with their jobs. This finding suggests that most individuals accommodate themselves to their chances and possibilities in life and in general do not maintain, as conscious aspirations, chances and opportunities not within their scope to realize. However, for many individuals, commitment to working is much deeper than commitment to their particular job. This is attested to by the high frequency with which people answer that they would change jobs if they inherited enough money to live comfortably without working. Many individuals, including those who say they are satisfied with their jobs, would switch to another job if they could, but few would stop working.

Further evidence that working is serving non-economic functions is found in the kinds of answers the men who want to keep working give to the question: "Suppose you didn't work, what would you miss most?" Over two-fifths respond with a general feeling that they would lose something important to their well-being if they did not work. Almost a third point directly to the social aspects of working (Table 4).

OCCUPATIONAL DIFFERENCE

The data presented so far indicate that working serves non-economic functions for the vast majority of employed men. Does it serve different functions, however, for people in different occupations? A sample of 401 men is not large enough to specify in detail the particular functions of work for men in all the various specific occupations. We can, however, examine the meaning of working and the type of satisfactions gained from

TABLE 4

Things Missed If Did Not Work by Those Who Would Want to Keep Working

Question: "Suppose you didn't work, what would you miss most?"

	Number	Per cent
General feeling		
Feeling of living, belonging, being part of something	6	3
Feeling of doing something important, worthwhile, feeling of self-respect	23	9
Feeling of interest, being interested	12	5
Feeling of doing something, would be restless	62	25
Total expressing general feeling	103	42
Specific things missed		
The kind of work I do	29	12
The people I know through or at work, the friends, contacts	77	31
Regular routine	16	6
Money	5	2
Other	2	1
Total mentioning specific things missed	129	52
Nothing missed	15	6
Total responding	247	100
Not ascertained	67	
Total would work	314	
Total would not work	79	
Not ascertained	8	
Total sample	401	

the job for certain broad classifications of occupations. The basic classification which we have used separates the occupations into two major categories and one "offset" category. The two major divisions which we shall use are (1) middle class occupations and (2) working class occupations. We have separated farming into a third category because of its unique features such as the fusion of work and non-work, the high degree of self-employment, the rural setting, and the like.

The middle class occupations differ from the working class ones on a variety of dimensions. There are substantial differences not only in terms of the characteristics of the people recruited to the jobs, but in terms of the content of the jobs themselves. The middle class occupations more frequently emphasize verbal and conceptual skills, while the working class occupations more frequently emphasize skilled use of the body. In addition, there are differences in object-relations. Thus a large segment of the middle class jobs involve dealing with people, while many of the working class jobs involve working with tools and machines. Thus while the primary classification of middle class and working class occupations may seem to stress differences in prestige and social status between the two sets of jobs, there is actually a whole pattern of differences, a complex of factors, which separates these two groups of occupations.

The types of occupations which we have considered middle class are: professional, managers employed by others, and sales. For professional and sales we have followed the Census classification,[5] but we have excluded self-employed managers and proprietors from our managerial classification, despite their inclusion in the Census system.[6] We have labeled the following occupations as working class: foremen, crafts and trades; machine-operators and semi-skilled; unskilled; and service. The occupations which we have not included in this analysis in addition to the self-employed managers are clerical and government service. These occupations appear to include some jobs which would be classified as working class and some which would be classified as middle class. Along with the farmers these two major classifications of middle class and working class with their sub-headings will form the basis of the occupational analysis.

The findings on the relationship between occupation and certain demographic characteristics for our sample are consistent with those reported by the Census. The men in middle class occupations are better educated, are more often white and Protestant and earn more money than those in the working class occupations. The largest contrasts occur between the "top" of the middle class occupations, the professions, and the "bottom" of the working class occupations, service.

Almost the entire group of farmers are self-employed, while nearly all of the other occupational groups are employed by others. The farmers are similar to those in working class jobs in terms of education and income, yet are even more likely to be Protestant than those in middle class jobs.[7]

These results confirm the idea that by grouping the occupations into middle class, working class, and farming, we have also grouped on a number of other variables. The broad occupational differences cannot, therefore, be interpreted as due to any single factor, but rather as due to a pattern of factors pertaining to the type of people, type of work, and type of situation or environment in which they live and work.

FUNCTION OF WORKING AND OCCUPATIONAL CLASS

The occupational groupings differ much more on the type of function that working plays for them, than they do on the degree to which it serves other functions than the economic one. Many individuals in middle class occupations emphasize the interest to be found in their jobs, and the sense of accomplishment which comes from work well done. On the other hand, the typical individual in a working class occupation emphasizes the necessity for some directed activity which will occupy his time, his mind and his hands. These conclusions are based on answers given to the question, "Why would you continue working?" asked of those who said they would continue to work even if they inherited money (Table 5).

For many of those in the middle class occupations working means having some-

thing interesting to do, having a chance to accomplish things and to contribute. Those in working class occupations view working as virtually synonymous with activity, the alternative to which is to lie around and be bored or restless. For the farmers working is also activity, but the demarcation between work and other areas of life is less sharp than it is for the working class respondents. As a result many farmers, particularly older farmers, are almost unable to consider a way of life which does not include work.

These differences between the occupational groupings correspond to differences in the content of the middle class and working class jobs. The content of the professional, managerial and sales jobs concerns symbols and meanings. Furthermore, the middle class job imposes a responsbility for an outcome, for successful sales, successful operation of a department, or successful handling of a legal case. Thus a life without working to a man in a middle class occupation would be less purposeful, stimulating and challenging. The content of working class jobs on the other hand, concerns *activity*. Working class occupations emphasize work with tools, operation of machines, lifting, carrying, and the individual is probably oriented to the effort rather than the end. Therefore, life without working becomes life without anything to do.

Of course the meaning which work has for the individual is not only affected by the general type of work which he does, but is also determined by the type of person he is. To some extent, at least, there may be selection into occupations so that the person going into a middle class job has a different social background from one going into a working class job. The different functions of work may to some extent be attributed to different early learning and socialization of those entering different occupations. Perhaps both the nature of the job and the nature of the job-holders operate together to produce a similarity of orientation toward the place of work in life among people in the same general type of job.

TABLE 5

Reasons for Continuing to Work by Occupation

| | *Number of Individuals Who Give as Reasons for Working:* | | | |
	Interest or Accomplishment	*To Keep Occupied*	*Other*	*Total*
Middle class				
Professional	13	8	3	24
Manager	6	5	4	15
Sales	6	8	4	18
Total middle class	25	21	11	57
Per cent	(44)	(37)	(19)	(100)
Working class				
Trades	6	44	15	65
Operatives	6	42	9	57
Unskilled	1	9	3	13
Service	1	7	1	9
Total working class	14	102	28	144
Per cent	(10)	(71)	(19)	(100)
Total farmers	6	22	6	34
Per cent	(18)	(64)	(18)	(100)
Total responding				235
Not ascertained				18
Total would work				253
Total would not work and not ascertained				73
Total sample				326[a]

Chi-square between classes = 31.77, significant at the .001 level. Chi-squares within middle and working classes are not significant.

[a]Clerical, self-employed managers, and government workers do not appear in this table.

OCCUPATIONAL DIFFERENCES IN JOB ATTITUDES

The major reason for working *at a particular job* may be monetary, even though the reasons for wanting to continue to work are not. The extent to which the job is important to the individual for other than monetary reasons is probably best indicated by his response to the question of whether he would continue in the same job if he no longer had to work to earn a living. If the employed man answered that he would want to keep working even if he inherited money, he was then asked: "Would you still keep on doing the same type of work you are doing now?" The answers to this question, presented in Table 6, indicate very clearly that the farming job and the middle class occupations, particularly the professional jobs, are much more important to their occupants than are the working class jobs to their occupants. More than two-thirds of the farmers and more than three-fifths of the men in the middle class occupations would want to continue in their present type of work even if they inherited enough money so that it was no longer necessary for them to work for a living.

From these results it seems clear that while men almost regardless of job are adjusted to the type of work they are doing, those who have the less interesting, less prestigeful and less autonomous jobs would most like to change their jobs if the opportunity were provided. The most common

TABLE 6

**Per Cent of Respondents Who Would
Continue to Work
and Per Cent Who
Would Continue on Same Job**

	N	Per cent Who Would Work	Per cent Who Would Continue in Same Type of Work
Middle class			
Professional	28	86	68
Manager	22	82	55
Sales	22	91	59
Total middle class	72	86	61
Working class			
Trades	86	79	40
Operatives	80	78	32
Unskilled	27	58	16
Service	18	71	33
Total working class	211	76	34
Total farmers	43	86	69
Total would work	253		
Total would not work, not ascertained	73		
Total sample	326[a]		
Chi-squares between classes		6.87	29.22
p less than		.05	.001
Chi-squares within middle class		.76	.79
		Not significant	Not significant
Chi-squares within working class		8.74	6.30
p less than		.05	.10

[a]Clerical, self-employed managers, and government workers do not appear in this table.

type of job suggested as a replacement for their present work is going into business for

themselves. Many of the men in the working class occupations said that they would like to go into business for themselves, although they often were not able to say what type of business they would want to go into. These answers seemed to indicate a desire for a more prestigeful, freer job than the one they now had; one which would not, however, require additional formal education and training. The way the man in the working class occupation thought about going into business for himself was consistent with his view of working as keeping occupied. There was no mention of obtaining a feeling of purpose or accomplishment from this imagined work. He carried over his already developed view of the meaning of work to this new imagined occupation.

We already mentioned that most people are satisfied with their present job. Table 7 shows that the men in the middle class occupations are more polarized in their answers to the question: "Taking into consideration all the things about your job (work), how satisfied or dissatisfied are you with it?" Those in the middle class occupations, particularly the managers, are more likely to give extreme answers. The explanation for this difference between the occupational groupings may lie partially in the greater importance of the content of the job to those in the middle class occupations and partially in the greater opportunity for personal satisfactions in the middle class jobs. Those in the middle class jobs, as a result, react more strongly either in a positive or negative way to the particular job. The man in a working class job, on the other hand, gets used to his job, adjusts himself to it, perhaps even resigns himself to it.

Perhaps the most interesting findings in this area of job satisfaction are those which indicate the degree to which people do adjust to the job conditions and opportunities which are available to them. People in different occupations do not vary as greatly in whether or not they are satisfied with their

TABLE 7

Per Cent Satisfied and Dissatisfied
with Their Jobs by Occupation

	N	Percentages			*Total*
		Very Satisfied	*Satisfied*	*Pro-con, Dissatisfied*	
Middle class					
Professional	28	54	36	10	100
Managers	22	23	41	36	100
Sales	22	46	36	18	100
Total middle class	72	42	37	21	100
Working class					
Trades	84	32	57	11	100
Operatives	80	25	60	15	100
Unskilled	24	25	54	21	100
Service	16	19	50	31	100
Total working class	204	27	57	16	100
Total farmers	41	29	56	15	100
Total responding	317				
Not ascertained	9				
Total sample	326[a]				

Middle Class is significantly more "polarized" than the other groups. Chi-square = 9.87, p less than .05.

[a]Clerical, self-employed managers, and government workers do not appear in this table.

jobs as they do in their reasons for their satisfaction. The managers mention salary much more frequently than do the professional and sales people who stress the content of the job itself. The crafts and trades group respond positively to the kind of work they do, while the unskilled mention money, and those in service occupations tend to give as reasons for satisfaction the fact that it is the only type of job they could get and that they like the people they work with and meet. Each of the occupations shows quite a different pattern of satisfaction sources. The general conclusion from these results combined with those on present level of satisfaction would seem to be that most people adjust to the jobs which they have, base that adjustment on the particular attributes of the job and the job situation. There appears to be a tendency for the individual to react positively to his work situation and to emphasize the favorable aspects of it.

SUMMARY AND CONCLUSIONS

Using interviews with a national sample of employed men, we have studied the extent to which working serves non-economic functions for the total population and the differential meanings of work and the job for those in different occupations.

The results indicate that for most men working does not simply function as a means of earning a livelihood. Even if there were no economic necessity for them to work, most men would work anyway. It is through the producing role that most men tie into society, and for this reason and others, most men find the producing role important for maintaining their sense of well-being.

To the typical man in a middle class occupation, working means having a purpose,
gaining a sense of accomplishment, expressing himself. He feels that not working would
leave him aimless and without opportunities
to contribute. To the typical man in a
working class occupation working means
having something to do. He feels that not
working would leave him no adequate outlet for physical activity; he would just be
sitting or lying around. To the typical
farmer, just as to the typical individual in a
working class occupation, working means
keeping busy, keeping occupied. But work
has a much more pervasive importance for
the farmer. The boundaries between work
and home life are not as sharp for him, and
life without work is apt to be difficult to
consider. These results confirm what other
studies, using other methods, have shown.

We are now going through a period of
readjustment of our institutions to the shortening of the work day and week and to
the early retirement of individuals from
their jobs. The development of means by
which individuals can gain the same feelings
which they now obtain from work through
substitute activities is one possible long-
range solution. Another, perhaps, is the development of methods by which individuals
might remain productive in their later years.
In either case it would seem necessary that
the occupation give the individual meaningful (in his own terms) and socially integrating activity.

[1]The same type of over-generalization of a
trend was found until recently in the writing on
the family. Since the family was changing (and
in some ways reducing) its functions, there was
some tendency to go to the extreme and predict
the dying out of the family altogether.

[2]This exploratory study was made possible
through cooperation with the Economic
Behavior Program of the Survey Research
Center. The short interview followed a longer
interview for that program on consumers'
expectations and plans and recent buying

experience. The interviewing was done in
September, 1953.

[3]A description of the Survey Research Cen-
ter sampling method will be found in *Research
Methods in the Behavioral Sciences*, L. Festinger
and D. Katz, editors, New York: The Dryden
Press, 1953, Chapter 5, "Selection of the
Sample" by L. Kish, especially pp. 230–235.
The general interviewing method used is
described in Chapter 8 of the same volume,
"The Collection of Data by Interviewing," by
C. Cannell and R. Kahn.

[4]Friedmann and Havighurst, studying five
occupational groups of men fifty-five or over,
found one-third to two-thirds of the men in
their occupational sample wanted to continue
working past sixty-five. Eugene A. Friedmann
and Robert J. Havighurst *The Meaning of
Work and Retirement*, Chicago: The University
of Chicago Press, 1954, p. 183. The approach
and findings of this book parallel at many
points those reported in this paper, although
the present authors were not aware of the
Friedmann, Havighurst research until after
this study was completed.

[5]The general occupational groupings used by
the Census and the specific occupations listed
under the various Census designations are to be
found in the *Alphabetical Index of Occupations and
Industries*, 1950 Census of Population, United
States Department of Commerce, Bureau of
the Census, Washington, D. C., 1950.

[6]While the managers employed by others
clearly fall into the middle class occupational
grouping, self-employed managers are a mixed
group. The initial coding has been in terms
of the Census classification and it would have
been necessary to go back and recode the
occupations. Thus while an owner of a realty
company would be in a middle class occupation, the operator of a gasoline station or a
restaurant worker who owns part of the
business would be more appropriately classified
in the working class occupations. The self-
employed managers were therefore excluded,
as were the other groups which would have
required recoding, the clerical and government service workers.

[7]The religious affiliation findings are probably the result of the pattern of immigration into
this country The non-Protestants (primarily
Catholics) were in general later immigrants,
when farm land was no longer so cheap nor as
easily available.

Psychoanalytic Conceptions of the Meaning of Work

WALTER S. NEFF, *New York University*

It is the aim of this paper to review what psychoanalysts have said about human work and to consider to what degree these comments lay the basis for an adequate theory of work behavior. My interest arises from the manifestly increasing concern of contemporary society with the problem of work adjustment.[1] There have always been people who find it very difficult or impossible to work and others whose work history is so unstable or erratic that the maintenance of gainful employment is a major life problem. But, until recently, this kind of life problem was not a matter of major concern for the psychiatrically oriented professional. It is true that, for some two decades, considerable attention has been paid to the vocational problems of the physically handicapped, but the focus of interest of most of the workers in this field has been primarily the limiting effects of the disability rather than the ability to work per se. Whatever is known, however, of the complexities of work motivation is derived largely from the field of rehabilitation, since the physically handicapped person — and the mentally and emotionally handicapped, as well — often presents a textbook case of the psychosocial consequences of relative unemployability. Increasing concern with the problems of the underprivileged, undereducated, and underemployed will require a much greater understanding of the psychodynamics of work.

Reprinted with the permission of author and publisher from the article of the same title in *Psychiatry*, 1965, *28*, 324–333.

By and large, the psychiatric literature on the psychodynamics of work is disappointingly meager. None of the major writings of psychoanalysts or psychiatrists makes more than a passing reference to this issue, and a great many do not mention it at all. This is not to say that the importance of human work has not been recognized. When Freud was asked what he considered the basic requirements of human existence, he answered, "To love and to work." However, an examination of the thousands of titles listed in a comprehensive index of psychoanalytic writings[2] has yielded less than a dozen papers relating to work or labor. Obviously, the student of psychopathology has been interested in other problems than those which directly bear upon the ability to work. Nevertheless, it is appropriate to begin by asking how work is perceived within the framework of psychiatric theory and practice.

FREUD ON WORK

Although work as a human activity has received little attention from psychoanalysis, it has not been totally ignored. Freud's remarks on work are scattered very sparsely through his writings, and are typically encountered as asides, set down as incidental observations. His evaluation of the importance of work in man's psychological economy is ambivalent. On the one hand, he argues that work is one of the two great spheres of human activity, without which human society cannot be understood. He says: "The communal life of human beings had . . . a two-fold foundation: the compulsion to work, which was created by external necessity, and the power of love. . . . *Eros* and *Ananke* have become the parents of human civilization. . . ."[3] In this sense, work is one of the forces which bind men to each other, and thus lay the basis for human society. Thus, he writes:

After primal man had discovered that it lay in his own hands, literally, to improve his lot on earth by working, it cannot have been a matter of indifference to him whether another man worked with him or against him. The other man acquired the value for him of a fellow-worker, with whom it was useful to live together.[4]

On the other hand, Freud obviously saw work not as a pleasurable activity to be sought, but as a painful burden to be endured. He states that "human beings exhibit an inborn tendency to carelessness, irregularity and unreliability in their work, and . . . a laborious training is needed before they learn to follow the example of their celestial models."[5] Work, for Freud — like all other aspects of adult life — involves a "renunciation of the instincts," entails giving up the pleasures of childhood, and means a life ruled by the *reality principle* rather than the *pleasure principle*. The only pleasures that can be involved in work are libidinous in origin, are modifications of Eros. Thus, he concludes that "collections of men are to be libidinally bound to one another. Necessity alone, the advantages of work in common, will not hold them together. But man's natural aggressive instinct, the hostility of each against all and of all against each, opposes this programme of civilization."[6] Elsewhere, he points out how the instinctual love which forms the nuclear family is modified and blunted in society to "aim-inhibited affection," which binds men and women together "in a more intensive fashion than can be effected through the interest of work in common."[7]

The role which Freud assigns to work is consistent with his general views of adult human functioning. Freud sees adult human behavior as the outcome of a long struggle between the parents and the child, which has on the parents' side the objective of socializing an asocial and amoral animal, and has on the child's side the objective of finding those modes of behavior which have the double aspects of meeting the demands of the parents and retaining some vestige of forbidden pleasures. Of course, neither party to the struggle plans its operations rationally, or with full consciousness. But the process of child development is a process of active, even oppressive, socialization in which the parents direct against the libidinal and aggressive instincts of the child all the massive force of their overwhelming authority and their greatly superior intelligence and maneuverability. In this unequal struggle, the child, faced by the terrible consequences of the loss of parental love and support, must succumb. Successful surrender involves the discovery of modes of behavior which satisfy the demands of the parents and, with good fortune, will retain some portion of the pleasures of unrestricted instinctual gratification. Had Freud written directly on this issue, he presumably would have said that work is one of the activities the human being develops as a means of coping with the inner and outer demands made upon him. The *manner* in which he works — or the guilt he may feel over not working — is a function of a complex set of feelings, attitudes, and ideas which develop as the child perceives, reacts to, and incorporates the parental models of behavior.

Freud's voluminous writings include very little more which bears upon work than the few remarks cited above. He was interested in the play of children and in artistic and creative work,[8] but he apparently did not find it necessary to record his observations on common, everyday work, assuming he ever bothered to reflect deeply upon it. Perhaps it was partly because he was struggling to solve problems which were far more painful to his patients than work incapacity or inefficiency, and partly because work was not perceived as a serious economic problem by his patients.

OTHER PSYCHOANALYTIC CONCEPTIONS OF WORK

The concern of many neo-Freudians with ego development and the process of adaptation has turned attention to somewhat different problems than those which preoccupied the classical Freudians. Erikson, for example, has tried to work out a theory of ego growth which includes crucial stages of development well beyond the crises of early childhood in which Freud was primarily interested.[9] Where Freud leaves his readers with the impression that the most important aspects of personality development are concluded by the time the child is five or six years old, with the resolution of the third stage of psychosexual development (the phallic stage), Erikson discerns later important stages of development through what Freud called the latency period (from the Oedipal period to the onset of puberty), and through early and late adolescence as well.

It is of particular interest to note here that one of Erikson's crucial later stages (he places it in the latency period) is the industry stage, in which the young person first begins to work out his attitudes toward work and achievement. Freud seems to imply that attitudes toward work and toward important persons encountered while working (peers, subordinates, supervisors, employers) are pretty much determined by the events of early childhood — the manner in which the person works out his relationships to the nuclear parents during the early childhood crises of oral, anal, and genital development. For Erikson, it would appear that the early childhood stages are necessary but not *sufficient* to account for adaptation to the demands of work. In extending

the scope of the experiences which play a formative role in personality development, Erikson by no means discounts the importance of early childhood. Certainly, the growing child must first meet and resolve the problems of weaning, sphincter-training, and early jealousy before he can begin to work out his relationships to schoolmates, teachers, and employers. It is certainly also true that an epigenetic view of development — to which Erikson subscribes — demands conceiving of the older child as meeting later experience with abilities and emotions already heavily influenced by earlier experience. But whereas the early Freudian view has led various of his followers to conclude that the events of early childhood are both necessary and sufficient to account for adult emotional life, Erikson seems to be saying that the affective stages of later childhood and adolescence are an essential part of development.

Hendrick has attempted to take account of human work in a manner which appears to stand midway between classical Freudian theory and modern ego theory. One of the questions he raises is concerned with the sources of the enormous amount of energy man has displayed in subduing and changing his natural environment.[10] Hendrick became convinced that Freud's two principles of mental functioning (the pleasure principle and the reality principle) were insufficient to account for the psychosocial activities of the total organism. Hendrick interprets Freud as saying that pleasure is available to the human organism in only two ways — either through direct gratification of the primary instinctual drives (the pleasure principle), or through an indirect and attenuated gratification achieved by the defense mechanisms which reality forces the ego to develop (the reality principle). For Hendrick, this conceptual structure is insufficient to explain the continuous and persistent efforts of the human animal to explore the world, understand it, and alter it to suit his convenience. Hendrick believes that, in addition to the primary pleasures achieved through gratification of the sexual and aggressive instincts, and the derivatives and transformations of these instincts which reality imposes during child development, there is a third source of primary pleasure: ". . .that. . .sought by efficient use of the central nervous system for the performance of well-integrated ego functions which enable the individual to control or alter his environment."[11] He calls these ego functions the *executant* functions and feels that psychoanalysis has overlooked them or taken them for granted.

Thus, Hendrick puts forward the thesis that there is a *work principle* which governs the operation of the executant functions. Following Freud's theorem that the source of all mental energy lies in the instincts, Hendrick posits a "mastery instinct" as the source of energy of the executant functions.[12] The pleasure in work, then, is a consequence of gratification of the instinct to master the environment. Hendrick sees his work principle as more than the set of defense mechanisms which comprise the reality principle. Sublimation, displacement, rationalization, and similar defenses may manifest themselves in work, but cannot fully account for work pleasure. Similarly, the repetition compulsion cannot account for many aspects of work activity, but appears only when the ego is inadequate.[13] However, Hendrick does not apply this interpretation to the infantile compulsion to practice, over and over again, certain sensory and motor integrations — a compulsion which disappears once mastery is achieved.

Lantos, a psychoanalyst who has been strongly influenced by Hartmann, Kris, and Loewenstein, has written two papers specifically on work.[14] She reminds her colleagues that in clinical practice disturbances of working capacity are second in importance only to disturbances of sexuality, but that very little attention has been paid to work in the psychoanalytic literature. In the earlier paper, she begins her observations on the dynamics of work by commenting on the play of children. Noting that children do not work, but adults do, she speculates that children's play involves two distinct kinds of pleasure. One she defines as pleasure in the function itself, which finds its source in pregenital autoerotic gratification. The second is pleasure in achievement, which, she says, "lies outside the activity itself." In the play of either children or adults, the first kind of pleasure is dominant; the second kind, if it has any part at all, is subordinate. Lantos believes that work is principally related to the second kind of pleasure. She contrasts work and play as follows:

The principle of playing means that what is done, is done for its own sake; gratification lies in the activity itself. The principle of working means that an action is not undertaken for its own sake, but for some other purpose, serving the ends of self-preservation: gratification lies not in the action as such, but in obtaining something by means of it.[15]

Thus, play and work are distinguished not by their content, but by their purpose. Mountaineering may be a very arduous activity, but it is play for the tourist and work for the guide.

Like Erikson, Lantos feels that the transition from pleasure in activity to pleasure in achievement takes place during the latency period, which is observed only in human beings — here she cites Freud's remark that animals reach adulthood without passing through a latency period. The association of the latency period with learning and education suggests that the educational process has, as one of its aims, the transformation of pleasure in activity to pleasure in achievement, although, of course, the former need not be wholly given up in acquiring the latter.

Finally, Lantos asks why it is that feelings of independence, freedom, and security are pleasurable, and points to their connection in most people with the ability to guarantee one's own existence by one's own achievements. She speculates that a child finds it natural to have his needs for self-preservation served by parents (or parental surrogates), but that an adult who is deprived of his work loses the essential condition of being an adult. Lantos relates the anxieties experienced by those who cannot or need not work to the feelings of fear arising from the fact that "the instinct of self-preservation is not transformed into life-supporting work."[16]

In her later paper, Lantos notes that Hendrick and Oberndorf agree with her chief contention — that work is a dynamically important activity for human beings. Lantos feels, however, that Hendrick goes too far in assuming a "work instinct." She returns to her earlier argument that work is related to the self-preservative instincts, and then elaborates this argument in terminology familiar to psychoanalytic ego psychology, redefining work as a "highly integrated ego activity serving self-preservation."[17] Work is specifically human and is related to the fact that the instinctual series is broken in man, with the interposition of mental activity between the instinctual need and the gratifying act. She sees pleasure in work achievement as an *ego* reaction, as distinct from libidinal pleasure, which is an *id* reaction. Since, in man, most of the objects of adult gratification are not obtainable *directly* (as in the instinctual sequence in animals), but must be worked for, the original energy available for instinctual acts "floats" into the ego. There it becomes desexualized and de-aggressivized ("neutralized," according to Hartmann[18]). In childhood, the energies which arise in the course of "breaking" the instinctual sequence are available for controlling and manipulating the environment.

In close similarity to Freud, however, Lantos feels that men do not work spontaneously. The work-related motive is self-preservation, "mediated by intelligence, reinforced by conscience."[19] In a final extension of her analysis, Lantos argues that two different forces impel men to work. One is an outer force — necessity — the initial origin of Freud's *reality principle*. The other is inner:

... internalized aggression is the ultimate guarantee of the maintenance of work and, therefore, of self-preservation. To quote Freud: "The ego has set itself the task of self-preservation."[20]

The source of this internalized aggression is the superego, and it is directed against the id impulses to be ruled by the pleasure principle.

Menninger and Oberndorf have written papers on work which appear to hew more closely to orthodox psychoanalytic views. Both men regard adult work as best understood in relation to the defensive activity of *sublimation*, through which the human adult may gratify his sexual and aggressive impulses in altered and socially acceptable forms. For Menninger, work is a sublimated mix of the strivings of the life and death instincts:

Of all the methods available for absorbing the aggressive energies of mankind, work takes first place . . . . The essential point is that in work, as contrasted with purposeless destruction, the aggressive impulses are molded and guided in a constructive direction by the influence of the creative (erotic) instinct.[21]

Reflecting on the meager attention psychoanalysts have paid to the problems of work, Menninger states flatly that ". . .three-fourths of the patients who come to psychiatrists are suffering from an incapacity of their satisfaction in work or their inability to work. In many it is their chief complaint."[22] He then asks why it is that work becomes dissociated from pleasure, finding the answer in insufficient eroticization of the aggressive element. Following Freud, he finds no reason to believe that work is pleasurable in itself, only that there are certain circumstances in which pleasure can become associated with work. As *external* conditions of work pleasure, he lists: (1) a minimum of compulsion, (2) positive group feelings among co-workers, (3) an absence of excessive discomfort or fatigue, (4) some pride in the product, and (5) some conviction that the work is useful and appreciated.

He also cites two *internal* conditions: relative freedom from guilt associated with pleasure, and relative freedom from neurotic compulsions to work or not to work. Menninger regards the two internal conditions of work pleasure as relating to solutions of the instinctual vicissitudes of early childhood, particularly those concerned with basic parent-child relationships.

Like Menninger, Oberndorf[23] invokes the mechanism of sublimation to account for both the activity of work and associated pleasure. Oberndorf specifically criticizes Hendrick's notion of the "mastery instinct," and also does not agree with Lantos' idea that work is related to self-preservation alone, because of "the close inclusion of many, perhaps all of the libidinal drives in work."[24] Oberndorf's main interest, however, is in clinical material, and he cites a number of instances in his own practice where work pathologies (over- or under-investment in work) are directly related to relationships with the parents. As an example, he describes a case in which a driving and aggressive mother with an ineffectual husband made such excessive demands for achievement upon her son that work as an ego-ideal took on a strong feminine quality which made it incompatible with his normal masculine strivings. He completes his case presentations with the following summary statement:

Persons who constantly regard work as something difficult and unpleasant are those who have not emerged from the necessity of immediate reward and who are reluctant to assume responsibility (self-support) inherent in maturity. The protraction of infantile pleasure or the necessity for its denial as one matures determines the overinvestment or underinvestment of libido in work. This interrelationship is a close and continuous one, and it seems futile to attempt to distinguish whether such libido is predominantly sexual or ego.[25]

Both Menninger's general theory of work and Oberndorf's clinical applications derive quite logically from Freud's view of the overwhelming importance of the infancy and early childhood determiners of adult behavior and will be examined in that connection below.

DISCUSSION

Disregarding the differences in these points of view for the moment, one can discern common themes among them. First, there is a heavy preoccupation with the instincts, both as a source of motivation and as a primary locus of the "psychic energy" available for human behavior. This is perhaps less characteristic of Erikson, who is anxious to build a bridge between psychoanalysis and modern social theory and is aware of the hostility of the latter to explicit reliance upon instinct as an explanatory hypothesis. Second, there seems to be a general supposition that the vicissitudes of work behavior in the adult may be entirely, or almost entirely, accounted for by the manner in which the affective processes are shaped by the early crises of interaction between the parents and the child. Again, Erikson is something of an exception but, as a consistent epigeneticist, he continuously emphasizes the powerful influence of earlier on later experiences. Thirdly, these writings appear to include meager references to the differential effects of society and culture on individual patterns of development. Here Freud is the outstanding exception, but there is some reason to believe that Freud's view of culture is unduly restrictive and one-sided. In commenting on these common themes, I shall suggest certain alternative hypotheses which, while retaining the valuable core of psychoanalytic thinking, may have the effect of preparing the way for a more comprehensive theory.

On the Instincts

It is well known, of course, that the later writings of Freud, and certainly those of many of his more contemporary followers ociety.[22] One has only to recall the pre-vailing attitudes toward work in classical Greece or feudal Europe, in which the conception prevailed that many kinds of work were ignoble and degrading activities, fit only for the slave, the serf, or the outlander. It is, of course, virtually a historical commonplace that notions that work is en-nobling, and even ethically and morally necessary, are only a few hundred years old and began to come into currency with the breakup of feudalism. Additionally, there are current impressions that the pres-ent pace of technological development is again threatening to make work a mean-ingless activity for a great many people and that this aspect of the Protestant ethic is beginning to lose its force. Whatever the case, it seems regrettable to the writer that the brilliant and sensitive insights contrib-uted by psychoanalytic theory are married to a single and rather restrictive model of human motivation.

On the Role of Early Psychosexual Development

The general tendency of psychoanalytic theory is to place heavy emphasis on the vicissitudes of the first few years of life, the period in which the child works out his basic relationships to the parents. In Freud's early formulation, the basic components of the emotional life are laid down by the time the child is five or six years old and constitute the overwhelmingly powerful, if unconscious, influences on later behavior. Thus, the adult reactions to authority fig-ures — the teacher, the employer, the po-litical leader — may be interpreted in terms of the responses of the young child to parental discipline. Various of the neo-Freudians have softened this principle some-what, arguing that the early experiences are the *necessary* but not necessarily the *sufficient* determiners of adult behavior, but, by and large, the weight given to the early determiners is a distinguishing feature of psychoanalytic theory.

While the principle of early determina-tion may contribute greatly to an under-standing of certain other phenomena of adult life, its usefulness appears to become more limited when applied to work. In different ways, Lantos and Erikson assign great importance to experiences encountered in later childhood, and Hendrick goes so far as to argue that work behavior is not derivable from early libidinal and aggres-sive experiences at all but has a different instinctual source. The clinical literature does not support such ideas unequivocally. Certainly there are cases, as Oberndorf indicated, in which the work attitudes of the adult seem wholly or largely determined by the child's relations with his parents. There are, however, numerous instances of frank psychotics, with symptoms clearly re-lated to early crises, but also with relatively unimpaired work capacity,[30] and, of course, there are severe neurotics who are mal-adapted in many life areas, but not necessarily in the area of work. Thus it seems useful to inquire whether the variables which influence behaviors vis-à-vis work are neces-sarily identical with, or even derivable from, the variables which influence the ability to live, to marry, to make friends. The affec-tive reactions mobilized by work need not be the same as those mobilized by other important life demands.

The chief point suggested by Erikson and Lantos is that the older child is confronted by a new set of life demands, quite different in quality from those which confronted him in his early years. It is true that the pre-latency child must incorporate many in-strumental activities: He must learn to feed himself, to put on his own clothing, to control and order his urinary and defecatory processes, and even to help in the manage-ment of the household. But it is during what Freud called the latency period that quite new tasks appear. He must begin to work out his relationships to nonfamilial figures and accept the authority of strangers. He must reduce his dependence on loved ones and begin to deal with the impersonal.

(the ego analysts), have tended to move away from major concern with the instincts and their transformations. Nevertheless, I think it is fair to maintain that psychoanalytic motivation theory is largely based on the model of drive-reduction. According to this model, the positive affects, such as pleasure or joy, are the consequences of drive-satiation, while negative affects such as pain or displeasure are experienced as a consequence of drive-arousal. In the nineteenth century and the early part of the twentieth, when it was customary to seek wholly biological explanations of human behavior, the drives in question were thought to be largely innate, and many investigators constructed long lists of human instincts.[26] But during the last few decades the classical instinct theory has come to be regarded as naive, and drive theorists now consider only one or two drives as primary — for example, sex and aggression — with all other drives being increasingly regarded as "secondary," "derived," or "learned." Nevertheless, if one is a consistent drive theorist, it is logical to infer the existence of some kind of drive, whether primary or secondary, whenever an affect is observed.

It is this sort of reasoning which leads Freud, Menninger, and Oberndorf to infer that any pleasure to be derived from working must flow from libidinal components in work behavior, and it is much the same mode of thought which Lantos utilizes in deriving the pleasures of work from gratification of the self-preservative instincts. Similarly, Hendrick's dissatisfaction with an account of work motivation in terms only of sex and aggression merely leads him to invent a "work instinct" or an "instinct of mastery," to account for the human animal's determined activities directed toward knowledge and control of his material and social environment. The moot point here is whether there are alternatives to the drive-reduction model which are at least equally plausible. In recent years, a number of writers have attempted to construct theories of motivation and learning which explicitly

depart from the drive-redu
An illustration is afforded
White.[27] The current effort
theory appear to arise fro
the bulk of human behavio
understood in social and cul
that the drive model is, at
mechanical or biological a
extreme form, this newer v
sionally falls into the pitf
relativism,[28] which tends to c
monalities at all in the hum
In most cases, however, the
this position simply insist th
largely a socialized and accult
that human motivation is e
chiefly sociocultural rather tha
According to this view, even se
in the human being should be
drive-determined only in part,
share of its motivation attribut
mores and cultural forces.

It must be admitted that
knowledge concerning human m
still so meager that neither of the
positions can be supported wi
evidence. Under these circumst
viduals will adhere to one or th
be dissatisfied with both, large
basis of idiosyncratic experience
sonal preference. However, it
noted that the psychosocial the
least as plausible as the drive t
though it suffers from less aut
spokesmen and from the lack of
tradition. In any event, it is nec
investigate the degree to which the
and pains that given people associ
various kinds of work — and even t
structure of the motivation to wor
derivable from cultural forces rath
from subtle transformations of
biological drives; following such in
tions the relationship between cult
fluences and biological drives can be
assayed. Certainly, work has mean
different things to people in differen
eties and means very different thi
people in different sectors of contemp

Despite the influence of relationships within the family on extrafamilial relationships, to a qualitatively different extent his life is organized around achievement rather than affection. He begins the long progression which society demands from him, the development from the dependent, playing child to the independent, working adult.[31] Thus, it may well be possible that certain important factors which influence the adult adjustment to work originate at later times and in other settings than those which characterize the earlier experiences in the nuclear family.

AN OVERVIEW

Even if one grants the possibility of certain of the theoretical alternatives touched on in the preceding section, the pychoanalytic observations on work must be seen as both stimulating and suggestive. Freud's conception of the uneasy and conflicted balance of work and love cannot be ignored by a comprehensive theory of work. Erikson is most illuminating in pointing out that not only does each phase of development have something of a unique central task to solve, but also that the coping processes of any given phase are influenced by the affects, cognitions, and response-patterns evolved in connection with prior phases. Again, while it seems gratuitous to assume a special work instinct, as Hendrick does, one can agree with him that work behavior appears to be too complex to be satisfactorily accounted for within the framework of psychosexual development. Similarly, while Lantos' speculations on the role of the self-preservative instincts are questionable, I am impressed by many of her comments on the distinctions between play and work, and on the importance of the latency period in the human being. Finally, the clinical observations of Menninger and Oberndorf serve as reminders that the domains of work and love are not entirely separable, but vary in their interconnectedness from person to person.

On balance, however, I have the impression that the sparseness of the psychoanalytic writings on work has permitted only a meager penetration into the complexities of the problem, leaving most questions unanswered. What are the social and cultural forces which interact with familial experiences to form the adult work personality? What is the relative weight of the psychosocial determiners compared to that of the earlier experiences? Can a comprehensive theory be developed which will account for the fact that many people are almost wholly alienated from the work subculture, yet appear to be reasonably adequate in other areas of ego functioning? Will such a theory equally well account for the converse? What is the treatment of choice for severe vocational maladaptation? Can amelioration of the inability to work best be achieved by reconstruction of the entire personality, or can a constructive and direct attack be made upon this particular life-sphere without necessarily attempting to solve the problems of other vital areas of adaptation? Finally, can the work personality be conceived of as possessing something of a semi-autonomous character, independent to a degree not only of the motives which play upon other areas of the personality but also possessing its own motivational structure?

While the answers to these questions are not easy to come by, it is likely that the current pressures on the helping professions will require that they be asked. It is likely also that the search for answers will require the devoted cooperation of many disciplines, including at least the fields of psychiatry, psychology, social work, sociology, and cultural anthropology.

[1]The launching by the Johnson administration of an official "war on poverty" has focused national attention on the fact that many people are making very inadequate adaptations to work. Although impairments or malformations of the ability to work have

in the past constituted a major problem of human adjustment, attempts to deal with this problem are now undergoing a change: The ability to work is increasingly being formulated as an issue related to mental health, although the relationship between the two areas is far from clear. Although the present efforts to establish new programs for finding work for most of the population are marked by considerable administrative and professional uncertainty, it seems likely that they will become a permanent feature of American life. An important question is the degree to which mental health experts — psychiatrists, social workers, psychologists, and so forth — are professionally prepared to play a role in these programs, assuming they are asked to do so.

[2]A. Grinstein, *The Index of Psychoanalytic Writings*, Vols. 1–5; New York Internat. Univ. Press, 1960.

[3]Sigmund Freud, "Civilization and Its Discontents," *Standard Edition of the Complete Psychological Works* 21: 64-145; p. 101.

[4]See footnote 3; p. 99.

[5]See footnote 3; p. 93.

[6]See footnote 3; p. 122.

[7]See footnote 3; p. 102.

[8]Sigmund Freud, "Creative Writers and Day-Dreaming," *Standard Edition of the Complete Psychological Works* 9: 143–153. "Formulations on the Two Principles of Mental Functioning," *Standard Edition of the Complete Psychological Works* 12: 218–226.

[9]Erik H. Erikson, "Identity and the Life Cycle," *Psychological Issues*, vol. 1; New York, Internat. Univ. Press, 1959. *Childhood and Society* (second edition); New York, Norton, 1963.

[10]This interest in the executive aspects of human behavior is reflected in McClelland's work on the "achievement motive" (David C. McClelland, John W. Atkinson, Russell A. Clark, and Edgar L. Lowell, *The Achievement Motive;* New York, Appleton-Century-Crofts, 1953). It is also emphasized in a major paper by White which marshals evidence against those theories of motivation that rely upon a drive-reduction model. White includes both Freud and Hull among proponents of the latter kind of theorizing. See Robert W. White, "Motivation Reconsidered: The Concept of Competence," *Psychological Review* (1959) 66; 297–333. For a criticism of White's

remarks on Freud, see David Rapaport, "On the Psychoanalytic Theory of Thinking," *Internat. J. Psychoanalysis* (1950) 31: 161–170. White has elaborated his ideas in an important recent monograph, "Ego and Reality in Psychoanalytic Theory," *Psychological Issues*, vol. 3, whole no. 11; New York, Internat. Univ. Press, 1963.

[11]Ives Hendrick, "Work and the Pleasure Principle," *Psychoanalytic Quart.* (1943) 12: 311–329; p. 311.

[12]Ives Hendrick, "The Discussion of the Instinct To Master," *Psychoanalytic Quart.* (1943) 12:516–565.

[13]See footnote 11.

[14]Barbara Lantos, "Work and the Instincts," *Internat. J. Psychoanalysis* (1943) 24: 114–119. "Metapsychological Considerations on the Concept of Work," *Internat. J. Psychoanalysis* (1952) 33: 439–443.

[15]See footnote 14, 1943; p. 118.

[16]See footnote 14, 1943; p. 118. In this connection, Kutner has observed that workers who are disemployed because of aging may often experience severe anxieties related to feelings of dependency and insecurity that they have not had since they were children. In speaking of the reactions of male workers, Kutner adds that for some of them the demand that they give up their work is equivalent to a demand that they change their sex. See Bernard Kutner, D. Fanshell, A. M. Togo, and T. H. Langner, *Five Hundred Over Sixty;* New York, Russell Sage Foundation, 1956

[17]See footnote 14, 1952; p. 118.

[18]Heinz Hartmann, *Ego Psychology and the Problem of Adaptation;* New York, Internat. Univ. Press, 1958.

[19]See footnote 14, 1952; p. 442.

[20]See footnote 14, 1952; p. 442.

[21]Karl A. Menninger, "Work as a Sublimation," *Bull. Menninger Clinic* (1942) 6: 170–182; pp. 171–173.

[22]See footnote 21; p. 177.

[23]C. P. Oberndorf, "Psychopathology of Work," *Bull. Menninger Clinic* (1951) 15: 77–84. Oberndorf's paper was presented at a staff forum of the Menninger Foundation, and it appears to serve the purpose of supplying clinical material in support of Menninger's views.

[24]See footnote 23; p. 78.

[25]See footnote 23; p. 84.

[26]See, for example, William McDougall,

Outline of Psychology; New York, Scribner, 1923.

[27]White has greatly elaborated his ideas of what he calls *effectance* in a recent monograph (see footnote 10, 1962), written as a contribution to psychoanalytic theory. His chief point is that the active efforts which human beings put forth to influence the environment and the "feelings of efficacy" which are the psychological accompaniments of such efforts are not derivable from the basic drives which Freud conceptualized as the sexual and aggressive instincts. Rather, he attempts to marshal evidence that effectance is an "independent ego energy" which is operative at least from the moment of birth and which prompts the organism to explore the properties of the environment. He thus departs somewhat further from the classical Freudian position than does Hartmann (see footnote 18), who merely wished to make a case for ego activities which reflect neutralized instinctual energy ("desexualized" and "deaggressivized").

[28]See, for example, Ruth Benedict, "Anthropology and the Abnormal," *J. General Psychology* (1934) 10: 59–82.

[29]In another paper, in preparation, the writer is examining the sociocultural origins of contemporary conceptualizations of work, both across cultures and within Western cultural history.

[30]Walter S. Neff, "The Rehabilitation Workshop as a Therapeutic Medium," *J. Jewish Communal Service* (1959) 36: 225–321.

[31]It can be argued that the distinctions suggested here are too sharp, that childhood play anticipates many of the features of adult work, that the instrumental activities of early childhood are not really different in kind from those of later childhood, and that social interactions outside of the family setting are largely similar to those within. To a certain extent, this argument has merit, since all life-activities display unity as well as diversity. But I think that the differences between demands and activities at different life periods will repay closer examination. Too much has been made, for example, of certain gross similarities between work and play. It is true that both require adherence to certain rules, that both involve competition and cooperation, and that both require certain levels of environmental mastery. But these two spheres draw on very different motivations and have quite disparate goals. Even very young children are quite capable of distinguishing play from work and use the language of "make-believe." The salesman who plays golf with a prospect largely for economic reasons is not really playing, as much of his subsequent behavior attests.

THE FUTURE OF WORK

This chapter refers to the changes which have appeared in the uses served by work. It may be appropriate to speculate on the manner in which work will continue to change, and the impact these changes may have on workers.

Piel (1961) has eloquently documented the changes which productive work has undergone as a result of the recent wholesale application of modern technology. He raises the question of what will happen to man when work is gone, and there is nothing but leisure. His conclusions hint darkly that the prospect is not a pleasant one.

In contrast to Piel, De Grazia (1960) analyzes roughly the same data and achieves a very different conclusion. He suggests that the crucial change is not in the amount of work to be performed, but in the kind of work, concluding essentially that we are in no danger. He believes that while there has been a loss in primary work, there has been no increase in idle leisure — that secondary work, such as traveling to and from primary work, part-time and unpaid work around the living place have expanded to fill in the open hours of the week.

While Piel and De Grazia both agree that the future promises less formal or primary work to be performed, neither has documented the changes which work has undergone in the present, and in which shape it may continue where automation is stalled from making its inroads. This change has been the division of labor for efficiency purposes, specializations of function, and ultimate present introduction of the paced, fractionated work of the assembly or production line. The last was introduced in practical form in the automobile plants of Henry Ford, following the earlier statements of the scientific management views of F. W. Taylor (1911). It did not occur without forewarning:

The man whose whole life is spent in performing a few simple operations, of which the effects too are, perhaps, always the same, or very nearly the same, has no occasion to exert his understanding, or to exercise his invention in finding out expedients for removing difficulties which never occur. He naturally loses, therefore, the habit of such exertion, and generally becomes as stupid and ignorant as it is possible for a human creature to become. The torpor of his mind renders him, not only incapable of relishing or bearing a part in any rational conversation, but of conceiving any generous, noble, or tender sentiment, and consequently of forming any just judgment concerning many even of the ordinary duties of life.

This quotation from Adam Smith's *Wealth of Nations* is elaborated in multitudinous observations of a French sociologist, George Friedmann (1961). Empirical evidence which follows along the conclusions of Smith and Friedmann may be found in books by Walker and Guest (1952), and in Blum (1953). Another book by Kornhauser and Freid (1965) publishes more recent data demonstrating the association between barely skilled workers performing low-level jobs and their dissatisfaction, ill mental health, and socialization problems. Similar findings are reported in Gurin, Veroff, and Field (1960).

REFERENCES

Blum, F. H. *Toward a Democratic Work Process*. New York: Harper & Row, 1953.
De Grazia, S. Tomorrow's good life. *Teachers College Record*, 1960, *61*, 379–385.
Friedmann, G. *The Anatomy of Work*. New York: Free Press, 1961.
Gurin, G., J. Veroff, and S. Field. *Americans View Their Mental Health*, New York: Basic Books, 1960.
Kornhauser, A., and O. M. Freid. *The Mental Health of the Industrial Worker*. New York: Wiley, 1965.
Piel, G. The future of work. *Vocational Guidance Quarterly*, 1961, *10*, 4–10.
Taylor, F. W. *The Principles of Scientific Management*. New York: Harper & Row, 1911.
Walker, C. R., and R. H. Guest. *Man on the Assembly Line*. Cambridge, Mass.: Harvard University Press, 1952.

OTHER RELEVANT ARTICLES

Weiss, R. S., and R. L. Kahn. Definitions of work and occupation. *Social Problems,* 1960, *8,* 142–150.

That the conceptions of work which Schrecker so elegantly illuminates are shared in the popular mind, is the essence of this study. Weiss and Kahn asked a number of men from varied socioeconomic statuses what distinguished work from what was not work, three fourths of them defined work either as activity which was not enjoyed, or as activity which was scheduled for paid for. Also, they found that persons whose work relates them directly to people tend to regard work in terms of opportunity for self-expression, recognition, and sense of competence, while the factory worker tends to be concerned only with whether pay and working conditions are as good as can be expected.

Tilgher, A. *Homo Faber: Work through the Ages.* (D. C. Fisher, translator) Chicago: Henry Regnery, 1958.

The early chapters of this work trace the change in the conception of work and its economic function from the time of the Greeks and Hebrews, through that of Luther and Calvin. At first, man thought himself condemned by the gods to drudgery and toil, and his word for work was derived from the same root as the word for sorrow. In early Christian times work gained respect, if not dignity, but not when performed for economic gain. Work was transformed into "calling" in the course of the Reformation, and finally prosperity was recognized by Calvin as a sign of being among the elect. Thus emerged our present concept of work, which Max Weber labeled, "the Protestant Ethic."

Breger, P. (Ed.). *The Human Shape of Work.* New York: Macmillan, 1964.

Breger has edited a collection of essays on the meaning of work in human society. In it he explores three ideologies of work: (1) that work is identity; fulfillment; (2) that work is oppressive, an indignity, that it threatens self identification — these should be recognized as kin to the Abraham and Adam concepts of Herzberg in his *Work and the Nature of Man* — and (3) that work is a gray region between these two poles, which man puts up with for the sake of other things which are more important. Breger contends that the first and second categories are shrinking, and are rapidly giving way to an expanding center category.

There is more material on the definition of work than is practical to include here. If the reader were to pursue the matter in further detail, the following references would help.

Gross, Edward. *Work and Society.* New York: Crowell, 1958.
Levy, Sidney. *The Meaning of Work.* Brookline, Mass.: Center for the Study of the Liberal Education of Adults, 1963.
Shimmin, S. Concepts of work. *Occupational Psychology,* 1966, *40,* 195–201.

Wrenn, C. Gilbert. Human values and work in American life. In H. Borow (Ed.), *Man in a World at Work*. Boston: Houghton Mifflin, 1964.

Definitions of other concepts relating to work, such as job, position, and the like, are well treated in Shartle, C. L., *Occupational Information*. (3rd edition) Englewood Cliffs, N. J.: Prentice-Hall, 1959.

Some references which reflect the differences in the meaning of work to varied and different persons are:

Dombush, S. M., and D. M. Heer. The evaluation of work by females. *American Journal of Sociology*, 1957, *63*, 27–29.

Herson, P. Personal and sociological variables associated with the occupational choices of Negro youth: Some implications for guidance. *Journal of Negro Education*, 1965, *34*, 147–151.

Hsu, F. L. K. Incentives to work in primitive communities. *American Sociological Review*, 1943, *8*, 638–642.

Love, E. G. *Subways Are for Sleeping*. New York: New American Library, 1959.

Lyman, Elizabeth L. Occupational differences in the value attached to work. *American Journal of Sociology*, 1955, *61*, 138–144.

Neff, W. S., and A. Helfand. A Q-sort instrument to assess the meaning of work. *Journal of Counseling Psychology*, 1963, *10*, 139–145.

Palmer, G. L. Attitudes toward work in an industrial community. *American Journal of Sociology*, 1957, *63*, 17–26.

Simpson, R. L., and I. H. Simpson. Occupational choice among career oriented college women. *Marriage and Family Living*, 1961, *23*, 377–383.

Thompson, A. S. *Homo laborans:* An analysis of the meaning of work. *Bulletin of the International Association of Applied Psychology*, 1963, *12*, (no. 2) 5–23.

Zytowski, D. G. Avoidance behavior in vocational motivation. *Personnel and Guidance Journal*, 1965, *43*, 746–750.

Additional understanding of the use man makes of work might be obtained by examining the effects of being deprived from work. Data of this kind are relatively rare, but discursive accounts are not. A few are:

Unemployment effects:
Bakke, E. W. *The Unemployed Man*. New York: E. P. Dutton, 1935.

———. *Citizens without Work*. New Haven, Conn.: Yale University Press, 1940.

———. *The Unemployed Worker*. New Haven, Conn.: Yale University Press, 1940.

Eisenberg, P., and P. F. Lazarsfeld. The psychological effects of unemployment. *Psychological Bulletin*, 1938, *35*, 358–390.

Ginzberg, E. *Grass on the Slag Heaps: The Story of the Welsh Miners*. New York: Harper & Row, 1942.

Jahoda, Marie. Incentives to work: A study of unemployed adults in a special situation. *Occupational Psychology*, 1942, *16*, 20–30.

Effects of retirement:

Friedmann, E. A., R. J. Havighurst, *et al. The Meaning of Work and Retirement.* Chicago: University of Chicago Press, 1954.

Kleemeier, R. W. *Aging and Leisure.* New York: Oxford University Press, 1961.

Resources concerning automation and the nature of work:

The Bulletin series of the Bureau of Labor Statistics published a bibliography of automation publications under the number 1319 in February, 1962. The series was to be continued yearly, but the only other issue has been number 1319-1, March, 1964. In addition, the Bureau has published irregularly in the Bulletin series reports of the impact of technological change in various industries. Summaries of research of this kind:

Faunce, W. A., E. Hardin, and E. H. Jacobson. Automation and the employee. *Annals of the American Academy of Political and Social Science*, 1962, *340*, 60–68.

Lipstreau, O. Automation and morale. *California Management Review*, 1964, *6*, 81–89.

Mann, F. C., and L. R. Hoffman. *Automation and the Worker.* New York: Holt, Rinehart and Winston, 1960.

Other important statements of a non-empirical nature include:

Technology and the American Economy, Report of the National Commission on Technology, Automation, and Economic Progress. Washington, D.C.: U.S Government Printing Office, 1966.

Bagrit, L. *The Age of Automation.* New York: The New American Library, 1965.

Diebold, J. *Automation: Its Impact in Business and Labor.* Washington, D.C.: National Planning Association, 1959.

Levenstein, A. *Why People Work: Changing Incentives in a Troubled World.* New York: Crowell-Collier Macmillan, 1962.

Markham, C. (ed.). *Jobs, Men, and Machines.* New York: Frederick A. Praeger, Publisher, 1964.

Phillipson, M. (ed.) *Automation: Implications for the Future.* New York: Vintage Books, 1962.

Silberman, C. E. *The Myths of Automation,* New York: Harper & Row, 1966.

PART II

The Nature of Occupations

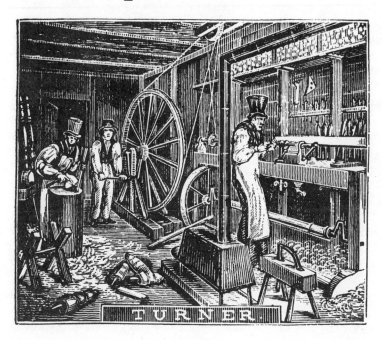

20,000 jobs! Twenty thousand jobs, known by thirty thousand titles, constitute the kinds of work in which American men or women may engage themselves, according to the 1966 edition of the *Dictionary of Occupational Titles.*

How is one to know them all? Are there some common attributes, some least-common denominators around which categories may be formed, so that the mind can combine them, and comprehend their similarities and differences?

These are the questions which have stimulated some of the first and continuing study of the attributes of work, which have in turn made possible the more sophisticated formulations of the underlying structure of occupations.

Chapter 2 relates some systems for classifying occupations, grouping them according to similar attributes, both by intuitive and empirical procedures. Few of them are demonstrated to be valid divisions, but their utility is apparent in some cases where occupations can be assigned to them with some agreement.

The perception of occupations and their attributes is the topic of Chapter 3. Since action relating to an occupation, most usually choice or rejection, has to be taken before any actual experience with them has been obtained, their qualities, as perceived rather than experienced, are important to be understood. A few studies of this kind are included.

At this point the reader should be aware of several problems which arise in the consideration of occupations. In general, they concern themselves with "frame of reference." In the case of the attributes of occupations, does one look at the requirements which the occupation has, or does one look at the attributes of the persons who hold those occupations? Put another way, does one study the person or the job?

Similarly, is the structure which is imposed on occupations by the classification systems suggested in Chapter 2 actually inherent in them? Or does it reside only in the observer?

Campbell (1966) has remarked on these questions. He speculates that perhaps men have arranged the world of work in the same way their interests are structured. This would suggest, for instance, that some men sell things not because there are things to be sold, but because they enjoy the activities of selling, or that the decline in farming occupations might have been all the faster were it not for persons who continue to want to farm.

No consistent frame of reference appears in the articles in this section. Rather, one or another is appropriate to the question under consideration. Thus, a study of ability differences in occupations is necessarily a study of the persons in them, while a study of the perception of an occupation may relate a quality which the occupation bestows upon the individual, rather than anything which he possesses himself.

THE DIFFERENTIAL PSYCHOLOGY OF OCCUPATIONS

The opportunity to speculate upon and build occupational classification schemes rests upon roughly a half century of study of the individual differences in occupations. The discussion which follows traces the development of ability measurement, and presents a few examples of studies of occupational differences in the non-cognitive domain.

It was clear to the Greek philosophers, and it is apparent now that persons who have different occupations differ in the amount and kinds of abilities they possess. It was always assumed to be so, but only in the twentieth century was it possible to demonstrate the differences with objective tests of ability. The greatest part of that testing is finished; occupational and personnel psychologists have turned to measures of interests, values, and personality and have improved on their predictions of entry and success.

Thus, there are few publications in the last ten years which provide any further evidence of the validity of a differential psychology of occupational abilities, which might be included here. Hence, a brief review of that evidence, with some examples of its scope, will be presented.

One of the first fairly systematic presentations of abilities of persons with diverse occupations stems from the wholesale testing with the Army Alpha during World War I. Fryer (1922) compiled Alpha scores for 96 occupations from about 3500 draft inductees, resulting in a table of mean scores and ranges, presented in descending order of ability. The data make clear the association of intelligence with occupational incumbency, and also that the ranges within any one occupation might be sufficiently wide to overlap with a substantial portion of the occupations ranked above and below. Fryer demonstrated that at least some persons in occupations which rank very low are more intelligent than a few individuals in occupations marked by the highest ability scores.

It was recognized too that intelligence was not the only ability which distinguished different occupations. As other kinds of abilities became testable, their contributions were included. An effort to expand the catalog of differences to several abilities is represented by the Minnesota Occupational Rating Scales (MORS), of Patterson, Gerken, and Hahn (1953).

The MORS rates 432 jobs for seven abilities: academic, mechanical, social intelligence, clerical, musical, artistic-graphic, and physical agility, on four-level scales. Unfortunately, the ratings do not represent empirical data, but rather the pooled judgment of a number of experts.

Similar ratings were undertaken for 4000 jobs in the Functional Occupational Classification Project (Fine, 1957). They included estimates of aptitudes, temperaments, interests, physical capacities, working conditions, and general educational development.

The trend which the MORS illustrates was further developed in the application of factored aptitude tests, of which the U.S. Employment Service's General Aptitude Test Battery (GATB) is representative. The GATB yields scores on eleven factors, and in the years of its use, patterns of scores relevant to success in a number of occupational groups have been developed empirically, supplying definitive evidence of the variation in amount and kind of abilities required in different occupations. The following table summarizes some of the findings into what are called Occupational Aptitude Patterns (OAP's).

An extension of the OAP is the Validity Information Exchange, instituted in 1953 in the journal *Personnel Psychology*, to report from many sources relationships between test scores of various kinds and success or placement criteria.

Adult Minimum Aptitudes Scores for 36 Occupational Types

Occupations	G	V	N	S	P	Q	K	F	M
1. Physician Engineer Programmer	125		115	115					
2. Accountant Auditor	115		115			105			
3. Teacher Tower controller Mortician	110	105	105						
4. Librarian Bank teller	105		110			105			
5. Dental hygenist Lithography Cameraman	105			95	100				
6. File clerk Claim adjuster	100	105				95			
7. Theater manager Bookkeeper	100	100	100						
8. X-ray technician Chemical technician	100	100		90					
9. Grocery checker Key punch operator Salesperson	95		90			95			
10. Cook Serviceman Cabinetmaker Diemaker	95			95					95
11. Auto mechanic Stereotyper	95			85				75	
12. Retail food manager Proofreader	95				95	100			
13. General clerk	90	90				100			
14. Waitress Bricklayer	90		95						75
15. Clothes designer Glazier	90			100	90				
16. Sheet-metal worker Stripper (photography)	90			100	90				
17. Still operator Coil assembler	85						70		75
18. Ward attendant Fork lift truck driver	80						90		80
19. Stock cleaner-truck driver Weigh station operator	80		80			80			
20. Millwright Plumber	80			75					85
21. Telephone operator Hairdresser	80				90		80		
22. Woodworking machine operator Sewing machine repair	75							75	80

Adult Minimum Aptitudes Scores for 36 Occupational Types

Occupations		GATB Test							
	G	V	N	S	P	Q	K	F	M
23. Calculating machine and comptometer operator Bookkeeping machine operator			95		100	105			
24. Electrician Radio repairman Pinsetting machine repairman			85	95				80	
25. Carpenter Painter			80	90					90
26. Weaver Watch repairman Cold and hot mill operator			85	90			85		
27. Power house engineer Welder Instrument assembler				80				90	85
28. Dental technician Turret lathe operator				75	75				75
29. Hosiery pairer Solderer					90			85	75
30. Pressman (printing)					85		85		100
31. Office machine serviceman Fancy stitcher (shoes) Shrimp-picker					85		80		80
32. Iron worker Nut sorter Apple packer					75			80	80
33. Merchandise packer Laundry bundler						90		80	85
34. Toy assembler Light bulb assembler							90	85	90
35. Sausage packer Garment folder Paper slitter operator							85	80	80
36. Typist Stenographer Typesetter	105					100	90		

Just as World War I provided the data to demonstrate occupational differences in intelligence, World War II provided an opportunity to follow up occupational entry and success from a test of various special abilities used for selecting Air Force pilots. This is reported in Thorndike and Hagen's *10,000 Careers* (1959).

Most recently, E. E. Ghiselli (1966) has published a herculean integration of the validities of tests for the prediction of occupational success, reflecting again that occupations differ in the amount and kinds of abilities they require of the individuals in them. Admitting the diverse sources of his validity coefficients, their potential to be unreliable and error-ridden, and the entirety of the problem of the criterion of performance, he nevertheless reduces the differential predictors of success to four general cognitive factors, and one noncognitive factor, and demonstrates that when one combines occupations into groups of functional similarity, they differ distinctly in relative content of the five factors.

The reader interested in further discussion of individual differences in occupations should be certain to read Tyler's Chapter 8 in Borow's *Man in a World at Work* (1964) and especially Roe's extensive summary of the cognitive and noncognitive attributes of a number of occupations in Chapters 13 and 20 of *The Psychology of Occupations* (1956).

Also, the U.S. Department of Labor (1966) has recently published a supplement to the *Dictionary of Occupational Titles* giving the physical demands, working conditions, and training time for a great number of occupations.

Individual differences in the noncognitive attributes of occupations are not without a history, too. The finding that men in a given occupation tend to have interests which distinguish them from men in general is the basis upon which Strong built the widely known Vocational Interest Blank, beginning in 1929.

And, the development of other tests and inventories of personality, interest, and attitude factors has had a corollary of occupational differentiation. Probably hundreds of reports exist. The few articles which are commented upon here could not hope to be exhaustive, nor perhaps even representative, but might show how traits vary at different levels of occupation, and how many varied traits can be shown to differ. Some of the lengthier presentations, a sampling of the unique, and other resources for finding reports are listed at the end of this introduction.

Matarazzo, Allen, Saslow, and Wiens (1964) have shown that policemen and firemen present homogeneous arrays of personal characteristics, which however, differentiate between them. For instance, on ten of the fifteen scales of the Edwards Personal Preference Schedule, they appeared to differ from adult males, while differing from each other on two. Similarly, they showed differences from the norm group means on three of the MMPI scales, but none between each other. They obtained much the same results on a number of the scales of the Strong Vocational Interest Blank, but were not differentiated on any variable of the Rorschach as scored by the Beck method.

At a different status level—mathematicians, poets, and psychologists—Hoffberg and Fast (1966) were able to find a number of distinctions in responses to the Thematic Apperception Test. Working from the same stream of thinking as is presented in the chapter of this book on the psychoanalytic conception of occupational determinants, they showed that the three occupational groups differed in their capacity and mode for expression of impulses as measured from their fantasy productions.

Gray (1963) differentiated groups of teachers, accountants, and engineers on both personal needs, and on the values of intrinsic satisfaction, prestige, and social rewards, yet another level of the noncognitive domain of attributes.

Finally, Dunnette (1957) was able to differentiate within one occupational group, engineers, employed in different functions by means of their Strong Vocational Interest Blank scale scores. Employing first a checklist of job duties to assign membership as one of (1) pure research, (2) applied research, (3) process and production, and (4) sales and service engineers, he found that each tended to obtain characteristic levels of scores on other scales of the Strong Blank than the engineering scale.

The list of studies of differences in occupational attributes most probably approaches infinity at present. Not all of them are valid studies, most likely, and some of them have little practical relevance. The reader who is interested will find many of them in the following journals: *Personnel and Guidance Journal; Journal of Counseling Psychology; Journal of Applied Psychology; American Sociological Review; American Journal of Sociology.*

In addition, one should consult the manuals of the familiar aptitude tests and such personality and interest inventories as: The Kuder Preference Record, Vocational; The Gordon Survey of Interpersonal Values; The Edwards Personal Preference Record; Cattell's 16 P.F. Test; The Minnesota Multiphasic Personality Inventory.

Some occupations have received "in depth" studies, not only of the characteristics of their occupants, but also of the rewards and demands the occupation possesses. A few are:

Eiduson, B. T. *Scientists: Their Psychological World.* New York: Basic Books, 1962.
Fichter, J. H., and S. J. Fichter. *Religion as an Occupation.* South Bend, Ind.: University of Notre Dame Press, 1961.
Glaser, B. G. *Organizational Scientists: Their Professional Careers.* Indianapolis. Bobbs-Merrill, 1964.
Janowitz, J. *The Professional Soldier.* New York: Free Press, 1960.
Lieberman, M. *Education as a Profession.* Englewood Cliffs, N. J.: Prentice-Hall, 1956.
Newcomer, Mabel. *The Big Business Executive: The Factors That Made Him.* New York: Columbia University Press, 1955.
Roe, Anne. *The Making of a Scientist.* New York: Dodd, Mead, 1953.
Smigel, I. *The Wall Street Lawyer.* New York: Free Press, 1964.
Warner, W. L., et al. *The American Federal Executive.* New Haven, Conn.: Yale University Press, 1963.
Wilson, L. *The Academic Man: A Study in the Sociology of a Profession.* New York: Oxford University Press, 1942.
Whyte, W. F. *Human Relations in the Restaurant Industry.* New York: McGraw-Hill, 1948.

Some fascinating ideas of other differentiations in occupational behavior are presented by Gross in his *Work and Society* (New York: Crowell, 1958). He notes the adaptation of ceremonies, distinctive garb and symbols and especially "argot."

In addition, the editor cannot resist including a few references which illustrate the scope of study of occupational differences:

Murphy, H. B. M. Personality and the vermiform appendix. *Journal of Health and Human Behavior*, 1966, 7, 153–162. Notes the differential incidence of appendectomies in varied groups of college majors related to occupational intentions.

Seltzer, C. C. Occupation and smoking in college graduates. *Journal of Applied Psychology*, 1964, *48*, 1–6.

Wagner, E. E. Exhibitionistic human movement responses of strippers: an attempt to validate the Rorschach M. *Journal of Projective Techniques and Personality Assessment*, 1965, *29*, 522–524.

See also the 1963, vol. 92, Fall issue of *Daedalus*, on the professions.

REFERENCES

Campbell, D. P. Review of the Minnesota Vocational Interest Inventory. *Personnel and Guidance Journal*, 1966, *44*, 854–858.

Dunnette, M. D. Vocational interest differences among engineers employed in different functions. *Journal of Applied Psychology*, 1957, *41*, 273–278.

Fine, S. A. USES occupational classification and the Minnesota Occupational Rating Scales. *Journal of Counseling Psychology*, 1957, *4*, 218–223.

Fryer, D. Occupational intelligence standards. *School and Society*, 1922, *16*, 273–277.

Ghiselli, E. E. *The Validity of Occupational Aptitude Tests.* New York: Wiley, 1966.

Gray, J. T. Needs and values in three occupations. *Personnel and Guidance Journal*, 1963, *42*, 238–244.

Hoffberg, C., and I. Fast. Professional identity and impulse expression in fantasy. *Journal of Projective Techniques and Personality Assessment*, 1966, *30*, 488–498.

Matarazzo, J. D., B. V. Allen, G. Saslow, and A. Wiens. Characteristics of successful policemen and fireman applicants. *Journal of Applied Psychology*, 1964, *48*, 123–133.

Paterson, D. G., C. d'A. Gerken, and M. E. Hahn. *Revised Minnesota Occupational Rating Scales.* Minneapolis, Minn.: University of Minnesota Press, 1953.

Roe, A. *The Psychology of Occupations.* New York: Wiley, 1956.

Thorndike, R. L., and E. Hagen. *10,000 Careers.* New York: Wiley, 1959.

Tyler, L. Work and individual differences. In H. Borow (Ed.), *Man in a World at Work*. Boston: Houghton Mifflin, 1964.

U.S. Department of Labor. *Selected Characteristics of Occupations*. Washington, D.C.: U.S. Government Printing Office, 1966.

Occupational Structure

level - field & enterprise

2

It is useful to know that occupations differ in various ways, but it is also appropriate to attempt to integrate what is known in to some kind of structure which might represent the diverse kinds of work. The value in this enterprise should be apparent. If the abilities and interests of a developing worker can be made explicit, then knowledge of similarities and communalities among occupations will provide him with the widest possible range from which to choose. From another perspective, if manpower shortages in one occupation should occur, the schemata of occupational structure would provide information for locating individuals who, by reason of training or slightly altered incentives, might be most easily induced to relieve the shortage.

Holland (1959) introduced a classification scheme some time ago, but did not, until the 1966 publication which leads this chapter, report a test of it independently of tests of his general theory of choice. His citation in this article of rules for logical classification should stand to evaluate every system which is represented in this chapter. He states that a category must be exhaustive, that it must not overlap with any other category, and that the principle of division must be the same for each category.

Other attempts to classify occupations into a structural scheme employ cognitive and affective dimensions, similar to the two major kinds of occupational differences presented in the previous chapter. Roe (1956) has classified occupations by level (the cognitive dimension) and by field (the affective). Her level dimension is called "complexity" because there seems to be no single factor presently measured by tests to represent it. Her fields are composed of a subjective compilation of the results of factor analyses of a number of interest inventories. Super, in his *Psychology of Careers*, has added a third dimension, enterprise, recognizing the preference of some persons for the locus of their occupation over the type of activity they perform. He suggests, for instance, that the civil engineer who works for the National Park Service may have a work place, associates, and routines quite different from a civil engineer who works for a construction company, who in turn will differ from one who has his own consulting office.

Evidence that Roe's system of occupational fields is a viable one, is given in her article with Hubbard, Hutchinson and Bateman. Using follow-up information on career changes as data, they demonstrate that changes are more likely to occur between adjacent fields.

Brender's efforts to provide a psychodynamic rubric for the classification of occupations follows. The dividing principle he elects is that of "intrinsic reward," as compared with Roe's fields of work, Super's fields of enterprise, and Holland's personality types.

An altogether different approach is represented by the Fine article describing the Functional Occupational Classification System. This system, reported first in 1958, appeared as a core of revision in the third edition of the *Dictionary of Occupational Titles* (1966). One dimension of the FOCS is rather coarse: the object of the work endeavor as things, people, or data. The other dimension is very finely and cleverly cut: it consists of transitive verbs representing how the object is dealt with. Although the three verbs on a single level differ, depending on their object, they are constituted as roughly the same level of difficulty. And, they are arranged in hierarchical fashion: performance at any given level denotes the ability to perform all of the lower levels. The FOCS system has been painstakingly developed, and although it has not received a test, it might be possible to align the Dunnette article reported in the introduction to this section as evidence that classification on the basis of function approaches the criteria of mutual exclusivity, at least.

REFERENCES

Holland, J. L. A classification for occupations in terms of personality and intelligence. *American Psychologist*, 1959, *14*, 376 (Abstract).

Roe, A. *The Psychology of Occupations.* New York: Wiley, 1956 (Chapter 11).

Super, D. E. *The Psychology of Careers.* New York: Harper & Row, 1957 (Chapter 3).

U.S. Department of Labor. *The Dictionary of Occupational Titles*, 3d ed. Washington, D.C.: U.S. Government Printing Office, 1966.

A Psychological Classification Scheme for Vocations and Major Fields

JOHN L. HOLLAND, *American College Testing Program*

When compared with the work on aptitude, interests and counseling, the psychological classification of vocations and fields of training has received relatively little direct study, although such problems plague both practitioners and researchers in education and social sciences. Usually we have struggled along with a variety of traditional classificatory schemes with all their defects — ambiguous definitions, overlapping categories, obscure rationales, and incomplete sets of categories. To illustrate, what fields belong in categories such as humanities, business or social sciences? What is the rationale for assigning history to "humanities" rather than to "social sciences"? How should a new field such as "computer science" be categorized? Some of these difficulties occur in traditional classification schemes because the schemes do not comply with the basic rules for logical classification. These rules are: "(1) a division must be exhaustive, (2) there must be no overlap across divisions, and (3) a division must proceed at every stage upon one principle, the *fundamentum divisionis*" (Cohen and Nagel, 1934).

The purpose of this report is to present several classification schemes for vocations and fields of study which, by following these logical principles, avoid some, but

Reprinted with the permission of the author and publisher from *Journal of Counseling Psychology*, 1966, *13*, 278–288.

not all, of the weaknesses inherent in earlier plans. Because of their rationale and method of construction, these new plans are expected to be useful in the conduct of censuses, vocational guidance, industrial selection, placement and research. Preliminary versions of these classifications have been reported earlier (Holland, 1959b; Astin and Holland, 1961).

The following sections summarize the rationale for establishing the classifications, the student data used in the construction of the classifications and the results attained when the rationale was applied to the relevant information obtained from large samples of college students.

RATIONALE

In a theoretical sense, the proposed schemes are based on the assumption that vocational choice is an expression of personality. Put another way, if we classify together people having similar vocational choices we are also classifying similar personalities together. Accordingly, the present schemes arrange vocations and major fields in terms of personality types and subtypes.

The present classification schemes, inasmuch as they use similar major groupings, were anticipated by those of Fine (1955) and Roe (1954). They also resemble the attempts to define by factor analysis the independent dimensions among vocations

(Vernon, 1949; Guilford, Christensen, Bond, and Sutton, 1954; Palmer and McCormick, 1961).

The instrument used in developing the present scheme is the Vocational Preference Inventory (Holland, 1965). Use of this instrument provides a psychological rationale for the interpretation of the classification, as the scales assess the major constructs in a theory of vocational choice and personality (Holland, 1959a, 1966). Both the inventory and the theory have undergone investigation so that the meanings attributed to scale scores and, consequently, the present classification scheme have some validity (Holland, 1962, 1963, 1964, 1965).

To apply the logical principles for a classification scheme to this instrument, we used the average interest inventory profiles of students aspiring to specific vocations and major fields. To illustrate, the profile formed by the Realistic, Intellectual, Social, Conventional, Enterprising and Artistic scales of the VPI for a sample of prospective physicists defined both the major class to which physicists belonged (the scale with the highest mean score), and the various subclasses to which physicists belonged (the scales with the second and third highest average scores). The assignment of major fields to classes was performed in the same way. Such a procedure results in groups and subgroups with an increasing degree of homogeneity as we proceed from one to six average scale scores as a basis for the formation of classes and subclasses. This occurrence is an especially desirable outcome because it enables a person to interpret the application of the classification to a problem with more reliability and validity than he may have otherwise.

This simple procedure, then, complies with the rules for logical classification: *All* fields and vocations studied are classified into one of six classes; each field and vocation is classified only in a *single* class or subclass. The principle for classification is always the *same* empirical procedure — average scores for six interest scales.

STUDENT INFORMATION

The basic data used in construction of the classification systems were obtained in two extensive surveys in which college freshmen took the Vocational Preference Inventory, indicated their choice of vocation and major field from coded lists (Abe, Holland, Lutz, and Richards, 1965), and responded to a number of other survey questions, ratings and scales.

The first survey was administered in the spring of 1964 to 12,432 college freshmen in 31 institutions, including 6 junior colleges, 7 undergraduate colleges and 18 universities. Table 1, in Abe et al. (1965), indicates the participating colleges and the number of students who responded to the survey.

The second survey was administered in the fall of 1964 to 10,646 students in nine institutions, including one junior college, four undergraduate institutions, and four universities.

Although these student samples are not precise representative samples, they appear to be reasonable approximations of the typical college freshman, especially the first sample (spring ACS, 1964). An attempt was made to assess all freshmen in each college. The percentage of respondents among colleges ranged from 22 to 96. The specific bias due to nonrespondents is not known. The following sections summarize our knowledge of the scales and assessment devices used in the present study.

Vocational Preference Inventory (Fifth Revision). This personality and interest inventory is composed entirely of occupational titles (Holland, 1965). To take the inventory, a student indicates which occupations he likes and dislikes. Scores on only the following 14-item scales were used: Realistic, Intellectual, Social, Conventional, Enterprising and Artistic. Reliabilities (Kuder-Richardson 20) range from .83 to .89 for 6289 male college freshmen and from .76 to .89 for 6143 females. For the present study, it is useful to interpret the VPI as an inventory of vocational interests. The VPI scales used and their "interest" interpretations are as follows:

Scale	Preference for:
Realistic	technical and skilled trades
Intellectual	scientific occupations
Social	teaching and helping occupations
Conventional	clerical occupations
Enterprising	supervisory and sales occupations
Artistic	artistic, musical and literary occupations

Preconscious Activity Scale. This is an a priori scale developed to measure Kubie's (1958) notion of preconscious activity as a process in creative performance (Nichols & Holland, 1963). The Preconscious Activity Scale is a 38-item true-false scale with reliabilities (KR 20) of .72 and .68 for male and female freshmen. The predictive and concurrent relationships of this scale with originality and interest measures imply that the Preconscious Activity Scale should be interpreted as an originality measure, especially in the fields of art, literature and music (Nichols & Holland, 1963).

Range of Competencies. From a list of 143 activities, students checked those they could do well or competently. These scales assume that a large number of abilities contribute to achievement generally and abilities in a particular field contribute to achievement in that field. Typical items from this list included: I have a working knowledge of *Robert's Rules of Order*, I can dance, I am a good cook, I can make jewelry, I can read blueprints, I can read Greek, I can operate a tractor, I can use logarithm tables, etc. Three judges categorized the items into several areas of competence: scientific, technical, governmental, athletic, business, social and educational, homemaking, arts, leadership and sales, and foreign language. Students were then scored for each kind of competency. KR 20's ranged from .38 to .87 for men and women.

Interpersonal Competency Scale. This a priori scale of 20 items was modeled after the work of Foote and Cottrell (1955). Having defined interpersonal competence as "acquired ability for effective interaction," they outlined a program of research to study this concept. Scale items simply poll the subject for those factors which Foote and Cottrell, believe to be conducive to, or typical of, interpersonal competency — good health, social experience, social competencies, positive self-regard. The KR 20's for male and female freshmen were .69 and .67, respectively.

Dogmatism Scale. This scale, developed by Rokeach (1956) to measure dogmatic and rigid thinking, consists of 40 true-false items concerned with beliefs and attitudes. (The first version by Rokeach is in multiple choice form.) The KR 20's were .77 and .75 for men and women.

Student Orientation Survey, Form C. Farber and Goodstein (1964) developed four a priori scales to assess the student orientations implied in Trow's student typology (1960). These scales are Academic, Collegiate, Non-conforming and Vocational. The a priori scales were revised by an internal consistency item analysis to develop homogeneous, 10-item scales. The KR 20's ranged only from .36 to .50 for men and women.

Other Descriptive Information. Students were polled for such background information as their educational and economic aspirations, their life goals, and their self-ratings. They were asked to indicate their choice of vocation and field of training. Students specified whether different life goals and achievements (such as, being a religious person, making a contribution to scientific knowledge, being happy and content) were "essential, very important, somewhat important or of little importance" to them. Using a list of traits and abilities such as originality, scholarship and conservatism, students rated themselves on a four-point scale — top 10%, above average, average and below average.

A VOCATIONAL CLASSIFICATION

Average VPI profiles, using the Realistic, Intellectual, Social, Conventional, Enterprising and Artistic scales, were calculated for the students aspiring to each vocation. Vocations were assigned first to one of six vocational classes (Realistic, Intellectual, Social, Conventional, Enterprising, Artistic), depending upon the highest average VPI scale obtained by its aspirants. Vocations were also assigned to subgroups *within* a vocational class, depending upon the second and third highest average VPI scale scores of its aspirants. Tables 1 and 2 present the vocational classes and subclasses which resulted from this simple sorting procedure for 5600 men and 5560 women.

In all tables, the codes for VPI scales are as follows: 1 equals Realistic, 2 equals Intellectual, 3 equals Social, 4 equals Conventional, 5 equals Enterprising and 6 equals Artistic. The reader will find it helpful to study Table 1 and the remaining tables by decoding the subgroups and applying the interpretations provided by the VPI and a closely associated theory (Holland, 1959, 1966).

TABLE 1

A Classification for *Men's* Vocations in Terms of a Theory of Vocational Choices
(N = 5600)

Vocation	VPI Code	N
Realistic Class		
Industrial Arts Education	123	50
Trade & Industrial Education	123	27
Forestry	123	105
Civil Engineering	125	185
Farming	125	61
Mechanical Engineering	125	152
Industrial Engineering	125	37
Architecture	126	83
Geography	1235	12
Agricultural Science	152	166

TABLE 1 (cont.)

Vocation	VPI Code	N
Intellectual Class		
Oceanography	213	9
Veterinary Science	213	120
Biochemistry	213	15
Botany	213	12
Zoology	213	33
Aeronautical Engineering	215	77
Chemical Engineering	215	94
Electrical Engineering	215	259
Engineering, General & Other	215	65
Military Service	215	80
Geology, Geophysics	216	19
Astronomy, Astrophysics	216	14
Chemistry	216	87
Physics	216	61
Engineering Science	216	44
Mathematics, Statistics	214	80
Metallurgical Engineering	2145	14
Medical Technology	2136	9
Other Biological Science Fields	231	36
Biology	231	55
Natural Science Educ.	231	86
Mathematics Educ.	231	138
Other Health Fields	236	14
Medicine	236	354
Dentistry	251	120
Pharmacy	253	51
Physiology	253	11
Physical Therapy	263	9
Anthropology	263	12
Social Class		
Physical Educ., Recreation & Health	312	272
Educ. of Exceptional Children	312	8
Elementary Educ.	325	116
Exp. & General Psych.	325	23
Social Work	325	19
History Education	352	202
Educational Psychology	352	9
History	352	57
Education, General & Other Specialties	356	22
Counseling & Guidance	356	36
Industrial & Personnel Psychology	356	17
Foreign Service	356	35

TABLE 1 (cont.)

Vocation	VPI Code	N
Sociology	3526	15
General Social Sciences	362	8
Theology, Religion	362	77
Clinical Psychology	362	42
Foreign Language Educ.	365	17
Conventional Class		
Business Education	435	23
Accounting	451	279
Finance	452	91
Enterprising Class		
Public Administration	534	19
Political Science	536	76
Purchasing	541	16
Sales	541	64
Economics	542	14
Other Business & Comm.	542	39
Management	543	360
Marketing	543	45
Law	563	288
Public Relations	564	40
Artistic Class		
Literature	623	10
Art	623	45
Speech	632	10
General Humanities	632	11
Philosophy	632	10
English, Creative Writing	632	42
Art Education	632	29
Music Education	632	63
Music	635	41
Drama	635	19
English Education	635	67
Journalism, Radio-TV, Communication	653	58
Other Fine & Applied Arts	652	10

Note. The total samples in Table 1 (5600 men) and 2 (5560 women) are about 10% smaller than the total samples assessed, because "undecided" students, fields with very small *N*'s, and non-responding students were not used in these analyses, Underlining indicates "tied codes" or groups having identical average scale scores on the VPI.

TABLE 2

A Classification for *Women's* Vocations in Terms of a Theory of Vocational Choices (*N* = 5560)

Vocation	VPI Code	N
Realistic Class		
None		
Intellectual Class		
Mathematics, Statistics	234	54
Medicine	236	79
Veterinary Medicine	236	16
Other Biological Sciences	236	21
Biology	236	40
Bio-chemistry	236	12
Zoology	236	13
Natural Science Education	236	45
Chemistry	236	25
Physics	261	7
Agricultural Science	263	15
Architecture	263	8
Social Class		
Pharmacy	326	15
Medical Technology	326	111
Mathematics Education	326	114
Clerical Work, Office Work	345	94
Business Education	345	89
Secretarial Science	346	267
Management, Business Adm.	356	22
Sales	356	25
Purchasing	356	55
Educational Psychology	356	15
Dentistry	362	32
Nursing	362	301
Other Health Fields	362	51
Clinical Psychology	362	48
Exp. & General Psych.	362	12
Political Science, Govt., Int. Relations	362	32
Theology, Religion	362	34
Physical Therapy	362	32
Speech	365	22
Elementary Education	365	1497
Foreign Language Educ.	365	117
English Education	365	306
Educ., General & Other Specialties	365	29
History Education	365	154
Physical Educ., Recreation & Health	365	239

TABLE 2 (cont.)

Vocation	VPI Code	N
Educ. of Exceptional Children	365	145
Home Economics Educ.	365	153
Counseling & Guidance	365	76
Sociology	365	34
History	365	24
Public Relations, Advertising	365	13
Law	365	32
Social Work, Group Work	365	140
Home Economics	365	184
Housewife	365	122
Conventional Class		
Accounting	435	42
Enterprising Class		
None		
Artistic Class		
Art	632	92
Art Education	632	93
Literature	632	22
English, Creative Writing	632	52
Music	632	43
Music Education	635	74
Drama	635	18
Other Fine & Applied Arts	635	11
Modern Foreign Language	635	42
Journalism, Radio-TV, Communication	635	57
Foreign Service	635	36
Library Science, Archival Science	635	32

When we look at Tables 1 and 2, it is clear that the main groups of vocations formed by our empirical procedure are generally consistent with many traditional classifications. In Table 1, for example, the industrial arts, some engineering specialties and agricultural fields fall in the same group, Realistic. Similarly, the physical and social sciences fall in the same group, Intellectual. Of equal interest, the subclasses usually appear to make psychological sense. Within the Intellectual group in Table 1, for instance, several subgroups were created: (a) an Intellectual-Realistic-Social group (Code

213), a life science subgroup composed of oceanography, veterinary science, biochemistry, botany and zoology; (b) an Intellectual-Realistic-Enterprising group (Code 215), an engineering-military science group; (c) an Intellectual-Realistic-Artistic group (Code 216) composed largely of physical sciences; (d) several Intellectual-Social groups (Codes 231, 236) composed of scientific-humanistic fields such as natural science education and medicine and (e) several smaller subgroups which can be intercepted in terms of the six VPI scale meanings.

The classification obtained for the vocations of women in Table 2 differs in several ways from the men's classification. No women's vocations were classified as either Realistic or Enterprising. The majority of women are classified as Social, whereas the majority of men are classified as Intellectual. With some notable exceptions, vocations are, however, generally classified in the same group by both male and female VPI profiles.

EXAMINATION OF THE CLASSIFICATION SCHEME

While the classification produced by the application of the rationale not only conforms with the logical principles of classification but also appears sensible, it is desirable to examine the classification by some formal tests. The present method of construction *should have* produced a plan with some desirable properties, but it does not *guarantee* such a plan. Accordingly several analyses were performed to secure answers to the following questions:

1. Is the classification scheme stable? It is possible that some classifications are unreliable, because many are based on a small number of students. For instance, vocations may be classified in different classes, when the scheme is applied to different samples of people.

2. When the classification system is applied (students being classified by their *choice of vocation* rather than by their *scores* on the VPI), do students possess the personal characteristics suggested by the VPI and its associated theory?

3. How homogeneous are the groups formed by the classification system?

The first test of the classification was performed to learn if the scheme had produced meaningful, homogeneous groups of students. For this analysis, the spring sample of male freshmen was classified according to their vocational choices. Then a simple analysis of variance was calculated for each of 24 self-ratings, life goals, competencies and personal traits. The outcome of this procedure, presented in Table 3 reveals several desirable characteristics of the classification: (1) the students in different classes do differ significantly on all variables ($p < .05$). The size of the F ratio is frequently large. The intra-class Rs computed from the basic data range from .004 to .19 and correspond to Pearson rs of .06 to .44. There is, then, considerable discrimination on many student characteristics across classes. (2) A review of the means for each student characteristic makes it clear that generally students possess the characteristics hypothesized in the theory.

The predicted highest mean on a given student trait is shown in italics. For example, the Realistic group (skilled trades and technical occupations) is highest on self-ratings of mechanical ability, number of claimed technical competencies and dogmatism. They are lowest in originality, popularity, understanding of others, social competencies, leadership competencies and interpersonal competency. Similar theoretically consistent and expected profiles were found for the other classes.

The second test of the classification was performed to learn if the classification produced similar results from sample to sample. For this analysis, students were classified according to their vocational choice, using the results obtained from the male freshmen in the spring sample (Table 1). A simple analysis of variance was then performed for each of the VPI scales. The same procedure was applied to the male freshmen in the fall sample.

The results of these analyses shown in Table 4 indicate that the classification produced similar discriminations in both samples. The high and low means are without exception associated with the appropriate class. The F ratios did not fall markedly from the spring to the fall samples so that it is reasonable to conclude that the classification is not dependent upon the idiosyncrasies of the spring sample, and that it has useful stability.

The third test of the classification was performed to learn how well the classification established for men in the spring sample worked when applied to women in the fall sample. The results of this test, using women's vocational choices categorized by the men's classification, are given in Table 5. The F ratios indicate that the VPI scales still discriminate significantly across classes but less efficiently for women than for men. The discriminant validities of the VPI scales are also appropriate except for the Intellectual Scale, which is higher for the Realistic than for the Intellectual class.

The final test of the classification system was an attempt to improve the classification of women's vocational choices. The first classification scheme established by using the women in the spring sample (see Table 2) created only four major classes, with the Social class containing a majority of the women in the sample. In an attempt to obviate these difficulties, a seven-category scheme was established by using the Intellectual, Conventional and Artistic classes and subdividing the large Social class into subtypes: Social-Intellectual, Social-Conventional, Social-Enterprising and Social-Artistic. The resulting classification is presented in Table 6. These results are not substantially more discriminating across groups than the results obtained by the

TABLE 3

The Homogeneity of the Classification Scheme for *Men*

Student Characteristics		1 Real (*N* = 879)	2 Int (*N* = 1981)	3 Soc (*N* = 975)	4 Conv (*N* = 393)	5 Ent (*N* = 961)	6 Art (*N* = 415)	*F*
Self-Ratings								
Originality	X̄	2.30	2.47	2.38	2.22	2.50	*2.83*	40.62
	SD	.68	.75	.72	.67	.73	.80	
Mechanical ability	X̄	*2.62*	2.42	1.97	2.07	2.09	1.85	90.78
	SD	.89	.91	.87	.83	.88	.87	
Popularity	X̄	2.35	2.42	*2.44*	2.46	2.56	2.36	9.56
	SD	.68	.72	.69	.66	.70	.71	
Understanding of others	X̄	2.56	2.73	*2.80*	2.64	2.83	2.83	17.18
	SD	.69	.73	.75	.68	.74	.75	
Math ability	X̄	2.35	*2.74*	2.02	2.40	2.07	1.85	150.25
	SD	.89	.92	.87	.82	.87	.87	
Conservatism	X̄	2.30	2.29	2.19	*2.33*	2.25	2.08	8.99
	SD	.68	.74	.72	.71	.76	.76	
Life Goals								
Inventing useful product	X̄	1.68	*1.74*	1.39	1.39	1.47	1.38	46.05
	SD	.82	.83	.70	.69	.68	.68	
Making theoretical contrib.	X̄	1.61	*2.10*	1.40	1.29	1.36	1.31	204.81
to science	SD	.77	.95	.70	.57	.67	.65	
Producing works of art	X̄	1.49	1.34	1.39	1.24	1.38	*2.10*	76.40
	SD	.85	.69	.72	.59	.72	1.17	
Becoming expert in finance	X̄	1.75	1.59	1.58	*3.03*	2.48	1.50	324.32
& comm.	SD	.84	.81	.82	.94	1.00	.77	
Being active in religious	X̄	2.73	2.57	*2.62*	2.74	2.48	2.44	9.28
affairs	SD	1.00	1.03	1.02	.94	1.03	1.06	
Having executive resp. for	X̄	2.39	2.26	2.26	2.76	*2.80*	2.10	79.94
others	SD	.83	.87	.87	.82	.88	.91	
Competencies								
Scientific	X̄	4.02	*5.02*	3.67	3.37	3.64	3.28	86.41
	SD	2.37	2.48	2.50	2.19	2.42	2.43	
Technical	X̄	*14.36*	13.17	11.26	12.00	12.32	10.49	76.54
	SD	3.71	4.41	4.44	4.21	4.50	4.71	
Business	X̄	1.71	1.86	1.81	*2.54*	2.48	1.87	53.82
	SD	1.28	1.35	1.34	1.31	1.37	1.37	
Social	X̄	4.97	5.50	*6.46*	5.51	6.27	6.38	37.08
	SD	2.97	3.00	2.85	2.93	2.84	2.91	
Artistic	X̄	5.90	7.34	7.54	5.80	7.98	*12.22*	79.22
	SD	5.14	5.84	5.72	5.09	5.96	6.09	
Leadership	X̄	3.74	4.33	4.39	4.31	*5.46*	4.87	32.79
	SD	2.97	3.07	3.00	3.05	3.15	3.14	

TABLE 3 (Cont.)

Student Characteristics		1 Real (N = 879)	2 Int (N = 1981)	3 Soc (N = 975)	4 Conv (N = 393)	5 Ent (N = 961)	6 Art (N = 415)	F
		Vocational Classes						
Personality and Attitudinal Scales								
Preconscious Activity (Originality)	X̄	15.36	17.33	17.26	13.41	15.74	*21.48*	139.47
	SD	4.84	5.04	4.95	4.34	5.03	5.40	
Dogmatism	X̄	18.15	17.65	17.60	*18.08*	17.32	17.21	2.83
	SD	5.78	5.74	5.96	5.86	6.00	5.84	
Academic Type	X̄	4.38	*4.65*	4.69	4.25	4.46	5.02	9.85
	SD	1.91	1.96	2.01	2.04	2.06	1.93	
Vocational Type	X̄	*5.35*	4.93	4.80	5.57	5.16	4.41	29.98
	SD	1.63	1.72	1.71	1.73	1.79	1.88	
Non-Conformist Type	X̄	3.06	3.14	3.30	3.04	3.46	*3.59*	11.08
	SD	1.66	1.69	1.74	1.59	1.76	1.91	
Collegiate Type	X̄	4.29	4.38	4.59	4.74	*4.85*	4.19	14.58
	SD	1.90	1.91	1.84	1.82	1.85	1.92	
Interpersonal Competency	X̄	10.48	11.05	*11.67*	10.98	11.96	11.16	22.79
	SD	3.30	3.42	3.32	3.32	3.22	3.48	

TABLE 4

Stability of the Classification Scheme from Sample to Sample for *Men*

VPI Scales		1 Real (N = 879)	2 Int (N = 1981)	3 Soc (N = 975)	4 Conv (N = 393)	5 Ent (N = 961)	6 Art (N = 415)	F
		Vocational Choices of Male Sample (Spring Freshmen)						
Realistic	X̄	*6.18*	4.63	3.85	3.96	3.41	2.92	85.03
	SD	3.59	3.53	3.45	3.50	3.36	3.14	
Intellectual	X̄	5.10	*7.61*	4.55	3.35	3.87	4.14	185.21
	SD	3.93	4.11	4.08	3.89	3.93	3.95	
Social	X̄	2.99	3.73	*7.16*	4.09	4.45	5.15	178.92
	SD	3.10	3.32	3.47	3.47	3.59	3.60	
Conventional	X̄	2.70	2.56	2.59	*8.15*	4.52	1.92	257.99
	SD	3.03	2.97	3.24	3.58	3.78	2.88	
Enterprising	X̄	3.63	3.50	4.56	6.61	*6.94*	4.22	186.73
	SD	3.27	3.19	3.39	3.42	3.33	3.41	
Artistic	X̄	2.29	3.35	3.99	2.39	3.68	*7.55*	144.86
	SD	2.74	3.63	3.70	3.09	3.67	3.61	

application of the men's classification to the same sample of women (see Table 5). This revision for women does, however, distribute women's vocational choices more evenly across categories.

AN EDUCATIONAL CLASSIFICATION

The procedure for establishing the classification for fields of study was identical to that for vocations. Average VPI profiles

TABLE 4 (Cont.)

		(*Fall Freshmen*)						
		(N = 624)	(N = 1819)	(N = 534)	(N = 239)	(N = 834)	(N = 295)	
Realistic	X̄	*5.59*	3.76	3.01	3.21	2.77	2.38	74.83
	SD	3.53	3.26	2.90	3.05	2.88	2.99	
Intellectual	X̄	5.25	*7.48*	4.64	3.04	3.26	3.40	189.95
	SD	4.04	4.02	4.13	3.41	3.60	3.62	
Social	X̄	2.61	3.33	*6.86*	3.24	4.03	4.59	124.74
	SD	2.84	3.13	3.64	3.16	3.36	3.65	
Conventional	X̄	2.70	2.33	2.13	*7.53*	3.95	1.43	164.97
	SD	3.17	2.70	2.97	3.32	3.67	2.56	
Enterprising	X̄	3.30	3.23	4.40	6.41	*6.60*	4.01	161.36
	SD	3.26	3.07	3.28	2.98	3.37	3.16	
Artistic	X̄	2.26	3.15	4.48	2.00	3.50	*7.22*	104.61
	SD	2.98	3.50	3.86	2.58	3.48	4.00	

TABLE 5

Application of *Men's* Vocational Classification to Vocational Choices of *Women*

		Vocational Classes						
VPI Scales		1 Real (N = 21)	2 Int (N = 807)	3 Soc (N = 1742)	4 Conv (N = 67)	5 Ent (N = 206)	6 Art (N = 623)	*F*
Realistic	X̄	*3.05*	1.57	1.05	1.51	1.08	1.29	14.21
	SD	2.85	1.98	1.63	2.10	1.95	1.87	
Intellectual	X̄	6.71	*6.60*	3.18	2.79	2.72	3.44	109.77
	SD	4.31	4.10	3.47	3.40	3.34	3.74	
Social	X̄	3.86	6.30	*8.69*	6.00	6.62	7.04	67.11
	SD	3.30	3.75	3.36	4.35	3.76	3.77	
Conventional	X̄	2.43	2.40	1.84	*7.12*	2.97	1.51	66.13
	SD	3.30	2.87	2.39	3.92	3.44	2.30	
Enterprising	X̄	3.00	2.51	3.27	3.96	*5.06*	3.53	31.73
	SD	3.06	2.55	2.76	2.63	3.04	2.88	
Artistic	X̄	5.00	4.81	5.54	3.40	5.65	*8.00*	49.18
	SD	4.09	4.08	4.32	4.03	4.08	3.97	

TABLE 6

Application of *Women's* Classification (Spring Sample) to *Women's* Vocational Choices (Fall Sample)

VPI Scales		1 Int (N = 359)	2 Soc-Int (N = 1136)	3 Soc-Conv (N = 220)	4 Soc-Ent (N = 87)	5 Soc-Art (N = 2091)	6 Conv (N = 27)	7 Art (N = 498)	F
					Vocational Classes				
Realistic	X̄	*1.72*	1.28	.75	1.31	1.08	1.69	1.33	10.14
	SD	2.09	1.91	1.26	2.06	1.68	2.46	1.79	
Intellectual	X̄	*7.42*	5.06	1.35	2.44	3.03	3.38	3.67	116.13
	SD	3.95	4.07	2.02	3.13	3.41	3.84	3.82	
Social	X̄	5.86	7.51	6.34	7.57	*8.42*	4.59	6.54	47.03
	SD	3.61	3.62	3.62	3.85	3.53	4.15	3.80	
Conventional	X̄	2.24	1.98	4.80	3.79	1.86	*9.03*	1.42	90.80
	SD	2.85	2.64	3.12	3.88	2.43	3.36	22.2	
Enterprising	X̄	2.35	2.76	3.50	*4.91*	3.35	3.66	3.52	19.04
	SD	2.43	2.64	2.67	3.22	2.76	2.29	2.95	
Artistic	X̄	5.11	5.03	3.16	5.54	5.48	3.41	*8.06*	46.77
	SD	4.10	4.21	3.68	3.89	4.29	3.62	3.94	

Note: Italics indicate expected highest mean among classes. Discrepancy in total N's between Tables 5 and 6 occurs because male classification scheme fails to categorize such vocational choices as "housewife," etc.

were calculated for students aspiring to each field, and fields were assigned to classes according to their highest average VPI scale score. Fields were also assigned to subgroups, according to the second and third highest average VPI scale scores of a field's aspirants. Tables (A and B) showing the classification of major fields created by this method for each sex can be obtained from the author.

In general, the classification for major fields is most remarkable for its similarity to the earlier classification developed for vocations. The majority of vocations and their related fields of training are given either an identical classification, or they differ only in the subgroup to which they have been assigned.

No empirical examination of the major field classification was made for several reasons. The similarity between the two systems suggested that we would obtain

similar results; earlier studies by Abe and Holland (1965a, 1965b) produced similar results on the same student characteristics for the spring sample, when the variation across vocations and major fields was calculated by a simple analysis of variance for each variable.

DISCUSSION

The present classifications have several weaknesses which are difficult to evaluate. More confidence could be placed in the classification if we had used employed adults for the vocational classification and college seniors for the educational classification. Similarly, much larger samples would result in the classification of more fields and vocations. On the other hand, the test of a classification lies largely in its usefulness in subsequent research and practice rather than in its particular method of construction.

The possible practical applications seem to be several. Occupational information files can be organized into special groups and subgroups. Such an organization would put student vocational interests and occupational materials in the same terms. For example, a student with an Intellectual-Realistic-Artistic "interest" code could go to a file of occupational materials for that code, and he could be easily directed to related coded material. His counselor would also have a theory for interpreting his profile and for suggesting relevant diagnostic information. In a similar fashion, placement and employment files could be organized according to the present system. Job classification plans could also be revised, and perhaps tried out, to explore the usefulness of the scheme.

The possible research applications appear numerous. The classifications can be used to categorize vocational and educational aspirations. And, depending upon his N, the researcher can use either the main groups alone or a number of subgroups as well. Equally important, he is more likely to obtain psychologically meaningful results, since he has used a classification scheme with some demonstrated homogeneity, whereas traditional schemes usually contain one or more heterogeneous categories of unknown origin with only an implicit rationale. The researcher has a simple, empirical method for the resolution of controversial classifications, or for the classification of new fields and occupations: using the VPI, he simply tests the sample in question, computes their average profile, and classifies the sample accordingly. In this way the present scheme can readily integrate new information about educational and vocational fields. The simple revisional possibilities of the scheme mean that anyone can add to the classification in a consistent way as he acquires information, without having to resort to judges or to his own iudgment, whose value is indeterminate.

Similar classification schemes could be established by using data obtained with the Strong and Kuder. The full exploration of that data might yield more useful categorizations. A few studies of this kind have been performed, but they have attracted little interest (Callis, Engram, and McGowan, 1954; McGowan, Callis, and Rybolt, 1962; Holland, Krause, Nixon, and Trembath, 1953).

In a recent paper, Cooley (1965) has proposed several methods for the development of vocational classification plans that are similar to the present method, and he has also argued for a classification scheme that would be useful in relating vocational theory to empirical research. His illustrations from biological classifications are a useful supplement to the logical principles of classification (Cohen and Nagel, 1934), although there is some overlap in the guidance each set of principles provides.

REFERENCES

Abe, C., and Holland, J. L. *A description of college freshmen:* I. Students who aspire to different major fields. Research Report No. 3. Iowa City: American College Testing Program, 1965. (a)

Abe, C., and Holland, J. L. *A description of college freshmen:* II. Students with different vocational choices. Research Report No. 4. Iowa City: American College Testing Program, 1965. (b)

Abe, C., Holland, J. L., Lutz, Sandra W., and Richards, J. M., Jr. *A description of American college freshmen.* Research Report No. 1. Iowa City: American College Testing Program, 1965.

Astin, A. W., and Holland, J. L. The Environmental Assessment Technique: a way to measure college environments. *J. educ. Psychol.,* 1961, *52*, 308–316.

Callis, R., Engram, W. C., and McGowan, J. F. Coding the Kuder Preference Record-Vocational. *J. appl. Psychol.,* 1954, *38*, 359–363.

Cohen, M. R., and Nagel, E. *An introduction to logic and scientific method.* New York: Harcourt Brace, 1934.

Cooley, W. W. The classification of career plans. Paper presented at APA convention, Chicago, 1965.

Farber, I. E., and Goodstein, L. D. Student orientation survey. Preliminary report, PHS research grant M-226, Univer. of Iowa, Iowa City, Iowa, 1964.

Fine, S. A. The structure of worker functions, *Personnel guid. J.,* 1955, *34,* 66–74.

Foote, N. N., and Cottrell, L. S. *Identity and inter-personal competencies.* Chicago: Univer. of Chicago Press, 1955.

Guilford, J. P., Christensen, P. R., Bond, N. A., Jr., and Sutton, M. A. A factor analysis study of human interests. *Psychol. Monogr.,* 1954, *68,* 4 (Whole No. 375).

Holland, J. L. A theory of vocational choice. *J. counsel. Psychol.,* 1959, *6,* 35–45. (a)

Holland, J. L. A classification for occupations in terms of personality and intelligence. *Amer. Psychologist,* 1959, *14,* 376 (Abstract) (b)

Holland, J. L. Some explorations of a theory of vocational choice: I. One- and two-year longitudinal studies. *Psychol. Monogr.,* 1962, *76,* 26 (Whole No. 545).

Holland, J. L. Some explorations of a theory of vocational choice and achievement: II. A four-year prediction study. *Psychol. Rep.,* 1963, *12,* 545–594. Southern Universities Press, 1963, Monograph Suppl. 4-V12.

Holland, J. L. Manual for the Vocational Preference Inventory. (6th rev.). Iowa City, Iowa: Educational Research Associates, 1965.

Holland, J. L. *The psychology of vocational choice: a theory of personality types and environmental models.* New York: Ginn, 1966.

Holland, J. L., and Nichols, R. C. Explorations of a theory of vocational choice: III. A longitudinal study of change in major field of study. *Personnel guid. J.,* 1964, *43,* 235–242.

Holland, J. L., Krause, A. H., Nixon, M. Eloise, and Trembath, Mary F. The classification of occupations by means of Kuder interest profiles: I. The development of interest groups. *J. appl. Psychol.,* 1953, *37,* 263–269.

Kubie, L. S. *Neurotic distortion of the creative process.* Lawrence, Kansas: Univer. of Kansas Press, 1958.

McGowan, J. F., Callis, R., and Rybolt, G. A. Coding the Kuder. Testing and Counseling Service Report, 1962, *16,* No. 3, Univer. of Missouri, Columbia, Missouri.

Nichols, R. C., and Holland, J. L. Prediction of the first year college performance of high aptitude students. *Psychol. Monogr.,* 1963, *77,* No. 7 (Whole No. 570).

Palmer, G. J., Jr., and McCormick, E. J. A factor analysis of job activities. *J. appl. Psychol.,* 1961, *45,* 289–294.

Roe, Anne. A new classification of occupations. *J. counsel. Psychol.,* 1954, *1,* 215–220.

Rokeach, M. Political and religious dogmatism, an alternative to the authoritarian personality. *Psychol. Monogr.,* 1956, *70,* No. 18 (Whole No. 425).

Trow, M. The campus viewed as a culture. In H. T. Sprague (Ed.), *Research on college students.* Boulder, Colorado: Western Interstate Commission for Higher Education, 1960.

Vernon, P. E. Classifying high-grade occupational interests. *J. abnorm. soc. Psychol.,* 1949, *44,* 85–96.

Job Changes and the Classification of Occupations

ANNE ROE, *Vocational Consultant, Tucson, Arizona*

W. D. HUBBARD

THOMAS HUTCHINSON, *California State College at Los Angeles*

THOMAS BATEMAN

In order to bring the structure of occupations into a framework which would make possible a psychologically meaningful study of them, Roe (1956) devised a new classification, using two sets of categories in an 8-by-6-celled table. The vertical set of categories, called Levels, indicates degrees of personal responsibility and autonomy, skill and training, decreasing from Level 1 to Level 6. The data to be presented in this paper do not refer to Levels, but to the horizontal set of categories, called Groups.

The Groups are subdivided according to the primary focus of activity in the occupation. These subdivisions are related to most factorizations of interest, although not identical with any of them. The Groups were ordered along a continuum believed to express the intensity and nature of the interpersonal relationships involved in the occupational activities, so that contiguous groups are more alike in this respect than non-contiguous ones. The arrangement was thought of as round, with Group VIII next to Group I as well as to Group VII. It is the arrangement of the Groups in a continuum that is under study in this paper.

This reading appeared as Part I of Studies of occupational history. Reprinted with the permission of the authors and publisher from *Journal of Counseling Psychology*, 1966, *13*, 387–393.

The Groups are as follows:

I. *Service:* These occupations are primarily concerned with serving and attending to the personal tastes, needs and welfare of other persons. Included are occupations such as social work and guidance, and domestic and protective services. The essential element is a situation in which one person is helping another.

II. *Business Contact:* These occupations are primarily concerned with the face-to-face sale of commodities, investments, real estate and services. The person-to-person relation is again important, but it is focused on persuasion to a course of action rather than on helping. The persuader will profit if his advice is followed; the advisee is supposed to.

III. *Organization:* These are the managerial and white collar jobs in business, industry and government — the occupations concerned primarily with the organization and efficient functioning of commercial enterprises and of government activities. The quality of person-to-person relations is largely institutionalized.

IV. *Technology:* This group includes occupations concerned with the production, maintenance and transportation of commodities and utilities. Here are occupations in engineering, crafts and the machine trades, as well as transportation and communication. Interpersonal relations are of relatively little importance, and the focus is on dealing with things.

V. *Outdoor:* This group includes the occupations primarily concerned with the cultivation, preservation and gathering of crops, of marine or inland water resources, of mineral resources, of forest products and of other natural resources, and with animal husbandry. Interpersonal relations are largely irrelevant.

VI. *Science:* These are the occupations primarily concerned with scientific theory and its application under specified circumstances other than technology. Even in scientific research (as in physics) that is not at all person-oriented as well as in such fields as psychology and anthropology, it is clear that there is a relationship to the occupations in Group VII, with some return to more specific personal relations in the medical groups that belong here.

VII. *General Cultural:* These occupations are primarily concerned with the preservation and transmission of the general cultural heritage. Interest is in human activities rather than in individual persons. This group includes occupations in education, journalism, jurisprudence, the ministry, linguistics and the subjects usually called the humanities. All elementary and high school teachers are placed in this group. At higher levels teachers are placed in Groups by subject matter — e.g., teachers of science in VI, of art in VIII, of humanities in VII.

VIII. *Arts and Entertainment:* These occupations include those primarily concerned with the use of special skills in the creative arts and in the field of entertainment. For the most part, the focus is on a relationship between one person (or a small group) and a more general public. The interpersonal relation is important but neither so direct nor of the same nature as that in Group I.

This ordering was arrived at without the benefit of any empirical evidence; there was none available at the time. If it is correct, however, this ordering should predict relationships among several occupational

choices of one individual and the probability of different kinds of changes in occupations during the course of a lifetime. That is, choices or changes should most often be within the same Group, next most often within contiguous Groups, and least often between the most widely separated Groups. Some checks of this sort have now been made.

Jones (1965) administered an Occupations Preference Inventory to 50 summer high school students, involving paired comparisons between occupations representative of all eight categories. (The Levels dimension was omitted.) A factor analysis indicated that about half of the total trace was explained in terms of two factors. On the basis of their relationships to scores on the Guilford-Zimmerman Temperament Scale, he interpreted these as I. person-oriented vs. non-person-oriented occupations; II. external (power, income, etc.) vs. internal (sense of accomplishment, helping others) goals. On a two-dimensional plot, the relationship of the Groups was the same as in the Roe model, except that Group VIII fell between Groups I and II instead of between Groups VII and I. (Fig. 1) Jones concluded that "the contiguity

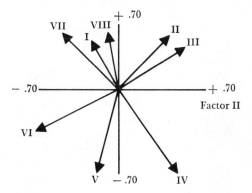

Factor I

FIGURE 1. Category relationships underlying the Roe classificatory scheme. (Length of test vectors equal to the square root of the test's total variance accounted for by the two dimensions.) From Jones.

of the occupational categories postulated by Roe is reflected in this sample of occupational preference data," and "the psychological thread of this contiguity is in large part orientation toward or away from people."

Crites (1962) asked 100 college students to rank the eight groups according to how much they require relationships with people as ends in themselves as the primary work activity. Groups IV, V and VI clustered at approximately the same value. Using Guilford's normalized rank method, the data yielded the following scale values:

Group	Scale Value
I, Service	7.90
VII, Cultural	6.60
II, Business Contact	6.20
III, Organization	5.60
VIII, Arts & Entertainment	5.20
V, Outdoor	4.60
IV, Science	4.50
VI, Technology	4.50

Crites felt it might be inappropriate to attempt to distinguish among Groups IV, V and VI with respect to an interpersonal relations continuum, but suggested an interpersonal relations scale corresponding to particular aspects of the major orientations, and arranged as above.

It is clear that both Jones and Crites agree with Roe that occupations can be ordered along a person-to-person interest continuum, although they differ in the exact ordering suggested. In both studies the subjects were students, and the data quoted are preferences or opinions.

This paper reports an attempt to determine the most appropriate arrangement of these occupational Groups through an investigation of actual changes in occupation over periods ranging up to 22 years. The data are from questionnaires filled out by 804 men who had been given a Strong Vocational Interest Blank some time between 1927 and 1933, and again in 1949,

when they also reported their occupational histories job by job. At the original contact 403 were undergraduates at Stanford, 245 were in the Graduate School of Business and 156 in other Stanford graduate schools. They clearly do not represent Stanford students in general, even less college graduates in general, but they do provide an opportunity to check the appropriateness of the arrangement of the classification since it should theoretically hold for any sizeable sample of a reasonable degree of generality. If a test of the "neighboring" hypothesis with this limited sample does not hold up, the hypothesis must be rejected; if it does hold up it cannot be considered proven for other samples, but it then clearly merits continued examination. In that case, analysis of occupational life histories of a large, randomly selected sample, including all educational levels would obviously be the next step. Even if the neighboring hypothesis is upheld, it does not necessarily follow that the arrangement does in fact reflect an interpersonal relations continuum, but only that some continuum is present. Just what that continuum is requires further study.

Every job listed by each man was coded by the Roe system. There were of course some complications. The time span includes both the depression years when many men took jobs outside their interests and below their capacities, and the war years. The effect of the depression would be chiefly to increase the likelihood of job changes of an extreme sort (i.e., contrary to the hypothesis of neighboring). War service, return to school, and illness were tabulated, but not recorded as job changes. Normal advancement within an organization was also not considered a job change.

For each subject, for each year, the job classification and the position of that job in his sequence of jobs was recorded (e.g., 1927, class VI, job 1; 1928, class VI, job 1; 1929, class IV, job 2, etc.). A computer program was developed by Hubbard which made it possible to compile a matrix of job changes, such as is shown in Table 1. Analy-

TABLE 1

A Frequency Count of All Job Changes Grouped According to the Roe Classification System

Group from Which Changed	Group to Which Changed								
	I	II	III	IV	V	VI	VII	VIII	Σ
I	4	3	6	2	0	0	1	0	16
II	3	38	76	12	0	1	9	3	142
III	4	62	571	42	9	10	28	6	732
IV	3	19	92	212	13	10	5	3	357
V	1	2	14	30	31	1	4	2	85
VI	2	0	5	11	1	91	1	0	111
VII	1	8	28	4	3	4	216	7	271
VIII	0	7	5	1	1	0	5	38	57
Σ	18	139	797	314	58	117	269	59	1771

sis of this matrix and all subsequent analyses were planned and carried out by Hutchinson.

A glance at the table suggests that job change is non-random. A statistical test of association of the table as it stands was inappropriate because of the low-frequencies in Group I. These frequencies were therefore combined with those of Group VIII (one of its neighbors). Chi square is 3631, which with 36 degrees of freedom, gives a p of less than .001. The coefficient of contingency is .820 (maximum for a 7×7 table is .926). These job changes, therefore, were non-random. The Group to which a member of this sample moved is associated with the one from which he moved.

If the "neighboring" hypothesis is correct, not only should the greatest frequencies be in the diagonal (top left to bottom right), as they are (68%), but the frequencies should decrease as the distance from the diagonal increases. A change from any Group to the one adjacent to it on either side, e.g., from II to I or from II to III, is a 1-step change. A 4-step change is the largest possible for eight less than .001. Even under these circumstances, then, the changes are not random.

Nevertheless, since there are almost as many 4-step changes as 3-step (instead of about half as many), the specific changes that were made merit inquiry. If they are concentrated in specific occupations within

TABLE 2

Observed and Expected Frequencies of Job Changes by Steps

	Steps					
	0	1	2	3	4	Σ
Expected Frequency	221.375	442.75	442.75	442.75	221.375	1771
% of Total	12.5	25	25	25	12.5	100.00
Observed Frequency	1201	340	104	64	62	1771
% of Total	67.815	19.198	5.872	3.614	3.501	100.00

the sample, it is possible that some occupation(s) would be more appropriately coded in a different Group. Interchanges between Groups III and VII account for 56 of the 62 changes (28 from III to VII and 28 from VII to to III). They are specified below:

Between law and administration (business or government)	24
Between teaching and business or government	
Level of teaching unknown 6	
High School 7	
Junior College 1	
College (not business subjects) 5	
	19
Change in level of teaching, from High School or Junior College to College	3
Between teaching (any level) and business administration of school	5
Between news editor and business	4
From business to translation	1
	56

These data suggest that the practice of law should perhaps be subdivided, with men in corporation law being classified in Group III rather than in Group VII. We are not sure that all of the 24 exchanges between law and administration are of men who were in corporate law from the start, but it is probable that most of them were. Some of those whose level of teaching is unknown may have been college teachers of business subjects, in which case they would have been classified in III in both teaching and business. Recoding of such changes would just about bring the number of 4-step changes down to half the 3-step changes.

The fact that the current arrangement of Groups seems to accord closely with the general hypothesis of neighboring does not preclude some other arrangement being better. For 8 groups there are 5,040 possible arrangements. We are looking for that order which maximizes our ability to predict to what job family a person is most likely to change if he leaves his present job family. We do not propose to check all 5,040 possibilities, but only to analyze what these data

would show if the Groups were rearranged to fit the suggestions of Jones or Crites. Table 3 shows the expected frequencies if the changes were in fact random, the frequencies for each of the three orders, and chi squares for goodness of fit for each. Since the order suggested by Jones is so similar to Roe's it is to be expected that the chi squares would differ very little, as is the case. Crites did not intend his arrangement to predict changes, but if the dimension he used is relevant to the structure of occupations it might be expected to. It clearly does not do so for this sample, to which, of course, our conclusions are limited. His very different arrangement does suggest, however, that although Roe's ordering of her categories is related to occupational changes in this sample, this ordering may not in fact be based on interpersonal relationships as she believed. An investigation of this point is now underway.

A further question concerns whether or not the Roe arrangement is a circumplex in Guttman's (1954) terms. This would require the probability that n-step changes would be the same whatever the starting Group. Unfortunately the frequencies in the different Groups are very different, but this inequality can be reduced to some extent by dividing the observed frequencies in Table 1 by the expected frequencies producing Table 4. For the model to be a circumplex the values in the diagonal must be the largest, with the remaining values dropping off rapidly as we move away from the diagonal and then rising again as the corner elements are approached. Although the data in Table 4 approximate this model, the correspondence is not perfect.

Another requirement for circularity is that shifting should be as likely in one direction as another — that moves from III to II, for example, should be as likely as from III to IV. Table 5 shows the observed and expected frequencies. A test for goodness of fit for this table gives chi square = 9.17 which with 3 degrees of freedom gives a p of less than .05. There is, then, a significant tendency for there to be more shifting to the

TABLE 3

The Frequency Distributions of 1, 2, 3 and 4 Steps of Change for Three Orders

Order	Steps 1	2	3	4	χ_3^2
Expected Frequencies	163	163	163	81	
Roe's I, II, III, IV, V, VI, VII, VIII	340	104	64	62	279
Jones' I, VIII, II, III, IV, V, VI, VII	334	113	58	65	263
Crites' I, VII, II, III, VIII, V, IV, VI	237	111	169	53	60

TABLE 4

The Observed Frequencies of Table 3 Divided by the Expected Frequencies of Table 3

Group	II	III	IV	V	VI	VII	VIII + I
II	3.41	1.19	.48	0	.11	.42	.97
III	1.08	1.73	.32	.38	.21	.25	.31
IV	.68	.57	3.35	1.11	.42	.09	.39
V	.30	.37	1.99	11.14	.18	.31	.81
VI	0	.10	.56	.28	12.41	.06	.41
VII	.38	.23	.08	.34	.24	5.25	.68
VIII + 1	1.75	.33	.23	.42	0	.54	13.24

eft than to the right, hence the matrix for this population of job changes is not a perfect circumplex.

TABLE 5

Observed and Expected Frequencies of the Sums of Left Step Changes and the Sums of Right Step Changes

Frequencies	Direction Left Steps			Right Steps		
	3	2	1	1	2	3
Observed	30	55	197	143	49	34
Expected	32	52	170	170	52	32

There are two complications: some subjects made more job changes than others (range is 0 to 9), and the frequencies in the different Groups are not equal. With a large number in Group III and a small number in Group II, the possibility of changes from III to II is greater than from II to III. Also if a second change is made, a subject who had changed from III to II is more likely to change back to III than to move to I. Our analysis has assumed that earlier changes had not affected the later ones. We would now hypothesize that for the first job change the probability of making a given step change to the left is equal to the probability of making the same distance change to the right (i.e., that an underlying circular model does exist); but that given a past history of working in another job family, the probability of these two changes will be unequal. This hypothesis will be examined in another paper.

Our general conclusion is that Roe's intention of placing her Groups in an ordered arrangement has been accomplished. For this sample, at least, when men change jobs they are most likely to change within one Group; and when they leave any Group the likelihood of their entering any other Group varies inversely with the distance of that Group from the original one. Two other orders suggested in the literature are shown to have less predictive power for this sample than Roe's order. Some evidence is adduced to suggest that the arrangement represents a genuine circumplex.

REFERENCES

Crites, J. O. An interpersonal relations scale for occupational groups. *J. appl. Psychol.*, 1962, *46*, 87–90.

Doyle, R. E. Career patterns of male college graduates. *Personnel guid. J.*, 1965, *44*, 410–415

Guttman, L. A new approach to factor analysis: the radex. In P. F. Lazarfeld (Ed.), *Mathematical thinking in the social sciences*. New York: The Free Press, 1954. Pp. 258–348.

Jones, K. J. Occupational preference and social orientation. *Personnel guid. J.*, 1965, *43*, 574–579.

Roe, Anne. *The psychology of occupations*. New York: Wiley, 1956.

Toward a Psychodynamic System of Occupational Classification

MYRON BRENDER, *Brooklyn VAOPC*

It is the purpose of this paper to explore a relatively untried approach to the task of occupational description and classification, to examine the potentialities of this approach for the development of a comprehensive and exhaustive classificatory scheme.

WHY ANOTHER SYSTEM OF OCCUPATIONAL CLASSIFICATION?

In a recent survey of the various kinds of occupational classifications in current use, Super (1957) identified the following: (a)

Reprinted with the permission of the author and publisher from *Journal of Counseling Psychology*, 1960, 7, 96–100.

Socioeconomic classifications. (b) Classifications based on the different intellectual requirements of various occupations. (c) Enterprise classifications in which groupings are made with regard to the setting or locale in which the occupation is pursued. (d) Composite classifications which take into account the ways in which occupations differ with respect to a variety of factors such as status, prestige, income, degree of authority exercised, degree of freedom of action permitted, etc. (*i.e.*, multi-dimensional classifications incorporating the concepts of level and field as well as enterprise). (e) Classifications structured in terms of types of roles and activities that are intrinsic to the various occupations (*i.e.*, classifications arranged on the basis of interests, or assumed modal personality types).

Save for the systems in the last category, and a few included in the category immediately preceding (notably Roe's two-dimensional classification [1956] and Super's three-dimensional modification thereof [1957]), none has been designed specifically to take into account the purely psychological aspects of the world of work. Of those few mentioned that do attempt to touch at least in part upon pertinent psychological factors, none deals adequately with the motivational facets of occupational psychology. Systems based on the concepts of modal personality type and interest patterns perhaps can be regarded properly as displaying an essential psychological orientation but the absence of an explicit concern with factors of human motivation limits their value.[1] It is with a view toward remedying such a deficiency that this proposal is advanced.

THE POSTULATES

The following is posited:[2]

1.   People work in order to gratify certain needs or motives. Conversely, all work is potentially capable of gratifying certain human needs.

2.   The need-gratifying potential immanent in all work can be analyzed into elements designated as *job satisfactions, job gratifications, job rewards*, or simply *rewards* or *satisfactions*.

3.   The various rewards immanent in all work activity can be separated grossly into two main categories: intrinsic and extrinsic rewards.[3] Intrinsic rewards may be defined as those satisfactions inherent in an occupation, which are unique to the work activities of that occupation, or to a small family of occupations related in that respect. By their very uniqueness they serve to characterize that occupation, or occupational family, and to distinguish it from all others.[4]

4.   Theoretically, it should be possible to classify people in accordance with their dominant motives. Similarly, it should be possible to cast them into groupings with

respect to the needs that they wish or expect to have gratified in their work. Groupings made on this basis should disclose appreciable differences among people both in terms of the needs, or need-patterns that characterize them and the degree of importance that they attach to having these needs gratified by the intrinsic and extrinsic rewards inherent in various occupations.

5.   It also should be possible to classify occupations, generally, in accordance with the types and degrees of rewards that are intrinsic to them.

6.   If occupations can be classified successfully along the dimension of intrinsic rewards, and if individuals can be sorted successfully into distinctive groups with respect to the principal needs they hope or expect to have gratified in their work, then a basis exists for the development of a new means of matching people and jobs.

7.   If it can be demonstrated that the intrinsic reward system of occupational description and taxonomy provides a firm basis for the development of a new technique for matching people and jobs, then its essential usefulness will have been adequately established and its creation amply justified.

THE INTRINSIC REWARD APPROACH TO OCCUPATIONAL TAXONOMY

By employing the concept of intrinsic reward or job satisfaction as a focal classificatory principle, it becomes possible to devise a feasible and psychologically meaningful system of occupational description and taxonomy.[5] An indispensible initial requirement of such a program is that there be available some procedure whereby the intrinsic job satisfaction immanent in each occupation can be identified and described. With appropriate modifications the standard techniques of job analysis and occupational description (Shartle, 1952) can be adapted for the task. Thus, by rational analysis and inference from existing job descriptions — or through revised job analyses which include data on intrinsic and extrinsic rewards obtained directly from the sampled opinions of experts and from workers in the various occupations — occupational descriptions could be rewritten to incorporate material pertinent to the dimension of intrinsic and extrinsic job satisfaction in different occupations. Material gathered in this way could then be used as a basis for arranging occupations into families in terms of the intrinsic job satisfactions held in common by all the members. Such taxonomic groupings having been accomplished, the data could then be assembled into a compendium resembling the *Dictionary of Occupational Titles* (1949). The format would provide for coding and indexing of entries arranged according to the intrinsic job reward designations of the constituent occupational families.

Illustrations of the Intrinsic Reward Approach

While the magnitude of the project obviously precludes any thorough or extensive treatment of the details of the procedure in this account, a few necessarily sketchy examples may serve to clarify.

WRITER Analyzing this occupation with an eye toward teasing out intrinsic need gratifications, it becomes apparent that a salient characteristic of this occupation — or more properly, family of occupations — is that it allows maximal gratification of the need for verbal expression. Consequently, to code or classify the occupation of writer with reference to intrinsic rewards one might list it initially under the rubric of expressive occupations, with the subcategory, verbal, and the code designation, *ir*-expressive, verbal (*i.e., intrinsic reward* — expressive, verbal).

Using a finer analysis, one might then decide that an additional break-down is desirable in order to incorporate a creative-reproductive dimension. Thus, one might adopt as the most general category, "*ir*-expressive"; as the first subcategory, "*ir*-expressive, verbal"; and as the second subcategory, "*ir*-expressive, verbal, creative" or "*ir*-expressive, verbal, reproductive." Taking the *ir*-expressive, verbal, creative classification, one might then proceed to list under this rubric the occupation writer, fiction and writer, non-fiction. Introducing yet a third subcategory, "*ir*-expressive, verbal, creative, imaginative or intellective" permits the listing of the professions of novelist, short-story writer, poet, playwright (stage, screen, TV, radio) and — by courtesy — comedy or gag-writer under the rubric of "*ir*-expressive, verbal, creative, imaginative"; and the professions of essayist, scholarly and scientific writer, journalist (commentator, political or news analyst, reporter, and possibly columnist) and perhaps technical writer under the rubric of "*ir*-expressive, verbal, creative, intellective."

Rather than continuing further into the minutiae of the system, a reversal of direction toward more comprehensive categories may prove equally illuminating.

Since writing is not the only occupational activity that gratifies the need for expression, the rubric of *expressive occupations* will be found to include within its compass the professions of musician, artist (graphic), actor, and dancer, as well as some of the occupations ordinarily classified among the humanities, and possibly a few usually grouped with the sciences. Hence, in the general category of expressive occupations, the profession of writer constitutes only a single subdivision among many others. This becomes even clearer if an intrinsic reward analysis of some of the other expressive occupations is attempted.

MUSICIAN This might be classified as "*ir*-expressive, musical, vocal, or instrumental, creative," with additional subdivisions as needed. A composer of vocal music (opera, songs, ballads, etc.) would be entered under the category *ir*-expressive, musical, vocal, creative, whereas a singer would be listed as "*ir*-expressive, musical, vocal, reproductive" (or performing). Similarly, the occupation of *Choreographer* would be classified as "*ir*-expressive, dance, creative" in contrast to the occupation *Ballet Dancer*, "*ir*-expressive, dance, reproductive" (or performing). Alternative groupings and assortments will be needed so that by consulting cross references it will be possible to find the occupation of ballet dancer also listed in the company of gymnast, athlete, lumberjack, stevedore and other occupations which in similar fashion provide intrinsically gratification of the need for vigorous physical activity.

CLINICAL PSYCHOLOGIST Turning from the arts, an analysis of this occupation might point up the following rewards: (a) Opportunity to assist in the healing of others, which places the occupation — along with medicine, dentistry, osteopathy, podiatry and chiropractic — in the palliative category, *i.e.*, "*ir*-palliative mental, reproductive" (or non-creative, inasmuch as techniques and procedures already established are being used). (b) Opportunity to teach the skills of the occupation to others, which places the occupation, together with all other teaching specialties, in the informative category, *i.e.*, "*ir*-informative, applicative" (or reproductive, in that what is being imparted is information acquired previously or by others rather than the results of one's own current original investigations). (c) Opportunity to engage in original research or investigation would locate the occupation, along with all other research specialities, in the inquisitive (or interrogative, or investigative) category, *i.e.*, "*ir*-investigative, scientific, social, applicative (or applied), behavioral, creative." Because the foregoing analysis is merely suggestive and illustrative rather than finished and definitive other intrinsic reward designations might be found to be preferable as the classification effort is improved and refined.

Super (1957, p. 313) asserts, "For the professional, work is its own reward . . . , for the semi-skilled, work is rewarding because it makes life possible. Stability for the professional is work-centered; stability for the semi-skilled is living-centered." Implicit in this contention is the hypothesis that for the worker at the semi-skilled and unskilled levels the principal gratifications in work are essentially extrinsic, *i.e.*, pleasant surroundings, affable associates, satisfactory remuneration, and reasonable hours. It would then follow that occupational description in terms of intrinsic reward has limited, or no applicability to occupations at the lower levels. Such an assumption is tested in an intrinsic reward analysis of the occupation of *Messenger-Delivery Boy* (dental laboratory).

The typical work duties of the delivery boy for a dental laboratory include calling for wax or plaster impressions of teeth at the offices of local dentists, transporting these impressions to the laboratory for processing, and returning the finished product to the office of the dentist. Except where special mailroom personnel is employed, the messenger also may be expected to devote part of his working time to packing, addressing and posting for shipment those completed articles that cannot be delivered personally.

Superficial intrinsic reward analysis of this occupation discloses at least the following gratifications inherent in the work: (a) Opportunity for gratification of the need for frequent change of the work environment. (b) Opportunity to gratify the need for at least limited personal contact with others. (c) Opportunity to gratify the need to master at least a limited and relatively simple body of knowledge (*i.e.*, postal zone rates, packing techniques, etc.) and to assume the meager responsibility attendant thereon.

With this in mind it now becomes possible to classify *Messenger-Delivery Boy* (dental laboratory) as "*ir*-sustentative (inasmuch as he sustains the efforts of the skilled and professional personnel of the laboratory), mobile, interpersonal" (or affiliative, or social, to indicate the interpersonal contact aspect of the occupation). This illustration, while admittedly brief and incomplete, is intended to demonstrate that at least in principle there need be no difficulty in constructing suitable intrinsic reward categories for use in classifying lower level occupations.

APPLICATION OF THE INTRINSIC REWARD SYSTEM

Application of the intrinsic reward scheme of occupational classification in personnel selection, placement and vocational counseling hinges upon the parallel development of similar procedures for assessing the vocational needs and expectations of the individual. This could be accomplished by means of appropriate adaptations of projective techniques, standardized interviews, or specially constructed questionnaires such as those used by Schaffer (1953). It might require the fresh invention of radically new techniques specifically designed to serve this purpose. In either case, the consequent matching of men and jobs with reference to the personal needs of the former and the intrinsic satisfactions inherent in the latter provides the vocational counseling movement with a psychodynamic approach to the successful meshing of the two.

IMPLICATIONS FOR RESEARCH

Using both the proposed intrinsic reward approach to occupational classification and the complementary technique of assessing and classifying individuals with respect to the gratifications they expect and desire from occupations, it should be possible to test the following hypotheses:

1. The more inclined the individual is to expect or demand extrinsic gratifications rather than intrinsic rewards from his work, the more likely he is to adapt himself with equal alacrity to a variety of different vocations and to experience equal satisfaction with most of them.

2. The more inclined the individual is to expect or demand intrinsic gratifications rather than extrinsic rewards from his work, the more likely he is to show himself adaptable only to a narrow range of occupations, or to a particular family of occupations, and the less apt is he to express satisfaction with any occupation not falling within the narrow range of his preference.

3. When both are satisfied in their occupational pursuits, the individual who receives intrinsic gratification from his work will experience more intense satisfaction than will the individual who seeks and obtains extrinsic gratification from his work.

4. When both are dissatisfied in their occupational pursuits, the individual who seeks but does not receive intrinsic reward from his work will experience stronger dissatisfaction than will the individual who seeks but does not receive adequate extrinsic gratification from his work.

5. Individuals suited by need and ability to enter higher level occupations will show themselves to be more inclined to seek intrinsic rewards from their work activities.

6. Individuals suited by need and ability to enter lower level occupations will show themselves more apt to seek extrinsic rewards from their work activities.

7. Intellectual differences will be found to be related to differences in the kind of vocational gratifications sought and expected. The higher his intelligence level, the more likely the individual will be to seek intrinsic satisfaction from his work.

8. Differences in individual and parental value systems will be found to be related to differences in the kind of vocational gratification sought and expected.

9. Social class, ethnic group, and perhaps racial differences will be found to be related to differences in vocational gratification expectations.

10. National differences will be found to be related to differences in vocational

gratification expectations only where the national differences reflect essential cultural differences. Nations that share a common cultural heritage as do the European nations, and more broadly the Western nations, will show little general significant difference among themselves with respect to vocational gratification expectations, but will differ appreciably in their vocational gratification expectations from the oriental nations. Westerners will show themselves to be more concerned with extrinsic rewards provided by work, whereas orientals will show greater interest in the intrinsic rewards inherent in work.

11. Nations with similar economic structures will show similar work gratification expectations, and will differ markedly in this dimension from nations with different economies. For example, industrialized nations will share a high common regard for the extrinsic gratifications provided by work, whereas agrarian and handicraft nations will share a high common interest in the intrinsic satisfactions available in work.

[1]Possibly it is this lack which is in part responsible for the distressingly ambiguous and often discrepant findings reported in studies investigating relationships between personality variables and aspects of vocational choice, achievement, and satisfaction (Super, 1957).

[2]Although the position taken in this paper recognizably will parallel in many respects that adopted by Schaffer (1953), the discussion

addresses itself to different issues than does his pioneering formulation.

[3]cf. Super's use of these terms (1957, p. 299).

[4]Variables such as opportunity for advancement, rate of advancement, salary, status, prestige, level of difficulty and level of complexity of work, as well as Schaffer's (1953) need areas of moral value scheme, affection and interpersonal relationships, dominance, recognition and approbation, economic security, independence, socioeconomic status, and dependance would, by this definition, be subsumed under the rubic of extrinsic satisfactions.

Illustrations of the variables to be subsumed under the rubric of intrinsic satisfactions will be presented in the main body of the text.

[5]Extrinsic rewards are ignored at this point because they are of no consequence in the system of occupational classification being developed here.

REFERENCES

Roe, Anne. A new classification of occupations. *J. counsel. Psychol.*, 1954, *1*, 215–220.

Roe, Anne. *The psychology of occupations.* New York: Wiley, 1956.

Schaffer, R. H. Job satisfaction as related to need satisfaction in work. *Psychol. Monogr.*, 1953, No. 364.

Shartle, C. L. *Occupational information.* Englewood Cliffs, N. J.: Prentice-Hall, 1952.

Super, D. E. *The psychology of careers.* New York: Harper, 1957.

United States Department of Labor. *Dictionary of occupational titles.* Washington: Government Printing Office, 1949.

The Functional Occupational Classification Structure

SIDNEY A. FINE, *W. E. Upjohn Institute for Employment Research*
CARL A. HEINZ, *United States Employment Service*

The new occupational classification structure of the United States Employment Service has begun to take shape [2, 8, 9]. It is exemplified by a three part, nine digit code. One part (three digits) classifies what workers do and reflects worker traits; a second classifies the work that gets done, that is, technologies; a third classifies materials, products, subject matter, and services, or what the jobs are mainly about. It is believed that this threefold approach to occupational classification will be equally useful in classifying job requirements and worker qualifications.

OBJECTIVES AND NEEDS

In its new occupational classification structure, the Employment Service wants a system that will effect the best use of the labor supply by exposing workers to the maximum number of jobs for which they can qualify and one that will make available for employer job orders the maximum number of qualified workers.

In addition, it is felt that the system should be:

1. *Simple:* Permit easy classification and coding of workers and quick location of their applications in the files.

Reprinted with the permission of the authors and publisher from *Personnel and Guidance Journal*, 1958, 37, 180–192.

2. *Communicable:* Easy to learn in a reasonably short training period.

3. *Adaptable:* Permit broad or narrow coding of workers' potential depending on the nature of the recruiting being carried on by employers.

4. *Flexible:* Allow for systematic addition of new classifications and removal of old without disturbing the coding system.

5. *Comparable:* The new system will have to provide for comparability with Census, Military, and ILO classifications for statistical purposes.

EIGHT COMPONENTS

In order for the new classification system truly to reflect "skills, knowledges, and abilities," it was determined that jobs should be analyzed according to the following eight components: Aptitudes; Interests; Temperaments; Physical Capacities; Working Conditions; Training Time; Industry; Work Performed.

The data developed on 4,000 jobs for all the components except Work Performed were published by the Bureau of Employment Security in 1956 as an interim source of occupational information [1, 7].

Although the data on Work Performed were not published, the principles determining the ratings on this component have been described in previous publications [3, 4, 6]. Samples of these ratings are shown in

TABLE 1

Work Performed Analysis of Selected Jobs

Job Title	Worker Functions	Work Field	MPSMS
Account-Classification Clerk	handling—COMPILING—taking instructions—helping	Accounting-Recording	Business Accounting
Airplane Hostess	manipulating—COMPILING—SERVING	Accommodating	Air Transportation Services
Airplane Pilot, Commercial	DRIVING-CONTROLLING—ANALYZING—speaking-signalling	Transporting	Air Transportation Services
Beauty Operator	PRECISION-WORKING—ANALYZING—SERVING	Accommodating	Beauty Services
Charge Floorman, Blast Furnace	DRIVING-CONTROLLING—comparing—taking instructions—helping	Melting	Metallic Minerals
Engineman	PRECISION-WORKING—ANALYZING—taking instructions-helping	Mechanical Fabricating-Installing	Aircraft and Parts
Plumber	PRECISION-WORKING—COMPILING—taking instructions—helping	Structural Fabricating-Installing	Plumbing and Heating Equipment

Table 1. Tables, 2, 3, and 4 show the Structure of Worker Functions, List of Work Fields, and a sample of the listing for Materials, Products, Subject Matter, and Services (hereafter referred to by the initials MPSMS) on the basis of which the ratings were made.

THEORY OF WORK PERFORMED

The theoretical approach to the Work Performed ratings is as follows: In order to understand the work performed on a job it is necessary to understand that what gets done is quite distinct from what the worker does, and both relate to a specific content. What workers do is done at various levels of complexity in relation to Things, Data, and People. All jobs involve some relation to all three. The ways in which workers function in relation to Things, Data, and People are unique and can be expressed in terms of separate hierarchies. In each hierarchy, the

functions proceed from the simple to the complex with each successive function conceived as including the simpler ones and excluding the more complex ones. Thus by selecting the appropriate function from each of the three hierarchies that describes what the worker does in a given job-worker situation, it is possible to show the totality of the worker's relationships to Things, Data, and People. The adopted sequence with which these functions are presented for a job is as in Table 1. Thus in the case of Account-Classification Clerk the functional relationship to Things is "Handling," the simplest in the hierarchy; the relationship to Data is "Compiling," occurring about the middle of the hierarchy; and the relationship to People, "Taking Instructions-Helping," is again the simplest in its hierarchy. Lower case and upper case are used in the present paper to show emphasis. In the original rating, the analysts distributed a total weight of 10 to all three functions to indicate relative importance of the functions.

Thus for the Account-Classification Clerk in Table 1 the weights assigned were 1-7-2. These weights explain why Compiling is in capitals and the other functions in lower case.[1]

The work that gets done is Accounting-Recording. The Work Field refers to the complex of specific methods, end results, and machines, tools, equipment, and work aids by which the worker functions as he does and is defined as below.

Definition of Work Field

RIVETING — 073

Fastening together parts by fitting a headed, malleable bolt, pin, or rod through previously bored holes and then hammering or pressing the shank end to form another head. Distinguish from fastening paper or similar light materials with paper "rivets," eyelets, grommets, or the like (*Folding-Fastening*).

Method Verbs	Explanatory Verbs	Misc. End Result Verbs
Bucking	Assembling	Attaching
Clinching	Fastening	Expanding
Dimpling	Joining	Flattening
Driving	Securing	Forming
Hammering	Uniting	Shaping
Squeezing		Spreading
Striking		

MACHINES, TOOLS, EQUIPMENT, AND WORK AIDS

Machines	Tools	Equipment	Work Aids
Combination	Air Hammer		Rivet
Pneumatic	Chisel		Collar
Riveting-and-	Compressed-		Rivets
Dimpling	Air Hold-		
Machine	ing-On-Tool		
Forming Press	Dolly Bar		
Pinch Riveter	Hammer,		
Pneumatic	Hand		
Hammer	Riveting		
Pneumatic Rivet	Hammer,		
Squeezer,	Portable		
Portable	Rivet Set		

Machines	Tools	Equipment	Work Aids
Riveting Machine	Rivet Set, Hand Sledge		

Note: Other Work Fields commonly or typically occurring in job definitions with the above-defined Work Field are: *Appraising, Bolting-Screwing, Boring, Heat Conditioning, Loading-Moving, Pressing-Forging.* In listing these, it is not intended to assert occupational similarity, although relationships may exist in varying degrees.

Finally, this work is most concerned with Business Accounting which thus designated (in this case a service) completes the analysis of Work Performed. Although each of the three parts of Work Performed is independently classified, each relates to Things, Data, and People in a different way and thus complements the others. Together, they are intended to provide a rather sharp focus on the level and technological area of functioning and knowledge involved.

A THREE PART CODE

A job-worker situation according to the system implicit in this new structure will have a three part, nine digit code.

Thus for the jobs in Table 1, the codes will be as follows:

Account-Classification Clerk	cNr–232–892
Airplane Hostess	fNS–291–857
Airplane Pilot, Commercial	HOt–013–857
Beauty Operator	IOS–291–901
Charge Floorman, Blast Furnace	Hlr–131–350
Engineman	IOr–121–572
Plumber	INr–101–544

Following the brief theoretical discussion above, the first part of the code reflecting Worker Functions (what the worker does) is made up of letters indicating the level of functioning and relative involvement of the worker with Things, Data, and People. In the case of Plumber, this part of the code "I" for Things, "N" for Data, and "r" for People tells us that this job-worker situation involves primarily Precision-Working and Compiling but also Taking Instructions-Helping. In the case of the Account-Classification Clerk, the code tells us that this job-worker situation is primarily Compiling but also Handling and Taking Instructions-Helping. Using Table 2, the reader can now interpret the Worker Functions for any of the other jobs.[2]

The second part of the code consists of three digits ranging from 000 through 299. It represents the Work Field as listed in Table 3.

The third part of the code also consists of three digits ranging from 300 through 999.[3] It represents the Material, Product (also Machine or Equipment), Subject Matter, or Service with which worker and technology are primarily involved. Table 4 shows the source of this code. This listing was developed from the Standard Industrial Classification of the Bureau of the Budget, The National Register of Scientific and Technical Personnel, and experience in rating the 4,000 jobs. As will be noted, these items are organized in groups of 10. The first item, ending in 0, is the general category for the group; items ending 1 through 8 are the specifics; and the items ending in 9 are "not elsewhere classified" or "miscellaneous" category for the group.

TABLE 2

Structure of Worker Functions*

Things	Data	People
	A Observing	
	B Learning	
C Handling	K Comparing	R Taking Instructions-Helping
D Feeding-Offbearing	L Copying	S Serving
E Tending	M Computing	T Speaking-Signalling
F Manipulating	N Compiling	U Persuading, V Diverting
G Operating-Controlling	O Analyzing	W Supervising, X Instructing
H Driving-Controlling	P Coordinating	Y Negotiating
I Precision Working	Q Synthesizing	Z Mentoring
J Setting Up		

Notes:

1. Each successive function reading down includes all those that precede it.

2. Feeding-Offbearing and Tending, Operating-Controlling and Driving-Controlling, and setting Up are special cases involving machines and equipment of Handling, Manipulating, and Precision Working respectively and hence are indented under them.

3. The hyphenated factors Feeding-Offbearing, Operating-Controlling, Driving-Controlling, Taking Instructions-Helping and Speaking-Signalling are single functions.

4. The factors separated by a comma are separate functions on the same level separately defined. They are on the same level because, although excluded from the one above it, usually one or the other and not both are included in the one below.

*Definitions for these functions available on request. They appeared in full in [2].

In effect, these are three separate classifications. However, they are not independent since the best understanding of each part of the code can be had only by keeping the three parts together. The need for the linking together is inherent in the concept of a job-worker situation as a dynamic and complex entity produced by the coordinates of three dimensions.

1. Worker Functions (what worker does in relation to Things, Data, People)

Information: Aptitudes, Interest, Temperaments, General Educational Development.

2. Work Fields (work that needs to be done)

Information: Machines, Tools, Equipment, Work Aids and end result when considered in conjunction with MPSMS.

3. Material, Product, Subject Matter, Service (MPSMS)

Information: Most relevant job content.

TABLE 3
Work Fields

001 — HUNTING-FISHING	091 — MASONING
002 — LOGGING	092 — LAYING
003 — CROPPING	093 — TROWELING
004 — MINING-QUARRYING-EARTH BORING	094 — CALKING
005 — BLASTING	
	101 — STRUCTURAL FABRICATING-INSTALLING
011 — LOADING-MOVING	102 — UPHOLSTERING
012 — HOISTING-CONVEYING	
013 — TRANSPORTING	111 — ELECTRICAL FABRICATING-INSTALLING
014 — PUMPING	112 — ELECTRONIC FABRICATING-INSTALLING
	121 — MECHANICAL FABRICATING-INSTALLING
021 — STATIONARY ENGINEERING	
	131 — MELTING
031 — CLEANING	132 — CASTING
032 — IRONING	133 — HEAT CONDITIONING
033 — LUBRICATING	134 — PRESSING-FORGING
	135 — DIE SIZING
041 — FILLING	136 — MOLDING
042 — PACKING	
043 — WRAPPING	141 — BAKING-DRYING
	142 — CRUSHING
051 — ABRADING	143 — MIXING
052 — CHIPPING	144 — DISTILLING
053 — BORING	145 — FILTERING-STRAINING-SEPARATING
054 — SHEARING-SHAVING	146 — COOKING-FOOD PREPARING
055 — MILLING-TURNING-PLANING	147 — PROCESSING-COMPOUNDING
056 — SAWING	
057 — MACHINING	151 — IMMERSING-COATING
	152 — SATURATING
061 — FITTING-PLACING	153 — BRUSHING-SPRAYING
062 — FOLDING-FASTENING	154 — ELECTROPLATING
063 — GLUING	
	161 — COMBING-NAPPING
071 — BOLTING-SCREWING	162 — SPINNING
072 — NAILING	163 — WINDING
073 — RIVETING	164 — WEAVING
	165 — KNITTING
081 — WELDING	
082 — FLAME CUTTING	171 — SEWING-TAILORING
083 — SOLDERING	

TABLE 3 (Cont.)

181 — ERODING	244 — ENGINEERING
182 — ETCHING	251 — RESEARCHING
183 — ENGRAVING	
	261 — WRITING
191 — PRINTING	262 — PAINTING
192 — IMPRINTING	263 — COMPOSING
	264 — STYLING
201 — PHOTOGRAPHING	
202 — DEVELOPING-PRINTING	271 — INVESTIGATING
	272 — LITIGATING
211 — APPRAISING	
212 — WEIGHING	281 — SYSTEM COMMUNICATING
221 — STOCK-CHECKING	291 — ACCOMMODATING
	292 — MERCHANDISING
231 — RECORDING	293 — PROTECTING
232 — ACCOUNTING-RECORDING	294 — HEALING-CARING
	295 — ADMINISTERING
241 — LAYING OUT	296 — TEACHING
242 — DRAFTING	297 — ENTERTAINING
243 — SURVEYING	

Thus, suppose the MPSMS part of the code is for aircraft engines. The three codes in Table 5 show the varying significance of this item.

Similar interdependence can be shown for the other two parts of the code [5]. Thus we have here a three dimensional system requiring the coordinates of all three dimensions properly to define and comprehend any specific job-worker situation.

THE SEARCH FOR GROUPS

Originally it was felt that sorting the ratings of the eight components according to patterns of similar requirements would produce groupings which would suggest a structure. Sorting the data in various combinations did indeed yield groupings. As expected, however, the groupings produced by sorting first for Aptitudes were not the same as those produced by sorting first for Physical Capacities or Interests. Each component had its own contribution to make and it was necessary to find a sort that would give an optimum grouping of the information

consistent with the systematic objectives outlined above.

The grouping and structural principles that came closest to doing this were those inherent in the Work Performed component, expecially the Structure of Worker Functions. In short, it was found generally true that jobs having common worker function patterns had, within reasonable ranges, common patterns of Aptitudes, Interests, Temperaments, General Educational Development, and to a lesser extent Specific Vocational Preparation. Physical Capacities and Working Conditions were not grouped by this approach.

Analysis of why the Worker Functions patterns should yield what appears to be groupings with optimum integration of worker trait information suggests that just as certain functions are peculiar to Things, to Data, and to People, similarly certain combinations of traits are primarily concerned with each of these three areas of activity. Since both functions and traits, particularly Training Time and Aptitudes, have scaling built into them, systematic changes in one are associated with changes in the other.

TABLE 4

Sample Section of Materials, Products, Subject Matter, and Services Classification*

080 FOOD STAPLES
081 Grain Mill Products
082 Meat Products, including Sea Food and Poultry
083 Dairy Products (Milk, Butter, Ice Cream and Cheese)
084 Bakery Products
085 Oils and Fats, Edible (Margarine, Shortening, Table Oils, etc.)
086 Sugar and Syrup (Cane, Beet, Maple Syrup, etc.)
087 Canned, Bottled, Frozen and otherwise-Preserved Foods
088
089 Food Staples, not elsewhere classified
140 LUMBER AND WOOD PRODUCTS
141 Logs, Rough Lumber, and Fuel Wood
142 Finished Lumber, Treated Wood, Shingles, and Cooperage Stock
143 Plywood and Veneer (Marquetry)
144 Prefabricated Wooden Buildings and Structural Members, Including Partitions (Stage Settings, except Scenery)
145 Millwork (Window and Door Frames; Doors; Mantels; Panel Work; Stairways; and Shutters)
146 Wood Fixtures (Shelving; Cabinets; Bar Fixtures; Butchers' Fixtures; Lockers; Display Cases, Racks, and Stands; and Telephone Booths)

TABLE 4 (Cont.)

147 Wooden Containers (Baskets; Laundry Hampers; Cigar Boxes; Crates; Cases; Shipping Drums; Barrels; Kegs, Box Shooks; and Wooden Trunk Slats)
148 Wooden Articles (Shoe Lasts; Hat Blocks; Mirror and Picture Frames; Kitchen Woodenware; Pipes; Toys; Pencils; Curtain Rods; Golf Clubs)
149 Lumber and Wood Products, not elsewhere classified (Excelsior; Caskets; Window and Door Screens and Weather Strip, Cork Products, etc.)
770 PERSONAL SERVICES
771 Barbering Services; Beauty Services
772 Lodging Services
773 Meal Services (Including both Food and Beverages; also Catering) except Domestic
774 Valet Services (Pressing, Alteration, Garment Repair; Shoe Repair, Shoe Shine, Hat Cleaning)
775 Laundry and Dry Cleaning Services
776 Child and Adult Care
777 Photographic Services
778
779 Personal Services, not elsewhere classified (Funeral Services; and Porter Services; Social Escort Services; Clothing Rental; Steam Baths)

*The final code numbers will run from 300 to 999.

TABLE 5

Varying Significance of Same Knowledge Area Code for Three Jobs

Job Title	Worker Functions	Work Field	MPSMS
Engine-Installation-Assembler Helper	Clr HANDLING—comparing—taking instructions —helping	121 Mechanical Fabricating-Installing	572 Aircraft and Parts
Engineman	IOr PRECISION-WORKING —ANALYZING—taking instructions—helping	121 Mechanical Fabricating-Installing	572 Aircraft and Parts
Salesman, Aircraft Engines	cNU handling—COMPILING —PERSUADING	292 Merchandising	572 Aircraft and Parts

When the Work Field and MPSMS designations are added to the Worker Function patterns, this tends to crystallize the essential nature of a group of jobs. In fact it becomes possible almost to guess some of the job titles from this threefold analysis. Hence the three parts of Work Performed are used as the basis for the proposed classification structure.

THE RESULTING STRUCTURES

In effect, the method of classifying jobs proposed produces several structures. Since each part of the three part code represents a different essential characteristic, it is possible to arrange jobs in a variety of ways. However, two arrangements are being considered initially by the Employment Service to determine their utility in meeting placement, counseling, and reporting needs.

Structure A (Table 8): This is an arrangement primarily by Worker Functions, with sub-groups by Work Fields and MPSMS. It is most directly relatable to an individual's potential in the areas of Aptitudes, Interests, Temperaments, and General Educational Development, suggesting that its main usefulness may be in counseling.

There are seven major groups in this arrangement, as shown in Table 6. These major groups, besides having widely different numbers of jobs, have varying numbers of sub-groups (see Table 6) ranging from simple and limited functional involvement to complex and major functional involve-

Table 6

Major Classification Group by Primary Worker Function Involvement Showing Sub-Groups and Number of Jobs in Major Groups (in Round Numbers)

Major Groups	Sub-Groups	No. of Jobs
Things	10	2,400
Data	20	300
People	6	90

Table 6 (cont.)

Major Groups	Sub-Groups	No. of Jobs
Things-Data	31	800
Data-People	35	200
People-Things	3	10
Things-Data-People	25	200
TOTAL	130	4,000

ment. Table 7 gives the Worker Function patterns and number of jobs for each of the sub-groups in the Things major group. The relative simplicity or complexity of the pattern is determined by the position of the primary functions in the Structure of Worker Functions — Table 2. It should be noted that the three functions of a pattern spell out the full scope of the demands of the job — what is included as well as excluded.

At present the emphasis is on differentiation. It may be that for practical purposes some groups with very few jobs, despite significant difference in trait requirements, will be consolidated.

In Table 8 is a partial illustrative listing (based on the 4,000) of one of the groups as it might appear in the final structure. Volume II and Part IV codes of the *Dictionary of Occupational Titles* are shown here only so that they may be compared with this new arrangement. Each such group will be preceded by a descriptive statement and profile summarizing the nature of the group. It has not been determined how these statements will be integrated in the final format.

As noted, each Worker Function group is divided first by Work Fields and then by MPSMS. These same Work Fields and MPSMS categories will appear in other Worker Function groups. However, since both the Work Fields and MPSMS also reflect varying involvements with Things, Data, and People, there are some rather systematic associations. For example, a Worker Function group predominantly concerned with People and Data will show such Work Fields as Researching, Healing-

TABLE 7

Worker Function Sub-Groups of the THINGS Major Group

			No. of Jobs
LEARNING	comparing computing	Speaking-Signalling	30
HANDLING	comparing	Taking Instructions-Helping Speaking-Signalling	430
FEEDING-OFFBEARING	comparing	Taking Instructions-Helping Speaking-Signalling	130
TENDING	comparing	Taking Instructions-Helping Speaking-Signalling	360
MANIPULATING	comparing	Taking Instructions-Helping Speaking-Signalling	380
OPERATING-CONTROLLING	copying comparing	Taking Instructions-Helping Speaking-Signalling	350
OPERATING-CONTROLLING	computing compiling	Taking Instructions-Helping Speaking-Signalling	270
DRIVING-CONTROLLING	comparing	Taking Instructions-Helping Speaking-Signalling	100
PRECISION-WORKING	comparing	Taking Instructions-Helping Speaking-Signalling	150
PRECISION-WORKING	computing compiling	Taking Instructions-Helping Speaking-Signalling	200
TOTAL			2,400

TABLE 8

SAMPLE OF STRUCTURE A — Jobs Primarily Involved With THINGS

Glr *t*	*G* *OPERATING-CONTROLLING*	*k* *Comparing*	*r, t* *Taking Instructions- Helping Speaking-Signalling*	
			Vol. II Code	*Part IV Code*
Work Field	*Materials, Products, and Subject Matter*			
Mining-Quarrying- Earth Boring 004	*Petroleum* DERRICKMAN (petrol. production) I		5-20.825	4-x2.494
	Coal CHAIN-MACHINE OPERATOR (bit. coal mining)		5-21.210	4-x2.494
	RADIAL MACHINE MAN (bit. coal mining)		5-21.210	4-x2.494
	SUMPER (bit. coal mining)		5-21.210	4-x2.494
Hoisting-Conveying 012 Pumping	*Coal* LOADER, MACHINE (anth. coal mining) *Petroleum*		7-21.410	6-x2.493

TABLE 8 (Cont.)

Glr t	G OPERATING-CONTROLLING	k Comparing	r, t Taking Instructions- Helping Speaking-Signalling	
			Vol. II Code	Part IV Code
	Work Field	Materials Products, and Subject Matter		
014	JACK-LINE MAN (petrol. production)		7-72.570	4-x2.102
	Electric Power and Light			
	SUBSTATION OPERATOR (light, heat, and power)		5-51.210	4-x6.188
	Gas Supply			
	GAS-PUMPING-STATION OPERATOR (light, heat, and power)		5-72.580	4-x2.102
	ODORIZATION MAN (light, heat, and power)		7-54.515	6-x4.601
	Water Supply and Irrigation			
	DAM MAN (petrol. refin.)		7-54.610	4-x2.102
	Chemicals, Inorganic and Organic			
	PUMPMAN, GAS PLANT (light, heat, and power)		5-72.925	4-x2.012
	Acids			
	ACID PATROLMAN (rayon and allied prod.)		4-51.030	4-x6.641
Stationary Engineering 021	*General Industrial Machinery, Prime Movers and Equipment Except Electrical*			
	COAL SHOOTER (any ind.)		7-54.711	6-x2.493
	COAL-SUBSTATION ATTENDANT (any ind.)		7-54.713	6-x2.608
	STATIONARY ENGINEER (any ind.)		5-72.010	4-x2.102
	Engine and Turbines			
	BREAKER ENGINEER (anth. coal mining)		5-72.010	4-x2.102
	DIESEL ENGINE OPERATOR, STATIONARY (any ind.)		5-72.210	4-x2.102
	ENGINEER (fish.)		0-88.25	4-x2.102
	GAS-ENGINE OPERATOR (any ind.)		5-72.945	4-x2.103
	ROTARY-RIG ENGINEMAN (petrol. production)		5-72.915	4-x2.100
	TIPPLE ENGINEER (bit. coal mining)		5-72.010	4-x2.102
	TURBINE OPERATOR (light, heat, and power)		5-51.102	4-x2.102
	WASHERY ENGINEER (anth. coal mining)		5-72.010	4-x2.102
	Pumps, Air and Gas Compressors, and Pumping Equipment			
	AIR-COMPRESSOR OPERATOR (any ind.)		7-72.580	4-x2.102
	AIR-COMPRESSOR-STATION ENGINEER (petrol. refin.)		5-72.944	4-x2.102
	COMPRESSOR OPERATOR (chem.)		5-72.924	4-x2.102
	GAS COMPRESSOR OPERATOR (any ind.)		5-72.920	4-x6.493
	GAS-LIFT ENGINEER (petrol. production)		5,72-920	4-x2.102
	GASOLINE-PLANT ENGINEER (petrol. production)		5-72.920	4-x6.693
	Blowers, Exhaust and Ventilating Fans			
	FAN ENGINEER (anth. coal mining; bit. coal mining)		5-72.010	4-x2.102
	Refrigeration Machinery and Air Conditioning Units			
	HUMIDIFIER ATTENDANT (textile; tobacco)		7-72.410	4-x2.102
	Electrical Motors, Generators, and Parts			
	POWERMAN (tel. and tel.) I		5-51.510	4-x6.188
	SWITCHBOARD OPERATOR (light, heat, and power)		5-51.130	4-x6.188

TABLE 9

SAMPLE OF STRUCTURE B — 021 Stationary Engineering

Producing and/or distributing heat, power, or conditioned air.

E — TENDING

285 — Domestic Steam and Hot-Water Heating Apparatus
021-Elr-285
    FIREMAN, LOW PRESSURE (any ind.)
307 — Industrial Boilers, Furnaces, and Ovens
021-Elr-307
    FIREMAN, TIPPLE (bit. coal mining)

G — OPERATING-CONTROLLING
302 — Engines and Turbines
021-Glr-302
    HOT MILL ENGINEER (iron & steel)
305 — Pumps, Air and Gas Compressors, Pumping Equipment
021-Glr-305
    COMPRESSOR ENGINEER, CAISSON (const.)
307 — Industrial Boilers, Furnaces, and Ovens
021-Glr-307
    FIREMAN, FAN (bit. coal mining)
333 — Electrical Motors, Generators, and Parts
021-Glr-333
    ENGINEMAN (any ind.) I
300 — General Industrial Machinery, Prime Movers and Equipment, Except Electrical
021-Gmr-300
    COAL SUBSTATION ATTENDANT (any ind.)
302 — Engines and Turbines
021-Gmr-302
    BREAKER ENGINEER (any ind.)
    TIPPLE ENGINEER (bit. coal mining)
    WASHERY ENGINEER (anth. coal mining)
305 — Pumps, Air and Gas Compressors, and Pumping Equipment
021 Gmr-305
    AIR-COMPRESSOR OPERATOR (any ind.)
    AIR-COMPRESSOR STATION ENGINEER (petrol. refin.)
    COMPRESSOR OPERATOR (chem.)
    GAS-LIFT ENGINEER (petrol. production)
    GASOLINE-PLANT ENGINEER (petrol. production)

306 — Blowers, Exhaust and Ventilating Fans
021-Gmr-306
    FAN ENGINEER (anth. coal mining; bit. coal mining)
305 — Pumps, Air and Gas Compressors, and Pumping Equipment
021-Gmt-305
    GAS-COMPRESSOR OPERATOR (any ind.)
300 — General Industrial Machinery, Prime Movers and Equipment, Except Electrical
021-Gnr-300
    COAL SHOOTER (any ind.)
    STATIONARY ENGINEER (any ind.)
302 — Engines and Turbines
021-Gnr-302
    DIESEL-ENGINE OPERATOR, STATIONARY (any ind.)
    ENGINEER (fish.)
308 — Refrigeration Machinery and Air-Conditioning Units
021-Gnr-308
    HUMIDIFIER ATTENDANT textile; tobacco)
333 — Electrical Motors, Generators, and Parts
021-Gnr-333
    POWERMAN (tel & tel.) I
    SWITCHBOARD OPERATOR (light, heat & power)
302 — Engines and Turbines
021-Got-302
    GAS-ENGINE OPERATOR (any ind.)
    ROTARY-RIG ENGINEMAN (petrol. production)
021-Gnt-302
    TURBINE OPERATOR (light, heat & power)

BO — LEARNING — ANALYZING
300 — General Industrial Machinery, Prime Movers and Equipment, Except Electrical
021-BOt-300
    CADET ENGINEER (water trans.)

CO — HANDLING — ANALYZING
330 — Electrical Machinery, Equipment, and Supplies
021-COt-330
    POWERHOUSE RUNNER (light, heat & power)

GO — OPERATING-CONTROLLING — ANALYZING

TABLE 9 (Cont.)

307 — Industrial Boilers, Furnaces, and Ovens	021-gPt-330
021-GOr-307	SYSTEM OPERATOR (light, heat, & power)
BOILER OPERATOR (any ind.)II	IO — PRECISION-WORKING — ANALYZING
GP — OPERATING-CONTROLLING — COORDINATING	300 — General Industrial Machinery, Prime Movers and Equipment, Except Electrical
330 — Electrical Machinery, Equipment, and Supplies	021-IOr-300
	MAINTENANCE ENGINEER (any ind.) I

Caring, Administering, and Teaching. These Work Fields are not likely to show up under the Things major group.

Structure B (Table 9): This arrangement is primarily by Work Fields, with sub-groups by Worker Functions, and MPSMS. It is most directly relatable to the technological area and level in which a worker has his major experience. Thus it may be most useful in placement of the experienced.

There are 95 such Work Fields. These are grouped by the coding system according to 30 areas of major technological relationships.

The incomplete listing for Stationary Engineering shows how this grouping might appear in a classification arrangement. As will be noted, it is particularly useful in understanding how a technology of a certain type (a) cuts across industrial lines and (b) calls for various levels of complexity at different times and places. Because of these reasons it is also particularly useful for study of the functional composition of an industry and the technological distribution of workers in a community.

APPLICATIONS

Let us examine this new classification approach with regard to the criteria set out at the start of this paper.

1. *Does this system permit easy classification and coding of workers and quick location of their applications in the files? Is it simple?*

At present it is necessary to go to the *DOT* in order to classify workers. It is necessary to locate first the title and then the description which most adequately fits the experience of the worker in order to obtain an appropriate code. Where such a description cannot be found, a tentative code needs to be assigned.

It may still be desirable to have such a system, or modification of it, particularly to locate information about jobs. However, such a system may not be necessary to classify and code workers. Instead, a coding folder containing the equivalent of Tables 2, 3, and 4 — namely, The Structure of Worker Functions, Work Fields, and MPSMS — may be all that is necessary. Using this coding folder, appropriate codes can be assigned from these lists by the interviewer after determining the appropriate area and levels at which the worker has been engaged. The job-worker situation may not be described in the *DOT*, but still it can be coded and made accessible in the files. For example, suppose a worker states he has been generating power (Work Field — Stationary Engineering) by Operating-Controlling (Primary Worker Function Involvement) a nuclear reactor (MPSMS). The coverage in the *DOT* may well include the Work Field and the Worker Function but not the MPSMS. However the appropriate three digit category in MPSMS is available (power generating equipment). Even if nuclear reactor is lacking as a specific, the three digit code ending in 9 can be assigned indicating this. The specific nuclear reactor can be added or may even be retained in the category ending in 9.

Inexperienced workers can be coded in terms of their potential as determined by interview. These codes utilize the same coding system except that some device, such as encircling the code, may be used to designate potential rather than experience. If only background information, such as schooling and test results, is available and inadequate interest, knowledge, or casual experience information is obtained, then it may be that only a Worker Function code can be assigned. Sometimes it may be possible to assign only one or another of the Work Field or MPSMS classifications depending on the information obtained. In these cases, such partial coding can help identify the placement problem.

In other instances, the potential of the inexperienced worker will warrant a code for a higher level training time job than is feasible for initial employability. In such instances, it would be desirable to assign the most reasonable code, properly indicating that it represents potential, and an additional related code reflecting entry opportunities necessary to attain goals.

A similar procedure may be useful in coding the untapped potential of experienced workers. They can be assigned a code to reflect their highest potential as well as their experience code, and this separate card can be filed in its appropriate place. Many approaches are possible to deal with the filing problem and possibly more than one will have to be used to meet varying circumstances. It seems clear from the foregoing that no single code, even the proposed three part, nine digit code, can express every person's complete vocational potential. The proposed code does relate a worker's experience or potential to the broadest area of qualification *for a single code*. However, where an individual worker has a potential that ranges over more than one Work Field (and perhaps broadly different ones), more than one major category of MPSMS, and entirely different emphases in Worker Functions, then several code numbers may be necessary.

Where only one card is used, some type of edge sorting device (as used in the Armed Services during the war) providing place for several codes can be used. Another approach may be the use of duplicate cards with the duplicates filed according to additional codes. For large offices, it may be practical to experiment with punched card machine sorting systems. Very effective methods have been devised by the Armed Services for keeping such systems up to date with a minimum of effort and clerical error.

2. *Is this classification system easy to learn in a reasonably short training period?*

This is difficult to ascertain prior to tryout. However, various types of orientation experience indicate that a single week of training including demonstration and exercise would be adequate, provided there has been previous training (now one week — 30 hours) in the Worker Traits part of the system. Selected individuals in government and private industry have been trained in brief periods with good results.

3. *Is this adaptable to broad or narrow coding of worker's potential?*

It is possible to use as much of the code as is called for by job orders. If an employer stresses simply type of person, usually for entry purposes, then it is possible to search the files only for Worker Function pattern. If he stresses Work Field experience or Subject Matter, then these codes can be searched. An employer's approach might vary not only with labor market conditions but with his needs for different kinds of jobs. Thus, the three part code, each part representing possibly varying needs, can serve an essential purpose in the placement process.

As noted in (1), ability to code a worker may vary with the amount of information available or obtainable. However, as a minimum it should be possible to classify and code a worker's functional potential for immediate employability.

4. *Will the system permit the addition of new and the dropping of old codes without disturbing the coding pattern?*

This will be completely possible since the proposed code is not sequential, that is, in series. It is a functional code reflecting information as it is obtained. The number of combinations and permutations is very much larger than the contemplated use. The coding of 4,000 jobs has developed most possibilities, leaving plenty of room for more.

5. *Will the system be comparable with other classification systems?*

Explorations in this area are in their early stages. However, a few observations can be made regarding the initial direction of our work.

The present two broad classifications most widely used to report trends, employment, and unemployment are the Census and *Dictionary of Occupational Titles*. The major groups for these two systems are listed below.

Census	DOT
0 Professional	0 Professional and Managerial occupations
1 Farmers	1 Clerical and Sales occupations
2 Managers	2 Service occupations
3 Clerical	3 Agricultural, Fishery, Forestry, and Kindred occupations
4 Sales	4 Skilled occupations
5 Craftsmen	5 Skilled occupations
6 Operatives	6 Semiskilled occupations
7 Service	7 Semiskilled occupations
8 & 9 Laborers	8 Unskilled occupations
	9 Unskilled occupations

These systems try to do two things at the same time — namely, reflect level of difficulty and type of work. For this purpose they use common terms that have socio-economic status connotations which tend to confuse the results of statistical reports. For example, should technicians be regarded as "skilled" or "craftsmen" or should they be regarded as "semiprofessional?" Their place should be established on the basis of the relative difficulty of the work, the training involved, and the need for this type of worker. The status question as to whether they are skilled or professional is important to the individual but is not material to an understanding of the manpower problem involved.

By means of the Scale of General Educational Development, all jobs can be placed in relation to each other according to a single scale of difficulty. There are six such levels.[4] The "Reasoning Development" part of this scale is shown as below.[5]

1. Apply principles of logical or scientific thinking to a wide range of intellectual and practical problems. Deal with non-verbal symbolism (formulas, scientific equations, graphs, musical notes, etc.) in its most difficult phases. Deal with a variety of abstract and concrete variables. Comprehend the most abstruse classes of concepts.

2. Apply principles of logical or scientific thinking to define problems, collect data, establish facts, and draw valid conclusions. Interpret an extensive variety of technical instructions, in books, manuals, mathematical, or diagrammatic form. Deal with several abstract and concrete variables.

3. Apply principles of rational systems[6] to solve practical problems. Interpret a variety of instructions furnished in written, oral, diagrammatic, or schedule form. Deal with a variety of concrete variables.

4. Apply common sense understanding to carry out instructions furnished in written, oral, or diagrammatic form. Deal with problems involving several concrete variables.

5. Apply common sense understanding to carry out detailed but uninvolved written or oral instructions. Deal with problems involving a few concrete variables.

6. Apply common sense understanding to carry out very simple instructions containing no more than two steps. Deal with standardized situations involving no more than two occasional variables.

The seven major groups on the horizontal coordinate delineate the types of work. No class names having "status" implications are used. The exploratory work now going on, with indications of favorable results, will apportion the various Worker Function patterns (about 130) to the levels of difficulty in advance, so that the reporting place of a job will be immediately apparent. For example, all jobs having the Worker Function patterns Glr, GMt, gMr, gMT, glT, GMT although falling in different major groups from the standpoint of their involvement with Things, Data, and People, would all be on the same level. Jobs involving such patterns are:

Profiling-Machine   Operator   (mach. shop) II
Fireman, Bisque Kiln (pottery & porc.)
Account Checker (clerical)
Cashier (clerical) I
Telephone Operator (clerical) I
Grocery Checker (ret. tr.)

WORK TO BE DONE

The immediate activities ahead are three-fold: (a) examination of the system by professional personnel to determine its soundness in relation to operating and over-all manpower needs, (b) try-out of the system in selected local employment offices under operating conditions, and (c) incorporation of the remaining 18,000 jobs (for which the ratings have already been made) into the system.

Many areas need to be investigated. Only a few can be mentioned here.

1. Is the conception of a job implicit in the Work Performed component acceptable? Such a conception may result in the recognition of considerably fewer than the present estimated "35,000" jobs in the American economy.

2. Are the present Worker Functions, Work Fields, and MPSMS categories adequate for special classification problems? Armed Services explorations to adapt these concepts to their systems could add materially to our understanding of them. In addition it would be helpful to get some thorough examination of the system by some industrial personnel offices.

3. Extensive research seems warranted as to the relation between the Worker Function patterns and trait data. The advantages of additional positive findings in this area, even to a limited extent, would help considerably in establishing patterns of traits rather than components as the basis for selection and placement.

[1] The same procedure is followed in the coding. Capital letters show primary involvement, lower case secondary or negligible involvement. Capital and lower case reflect the weight distributions.

[2] It should be noted that the first place of this code runs from C to J, the second place from K to Q, the third place from R to Z. B for Learning can appear in any of the three columns; A for Observing is not used in coding job-worker situations.

[3] This code frequently overlaps with industrial designation particularly where industries are designated by specific materials, products, or services, and with titles in the case of subject matter. Sometimes, for some of the crafts it overlaps with the Work Field.

[4] The original scale contains seven levels. The last two levels have been combined for this reporting purpose.

[5] There are two other parallel scales, one for mathematical development and one for language development, which are used to help place a job on its proper level.

[6] Examples of "principles of rational systems" are: bookkeeping, internal combustion engines, electric wiring systems, house building, nursing, farm management, ship sailing.

REFERENCES

1. Estimates of worker trait requirements for 4,000 jobs as defined in the *Dictionary of occupational titles*. Washington, D. C.: Department of Labor, Bureau of Employment Security, 1956.

2. Fine, S. A. A pilot study to develop a functional classification structure of occupations. Paper read at APA Convention, Chicago, Sept., 1951.

3. Fine, S. A. Functional job analysis. Paper read at APA Convention, New York, Sept., 1954. Also, *Personnel Admin. & Industr. Relat.*, Spring, 1955.

4. Fine, S. A. A structure of worker functions. *Personnel Guid. J.*, 1955 *34*, 66–73.

5. Fine, S. A. A re-examination of transferability of skills I & II. *Monthly Labor Rev.*, July & August, 1957.

6. Fine, S. A., and Newman, J. A note on Thorndike's preference blank for psychologists. *Amer. Psychologist*, July, 1956.

7. Fine, S. A., and Heinz, C. A. The estimates of worker trait requirements for 4,000 jobs. *Personnel Guid. J.*, 1957, *36*, 168–174.

8. Studdiford, W. S. A functional system of occupational classification. *Occupations*, 1951, *30*, 37–42.

9. Studdiford, W. S. New occupational classification structure. *Emplmt. Secur. Rev.*, Sept., 1953.

OTHER RELEVANT ARTICLES

The following are abstracts of articles relevant to the topic of this chapter:

Morris, R. G., and R. J. Murphy. The situs dimension in occupational structure. *American Sociological Review*, 1959, *24*, 231–239.

The sociological equivalents of Roe's levels and fields are status and situs, respectively. The authors of this article review various attempts at categorization, criticizing both the efforts of psychologists and sociologists. They develop ten categories of occupations based on what things must be done in society. A minor test of the system was obtained by asking college students to classify a number of occupations in the categories. Aside from finding ambiguity in the dimensions of situs, they concluded that some occupations involved secondary roles which made classification difficult, and that there were misunderstanding or misperceptions by the public as to what an individual actually does in an occupation.

Palmer, G. J., and E. J. McCormick. A factor analysis of job activities. *Journal of Applied Psychology*, 1961, *45*, 289–294.

This study developed a checklist of worker activities to describe a number of jobs. This data was then subjected to a factor analysis in order to identify the dimensions of job activities. They considered four general factors to describe adequately the domain of activities in the jobs which were described. Factor I indicated that the greatest difference in jobs lies in decision-making and mental activities. Factor II concerned differences in physical activities. Factor III referred to varied sources and methods of communications for originating, relaying, or receiving information required in the performance of jobs. Factor IV suggested knowledge or skill in the use of mathematics, perhaps relating to manual and computational routines. These findings might be compared to the more intuitive classification schemes.

Another general review of occupational classification, especially early attempts, is Shartle's Chapter 13 in Borow, H. (Ed.) *Man in a World at Work*, Boston: Houghton Mifflin, 1964, and also Shartle's most recent edition of his book, *Occupational Information*, Englewood Cliffs, N.J.: Prentice-Hall, 1959.

Super's Chapter 3 of *The Psychology of Careers*, New York: Harper & Row, 1957, is another general review, containing a complete presentation of his "enterprise" dimension.

See also the first report on functional classification:

Fine, S. A structure of worker function. *Personnel and Guidance Journal*, 1955, *34*, 66–73.

and other incidental articles:

Glick, P. Three-dimensional classification system of the occupations of college graduates. *Vocational Guidance Quarterly*, 1966, *14*, 130–135.

Osipow, S. H. Consistency of occupational choices of Roe's classification of occupations. *Vocational Guidance Quarterly*, 1966, *14*, 285–286.

Studdiford, W. S. A functional system of occupational classification. *Occupations*, 1951, *30*, 37–42.

Factor analytic efforts to define the structure of work activity (as contrasted with the more rationalistic efforts presented) include:

Coombs, C. H., and G. A. Sattler. A factorial approach to job families. *Psychometrica*, 1949, *14*, 33–42.

Guilford, J. P., P. R. Christensen, N. A. Bond, and M. A. Sutton. A factor analysis of human interests. *Psychological Monographs*, 1954, *68*, 4 (Whole Number 375).

Vernon, P. E. Classifying high grade occupational interests. *Journal of Abnormal and Social Psychology*, 1949, *44*, 85–96.

Perceptions
of Occupations

3

It is appropriate that occupations be clearly understood by counselors and personnel workers, who need to be experts in occupational behavior. But how are occupations understood and seen by persons who need only briefly to be expert — mainly at the time of their choice or entry into a work role? What are the layman's perceptions of the attributes of various occupations? These questions have received some attention in the occupational behavior literature, and a survey of those articles constitutes the content of this chapter.

There is an assortment of occupational attributes which may be the objects of subjective perceptions. One which has been of continuing interest to sociology is prestige. Clearly, prestige is not residual in persons who have different occupations, but rather seems to be conferred upon the occupation-holder by others. Attributes in a similar category of rewards might include power or influence, independence, security, and might range through the entire catalog of reasons people find for preferring one kind of work over another.

Another perspective is represented by the perception that occupations demand certain behavioral inputs or attributes — great sacrifice, devotion, or altruism, or that they require risk to life or limb.

Occupations may also be subjectively appraised in terms of the qualities of the people in them — their "image," if one prefers. One major study of this type has been undertaken.

The technique of measurement of perceptions also merits a brief comment. The most widely used procedure is the Semantic Differential, but it is used with varying degrees of validity. Personality and interest inventories may also be employed in this service. Since they are chiefly inventories of self-perceptions, a modification of their instructional set will convert them to measures of other-perception. Some caution about the validity of this procedure ought to be observed, but is rarely.

The first article in Chapter 3 stands for the numerous studies of occupational prestige. It includes the substance of the classic North-Hatt 1947 study of occupational prestige, and adds evidence on the nature of stability and change in this phenomenon over about fifteen years. The portion which recapitulates studies of prestige before 1947 has been omitted.

A discussion of the concept of occupational difficulty is next. This concept is not typically the object of study, but it should gain importance as our models of occupational choice develop.

That perceptions of occupations are affected by their titles and descriptions is the thesis of Osipow's article. He demonstrates, as might be expected, that job titles do make a difference in others' regard.

The Triandis article should be of interest because it compares the two sides of the occupational coin: jobs and people. Further, since perceptions are thought to be influenced not only by the cues the object produces, but also by the nature of the perceiver, ratings of the same object by differing status groups are compared. Note also the method Triandis uses to generate the scales of measurement.

Last of all is one of several reports from a larger study by Beardslee and O'Dowd. In it, ratings are made of the job occupant, not only in terms of the kind of working person he is, but also of attributes of his personal life — his politics, his mental health, his marriage situation, and so forth.

If, indeed, vocational behavior is structured and actualized on the basis of some portion of perception, as opposed to real experience, considerably more study of the perception of occupations is appropriate, and some terms which account for it must be woven into our conceptualizations of the activity of pursuing a career.

Occupational Prestige
in the United States, 1925–1963

ROBERT W. HODGE

PAUL M. SIEGEL

PETER H. ROSSI, *National Opinion Research Center*

The research reported in this paper represents an attempt to add historical depth to the study of the prestige of occupa-

Reprinted with the permission of the authors and publisher from *American Journal of Sociology*, 1966, 72, 286–295.

tions in the United States. It reports mainly on a replication conducted in 1963 of the National Opinion Research Center's well-known 1947 study of the prestige positions accorded to ninety occupations by a national sample of the American adult population.[1] . . .

The prestige hierarchy of occupations is perhaps the best studied aspect of the stratification systems of modern societies. Extensive empirical studies have been undertaken in a variety of nations, socialist and capitalist, developed and underdeveloped. Intensive analyses have been undertaken of results of particular studies searching for the existence of disparate prestige hierarchies held by subgroups within nations.[2] Despite rather extensive searches conducted by a variety of techniques, it appears that occupational-prestige hierarchies are similar from country to country and from subgroup to subgroup within a country. This stability reflects the fundamental but gross similarities among the occupational systems of modern nations. Furthermore, knowledge about occupations and relatively strong consensus on the relative positions of occupations are widely diffused throughout the populations involved.

The consensus within and among populations on the prestige positions of occupations leads one to expect that there will be considerable stability over time in the positions of particular occupations. Industrialization has proceeded to different points in the several countries whose prestige hierarchies have been studied without seriously affecting the relative positions of occupations in the countries involved. Cross-sectional comparisons between different countries at different stages of industrial evolution suggest that it would be erroneous to expect any considerable change in the *prestige* structure of a single country over time, even though that country might be experiencing appreciable changes in *occupational* structure. We can only expect to observe changes on the order of those previously found between two nations at different stages of economic development.

On the other hand, there are cogent reasons for expecting that changes in occupational structure will be reflected, at least ultimately, in corresponding changes in the prestige positions of occupations. The prestige position of an occupation is apparently a characteristic generated by the way in which the occupation is articulated into the division of labor, by the amount of power and influence implied in the activities of the occupation, by the characteristics of incumbents, and by the amount of resources which society places at the disposal of incumbents. (Other factors are undoubtedly at work, but these are the most obvious.) Hence, as occupations shift in these respects over time, corresponding adjustive shifts in prestige positions can be anticipated.

Considerable changes have occurred since 1947 in the occupational structure and labor force of the United States. The long-term trend in the growth of professional and scientific occupations persisted and was even accelerated during this period. Governmental and popular concern over the numbers and quality of our professional and technical manpower was expressed in a great expansion of our universities as well as in more attention being given lower levels of schooling. The proportion of the labor force devoted to agricultural pursuits declined along with unskilled and heavy labor components. This was also the period during which automation continued to expand, raising a serious question as to whether the American labor force could absorb both workers freed from jobs eliminated by technological progress and the large cohorts of postwar births now beginning to enter the labor force. Mention must be made of the stepped-up drive for equality on the part of Negroes, although we cannot tarry here to examine it. The question at issue is whether changes in the occupational structure have been reflected in shifts in the prestige of occupations between the two points in time.

On the basis of our empirical knowledge concerning the stability under a variety of conditions of the hierarchy of occupational prestige, we can support an expectation that there will be relatively few changes in the positions of occupations as we proceed from the 1947 to the 1963 study. On the basis of what seems to be a reasonable model of how these prestige positions have been generated, we expect somewhat more in the way of changes. Neither point of view produces very precise expectations for we need to know what is an acceptable level of stability (or change) either to conform to or to negate each expectation.

One further problem plagues interpretation of any comparisons such as this study envisages: Consider a set of occupational titles for which we have an aggregate prestige rating at two points in time; the difference between these ratings can be attributed either to a general increase in the amount of prestige in the occupational system or to an increase in the prestige of the aggregate of occupations in the set and a corresponding decrease in the prestige of some occupations not in the set. There is no conceivable way of choosing between these interpretations with the present data.

In view of the large number of professional occupations included in the NORC list, it may well be the case that in the aggregate the ninety occupations stood higher in the prestige hierarchy in 1963 than in 1947. If prestige is regarded as a "commodity" that behaves like the payoff in a "zero-sum" game, then, to be sure, what one set of occupations gains another must lose. But the NORC titles might get higher ratings in 1963 than 1947 because there is, all told, a greater amount of prestige in the system. If the latter is the case, the ninety NORC titles may get higher ratings and at the same time a smaller share of all prestige and a lower place in the total prestige hierarchy.[3]

These remarks are perhaps sufficient to alert the reader to the ambiguities which characterize the study of occupational prestige. Indeterminacies encountered in the study of a set of occupations are, of course, duplicated when the focus is upon a single occupation. It is for this reason that our focus is largely on the ordering of the ninety NORC occupational titles in two time periods and not upon changes in the prestige of particular occupations. All indications of changes in occupational prestige revealed here are of necessity relative to the set of ninety titles under consideration. These occupations exhaust our universe, and changes in their prestige are assumed to indicate restructuring of the relative prestige of the occupations under consideration.

METHODS AND PROCEDURES

A small-scale replication of the 1947 study was undertaken in the spring of 1963. In order properly to compare the replication with the original, it was necessary to replicate the study using procedures as nearly identical as possible with those of the earlier study. The same question was used to elicit ratings, and the ninety job titles were rated in the same orders (using rotated blocks) in the same way. Most of the items (with the exception of those that were historically obsolete) were repeated. Even the sample was selected according to the outmoded quota sampling methods employed in 1947. The few new items included in the restudy were placed in the questionnaire after the occupational ratings.

Because of the stability of prestige positions of occupations from subgroup to subgroup in the 1947 study, it was felt that a relatively small national sample would be sufficient for the replication. In all a total of 651 interviews was collected according to quota sampling methods from a national sample of adults and youths.[4]

As in the 1947 study, occupational ratings were elicited by asking respondents to judge an occupation as having *excellent, good, average, somewhat below average,* or *poor* standing (along with a "don't know" option) in response to the item: "For each job mentioned, please pick out the statement that best gives *your own personal opinion* of the *general standing* that such a job has."

One indicator of prestige position is the proportion of respondents (among those rating an occupation) giving either an "excellent" or a "good" response. Another measure which can be derived from a matrix of ratings by occupation requires weighting the various responses with arbitrary numerical values: We can assign an excellent rating a numerical value of 100, a good rating the value of 80, an average rating the value of 60, a somewhat below average rating the value of 40, and a poor rating the value of 20. Calculating the numerical average of these arbitrarily assigned values over all respondents rating the occupation yields the NORC prestige score. This latter measure has received rather widespread use despite arbitrariness in the numerical weights assigned to the five possible ratings.[5]

The ratings and derived scores for each of the ninety occupations obtained in 1947 and in 1963 are shown in Table 1. We

TABLE 1

Distributions of Prestige Ratings, United States, 1947 and 1963

Occupation	1963		1947	
	NORC Score	Rank	NORC Score	Rank
U.S. Supreme Court justice	94	1	96	1
Physician	93	2	93	2.5
Nuclear physicist	92	3.5	86	18
Scientist	92	3.5	89	8
Government scientist	91	5.5	88	10.5
State governor	91	5.5	93	2.5
Cabinet member in the federal government	90	8	92	4.5
College professor	90	8	89	8
U.S. representative in Congress	90	8	89	8
Chemist	89	11	86	18
Lawyer	89	11	86	18
Diplomat in the U.S. foreign service	89	11	92	4.5
Dentist	88	14	86	18
Architect	88	14	86	18
County judge	88	14	87	13
Psychologist	87	17.5	85	22
Minister	87	17.5	87	13
Member of the board of directors of a large corporation	87	17.5	86	18
Mayor of a large city	87	17.5	90	6
Priest	86	21.5	86	18
Head of a department in a state government	86	21.5	87	13
Civil engineer	86	21.5	84	23
Airline pilot	86	21.5	83	24.5
Banker	85	24.5	88	10.5
Biologist	85	24.5	81	29
Sociologist	83	26	82	26.5
Instructor in public schools	82	27.5	79	34
Captain in the regular army	82	27.5	80	31.5
Accountant for a large business	81	29.5	81	29
Public school teacher	81	29.5	78	36
Owner of a factory that employs about 100 people	80	31.5	82	26.5

TABLE 1 (Cont.)

Occupation	1963		1947	
	NORC Score	Rank	NORC Score	Rank
Building contractor	80	31.5	79	34
Artist who paints pictures that are exhibited in galleries	78	34.5	83	24.5
Musician in a symphony orchestra	78	34.5	81	29
Author of novels	78	34.5	80	31.5
Economist	78	34.5	79	34
Official of an international labor union	77	37	75	40.5
Railroad engineer	76	39	77	37.5
Electrician	76	39	73	45
County agricultural agent	76	39	77	37.5
Owner-operator of a printing shop	75	41.5	74	42.5
Trained machinist	75	41.5	73	45
Farm owner and operator	74	44	76	39
Undertaker	74	44	72	47
Welfare worker for a city government	74	44	73	45
Newspaper columnist	73	46	74	42.5
Policeman	72	47	67	55
Reporter on a daily newspaper	71	48	71	48
Radio announcer	70	49.5	75	40.5
Bookkeeper	70	49.5	68	51.5
Tenant farmer—one who owns livestock and machinery and manages the farm	69	51.5	68	51.5
Insurance agent	69	51.5	68	51.5
Carpenter	68	53	65	58
Manager of a small store in a city	67	54.5	69	49
A local official of a labor union	67	54.5	62	62
Mail carrier	66	57	66	57
Railroad conductor	66	57	67	55
Traveling salesman for a wholesale concern	66	57	68	51.5
Plumber	65	59	63	59.5
Automobile repairman	64	60	63	59.5
Playground director	63	62.5	67	55
Barber	63	62.5	59	66
Machine operator in a factory	63	62.5	60	64.5
Owner-operator of a lunch stand	63	62.5	62	62
Corporal in the regular army	62	65.5	60	64.5
Garage mechanic	62	65.5	62	62
Truck driver	59	67	54	71
Fisherman who owns his own boat	58	68	58	68
Clerk in a store	56	70	58	68
Milk route man	56	70	54	71
Streetcar motorman	56	70	58	68
Lumberjack	55	72.5	53	73
Restaurant cook	55	72.5	54	71
Singer in a nightclub	54	74	52	74.5

TABLE 1 (Cont.)

Occupation	1963		1947	
	NORC Score	Rank	NORC Score	Rank
Filling station attendant	51	75	52	74.5
Dockworker	50	77.5	47	81.5
Railroad section hand	50	77.5	48	79.5
Night watchman	50	77.5	47	81.5
Coal miner	50	77.5	49	77.5
Restaurant waiter	49	80.5	48	79.5
Taxi driver	49	80.5	49	77.5
Farm hand	48	83	50	76
Janitor	48	83	44	85.5
Bartender	48	83	44	85.5
Clothes presser in a laundry	45	85	46	83
Soda fountain clerk	44	86	45	84
Sharecropper—one who owns no livestock or equipment and does not manage farm	42	87	40	87
Garbage collector	39	88	35	88
Street sweeper	36	89	34	89
Shoe shiner	34	90	33	90
Average	71		70	

present the findings in such detail because of their intrinsic interest. However, the bulk of the analysis contained in this paper is more concerned with characteristics of the distributions of these ratings than with the positions of particular occupations.

CONGRUITIES IN OCCUPATIONAL PRESTIGE: 1947–1963

The major result of the 1963 restudy is dramatically summarized in the product-moment correlation coefficient of .99 between the scores in 1947 and the scores in 1963. The linear regression of the 1963 on the 1947 scores is given by

$$Y = 0.97X + 2.98,$$

a result which indicates that there are very little regression toward the mean and a slight net upward shift in scores.[6] (Here and elsewhere in the text boldface symbols are used to represent regression estimates.)

The high over-all correlation in the total set of occupations is matched by high correlations within subsets of occupations. If we group occupations into professional occupations, other non-manual occupations, and manual occupations, as in Table 2, we can see that the regression lines within the three groups are quite similar.[7]

The very slight effect of grouping occupations is shown again in Figure 1, where the three within-group regression lines are plotted over the range of the 1947 NORC scores contained within each group. The three lines nearly coincide over the observed range of the NORC scores and do not appreciably depart from the line $Y = X$ (where the 1963 and the 1947 scores are equal).

The gross similarity between the 1947 and the 1963 NORC scores tends to overshadow some interesting small changes revealed by the data. Thus, in Figure 1 the regression line for blue-collar occupations

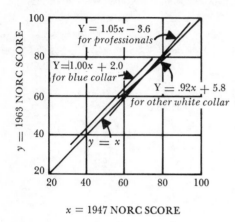

$$Y = 1.05x - 3.6$$
for professionals

$$Y = 1.00x + 2.0$$
for blue collar

$$Y = .92x + 5.8$$
for other white collar

$$y = x$$

$y = $ 1963 NORC SCORE— (vertical axis)

$x = $ 1947 NORC SCORE

FIGURE 1. Regressions of 1963 NORC score on 1947 NORC score within occupational groups.

lies above (and, in fact, parallels) the line $Y = X$. Consequently, one infers that all blue-collar occupations had slightly higher scores in 1963. For professionals and other white-collar workers, however, the picture is more complex, since the within-group regression lines for these two broad groupings cross over the line $Y = X$. Consequently, in the case of professionals, those particular occupations with the highest

prestige scores in 1947 (largely scientific and free professional occupations) slightly increased their scores, whereas those professional occupations with relatively low prestige in 1947 (marginal professional occupations such as "singer in a nightclub") receive somewhat lower scores. Among "other white-collar occupations" the situation is reversed. That is, from the within-group regression line we see that the other white-collar occupations with highest prestige in 1947 (largely managerial and political occupations) tended on the average to decline slightly, whereas lower white-collar occupations slightly increased in prestige.[8]

One other point is brought out sharply by Figure 1 and deserves mention. Since the within-occupational-group regression lines are plotted only for the range of 1947 scores observed within the group, one can easily see the appreciable overlap in scores between professional, other white-collar, and blue-collar occupations. Although these divisions are often employed by social scientists as though they represented fundamental class barriers,[9] Figure 1 makes clear that no such barrier can be detected on the basis of occupational prestige. The cleavage between white-collar and blue-collar — if it exists at all — is based not so much upon matters of societal evaluation as perhaps upon the character of dress and work in the three groups.

All in all the preceding results indicate a striking similarity between the structure of

TABLE 2

Regressions within Subsets of Occupations

Occupation Group	Regression Coefficient	Regression Constant	Correlation
Total, all occupations ($n = 90$)	0.97	2.98	.99
Professional, including one title duplicated for validation purposes ($n = 33$)	1.05	−3.61	.96
One non-manual occupations ($n = 21$)	0.92	5.85	.98
All manual occupations, including one craft occupation duplicated for validation purposes and two military titles ($n = 21$)	1.00	2.00	.99
Farm occupations ($n = 4$); not computed			

the 1947 and the 1963 NORC scores. While we shall subsequently document a number of systematic shifts in the prestige of specific occupational groups, it is abundantly clear that these shifts are small and did not produce any substantial re-ordering of the relative prestige of the ninety occupations under consideration here.

There are several good reasons for this observed stability. First, relative differential educational requirements, monetary rewards, and even something as nebulous as the functional importance of occupations are not subject to rapid change in an industrial society.[10] Second, any dramatic shifts in the prestige structure of occupations would upset the dependency which is presumed to hold between the social evaluation of a job, its educational prerequisites, its rewards, and its importance to society. Finally, instabilities would further ambiguities or status inconsistencies if the prestige structure were subject to marked and rapid change. Indeed, the meaning of achievement, career, seniority, and occupational mobility would be fundamentally altered if occupational prestige were subject to large-scale changes. No small amount of intragenerational mobility between prestige classes would, for example, be induced solely by the changing structure of occupational prestige *even though individuals did not change their occupations over time.*

KNOWLEDGE ABOUT OCCUPATIONS AND OCCUPATIONAL RATINGS

Occupations vary in their visibility to wide segments of the members of a society. To capture the extent to which such knowledge is distributed throughout the American population, one of the options on the NORC rating scales was "I don't know where to place that one." "Don't know" responses of this sort may indicate ignorance about an occupation and/or ambivalence about its location in the hierarchy of prestige. Given the pattern of heavier proportions of "don't

know" responses for the more esoteric occupations (see Table 1), it would appear that such responses indicate primarily lack of knowledge rather than ambivalence.

Knowledge about occupations has increased markedly over the period 1947–63. The correlation between proportions "don't know" for the two periods is .85, with the linear regression of 1963 proportions on 1947 proportions represented by

$$Y = 0.29X + 0.62.$$

The "don't know" percentages were considerably less in 1963 as compared with 1947, and for only one occupation did the percentage increase during the period. Since the correlation between percentage "don't know" for the two periods was very high, occupations receiving high proportions of "don't knows" in 1947 also received high proportions in 1963, even though the average proportion "don't know" for the entire group of occupations dropped.

Inspection of the scattergram of the 1963 and 1947 percentages "don't know" for the ninety occupations reveals that the results reported above are strongly affected by the inclusion of "nuclear physicist" which elicited a very large proportion of "don't know" responses in 1947. Omitting "nuclear physicist," the regression of the 1963 percentage "don't know" on the 1947 percentage "don't know" over the remaining eighty-nine occupations becomes

$$Y = 0.44X + 0.26,$$

and *r* increases to .91. While these results lead to much the same interpretation as those reported above, they do call attention to the remarkable change in knowledge about the prestige rating of "nuclear physicist." In 1947, 51 per cent of all respondents did not know where to place "nuclear physicist," but by 1963 this figure had dropped to 10 per cent.

Insights into the quality of information about occupations held by respondents can be gained from responses to a supplementary question included in both the 1963 and the 1947 studies. Respondents were asked: "A good many people don't know exactly what a *nuclear physicist* does, but what is your *general* idea of what he does?" In 1947 only 3 per cent of all respondents supplied a "correct" answer by indicating that a nuclear physicist "investigates the properties of the nucleus of the atom, breaks down nuclear or atomic energy, studies the innermost part of the atom, works on nuclear fission" or some similar description of the subject matter of nuclear physics. In 1963, only 2 per cent of respondents provided a correct answer of the kind indicated above. In response to this item in 1947, 55 per cent of the respondents claimed they "did not know" what a nuclear physicist was, while in 1963 this figure had dropped to 25 per cent. Thus, while there is no indication that more persons "knew" in a precise way what a nuclear physicist does, there were considerably more persons in 1963 who were willing not only to rate "nuclear physicist" but to provide indications — such as "works with atomic bomb," "runs Cape Kennedy," "is a laboratory worker," or "does atomic research" — of their impression of what a nuclear physicist does. Many of these indications are vague and erroneous, but they apparently provide a sufficient basis for respondents to draw inferences about the general standing of nuclear physicists. Thus, it appears that respondents are willing to evaluate occupations without a clear and well-defined idea of the duties involved in their performance.

The situation of the nuclear physicist suggests an hypothesis to which we will pay some attention. As it turned out the 1947 NORC score for "nuclear physicist" was 86, while the 1963 score was 92. Thus, an increase in the standing of "nuclear physicist" accompanied the remarkable increase in the proportion of respondents willing to rate the occupation. One may presume that the frequent mention of nuclear physicists in the press between 1947 and 1963 contributed to the increased will-

ingness of respondents to give their impressions of the occupation. The particular hypothesis which concerns us is that publicity enhances prestige. The case of nuclear physicist and several other occupations suggests that there may be some truth to this hypothesis. Here we can examine whether changes in the ability to rate occupations (as indicated by the proportion of "don't know" responses), which should be a consequence of publicity, affect occupational standings.

Most of the ninety NORC occupations were already well-known in 1947, so that little if any change in the ability of respondents to rate them could be expected. We consider, therefore, only those twenty-five NORC occupations which in 1947 had 5 or more per cent of respondents refusing to rate them. The correlation between changes in percentages "don't know" between 1947 and 1963 with changes in prestige scores for this subset of occupations is .48.[11] Thus, for this subset of occupations for which there was some room for the diffusion of knowledge, the expected positive relationship between decreases in the percentage "don't know" and score increases apparently holds.[12]

[1]The replication was undertaken as the first stage of a larger project supported by a National Science Foundation grant (NSF G85, "Occupations and Social Stratification") aimed at providing definitive prestige scores for a more representative sample of occupations and at uncovering some of the characteristics of occupations which generate their prestige scores. The replication was undertaken as the first step in the research program to determine whether appreciable shifts occured in prestige scores in the time period 1947–63 so that the effects of improvements in technical procedures could be sorted out from effects of historical changes in any comparisons which would be undertaken between the 1947 study and the more definitive researches presently under way.

[2]See, e.g., Kaare Svalastoga, *Prestige, Class and Mobility* (Copenhagen: Glydendal, 1959),

pp. 43-131; C. A. Moser and J. R. Hall, "The Social Grading of Occupations," in D. V. Glass (ed.), *Social Mobility in Britain* (London: Routledge & Kegan Paul, 1954), pp. 29–50; and Albert J. Reiss, Jr., Otis Dudley Duncan, Paul K. Hatt, and Cecil C. North, *Occupations and Social Status* (New York: Free Press of Glencoe, 1961). The last-mentioned volume contains the major analyses of the 1947 North-Hatt-NORC study of occupational prestige.

[3]This point is perhaps more clearly illustrated with a more familiar commodity: money income in dollars. It is fairly easy to see how a group could receive a smaller proportion of all income over time, but at the same time have greater income because there is more income to spread between groups.

[4]Justification for our claim that 651 cases suffice to give a reliable intertemporal comparison can be derived from examination of sampling error estimates based on the assumption of a random sample. Such estimates indicate that confidence limits at the 0.90 level for $p = 0.50$ and $N = 651$ are 0.47 and 0.53. For $N = 60$ (smaller than any subgroup used in this paper) the corresponding error estimates are 0.39 and 0.61. Thus for even relatively small subgroups any dramatic changes are likely to be detected, although it must be clearly understood that error estimates for quota sampling are only approximated by assuming that formulas for random samples apply.

[5]The reader will observe that the correlation between the two ways of ordering occupations need not be unity. Of the two measures mentioned above, the proportion of excellent or good ratings enjoys some advantages over the NORC prestige scores. Its range and variance are somewhat larger than the NORC prestige scores, which tend to obscure differences between occupations in the middle of the prestige hierarchy. However, the two measures are, in fact, highly intercorrelated ($r = .98$) and the advantages of the proportion of excellent or good ratings over the NORC prestige scores are largely statistical in nature. Throughout this paper, the bulk of our analysis employs the NORC prestige scores — a decision based largely on the wide use and popularity of the prestige scores derived from the original 1947 study.

[6]When the NORC scores are ranked, we find a Spearman rank-order correlation of .98 between the 1947 and 1963 ranks.

[7]The hypothesis that a common regression line fits all groups may be rejected at the 0.07 level of confidence, as indicated by the F-ratio resulting from an analysis of covariance.

[8]There is a slight increase in the ability of the within-group regression lines to predict the direction of changes in scores between 1947 and 1963, as compared with the regression line for the total set. Correct predictions about the directions of change can be made by the overall regression in 60.5 per cent of the cases and by the within-group regression lines in 62.8 per cent of them, an increase in efficiency of 5.8 per cent.

[9]This is, e.g., the major distinction employed in a recent comparative study of occupational mobility (Seymour Martin Lipset and Reinhard Bendix. *Social Mobility in Industrial Society* [Berkeley: University of California Press,1959]).

[10]For a discussion of this point see Otis Dudley Duncan, "Properties and Characteristics of the Socio-economic Index," in Reiss *et al., op. cit.*, pp. 152–53. A correlation of .94 was found between an aggregate measure of the income of an occupation in 1940 and a similar indicator in 1950; a correlation of .97 was found between the proportion of high-school graduates in an occupation in 1940 and the same measure in 1950.

[11]The regression of the change in the percentage "don't know" on the change in prestige scores is given by $Y = 0.16X - 0.11$.

[12]However, "nuclear physicist," which shows the most dramatic change in "don't knows," falls among these twenty-five occupations. Upon exclusion of this occupation, we find that for the remaining twenty-four occupations r falls to .33. On the other hand, the regression slope is two-thirds again as large since for the twenty-four occupations under consideration, $Y = 0.27X - 0.61$. Thus, whether elimination of "nuclear physicist" upsets the observed relationship between decreases in the proportion "don't know" and score changes depends on whether you take the point of view of regression or of correlation. On the one hand, the variance around the regression line is greater, but on the other hand, score changes increase more rapidly with decreases in the percentage "don't know." In any case, for the twenty-four occupations, we have found some evidence, albeit slight, in support of the predicted positive association between score changes and shifts in public knowledge of occupational standings.

Occupational Difficulty

DONALD G. ZYTOWSKI, *Iowa State University*

For reasons which will become clear in the chapter on the decision-making model of relating determinants to choices, a brief discussion of the perception of occupational difficulty is included here.

Most persons are able to estimate how hard it is to attain some given occupational role: the difficulty of passing the prerequisite courses for entrance into medical school is well known, for example. Despite this, there has been no systematic study of popular conceptions of the difficulty of attaining various occupational roles. In one study Mahone (1960) asked college students to estimate how many of themselves out of one hundred typical students had the ability to attain a number of different occupational goals. He found, as examples, that his subjects felt that only 7 out of 100 had the ability to become medical specialists, while 72 could be clerks. Of most importance was the finding that these difficulty estimates correlated .85 with prestige rankings obtained in national surveys.

That the correlation between the excellence an occupation demands and the prestige it confers is not perfect, affords the possibility that a few occupations would show visible discrepancies in the two perceptions. This finding was almost incidental to a study by Bernstein and his colleagues (1963) but is of interest to this discussion. They found, for instance, that the occupations of corporation board member, banker, and clergyman were afforded higher ranking prestige than competence demanded, while nuclear physicist, chemist, and college

Prepared especially for this volume.

professor required more competence relative to their prestige values.

On further consideration, it is also possible to conceive of occupations which differ in whether successful attainment or successful performance is more difficult. Most persons would agree that it is not difficult to find an opportunity to drive a race car, but exceedingly difficult to become a successful driver. Conversely, it might be conceded that attaining the role of a physician is generally regarded as equivalent to success, but it is not easy to attain the role.

At the same time, within the medical specialties, the difficulty of normal practice may be perceived as differing. The dermatologist is sometimes accused of the easy life: no emergency calls, no night work, no hospital visits. The obstetrician, on the other hand, is regarded as a hard worker, whose occupation demands many sacrifices.

Madden (1962) has studied the attributes of work which make it difficult, and concluded that a global concept of difficulty is inadequate. From data obtained in the military service, he catalogued nine reasons for task difficulty as follows:

1. Pressure — Insufficient time to do the work properly, rapid change in how work is performed, responsibility for expensive equipment.

2. Working conditions — Extremely strenuous work, dirty work, etc.

3. Attention — Work is very complex, requires great precision, mistakes are very costly.

4. Interpersonal relations — Work makes receiving or giving supervision difficult, or relations with peers.

5. Frustration — Improper tools, information, parts, supplies not regularly available.

6. Training — Training was not adequate, performer has to learn too much on the job.

7. Regulations, Information — Conflicting instructions, lack of information, or ambiguous.

8. Forms — Too detailed or time consuming, hard to get information for them.

9. Aptitude — Job calls for performance for which incumbent is not apt.

A great deal more study of the difficulty of occupational performance, success, and attainment would be appropriate. According to Jules Henry (1963) adolescents are frequently discouraged from pursuing idealistic goals by perceptions (correct or not) of this kind. More accurate assessment of this variable would be a contribution to opportunity for rational and deliberate occupational development.

REFERENCES

Bernstein, E., R. Moulton, and P. Liberty. Prestige vs. excellence as determinants of role attractiveness. *American Sociological Review*, 1963, *28*, 212–219.

Henry, Jules. *Culture against Man*. New York: Random House, 1963.

Madden, J. M. What makes work difficult? *Personnel Journal*, 1962, *41*, 341–344.

Mahone, C. H. Reported in Atkinson, J. W. *An Introduction to Motivation*. Princeton, N.J.: Van Nostrand, 1964.

Perceptions of Occupations as a Function of Titles and Descriptions

SAMUEL H. OSIPOW, *Pennsylvania State University*

Recently there have been a number of attempts to use occupational titles in the study of career development. One such attempt has used attitudes toward career titles as a means of personality assessment (Holland, 1958; 1960; 1961). Another examined the occupational perceptions of a group homogeneous in interests and goals (McCabe, 1960). A third studied the images held by college students of several highly visible

Reprinted with the permission of the author and publisher from *Journal of Counseling Psychology*, 1962, *9*, 106–109.

occupations (O'Dowd and Beardslee, 1960). The results of these studies suggest that there is a wealth of stimulus value in occupational names that would be worthwhile developing. For example, the problem of the degree to which career choices are influenced by the perceptions of occupational titles is of significance to the counselor. Also of interest is the degree to which these initial perceptions are altered by additional information, even of a minimal nature. The present experiment was designed to study the role that job titles in interaction with descriptions play in occupational perceptions.

The Dollard and Miller (1950) formulation of the cue-producing properties of labels may be used in investigating the stimulus value of occupational names. For example, Di Vesta and Bossart (1958) found that attitudes toward an issue varied depending upon whether the issue was identified to the *S*s as either an economic, ethical, or social situation. Since career preferences may be considered to be specialized forms of attitudes, it would seem reasonable to expect that attitudes toward careers would be influenced in a similar manner. That is, the associative components of job titles should influence resulting job preferences.

THE PROBLEM

To test the assumptions of the just preceding sentence, it was predicted that *S*s would differ in their attitudes toward a pair of specific job titles (for the same occupation) when no job description was available. The specific prediction was that these differences would hold along the *evaluative, potency,* and *activity* dimensions of meaning. Since the addition of the same description for both job titles should reduce the difference between the subsequent associative components, it was also predicted that these differences in attitudes would not exist along the potency and activity dimensions of meaning when job descriptions were given; the difference in attitude along the evaluative dimension was predicted to persist under "description" conditions because this dimension was expected to be present mainly in the job title rather than the description.

METHOD

*S*s were 96 university students enrolled in an adolescent psychology course. (Six additional *S*s were discarded for failure to use the questionnaire properly.) They were first given preliminary instructions in the use of the semantic differential (Osgood,

Suci, and Tannenbaum, 1957). They were then instructed to respond to the polar words on the questionnaire as they felt the words described the job in question.

There were 15 semantic differential items to which they were to respond, five loaded on the evaluative dimension of meaning, five loaded on the potency dimension, and five on the activity dimension (Osgood, et al., 1957). The following are examples of evaluative, potency, and activity items respectively:

clean......—:—:—:—:—:—:—......dirty
large......—:—:—:—:—:—:—......small
fast.......—:—:—:—:—:—:—......slow

*S*s were randomly divided into four groups of 24 students each. Group I evaluated the job of building superintendent with no description, Group II rated building superintendent with a description, Group III rated janitor without a description, and Group IV responded to janitor with a description. The descriptions used were identical and were based on those given for these occupations in the *Dictionary of Occupational Titles* (1949). Consequently, the only difference between the stimuli presented to Groups II and IV was in the title, as was the only difference between the stimuli given to Groups I and III. Comparisons of the ratings made by Groups I and III would provide information about the differences in perception stimulated by the two job titles alone, while comparisons of ratings of Groups II and IV would allow inferences to be drawn about the effect of the identical job descriptions on perceptions of the two job titles.

RESULTS

Table 1 summarizes the analysis of variance based on the responses of the four groups along the three dimensions of meaning. It can be seen that a significant difference in rating occurred along the evaluative dimension.

The results of a comparison of the individual group means in evaluative rating are shown in Table 2. The mean evaluative rating given by Group I differed significantly from those ratings given by Groups II, III, and IV at the .05 level of confidence. The results of the Bartlett test for homogeneity of variance indicated that the samples came from a population with a common variance.

TABLE 1

Analysis of Variance of Evaluative Activity, and Potency Meaning

Dimension	Source	df	MS	F	p
Evaluative	Between Groups	3	66.03	5.26	<.01
	Within Groups	92	12.55	—	—
	Total	95	—	—	—
Activity	Between Groups	3	30.94	2.66	>.05
	Within Groups	92	11.48	—	—
	Total	95	—	—	—
Potency	Between Groups	3	44.78	16.83	<.01
	Within Groups	92	2.66	—	—
	Total	95	—	—	—

TABLE 2

Difference between Group Means on the Evaluative Dimension

Group	II	III	IV
I	*3.84	*2.46	*3.34
II	—	1.38	0.50
III	—	—	0.88

*Significant at the .05 level.

Turning back to Table 1 and examining the F for the analysis of variance for the potency dimension, it can be seen that it is significant at the .01 level of confidence.

Here, however, the results of the Bartlett test suggested that the population variances differed. This means that the population variances may have contributed to the overall mean differences that were found. Lindquist (1953) suggests that where the heterogeneity of variance is not extreme the F ratio may still be valid, provided the underestimation of the probability that results is taken into account. However, the ordinary t test would not be equally valid. Consequently, the differences between the means of the groups were tested with the Cochran-Cox test (1950). This method was the basis of the significance tests shown in Table 3, which compares the differences in group means on the potency dimension. It may be seen that Group I differed significantly from Groups III and IV, and that the mean potency rating by Group II differed from that of Group III at the .05 level of confidence.

TABLE 3

Difference Between Group Means on the Potency Dimension

Group	II	III	IV
I	0.67	*3.08	*1.92
II	—	*2.41	1.25
III	—	—	1.16

*Significant at the .05 level.

DISCUSSION

It was predicted that Ss would differ in their attitudes toward a specific pair of job titles when no description was provided. Differences were found under "no description" conditions along the potency and evaluative dimensions but not along the activity dimension. The direction of the difference on the potency and evaluative dimensions suggests that building superintendent is perceived as a more potent (illustrated by such words as large, strong, heavy, thick, and deep) and positive (clean, honest, valuable, pleasant, and fragrant) job than is janitor.

It was also predicted that the differences in attitude would not exist along the potency and activity dimensions when descriptions were given but that the difference along the evaluative dimension would persist. This prediction was not confirmed. Instead, the findings indicate that, along the potency and evaluative dimensions, the descriptions eliminated the difference in perception that apparently existed as a result of the titles alone.

It is interesting to note that building superintendent was perceived more negatively along the evaluative dimension when a description was given than when it was not. This suggests that the title itself provided some desirable cues which were counterbalanced in the group that received the description. This might also indicate that a more accurate perception existed for the work of janitor than for building superintendent.

These results suggest that the semantic differential method may be useful in the study of occupations. The counselor might use it as an aid in understanding his clients. Furthermore, the analysis of occupations along the dimensions of meaning could provide useful occupational information; however, an atlas related to the meaning of careers along the lines of the occupational images described by O'Dowd and Beardslee (1960) would be essential. The findings also suggest the hypothesis that vocational choice behavior is likely to be influenced by the perception of the verbal labels used to identify jobs.

SUMMARY

The semantic differential was used to test the prediction that differences in attitudes toward a pair of specific job titles for the same occupation would exist when no job description was provided and that these differences would persist along the evalua-

tive dimension of meaning alone when descriptions were provided.

Ninety-six students in adolescent psychology were instructed to rate one of two jobs on 15 pairs of polar words. Half the *S*s had descriptions for the jobs, half did not.

Differences in attitude toward the job titles were found on the evaluative and potency dimensions of meaning under "no description" conditions. Neither of these differences appeared under "description" conditions.

The results suggest that there are likely to be differences in perceptions of careers along various dimensions of meaning when the stimuli are presented in the form of specific job titles. The results further suggest that these differences may be reduced by the presentation of minimal occupational descriptions.

REFERENCES

Cochran, W. G., and Cox, Gertrude M. *Experimental designs.* New York: Wiley, 1950.

Dictionary of occupational titles. U.S. Employment Service, Washington, D.C.: U.S. Government Printing Office, 1949.

Di Vesta, F. J., and Bossart, P. The effects of sets induced by labeling on the modification of attitudes. *J. Pers.*, 1958, *26*, 379–387.

Dollard, J., and Miller, N. *Personality and psychotherapy.* New York: McGraw-Hill, 1950.

Holland, J. L. A personality inventory employing occupational titles. *J. appl. Psychol.*, 1958, *42*, 336–342.

Holland, J. L. The relation of the Vocational Preference Inventory to the Sixteen Personality Factor Questionnaire. *J. appl. Psychol.*, 1960, *44*, 291–296.

Holland, J. L. Some explorations with occupational titles. *J. counsel. Psychol.*, 1961, *8*, 82–85.

Lindquist, E. F. *Design and analysis of experiments in psychology and education.* Boston: Houghton Mifflin, 1953.

McCabe, S. P. Occupational stereotypes as studied by the semantic differential. *Amer. Psychologist*, 1960, *15*, 454.

O'Dowd, D. D., and Beardslee, D. C. College student images of a selected group of professions and occupations. U.S. Office of Education, Co-operative Research Project No. 562(8142), Wesleyan University, Middletown, Connecticut, 1960.

Osgood, C. E., Suci, G. J., and Tannenbaum, P. H. *The measurement of meaning.* Urbana, Ill.: Univer. Illinois Press, 1957.

Differential Perception of Certain Jobs and People by Managers, Clerks, and Workers in Industry

HARRY C. TRIANDIS, *University of Illinois*

The recent development of the semantic differential by Osgood and his associates (Osgood, Suci, and Tannenbaum, 1957) has provided a procedure of great simplicity and flexibility for the study of the frames of reference of industrial subjects. *S*s are required to rate a series of *concepts* on a series of *scales*. The means of the ratings for a given group provide information about the group frame of reference. Weaver (1958) compared the meaning of 10 concepts for members of management and labor leaders and found significant differences in the meanings of the concepts "the closed shop," "grievance," "the labor movement," "working during a strike," "labor in politics," and other concepts, between the two groups. The present study describes the use of the semantic differential for the study of how certain jobs and certain people are perceived by various groups of industrial *S*s.

Reprinted with the permission of the author and publisher from *Journal of Applied Psychology*, 1959, *43*, 221–225.

METHOD

Technical Note

Osgood and his associates used mostly college students as *S*s. The writer's attempt to use the semantic differential with workers suggested that these *S*s find it extremely difficult to respond to "unusual" combinations of concept and scale (e.g., Joe Dow rated on *angular-rounded*). For this reason, special differentials for jobs and for people were developed. The procedure for the development of the differentials was as follows: First, 12 triads of jobs and 12 triads of people were presented to 105 industrial *S*s (20 workers, 30 male clerks, 30 female clerks, and 25 managers). The *S*s were asked: "Which one of these three jobs (people) is different from the other two and why?" (e.g., triad: teacher, welder, clerk. Response: teacher is *professional*, or welder is *manual*, or clerk is *routine worker*). "What is the opposite of this characteristic?"

(e.g., *unprofessional*, or *white collar;* or *variable*). The lists of the characteristics obtained from the various groups of *S*s differed from each other. An analysis of these lists has been published elsewhere (Triandis, 1959). A stratified random sample of the characteristics so obtained constituted 28 scales of each of the semantic differentials. An additional 10 scales were selected from Osgood, Suci, and Tannenbaum (1957), so as to represent the seven factors of their semantic differential factor analysis. The sheets of paper used for this test could accommodate only 38 scales. The differentials and the instructions that were finally used may be found in Triandis (1958, pp. 296–298).

Procedure

The two 38-scale semantic differentials, one for jobs and one for people, which were developed as is described above, were administered to 156 *S*s. Usable answers were received from 5 members of the company's executive committee, 14 department managers, 18 section managers, 32 female clerks, 28 male clerks, and 55 workers. The *S*s rated five jobs (welder, teacher, vice-president, personnel director, and clerk) in counterbalanced order on the semantic differential. In addition they rated their supervisors, the company's personnel director, the boss of their supervisor, the vice-president of their division, a "fellow at work whom you like," and "an effective manager you have known well and who is not the same as any of the people already rated."

RESULTS AND DISCUSSION

The means of the ratings of the various jobs and people on the 38 scales of the semantic differential, for groups consisting of upper managers, lower managers, female clerks, male clerks, and workers, can be found elsewhere (Triandis, 1958). Limitations of space do not permit complete presentation of the findings. A general observation, however, is possible; the means of the various groups on most of the scales of the differential are very similar. Against this background of similarity, however, it is possible to note several important differences.

Differences in the Perception of People

A comparison of the two "*ideal*" concepts, the workmate and the manager, reveals great consistency between the groups and between levels of each of the divisions. Both ideals are considered *successful*, though the manager is a little more successful than the workmate. The ideal manager is *purposeful*, while the workmate does not have this trait. Both are *easy to understand, stable, educated, kind, ambitious*, though the manager is a little more ambitious than the workmate; *gracious*, though the workmate a little more than the manager; *receptive, capable, active, colorful, cooperative, original*, though the manager a little more than the workmate; *experienced, young, friendly, intelligent, aggressive*, though the manager a little more than the workmate; *skilled, progressive, powerful*, though the manager a little more than the workmate; *sociable, very concerned with public relations, like traveling, good-humored, self-made*, and just slightly *emotional*. The workmate's *pay* is average, the manager's high. The manager is more talkative. The workmate does not have too many headaches on the job, the manager does. Finally, the workmate is more *satisfied* than the manager; the latter is at times very *dissatisfied*.

The Characteristics of the Successful and Unsuccessful Supervisors

In this section we will undertake to answer the following question: Suppose there are two department heads who are considered as successful and relatively unsuccessful respectively by *their* supervisor (a vice-president). How are these two men perceived by their subordinates? Let us call them Mr. Effective (E), and Mr. Ineffective (I). Both are perceived as being *successful*. E is perceived to be more *purposeful* than I. But I is *easier to understand*. Both are *stable, educated, ambitious, strong, capable, active, quiet, colorful, cooperative, conventional, get high pay, experienced, young, intelligent, satisfied, aggressive, fast, skilled, progressive, powerful, sociable,* and share most of the other characteristics in equal amounts, yet E is *crude* while I is *gracious*, E is *assuming*, and I *unassuming*, E is *stubborn*, and I is *receptive*, I is more *friendly* and *good humored*, E is more *unfriendly* and *bad humored*. In short, I is closer to the picture of the ideal manager of most groups, while E is more instrumental and task-oriented. We might conclude, then, that the particular vice-president is more task-oriented than employee-oriented. Three out of four of the vice-presidents of this company were similarly task-oriented.

Another comparison considered the profiles of 11 department heads who are well liked and 3 department heads who are disliked by their subordinates. The disliked department heads were perceived as being *more difficult to understand, cruel, crude, stubborn, uncooperative, inexperienced, unfriendly, dissatisfied,* and *assisted*.

The Meaning of the Similarity between the Perception of the "Actual" and the "Ideal" Supervisor

It is reasonable to expect that the greater the similarity between the profiles of the actual and the *ideal* supervisors, the more will be the liking of the subordinate for the supervisor. This would imply that *S*s like those people who perform their role in society in such a way that their behavior approaches the ideal expected behavior for the particular role, as the latter is perceived by the *S*s. To test this view, the similarity in the profiles of the actual and the ideal supervisors was correlated to ratings of liking of the supervisor on a Thurstone-type successive intervals scale (Edwards, 1957,

pp. 120–145). The profile similarity was computed as follows:

$$S_p = 1 - \frac{\sum_{1}^{n} d^2}{36.\ n} = 1 - \frac{D^2}{36n}$$

where d is the difference between the perception of the actual and the ideal supervisors on one of the n scales of the semantic differential. D is the same as the D-statistic used by Osgood et al. and others. In our case $n = 38$. The 36 is a constant which comes from the fact that a 7-point scale was used.

The Pearson r coefficients between S_p and L (liking for the supervisor) were as follows: For 42 managers and top clerk $r = .73$ ($p < .0001$); for 50 clerks $r = .58$ ($p < .001$); and for 50 workers $r = .54$ ($p < .001$). We conclude that our hypothesis about the relationship of "ideal" and actual behaviors to liking is confirmed.

Differences in the Perception of Jobs

There is a tendency for the workers to perceive a Welder's Job as involving more *experience*, and being more *desirable, important, responsible, alert, difficult, professional, executive, creative, skilled,* and *doing more things*, as well as less *routine*, as compared to the other groups. In other words, there is a tendency to idealize, or overevaluate, this factory job. This suggests that any tendency of management to minimize the importance of this job will be perceived as offensive. This finding is consistent with a case study by Whyte (1956) in which it was shown that a vice-president's remark that a certain skilled job was "just a watchman's job" was so infuriating to the workers that they joined the C.I.O. in large numbers. The findings suggest that management ought to consider the tendency of workers to value their jobs more than management values them, in its communications to them. In the case of clerks, rating a Clerk's Job, however, the data did not reveal any tendency towards overevaluation.

Osgood et al. (1957, p. 244 ff.) have described how the data from the semantic differential can be used to compute distances between concepts. The greater the *D*-statistic, or distance between two concepts, the more different the two concepts seem to be to the *S*s doing the judging on the semantic differential. Osgood's procedure was used to determine the distances between the five jobs studied in our field project. The *D*-matrix is shown in Table 1. Two-dimensional drawings of the three-dimensional forms constructed from the *D*-matrix are shown in Fig. 1.

The only major difference in the perception of the five jobs from group to group, as revealed by Fig. 1, is in the position of a Clerk's Job relative to the other jobs. The workers view it in rather "exalted" terms, the top managers see it as the most different job as compared to the prestigeful Vice-President's Job. Perhaps the large number of dissatisfied clerks in the particular company is due to this perception of top management. Approximately 30% of the clerks dislike their supervisors; this percentage is quite high for this company.

It is interesting to notice that the most meaningful way to represent the job percep-

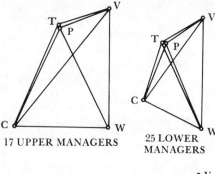

17 UPPER MANAGERS   25 LOWER MANAGERS

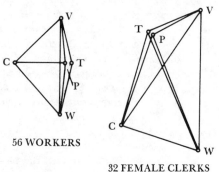

56 WORKERS   32 FEMALE CLERKS

FIGURE 1. Relationships between five jobs as viewed by different groups. (Note: V stands for Vice-President's job; P, Personnel Director's job; T, Teacher's job; C, Clerk's job; W, Welder's job.)

TABLE 1

D Matrix for the Perception of Five Jobs by Five Groups[a]

Distance Between	Top Mgrs. ($N = 17$)	Low Mgrs. ($N = 25$)	Female Clerks ($N = 32$)	Male Clerks ($N = 33$)	Worker ($N = 56$)
Welder's Job and Clerk's Job	62	55	48	59	51
Welder's Job and Teacher's Job	64	56	68	63	50
Welder's Job and Personnel Director's	68	60	69	63	61
Welder's Job and Vice-President's Job	76	65	74	73	66
Clerk's Job and Teacher's Job	66	54	63	64	54
Clerk's Job and Personnel Director's	69	55	60	60	51
Clerk's Job and Vice-President's Job	84	66	70	75	58
Teacher's Job and Personnel Director's	37	36	58	40	46
Teacher's Job and Vice-President's Job	44	41	50	49	45
Personnel Director's and Vice-President's Job	37	35	45	43	45

[a]All distances adjusted so that the same $N(N = 17)$ is used throughout.

tions of these groups is to draw a perpendicular line between a Welder's and a Vice-President's Job. It means that the most significant variable in the perception of jobs is the *level* of the job.

It is also interesting to note that the managers make finer discriminations between jobs than do the workers. This is seen from the fact that the *D*s obtained from the top managers are consistently higher than the *D*s obtained from the workers.

The Perception of the Man and the Job

To what extent does the man determine the perception of a job, and the job the perception of the man doing it? This is a complex question. We have only made a beginning towards answering it, but we did collect some data that are interesting.

The 155 employees who participated in the study rated Mr. T., the Personnel Director, also the Personnel Director's Job on the semantic differential. The reader will recall that the semantic differential for people and the one for jobs were not the same. Nevertheless, we did have a few scales which were equivalent.

Job S.D. Scales	People S.D. Scales
Evaluative	
High-low position	Successful-unsuccessful
Requires much-no education	Educated-uneducated
Requires much-no experience	Experienced-inexperienced
High-low pay	Gets high-low pay
Sociable-unsociable	Sociable-unsociable
Requires much-no intelligence	Intelligent-unintelligent
Clean-dirty	Gracious-crude
Good-bad	Good-bad humored
Potency Scales	
Heavy-light	Weak-strong
Important-unimportant	Powerful-powerless
Activity Scales	
Active-passive	Active-passive

Osgood et al. (1957, p. 91) *D*-scores were obtained from the discrepancies in the ratings of these corresponding scales. The reader will notice that the scale correspondence is not very close. The *D*-scores that were computed were very small. This is rather remarkable in view of the very rough correspondence between the scales. It appears that the perceptions of the job and the man are very closely interrelated. The job acquires the characteristics of the man and the man the characteristics of the job.

From consideration deriving from Osgood et al. (1957), on the reliability of the semantic differential, we conclude that, for our particular case, a *D* smaller than 48 means that there is complete fusion of the job and the man. For 80% of the top management, 62% of the middle management, 68% of the lower management, 47% of female clerks, 58% of the male clerks, and 56% of the workers there was such *complete* fusion.

A reasonable hypothesis, it seemed, was that if a person had never had any experience with personnel men, in other words if he never worked before in a setting in which there was a personnel man, this fusion between job and man doing the job would be even more complete. Surprisingly, this hypothesis cannot be supported by the data. In fact, if there is a relationship it runs in the opposite direction ($p < .25$, chi square, two-tail test).

SUMMARY

Five jobs and 6 people were rated on 38 scales of corresponding semantic differentials by 156 *S*s representing various groups in industry. The differences in the perception of the jobs and the people are discussed.

REFERENCES

Edwards, A. L. *Techniques of attitude scale construction.* New York: Appleton-Century-Crofts, 1957.

Osgood, C. E., Suci, G. J., and Tannenbaum, P. H. *The measurement of meaning.*
Urbana: Univer. Illinois Press, 1957.

Triandis, H. C. Some cognitive factors
affecting communication. Unpublished
doctoral dissertation, Cornell Univer.,
1958.

Triandis, H. C. Categories of thought of
managers, clerks, and workers about jobs

and people in industry. *J. appl. Psychol.*,
1959, *43*, in press.

Weaver, C. H. The quantification of the
frame of reference in labor management
communication. *J. appl. Psychol.*, 1958,
42, 1–9.

Whyte, W. F. Engineers and workers: A
case study. *Hum. Organization*, 1956, *14*,
3–12.

The College-Student Image
of the Scientist

DAVID C. BEARDSLEE, *Oakland University, Rochester, Michigan*
DONALD D. O'DOWD, *Oakland University, Rochester, Michigan*

The image of the scientist among high school students has been studied in detail in recent years. Remmers and Radler (*1*) have reported on some beliefs of teen-agers about scientists, and Mead and Metraux (*2*) have summarized the image of the scientist revealed in essays produced by a large sample of high school students.

The beliefs of college students about the scientist are also of interest. Many students entering college seriously consider careers in science, and college students will eventually constitute an influential segment of the citizens whose views make up the public response to science.

Exploration of the college-student image of the scientist was initiated in a series of unstructured interviews with college undergraduates at Wesleyan University (*3*). In these interviews, students described the scientist as being dedicated to his work and carrying it out with heroic devotion at the

expense of concern with public affairs and even family responsibilities. The scientist was described as unsociable, introverted, and possessing few, if any, friends. Some students referred spontaneously to his high intelligence; others were more impressed by the precision of his thinking and the objectivity (that is, lack of emotional involvement) with which he handles most personal and professional problems. Two telling comments represent the common response of undergraduate men to the scientist. One student volunteered, "I wouldn't care to double-date with a scientist," and another student commented, "maybe it's not a good idea for him [the scientist] to be married." A number of students were impressed by the scientist's apparent need to proceed in his work regardless of other demands on his time. In general, the college students revealed in these interviews beliefs similar to those found among high school students. The scientist, to use the student phrase, "is not well rounded."

In order to pursue further the subject of the student image of the scientist, a series of

Reprinted with the permission of the publisher
from the article of the same title in *Science*, 1961,
133, (March) 997–1001.

three successive questionnaires was designed and used in testing. A fourth version of the questionnaire was selected as the main instrument for an empirical study. It contained materials derived from the interviews and from standard questionnaires and scales developed in the earlier versions. In the questionnaire students were asked to indicate the appropriateness of a series of terms to each of 15 occupations, including that of scientist (*4*). The terms were arranged in two-ended, seven-point rating scales of the following form (*5*):

1. wealthy —:—:—:—:—:—:—
                                                          not well-to-do
2. optimistic —:—:—:—:—:—:—
                                                          pessimistic
3. excitable —:—:—:—:—:—:—   calm

This design makes it possible not only to determine absolute values for characteristics attributed to the scientist but also to obtain an estimate of the standing of the scientist relative to individuals in other occupations.

The questionnaire was given to undergraduate men and women in four colleges in the northeastern United States: Wesleyan University, a second small and highly selective men's liberal arts college, a highly selective private women's college, and the college of arts and sciences of a state university (*6*). At each college, probability samples of freshmen and seniors were chosen. Over 90 percent of the students selected at three of the four colleges returned completed questionnaires. At the second men's liberal arts college, all of the freshmen but only two-thirds of the seniors completed the questionnaire. Data from these seniors were not used in many of the following analyses. In all, about 1200 students were included in this phase of the study (*7*).

IMAGE OF THE SCIENTIST

It is possible to present a composite picture of the scientist from the responses

obtained. Students from all of the colleges, both men and women, freshmen and seniors, were in sufficient agreement to justify a summary of the characteristics attributed to the scientist by all groups. There is clearly a well-defined stereotype of the scientist among college students as well as among high school students. In the following summary, the rating of the scientist relative to individuals in other occupations is considered.

The scientist, according to college students, is outstanding in several respects. Students see him most prominently as a highly intelligent person with a strong tendency to be both individualistic and radical in personal and social outlook. At the same time, the scientist is seen as socially withdrawn; he is indifferent to people, retiring, and somewhat depressed, and he rates low in social popularity. In over-all sociability the scientist rates lowest among individuals in the 15 high-level occupations. It is therefore not surprising that he is believed to have a relatively unhappy home life and a wife who is not pretty. There is an air of strangeness about him; he is hard to like and comprehend. He is respected for his great contribution to society, but he is not the kind of person one can easily get to know.

The scientist is believed to be highly intelligent but not interested in art. He is both self-sufficient and persevering. He focuses his powers in a rational and sensitive pursuit of answers to nature's mysteries. He is rated as reasonably successful and as having ample opportunity to advance in his field. At the same time he is seen as having only modest wealth. It appears that the scientist could exploit his situation to secure wealth and status, but he is so devoted to his work that he is satisfied with a modest income.

The scientist is moderately confident, optimistic, and realistic in his approach to life. He has power in public affairs yet is given only a moderately high score on responsibility. When combined with his radicalism, this finding suggests that there are grounds for an anxious public to become suspicious of his loyalty. After all, he has few friends, great determination, and an unusual set of values.

Rather surprisingly, the scientist is scored relatively low on stability, caution, and calmness. It appears that he has difficulty controlling his impulses. This is consistent with the picture of his radicalism. He is coldy intellectual in some spheres of his life — mainly in his work — and he is emotional in his response to social and political appeals.

The complexity of the scientist's nature must account for his being considered mildly interesting and colorful. He is thought to be very valuable to society and to derive very great personal satisfaction from his work. If one were to study his recreational habits one would find him most frequently at chess, rarely playing bridge, and never playing poker.

In summary, there emerges a picture of the scientist as a highly intelligent individual devoted to his studies and research at the expense of interest in art, friends, and even family. The scientist derives great personal satisfaction, a sense of success, reasonably high status in the community, and a modest income from his work. He serves mankind in a selfless way, almost unaware that he is doing so; he serves others by serving himself.

In public matters the scientist is influential, but he may be somewhat naive. He is extreme in his views on social matters, and he tends to become emotionally involved with issues outside his realm of professional competence. The scientist is coldly intellectual in his professional area but excitable in the public political sphere. He is clearly an intellectual, but unlike "eggheads" in the humanities, he is characterized by a vigorous and directed use of his intelligence. The image conveys a sense of strength of personality, but it is a little extreme, a little strange, somewhat contradictory, and, therefore, hard to comprehend.

COMPARISON WITH IMAGES OF THE NONSCIENTIST

An estimate of the similarity of the scientist image with the images of individuals in 14 other occupations was obtained by correlating the mean scores obtained on 48 scales for the scientist and for people in these other occupations. The data from a subsample of the students tested were used to obtain the correlations presented in Table 1.

TABLE 1

Correlation of the Profile of the Scientist with Profiles of Individuals in Other Occupations

Occupation	Correlation
College professor	+.77
Engineer	+.53
Artist	+.51
School teacher	+.49
Doctor	+.44
Lawyer	+.41
Social worker	+.30
Accountant	−.03
Business executive	−.03
Industrial manager	−.03
Personnel director	−.18
Sales manager	−.25
Office supervisor	−.29
Retail store manager	−.29

These data reveal that the scientist is believed to have much in common with the college professor. The similarity of ratings for the scientist and engineer was predictable, but the correlation with ratings for artist and school teacher had not been clearly foreseen. This correlation stems primarily from the students' grouping of all these roles as intellectual roles. It is clear that the students believe that scientists do not share many attributes with individuals in any of the business and industrial occupations.

Comparison of the image of the scientist with that of the college professor reveals some interesting differences between these roles that are often filled by the same person.

Both occupations are entered by men of high intelligence with personality characteristics represented by high scores on *self-sufficient* and *persevering*, middle values on *strong, active, confident,* and *self-assertive,* and low scores on *stable* and *adaptable in habits.* Both professions are believed to attract men who are, to a high degree, radical and individualistic. Members of the two professions differ in that the scientist is thought to lack the artistic interest, good taste, and sensitivity of the college professor. The scientist is not a cultured intellectual, while the college professor attains the highest score in this dimension. Moreover, the scientist is, to a striking degree, less interested in people and less sociable and popular than the college professor. The professor is interested in people and quite successful with them. The scientist is neither drawn to people nor socially attractive. Finally, the scientist is less interesting and colorful than the college professor. The scientist is scored above the college professor on two components of what might be called "material opportunity" — that is, wealth and the opportunity for advancement. The scientist has a more markedly active, persevering, and rational approach to life and work than the professor. In summary, the scientist has greater wealth and opportunity than the professor and a more forceful approach to intellectual problems. However, in the very important areas of social sophistication and esthetic interests the college professor leads the scientist by a wide margin.

When the full range of occupation profiles is considered, the scientist and the engineer have a good deal in common. In terms of strength and competence, as indicated by middle values on such items as *active, confident, strong, hard, self-assertive,* and *realistic about life,* they have very similar scores. Competence in either field connotes a reasonable degree of success, social status, and power in public affairs. The scientist differs from the engineer in that he is believed to be more intellectual and less conformist in personal behavior and political viewpoint. The scientist also is rated higher than the engineer in concern with esthetic matters, in spite of the relatively low rating of the scientist in the realm of cultural interests. The scientist is considered more persevering, self-sacrificing, and valuable to society, as well as more interesting and colorful. On the other hand, the engineer has two clear advantages over the scientist. First, the engineer is more concerned with people. He is a sociable, popular fellow as compared with the scientist. Secondly, the engineer is considerably wealthier, and he is a more "regular guy" than the scientist. This latter characteristic is indicated by the higher scores for the engineer on *clean cut, plays poker,* and *has good taste* (taste in clothes, house, car, and so on), and the engineer is believed more likely to have a pretty wife. In conclusion, then, the engineer is thought to be less of an "egghead" than the scientist. He is less intelligent, less nonconforming, less sensitive esthetically, and less valuable to society. At the same time, the engineer is a more normal, healthy American male, with somewhat the same traits of character as the scientist but with little of the scientist's tendency to go to extremes in behavior or emotional commitment. To summarize, engineers are "Simonized scientists," to bend a phrase recently reported in a national magazine.

RELATION OF EXPERIENCE TO IMAGE

The student responses were analyzed to determine whether the life experiences and current status of the students were associated with different beliefs about occupations. It was found in comparing the scientist image held by men with that held by women and the image held by students in private as against public colleges, by freshmen as against seniors, by students from different socioeconomic backgrounds, by students from professional as against business families, and by students from different types of communities, that these groups do not differ in their beliefs about the scientist. This is clearly a stable image that is shared widely among college students with varied histories and experience.

In a study parallel to the one under consideration, 41 entering Wesleyan freshmen who indicated an intention to become scientists were compared with all the freshmen who planned to be active in other careers (*8*). Those who intended to be scientists had a more favorable image of both the scientist and the engineer than the remainder of the newly arrived freshmen. The would-be scientists, as compared to the other freshmen, viewed the scientist as more colorful and interesting, of higher social status, more successful, more sensitive to art, and of a more sociable temperament. In absolute terms, the men wishing to enter the field of science rated the scientist quite high in material and social success and in esthetic interests, while they considered him moderately concerned with people. The scientist, as seen by these students, is interesting and colorful. Moreover, as compared with the non-science students, the science students had an image of the engineer that was closer to their image of the scientist. They viewed the engineer as more individualistic, persevering, and capable of deriving satisfaction from his work than did non-science students. In general, the engineer was seen as being more a man of parts by the pre-science students.

There is also evidence in the data that students on entering college have a more favorable view of the scientist than students who have already spent a semester in college. The new students have a more favorable view than second-semester freshmen of the intellectual ability, artistic concern, and success of the scientist.

FACULTY MEMBERS' VIEW

A group of 27 college teachers of science at Wesleyan University were asked to respond to the same questionnaire that was given to the students. These men were a random sample of the science faculty. It is quite clear that the word *scientist* has similar connotations for them and for students. There was a correlation of $+.91$ between the average values attributed to the scientist by the Wesleyan students and by members of the science faculty on a group of 21 scales to which responses were made by both groups. The main differences between the two groups were, first, that the students attributed much more influence in public affairs to the scientist than the science teachers did, and, second, that members of the science faculty saw the scientist as more interested in art. Otherwise, the two groups were in close agreement.

Within the ranks of college teachers at Wesleyan, members of science and of social-science faculties are in almost complete agreement on the scientist image. On the other hand, faculty members in the humanities are more complimentary to the scientist than are the teachers of science or social science. A random sample of 23 teachers of the humanities rated the scientist quite high in material and social success and considered him more calm and more sociable than the science teachers did. The wordly success of the scientist seemed more impressive to teachers of the humanities than it did to teachers of the sciences.

OCCUPATIONAL PREFERENCES

Students participating in the main study were asked to indicate the degree to which they would like to enter each of the 15 occupational fields if barriers related to expense, length of training, and native ability were removed. In other words, a male student was directed: "rate each occupational position in terms of how much you would like to be in it if you could be in any occupation you wanted." The data revealed that a group of four occupations — those of college professor, lawyer, doctor, and business executive — were considered most desirable, in that order. The occupations of scientist and school teacher came next in order in a second grouping, at some distance from the first. A rather large gap appeared between this and the next grouping, the occupations of engineer and personnel director. When women were asked to estimate the attractiveness of these occupations for men, they also ranked the scientist in the fifth position. However, when college women were asked to name the single occupation for a future husband that would be most pleasing to them, only 3 percent indicated scientist. Approximately 20 percent of the women wished their husbands would be doctors, and another 20 percent selected the profession of lawyer.

STEREOTYPES
OF SPECIALIZED SCIENTISTS

In studies of the ranking in prestige of professions and occupations, the ranking of the term *scientist* differs from that of terms such as *chemist* or *biologist*, which describe scientists in specific fields (*9*). In view of this finding, an exploratory study was designed to elicit the images of biologist, chemist, and physicist (*10*). A small number of Wesleyan students were asked, in an interview, for their impressions of the personality, family life, status, social life, and motivations of men in each scientific field. Although the sample was small and unsystematically chosen, the agreement among students was so great as to suggest that the findings are of general significance. The stereotype of the specialized scientist in each case was more favorable than the image of scientist that was revealed in other interviews. According to these stereotypes the scientists in designated fields are more wealthy and successful, have richer social lives and more rewarding family lives, and are more pleasant and outgoing people than the "scientist" considered apart from his field. The biologist is the most normal of the scientists in the sense that he approaches most closely the American ideal, and to the physicist are attributed

many of the negative qualities that emerged in the interviews concerned with the generalized "scientist." The chemist falls between the two extremes.

CONCLUSIONS

These data suggest that there exists among college students a readiness to respond to the word *scientist* in a complex and differentiated manner. There is wide agreement concerning the image of the scientist among various classifications of men and women students in the Northeast. Members of one college faculty share this image with their students. The image is the same for freshmen as for seniors. It is safe to assume that the outlines of the image are the same for students at many colleges and for many college-educated adults. It is quite likely that the image is shifted somewhat in the first few months of a student's college career, but it is obviously not markedly changed. The image of the scientist among college students resembles in many ways the image held by high school students, as reported by Mead and Metraux (*2*).

The specific features of the scientist image are important for several reasons. First, the image reveals the students' beliefs about the personality of the scientist and the style of life associated with a career in science. It means to the potential recruit that, if he selects science, he should have a certain set of personal qualities and can expect a particular kind of social life and certain types of personal associates, and it implies that the kind of life he will live is greatly limited by his work. If these features of the life of the scientist do not fit with the student's beliefs about himself or his hopes for the future, he is likely to be wary of committing himself to a career in science. At the same time, of course, the image influences the behavior of the student who has chosen science and leads him to develop those aspects of his character most in keeping with the stereotype of the scientist.

In short, the image has the effect of recruiting a certain type of person and discouraging others. This limits the range of people likely to consider the field, and it restricts the variety of basic talents available to science. Second, the public reaction to science, scientists, and the contributions of scientific research is likely to be colored by this image. This is particularly true in areas where arguments center around the generalized role of science. For example, the role of scientists in government or the advisability of admitting scientists to positions of high responsibility are issues frequently discussed in general terms. It may even be that the negative reaction of college students to courses in "general science" is attributable in part to the attitudes tapped by the word *science*.

The strong features of the image of the scientist are his high intelligence and his driving concern to extend knowledge and to discover truth. His work is of great value to mankind, and it brings him both a sense of satisfaction and a fair measure of success. The weaknesses in the image are many and disturbing. The scientist is seen as basically uninterested in people and unsuccessful with them. To the contemporary student, a person who does not care for people is suspiciously out of touch with life. The scientist is not interested in art — he has eschewed the life of the spirit that gives breadth and vitality to the life of the mind. Further, the scientist is a nonconformist and a radical, as well as a person with only moderate control of his impulses. These features suggest that college students possess beliefs that can easily be played upon to indict the scientist in times when loyalty is an issue of public concern. The undesirable aspects of this picture of the personal and intellectual life of the scientist make the role hard to accept in spite of the attractiveness of the work and the social contributions of the scientist.

The attractiveness of a scientific career in an abstract sense is clearly indicated by the high rank given it by men in statements concerning what they would like to be. Yet, surprisingly, few women wish to marry a scientist. It must be that, for men, the intellectual status, success, and material well-being of the scientist outweigh the many disadvantages of the scientist image. On the other hand, a woman married to a scientist must accept his personal qualities while benefiting very little in a direct way from the nature of his job.

Students clearly prefer the personality, social opportunities, and style of life of the college professor to those of the scientist. The scientist's only asset, by comparison with the professor, lies in the rewards associated with the work, and the differential is not great. The engineer and the scientist offer relatively interesting alternatives. The scientist is seen as an intellectual, with little capacity for social interchange; the engineer is a more normal "organization man," aiming at a nine-to-five existence, with an interest in good fellowship. It would seem that a student of science who could achieve the requisite training would be strongly drawn to college teaching with its richer, more humane connotations. On the other hand, the attractions of science and of engineering would seem to balance, with a person's view of himself playing an important role in his choice of one or the other.

It is interesting that students intending to pursue careers in science should have a more favorable image of the scientist than their colleagues who are planning other careers. It is not known whether commitment to a field changes the image or whether those with a more favorable image are drawn to the field. Probably both of these processes contribute to this difference.

It is comforting to find that scientists who are identified with their particular specialties are perceived as relatively normal people. These findings indicate that monolithic "science" is a source of concern to many sensitive citizens. On the other hand, men with professional specialties are considered more human, loyal, and comprehensible than "the scientist."

SCIENCE AS A WAY OF LIFE

The standard contemporary response to the finding that a product presents a "bad" image to the public is to turn for assistance to a team of public relations men who are instructed to change the image. To change an image as well developed and as widespread as the image of the scientist appears to be a most discouraging undertaking. This image is imbedded in a system of other stereotypes with which people, even highly educated people, structure their social world. To eliminate the unfavorable connotations from *scientist* would require a brilliantly conceived long-term campaign of confrontation through mass media and of educational innovation that is not likely to be undertaken. But is a massive campaign to alter this image appropriate? Scientists themselves, as well as their faculty colleagues, agree upon the essential features of the image. If it does represent, even in a distorted and exaggerated fashion, the characteristics of American scientists, it may be that to use publicity techniques would not only fail to hide the reality that lies behind the image but might also be dishonest.

Our studies give no data as to the actual (as distinguished from the perceived) characteristics of scientists. Yet C. P. Snow (*11*) has argued that indeed scientists *are* less interested than most educated men in esthetic matters and social affairs. Perhaps "the discipline" of science *does* narrow a man's interests, does create a group who do not meet the cultural ideal of the broadly educated man. If so, the "solution" is not to be found in an aping of Madison Avenue but, as Snow has also argued, in a more general appreciation on the part of the intellectual community of the demands the scientific mode of though makes upon anyone, professional scientist or not, who seeks an objective understanding of the world around him. Perhaps, also, scientists have "over-conformed" to their own image of what a scientist is, and perhaps the reality can change as more of them develop the broader interests and cultural appreciation constantly called for by liberal educators.

A final stance for the scientist consists in recognition of the possibility that to be a scientist is indeed to be different. The studies of Roe (*12*) and of Thorndike and Hagen (*13*) have shown that scientists tend to have characteristic developmental histories and personality structures. It may be that in order to do their work, recruits to scientific careers require some of the qualities which, in extreme form, appear in the stereotype of the scientist. If so, cannot the scientist accept this and get on with his work?

REFERENCES

1. H. H. Remmers and D. H. Radler, *The American Teenager* (Bobbs-Merrill, Indianapolis, 1957).

2. M. Mead and R. Metraux, *Science 126*, 384 (1957).

3. E. W. Harbinger and A. LaCava, Wesleyan undergraduates, assisted us in this study. The research was carried out under a contract with the U.S. Office of Education, Department of Health, Education, and Welfare, Additional support was provided by the Faculty Research Committee of Wesleyan University.

4. The occupations that were studied are listed in Table 1.

5. The form of the questionnaire and some of the scales are taken from the work of C. E. Osgood [for example, C. E. Osgood, G. J. Suci, P. H. Tannenbaum, *The Measurement of Meaning* (Univ. of Illinois Press, Urbana, 1957)].

6. The data were collected during 1958 and 1959.

7. A summary of the entire study appears in "College Student Images of a Selected Group of Professions and Occupations," *Final Report, Cooperative Research Project No. 562, U.S. Office of Education* (Wesleyan University, Middletown, Conn., 1960).

8. This study was made by D. H. Bogart, a Wesleyan student.

9. National Opinion Research Center, in *Class, Status, and Power*, R. Bendix and S. M. Lipset, Eds. (Free Press, Glencoe, Ill., 1953).

10. The interviews were conducted by E. W. Harbinger, of Wesleyan.

11. C. P. Snow, *The Two Cultures and the Scientific Revolution* (Cambridge Univ. Press, New York, 1959).

12. A. Roe, *The Psychology of Occupations* (Wiley, New York, 1956).

13. R. L. Thorndike and E. Hagen, *Ten Thousand Careers* (Wiley, New York, 1959).

OTHER RELEVANT ARTICLES

The following are abstracts of articles relevant to the topic of this chapter:

Grunes, W. F. On perception of occupations. *Personnel and Guidance Journal*, 1956, *34*, 276–279.

————. Looking at occupations. *Journal of Abnormal and Social Psychology*, 1957, *54*, 86–92.

These two articles report the results of an experiment in which high schoolers were asked to group fifty-one occupations in categories of their own subjective choosing. Data were compiled on each job showing the other jobs it was grouped with and the reasons for the group offered by the subject. For instance, "doctor" was most frequently associated with the jobs of nurse, college professor, teacher, engineer, and so forth, and was listed under titles as "much education," "lot of money," "social skills," "good looking," and the like.

In this way the subjects' perceptions of the structure of occupations was elicited, contrasting with the expert judgment of occupational structure presented in the previous chapter. Grunes found that four main clusters could be formed, differentiated by characteristics of prestige, amount of education required, verbal skill content, business setting, amount of physical labor, and social skills. Three clusters overlapped to an extent that the overlaps were considered distinct subgroups, reflecting outdoor versus indoor physical labor, and business occupations which require less education. A few occupations of the fifty-one rated could not be placed with the system of interrelated clusters, but formed independent ones representing glamour and adventure.

Grunes also found that the association of various jobs within clusters and consciousness of various dimensions by the subjects were influenced by their family's socioeconomic status and by the region of their residence.

Porter, L. W. Self-perceptions of first level supervisors compared with upper-management personnel and with operative line workers. *Journal of Applied Psychology*, 1959, *43*, 183–186.

This article illustrates the use of adjective checklists to obtain descriptions of a given worker, foremen, for comparison with the self descriptions of workers at higher and lower levels of work. The findings may be summarized as showing the foreman to perceive himself as cautious, conservative, and restrained compared to workers above and below him in the hierarchy of management. Porter interprets this as a result of their peculiar position of being formally and psychologically in-the-middle, or between the extremes in formal positions in their organizations.

The references in Porter's article contain a number of his other studies of workers' perceptions of themselves.

Another characteristic of occupations has been identified by Rosenberg (*Occupations and Values*, New York: Free Press, 1957). That is their permeability as occupational choices, as reflected by the frequency with which college students change in and out of them, and the proportion of late entrants to early entrants. Such choices as engineering, architecture, and medicine are the early chosen ones, while advertising, government service, business and the like are decided upon later.

Selected additional resources to accompany the articles in this chapter are:

Caplow, T. *The Sociology of Work*. Minneapolis, Minn.: University of Minnesota Press, 1954. Includes a chapter on the measurement of occupational status.
Slocum, W. L. *Occupational Careers*. Chicago: Aldine Publishing Co., 1966. Also includes a chapter on occupational status.
Davis, K. *Human Society*. New York: Macmillan, 1949. Has material on the dimensions and correlates of prestige.
Simpson, R. L., and Ida Simpson. Correlates and estimation of occupational prestige. *American Journal of Sociology*, 1960, *66*, 135–140.

The prestige not only of occupations, but of other objects relating to occupational goals has been studied:

Campbell, R. E. The prestige of industries. *Journal of Applied Psychology*, 1960, *44*, 1–5.
McTavish, D. G. The differential prestige of situs categories. *Social Forces*, 1962, *41*, 363–368.
Reiss, A. J. *Occupations and Social Status*. New York: Free Press, 1961.
Zytowski, D. G. An exploration of the prestige values of college majors. *Vocational Guidance Quarterly*, 1966, *15*, 46–49.

Other modes of occupational perception are described in the following articles:

Broom, L., and J. H. Smith. Bridging occupations. *British Journal of Sociology*, 1963, *14*, 321–324. This article identifies certain occupations in terms of their bridging quality — their ability to facilitate or enable social mobility.
Havighurst, R. J. Youth in exploration and man emergent. In Borow, H., (Ed.) *Man in a World at Work*. Boston: Houghton Mifflin, 1964. On pages 226–227 a presentation is made of occupations as either ego-involving or society maintaining.
Mack, R. W. Occupational ideology and the determinate role. *Social Forces*, 1957, *36*, 37–44. Mack proposes that occupations are variable in the degree to which they define mobility and status, and role expectations for attainment and performance.

Super, D. E. Occupational life spans and output curves. (Chapter 4 of *The Psychology of Careers*, New York: Harper & Row, 1957) Describes careers in terms of early, normal, and late entry and leaving. A typical early-entry career is bootblack, a late-entry career would be judge; contrasting with an early-leaving career of athlete, or airline stewardess, and late-leaving of night watchman.

Additional studies of occupational images are:

Clive, Lois. Relationship of values to the perception of activities involved in an occupation. *Journal of Counseling Psychology*, 1964, *11*, 262–266.

Davidson, H., F. Reissman, and E. Meyers. Personality characteristics attributed to the worker. *Journal of Social Psychology*, 1962, *57*, 155–160.

Dipboye, W. J., and W. F. Anderson. Occupational stereotypes and manifest needs of high school students. *Journal of Counseling Psychology*, 1961, *4*, 296–304.

Gonyea, G. G. Job perceptions in relation to vocational preference. *Journal of Counseling Psychology*, 1963, *10*, 20–26.

Schutz, R. A., and D. H. Blocher. Self-concepts and stereotypes of vocational preferences. *Vocational Guidance Quarterly*, 1960, *8*, 241–244.

Ulrich, Gretchen, J. Hecklik, and E. C. Roeber. Occupational stereotypes of high school students. *Vocational Guidance Quarterly*, 1966, *14*, 169–174.

Walker, K. F. A study of occupational stereotypes. *Journal of Applied Psychology*, 1958, *42*, 122–124.

Webb, S. C. and Audry Frush. Qualities that differentiate dentists and physicians. *Personnel and Guidance Journal*. 1965, *43*, 702–706.

The dimensionality of job perceptions, a topic related to the preceding material on the structure of occupations, is represented by:

Goneya, G. G. Dimensions of job perceptions. *Journal of Counseling Psychology*, 1961, *8*, 305–311.

Reeb, M. How people see jobs: a multidimensional analysis. *Occupational Psychology*, 1959, *33*, 1–17.

The Beardslee and O'Dowd article is abstracted from their larger report, College student images of a selected group of professions and occupations. Final Report, Cooperative Research Project No. 562, U.S. Office of Education, Wesleyan University, Middletown, Connecticut, 1960.

Other articles issuing from the same study are:

Beardslee, D. C., and D. D. O'Dowd. Students and the occupational world. In Sanford, N. (Ed.) *The American College*.

O'Dowd, D. D., and D. C. Beardslee. The image of the college professor. *American Association of University Professors Bulletin*, 1961, *47*, 216–221.

———, and ———. The student image of the school teacher. *Phi Delta Kappan*, 1961, *42*, 250–254.

PART III

A Developmental Concept of Vocational Behavior

MARINER

A Developmental Concept
of Vocational Behavior

4

Today, no one would quarrel with a concept of vocational behavior as having important developmental qualities. But from the turn of this century until the nineteen-fifties, the attention of the vocational psychologist was on the non-developmental, the point-in-time "vocational choice." Antecedents to this event were assumed, but were not integrated into it, nor were subsequent events to it. The important event of vocational behavior occurred when the prospective worker made some assessment of his abilities and inclinations, and chose some occupation from the opportunities available, which he felt promised him greatest success or satisfaction.

The time at which the crystallized choice typically occurred was known, as were some maturational characteristics of interests, but stages of development, the tasks essential to them, and the determinants of development had not been linked together in any integrated fashion.

This chapter concerns itself with statements of varied aspects of the developmental character of vocational behavior: general ones, stages and patterns of development, and the concept of maturity, plus whatever evidence there is available to support them.

Beilin (1955) suggests that theories of vocational development are special cases of general developmental theory, and that they should possess certain desidirata as such. The reader may evaluate the papers in this chapter from the discussion of Beilin's points which follow.

General developmental theory specifies a number of characteristics. The first, Beilin says, is almost too obvious: that development is a continuous process. Yet until only recently, vocational development was not conceived as continuing beyond the choice of an occupation. Presently Super is investigating its process beyond that point. The next specification is that developmental process is irreversible; that the same set of conditions cannot exist in two samples of a process taken at different times. Further, developmental process must be differentiable into patterns, and in any time span some aspect of development should be pre-eminent.

That which is best known is the process of arriving at a vocational choice, and although there is disagreement on when this developmental task is essentially begun, it can be assumed to have ceased when the individual seems established in an occupation.

If normal development is continuous and irreversible, then a concept of maturity is viable, reflecting the stage of development at which an individual stands. Specification of what comprises mature vocational behavior has been trouble-some, especially after entry into an occupation or career, for it is not certain what the developmental tasks after that time are.

The first article in this chapter is Super's original statement of his views on vocational behavior. In it, he reviews the earlier statement of Ginzberg, Ginsburg, Axelrad, and Herma (1951), and documents some of his reasons for an expansion of it. Super also provides a postulate to explain the mechanism of vocational choice, which is enlarged upon in a subsequent chapter of this book.

This is followed by Tiedeman's more microscopic examination of the "process" of choice and his comments on vocational life patterns. Aside from the stages of the decision, Tiedeman also elaborates on the interdependence of the many deci-sions which go into the developmental process, and remarks on the importance of the arrangement of positions in the work history.

Yet another outline of the stages of vocational development is offered by Hershenson, for the purpose of trying to integrate existing theories and provide hypotheses which may be tested. No tests of it have been accomplished which might be included in this chapter.

In order that the reader may compare Hershenson's conception of life stages with those of other commentators, tables are included showing vocational stages as seen by Super, by Havighurst, and by Miller and Form.

The next several papers concern themselves with vocational maturity. Super initiated the concept in a (1955) article, and presented findings from an extensive study of the vocational maturity of ninth-grade boys (Super and Overstreet, 1960). In this study, they rated interviews for a number of indices of maturity, reduced them to five general factors, and related these five expressions of maturity to various external influences and determinants.

Most recently Crites has developed a self-report measure of vocational maturity. A substantial excerpt from this monograph is included here, reporting the success with which he selected items to constitute the inventory, and some findings relative to its development. Most of the discussions of methodology and con-ceptualization have been omitted, not because they lack value, but simply for reasons of economy of space. The reader is urged to read the entire report if the topic is of interest to him.

O'Hara and Tiedeman, in the following paper, demonstrate how the self-concept becomes more distinct as the person matures. This is in line with the principle that the person's system differentiates as it develops. They further endeavor to identify the boundaries of stages in the developmental sequence and their essential tasks.

The final report of research employs a slightly different concept of vocational maturity, one which appeared at a time just prior to the trial stage of Super. It identifies three levels of certainty of vocational choice, and investigates some correlates of each. There are other concepts related to this level of development, such as anticipated occupational frustration, and maturation of work values, references for which are presented at the end of this chapter.

It is here that this book aligns with a developmental view of vocational behavior. Its middle chapters are devoted to broad examinations of the crucial task or stage in that development: choice or entry and their determinants. The book returns to the cross-sectional frame of reference again when it considers worker satisfaction and performance.

REFERENCES

Beilin, H. The application of general developmental principles to the vocational area. *Journal of Counseling Psychology*, 1955, 2, 53–57.

Ginzberg, E., J. W. Ginsburg, S. Axelrad, and J. L. Herma. *Occupational Choice*. New York: Columbia University Press, 1951.

Super, D. E. Dimensions and measurement of vocational maturity. *Teachers College Record*, 1955, 57, 151–163.

————, and P. L. Overstreet. *The Vocational Maturity of Ninth-Grade Boys*. New York: Teachers College Columbia University, Bureau of Publications, 1960.

A Theory
of Vocational Development

DONALD E. SUPER, *Teachers College, Columbia University*

Two and one-half years ago a colleague of mine at Columbia, Dr. Eli Ginzberg, an economist, shocked and even unintentionally

Reprinted with the permission of the author and publisher from the *American Psychologist*, 1953, *8*, 185–190.

annoyed many members of the National Vocational Guidance Association by stating, at the annual convention, that vocational counselors attempt to counsel concerning vocational choice without any theory as to how vocational choices are made. A year later Dr. Ginzberg published his monograph on *Occupational Choice*, in which he stated:

Vocational counselors are busy practitioners anxious to improve their counseling techniques ... the research-minded among them devote what time they can to devising better techniques. They are not theoreticians working on the problem of how individuals make their occupational choices, for, though they have no bias against theory, they have little time to invest in developing one (10, p. 7).

Ginzberg continues, apropos of the fields of psychology and economics:

there are good reasons why the problem [of how occupational choices are made] has not been a focus of investigation for psychology or economics.... The process has roots in the interplay of the individual and reality, and this field is only now beginning to be included in the boundaries of psychological inquiry. The obverse formulation applies to economics, which as a discipline concentrates on a detailed analysis of reality forces and satisfies itself with a few simplified assumptions about individual behavior (10, p. 7).

These conclusions were based partly on a review of the research literature which I did at his request, and partly on a number of discussions in which he, his research team, and I participated. Consequently, I have a feeling of responsibility, not for the conclusions which he drew, but for drawing my own conclusions and for sharing them with my colleagues in psychology and guidance.

BASIS OF GINZBERG'S CRITICISMS It may help to point out that Ginzberg's conclusions were based on a review of the research literature which was designed to provide answers to specific questions asked by his research team in order to help them plan their own research project. What synthesizing of results I did was undertaken to answer these questions. I did not attempt to answer the question "What theories underlie the principles of vocational guidance now generally accepted by practitioners?"

But I do agree with his analysis of the situation with regard to theory construction: we have done relatively little of it, and for the reasons he has suggested. However, this does not mean that we have operated without theory. It is the principal purpose of this paper to set forth a theory of vocational development, a theory inherent in and emergent from the research and philosophy of psychologists and counselors during the past two decades. But first I should like, as a help in formulating a more adequate theory, briefly to present the theory of occupational choice put forth by Ginzberg and his associates, to show how each of its elements had already been set forth by psychologists doing research in this field, and to point out some of its limitations.

THE GINZBERG THEORY

As Ginzberg, Ginsburg, Axelrad, and Herma summarize their theory of occupational choice, it contains four elements:

1. *Occupational choice is a developmental process which typically takes place over a period of some ten years.* This theory of Ginzberg's, it should be noted, is one of the points made by the official statement of the *Principles* and *Practices of Vocational Guidance* [33], first formulated by the National Vocational Guidance Association 25 years ago, it is a point stressed by Kitson in his *Psychology of Vocational Adjustment* [14], published in 1925, and, in 1942, in my own *Dynamics of Vocational Adjustment* [29] several pages are devoted to a discussion of the fact that "choosing an occupation ... is a process which ... may go on over a long period."

2. *The process is largely irreversible:* experience cannot be undone, for it results in investments of time, of money, and of ego; it produces changes in the individual. This second theory of Ginzberg's is clearly implied in Charlotte Buhler's 20-year-old theory of life stages [5], in Lehman and Witty's equally old studies of play interests [15], in Pressey, Janney, and Kuhlen's 13-year-old discussion of adolescent and adult development [20],

and in my own 10-year-old text on vocational adjustment [28].

3. *The process of occupational choice ends in a compromise between interests, capacities, values, and opportunities.* This third theory of Ginzberg's is well illustrated in the practices of individual diagnosis developed by the Minnesota Employment Stabilization Research Institute 20 years ago and described by Paterson and Darley [19]; it was further demonstrated and described by the Adjustment Service experiment 17 years ago [2]; and it is basic to presentations of the use of diagnostic techniques in texts such as Bingham's [3] and mine [29], both of which appeared before the completion of Ginzberg's study. In fact, Frank Parsons [18], in 1909, discussed vocational counseling as a process of helping the individual to study both himself and possible occupational opportunities, and to work out a compromise between his abilities, interests, and opportunities. He called this last process "true reasoning."

4. Ginzberg's final theoretical formulation is that *there are three periods of occupational choice:* the period of *fantasy* choice, governed largely by the wish to be an adult; the period of *tentative* choices beginning at about age 11 and determined largely by interests, then by capacities, and then by values; and the period of *realistic* choices, beginning at about age 17, in which exploratory, crystallization, and specification phases succeed each other. Those who are acquainted with Lehman and Witty's early research in the change of interest with age [15], with Strong's more searching work [25] in the same area, with Sisson's research in the increasing realism of choice with increasing age [23], with Charlotte Buhler's research in life stages [5], and with the use made of these data by Pressey [20] or by me [28], will find these three choice periods familiar. The special contribution of Ginzberg and his associates is the postulation of the successive dominance of interests, capacities, and values as determinants of choice before reality begins to play a major role.

It is easy, and perhaps even rather petty, thus to take a theoretical contribution and demonstrate its ancestry, showing that there is nothing particularly original about it. This is, undoubtedly, the normal reaction to claims of originality. But originality is more generally the result of a rearrangement of the old than the actual creation of something new: the rearrangement is original because it brings out details or relationships which have been missed or points up new applications. Ginzberg's theory is indeed an important contribution, this seems clear to me, at least, as I recollect the struggle I had in writing parts of my *Dynamics of Vocational Adjustment* (a struggle which resulted from the lack of a theoretical structure and from inadequate research), and as I work on its revision in the light, among other things, of Ginzberg's theoretical formulation and the thinking which it has stimulated. I have used this critical approach to Ginzberg's work in order to demonstrate that we have not entirely lacked a theoretical basis for our work in vocational guidance, and to show that the elements of theory on which we have based our practice have been sound, at least in that they have foreshadowed the elements which one group of theorists used when they went about constructing a theory of occupational choice.

Limitations of Ginzberg's Theory

But this is not the whole story. Ginzberg's theory is likely to be harmful because of its limitations, limitations other than those of research design and numbers in his basic study.

First, it does not build adequately on previous work: for example, the extensive literature on the nature, development, and predictive value of inventoried interests is rather lightly dismissed.

Second, "choice" is defined as preference rather than as entry or some other implementation of choice, and hence means different things at different age levels. To the 14-year-old it means nothing more than preference, because at that age the need for realism is minimized by the fact that the preference does not need to be acted upon until the remote future. To the 21-year-old student of engineering, on the other hand, "choice" means a preference which has already been acted upon in entering engineering school, although the final action will come only with graduation and entry into a job. No wonder that reality plays a larger part in choice at age 21, when, unlike choice at age 14, it is by definition a reality-tested choice!

A third defect in Ginzberg's theory emerges from these different meanings of the term "choice" at different ages: it is the falseness of the distinction between "choice" and "adjustment" which he and his research team make. The very fact that choice is a continuous process going on over a period of time, a process rather far removed from reality in early youth but involving reality in increasing degrees with increasing age, should make it clear that there is no sharp distinction between choice and adjustment. Instead, they blend in adolescence, with now the need to make a choice and now the need to make an adjustment predominating in the occupational or life situation.

Finally, a fourth limitation in the work of the Ginzberg team lies in the fact that, although they set out to study the process of occupational choice, and although they properly concluded that it is one of compromise between interests, capacities, values, and opportunities, they did not study or describe the compromise process. Surely this is the crux of the problem of occupational choice and adjustment: the nature of the compromise between self and reality, the degree to which and the conditions under which one yields to the other, and the way in which this compromise is effected. For the counseling psychologist's function is to help the individual to effect this compromise. He must not only know the factors which must be compromised and how these have been compromised in the experience of others,

but also the dynamics of the compromising process, so that he may facilitate this process in his counselee with constructive results.

ELEMENTS OF ADEQUATE THEORY OF VOCATIONAL DEVELOPMENT

An adequate theory of vocational choice and adjustment would synthesize the results of previous research insofar as they lend themselves to synthesis; it would take into account the continuity of the development of preferences and of the differences in the stages, choices, entry, and adjustment; it would explain the process through which interest, capacities, values, and opportunities are compromised. The second part of this paper will be devoted to a sketch of the main elements of such a theory of vocational development as they appear in the literature, and the third and final part will consist of an attempt to synthesize these elements in an adequate theory. The term "development" is used rather than "choice," because it comprehends the concepts of preference, choice, entry, and adjustment. There seem to be a dozen elements to a theory of vocational development: they are taken up in sequence.

Individual Differences

One of the basic elements of a theory of vocational development has been the theory of individual differences, a cornerstone of modern educational and vocational psychology. Kitson based much of his early *Psychology of Vocational Adjustment* [14] on this theory and on the findings on which it was based. It was essential to the work of the Minnesota Employment Stabilization Research Institute [19]. It is surely unnecessary to document the fact of individual differences in aptitudes, interests, and values, or the significance of these differences for vocational development.

Multipotentiality

A second basic element of theory has been the concept of the occupational multi-potentiality of the individual. It was first documented for intelligence by Army psychologists in World War I, and was stressed by Kitson in his early textbook. It was documented for interests by Strong's work on the classification of occupational interests [26]. It is a well-established fact and a basic assumption of vocational counseling that each person has the potential for success and satisfaction in a number of occupations.

Occupational Ability Patterns

The existence of occupational ability patterns, that is, the fact that abilities and interests fall into patterns which distinguish one occupation from another, was established by the Minnesota Employment Stabilization Research Institute [19] and has been confirmed in other studies, particularly those of the United States Employment Service [8]. People have been found to prefer, enter, remain in, like, and succeed most consistently in occupations for which they have appropriate patterns of traits. The theory of the patterning of aptitudes and interests within individuals and within occupational families and the significance of this patterning for choice, entry, and adjustment are widely accepted and applied by counselors and psychologists today.

Identification and the Role of Models

Much has been made of the importance of identification with parents and other adults in individual development by psychoanaly-

tically oriented writers, and this concept is widely used by counseling psychologists regardless of orientation. It has been little documented, however, in psychological research in the vocational choice and adjustment process. The work of Friend and Haggard [9] and a study by Stewart [1] do, however, provide some objective basis for the theory that the childhood and adolescent identifications play a part in shaping vocational interests, and also provide role models which facilitate the development and implementation of a self-concept, provided that the required abilities and opportunities are present.

Continuity of Adjustment

The continuity of the adjustment process was stressed by Kitson in his 1925 textbook as a result of his analysis of the careers of men whose success was attested to by being listed in *Who's Who in America*. The fact that adolescents and adults face a succession of emerging problems as they go through life, and that some of these problems are peculiar to the various life stages, was brought out by the studies of life stages made by Charlotte Buhler [5] and by those of occupational mobility conducted by Davidson and Anderson [7], Strong [26], and Miller and Form [16]. And theories of the development of interests have been formulated by Carter [6] and by Bordin [4], theories which I modified slightly in my book on testing and upon which I drew in describing the process of vocational choice and adjustment in a speech first made at Ft. Collins, Colorado, in 1949, revised several times, and later published in the journal *Occupations*, under the title of "Vocational Adjustment: Implementing a Self-Concept" [30]. These formulations are drawn on again as the cement for the various elements which need to be brought together in a theory of vocational development and as an explanation of the process of compromise between self and reality.

Life Stages

The work of psychologists and sociologists in describing the stages through which growth and development proceed, and in showing how these stages bear on the process of vocational choice and adjustment, has already been referred to. It was drawn on heavily in the text by Pressey, Janney, and Kuhlen [20], in my own first text [28], in Ginzberg's research [10], and in a recent text on *Industrial Sociology* by Miller and Form [16] which is as important for its original contribution and synthesis as it is annoying for its bias against anything that does not conform to sociology as they conceive of it. Buhler's theory of development through the exploratory, establishment, maintenance, and decline stages is translated into occupational terminology by Miller and Form, who also documented the theory for American careers, while Ginzberg, Ginsburg, Axelrad, and Herma have developed in more detail the phases of the exploratory stage. This latter theory needs confirmation with a large sample and more objective procedures, in view of Small's [24] recent failure to confirm it with a somewhat different adolescent sample, but the general theory of life stages is basic to vocational guidance and will be drawn on heavily in my attempt at synthesis.

Career Patterns

The formulation of a theory of career patterns resulted from the occupational manifestations of life stages first documented by Davidson and Anderson [7], added to for a select group by Terman's genetic studies of gifted persons [31], and then pointed up by Ginzberg and his associates [10] and by Miller and Form [16]. Career pattern theory appears to be a key element in the theoretical basis of vocational guidance, for it gives the counselor basic assumptions concerning the social, educational, and occupational mobility of his counselees, and it enables him to foresee types of problems which a given

client is likely to encounter in establishing a career.

Development Can Be Guided

Another basic element in a theory of vocational development is the theory that development through the life stages can be guided. Although there is ample evidence that ability is to some extent inherited, and that personality too has its roots in inherited neural and endocrine make-up, there is also good evidence that manifested aptitudes and functioning personality are the result of the interaction of the organism and the environment. It is a basic theory of guidance as we know it today that the development of the individual can be aided and guided by the provision of adequate opportunities for the utilization of aptitudes and for the development of interests and personality traits.

Development the Result of Interaction

That the nature of the interaction between the individual and his environment is by no means simple has been brought out by a variety of investigations ranging from studies of the effects of foster homes and of education on intelligence [17] to evaluations of the effects of occupational information and of test interpretation on vocational plans and on self-understanding [13]. The realization of this fact and the acceptance of this principle have led to a greater humility in our claims for counseling and to a greater degree of sophistication in our use of guidance techniques.

The Dynamics of Career Patterns

The interaction of the individual and his environment during the growth and early exploratory stages, little understood though the process actually is, has been much more adequately investigated than has this same process during the late exploratory, establishment, and maintenance stages. We still know relatively little about the dynamics of career patterns. Terman's work [31] tells us something about the role of intelligence, Strong's [26] about interests, and Hollingshead's [11] about social status, but no adequate studies have been made of the interaction of these and other factors in determining whether the individual in question will have a career pattern which is typical or atypical of his parental socioeconomic group. It was partly with this objective that an investigation known as the Career Pattern Study was launched in Middletown, New York, last year.

Job Satisfaction: Individual Differences, Status, and Role

Early theories of job satisfaction stressed the role of intelligence and interest in adjustment to the occupation or to the job, building on studies of the relationships between these traits and occupational stability such as those made by Scott [22, ch. 26] and by Strong [26]. More recently other investigations such as the Hawthorne [21] and Yankee City studies [32], anticipated in this respect by Hoppock's work [12] and by a minor study of mine [27] in job satisfaction, have played up the importance of the status given to the worker by his job, status both in the sense of group membership or belongingness and of prestige.

While researchers interested in the role of one kind of factor or another have tended to emphasize the signal importance of that type of factor, there is nothing inherently contradictory or mutually exclusive in these findings. They can all be included in a comprehensive theory of job satisfaction or work adjustment. This is the theory that satisfaction in one's work and on one's job depends on the extent to which the work, the job, and the way of life that goes with them, enable one to play the kind of role that one wants to play. It is, again, the theory that vocational development is the

development of a self concept, that the process of vocational adjustment is the process of implementing a self concept, and that the degree of satisfaction attained is proportionate to the degree to which the self concept has been implemented.

Work Is a Way of Life

This leads to a final theory, one that has been more widely accepted and stressed by sociologists than by psychologists, but familiar to most counselors and considered basic by some writers in the field. This is the theory that work is a way of life, and that adequate vocational and personal adjustment are most likely to result when both the nature of the work itself and the way of life that goes with it (this is, the kind of community, home, leisure-time activities, friends, etc.) are congenial to the aptitudes, interests, and values of the person in question. In the estimation of many, this is a basic element in a theory of vocational development.

A THEORY OF VOCATIONAL DEVELOPMENT

Now that we have surveyed the diverse elements of a theory of vocational development, there remains the final task of organizing them into a summary statement of a comprehensive theory. The theory can be stated in a series of ten propositions:

1. People differ in their abilities, interests, and personalities.

2. They are qualified, by virtue of these characteristics, each for a number of occupations.

3. Each of these occupations requires a characteristic pattern of abilities, interests, and personality traits, with tolerances wide enough, however, to allow both some variety of occupations for each individual and some variety of individuals in each occupation.

4. Vocational preferences and competencies, the situations in which people live and work, and hence their self concepts, change with time and experience (although self concepts are generally fairly stable from late adolescence until late maturity), making choice and ajdustment a continuous process.

5. This process may be summed up in a series of life stages characterized as those of growth, exploration, establishment, maintenance, and decline, and these stages may in turn be subdivided into (*a*) the fantasy, tentative, and realistic phases of the exploratory stage, and (*b*) the trial and stable phases of the establishment stage.

6. The nature of the career pattern (that is, the occupational level attained and the sequence, frequency, and duration of trial and stable jobs) is determined by the individual's parental socioeconomic level, mental ability, and personality characteristics, and by the opportunities to which he is exposed.

7. Development through the life stages can be guided, partly by facilitating the process of maturation of abilities and interests and partly by aiding in reality testing and in the development of the self concept.

8. The process of vocational development is essentially that of developing and implementing a self concept: it is a compromise process in which the self concept is a product of the interaction of inherited aptitudes, neural and endocrine make-up, opportunity to play various roles, and evaluations of the extent to which the results of role playing meet with the approval of superiors and fellows.

9. The process of compromise between individual and social factors, between self concept and reality, is one of role playing, whether the role is played in fantasy, in the counseling interview, or in real life activities such as school classes, clubs, part-time work, and entry job's.

10. Work satisfactions and life satisfactions depend upon the extent to which the individual finds adequate outlets for his abilities, interests, personality traits, and values; they depend upon his establishment in a type of work, a work situation, and a way of life in which he can play the kind of role which his growth and exploratory experiences have led him to consider congenial and appropriate.

REFERENCES

1. Barnett, G., Handelsman, I., Stewart, L. H. and Super, D. E. The Occupational Level scale as a measure of drive. *Psychol. Monogr.*, 1952, *65*, No. 10 (Whole No. 342).

2. Bentley, J. H. *The adjustment service.* New York: American Association for Adult Education, 1935.

3. Bingham, W. V. *Aptitudes and aptitude testing.* New York: Harper, 1937.

4. Bordin, E. S. A theory of vocational interests as dynamic phenomena. *Educ. psychol. Measmt.*, 1943, *3*, 49–66.

5. Buhler, Charlotte. *Der menschliche Lebenslauf als psychologisches Problem.* Leipzig: Hirzel, 1933.

6. Carter, H. D. Vocational interests and job orientation. *Appl. Psychol. Monogr.*, 1944, No. 2.

7. Davidson, P. E. and Anderson, H. D. *Occupational mobility.* Stanford: Stanford University Press, 1937.

8. Dvorak, Beatrice. The new U.S.E.S. General Aptitude Test Battery. *Occupations*, 1947, *25*, 42–49.

9. Friend, J. G. and Haggard, E. A. Work adjustment in relation to family background. *Appl. Psychol. Monogr.*, 1948, No. 16.

10. Ginzberg, E., Ginsburg, S. W., Axelrad, S. and Herma, J. L. *Occupational choice.* New York: Columbia University Press, 1951.

11. Hollingshead, A. B. *Elmtown's youth.* New York: Wiley, 1949.

12. Hoppock, R. *Job satisfaction.* New York: Harper, 1935.

13. Johnson, D. G. The effect of vocational counseling on self-knowledge. Unpublished doctor's dissertation, Teachers College, Columbia University, 1951.

14. Kitson, H. D. *Psychology of vocational adjustment*. Philadelphia: Lippincott, 1925.

15. Lehman, H. C. and Witty, P. A. *Psychology of play activities*. New York: Barnes, 1927.

16. Miller, D. and Form, W. *Industrial sociology*. New York: Harper, 1951.

17. National Society for the Study of Education, G. M. Whipple (Ed.). *Intelligence: its nature and nurture*. Bloomington, Ill.: Public School Publishing Co., 1940.

18. Parsons, F. *Choosing a vocation*. Boston: Houghton Mifflin, 1909.

19. Paterson, D. G. and Darley, J. G. *Men, women, and jobs*. Minneapolis: University of Minnesota Press, 1936.

20. Pressey, S. L., Janney, J. E. and Kuhlen, R. G. *Life: a psychological survey*. New York: Harper, 1939.

21. Roethlisberger, F. J. and Dickson, W. J. *Management and the worker*. Cambridge: Harvard University Press, 1939.

22. Scott, W. D., Clothier, R. C. and Mathewson, S. B. *Personnel management*. New York: McGraw-Hill, 1931.

23. Sisson, E. D. An analysis of the occupational aims of college students. *Occupations*, 1938, *17*, 211–215.

24. Small, L. A theory of vocational choice. *Vocat. Guid. Quart.*, 1952, *1*, 29.

25. Strong, E. K., Jr. *Change of interest with age*. Stanford: Stanford University Press, 1931.

26. Strong, E. K., Jr. *The vocational interests of men and women*. Stanford: Stanford University Press, 1943.

27. Super, D. E. Occupational level and job satisfaction. *J. appl. Psychol.*, 1939, *23*, 547–564.

28. Super, D. E. *Dynamics of vocational adjustment*. New York: Harper, 1942.

29. Super, D. E. *Appraising vocational fitness by means of psychological tests*. New York: Harper, 1949.

30. Super, D. E. Vocational adjustment: implementing a self-concept. *Occupations*, 1951, *30*, 88–92.

31. Terman, L. M. and Oden, M. H. *The gifted child grows up*. Stanford: Stanford University Press, 1947.

32. Warner, W. L. and Low, J. D. *The social system of the modern factory*. New Haven: Yale University Press, 1947.

33. *Principles and practices of vocational guidance*. Cambridge, Mass.: National Vocational Guidance Association, 1927.

Decision and Vocational Development: A Paradigm and Its Implications

DAVID V. TIEDEMAN, *Harvard University*

For almost 50 years the vocational psychologist has attempted to view vocational development through the keyhole of *success*

Reprinted with the permission of the author and publisher from *Personnel and Guidance Journal*, 1961, *40*, 15–21.

in educational and vocational endeavors. Career is practically invisible from that angle of vision. The career is more apparent in relation to vocational *interests*. Still more of career is apparent in relation to educational and vocational *choices*. Ultimately, however, we must view career in terms of vocational *development* as Professor Super does in his recent text [*1*] on the subject.

Super's writings about vocational development [*1–3*] provide a clear outline of its process and its investigation. However, we still need an explicit statement of the process of *decision* in vocational development. The structure of decision must be specified before investigations of the theory of vocational development can enter new phases.

DECISION AND VOCATIONAL DEVELOPMENT

The compromise inherent in discovering and nourishing the area of congruence of person and society as expressed in an individual's vocational behavior is effected within a set of decisions. The set of decisions and the context of relevance for the anticipation and implementation of each constitutes the essence of vocational development. The purpose of this article is to attempt a formal statement of this proposition, a statement sufficiently specific to make it amenable to investigation.[1] The structure is represented symbolically in Figure 1, but needs further elaboration.

The analysis of vocational development is oriented by each of several *decisions* with regard to school, work, and life which a person makes as he matures. With regard to *each* decision, the problem of deciding may be profitably divided into two *periods* or aspects, a period of anticipation and a period of implementation or adjustment.

I. *The Period of Anticipation.* Anticipatory behavior may itself profitably be analyzed into subaspects or *stages*. Relevant stages are those of exploration, crystallization, and choice. During exploration, activities are somewhat random and probably very acquisitive. As *patterns* begin to emerge in the form of alternatives and their consequences, we speak of crystallization. Finally, with clarification and commitment, choice occurs and the person begins to organize or

to specify in preparation for the implementation of his choice. More specifically, each stage may be considered as follows:

Stage IA: Exploration: In exploration a number of different alternatives or possible goals (g_{1j}) are considered.[2] Relevant goals are those which can possibly be attained from the opportunities associated with the decision under consideration. The alternatives or goals *set* the field (f_{1j}) for choice; they specify the context in which choice emerges. The intended image is that of an open mind considering various purposes or goals. Conditions of relevance are given *order and meaning* only in relation to the goal. Hence the high saliency of the goal for understanding of the associated field. At this stage, fields are relatively transitory, highly imaginary (perhaps even fantastic), and not necessarily related one to the other. They are possibly a relatively unassociated set of possibilities and consequence. In exploration, a person probably reflects at least upon his aspiration, opportunity both now and in the future, interest, capability, distasteful requirements that still could be tolerated, and societal context for himself and his dependents. These are relevant aspects of the field set by each goal [*i.e.*, g_{1j} (f_{1j})]. In short, a person attempts to take the measure of himself in relation to each alternative as he senses it. The *structural* components of this so-called "measure" and further specification.

Stage IB: Crystallization: The "measures" are probably accessible only in terms of organization or order, O_1 [g_{1j} (f_{1j})], of all relevant considerations in relation to each of the goals. (g_{1j}). This order is an aspect of crystallization. Crystallization is not irreversible, however. Sequences of tentative crystallizations, new explorations, and recrystallizations can be a part of this process.

Parenthetically, it is well to remember that each stage is intended to represent a *discrete* change in the condition of the decision. The *quality* of the decision is different at one stage than at an earlier one. In a sense, a metamorphosis takes place. The

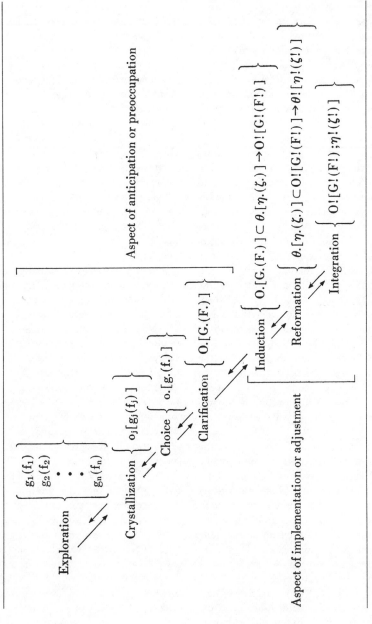

FIGURE 1. A paradigm of the process of decision.

Legend:

g_j, G_j represents goal when conceived and then clarified $(j = 1, 2, \ldots, n)$

f_j, F_j represents psychological field when conceived and then clarified $(j = 1, 2, \ldots, n)$

n (the analogue of g) represents goal the group holds for person

ζ (the analogue of F) represents the psychological field defined by the group

o_j, O_j represents organization as conceived and then clarified

θ_j represents the analogue of O_j in the group, that is, the cumulative effect of the O_j's of the group members.

former elements are there but the new stage changes the *character* of considerations with regard to a previous stage. These conditions are represented by discrete stages and names in the paradigm. The metamorphosis is neither instantaneous nor irreversible, however. Hence, a representation of this process by double arrows. ($\rightleftarrows$). Advance and retreat is possible at any stage and neither is necessarily limited to contiguous stages. Advance ordinarily eventually predominates, however. Therefore, the advancing is represented as the longer arrow.

Stage IC: Choice: As crystallizations stabilize, choice or decision becomes imminent. With choice, a particular goal, and its relevant field g_1. (f_1.) say, orients the behavioral system of the person of relevance for his vocational development. This goal may be elected with varying degrees of certainty and its motive power will vary as a result. Therefore, the "power" of this orientation is probably a function of the complexity and of the antagonism of alternatives involved in the ultimate crystallization. Furthermore, the degree of "rationality" generally available to the person in the matter of this decision will also affect the motivating power of the resulting resolution of alternatives. Some conditions of emotionality in relation with the decision will strengthen it; others will weaken the decision.

Stage ID: Specification: Choice readies the individual to act upon his decision. In the relative tranquility prior to his initiation, however, the individual has opportunity further to specify his anticipated position. An elaboration and perfection of the image of the future ensues.[3] Specification probably not only perfects the image of self in position but also dissipates some of the former doubts concerning the decision. Otherwise it will result in a return to a more primitive stage of the process. Such specifications probably create potentials for action in circumstances of high relevance for their realization. Consider, for instance, the college student who has crystallized his college major. His sub-

sequent specifications ordinarily create a potential directing his behavior for quite some time.

II. *The Period of Implementation and Adjustment.* Imaginative concerns come face to face with reality on the day of initiation of implementation; a stage of *induction* begins. Superiors and colleagues associated with the position a person elects to fill start the process of perfecting their expectations for him. Eventually, however, a person ascertains that he is accepted; he "arrives," so to speak. A *transition* or metamorphosis occurs. The primary mode of reaction is no longer responsive; it becomes assertive. As the need for assertiveness subsides, however, a stage of maintenance ensues; status quo reigns as possible. Equilibrium is re-established. These three stages of this period of implementation may be further specified as follows:

Stage IIA: Induction: Eventually experience starts and induction occurs. The individual field organized by the person's goal comes into operating interaction with society's (*i.e.,* school or employer) related but not identical goal and field.[4] During induction, the person's primary orientation of relevance for his goal is receptive. This condition is represented in Figure 1 by noting that the individual's goal and field *assimilatively* become a part of the region (represented symbolically as $\subset$) of the position the person is electing to fill. This process leads to a further perfection of individual goal and field, G_1'. (F_1.') say. (A ready assimilation of individual goal and field into the group purpose of relevance for the position is probably a necessary aspect of "success.")

Stage IIB: Transition: With the gaining of confidence that one has been successful, a new phase starts: transition. In transition, the primary orientation of relevance for the goal becomes assertive. The group goal and field $[\eta_1. (\xi_{.1})]$ is attacked in order to make it a part (against represented by $\subset$) of the modified goal and field of the person. If the individual is successful the group goal and field is modified, *i.e.,* becomes η_1'. (ξ_1.).

(Stage IIC: Maintenance: With modification of both the individual and group goals and fields, the maintenance phase is initiated. Both partners of the interaction strive to keep the resulting organization) (represented as $0_1'$ $[G_1.'$ $(F_1'.);$ $\eta_1'.$ $(\xi_1'.)])$. (The individual is satisfied, at least temporarily. The group considers him successful also. Of course, the person is likely to have an image of himself as successful in these circumstances, too. Maintenance is not unalterable; it is merely a condition of dynamic equilibrium. A new member joining the social system, new strivings of existing members of that system, or a quickening of the strivings of the person himself may disturb the status quo at any time. Such disturbances, *as elected by the person* or as forced upon him, contribute either to his vocational development or disintegration.)

DEPENDENT DECISIONS AND VOCATIONAL DEVELOPMENT

The described process of deciding upon a course of action and of implementing that decision in a manner intended to perfect idiosyncratic interests in a collaborative relation of interests is *possible* in each decision of relevance for vocational development. The course of events of relevance to decision may be unfolding with regard to *several* decisions simultaneously, however. Man can reflect these particular matters into systems permitting organization of diverse sets. *It is these systems of secondary (or perhaps of more comprehensive) order that specify vocational development.* Therefore, let us speculate about the structure within which those data may be comprehended.[5]

Consider, for instance, an embryo physician as a freshman in college. He is probably still in a stage of induction with regard to his college choice, may be specifying his choice of a medical school while tentatively crystallizing with regard to an area of specialization in medicine, and also exploring with regard to a place to practice medicine.

Vocational development then is self-development viewed in relation with choice, entry, and progress in educational and vocational pursuits. It is a process occurring over *time* in man who is capable of anticipation, experience, evaluation, and memory. Man is aware of some of the relevant conditions but not of others although, in the latter case, his behavior may well be quite consistent with another person's suppositions concerning such conditions.

Hence, vocational development not only occurs within the context of a single decision; vocational development ordinarily occurs within the context of several decisions. Man both remembers and imagines. Therefore, crystallization in relation to selection of the first goal which led to organization 0_1 can progress in some relation with tentative crystallizations concerning a second goal, g_{2j}, or even of a third, g_{3j}, or later goal. In fact, the discovery of dependencies among the several decisions hinges upon anticipatory behavior emerging in relation with several goals rather than with one alone. Similarly, traces of earlier considerations and evaluations of experience are ever present in any later mode of thought or of action. Hence after-effects of all former stages with regard both to a particular decision and all earlier ones are ever present in a current stage with regard to a special decision.

The *anticipations* at a given time with regard to one or more decisions *can* influence a person's mode of action with regard to: (1) a particular decision now in question; (2) those earlier decisions whose drama is not yet completed; and (3) those later decisions that are as yet either being considered or are not yet fulfilled. Similarly, experience related to a present decision and prior ones influences development of later events. These contingencies of evaluation of experience and of imagining of the future are probably most relevant to the matters of *organizations* of self as represented in the stages of crystallization and maintenance. The organization of self experienced in the maintenance stages of several decisions hopefully improve in quality and in the satisfaction they offer the person as his life progresses.

The aim of vocational counseling is to enhance the operation of reason in this dynamic process of vocational development and to free the person for progress in taking and acting upon a particular decision as well as in viewing decisions in relation with those taken and those possible. In this way, the counselor hopes to bring each client in his responsibility to view his educational and vocational decisions as a means-ends chain; that which is an end at an earlier time is to become a means for a later goal. Behavior is to become purposeful; evaluation is to become more meaningful; and an elaboration of self is to ensue. No goal is to become so compelling that it either destroys judgment in situations of conflicting goals or cannot give way to a later, and more fulfilling, goal.

THE PATTERN OF LIFE
AND VOCATIONAL DECISIONS

The study of vocational development requires a specification of the context of decision in relation to the purposes a person hopes to realize in life through the vocational expression of himself. A slight approximation of the *nature* of these decisions is already possible from consideration of the structure of man, school, and work which limits man's vocational development. Such a specification is attempted in Figure 2 where definite physical and social limitations upon career development are represented in relation with the life span.

Figure 2 suggests the validity of the characterization of vocational development which Super [*1*] has derived. Considerable exploration takes place in adolescence. Taking up work immediately after leaving a school is a major problem in transition. Trial of work (*i.e.*, the failure to pass beyond induction with regard to a series of job decisions) followed by establishment (transi-

tion in Figure 1), maintenance and decline (a phase not considered in Figure 1) seems a good characterization of the higher order effect of the *inter-dependent* career decisions. First there is mostly exploration, crystallization, choice, and specification. Next there is mostly a series of inductions. Then there may be several transitions. Finally, maintenance may dominate. Of course, there is ultimately disengagement from work in what to Super [*1*] is decline. If career has been truly consummated, however, this is an earned respite enjoyed in integrity. Man has surmounted his environment rather than the reverse.

NEEDED RESEARCH
IN VOCATIONAL DEVELOPMENT

We are considering then a process of evolving and of acting upon a conception of self as it is expressed through vocational behavior. The evolution transpires through a series of decisions. Each decision potentially consists of seven distinct phases. Each decision is also to be considered in relation with a wider context of past and future decisions leading to the presentation of career before the world in pride and in confidence. Hence vestiges of previous organizations of self gradually dissolve into newer and more overarching organizations of self. The career evolves in a time pattern in intimate association with the evolution of other aspects of life. So how do we "research" this *second-order* process of decision which is vocational development?

First of all, we need to tune in more on people's *thoughts* about themselves in relation to study, work, and life. That is, we need to address informants to the structure of decision in which we are interested and to encourage them to talk to us about it. From these talks about self we must learn how field solidifies with goal. We must discover the content of field in relation to various goals.

FIGURE 2. Staging of study and work discontinuities.

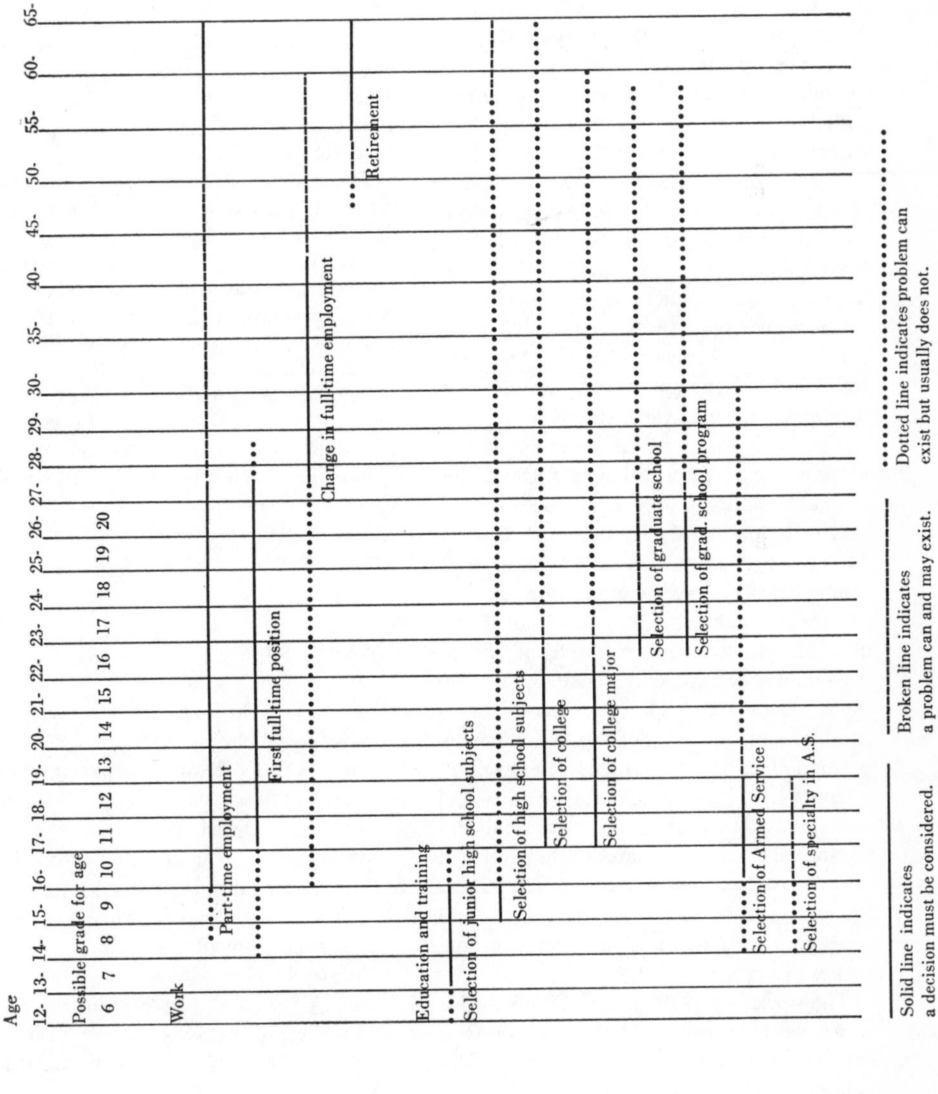

Solid line indicates
a decision must be considered.

Broken line indicates
a problem can and may exist.

Dotted line indicates problem can
exist but usually does not.

Next we must discover the *organization* of exploratory conceptions that precipitate crystallization and choice. Modes of reaction in induction, transition, and maintenance are also matters we should collect, ponder upon, order, and learn to use in anticipating relevant matters of vocational development.

Second, as we study vocational development from an internal, genotypic frame of reference we must do so in a manner that permits verification of our speculations. Our efforts need not embrace empiricism so fiercely that the object of our regard, self, is utterly ignored, however. Rather we must learn to use that "self" in specified ways. Why don't we let the self establish its own classification of occupations for us, for instance? Our predictions of choice would probably be greatly improved by this simple substitution of frame of reference. The result could still be articulated with *our* opinion of the world and thus verified.

The final aspect of my comment is that we must use a new criterion in the investigation of vocational development. For me, that criterion should be the work history. The three genotypic elements of a work history are: (1) the *kinds* of positions chosen: (2) their *sequence;* (3) the *duration of stay* in each. Much of our research on choice, personality, occupational classification, and some of our research on interests needs consideration in relation to the kind of position chosen. The residue of research on interests and all of our research on successful and satisfactory pursuit of educational and vocational endeavors relates to the matter of duration or implementation of choice. Finally, our emerging research on vocational development is of direct relevance to the matter of sequence of choice.

The work history then is the reality with which we must relate the considerations of career as career is understood through dependent decisions about school and work. This spreading of a life across the record of a work history *is* the vocational development about which we must always strive to formulate definite and verifiable propositions.

[1]It must be remembered that this is merely a paradigm. I believe that the paradigm has important correspondence with the available data of vocational development. Considerable study of this paradigm is still needed before it can be fully accepted, however.

[2]Since we are attempting a fairly explicit notation, two subscripts are necessary to specify the designated goals. The first subscript (1 in this case) refers to all goals of relevance to the first decision problem. The second subscript, j, denotes the several (in fact j can take values 1 to n_1) possible goals or alternatives conceived in relation to the first problem of decision. A companion symbol will also be used to specify the variability possible with the field (f_{1j}) called to mind by each goal. At a later time we shall wish to note that a *specific* one of the n_1 goals g_{1j} is now relevant. We shall denote that condition by replacing j by a dot (.), *i.e.*, g_1. (f_1.).

[3]We denote this elaboration by similar but not identical symbols, *i.e.*, G_1. (F_1.).

[4]Since this goal and field is usually related but not identical, we denote it by the Greek analogues of our Latinized notation, viz. η for G and ξ for F. Thus we write η_1. (ξ_1.) for this aspect of our conception.

[5]An explicit notational statement of this structure is available upon request.

REFERENCES

1. Super, Donald E. *The psychology of careers.* New York: Harper & Bros., 1957.
2. Super, Donald E., and Bachrach, Paul B. *Scientific careers and vocational development.* New York: Teachers College, Columbia University, Bureau of Publications, 1957.
3. Super, Donald E., Crites, John O., Hummel, Raymond C., Moser, Helen P., Overstreet, Pheobe L., and Warnath, Charles F. *Vocational development: a framework for research.* Career Pattern Study Monograph 1. New York: Teachers College, Columbia University, Bureau of Publications, 1957.
4. Tiedeman, David V., O'Hara, Robert P., and Matthews, Esther. *Position choices and careers: elements of a theory.* Cambridge, Mass.: The Senior Author (13 Kirkland Street), 1958. (Mimeographed.)

A Life Stage Vocational Development System

DAVID B. HERSHENSON, *Illinois Institute of Technology*

Marx (1963, p. 43) defined a "system" as "an organization and interpretation of the data and theories of a subject matter with emphasis upon a particular methodology (metatheory) and working assumptions (postulates)." The aim of this paper is to present a life stage vocational development system, that is, an organization of vocational development theories within a life stage framework. While the most immediate influence on the development of the system proposed here has been the on-going work of Roth, Berenbaum, and Hershenson (1967) on a developmental theory of psychotherapy, many prior personality theorists have conceptualized personality development in terms of a series of life stages, although they have differed widely on the number of stages involved and the basis for defining them. Murphy (1947) posited three stages (global, differentiated, and integrated), while Sullivan (1947) delineated seven (infancy, childhood, juvenile era, preadolescence, early adolescence, late adolescence, and maturity). Freud (1933) defined the stages in his theory on the basis of the body zone to which the most libidinal energy was then cathected (oral, anal, and genital), while Buehler (1933) defined the stages in her theory primarily on the basis of the socio-economic expectations of the individual (growth, exploration, establishment, maintenance, and decline). Erikson

Reprinted with the permissing of the author and publisher from *Journal of Counseling Psychology*, 1968, *15*, 23-30.

(1963), utilizing both physiological and societal considerations, posited eight stages (oral-sensory, muscular-anal, locomotor-genital, latency, puberty and adolescence, young adulthood, adulthood, and maturity). Clearly, the rationale for defining life stages for any personality theorist is determined by the focal constructs of his theory. Thus, Murphy and Buehler, being more concerned with adult behavior, gave less detailed analysis to the pre-adolescent period than did Freud or Sullivan, for whose anamnestic-therapeutic theories the events of early childhood are central.

Beilin (1955) has pointed out the relevance of the principles of developmental psychology to vocational development theory-building. Consistent with this, several vocational development theorists have utilized the life stage concept. Ginzberg *et al.* (1951) suggested the definition of three stages in the occupational choice process: fantasy (below age 11), tentative (ages 11 to 17), and realistic (above age 17). Super *et al.* (1957), utilizing Buehler's system, defined five stages of vocational development: growth (conception to age 14), exploration (ages 15 to 24,) establishment (ages 25 to 44), maintenance (ages 45 to 64), and decline (age 65 and above). Havighurst (1964) has posited six stages of vocational development: identification with a worker (ages 5 to 10), acquiring the basic habits of industry (ages 10 to 15), acquiring identity as a worker in the occupational structure (ages 15 to 25), becoming a productive person (ages 25 to 40), maintaining a productive society (ages 40 to 70), and contemplating a productive and responsible life (age 70 and above), While only Ginzberg set out to focus on it, all three theorists devoted their most detailed attention to the period between the ages of 10 and 25, the period of occupational choice. However, Super and Havighurst, being concerned with vocational development as a life-long process, both went on to define three life stages beyond the age of twenty-five. It might be noted that Miller and Form (1951), working in the field of industrial sociology, also posited a series of career development stages for use in their work.

One may ask why, in the light of the profusion of vocational development theories (and even of life stage vocational development theories), any further proliferation of theories is warranted. Several answers may be given. First, one may question the formal adequacy, as theories, of most existing vocational development theories. This criticism, of course, is not unique to the vocational development area, but may be leveled against all past psychological theory-building efforts, with the possible exception of the atheoretical theorizing of the Skinnerians. For the purposes of this paper, however, past vocational development theories will be accepted, prima facie, as theories. As has been stated, the aim of this paper is to locate existing vocational development theories within a consistent framework. Thus, this system should serve to integrate existing theories rather than to proliferate more.

Secondly, this system was developed with two specific considerations in mind, its amenability to empirical testing and its relevance to vocational counseling practice. It may be noted that any progress this system may make toward both these goals simultaneously stems from the inclusion within it of a number of already existing vocational development theories, most of which individually are oriented toward one or the other of these goals.

The essential premise of the system proposed here is that the vocational develop-ment process may be considered as a series of sequential stages. As may be seen in Table 1, five stages are specified: social-amniotic, self-differentiation, competence, independence, and commitment. The character of each of the stages will be spelled out below, following a discussion of the general principles of the system. However, it may be stated here that the stages are differentiated on the basis of the primary way in which energy (both physical and psychic) is utilized. Each successive way of utilizing energy is behaviorally reflected in a concomitant vocational mode.

Two basic assumptions are made concerning the stages. First, the sequential nature of the stages, rather than the chronological age at which they most typically occur, is central. Thus, for research or counseling purposes, one should look at the stage at which the person is actually functioning rather than comparing him to what most people of his age typically do. Naturally, maturational and social forces tend to set, roughly, minimum ages at which successive stages can occur. For example, one cannot have significant self-differentiation until sufficient language development has occurred; certain levels of fine muscle control are necessary for competence; and one needs to have available choices between alternatives (rather than just choices of the "go–no go" variety) before one can assert positive independence. However, conversely, chronological maturity does not imply necessary vocational development to the same level, as may be seen in the 50-year-old, back-ward, chronic psychotic, who may still be asking the question "Am I?" It may be noted that Ginzberg (1951) also posited the primacy of pattern over chronological age in developing his theory, although he devoted considerable energy to specifying age-defined benchmarks. The second assumption about the stages is that each one sets the limiting conditions for the subsequent ones. For example, individuals born into lower class and into middle class subcultures will probably experience different play environments and develop different values and work orientations. Likewise, what one will do must be chosen from among the things which one can do. (For more detailed discussion of this, see Hershenson and Roth, 1966.)

Another assumption of the system concerns motivation. It is assumed that both growth and deficit motivation exist throughout the life span. However, the two are not independent of each other. As deficits are overcome, further growth is promoted; and as growth trends press forward, there is increased pressure to make up deficits. Further, no distinction is made between physical and psychic energy. To make such a distinction would merely serve to perpetuate the errors of Cartesian dualism and would add nothing to the system proposed here.

Finally, it should be noted that the definition of five stages for this system is relatively arbitrary. As was pointed out above, the nature of the focal constructs in life stage theories tend to determine the number and definition of their stages. Hence, the stages defined in this system may only be defended on the basis of their convenience for handling the constructs proposed here.

Now one may proceed to a more detailed consideration of the five stages, as presented in Table 1. In Table 1, the far left-hand two columns, headed "Freud-Stage" and "Erikson-Issue," are provided as reference points for the next column, the "Vocational Development Stage". As has been noted above, the vocational development stages are posited as sequential, rather than age-related. Therefore, the concepts of Freud and Erikson should be viewed more for their dynamic content than for the age periods they encompass. (As both age and the life stages are sequential, one naturally tends to seek modal age-ranges for each stage. However, as these are not necessary for the construction or operation of the system proposed here and as no empirical evidence on the matching of age-ranges to the stages exists, efforts have been made to keep age and stage separate for at least the present discussion.) Following the columns headed "Energy Utilization" and "Vocational Mode," the meaning of which were discussed earlier in the paper, is a column headed "Vocational Question." This represents the vocationally-relevant issue for resolution during that stage. Clinically, this may be thought of as the underlying problem raised by the client to the vocational counselor (although, as frequently occurs in clinical practice, it may not be the presenting problem). The next two columns, "Measurement Construct" and "Typical Measures," suggest stage-relevant areas for testing, for diagnostic and research purposes. Thereby, questions such as whether interests actually do stem from abilities or whether job satisfaction follows from working in a field in which one has strong interests can be looked at empirically. Naturally, not all of the measures can or should be taken during the stage to which they refer. For example, most people are beyond the social-amniotic stage before they are able to cope with a paper-and-pencil "Trust" scale. However, from a research standpoint, the developmental sequence reflected in the measurement constructs is still open to testing later in life; and from a counseling standpoint, relatively few pre-verbal clients present themselves for vocational counseling or testing. Finally, the right-hand column lists a number of those vocational theorists whose theories are most relevant to that vocational development stage. Now the stages may be looked at individually.

The first stage, the social-amniotic, stretches from conception to the time that the muscles at both ends of the digestive tract are pretty much under voluntary control, that is, until speech and sphincter control are established. In its post-natal segment, this period would be roughly equivalent to Freud's oral and anal expulsive stages. (While it is not the purpose of this system to organize information about behavior outside of the vocational development area, it might be noted in passing that the inclusion of the anal expulsive with the oral stage in one developmental stage may provide a more adequate model for understanding the incontinence of many regressed psychotics than does the traditional psycho-analytic division into oral and anal stages.) The social-amniotic stage includes the prenatal period, thus taking into account the factors of genetic inheritance and prenatal environment (mother's diet, health, anxiety level, and other such factors which influence fetal development). Thus, a child born with a congenital heart defect generally could not become an athlete. The name "social-amniotic" was chosen in order to imply the continuity between the prenatal and early post-natal life. In a way, the social setting into which the infant is born surrounds him as did the amniotic fluid of his prenatal environment. Both serve to cushion him and to set the limits of his "life-space." Certainly, this is the stage during which the individual is most passive, yet this is a highly significant stage in that it most decisively sets the limits on the course of development during subsequent stages. The differences in one's vocational future, depending on whether one spent one's social-amniotic stage in a wealthy, white, suburban environment or in a poverty level, Negro ghetto environment, are too clear to require spelling out. During this stage, energy is utilized mainly for awareness, for soaking up the inputs from the environment, that is, primarily from the family, which to some degree reflects the subculture and culture of which it is a part. Out of this stage must come the individual's affirmation of his own existence, as would be reflected in positive responses to a "trust" scale. Conversely, poor socialization experiences should be reflected in high scores on an "anomie" scale. The vocational development theorists who are most relevant to this period are: (1) those who focus on the individual's social background factors, such as Lipsett (1962), (2) those who focus on family atmosphere, such as Roe (1957), and (3) those who focus on the vocational sequelae of very early introjections, such as Bordin, Nachmann, and Segal (1963). These theories tend to emphasize the vocational con-sequences of early environments in which the individual finds himself. In them, the individual assumes a more passive role in arriving at his career choice than he does in the theories relevant to later stages. This is consistent with the passive posture which characterizes the social-amniotic stage.

Having absorbed a sense of being which is consistent with one's background and having developed sufficient language to confront the issue of "me" versus "not me," the person may go on to differentiate himself as an individual. This process of differentiation of the self out of the social context was analyzed as long ago as G. H. Mead (1934) and as recently as Nevitt Sanford (1966). Having absorbed from his environment during the social-amniotic stage, the individual now seeks to assert himself, to become an individuated figure in his environment. Energy, thus, is now used more for control. At first, control is focused on his own body, and once the achievement of this is under way, the focus moves toward control of the environment. Early behavioral evidence of this process includes such phenomena as the "no"-gesture, locomo-tion, sphincter control, and block-stacking in toddlers. Evidence of the later shift may be seen in the movement from parallel to cooperative play. (Classical Freudians might argue that the oral sadistic stage, rather than the anal retentive, represents the transition from passive to effective. How-ever, it may be argued against this that the infant's biting is primarily a reflex to the pain of teething and that it is used more as a way of feeling or assessing objects (aware-ness) than of controlling them.) Out of the successes and rebuffs of the play experiences of this stage, the individual comes to a preliminary answer to the question, "Who am I?" The play experiences, it should be noted, include play with objects, play with people, and role play. The answer to the vocational question is measurable in terms of such constructs as affective self-concept, attitudes, and values. The limiting effect of the social-amniotic milieu on the outcome of this stage should be self-evident. The vocational development theories which are most relevant to this stage are those which focus on the self-concept as the basis for vocational choice and development, such as the theories of Bordin (1943) and Super (1957). Further, work directed toward spelling out the vocational implications of early attitudinal patternings, such as that of Tyler (1955; 1961) bears on this stage.

Having differentiated himself as an individual from his background context, the person seeks to manipulate his environment effectively. The term "Competence," taken from White (1960), seems best to characterize the process during this stage. Having gained control of his own individuated entity, the person can seek to locate the limits of competence of this entity, that is, to discover what he can (and cannot) do. The attitudes and values developed during the self-differentiation stage determine the areas in which the person will seek to develop competences. Much of the available evidence concerning the relationship between self-differentiation and competence is in the academic achievement area [for example, Fink (1962) and Shaw and Alves (1963)], Naturally, many individuals reach this stage during their school years, and the "work" (the directed energy) referred to in Table 1 is often school-work. While many of these studies indicate a positive relationship between self-concept and abilities, there is still not sufficient evidence to indicate a causal relationship between them. In addition to White, discussed above, the vocational development theorists most relevant to this stage are those who focus on the empirical effects of abilities on vocational development, such as Flanagan *et al.* (1962); and those who are concerned with the person's internal concept of his abilities as related to his vocational development, for example, Alfred Adler (1938) and Holland (1959).

Having learned what he can do, the person must then decide which, among these things, he will do. Energy, having

been shown to be capable of direction during the competence stage, is now directed toward a goal the person has selected. Vocationally, this goal may be called an occupation. It should be pointed out that the occupation may be schooling, social deviance, or inactivity, as well as being a job. This stage has been called the stage of independence because it represents the first opportunity for choice among real, available alternatives; it is the first time that will enters the vocational process. This was reflected in the wording of the vocational question, "What *will* I do?" The measurement construct for this stage is interests, either verbalized or inventoried. McArthur and Stevens (1955) have demonstrated that the two do not necessarily tap the same phenomena. Research must be done on the relevance of each of the sorts of interest measures. It has been suggested by some writers (for example, Ginzberg, 1951) that interests precede abilities. Generally, the sorts of vocational "interests" to which these writers allude are the early "fireman-jet pilot" sort of occupational role-play of young children. However, it appears, on closer inspection, that these "interests" are not really occupational, although they may be pre-vocational. They are early attempts at control, and lack any goal-directedness. Clearly, the capacity for directedness must precede goal-directedness; therefore, occupational interest must follow the development of competence. A considerable amount of empirical evidence of a relationship between abilities and interests exists, among the best of which is the study by Wesley, Corey, and Stewart (1950). However, here again, sufficient evidence to allow the attribution of a causal relationship is not now available. Vocational development theories which are relevant to the stage of independence are those which focus on occupational choice-making as a decisional process, such as the theories of Ziller (1957), Tiedeman (1961) and Hilton (1962).

Having made a choice (or at least having attained the capacity to make a choice), the issue of the individual's involvement

TABLE 1

Life Stages of Vocational Development

Freud: Stage	Erikson: Issue	Vocational Development Stage	Energy Utilization	Vocational Mode	Vocational Question	Measurement Construct	Typical Measures	Relevant Vocational Theorists
(birth) Receptive	(birth) Basic trust	(conception) Social-amniotic	Awareness	Being	Am I?	Socialization to: 1. Culture	Family S.E.S. "Trusts" scale "Anomie" scale	Social psychological: e.g. Lipsett
ORAL Sadistic						2. Family	Cultural conformity measures	(1962) Roe (1957) Bordin, Nachmann, and Segal (1963)
Expulsive								
ANAL	Autonomy					Affective self-concept Attitudes Values	Who are you? Adjective checklist Q-sort	Bordin (1943) Super (1957) Tyler (1955; 1961)
Retentive								
GENITAL	Initiative	Self-differentiation	Control	Play	Who am I?		Allport-Vernon Stern Activities Index Values Invent.	
Oedipal Resolution								

TABLE 1 (Cont.)

Freud: Stage	Erikson: Issue	Vocational Development Stage	Energy Utilization	Vocational Mode	Vocational Question	Measurement Construct	Typical Measures	Relevant Vocational Theorists
LATENCY Puberty	Industry	Competence	Directed	Work	What can I do?	Abilities	D.A.T. G.A.T.B. Miniature tasks TOWER	Adler (1938) Holland (1959) White (1960) Flanagan (1962)
ADOLESCENCE	Identity Intimacy	Independence	Goal-directed	Occupation	What will I do?	Interests	Verbalized Kuder S.V.I.B. O.I.I. (Lee-Thorpe) M.V.I.I.	Decision theories: Ziller (1957) Tiedeman (1961) Hilton (1962)
MATURITY	Generativity Ego Integrity	Commitment	Invested	Vocation	What meaning does what I do have for me?	Satisfaction	Verbalized Questionnaire Critical incident	Existential: Simons (1966) Herzberg (1959)

with his choice becomes focal. For an occupation to become a vocation, commitment to it is necessary, that is, energy must be totally invested in it. This stage represents the culmination of the vocational development process. It may be noted in Table 1 that this stage encompasses three of Erikson's stages. However, it appears that the focal issues of intimacy, generativity, and ego integrity may all be summed up as commitment (commitment to a partner, commitment to one's offspring, and commitment to life, respectively). The vocational question concerns the meaning one's work has for one. The measurement construct is satisfaction, but this should be interpreted broadly. One aspect of this process is similar to one of Allport's (1937) elements of maturity, the extension of self. Thereby, the issue of energy investment may be conceptualized: the greater the individual's maturity, the greater the likelihood of involvement in his work. However, the issue of vocational commitment may also be viewed as primarily an existential one, and therefore vocation development theories concerned with this philosophy (Simmons, 1966) are relevant to this stage. Likewise, the empirical work of Herzberg *et al.* (1959) is of value in conceptualizing commitment during this period. For this stage, also, many studies indicate a relationship between occupational interests and satisfaction, for example, the work of Lipsett and Wilson (1954). However, here again, causality remains to be demonstrated.

It would appear that the focus of research activities suggested by this system should be on the sequential nature of the stages. Evidence of relationship between adjacent stages already exists, and evidence of the processes within each stage may be drawn from existing research based on the vocational development theories cited as relevant to that stage. Perhaps some of the questionable findings of much of the past research in this field stem from looking for relationships separated by too many stages. Thus, Roe and her students (Roe and Siegelman, 1964) have been much more successful in demonstrating the relationship between family atmosphere and person-versus-thing-orientation (social-amniotic and self-differentiation issues, in adjacent stages) than they have been in demonstrating the relationship between family atmosphere and specific career field chosen (social-amniotic and independence issues, separated by two intervening stages).

This system has implications for vocational counseling practice, as well. Probably the most basic of these is the need for the counselor to be aware of the stage at which the client is functioning. Thus, one cannot do *vocational* counseling until the client has shown the capacity to make choices and engage in goal-directed activities. Likewise, one cannot do *occupational* counseling (the activity which currently is most frequently performed under the name of "vocational counseling") until the client as demonstrated the capacity to work and has realistic choices to consider. Should the client not have reached that stage, the counselor can only do "pre-occupational counseling" in order to help the client progress to the stage where he can meaningfully deal with occupational issues. Thus, the first task of the "vocational counselor" is diagnosing the level at which the client is operating. For this, tests are frequently of less value than interview data. The caveat must be issued to look behind the client's presenting question to determine his level. Thus, the client who comes for vocational counseling around the issue of whether to be an engineer or a musician may, among other alternatives, be reflecting either a conflict between two real competences or a lack of clear self-differentiation. The counselor must be aware of which of these it is before he can offer appropriate help. No progress would be made if the counselor proceeded to approach the question as a decisional issue when the underlying self-concept issue was still unresolved.

This system, in turn, has implications for the professional role definition of the counselor. Two alternative roles are possible. He may focus on one stage of development and refer clients at all other stages out. Thus, he may be a "self-differentiation counselor," a "competence counselor," an "occupational counselor," or a "vocational counselor." On the other hand, he may be eclectic and work with all stages, helping the client to arrive at the goal of vocational adequacy, no matter how many stages away that is. Research on techniques for helping clients at each stage and on which professional role model is more effective remains to be done. Appropriate settings for such research would include counseling centers and sheltered work-shops. For adequate testing of the system as a whole, however, longitudinal studies are needed.

REFERENCES

Adler, A. *Social interest*. London: Faber and Faber, 1938.

Allport, G. W. *Personality: A psychological interpretation*. New York: Holt, 1937.

Beilin, H. The application of general developmental principles to the vocational area. *J. counsel. Psychol.*, 1955, *2*, 53–57.

Bordin, E. S. A theory of vocational interests as dynamic phenomena. *Educ. psychol. Measmt*, 1943, *3*, 49–65.

Bordin, E. S.; Nachmann, B.; and Segal, S. J. An articulated framework for vocational development. *J. counsel. Psychol.*, 1963, *10*, 107–117.

Buehler, C. *Der menschliche Lebenslauf als psychologisches Problem*. Leipzig: Hirzel, 1933.

Erikson, E. H. *Childhood and society*. (Second edition) New York: Norton, 1963.

Fink, M. B. Self concept as it relates to academic underachievement. *Calif. J. educ. Res.*, 1962, *13*, 57–62.

Flanagan, J. C.; Dailey, J. T.; Shaycoft, M. F.; Gorham, W. A.; Orr, D. B.; and Goldberg, I. *Design for a study of American youth*. Boston: Houghton Mifflin, 1962.

Freud, S. *New introductory lectures on spychoanalysis*. New York: Norton, 1933.

Ginzberg, E.; Ginsburg, S. W.; Axelrad, S.; and Herma, J. L. *Occupational choice*: An approach to a general theory. New York: Columbia Univ. Press. 1951.

Havighurst, R. J. "Youth in exploration and man emergent." in Borow, H. (ed.) *Man in a world at work*. Boston: Houghton Mifflin, 1964.

Hershenson, D. B., and Roth, R. M. A decisional process model of vocational development. *J. counsel. Psychol.*, 1966, *13*, 368–370.

Herzberg, F.; Mausner, B.; and Snyderman, B. B. *The motivation to work*. (Second ed.) New York: Wiley, 1959.

Hilton, T. L. Career decision-making. *J. counsel. Psychol.*, 1962, *9*, 291–298.

Holland, J. L. A theory of vocational choice. *J. counsel. Psychol.*, 1959, *6*, 35–44.

Lipsett, L. Social factors in vocational development. *Personn. guild. J.*, 1962, *40*, 432–437.

Lipsett, L., and Wilson, J. W. Do suitable interests and mental ability lead to job satisfaction? *Educ. psychol. Measmt*, 1954, *14*, 373–380.

Marx, M. H. *Theories in contemporary psychology*. New York: Macmillan, 1963.

McArthur, C., and Stevens, L. B. The validation of expressed interests as compared with inventoried interests: A fourteen-year follow-up *J. appl. Psychol.*, 1955, *39*, 184–189.

Mead, G. H. *Mind, self and society*. Chicago: Univ. of Chicago Press, 1934.

Miller, D. C., and Form, W. H. *Industrial sociology*. New York: Harper, 1951.

Murphy, G. *Personality: a biosoical approach to origins and structure*. New York: Harper, 1947.

Roe, A. Early determinants of vocational choice. *J. counsel. Psychol.* 1957, *4*, 212–217.

Roe, A., and Siegelman, M. *The origin of interests*. Washington, D.C.: Amer. Personnel and Guid. Assn., 1964.

Roth, R. M.; Berenbaum, H. L.; and Hershenson, D. B. The developmental theory of psychotherapy: A systematic eclecticism. Paper in preparation, 1967.

Sanford, N. *Self and society*. New York: Atherton, 1966.

Shaw, M. C., and Alves, G. J. The self concept of bright academic underachievers. *Personn. guid., J.*, 1963, *43*, 401–403.

Simons, J. B. An existential view of vocational development. *Personn. guid. J.*, 1966, *44*, 604–610.

Sullivan, H. S. *Conceptions of modern psychiatry.* Washington, D.C.; William Alanson White Foundation, 1947.

Super, D. E.; Crites, J. O.; Hummel, R. C.; Moser, H. P.; Overstreet, P. L.; and Warnath, C. F. *Vocational development: a framework for research.* New York: Teachers College, 1957.

Tiedeman, D. Decision and vocational development: A paradigm and its implications. *Personn. guid. J.*, 1961, *40*, 15–20.

Tyler, L. E. The development of "vocational interests": the organization of likes and dislikes in ten-year-old children. *J. genet. Psychol.*, 1955, *86*, 33–44.

Tyler, L. E. Research explorations in the realm of choice. *J. counsel. Psychol*, 1961, *8*, 195–201.

Wesley, S. M.; Corey, D. Q.; and Stewart, B. M. The intra-individual relationship between interest and ability. *J. appl. Psychol.*, 1950, *34*, 193–197.

White, R. W. "Competence and the psychosexual stages of development." in Jones, M. R. (ed.) *Nebraska symposium on motivation.* Vol. VIII. Lincoln: Univ. of Nebr. Press, 1960.

Ziller, R. C. Vocational choice and utility for risk. *J. counsel. Psychol.* 1957, *4*, 61–64.

Vocational Life Stages

DONALD SUPER, *Teachers College, Columbia University*

1. *Growth Stage* (Birth–14). Self-concept develops through identification with key figures in family and in school; needs and fantasy are dominant early in this stage; interest and capacity become more important in this stage with increasing social participation and reality-testing. Substages of the growth stage are:

a. Fantasy (4–10). Needs are dominant; role-playing in fantasy is important.
b. Interest (11–12). Likes are the major determinant of aspirations and activities.

Reprinted by permission of the author and publisher from D. E. Super, *et al., Vocational Development: A Framework for Research*, New York: Teachers College, Columbia University Bureau of Publications, 1957.

c. Capacity (13–14). Abilities are given more weight, and job requirements (including training) are considered.

2. *Exploration Stage* (Age 15–24). Self-examination, role tryouts, and occupational exploration take place in school, leisure activities, and part-time work. Substages of the exploration stage are:

a. Tentative (15–17). Needs, interests, capacities, values, and opportunities are all considered. Tentative choices are made and tried out in fantasy, discussion, courses, work, etc.
b. Transition (18–21). Reality considerations are given more weight as the youth enters labor market or professional training and attempts to implement a self-concept.

c. Trial (22–24). A seemingly appropriate field having been located, a beginning job in it is found and is tried out as a life work.

3. *Establishment Stage* (Age 25–44). Having found an appropriate field, effort is put forth to make a permanent place in it. There may be some trial early in this stage, with consequent shifting, but establishment may begin without trial, especially in the professions. Substages of the establishment stage are:

a. Trial (25–30). The field of work presumed to be suitable may prove unsatisfactory, resulting in one or two changes before the life work is found or before it becomes clear that the life work will be a succession of unrelated jobs.

b. Stabilization (31–44). As the career pattern becomes clear, effort is put forth to stabilize, to make a secure place, in the world of work. For most persons these are the creative years.

4. *Maintenance Stage* (Age 45–64). Having made a place in the world of work, the concern is now to hold it. Little new ground is broken, but there is continuation along established lines.

5. *Decline Stage* (Age 65 on). As physical and mental powers decline, work activity changes and in due course ceases. New roles must be developed; first that of selective participant and then that of observer rather than participant. Substages of this stage are:

a. Deceleration (65–70). Sometimes at the time of official retirement, sometimes late in the maintenance stage, the pace of work slackens, duties are shifted, or the nature of the work is changed to suit declining capacities. Many men find part-time jobs to replace their full-time occupations.

b. Retirement (71 on). As with all the specified age limits, there are great variations from person to person. But, complete cessation of occupation comes for all in due course, to some easily and pleasantly, to others with difficulty and disappointment, and to some only with death.

Stages of Vocational Development

ROBERT J. HAVIGHURST

I. *Identification with a Worker* (Age 5–10)
Father, mother, other significant persons.
The concept of working becomes an essential part of the ego-ideal.

II. *Acquiring the Basic Habits of Industry* (Age 10–15)
Learning to organize one's time and energy to get a piece of work done. School work, chores.
Learning to put work àhead of play in appropriate situations.

III. *Acquiring Identity as a Worker in the Occupational Structure* (Age 15–25)

Reprinted with the permission of the publisher from p. 216 of H. Borow, (Ed.) *Man in a World at Work*, Boston: Houghton Mifflin, 1964.

Choosing and preparing for an occupation.

Getting work experience as a basis for occupational choice and for assurance of economic independence.

IV. *Becoming a Productive Person* (Age 25–40)
Mastering the skills of one's occupation. Moving up the ladder within one's occupation.

V. *Maintaining a Productive Society* (Age 40–70)
Emphasis shifts toward the societal and away from the individual aspect of the worker's role. The individual sees himself as a responsible citizen in a productive society. He pays attention to the civic responsibility attached to his job. He is at the peak of his occupational career and has time and energy to adorn it with broader types of activity.

He pays attention to inducting younger people into stages III and IV.

VI. *Contemplating a Productive and Responsible Life* (Age 70+)
This person is retired from his work or is in process of withdrawing from the worker's role. He looks back over his work life with satisfaction, sees that he has made his social contribution, and is pleased with it. While he may not have achieved all of his ambitions, he accepts his life and believes in himself as a productive person.

Vocational Developmental Stages

D. C. MILLER

W. H. FORM

I. *Preparatory — Birth — Age 14*
Pre-school
Socialization, work role taking within the home, modeling after parents.
Experience with work tasks in the home is acquired, roots of work habits developed.
In-school
Further socialization. Character, personality and values emerge. Secondary work models observed.

II. *Initial — 14 — End of formal or full-time education*
Dependence upon home is weakened. Indoctrination of work values of responsibility, willingness to work hard, get along with people, handle money, etc.
Adjust aspiration to realistic level. Acquire technical and social skills relevant to job performance. Adjust to a worker culture.

III. *Trial — From school leaving — Age 34*
Select permanently a satisfying job. Develop a career orientation: ambitious, responsive, fulfilled, confused, frustrated, or defeated.

IV. *Stable — 35 to retirement*
Settling down in an occupation. Establishing social roots in work plant and community. Progress to highest achievement level attainable.

V. *Retired — Retirement to death*
Adjust to non-work. Shift from work to home interests, change in status, change in friendship patterns, security, and health.

Adapted by the editor from Chapters 15–20 of D. C. Miller and W. H. Form, *Industrial Sociology*, New York: Harper and Bros., 1951.

Measurement of Vocational Maturity in Adolescence

JOHN O. CRITES, *University of Iowa*

THE VOCATIONAL DEVELOPMENT INVENTORY: CONTENT AND DESIGN OF THE ATTITUDE TEST

The Vocational Development Inventory (VDI) has been conceived and constructed to measure more completely than previous procedures the behavior domains of choice competencies and attitudes in vocational maturity, which are assessed respectively by two subtests — the Competence test and the Attitude test. The Competence test will be dealt with in greater detail in later reports, but is briefly described here so that it can be contrasted with the Attitude test and thus sharpen the theoretical definition of the latter. In its first experimental form the Competence test consists of five parts, each of which is comprised of 30 multiple-choice items with from three to five foils. Part I is the Problems test, which is designed to measure the ability to resolve conflicts between the factors in vocational choice. Part II is the Planning test, in which the task is to order scrambled series of steps leading to various vocational goals. Part III is the Occupational Information test, which includes items on job duties and tasks, trends in occupations, and future employment opportunities. Part IV is the Self-Knowledge test and is scored against standardized test information for accuracy of

Abridged from and reprinted with the permission of the author and publisher from the monograph of the same title from *Psychological Monographs*, 1965, *79*, Whole Number 575.

estimated vocational capabilities. Part V is the Goal Selection test, the items of which require the examinee to choose the "best" (most realistic) occupation for a hypothetical individual who is described in terms of his aptitudes, interests, and personality characteristics. The functions or processes which are supposedly involved in taking the Competence test, then, are largely what might be designated as comprehension and problem-solving abilities as they pertain to the vocational choice process.

In contrast, the Attitude test was designed to elicit the attitudinal or dispositional response tendencies in vocational maturity which are nonintellective in nature, but which may mediate both choice behaviors and choice aptitudes. The items for this test were developed from a combination of the best features of the empirical and rational methods of test construction. The empirical approach to item selection has the advantage that only items which are valid in differentiating between criterion groups, and which are properly cross-standardized, are selected for the test (Meehl, 1945). But, it has the distinct disadvantage, particularly in measures of constructs, of including items which are sometimes phenotypically nonsensical (Travers, 1951), such as the Minnesota Multiphasic Personality Inventory item "I think Lincoln was greater than Washington," which differentiates between several dissimilar criterion groups and normals for no apparent reason. Jessor and Hammond (1957) have observed:

If one is concerned only with the predictive validity of a test, the matter of item content is relatively unimportant, for the empirical item-criterion correlations provide criteria for the final selection of items. However, when a test-developer insists that his purpose includes more than the prediction of a particular criterion performance and that the test items are intended to be indicators of a construct, then item content becomes highly important, and item-criterion correlations only are insufficient . . . . Therefore, test items which are intended to indicate a construct should be selected by rational (rather than intuitive) means [p. 164].

The basic difficulty with the rational approach, however, is that items which are empirically nonvalid for the construct they are supposed to measure, because they do not correlate with behavior-relevant variables (American Psychological Association, 1954), are often retained in a test solely on the basis of their content or "face" validity, as in the case of the Bernreuter Personality Inventory (Landis and Katz, 1934; Landis, Zubin, and Katz, 1935). Another problem in rational test development is the confusion which has arisen over what is meant by a "construct" (Bechtoldt, 1959). The term has been used in at least two quite different ways: first, to refer to an internal state or condition of the organism, such as anxiety, which may be inferred from test responses and which may be thought of as more or less hypothetical in nature; and, second, to denote a pattern of interrelationships among a set of variables which is differentiable empirically from other patterns or variables, as in factorial and similar types of multivariate analysis (Cronbach and Meehl, 1955). The first meaning of construct is exemplified by the mental processes which the Competence and Attitude tests were designed to measure, and the second meaning is illustrated by the predicted moderate positive correlations among the dimensions of vocational maturity. In other words, choice competencies and attitudes are seen as hypothetical variables which are inferable from verbal test behavior, whereas the construct of vocational maturity can be viewed as a behavioral syndrome defined by the empirical relationships among the variables which comprise it. If these distinctions are made, and standardization and validation data are gathered accordingly, it would seem that the most reasonable approach to test construction would be one which incorporates the merits of both the empirical and rational methods and avoids their shortcomings. Such a strategy was followed as much as possible in the design of the Attitude test.

To establish the rational or "logical validity" (Jessor and Hammond, 1957) of the Attitude test the general model for writing items proposed by Flanagan (1951) was followed, with some minor modifications. This model outlines three steps in item construction:

1. Description of the behavior (the definition, delimitation, and illustration of the variety and scope of the actions included in the items). The behavioral descriptions and definitions which were used in writing items for the Attitude test are listed in Appendix A. Considering the possible universe of choice attitudes, these particular dimensions appear to be a fairly representative sample, having been selected from various statements of vocational development theory and inferred from relevant research findings (Ginzberg et al., 1951; Small, 1953; Super, 1957).

2. Analysis of the behavior (the classification of a specific behavior or item with respect to other behaviors and hypotheses about its generality and predictability). For each dimension in Appendix A from 10 to 25 items were written on the assumption that the behavior stated in the item would mature with increasing age (or grade). In other words, the research hypothesis for each item was that it would be consistently and systematically (monotonically) related to age (or grade). The items were written so as to maximize their relationships to age (or

grade) and to minimize their association with other variables, such as sex differences, socioeconomic status, and urban-rural residence. The goal was to devise items which were as generally applicable as possible.

3. Formulation of item specifications (decisions about the type of item content and response format appropriate to measure the specified behaviors). Two variables were experimentally manipulated in order to determine their effects upon the power of the items to differentiate between age (or grade) levels. First, some question has been raised whether self-report items should be written in the first or third person singular, the argument being that the latter may be more subtle and hence more valid (Guilford and Zimmerman, 1949). Consequently, some items ("Sometimes I wish I never had to work") were written in the more personal grammatical form, and others ("Work is drudgery") were stated in the more impersonal form. Second, the response format of the Attitude test was also varied. In one version, a 5-point Likert rating scale was used to indicate degree of item endorsement, whereas in the other only dichotomous "true-false" options were presented.

The experimental design for the Attitude test is summarized in Figure 1 which shows the various combinations of item type and response format. In accordance with this design, each test booklet was divided into two parts (1 and 2), with the items in the first half being stated in the third person singular and those in the second half in the first person singular. From a pool of approximately 1,000 items, 50 items were selected for each part of the booklet, making a total of 100 items for the initial standardization. This set of items was administered in two different forms (I and II), with the following instructions:

Form I:

Listed below are a number of statements about occupational choice and work. Read each statement and indicate on the separate answer sheet the extent to which you agree with the statement. Mark in the appropriate column on the answer sheet whether you "strongly disagree," "disagree," "neither disagree nor agree," "agree," or "strongly agree" with the statement.

Form II:

Listed below are a number of statements about occupational choice and work. Read each statement and indicate on the separate answer sheet the extent to which you agree with the statement. If you agree or mostly agree with the statement, place a mark in the column headed "T" on the answer sheet. If you disagree or mostly disagree with the statement, place a mark in the column headed "F" on the answer sheet.

Both International Business Machine (IBM) and Measurement Research Center (MRC) answer sheets, which have provisions for either scaled or true-false responses, have been used in administering the Attitude test, but the MRC answer sheet can be punched directly on to cards or reproduced upon magnetic tape and consequently has been considered to be preferable for large sample data processing.

RESPONSE FORMAT

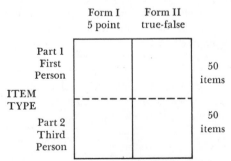

FIGURE 1. Experimental design for variation of item type and response format of the Attitude test.

STANDARDIZATION PROCEDURE FOR THE ATTITUDE TEST

Data Collection

To evaluate the "empirical validity" of the Attitude test, at least in so far as its items might be related to age (or grade), the experimental design in Figure 2 was replicated with male and female subjects at each of the age and grade levels shown in Figure 3. Grade as well as age was used as a criterion of vocational development, since it may be that the significant changes which occur in the maturation of vocational behavior are more closely associated with the impact of the educational system upon the individual than the mere passage of time. Not only is the school a major agent of socialization, but it also institutionalizes the developmental tasks, such as choice of a life's work, which society expects the individual to accomplish successfully at certain designated points in time (Havighurst, 1953; Super and Bachrach, 1957). The age or grade at which vocational developmental tasks are first encountered has not been determined empirically, but Ginzberg, Ginsburg, Axelrod, and Herma (1951) have hypothesized that the choice process probably begins sometime during the later elementary school years. Consequently, the items of the Attitude test were written so that children in the fifth and sixth grades could read and understand them. That this objective was largely achieved is indicated by a reading difficulty level for the inventory of 5.9595 in grade units, as calculated by the Dale and Chall (1948) formula for predicting readability. This value is inflated considerably by the use of the word "occupation" in many of the items, which is not included in the Dale list of familiar words for fourth graders. When the formula is computed without "occupation," the value is 5.1700, which is only slightly above the fourth-grade level. Since *occupation* was defined for the subjects in the lower grades, the smaller Dale-Chall value would seem to better represent the reading difficulty of the Attitude test.

The test was administered on a group basis during the 1961–62 academic year in selected schools of the Cedar Rapids, Iowa, elementary and secondary system. This city was chosen as the base-line community for standardizing the Attitude test not only because of practical considerations, such as the cooperation and interest of the school counselors and officials, but also because Cedar Rapids, with a population of approximately 92,000 in the 1960 census, has a fairly diversified economy and representative social structure. There are both large and small commercial and industrial concerns in the area, and the schools draw students from all socioeconomic levels. In selecting schools for the initial administration of the Attitude test, an effort was made to represent as closely as possible the various high and low rent districts of the city. At the elementary and junior high school levels, this objective was more satisfactorily achieved than it was at the senior high school level. Five elementary and two junior high schools were chosen by school officials, on the basis of previous studies and their personal knowledge, as representative of the system as a whole at these levels, but only one of the two senior high schools was selected for the first testing, due to problems of scheduling and time. As a consequence, the senior high school data may be somewhat biased, but this will not be known until they can be compared with results from the other high school, which was subsequently tested in 1963. Also, it should be noted that data were collected in the senior high school in the fall, whereas they were obtained in the other schools during the spring.

Sampling Design

The plan for sampling the subjects within the schools where the testing was conducted is diagrammed in Figure 2. At each age and grade level the limits of which were essen-

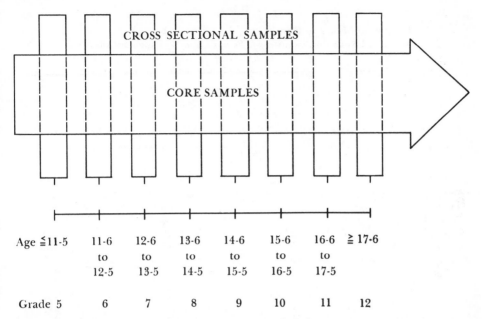

FIGURE 2. Sampling design for standardization of the Attitude test.

tially the same, a cross-sectional sample was designated for testing at any given point in time. Usually, this sample consisted of all students who were in attendance on the day the Attitude test was administered. The core samples, which will be followed up and tested from year to year, are comprised of those students who continue in the school system or who can be contacted after they drop out or graduate. On successive years, the cross-sectional samples will most likely change, due to students transferring in and out of the system, but the core samples will remain the same. Data on the latter will not only be used to standardize the Attitude test longitudinally but also to identify possible developmental stages in choice attitudes and to determine whether the test predicts vocational adjustment after occupational entry.

The Ns for the 1961–62 testing are given in Table 1. For some of the age intervals, notably the youngest and the oldest, the Ns are smaller than would have been desirable, particularly when the sexes are considered separately. Much the same can be said about

the lowest and highest grade levels, although their Ns are somewhat larger than those for age. The Ns for Form I for both the age and grade breakdowns are smaller than the Ns for Form II, since not as many subjects were needed to compute stable means from the 5-point rating scales of Form I as were required for stable percentages based upon the true-false responses to Form II. In general, the Ns were adequate for the analyses which were made for the initial standardization of the Attitude test but it should be cross-standardized on additional samples to increase the Ns at certain age and grade levels; and plans have been made to do this in the near future (Crites, 1964).

Analysis of Data

The analysis of the age and grade data was accomplished in three steps. First, the responses to each form of the Attitude test were analyzed separately by sex and then for the total group in a simple randomized design (Lindquist, 1953), where the be-

TABLE 1

Number of Male and Female Subjects Stratified by Age and Grade in the Standardization Samples for Forms I and II of the Attitude Test
(1961–62)

Age	Form I			Form II		
	Male	Female	Total	Male	Female	Total
≤11-5	30	25	55	59	78	137
11-6 to 12-5	40	24	64	94	80	174
12-6 to 13-5	20	24	44	296	312	608
13-6 to 14-5	14	9	23	324	304	628
14-6 to 15-5	31	51	82	408	413	821
15-6 to 16-5	37	51	88	116	113	229
16-6 to 17-5	47	56	103	83	70	153
≧17-6	26	30	56	45	27	72
Total			515			2822
Grade						
5	37	30	67	88	95	183
6	38	21	59	91	65	156
7	22	22	44	329	336	665
8	15	11	26	318	289	607
9	10	17	27	362	345	707
10	33	54	87	79	137	216
11	40	59	99	79	60	139
12	58	68	126	80	69	149
Total			535			2822

Note. In some instances, the Ns for certain analyses were slightly different than those given in this table, since some subjects, for one reason or another, were unable to complete their tests. Also, the Form I Ns for age and grade are not exactly the same, whereas those for Form II are, because of differences in key punching errors in processing the answer sheets.

tween-subjects factor was either age or grade. For Form I numerical values of 1–5 were assigned to the points on the rating scale, so that 1 indicated "strongly disagree" and 5 corresponded to "strongly agree"; for Form II numerical values of 1 and 2 were given to true and false, respectively. Items were retained for further statistical evaluation, if their F values from the analysis of variance reached or exceeded the .01 level. Second, for these items separate t tests between adjacent age or grade means were made to determine whether they increased or decreased monotonically. If an item mean for a given age or grade level was significantly greater or less than the other means at the .05 level, then the item was rejected as not meeting this criterion for a measure of a developmental variable. Rank-order correlations (rho) were also computed between the item means and age/grade to gain an impression of how strong the relationships were. Finally, the items which survived this process of elimination were scored with a key based upon the mean responses of twelfth graders, and average vocational maturity scores were computed for each grade. Also, the percentages of overlap in the score distributions of the grades were determined to estimate the discriminating power of the total vocational maturity score. In addition to these main analyses, certain supplementary ones were conducted which employed standard statistical methods, such as chi-square tests and product-moment correlations.

RESULTS AND CONCLUSIONS*

The data from the age and grade analyses, and a comparison of these, for response format and item type are presented first on the total sample. The findings on sex and school differences, which were negligible, are then reported. Finally, the results obtained from analyses of the total Vocational Maturity (VM) scale for the Attitude test are summarized and discussed.

Age Analysis

CONCLUSIONS   There are three major conclusions which can be drawn from the results of the age analyses. First, irrespective of variations in response format and item type, it is evident that responses to certain verbal statements of vocational attitudes and concepts, which are theoretically relevant to the choice of an occupation, are monotonically related to age during the adolescent years. Second, the true-false item format for such verbal statements appears to be preferable to item scaling in differentiating between subjects grouped according to age intervals which range from $\leq$ 11-5 to $\geq$ 17-6. And, third, there are no statistically demonstrable differences in the numbers of consistently age-related items which are written in the first and third person singular.

*Editor's note: In the interests of space economy, the results have been omitted here, and only the conclusions and further discussion are included. The interested reader is urged to obtain the entire monograph from the American Psychological Association.

Grade Analysis

CONCLUSIONS   In general, the conclusions which can be drawn from the grade analyses are much the same as those which were supported by the age analyses. Responses to verbally stated vocational behaviors change systematically and consistently from grade to grade, instructions to answer items as either true or false give better discrimination between grades than scaling instructions, and item type has no reliable effect upon differentiation between grades. On the basis of these results, and those from the age analyses, it was decided to conduct any further analyses of items only on data obtained with Form II, with no distinction being made between items written in the first and third grammatical styles.

Further Item Analyses

ITEM DIFFERENTIATION   Although most theories of vocational development (e.g., Ginzberg et al., 1951; Super, 1953, 1957) assume that age is the time dimension along which changes in vocational behavior occur, it is quite possible, as mentioned previously, that grade units may be equally, or even more, significant as the criteria of increments and stages in vocational maturity, since they correspond more closely to various aspects of development in general — educational, personal, and social. Chronological age may correlate more highly than grade with physical, and possibly intellectual, development but not necessarily with behaviors which are influenced more by learning than by heredity. Within a given grade, both younger and older students are expected to cope with the same developmental tasks and acquire the same types of capabilities, whether these involve problem-solving abilities or interpersonal competencies. Consequently, it would not be psychologically unreasonable to expect that item differentiation between grades might be equal to or even greater than that between age intervals.

This hypothesis was not testable statistically on the data of the present study, because most of the items which differentiated between age and grade levels were the same, and consequently they could not be classified into independent categories for purposes of comparison. A meaningful logical analysis of the age and grade differences in item differentiation can be made, however, by noting what the content was of those items which were related to one variable but not the other. The most clear-cut difference was for items which had to do with conceptions of the vocational choice process, such as "It's probably just as easy to be successful in one occupation as it is in another" and "There is only one occupation for each individual." Six times as many of these items were related to grade only as were associated with age only. Similarly, four times as many indecision items, such as "I really can't find any occupation that has much appeal to me," were independent functions of grade as compared with age. About twice as many work value items were contributed by grade alone. Why these particular item dimensions vary with grade but not with age may be due to the effects of a number of factors in addition to the impact of the educational system upon vocational development. But whatever the influence of other variables is, it would appear to be less significant than school experiences. Otherwise, age would have produced greater item differentiation than grade. Consequently, grade was used as the criterion for item selection.

TRENDS IN ITEM RESPONSES One finding which emerged from an inspection of the plots of Form II item means across grade levels was that most of them followed a curve from predominantly true responses in the elementary grades to predominantly false responses in the senior high grades. Of the 50 items in Form II which were monotonically related to grade, 43 were increasing functions from true to false, and only 7 were decreasing functions from false to true.

It might be argued from these trends that they indicate the operation of an extraneous response set were it not for two considerations. First, most of the items in the Attitude test are worded in such a way that a true response to them would be a less vocationally mature one. Illustrative items are: "A person can do anything he wants as long as he tries hard" and "I know very little about the requirements of occupations." The rationale for constructing items which primarily expressed vocationally *immature* attitudes, behaviors, and concepts, rather than mature ones, was that indiscriminate or generalized tendencies to endorse items as true would be counteracted and would not result in spuriously high vocational maturity scores. Second, some items were stated so that their content would be expected to elicit a true response as the more vocationally mature behavior, and it was among these that the items with decreasing functions of grade were found. Examples of such items are: "Choose an occupation, then plan to enter it" and "In making an occupational choice, you need to know what kind of person you are." Thus, the differential response trends to the two types of item content, with the mature items serving as a control on the immature items, may indicate that the tendency to answer items true in the lower grades is less an effect of test response set than it is degree of vocational development.

Another aspect of the trends in item means over grade levels was the extent to which the curves proceeded through discernible stages and the points at which these stages occurred. By defining a *stage* as a significant difference (.01 level) between adjacent item means for two grades, it was possible to classify the item trends into several different groups: first, out of the 50 items in Form II which were monotonically associated with grade, there were 10 which exhibited continuous curves with no significant "breaks" between grades. That is, there were no stages, as defined, in the trends for these items. Second, there were 20 items with one stage, 10 of which occurred between the sixth and seventh grades and 4 between the ninth and tenth grades. In other words, the steps in the educational ladder between elementary and junior high school and between junior high school and senior high school appear to be related to many of the stages which take place in vocational development. Third, there were 15 two-stage items, of which 10 had breaks between the sixth and seventh grades in conjunction with some other combination of differences between adjacent grades, 1 of these being between the ninth and tenth grades. Again, then, there is evidence of stages at the major transitional points in the educational system, particularly between the elementary and junior high school levels. Finally, 5 items had as many as three stages, but they did not conform to any particular pattern, other than that 3 of them had a stage between the sixth and seventh grades and 2 between the ninth and tenth grades. Thus, the most provocative finding from the analysis of stages in the item trends was that a total of 30 out of 50 items had stages which corresponded to the basic divisions in the educational structure.

A supplementary analysis which was performed on the trends in item responses was occasioned by the change observation that there were four items which would have met the "monotonic" criterion had it not been for a reversal in the curves of the item means in the eleventh and twelfth grades. In other words, these two grades had means on the four items which were significantly *less than* the tenth grade — and in three instances they were lower than the seventh, eighth, and ninth grades. In fact, they were more like the fifth and sixth grades. Why? When the content of the items was examined, it became apparent that they expressed a common attitude or feeling about making a vocational choice and planning for the future. The items were the following:

1. "I often wish that someone would just tell me what to do instead of having to choose an occupation by myself."

2. "You can wait to choose an occupation until after you have finished your schooling."
3. "If you do the best you can now, the future will take care of itself."
4. "Sometimes I wish I never had to work."

Each item refers to a desire to avoid the personal responsibility involved in selecting and committing oneself to a course of action which will lead to eventual occupational entry and a life of work. By responding to these items more as younger children did, the eleventh and twelfth graders in the sample, who were on the threshold of leaving the familiar and secure environment of the school, belied their anxiety and concern about venturing forth into a world which held unknown or uncertain prospects for them. In effect, what they did was to react to their apprehensions by *regressing* to modes of response which are more typical of earlier stages of vocational development.

DEVIATION ITEMS An unexpected phenomenon which was discovered through an inspectional analysis of the graphs for the item means was that certain items, a group of 10 in all, had two characteristics in common: first, they were not related to either age or grade; and, second, at each age or grade level 20% or less of the sample endorsed the items as either true or false, depending upon the direction of the predominant response. In other words, these items did not meet one of the necessary conditions for the measurement of vocational maturity *and* they were answered in a particular way by only a very small segment of the total sample. As a result, they were named the deviation response, or D, items, and the hypothesis was formulated that they may measure a maladjustment factor, as Berg (1959) has proposed. Additional data on the Deviation scale and its relationship to vocational maturity are presented and discussed below.

Sex Differences

Males and females differ on most non-intellective measures, as well as a few intellective ones, and consequently it was expected that they would differ in their responses to the Attitude test, but not as little as they actually did. There were only four items which differentiated between age and grade differently for the sexes. The following two items were related to both age and grade for males but not females: "There are so many factors to consider in choosing an occupation, it is hard to make a decision" and "If you have some doubts about what you want to do, ask your parents or friends for advice and suggestions." Conversely, these two items differentiated between age and grade for females but not males: "When it comes to choosing an occupation, I'll make up my own mind" and "I want to continue my schooling, but I don't know what courses to take or which occupation to choose." Whether the sex differences on these items are reliable ones which can be replicated will have to be determined in the cross-standardization of the Attitude test. About the most that can be concluded now is that the available data indicate only a few differences between males and females in the vocational attitudes and concepts which they endorse as self-descriptive. Evidently, sex is not a very significant factor in the maturation of these verbal aspects of vocational development.

Total Score Analyses

THE VM AND D SCALES Once the 50 items in Form II which were monotonically related to grade had been identified, they and the deviation items were scored for each subject in the sample to obtain total VM scores and D scores. For the VM scale it is noteworthy that, as mentioned previously, most of the items are keyed in the false direction for a higher vocational maturity score, and consequently the effect of any acquiescence response set associated with indiscriminate true endorsement of items should be reduced. The distributions of VM

TABLE 2

Means and Standard Deviations of Total VM and D Scores
for Males and Females Combined in Grades 5 through 12
(1961–62)

	Scale			
Grade	VM		D	
	M	SD	M	SD
5 ($N = 188$)	26.86	5.88	1.78	1.40
6 ($N = 150$)	29.26	5.74	1.70	1.43
7 ($N = 657$)	33.25	5.65	1.21	1.18
8 ($N = 601$)	35.07	5.44	1.11	1.10
9 ($N = 703$)	36.50	4.82	.98	.91
10 ($N = 213$)	37.81	4.58	1.17	1.02
11 ($N = 131$)	37.16	4.72	1.06	1.08
12 ($N = 143$)	39.00	4.00	1.02	1.03
Total ($N = 2786$)	34.64	6.03	1.18	1.13

scores were plotted on normal probability paper for each grade and the total sample, and they were shown to be essentially normal, the greatest departures being at the eleventh- and twelfth-grade levels, as was expected from the way in which the items were selected. For the D scale the distributions were highly positively skewed, since there were only a few subjects who answered many of these items in the keyed direction, which was directly opposite to that of the majority response. The means and standard deviations for the VM and D scales are summarized for each grade and the total sample in Table 2. The VM means increase from one grade level to another, with the possible exception of the eleventh grade where there is a slight leveling off, and the standard deviations decrease slightly in the upper grades. The D means are somewhat larger in the elementary grades, and there is greater heterogeneity at this level than later on.

The vocational maturity of the total sample is just about at the eighth grade level, as indicated by the mean of 34.64 in Table 2, which is approximately at the mid-point of the span between the fifth and twelfth grades. The mean and standard deviation of

the fifth grade would suggest that there is considerable "floor" under the Attitude test, since 98% of the fifth graders had scores above 15, and the lowest possible score is 0. The effective lower limit for the inventory has probably been reached, however, due to the reading difficulty of the items which is on the fifth-grade level. The "ceiling" for the Attitude test would appear to be adequate for subjects in secondary school, since only 1% of the twelfth graders had a score as high as 47 out of a possible 50; but it remains to be seen whether it can be used with older subjects who might be in college, technical school, or other types of post-high-school training.

OVERLAP BETWEEN GRADES ON VM One criterion of the effectiveness or utility of any instrument which purports to differentiate between groups or points on a continuum is the extent to which a low percentage of score overlap is achieved. Although there are several different methods for computing percentage of overlap (Strong, 1943), one of the most meaningful takes the median of the score distributions to be compared as the cut-off or dividing point between them. In Figure 4 this procedure was followed to determine how much overlap there was be-

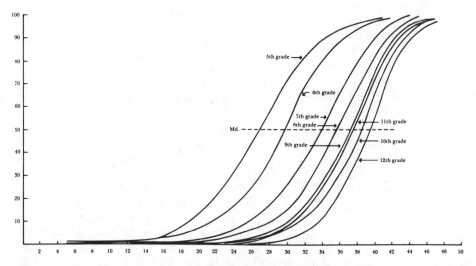

FIGURE 3. Cumulative percentage ogives of total VM scores for Grade 5 through 12.

tween grades in total VM scores. Cumulative percentage ogives were plotted against VM score for each grade, and then percentages of overlap were read from the graph for any combination of two grades by determining the percentage of scores above the point on the ogive of a given grade which corresponds to the median of the next higher grade. For example: the median of the seventh grade is a VM score of 34. The ordinate through this point intersects the ogive for the sixth grade at the eightieth percentile. The difference between this point and the upper end of the ogive is 20%, which is the amount of overlap between the VM score distributions of these two grades.

The percentages of VM score overlap for all possible pairs of grades are summarized in Table 3. The diagonal percentages are for adjacent grades, and they are all in the 30s, with the exception of the eleventh grade. As its ogive shows in Figure 3, the eleventh grade in this sample was atypical, since it was less like the twelfth grade in its VM score distribution than was the tenth grade. Whether this phenomenon is a function of biased sampling at the eleventh-grade level or the normal course of voca-

TABLE 3

Percentages of Overlap of Total Scores between Grades 5 through 12 with the Median as a Cut-Off Point
(1961–62)

Grade	Grade							
	5	6	7	8	9	10	11	12
5		30	11	7	4	3	4	2
6			20	13	8	5	7	3
7				38	25	17	24	12
8					37	28	34	21
9						38	47	38
10							50	40
11								32
12								

tional development during this period of high school needs to be studied further. That the sampling would be biased at just this one grade level, however, seems unlikely since exactly the same sampling procedures were used for the eleventh grade as were followed for the other grades. For the latter there is a definite tendency for the percentage of overlap to be larger in the upper grades, but this may be an artifact of the ceiling imposed by the method used to select items. If the scoring key had been based upon the responses of college seniors, the differentiation among Grades 9 through 12 might have been greater. It is also possible, however, that the twelfth grade represents the end point in the development of the vocational attitudes measured by the Attitude test and that an asymptote has been reached beyond which further differentiation would not be expected.

VM AND D SCALE CORRELATIONS In addition to the above analyses, it was of particular interest to compute the correlations of VM and D with age and grade and with each other, for several reasons. If the Attitude test measures individual differences in vocational maturity, which is a developmental variable, then the VM total scores for groups should be highly related to age and grade, as they are; but VM total scores for individuals should be only moderately positively correlated with age and grade. If they are too highly associated with these variables, then the Attitude test would be little more than an inefficient measure of age and grade. The actual product-moment r's, based upon the total sample of 2,784 subjects, were as expected, being .385 between VM and age and .463 between VM and grade, both of which were significant beyond the .001 level. Also, the value of t for the significance of the difference between these r's, which was 10.82, exceeded the .001 level with 2,781 degrees of freedom (Walker and Lev, 1953). In this analysis, the correlation of age with grade was $r = .908$. For D the predicted relationships with age and grade

were low ones, since one of the defining criteria for the deviation items was that they should be unrelated to these variables. The obtained r's for D with age and grade were $-.128$ and $-.159$, respectively, both of which were significant at the .001 level, with 1,931 degrees of freedom. Finally, the r for VM and D, with the same degrees of freedom, was $-.200$, which again was significant beyond the .001 level. In terms of the ways in which the two scales are scored, this low negative correlation means that the subjects who are less vocationally mature tend to be more deviant in their responses — and possibly, therefore, more maladjusted.

CONCLUSIONS When it is considered that the Attitude test must differentiate both (a) between groups of subjects at different grades and (b) between different subjects at the same grade in order to measure individual differences in vocational development, the standard deviations in Table 2 the percentages of overlap in Table 3, and the correlations of VM with age and grade, as well as with D, are encouraging. Together, these data indicate that the Attitude test measures behaviors which are highly enough related to age and grade that they are developmental in nature, but not so highly related that they are the same as age and grade.

REFERENCES

American Psychological Association. Technical recommendations for psychological tests and diagnostic techniques. *Psychological Bulletin*, (Suppl.) 1954, *51* (No. 2, Part 2).

Bechtoldt, H. P. Construct validity: A critique. *American Psychologist*, 1959, *14*, 619–629.

Berg, I. A. The unimportance of test item content. In B. M. Bass & I. A. Berg (Eds.), *Objective approaches to personality assessment*. Princeton, N. J.: Van Nostrand, 1959. Pp. 83–99.

Crites, J. O. Proposals for a new criterion measure and improved research design. In H. Borow (Ed.), *Man in a world at work*. Boston: Houghton Mifflin, 1964.

Cronbach, L. J., and Meehl, P. E. Construct validity in psychological tests. *Psychological Bulletin*, 1955, *52*, 281–302.

Dale, E., and Chall, Jeanne S. *A formula for predicting readability.* Columbus, O.: Bureau of Educational Research, Ohio State University, 1948.

Flanagan, J. C. The use of comprehensive rationales in test development. *Educational and Psychological Measurement*, 1951, *11*, 151–155.

Ginzberg, E., Ginsburg, S. W., Axelrad, S., and Herma, J. L. *Occupational choice*. New York: Columbia Univer. Press, 1951.

Guilford, J. P., and Zimmerman, W. S. Manual for the Guilford-Zimmerman Temperament Survey. Beverly Hills, Calif.: Sheridan Supply, 1949.

Havighurst, R. J. *Human development and education*. New York: Longmans, Green, 1953.

Jessor, R., and Hammond, K. R. Construct validity and the Taylor Anxiety Scale. *Psychological Bulletin*, 1957, *54*, 161–170.

Landis, C., and Katz, S. E. The validity of certain questions which purport to measure neurotic tendencies. *Journal of Applied Psychology*, 1934, *18*, 343–356.

Landis, C., Zubin, J., and Katz, S. Empirical evaluation of three personality adjustment inventories. *Journal of Educational Psychology*, 1935, *26*, 321–330.

Lindquist, E. F. *Design and analysis of experiments in psychology and education*. Boston: Houghton Mifflin, 1953.

Meehl, P. E. The dynamics of "structured" personality tests. *Journal of Clinical Psychology*, 1945, *1*, 296–303.

Small, L. Personality determinants of vocational choice. *Psychological Monographs*, 1953, *67* (No. 1, Whole No. 351).

Super, D. E. A theory of vocational development *American Psychologist*, 1953, *8*, 185–190.

Super, D. E. *The psychology of careers.* New York: Harper, 1957.

Super, D. E., and Bachrach, P. B. *Scientific careers and vocational development theory.* New York: Teachers College, Columbia University, Bureau of Publications, 1957.

Travers, R. M. W. Rational hypotheses in the construction of tests. *Educational and Psychological Measurement,* 1951, *11,* 128–137.

Walker, Helen M., and Lev, J. *Statistical inference.* New York: Holt, 1953.

Vocational Self Concept
in Adolescence

ROBERT P. O'HARA, *Boston College*

DAVID V. TIEDEMAN, *Harvard University*

SELF CONCEPTS
AND OCCUPATIONAL CHOICE

The process of occupational choice may be characterized as that of developing a vocational identity. The "Self" is the central concern of identity. The concepts of identity and self are intuitively satisfying means of attributing motivation for occupational choice to the person choosing.

Super and his associates say that the self concept "seems to lend itself admirably to the formulation of broad principles explanatory of occupational choice and vocational adjustment" (Super, *et al.*, 1957). They do, however, express some doubt about the merit of using the term self concept because of the difficulties encountered in making the term operational. Despite their doubts they formulate the general principle: "Self concepts begin to form prior to adolescence, become clearer in adolescence and are translated into occupational terms in adolescence."

Reprinted with the permission of the authors and publisher from *Journal of Counseling Psychology,* 1959, *6,* 292–301.

In an attempt to give an empirical formulation to self concept theory in the realm of vocational development, we have defined self concept as *an individual's evaluation of himself.* Using this definition we have investigated the areas of aptitude, interest, social class, and values. Previous research has shown that these areas are important in the development of careers. The research reported here not only measures the individual's standing in these four areas but adds a further dimension — a measure of the person's *ability to evaluate his standing.* Such a dimension is essential to an understanding of the way in which a person solves the occupational choice problem which he is facing. Hence it was felt that analysis of the evaluations individuals had of themselves in these areas would further illuminate the influence of these factors in occupational choice.

The relative independence of the dimension we are considering is apparent from several related studies. In the area of aptitude, inventoried assessment is only moderately related to self evaluation of aptitude (Arsenian, 1942; Brinn, 1956; Coffee, 1957; Matteson, 1956). "In terms of common elements, perhaps no more than between 25 and 50 per cent of the factors associated with expressed interests are associated with measured interest," according to Berdie (1950). This conclusion seems valid also for the areas of social class (Hollingshead, 1949; McArthur, 1954; McArthur and Stevens, 1955) and values as well (Stanley, 1951).

The above studies merely indicate that some awareness of vocationally-relevant attributes does exist during adolescence and early adulthood. None of them investigated the *clarification* of self concepts implied in Super's proposition. A study by Schulman (1955) and another by Anderson (1948) do provide evidence on this score in the areas under consideration. However, the two studies are limited to single areas, and each deals with a different set of fine points.

STAGES IN THE CLARIFICATION OF SELF CONCEPTS

In 1951, Ginzberg, Ginsburg, Axelrad and Herma set forth the theory that occupational choice progresses through three periods: fantasy choice, tentative choice, and realistic choice. The tentative choice period is subdivided into four stages: interest, capacity, value, and transition. Each of these names designates an element presumably dominant in occupational choice at a particular time. Ginzberg emphasized the developmental nature of his findings. He says that boys pass through the stages in the above order within rather regular age limits; interests, 11–12; capacities, 13–14; values, 15–16; transition, 17–18. Data for his study were derived from intensive analysis of interviews of eight individuals at each of eight periods in the educational process, starting with the sixth grade in elementary school, through the eighth, tenth, and twelfth grades in high school, freshman and senior years in college, first year graduate study and advanced graduate study.

In defining the stages of interest, capacity, value, and transition in the period of tenta-

tive choice, Ginzberg uses two approaches. The first approach involves the concept of maturity. However, little research evidence is presented for determination of the stages in explicit terms of maturity or quality of the subject's statements about his occupational choice.

The second approach to stages is found throughout Ginzberg's consideration of the tentative period. The criteria for the stages in this period are those factors which the interviews reveal to be the *basis for choice* by the boys at each age level.

Figure 1 represents graphically the stages of interest, capacity and value as enunciated by Ginzberg. All factors are present to awareness at all stages. At three grade levels the awareness comes into focus on one factor and this factor is used as the basis for making vocational choices during that period. Ginzberg made no effort at graphical presentation of his periods and stages. Hence our representation may do injustice to Ginzberg's ideas even though we have tried to present his words pictorially as faithfully as we can.

Whether our representation of Ginzberg's periods and stages is accurate or not, the fact remains that we have been unable to locate any work on the mathematical representation of the "periods" or "stages" of vocational development. The expression in the mathematical idiom of phases of development supposedly relevant for occupational choice is one of the major purposes of this study.

Although the concepts of "period" and "stage" are frequently used in regard to career development, they are difficult to define. However defined though, both words ordinarily connote a time interval in which something is prevalent which is not prevalent at another time. Thus, "period" and "stage" suggest discreteness, dominance, and irreversibility. Discreteness is indicated in Figure 1 by the precipitous change in the line for an area of discourse when it becomes the basis for choice. Dominance is implied when a line for an area exceeds lines for

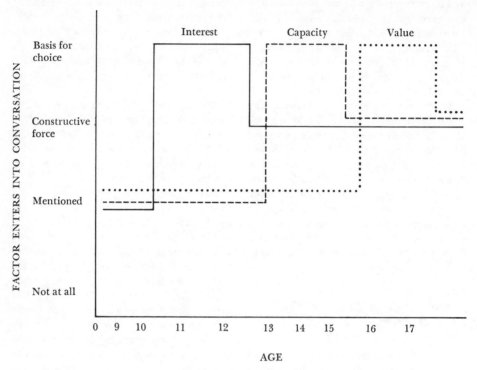

FIGURE 1. Stages in the tentative period. (After Ginzberg, 1951.)

other areas, i.e. when the area becomes the basis for choice. Irreversibility suggests that a line, once advanced, never recedes. Ginzberg is not clear about irreversibility in this sense. He suggests that earlier considerations remain "constructive forces" in the differentiation of occupational intent but implies that they never again reach the eminence of being the sole "basis for choice" once having been so. To us this implies the *reversibility* depicted in Figure 1. Adolescent imbalance causes an element to be the sole basis for choice but, having been so, the element returns to the more mature position of being a constructive force operating simultaneously with others to effect differentiation of occupational choice. This may result from an adolescent's increasing *ability to estimate* the reality of his interests, aptitudes, and values through his widening experience in school and work.

SEMANTIC PERSPECTIVE

This investigation relates the subjects' estimates of their present status with regard to aptitudes, interests, social class, and values to assessments of their standing in each of these categories as revealed by tests or statements of preference.

In the area of *aptitude* the following five scales of the Differential Aptitude Test: Form A, (Bennett, Seashore, and Wesman, 1947) were used: verbal reasoning, numerical ability, mechanical reasoning, space relations, and abstract reasoning. The ten scales of the Kuder Preference Record, Vocational, Form CH (Kuder, 1948) delimited the area of interests. The Home Index of Gough (1949) defined the area of social class. A modification of the Study of Values (Allport, Vernon, and Lindzey, 1951) which provided scales in each of the six areas of this inventory, was the setting for the study of general values. The Work Values Inventory (Super, 1955) distinguished the area of work values.

For every variable, the self estimate requested was oriented by adaptation of the definition provided by the test or inventory. A copy of the self estimate questionnaire used is available upon request. The questionnaire gives the actual definitions of variables for which subjects provided self-estimates. Authors' definitions of variables were followed as exactly as possible.

SUBJECTS

Data were collected at a private Catholic day school in Boston staffed by the Fathers and Scholastics of the Society of Jesus (Jesuits). There were 1021 boys in the sample, 160 Seniors, 264 Juniors, 276 Sophomores, and 321 Freshmen. The four grades are homogeneous by sex, intelligence, and religion by virtue of administrative policy. Our data revealed that the boys in the several grades also had similar distributions of verbal ability, numerical ability, and social class. The tests of this study were administered over a period of a week and a half in the latter part of March, 1958. Each boy contributed 8 hours of his time providing data.

Admission to the school is competitive and selective. As a result, the classes are above average in scholastic aptitude, yet a fairly high fraction of the boys who are admitted leave before graduating. The attrition, however, was independent of verbal ability and of social class in this sample.

ANALYSIS

Results are summarized by *grade* since grade was the sampling unit of this investigation. Strictly speaking, development should

be expressed as a function of *age*. Age was *not* the unit of sampling in this case, however, because the necessary complicated administrative arrangements did not yet seem justifiable. In addition, although we had no way to substantiate the supposition, we felt that clarification of self knowledge in these vocationally relevant areas is a function of the curriculum more than it is a function of length of life. These considerations dictated choice of *grade* as the unit of development *for this investigation*.

Ours is the cross-sectional method of studying development. With this method, tests of significance are made relative to the variations of individuals around the parameters one is interested in testing rather than relative to the variations within individuals. If this less sensitive test permits rejection of the null hypothesis, one may be assured that the more sensitive test available from longitudinal data would reject the same null hypothesis.

For the data of each grade, the relationships between self estimates and estimates provided through inventories are summarized for each area (aptitude, interest, general values, and work values) by means of the canonical correlation coefficient (Hotelling, 1935). These canonical correlation coefficients give in each case the maximum correlation between a *linear* composite of the self estimates in an area and a linear composite of the estimates provided through the analogous inventory. Clearly, nonlinear composites of either or both of the estimates provided by rating and test can be more highly correlated than the linear composites investigated. However, relating linear composites introduces sufficient complexity into the current state of our knowledge of the clarity of perception of vocationally relevant attributes.

Since the social class area provided only a single estimate from both self and test, these estimates were related by means of the product moment correlation coefficient which is the analogue of the canonical correlation for this class of data.

DEVELOPMENT OF KNOWLEDGE OF SELF IN VOCATIONALLY RELEVANT AREAS

Figure 2 depicts over-all relationships between self estimates and test estimates for each of the four grade levels in the five areas: aptitude, interest, social class, and general and work values. The correlations themselves are given in Table 1.

Except for the area of social class, the increasing congruence of self estimates and test estimates with increasing grade level is apparent from a glance at Figure 2. Since we knew of no test for the significance of the difference in canonical correlations at the time of this investigation, we could not

TABLE 1

Correlations of Test Scores and Self Ratings by Grade

	Fresh. ($N =$ 321)	Soph. ($N =$ 276)	Jun. ($N =$ 264)	Sen. ($N =$ 160)
Aptitudes	.44	.50	.59	.69
Interests	.70	.81	.79	.83
Social Class*	.42	.29	.42	.35
General Values	.56	.59	.63	.63
Work Values	.69	.67	.71	.84

*Product moment correlations. All others are canonical correlation coefficients n explanation given in text.

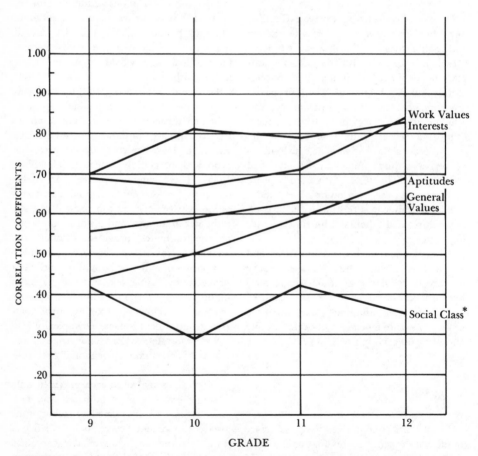

FIGURE 2. Correlations of test scores and self estimates by grades. (*Product moment correlations. All others are canonical correlation coefficients.)

determine whether the trends for interests, work values, and aptitudes were significant or not. In view of the large number of subjects and of the characteristics of the three curves, however, it seems likely that at least these three trends are significant. The trend for general values is perhaps not significant but manifests the same upward tendency. Congruence in the social class area does not seem to increase appreciably in these grades.

There is a test of significance of the difference between zero-order correlation coefficients and this test was applied to the difference between the correlation of self estimate and test estimate for the ninth-grade data and for the twelfth-grade data as obtained on each of the variables of the several areas. As is indicated in Table 2, 17 of the 37 correlations differed significantly from hypothesized equivalence at

TABLE 2

Tests of Equivalence of Ninth and Twelfth Grade Correlations for Each Variable of Each Area

Area	Number of Variables	Number of rejections* of $H: \rho_9 = \rho_{12}$ in which	
		$r_9 > r_{12}$	$r_9 < r_{12}$
Aptitude	5	0	2
Interest	10	0	6
Social Class	1	0	0
General Values	6	0	4
Work Values	15	0	5
Totals	37	0	17

*.05 level of significance.

the .05 level of significance and the difference indicated that the correlation among twelfth-grade data exceeded that among ninth-grade data. In no variable did the ninth-grade correlation exceed the twelfth-grade correlation significantly. Further study of Table 3 should convince one that, in general, estimates of these vocationally-relevant attributes are better differentiated

by twelfth-grade boys than by ninth-grade boys since 26 of the 37 favored the twelfth grade. The progress of these changes over the four grades is reported in Table 3.

A canonical correlation is at least as high as the largest of the zero-order correlations entering into its computation. Hence the high proportion of rejection of the hypothesized equivalence of ninth and twelfth-grade correlations reported in Table 2 suggests that the ninth and twelfth-grade canonical correlations reported in Table 1 are significant, particularly since the diminution of degrees of freedom contingent upon the fitting of constants in the computation of the canonical correlations is small relative to the sample sizes of the two grades.

Figure 2 also reveals that the relative *order* in the relationship between self estimates and test estimates of the several areas is approximately the same for the first three years of high school. Interest test scores are most highly related to their respective self ratings with correlations for work values, general values, aptitudes and social class following in that order. Only in the twelfth grade is the order changed. By the senior year the relationship of aptitudes to self ratings of aptitudes surpasses that of general values to self ratings of those values.[1]

To this point then, the analysis of the data clearly reveal that self concepts in the areas of interests, aptitudes, and work and general values are clarified as boys pass through grades nine to twelve.

STAGES IN THE CLARIFICATION OF VOCATIONAL SELF CONCEPTS

A major purpose of this investigation was to assess evidence for the existence of *stages* in the development of occupational choice within the context of congruity of self estimates and test estimates of vocationally relevant attributes. At the outset we suggested that "period" or "stage" should connote discreteness, dominance, and/or irreversibility. Therefore, let us now consider Figure 2 in these terms.

TABLE 3

Correlation of Self Estimate and Test Estimate by Area and Grade

Area	Variable	Grade 9	Grade 10	Grade 11	Grade 12
Aptitude	Verbal Reasoning	.30	.26	.31	.26
	Numerical Ability	.32	.40	.43	.51
	Mechanical Reasoning	.26	.38	.41	.58
	Space Relations	.24	.24	.26	.18
	Abstract Reasoning	.19	.08	.03	.13
Interest	Outdoor	.50	.48	.47	.50
	Mechanical	.49	.58	.57	.66
	Computational	.58	.60	.60	.69
	Scientific	.51	.54	.46	.68
	Persuasive	.24	.53	.48	.32
	Artistic	.59	.48	.43	.50
	Literary	.41	.43	.54	.57
	Musical	.59	.63	.61	.65
	Social Service	.44	.45	.60	.60
	Clerical	.32	.32	.37	.50
Social Class	Social Class	.42	.29	.42	.35
Values, General	Theoretical	.19	.16	.10	.18
	Economic	.22	.30	.25	.44
	Aesthetic	.32	.37	.43	.46
	Social	.19	.37	.46	.45
	Political	.28	.36	.27	.28
	Religious	.23	.31	.32	.46
Values, Work	Creative	.42	.50	.45	.57
	Aesthetic	.39	.36	.44	.39
	Planning	.19	.25	.25	.28
	Theoretical	.33	.27	.32	.40
	Variety	.44	.37	.52	.47
	Independence	.27	.34	.33	.30
	Supervision	.12	.10	.14	.09
	Work Conditions	.15	.07	.22	.20
	Associations	.24	.18	.19	.35
	Way of Life	.23	.33	.35	.40
	Social Welfare	.46	.55	.57	.61
	Security	.28	.28	.35	.48
	Material	.38	.38	.52	.56
	Prestige	.23	.31	.19	.35
	Mastery	.08	.07	.07	.04

Criterion of Discreteness

Some developments are characterized by surges which are followed by quiescence during which gains are consolidated. De- velopment of this nature, when represented by a growth function, is indicated by a line, parallel to the time axis for a period, which rises sharply from time to time without regression. These surges are indicative of some kind of discreteness in the growth function. It is unclear, however, whether the stage should be denoted by the sequence, surge followed by quiescence, or quiescence followed by surge. It is a matter of whether a stage involves anticipation or not and also of whether consolidation must be included or not. Because of this ambiguity, *we shall refer only to the surge itself as a stage.*

Figure 2 indicates possible nonlinearity in the progress of clarification of self knowledge. *Setting consideration of sampling variability aside* momentarily, the relationship of self estimates to test estimates in the interest area is best represented as a parabolic function of grade: were a parabola to be fitted to the data for interest, it would curve *markedly* in the range from grade 9 to grade 10 and start to become asymptotic to the grade axis even within the range indicated. This suggests some form of discreteness in the differentiation of interest, sampling considerations being ignored, with an *interest stage* that seems to *terminate* by grade 10. Our data do not permit inference of the grade at which this possible stage originates.

The area of work values also approximates a parabolic function when possible sampling variations are ignored. The function, however, seems to be the mirror image of that of interest. In the work values area, the developmental function will be approximately asymptotic to the grade axis in grades 9–11 and curve upward markedly between grades 11 and 12. Ignoring sampling variation then, work values become more differentiated through grade 12. This may well be a *secondary* phase for the differentiation of work values. Since the asymptote defined by the range *of these data* is relatively high for the area, there must be an earlier grade at which *primary* differentiation of these work values occurs in order for the relationship to have reached .69 by grade 9. We might speculate also that periods of gestation are required before surges of progress in awareness of self concepts can occur.

If sampling variations are completely ignored, progress in the differentiation of general values is also a parabolic function. The function, when fitted, would have a shallower curve than would those for interests and work values. This would suggest that progress in the development of general values is continuous through grades 9 and 10 and that a plateau in progress occurs in grades 11 and 12. Our data would then suggest that the stage of differentiation of general values is in progress through grades 9 and 10.

Since the surges of progress in differentiation of general values are not as precipitous as they are for the differentiation of work values and interest, we are inclined to consider the apparent surge in the general values curve attributable to sampling variation. In this case progress in the differentiation of general values is more likely a straight line within this range of data. *In this event, we would characterize differentiation of general values as that of continual progress rather than as that of a stage.*

Sampling variation notwithstanding, progress in differentiation of perceptions of aptitude is definitely linear rather than parabolic. *Within this grade-range there is not an aptitude stage* of differentiation of perceptions. Rather there is continual progress in the attainment of differentiated perceptions of aptitude.

The correspondence of self ratings and inventory estimates of social class seems to reflect only sampling variation about a line of zero slope. There seems to be no gain in awareness of social class in these grades.

Criterion of Dominance

The criterion of dominance in the definition of a stage usually implies that one aspect overrides another or others. Ginzberg (1951) says that interests, aptitudes and values dominate boys' talk about their occupational choices in that order. This research interprets dominance in terms of the *ability of the boys to estimate* their interests, aptitudes, values, and social class. According to this interpretation, congruence of self estimates and test estimates is greatest in the area of interest throughout the grade-range except in grade 12 when it is tied by the area of work values. In addition, maximum congruence is achieved earliest in the area of interest, namely in grade 10. Throughout grades 9 through 12, congruence of estimates in the areas of interest and work values eclipses congruence of estimates in the area of general values and aptitudes.

Congruence in the aptitude area is singularly low in grades 9, 10, and 11 when pupils are presumably making a number of tentative decisions about work which we would prefer to have based upon accurate perceptions of capability. Only in grade 12 does congruence in the area of aptitude exceed that in any area and then only that of the area of general values. This unawareness of aptitude in these grades may explain why assessments of aptitude predict curriculum choice only poorly in junior high school and high school (e.g., Cass, 1956; Kugris, 1956).

Criterion of Irreversibility

A third connotation of stage is that of irreversibility. In the sense that the congruence of self-estimates and test-estimates is a monotonic increasing function of grade, our data provide concrete evidence that the developmental function in each of the areas except that of social class is irreversible. Only in this connotation of stage do general values and aptitudes emerge as stages. Awareness of social class does not regress but neither does it progress.

The increasing ability to evaluate these vocationally-relevant factors could be responsible for the reversibility in the stages as outlined by Ginzberg earlier. The imbalance which resulted in one factor being the sole basis for choice is gradually redressed under the force of the always increasing clarification of vocationally-relevant self concepts so that at the end of the tentative period all factors become constructive forces in the career development process. The grade

limitation of our data does not allow us to estimate at what future point the ability to evaluate these factors converges. However, we feel that the location of this point is important for the estimation of vocational maturity. However, it may well be that there is no point of convergence but that there always remains a differential hierarchy of ability to evaluate one's self in these areas.

GENERALIZATION

Our purpose has been to establish empirically the existence of clarification of self concepts in areas of relevance to vocational choice, and through study of this clarification to introduce more precise means of identifying and describing the stages of occupational choice. Our contribution lies both in the methods we have introduced and in the conclusions drawn from the analysis of our data. The method opens a way for other investigations which are necessary before our conclusions are generalizable.

Dominance of areas was investigated by comparison of the general *level* of the congruence of test-estimates and self-estimates as revealed by canonical correlation. Irreversibility was equated with the monotonic increasing nature of the function relating congruence of estimates and grade level. Finally, a stage was taken to be represented by a monotonic increasing, nonlinear function whose level exceeded that of other functions at some time.

The above definitions were applied to the self-estimates and test-estimates provided by 1021 boys in attendance at a private Catholic day school in Boston. From the milieu of an academically well-qualified Catholic boy living in Greater Boston and receiving his education in the scholastic tradition of the Jesuits, *our data indicate increasing clarification of self concepts in four vocationally relevant areas. Further, our data identify an interest stage seemingly terminated by grade 10 and a work-values stage probably proceeding through a secondary phase in grade 12.* Differentiation of perception in the areas of aptitude and of general values progresses continuously and concomitantly with differentiation in the areas of interest and work values. No clarification of social class occurs during high school.

These data in no way contradict the stages of development proposed by Ginzberg. Ginzberg identified his stages in the *talk* of boys who were asked to consider themselves in relation to school and work. Interest, aptitudes, and values became a part of this talk, in that order, as he moved from boys in grades 8 and 9, to boys in grades 10 and 11, and to boys in grade 12. Our data do, however, indicate that this sequence is not applicable to the *quality* of estimates of vocationally-relevant attributes. A difference of particular importance is that reporting the *quality* of estimates of aptitude. *Aptitude is relatively poorly perceived throughout grades 9 through 12 even by academically able boys.*

[1]As in the case of multiple correlation, canonical correlation tends to increase with an increase in the number of variables. The patterning of the canonical correlations in relation to the numbers of variables entering into each causes us to consider this an unlikely explanation of the results, however.

REFERENCES

Allport, G. W., Vernon, P. E., and Lindzey, G. *A study of values* (rev. ed.). Boston: Houghton Mifflin, 1951.

Anderson, Rose G. Subjective ranking versus score ranking of interest values. *Personnel Psychol.*, 1948, *1*, 349–355.

Arsenian, S. Informing college freshmen of their test scores." *J. educ. Psychol.* 1942, *33*, 291–302.

Bennett, G. K., Seashore, R. G., and Wesman, A. C. *Differential aptitude tests.* New York: The Psychological Corp., 1947.

Berdie, R. F. Scores on the Strong Vocational Interest Blank and the Kuder Preference Record in relation to self ratings. *J. appl. Psychol.*, 1950, *34*, 42–49.

Brinn, O. G., Jr. College grades and self-estimates of intelligence. *J. educ. Psychol.*, 1956, *45*, 477–484.

Cass, J. C. Prediction of curriculum choice in Maine secondary schools. Unpublished Ed.D. dissertation, Harvard Graduate School of Education, 1956.

Coffee, J. Occupational realism: an analysis of factors influencing realism in the occupational planning of male high school seniors. Unpublished doctoral dissertation, Graduate School of Education, Harvard Univer., 1957.

Ginzberg, E., Ginsburg, S. W., Axelrad, S., and Herma, J. L. *Occupational choice.* New York: Columbia Univer. Press, 1951.

Gough, H. G. A short social status inventory. *J. educ. Psychol.*, 1949, *40*, 52–56.

Hollingshead, A. E. *Elmtown's youth.* New York: Wiley, 1949.

Hotelling, H. The most predictable criterion. *J. educ. Psychol.*, 1935, *26*, 139–142.

Kuder, G. F. *Kuder Preference Record — Vocational — Form CH* Chicago: Science Research Associates, 1948.

Kugris, Violet. A study of the allocation of differential aptitudes to various high school curricula in terms of pupil choice and counselor opinion. Unpublished Ed.D. Dissertation, Harvard Graduate School of Education, 1956.

McArthur, C. Long-term validity of the strong test in two sub-cultures. *J. appl. Psychol.*, 1954, *38*, 346–353.

McArthur, C., and Stevens, Lucia B. The validation of expressed interests as compared with inventoried interests: a fourteen-year follow-up. *J. appl. Psychol.*, 1955, *39*, 184–189.

Matteson, R. W. Self estimates of college freshmen. *Personnel guid., J.*, 1956, *34*, 280–284.

Schulman, J. A comparison between ninth and twelfth grade students on self estimates of abilities and objective scores on the Differential Aptitude Tests. Unpublished Doctoral dissertation, New York Univer., 1955.

Sinnett, E. R. Some determinants of agreement between measured and expressed interest. *Educ. psychol. Measmt.*, 1956, *16*, 110–118.

Stanley, J. C. Insight into one's own values. *J. educ. Psychol.*, 1951, *42*, 339–408.

Super, D. E. *Notes on Career Pattern Study Tests.* New York: Columbia Univer., February, 1955. (Mimeographed.)

Super, D. E., *et al. Vocational development: A framework for research.* New York: Columbia Univer. Bureau of Publications, 1957.

Vocational Certainty and Indecision in College Freshmen

JEFFERSON D. ASHBY, *Pennsylvania State University*

HARVEY W. WALL, *Pennsylvania State University*

SAMUEL H. OSIPOW, *Pennsylvania State University*

An aspect of the vocational choice process of interest to counselors involves the implications that specific personality traits have on making vocational decisions. In counseling, for example, it is not uncommon to encounter a student who experiences excessive difficulty in making any kind of decision, whether it be selecting a tie that goes well with his suit, a girl to date, a college to attend, or a career to embark upon. Such a characteristic may reasonably be considered to be part of a larger personality pattern. Such a pattern would necessarily have implications for the vocational decisions of an individual.

Some research about behavioral styles having implications for vocational decisions has been conducted by Ziller (1957), Lindgren (1962), and Couch and Keniston (1960), but many relationships between personality traits on the one hand and vocational behavior on the other remain unclear. For example, the question of how an individual approaches decision-making as a func-

Reprinted with the permission of the authors and publisher from *Personnel and Guidance Journal*, 1966, *44*, 1037–1041.

tion of personality patterns assumes considerable importance. Holland and Nichols' research with the general problem of indecisiveness (1964) is relevant to such a discussion. His results suggest that such a general trait exists, that it can be predicted on the basis of high school activities, and that it has implications for the kinds of decisions that people make. Furthermore, from his data one may make inferences about the way such a trait develops.

In addition to personality styles, it is of interest to know in what way background factors are similar or different for those who are vocationally decided and undecided. Such background data could clarify the forces that are important in shaping a person's general approach to decision-making.

The research reported in this paper grew primarily out of the investigators' daily confrontation with problems presented by students who were attempting to make sound educational and vocational choices. The major objective was an attempt to develop an understanding of the personality and demographic factors that differentiate vocationally decided from vocationally undecided students. The study was aimed at exploring the background, personality, and college performance of undecided students in comparison with freshmen who began college with a vocational objective clearly in mind.

METHOD

Sample

The subjects in this study were students entering their first term as freshmen at The Pennsylvania State University (PSU). The Decided (D) *S*s, 81 males and 27 females, were students who expressed considerable certainty about their educational-vocational plans and were enrolled in curricula oriented toward some relatively clear field, such as business, engineering, teaching, the liberal arts, etc.

The Undecided (U) subjects, 26 males and 3 females, were students who had difficulty in identifying an entry program in the university and chose instead to begin their university studies enrolled in the Division of Counseling. The Division of Counseling, which possesses administrative functions like that of a college in the university, permits wide flexibility in student scheduling during the early period of college work, in the expectation that undecided students will be able to clarify their goals during such an exploratory period. Although the students in the U group had some vague ideas about what they might like to do, none felt sufficiently certain of their plans to officially commit themselves to a specific program, and all identified themselves as uncertain or undecided about their educational-vocational plans.

A third group, called Tentative (T) was identified. This group, composed of 79 males and 12 females, possessed some educational-vocational goal with a moderate degree of certainty, but had some reservation about the goal which led them to choose to begin their college studies in the

Division of Counseling. While they were not uncertain in the same manner as the Undecided *S*s, they were clearly not committed to a course of study as were the D group.

Material and procedures

Prior to enrollment in the university, all freshmen provide the Division of Counseling with considerable data concerning their interests, abilities, and achievements. Out of this pool of information, the following were chosen for comparison: the Strong Vocational Interest Blank (SVIB); the Bernreuter Personality Inventory (BPI); selected items from a Personal Information Blank (PIB) which included academic aspiration, number of siblings, and birth order; the PSU Academic Abilities Test; the PSU English Placement Test; the PSU Mathematics Test; the size of the student's high school class, the student's grade-point average (GPA) through 11th grade; his SAT verbal and quantitative scores; his parents' income reported in five categories (below $3,000, between $3,000–6,000, $6,000–9,000, $9,000–12,000, and over $12,000); his father's and mother's education; and first term GPA at Penn State.

In addition to the above information, prior to their enrollment at PSU all the subjects were required to rate themselves according to a set of six personality descriptions based on Holland's (1962) personality types. Holland (1962) proposes that there are six general orientations to life, which he calls the Realistic (R), characterized by strong, masculine attention to concrete rather than abstract problems; the Intellectual (I), emphasizing understanding, and ambiguous and abstract work tasks; Social (S), where individuals are oriented toward the humanistic, feminine sociable approach to life; Conventional (C), focusing on well-defined technical activities with a minimum of interpersonal and physical requirements; the Enterprising (E), characterized by exploitative relations with others; and the Artistic (A), where individual and artistic expression is the chief mode of behavior. (See Osipow, Ashby, and Wall [1965] for details about the descriptions used to identify the types in the study.) Each student was instructed to read the descriptions, then rank them with respect to the order in which he felt they adequately described him, and then to rate each of the descriptions on a 1 to 5 scale with respect to the degree to which he felt the vignette was an accurate description of him (one was very dissimilar, five was very similar). These ratings were also used in comparing the three decision groups.

The SVIB group scores were based on a conversion of the letter grades each male S obtained on the SVIB occupational scales. The conversion represented an approximation to the appropriate raw score for that letter grade, thus permitting the computation of scores for the seven SVIB groups. The seven groups were as follows: Group I, general professional (including biological scientist, doctor, dentist, veterinarian, clinical psychologist, architect, and artist); Group II, science and engineering (chemist-physicist, engineer, mathematician, and experimental psychologist); Group III, practical (farmer, carpenter, forest service

TABLE 1

Comparisons between Decision Groups and Summary of Analyses of Variance

	Group			
Variable	D	T	U	F
Personality Ratings				
Realistic	2.45	2.52	2.41	0.13
Intellectual	3.04	2.59	2.59	5.27**
Social	2.38	2.10	1.97	2.41
Conventional	2.46	2.59	2.62	0.45
Enterprising	2.84	2.84	2.72	0.14
Artistic	2.40	2.01	2.10	3.05*
Bernreuter Scores				
Dominance	4.31	4.25	4.93	1.56
Submissiveness	5.41	5.46	6.03	1.33
Dependence	4.80	4.63	5.83	4.48*
Academic Aspiration	1.94	1.98	1.79	0.71
PSU Academic Abilities	154.53	141.81	150.17	6.51**
PSU Math Exam	27.27	24.66	24.31	2.24
PSU English Exam	73.30	64.32	71.76	7.88**
SAT-V	538.41	498.40	520.72	5.96**
SAT-Q	580.53	556.16	580.24	2.61
High School Index	3.15	2.82	2.87	11.07**
1st Term GPA	2.60	2.22	2.56	6.85**
High School Size	308.40	289.43	290.52	0.18
Parents' Income	3.30	3.66	3.62	1.90
Father's Education	12.94	12.75	13.00	0.06
Mother's Education	11.69	12.23	11.86	0.71
Number of Siblings	3.00	2.92	3.14	0.25
Birth Order	1.79	2.00	1.69	1.16

*p < .05; **p < .01; df = 2 and 225.

man, and math-physical science teacher);
Group IV, social service (social science
teacher, YMCA physical director, personnel
manager, public administrator, YMCA
secretary, guidance counselor, and min-
ister); Group V, business (accountant, office
worker, purchasing agent, banker, industrial
relations, and pharmacist); Group VI, sales
(sales manager, life insurance salesman, and
real estate salesman); and Group VII,
literary (advertising man, author-journalist,
and lawyer).

RESULTS

Table 1 summarizes the results of the
comparison of the three groups on all 23
variables. The resulting *F* tests indicate that
scores on several of the variables are different for the three groups. Inspection of some
of the means of the three groups is sufficient
to reveal where the sources of the differences
lie, but in several instances inspection is not

TABLE 2

**Two Way Comparisons between Significant
Variables**

Variable	Groups Compared	*t*
Artistic	D versus U	1.16
Dependence	D versus U	2.68**
HSI	D versus U	2.92**
PSU Acad. Abil.	T versus U	1.51
PSU English Exam	T versus U	2.11*
SAT-V	T versus U	1.29
First term GPA	T versus U	2.03*

**p < .01; *p < .05

sufficient to do so. Thus, several *t* tests were
computed to compare the means of groups
where the extent of the differences was not
evident by inspection. The results of these *t*
tests are summarized in Table 2. Examining

Table 1 and 2 together indicates that Group
D is different from both Groups T and U
on the Intellectual rating, and different from
Group T on the Artistic rating. A difference
is also evident on the Dependence scale of
the BPI, in this case showing that the U
Group scores significantly higher on the
Dependence scale than the D and T Groups.

With respect to achievement variables,
differences appear on the PSU Academic
Abilities test, the PSU English Exam, the
SAT-Verbal, the high school index, and the
first term GPA at PSU. Thus, the D group
earned significantly higher high school
grades than the U and T groups, significantly
higher scores on the PSU Academic Abilities
test than the T Group, and significantly
higher scores on the verbal portion of the
SAT than the T Group. Both the D and U
Groups scored higher on the PSU English
Exam and earned higher grades their first
term at PSU than did the T Group. No
differences appeared on the family-school
variables.

The results of a discriminant analysis
comparing the three decision groups on all
23 variables produced a Wilks lambda of
0.693 (p < .01).

It seemed reasonable to separate the 23
variables into three groups and further
evaluate the separation between them by
discriminant analysis. The results indicated
that on the Personality variables (based on
Holland personality ratings, BPI scores, and
academic aspiration) no differences were
likely (Wilks lambda = 0.874 p > .05).
On the family and school back ground
variables (high school size, parents' income,
father's and mother's education, number of
siblings and birth rank) again, no differences
were likely between the three groups (Wilks
lambda = 0.949, p > .05). However, in the
analysis of the aptitude-achievement variables (PSU English, mathematics, and academic ability tests, SAT verbal and quantitative, and high school and college GPS's)
the resulting Wilks lambda of 0.843 (p <
.001) indicated that the three groups could
be differentiated along the dimensions of

academic achievement and ability. A notable finding is that despite the heavy weighting of differences in the achievement area as opposed to the personality and family-school areas, the differences between the three decision groups were heightened when all 23 variables were studied simultaneously.

Table 3 summarizes the comparison of the SVIB group scores for the male subjects in the three decision groups. This analysis failed to reveal any differences in SVIB patterns, either individually by SVIB group or as a result of the discriminant analysis (Wilks lambda = 0.917, $p > .05$).

TABLE 3

Comparison between Decision Groups on SVIB Group Scores

	Decision Group			
SVIB Group	D	T	U	F
I	2.07	1.99	1.89	0.52
II	2.80	2.83	2.62	0.24
III	2.72	2.86	2.93	0.37
IV	2.11	2.15	1.80	1.28
V	2.57	2.47	2.49	0.28
VI	2.15	2.09	2.01	0.17
VII	1.98	1.83	1.81	0.61

DISCUSSION

Several important differences of note appear to exist between the three kinds of students compared in this investigation. The evidence for the academic superiority of the Decided and Undecided groups over the Tentative group appears clear. The T group's high school average, PSU Academic Abilities Test score, and SAT-V score are lower than the D Group, and its score on the PSU English Exam and first term GPA are lower than both the D and U Groups. These differences may well be related to the nature of the uncertainty the T group expresses upon entrance to college. It will be recalled that the differentiating feature of the T and U Groups was the fact that the T group individuals all had some educational-vocational goal but did not pursue it immediately upon college entrance because they possessed some reservation about it, while the *S*s in the U group possessed only the vaguest of notions of what studies they wished to follow. In light of the findings, it is not unreasonable to infer that the T *S*s had good reason to possess reservations about their plans, i.e., significant academic deficiencies. They feared they would do poorly, and, in fact, they performed at a lower level than the others.

The nature of the U group's uncertainty appears to have different antecedents. The clue in this case is the finding that the U group scores significantly higher on the Dependency scale of the BPI than the other groups. Thus, the U *S*s are capable enough, but for some reason need extra support and encouragement in working out their plans. Perhaps the U group has more at stake than the T group does.

The absence of relationships between the degree of career decisiveness and SVIB group scores carries the implication that failure to express and implement a vocational-educational decision at the time of college entrance is not related to lack of clarity of interests as they are ordinarily conceptualized. A counselor examining SVIB profiles would be unable to differentiate the clearly decided *S*s from the tentative and undecided ones.

Holland and Nichols (1964) discuss correlates of achievement of undecided students. They found that a tendency to change educational and vocational plans was associated with achievement and creativity. Such does not appear to be the case in this study. The T group clearly does not perform at an exceptional academic level; while the U group does well, the question of unusual creativity remains open. One feature that might account for the apparent discrepancy between Holland and Nichols' findings and those reported in this paper is that they studied National Merit finalists, clearly an unusual college group, while the *S*s in this study possessed abilities more typical of college freshmen in general.

The results indicating the greater dependence of the U Group than the T or D groups is consistent with Holland and Nichols' inference that indecisive students are oral dependent personalities,

The nature of the differences found between the T and U *S*s carry some significant implications for counselors working with college students on questions of vocational or educational uncertainty. The particular antecedents of the indecisiveness assume importance in the selection of counseling procedures. Thus, the treatment of preference for the T group would be procedures aimed toward either development of a choice consistent with preparation, remedial work, or some combination of the two, while for the U group, the preferred treatment would focus on the student's dependency.

REFERENCES

Couch, A., and Keniston, K. Yeasayers and naysayers: agreeing response set as a personality variable. *J. abnorm. soc. Psychol.*, 1960, *60*, 151–174.

Holland, J. L. Some explorations of a theory of vocational choice: I. One- and two-year longitudinal studies. *Psychol. Monogr.*, 1962, *76*, 26 (whole No. 545).

Holland, J. L., and Nichols, R. C. The development and validation of an indecision scale: the natural history of a problem in basic research. *J. counsel. Psychol.*, 1964, *11*, 27–34.

Lindgren, H. C. Age as a variable in aversion toward food and occupations. *J. consult. Psychol.*, 1962, *26*, 101–102.

Osipow, S. H., Ashby, J. D., and Wall, H. W. Personality types and vocational choice: a test of Holland's theory. *Harvard studies in career development, No. 37.* Center for Research in Careers. Harvard Graduate School of Education, Cambridge, Mass., April, 1965.

Ziller, R. C. Vocational choice and utility for risk. *J. counsel. Psychol.*, 1957, *4*, 61–64.

OTHER RELEVANT ARTICLES

The following are abstracts of articles related to the topic of this chapter:

Form, W. H., and D. C. Miller. Occupational career pattern as a sociological instrument. *American Journal of Sociology*, 1949, *54*, 317–329.

The authors identified three types of work periods: initial, consisting of jobs held before formal education is complete, trial, which are jobs taken in an exploratory and uncommitted sense, and stable, which is defined as a job on which the worker has continued for more than three years. Various combinations of these periods in a worker's history are called secure or insecure patterns, the latter being marked by repeated returns to trial periods after initial or stable periods. They then analyzed the employment histories of a representative stratified sample of Ohio workers. Among other things, they found that secure work patterns were less frequent in the lower socioeconomic occupational classifications, and that among those who achieved secure patterns, initial jobs tended to be at lower levels than trial and stable jobs. They found also that the type of occupational pattern was strongly associated with the worker's social background.

Doyle, R. E. Career patterns of male college graduates. *Personnel and Guidance Journal*, 1965, *44*, 410–414.

Doyle examined the early work histories of college graduates, finding that 70 percent of them convert their initial jobs to stable ones, 25 percent have one or more exploratory jobs before finding a stable one, and that the remaining 5 percent have not in five to ten years found a stable occupation. Doyle attempted without success to relate a number of predictors from the school and personal history of the alumni to the type of pattern each exhibited.

The selections included in this chapter on the developmental concept of career behavior represent only a few of numerous articles available. Additional references, which the reader may consult in order to gain further information on any phase, are listed herewith.

Two basic references of Ginzberg are:

Ginzberg, E., S. Ginsburg, S. Axelrad, and J. L. Herma. *Occupational Choice: An Approach to a General Theory*. New York: Columbia University Press, 1951.
———. Toward a theory of occupational choice. *Personnel and Guidance Journal*, 1952, *30*, 491–494.

A lengthier exposition of Super's views on development are contained in his books:

Super, D. E. *The Psychology of Careers*. New York: Harper & Row, 1957.
———. *Dynamics of Vocational Adjustment*. New York: Harper & Row, 1942.

A general discussion considering the essential nature of vocational development is:

Super, D. E. Vocational development: The process of compromise or synthesis. *Journal of Counseling Psychology*, 1956, *4*, 249–253.
———. Some unresolved issues in vocational development research. *Personnel and Guidance Journal*, 1961, *40*, 11–15.

Another important statement on the developmental character of career behavior is:

Tiedeman, D. V. and R. P. O'Hara. *Career development: Choice and integration*. New York: College Entrance Examination Board, 1963.

Some reports relevant to career patterns are:

Abu-Laban, B. Social origins and occupational career patterns of community leaders. *Sociological Inquiry*, 1963, *33*, 131–140.
Ginzberg, E., and J. L. Herma. Patterns of career development (Chapter 5 of) *Talent and Performance*. New York: Columbia University Press, 1964.

Hall, O. The stages of a medical career. *American Journal of Sociology*, 1948, *53*, 327–336.

Super, D. E., et al., *Vocational development: A framework for research.* New York: Teachers College, Columbia University Bureau of Publications, 1957.

————. Career patterns as a basis for vocational counseling. *Journal of Counseling Psychology*, 1954, *1*, 12–20.

Wilensky, H. L. Orderly careers and social participation: The impact of work history on social integration in the middle mass. *American Sociological Review*, 1961, *26*, 524–539.

References relevant to the concept of vocational maturity include:

Borow, H. Vocational development research: Some problems of logical and experimental form. *Personnel and Guidance Journal*, 1961, *40*, 21–25.

Lohnes, P. R. Markov models for human development research. *Journal of Counseling Psychology*, 1965, *12*, 322–327.

Additional material on vocational maturity and its correlates are:

Carlin, L. O. Vocational decisions and high school experiences. *Vocational Guidance Quarterly*, 1960, *8*, 168–170.

Crites, J. O. Ego-strength in relation to vocational interest development. *Journal of Counseling Psychology*, 1960, *7*, 137–143.

Dilley, J. S. Decision-making ability and vocational maturity. *Personnel and Guidance Journal*, 1965, *43*, 423–427.

Hall, D. W. The Vocational Development Inventory: A measure of vocational maturity in adolescence. *Personnel and Guidance Journal*, 1963, *41*, 771–775.

Mathewson, R. H., and J. W. Orton. Vocational imagery and vocational maturity of high school students. *Journal of Counseling Psychology*, 1963, *10*, 384–388.

Nelson, A. G. Vocational maturity and client satisfaction. *Journal of Counseling Psychology*, 1956, *3*, 254–256.

Material on vocational maturity at other developmental stages includes:

Brunkan, R. J. Perceived parental attitudes and parent identification in relation to problems in vocational choice. *Journal of Counseling Psychology*, 1966, *13*, 394–402.

Glick, P. J. Occupational values and anticipated occupational frustration of agricultural college students. *Personnel and Guidance Journal*, 1964, *42*, 674–679.

————. Anticipated occupational frustration: A follow-up report. *Vocational Guidance Quarterly*, 1965, *13*, 63–66.

Kahoe, R. D. Motivational-hygiene aspects of vocational indecision and college achievement. *Personnel and Guidance Journal*, 1966, *44*, 1030–1036.

Marr, Evelyn. Some behaviors and attitudes relating to vocational choice. *Journal of Counseling Psychology*, 1965, *12*, 404–408.

Singer, S. L. and B. Stefflre. Age differences in job values and desires. *Journal of Counseling Psychology*, 1954, *2*, 89–91.

Wagman, M. M. Sex and age differences in occupational values. *Personnel and Guidance Journal*, 1965, *44*, 258–262.

Currently, there are under way three major longitudinal studies of career behavior of selected groups of individuals from which reports appear periodically. Some are listed below under the major investigator:

Super's Career Pattern Study:

Super, D. E., et al. *Vocational Development: A Framework for Research*. New York: Teachers College, Columbia University, Bureau of Publications, 1957.

———, and Phoebe Overstreet, *The Vocational Maturity of Ninth Grade Boys*. New York: Teachers College, Columbia University, Bureau of Publications, 1960.

Flanagan's Project Talent:

Flanagan, J. C., et al. *Design for a Study of American Youth*. Boston: Houghton Mifflin, 1962.

———, et al. *The American High School Student*. Pittsburgh: Project Talent Office, University of Pittsburgh, 1964.

Gribbons and Lohnes Career Development Study:

Gribbons, W. D. and P. R. Lohnes. Relationships among measures of readiness for vocational planning. *Journal of Counseling Psychology*, 1964, *11*, 13–19.

———, and ———. Predicting five years of development in adolescents from readiness for vocational planning scales. *Journal of Educational Psychology*, 1965, *56*, 244–253.

———, and ———. Validation of vocational planning interview scales. *Journal of Counseling Psychology*, 1964, *11*, 20–26.

———, and ———. Shifts in adolescents vocational values. *Personnel and Guidance Journal*, 1965, *44*, 248–252.

———, and ———. Occupational preferences and measured intelligence. *Vocational Guidance Quarterly*, 1966, *14*, 211–214.

Gribbons, W. D., S. Halperin, and P. R. Lohnes. Applications of stochastic models in research on career development. *Journal of Counseling Psychology*, 1966, *13*, 403–408.

PART IV

The Determinants
of Occupations
and Careers

DYER.

Before presenting the several chapters which describe the variations in thinking on the determinants of careers, it is appropriate to build some foundation for their careful consideration. This will be undertaken through these introductory remarks and by means of Hewer's paper, which follows.

First of all, the many chapters representing differing points of view in the section should not suggest that we are abandoning the developmental framework which we adopted in the preceding section. Rather, the intention now is to consider the choice of career without notice for time, trying to organize the factors which determine or at least influence choice.

The material in the previous chapter suggests that for some individuals, occupational choice is synonymous with career choice. For some it is clearly not; to whatever extent it is, we are able to say "determinants of occupations and careers" without explanation. But it should be realized that in many cases, choice of occupation, occupation, and career are different events, with different determinants.

In this section, the terms "choice of occupation," "preference," and "entry" are used as essentially equivalent. Vroom, in his *Work and Motivation* (1964), does a careful job of distinguishing between those concepts, suggesting that a choice differs from a preference in that the chooser believes he has a realistic chance of gaining entry to the chosen occupation, and may have taken a first step toward attaining it. As much as individuals are unsuccessful in attaining their chosen occupations amounts to the difference between choice and entry. He also says that if (as is not the case) all people choose the occupation they prefer and all succeed in entering it, the distinctions are made unimportant. It should be understood, however, that some of the papers included in this section may refer to only one of these three aspects of occupational behavior, while others may provide postulates which link them.

Another point of difference in the theories presented is in the treatment they give to two aspects of the determinants of vocations. One is what is conceived of as determinants — that is, interests, self-concepts, geography, needs, and the like, and their manner of organization. The other aspect is the specification of how any of these determinants link to the vocational preference, choice, or entry which is prominent in their theory, that is, whether the mechanism is need reduction, sublimation, expression of self, or some other factor.

Finally, it might be pointed out that although the papers are organized into chapters which contain essentially one theoretical statement, they occasionally provide evidence for another. For instance, Galinsky confirms his psychoanalytic hypothesis, but also shows that his clinical psychology students had warmer, closer relationships to their mothers than physics students, confirming Roe's point of view, to a degree. Perhaps, then, we ought to regard each theoretical position as a metaphor of another — that each position illuminates differing sides of the same determinants.

REFERENCE

Vroom, V. H. *Work and Motivation*. New York: Wiley, 1964.

What Do Theories of Vocational Choice Mean to a Counselor?

VIVIAN H. HEWER, *University of Minnesota*

Within the last half century, social scientists have become increasingly concerned with factors underlying the occupational choices of individuals at all levels of society. Some may argue that the individual does not exercise any choice, that social and economic conditions will determine what he will do to earn his living. Others believe that the individual does exert a choice.

More specifically, sociologists, economists, and psychologists have written about vocational choice. Sociologists, such as Miller and Form (1951) and Caplow (1954), stress forces in our social structure as the major determinants of occupational choice, economists such as Harris (1949) stress manpower economics, and psychologists are largely concerned with the individual, his traits and needs. In addition to contributions from members of the separate disciplines, there have been two major interdisciplinary contributions. One group — Ginzberg, Ginsburg, Axelrad, and Herma (1951), an economist, psychiatrist, sociologist, and psychologist respectively — committed themselves to an approach, at least, to a general theory of vocational choice if not to a theory. Another group — Blau, Gustad, Jessor, Parnes, and Wilcock (1956), a sociologist, two psychologists, and two economists, respectively — have developed

Reprinted with the permission of author and publisher from the article of the same title, in *Journal of Counseling Psychology*, 1963, *10*, 118–125.

what they call a conceptual framework for studying occupational choice. They stress that their contribution is not a theory, but merely an attempt to concern themselves with the vast array of determinants of occupational choice.

The vocational counselor has a responsibility to use the relevant research findings of social scientists in his practice. He should also seek constantly for insight into man's behavior and, most crucially, for insight into the motivations of this behavior. This paper is concerned with the meaning for a vocational counselor of the findings and speculations of sociologists and psychologists about vocational choice. It is particularly concerned with the meaning of theories of vocational choice to a counselor.

IS A THEORY OF VOCATIONAL CHOICE POSSIBLE?

Although very few of the social scientists who have studied the determinants of vocational choice have characterized their contributions as theory, others have presented their findings, suggestions, and interpretations as having sufficient causal interrelationship to be called a theory. It is not the concern of this paper to discuss the characteristics of a theory, but a few statements are necessary to evaluate the current status of vocational choice theory as theory.

The basic purpose of theory is to explain the meanings underlying a set of descriptive principles growing out of an array of data. Because there have been many data collected about the choice of an occupation, social scientists have become impatient to understand the causal interrelationships underlying these data that lead to the occupational placement or choice of an individual. It does not appear reasonable at this point, however, to construct a valid theory of vocational choice because of two factors.

First, there is a need for further information about cultural and economic forces which may be assumed to have an impact on vocational choice. For example, the effects on choice of economic cycles and of the changing socio-economic class structure in this country are not well understood. Secondly, it may not be possible to theorize about the process of vocational choice. Because of a lack of logical interrelationships, empirical data from sociology, psychology, and economics may not lend themselves to the development of a series of constructs. The social, individual, and economic determinants of choice may be disparate events, operating in their own ways to effect the vocational choice of the individual. The student in search of a vocation may have to consider all of these factors as he chooses a vocation, but he may never be able to relate them in a systematic fashion.

CONTRIBUTIONS FROM SOCIOLOGISTS

The emphasis in the sociology of work or occupational sociology has been, among other things, on causes of occupational differentiation or the selection of different jobs by members of society, the social organization of workers within an industrial plant, and the role of the worker in his own work group. Sociologists have also considered the dynamics of vocational choice and comment about it, although briefly.

In one of the first books on occupational sociology, Miller and Form (1951) in a brief discussion of occupational choice, state that accident is the deciding factor in the determination of the occupation of most workers. The accident is the accident of birth which establishes family, race, nationality, social class, residential district, and to a great extent educational and cultural opportunity. The range of occupations that an individual will consider in choosing his vocational goal is determined largely by the status expectations of the social class to which he belongs. Miller and Form also believe that the process of trial and error determines the vocational goals of more individuals than does vocational counseling.

Caplow (1954), discussing vocational choice in his book entitled *Sociology of Work*, comments that we know little of how people choose their vocations. Although he also believes that error and accident play a large part, he discusses several selective factors which operate to determine vocational choice.

Parents influence occupations of their children by the direct inheritance of the father's occupation, but Caplow presents no systematic evidence as to the extent to which this occurs. He states that almost all farmers are recruited from farmer's sons. Direct inheritance of a father's occupation will most likely occur among those occupations which require capital investment or childhood participation; both of these elements are found in farming. Parents, particularly of the middle class, project their ambitions on their children, want them to be mobile upward socially through education, and reject the semiskilled and unskilled occupations. Like Miller and Form, Caplow also believes that children "inherit" the occupational level of their parents and they choose a vocation within a restricted range of occupations that is acceptable to a given class.

Formal education obviously operates to determine vocational choice. Caplow suggests that students who drop out of school before completing high school are restricted to manual work or the insecure white collar fringe, the semiskilled, unskilled, service and minor clerical occupations. He also discusses vocational guidance as a selective factor determining career choice. Thus Caplow, like Miller and Form, puts heavy emphasis on the effect of social status on occupational choice.

The conclusions of one other sociologist are important. A. B. Hollingshead in his study, *Elmtown's Youth* (1941), supports with research data his beliefs that the choice of a vocation is related to social status. He concludes that adolescents choose jobs which are a reflection of their experiences in the class in which they were born, and tend to limit the scope of jobs from which they choose to their class position in society. They thus unconsciously choose their occupations in such a way that they occupy the same socio-economic level as their parents.

Thus Hollingshead reaches the same conclusion as Miller and Form and Caplow, that in a study of the determinants of vocational choice, class status is important. The counselor may ask for evidence to support this conclusion beyond Hollingshead's research which was concerned with the plans of youth. In a study in which attempts were made to draw a national sample, Jenson and Kirchner (1955) report supporting data and conclude that sons do tend to follow the general type of the father's occupation.

DIFFERENCES BETWEEN SOCIOLOGISTS AND PSYCHOLOGISTS

Before the contributions of the psychologists are considered, it may be well to point out some differences in the points of view of these two disciplines. The psychologist is concerned not only with those determinants of vocational choice that explain the distribution of individuals broadly in the labor market which appears to be the concern of the sociologists, but also with individual variation within a given social class. The psychologist is concerned not only with the

level of choice of the upper middle class but also with determinants of vocational choice within the level. For example, he may know that sons of fathers who are professional men will generally choose a profession or an occupation in the upper levels of management, but the psychologist is concerned with what determines which profession the son chooses. What determines whether a young man will be a physician or lawyer, a carpenter or an electrician, a truck driver or a punch press operator? Secondly, the psychologist is concerned with individual variables that cause vertical mobility. Thirdly, the psychologist places emphasis on individual variability and dynamisms as related to vocational choice; the sociologist places emphasis on group variability.

CONTRIBUTIONS OF PSYCHOLOGISTS

Much of what is known about vocational choice comes from research done by psychologists. Although most of this research was not directly related to personality theory, their contributions will be discussed within this context. Because the vocational choice and the vocational life of an individual is an expression of the total personality, a vocational counselor can seek understanding of an individual in any one or all of the ways suggested by personality theorists. He can interpret the dynamics of vocational choice using psychoanalytic theory, self theory, need theory, or any of the other personality theories.

The basic problem in personality theory is to explain "motivation or the underlying impellents of behavior," according to Hall and Lindzey (1957, p. 7) in their book on *Theories of Personality*. Much of the early research in vocational psychology was directed at the assessment of aptitudes and interests with no effort to give a dynamic interpretation to these findings by drawing on motivational theory. Increasingly, vocational psychologists are turning to personality theory to explain the motivational aspects of vocational choice. For example, Anne Roe (1956) placed motivational and personality theory at the core of her explanation of vocational choice in her emphasis on Maslow's hierarchy of prepotent needs. Hilton (1962) has related career decision-making to Festinger's theory of cognitive dissonance (1958). It may be helpful to relate personality theory to vocational choice theory in another way.

In a recent book entitled *Psychology of Adjustment* (1961), Smith, following the writings of Gardner Murphy, has suggested that there are three broad approaches to personality theory: trait, structural, and adjustment. (The vocational choice emphasis of this paper will be on the trait and structural categories in addition to the developmental approach.) In explaining the adjustment approach, Smith states, "A personality is a structured organism-environment field, each aspect of which stands in a dynamic relation to each other aspect. There is organization within the organism and organization within the environment, but it is the cross organization of the two that is investigated in personality research" (1961, pp. 29–30). The adjustment view stresses the interaction between the person and his environment. Lewin is an example of this group.

Trait Theory

Smith states, "A personality is a distinguishable individual, definable in terms of a qualitative and quantitative differentiation from other such individuals" (1961, p. 29). In other words, a person can be understood in terms of his traits which are behavior manifestations of the individual. He can be described as bright, dull, sensitive, crude, loving, hostile, warm, cold, introverted, extroverted, psychotic, neurotic.

In both vocational counseling and vocational psychology, much of what is known

and used today has been contributed by trait psychologists. The basic proposition underlying the trait and factor theory is that people differ in their traits and jobs differ in their requirements. If the traits of people and requirements of jobs can be isolated and measured or quantified, it will be possible to match people with jobs. This is a deceptively simple statement that has caused a lot of controversy, but it is essentially a correct statement of this position. Vocational counselors give tests to get quantitative estimates of the counselee's traits. The counselee is concerned about the options he has in making a vocational choice; can he succeed in getting into medical school, does he have the ability for the graduate training required to be a vocational counselor, will he find drafting too sedentary, is he too shy and diffident to consider sales? Probably in most vocational and educational counseling, whether in high school, college, the employment service, or the community agency, this matching process is essentially what goes on.

During recent years there have been criticisms of the trait and factor theory of vocational choice. Among these, two will be noted:

1. There is doubt that the trait and factor theorists are able to describe a personality in all of its dimensions. There are several indications of concern, suggesting a need for a broad taxonomy or description of the personality.

Brayfield, speaking of unresolved issues in differential psychology, comments, "The most pressing is the need to create a comprehensive and occupationally meaningful taxonomy of the individual" (1961, p. 45). He then refers to a discussion of this same problem by Jenkins and Lykken in a chapter in the 1957 *Annual Review of Psychology* (1957). Their summary statement is, ". . . (a) that the current literature betrays a continuing neglect by psychologists of the problems of taxonomy and (b) that the taxonomic endeavor requires resourcefulness and versatility both in theory and methodology within the framework of the 'construct validity' approach" (1957, p. 107).

Murray of Harvard, in giving the recent Richard M. Elliot lecture at the University of Minnesota, commented that psychologists have moved too quickly to a sophisticated level of research methodology without undertaking the conventional (or traditional) preliminary task of careful description and classification of the entities or personalities with which it is concerned.[1]

An important research effort in the direction of personality description is one in progress in the division of Clinical Psychology of the Medical School of the University of Minnesota under the direction of Paul Meehl (1960) and others.

2. A second criticism of the trait and factor theory as related to vocational psychology is that it does not make a definite statement about motivation. Trait and factor theorists have dealt with motivation, but the theoretical explanation of motivation, as proposed by such trait and factor theorists as Cattell and Eysenck, has not been in a context of vocational choice and adjustment. Nevertheless, in spite of the complexity of the theoretical problem, the vocational counselor has at his disposal tools which will help him understand the motivation and goals of the individual. Vocational psychologists generally rely on vocational interest measurement to assess the individual's motivations.

Tiedeman and O'Hara in a recent paper say, "For years vocational psychologists have relied upon interests and values to detect inclinations toward vocational goals" (1962). Later these writers comment that they believe interest and value measurement "both really portray the result of ordering phenomena of relevance to one's life situation" (1962). Leona Tyler is concerned with choice in her current research. In a recent article she states, "that the core of individuality consists of a person's choices and the way he organizes them" (1961, p. 195). And, again, later, "I have come to feel that this

realm of choice is our peculiar heritage. The question people have brought to counselors of all kinds from time immemorial is: What shall I do" (1961, p. 201). She sees understanding the choices of a person as understanding the person as peculiarly individual, and believes that interest measurement such as Strong's gets at common components. Brayfield comments, "We have, in the work on vocational interest, the most substantial and significant work on personality in the history of psychology" (1961, p. 32).

Thus, interest measurement is concerned with the motivations of the individual, but this motivational structure is not related to any single personality theory. Darley and Hagenah state this well when they say, "Although we may conclude that interest phenomena now take their places within the boundaries of motivational and personality theory, it is quite evident that no single theory of motivation or personality development exists to encompass the phenomena" (1955, p. 188). Later they state, "For it is our major thesis now that occupational choice and measured occupational interests reflect, in the vocabulary of the world of work, the value systems, the needs, and the motivations of individuals" (1955, p. 191). One more point is of concern before we leave interest. The etiology of interest is not known. Anne Roe (1957) has suggested that the origin of interest may be related to childhood experiences and relations to parents but evidence from research studies designed to test this hypothesis is mixed. An understanding of the origin or etiology of interest and choice may eventually give the best understanding of vocational choice and its theoretical implications.

Structural Theories

In describing the structural approach to personality, Smith states, "A personality is a structured whole, definable in terms of its own distinctive structural attributes. The structural view stresses the dynamic organization of traits within the person" (1961, p. 29). Three structural theories related to vocational choice will be reviewed.

1. *Psychoanalytic Theory.* There have been some students of vocational psychology who believe vocational choice can be best understood if personality is viewed in a psychoanalytical framework (Super and Bachrach, 1957). Segal, reporting research related to this theory, views vocational choice as an expression of the personality and states, "Psychoanalytic concepts such as identification, the development of defense mechanisms, and the theory of sublimation, can be used to gain insight into the personality characteristics of individuals who made a specific vocational choice" (1961, p. 202). More recently, Galinsky (1962) reports research on vocational choice, testing hypotheses derived from psychoanalytic theory.

2. *Need Theory.* Anne Roe, in her recent book on *The Psychology of Occupations* (1956), pointed out that needs, whether at the conscious or unconscious level, are the major determinants of vocational choice. She subscribed to the need theory of Maslow and emphasized the hierarchy of prepotency among needs. Research studies based on the relationship of needs to vocational psychology are Centers (1948), Schaffer (1953), and Merwin and DiVesta (1959).

3. *Self-concept Theory.* The third vocational choice theory concerned with a structural approach to personality is that of the self. Basically, the self is a differentiated part of the total phenomenal field; it is the awareness one has of one's being. The dynamic aspect of the self concept theory is the striving for self-actualization just as the dynamic feature of the needs theory is found in striving for their satisfaction. Super (1957), one of the major proponents of this theory, believes that the individual obtains a degree of satisfaction from his work which is proportionate to the degree to which he has been able to implement his self concept. The research of O'Hara and Tiedeman (1959) draws hypotheses from self-theory.

Developmental Theory

The development of the personality is one area of emphasis among personality theorists. Thus, it is not surprising that a group of vocational psychologists have come to view vocational choice, an expression of the total personality, within a developmental framework. This group believes that the choice of a vocation is not a single event that takes place at a certain time, but that it is the result of a developmental process. In fact, all of an individual's vocational behavior including vocational choice becomes more meaningful when viewed longitudinally.

Developmental theory should probably not be viewed as a motivational theory. Super (1957), who has contributed much of the thinking and research on developmental theory, apparently accepts self-theory to explain motivation. Drawing in part on the work of Buehler (1933), Super (1957) has proposed five vocational life stages: growth, exploration, establishment, maintenance, and decline. The exploration period is probably the period most counselors are concerned with, for it is then the adolescent explores his potentialities through school and part-time work. In a research study concerned with self concept and developmental theory, O'Hara and Tiedeman (1959) report evidence for a developing self concept.

INTERPRETATION

What do these findings, speculations, and theories mean to me as a practicing vocational counselor in a college? It is well to emphasize the concern of this paper is with vocational choice theory and not with counseling theory and methodology.

1. From the sociologists, I have learned that I must pay attention to the social class of my clients, for their social origins may

indicate the range of occupations they are willing to consider. I should also be sensitive to the effect of vertical mobility on students, an effect which has been described as neurotogenic. Students who come from upper middle class families and who are not bright enough to get through college may suffer from anxieties due to threat of loss of social status. Very bright lower class students may be frightened by their possible change in status, and may not want to leave the way of life of their families.

2. From the economists, I have learned that the demands of our labor market are such that not everyone has the privilege of choosing a vocation. Some are forced into certain types of occupations because no other way of earning their livings is available to them.

3. From the psychologists, I have learned many things.

The Trait Theorists

Of all the theories dealing with vocational choice, I believe that in my work in assisting college students explore their vocational choices the trait and factor theorists have been most helpful to me because:

1. They have developed good tools for the assessment of aptitudes and abilities. One of the most powerful determinants of man's place in the occupational hierarchy is his intelligence. I think we can now do a competent job of assessing how bright an individual is with the tools we have.

2. They have given me good interest tests so I can understand the goals and motivations of the individual. They have taught me that interest is a stable trait, that man's interests persist over the years, that interest has lifetime meaning in choosing a vocation.

3. They have helped me understand jobs and their requirements in relation to the person.

4. They are increasingly helping me understand the impact of the style of the individual's interpersonal relations on his vocational choice.

What else would I like from the trait and factor theorists? (a) A better understanding of all the dimensions of the personality and the impact of these dimensions on vocational choice; (b) A better understanding of the meaning of choice to an individual so I can understand his goals and motivations; and (c) Continued exploration and search for the etiology of vocational interest.

The Structural Theorists

They have helped me largely to speculate about motivational theory in vocational choice. Eventually more of the major personality theories may be linked to vocational choice theory. I trust that from these speculations hypotheses will develop which will lend themselves to evaluation in research.

The Development Theorists

As a college counselor, I know many of the students I deal with are in an exploratory period and their vocational choices should be dealt with in a developmental framework. Many of them must change their plans because of inability to cope with the academic competition or because of lack of interest in their current choices. This developmental process calls for careful follow-up of counselees so assistance may be given, if needed, during this period of growth. I wonder whether within this developmental context of vocational choice, learning theory could explain motivation. That is, in the process of vocational development, can the direction the individual takes at any given choice point be explained by learning theorists? My experience has taught me that among college students grades can act as powerful rewards, influencing educational and vocational decisions.

MY PERSONAL BELIEFS

I believe that vocational choice should be viewed developmentally, that personality theory can help me speculate about motivation, but that the vocational choices available to an individual are determined by his traits.

From all of this I have developed a deep respect for the complexity of every human being — "Every person is in some very general aspects like every other person, in some less general aspects like some other persons, and in some particular aspects like no other person."[2] Because of this great complexity, I must have patience and take time with my counselees so they can resolve what they want to be. Because I know, too, that I am different, I know how meaningless it is for me to impose my values and my way of life on them.

[1]Murray, H. A. In a personal communication concerning the Richard M. Elliott address, University of Minnesota, 1962.

[2]Murray, footnote 1.

REFERENCES

Blau, P. M., Gustad, J. W., Jessor, R., Parnes, H. S., and Wilcock, R. C. Occupational choice: a conceptual framework. *Industrial labor relat. Rev.*, 1956, 9, 531–543.

Brayfield, A. H. *Vocational counseling today.* In E. G. Williamson (Ed.), *Vocational counseling — A reappraisal in honor of Donald G. Paterson.* Minneapolis: Univer. of Minn. Press, 1961, 22–59.

Buehler, Charlotte, *Der menschliche lebenslauf als psychologisches problem.* Leipzig: Hirzel, 1933.

Caplow, T. *The sociology of work.* Minneapolis: Univer. of Minn. Press, 1954.

Centers, R. Motivational aspects of occupational stratification. *J. soc. Psychol.*, 1948, 28, 187–217.

Darley, J. G., and Hagenah, Theda. *Vocational interest measurement.* Minneapolis: Univer. of Minn. Press, 1955.

Festinger, L. The motivating effect of cognitive dissonance. In G. Lindzey (Ed.), *Assessment of human motives.* New York: Grove Press, 1958, 65–86.

Galinsky, M. D. Personality development and vocational choice of clinical psychologists and physicists. *J. counsel. Psychol.*, 1962, 9, 299–305.

Ginzberg, E., Ginsburg, S. W., Axelrad, S., and Herma, J. L. *Occupational choice: an approach to a general theory.* New York: Columbia Univer. Press, 1951.

Hall, C. S., and Lindzey, G. *Theories of personality.* New York: Wiley, 1957.

Harris, S. E. *The market for college graduates.* Cambridge: Harvard Univer. Press, 1949.

Hilton, T. L. Career decision-making. *J. counsel. Psychol.*, 1962, 7, 291–298.

Hollingshead, A. B. *Elmtown's youth.* New York: Wiley, 1941.

Jenkins, J. J., and Lykken, D. T. Individual differences. In P. R. Farnsworth and Q. McNemar (Eds.), *Annu. Rev. Psychol.* Palo Alto: Annual Reviews, Inc., 1957, 79–112.

Jenson, P. G., and Kirchner, W. K. A national answer to the question, do sons follow their father's occupations? *J. appl. Psychol.*, 1955, 39, 419–421.

Meehl, P. E. The cognitive activity of the clinician. *Amer. Psychologist*, 1960, 15, 19–27.

Merwin, J. C., and diVesta, F. J. A study of need theory and career choice. *J. counsel. Psychol.*, 1959, 6, 302–309.

Miller, D. C., and Form, W. H. *Industrial sociology.* New York: Harper, 1951.

O'Hara, R. P., and Tiedeman, D. V. Vocational self concept in adolescence. *J. counsel. Psychol.*, 1959, 6, 292–301.

Roe, Anne. Early determinants of vocational choices. *J. counsel. Psychol.*, 1957, 4, 212–217.

Roe, Anne. *The psychology of occupations.* New York: Wiley, 1956.

Schaffer, R. H. Job satisfaction as related to need satisfaction in work. *Psychol. Monogr.,* 1953, *67,* No. 14, (Whole No. 364).

Segal. S. J. A psychoanalytic analysis of personality factors in vocational choice. *J. counsel. Psychol.,* 1961, *8,* 202–210.

Smith, H. *Psychology of adjustment.* New York: McGraw-Hill, 1961.

Super, D. E. *The psychology of careers.* New York: Harper, 1957.

Super, D. E., and Bachrach, P. B. *Scientific careers and vocational development theory.* New York: Bureau of Publications, Teachers College, Columbia Univer., 1957.

Tiedeman, D. V., and O'Hara, R. P. Differentiation and integration of career development. Harvard Studies in Career Development. No. 23. Unpublished paper (CEEB Grant), 1962.

Tyler, Leona. Research explorations in the realm of choice. *J. counsel. Psychol.,* 1961, *8,* 195–201.

Self-Expression
as an Occupational
Determinant

5

The title of this chapter is perhaps not entirely apt. It attempts to convey the idea that a man's occupation or career is an expression of himself — something internal, global, and dynamic which, without benefit of explicit labels, he seeks to find expression for in his occupational behavior. Super's construct, "Vocational choice is the implementation of a self-concept," is clearly illustrative of this point of view. Other terms which associate themselves with this frame of reference are ego- or identity development, self-concept or self-actualization theory.

The first paper presented in this chapter is Super's elaboration of the role of the self-concept in vocational behavior. He first reviews the construct, self-concept, and how it has been employed in research on vocational development. He concludes from research to date that occupational preference, and success and satisfaction with performance may be predicted from agreement between a person's self- and occupational concept. More important, though, Super specifies that the self-concept develops too; that there are stages of formation, translation and implementation.

It is in the second paper that a model for the translation of the self-concept into occupational concepts is described by Starishevsky and Matlin. They specify a number of "metadimensions" of self-concepts such as complexity, structuring, realism, and the like. In addition, they suggest that the best method of obtaining the self-concept is by means of Kelly's Role Construct Repertory Test. In essence, this technique permits the individual to make a number of self-descriptive statements, but allows him to choose which ones he will use and how he uses and interrelates them.

While Super outlines evidence that the self-concept does predict occupational role attainment, none of the investigations he cites employs the idiographic approach which the Role Construct Repertory Test allows. The next article, by

Oppenheimer, demonstrates that self-concept statements obtained by this methodology are as valid predictors as those obtained by the more usual adjective checklist and Q-sort techniques.

However, Korman's study, presented next, seems to suggest some caution to be applied in the interpretation of Oppenheimer's and similar findings. He shows that the relationship between self-concept and occupational choice is more tightly linked when the person's concept of himself includes a high level of self-esteem. Korman suggests that low self-esteem persons tend to be more accepting of non-satisfying states of affairs, at least within the realm of occupational behavior, or that they are likely to seek less reward for a similar situation than persons possessing much self-esteem.

Self Concepts
in Vocational Development

DONALD E. SUPER, *Teachers College, Columbia University*

In expressing a vocational preference (Super, 1951), a person puts into occupational terminology his idea of the kind of person he is; that in entering an occupation, he seeks to implement a concept of himself; that in getting established in an occupation he achieves self actualization. The occupation thus makes possible the playing of a role appropriate to the self concept.

This conceptualization of the vocational development process was stimulated by the theory of the development of vocational attitudes which Carter (1940) derived from his research in interests in adolescence, by the theory of vocational interests as reflections of the self concept and of occupational stereotypes which Bordin (1943) developed as a result of work with Strong's Vocational Interest Blank, from the revival of interest

Reprinted with the permission of author and publisher from *Career Development: Self Concept Theory.* New York: The College Entrance Examination Board, 1963, Pp. 1–16.

in self theory which dates from Lecky's (1945) treatise (first circulated in the mid-thirties) and Allport's (1943) rediscovery of the ego in psychology. In recent years the interest of personality theorists, social psychologists, clinical psychologists, and counseling psychologists in the psychology of the self and in self concepts has been lively and productive. Reviews of the literature on the measurement of the self concept by Crowne and Stephens (1961) and by Strong and Feder (1961), and in particular Wylie's (1961) critical review of the research literature, are evidence of this fact, as is Wrenn's (1958) earlier review.

It is remarkable, however, that communication on self theory between personality, social, and clinical psychologists, on the one hand, and counseling psychologists on the other, has evidently been a one-way affair. Even among counseling psychologists some seem to have listened exclusively to their personality-oriented colleagues, while others have been interested not only in personality development and treatment but also in the important self-organizing and self-actualizing social roles provided by occupations. These latter have, accordingly, looked also to vocational psychology as a source of ideas and of data.

Wrenn's (1958) review of the literature on the self concept in counseling neither mentions the topic of vocational choice and adjustment, nor cites any of the literature on self concepts in vocational development. Strong and Feder's (1961) review of the measurement of the self concept also neglects the subject of vocational development. Yet both papers were prepared by counseling psychologists who were presumably familiar with the literature on the development of vocational interests as a function of the self, and who knew that interest inventories have been interpreted in self-concept terms. Wylie's (1961) very thorough and scholarly review of the literature does not index the terms occupation, vocation, and work, and does not refer to the research and theories of Carter and Bordin, or to more recent work on the self concept by vocational psychologists. These are strange omissions, for various sociologists (Caplow, 1955; Hughes, 1958; Miller and Form, 1951), and some psychologists (Tyler, 1951; Darley and Hagenah, 1955; Roe, 1956; Super, 1957) have noted that work roles are among the most important in modern society and provide a focus for the study of self concepts and of the processes of development of selfhood. The vocational manifestations of selfhood have not been studied for as long, nor with as much success, as have other aspects; but the topic has not been neglected and there is a growing literature on the subject, accompanied by an even more lively interest.

THE LITERATURE
IN BRIEF PERSPECTIVE

The work of Carter and Bordin was well received, and is frequently referred to in the literature on vocational interest inventories. Bordin's theory generated one or two studies after World War II, studies in which he and others tested hypotheses derived from his theory (for example, Bordin and Wilson, 1953). The impact was limited, however, to test interpretation.

In the same year in which my paper linking self concept to vocational development theory appeared, Leona Tyler (1951) published a paper on the relationships of aptitudes and interests in young children in which she made use of self concept theory to explain her finding. Tyler (1955) followed up this study with more data on the development of interests in these same children as they grew older, building her theory of vocational development around the concept of identity. The elements identified (Super, 1953) as essential to a theory of vocational development included self concept development and vocational self actualization. Torrance (1954) then described the use of self concept data in the educational counseling of college students. Tyler and Tiedeman summarized their thinking on self concept and identity development in vocational choice in working papers drawn on by the Scientific Careers Project (Super and Bachrach, 1957), and use was made of the self concept as the organizing element in *The Psychology of Careers* (Super, 1957). Subsequent years have shown a burst of production on the vocational manifestations of the self concept, with three or four research papers published each year.[1]

There were good reasons for the rapid rise of self-concept theory to popularity in vocational guidance and counseling psychology in America, even though the realization of the relevance of self development to vocational development seems to have been limited to counselors. The post-war years constituted a period of great interest in personality theory and its implications for education, vocational guidance, and personnel selection and training. Furthermore, vocational psychology had become a somewhat static and therefore intellectually unrewarding field, in which it seemed that progress was to be made only by the standardization of available tests for more occupations and by the classification of more occupations according to existing methods. The analysis of personal and occupational aptitude and interest profiles which, in the General Aptitude Test Battery of the U.S. Employment Service and in Strong's Vocational Interest Blank, had become the acme of practical psychometric perfection, often appeared to be a mechanical matching of men and occupations which was incompatible with the dynamic concepts of personality development and adjustment which in these years challenged psychologists, counselors, and teachers (Borow *et al.*, 1959; Brayfield, 1961; Super, 1957, chap. 12-13). Vocational guidance was declining as guidance emphasizing personal adjustment dominated pupil personnel work in the schools and in the professional associations; vocational psychology suffered as counseling psychology felt a clinical emphasis; and personnel psychology proved to be the refuge of vocational psychologists who were still interested in aptitudes and interests. But beginning in about 1951 the conceptualization of occupational choice as the process of implementing the self concept began to bridge the gap between personality theory and vocational psychology. The picturing of the vocational counselor's task as helping a person to formulate an adequate idea of himself, and to find a role appropriate to the kind of person he conceives himself to be and seeks to become, added depth and meaning to the work of vocational guidance. It was small wonder that these formulations became popular among counseling psychologists and vocational counselors.

THE NATURE AND FUNCTION OF THEORY

Among vocational choice theorists and would-be theorists, however, the self concept theories of vocational development were criticized as incomplete, or as parts of theories which are vague and unable to generate testable hypotheses. Holland (1959) thus described these efforts at theorizing as so general in statement that they are of negligible value for integrating present knowledge or stimulating further research. The Career Pattern Study staff (Super *et al.*, 1957) had two years previously commented on "the difficulty of testing hypotheses concerning the self concept (in vocational development), even though it seems to lend itself admirably to the formulation of broad principles explanatory of occupational choice and vocational adjustment." We thus recognized the difficulties to which Holland alluded, but accepted them as difficulties which would be overcome as work progressed rather than treating them as deterrents to further work. It was made clear that self concept theory was viewed as dealing with just one aspect of vocational development (Super, 1953, 1957); it seemed necessary to develop these segmental theories before a sound general theory could be worked out in any detail. Editorializing on later theories of vocational choice, which then seemed to be sprouting like mushrooms after a rain, Wrenn (1959) wrote: "What troubles me is not the number or variety of theories intended to throw light upon the psychological nature of vocational choice, rather it is the lack of research sophistication implied. The value of a theory lies not only in its psychological or other rationale . . . but in its capacity to generate research." Wrenn, like Holland, even more than the Career Pattern Study staff, had serious doubts about the ability of self-concept theory to generate testable hypotheses and thus to result in good research.

Holland and Wrenn seem to have missed two important points. First, early in the development of a field of knowledge facts are scarce, scattered, unconnected, and ill-established. Any attempt to organize them in a meaningful way (that is, to construct a theory) is bound to result in something vague, general, and highly tentative, or in segmental, limited theories which may be so limited and so unconnected as to seem unworthy of the name of theory. But if research is to be something more than trial and error, such vague or limited theorizing must be done to provide a basis for further work. Second, the vague, segmental theories pertaining to self concepts in vocational development *have* generated research, and some of these researches have confirmed while others have led to the refinement of various elements of the theory.

RESEARCH ON SELF CONCEPTS IN VOCATIONAL DEVELOPMENT

In view of Carter's and Bordin's theoretical formulations it would be possible to view all studies of vocational interest inventories as investigations of self concepts in relation to vocational interests, and, when the study is longitudinal or deals with several different cross-sections, to relate self concepts to vocational development. One would then conclude that the self concepts of adolescents are expressed in terms which have vocational significance, are rather stable over the adolescent and adult years, become somewhat more social during adolescence, predict adult occupation rather well but better in the case of middle and upper-middle-class boys than in that of upper-class boys who respond more to family pressures than to self-actualization needs, and are related to occupation engaged in but not as a rule to degree of success in the chosen occupation.

But it may be argued that an interest inventory score is not a measure of the self concept, despite the fact that it involves self-reports and self-description. Since an inventory is in effect an inventory of self-reported likes and dislikes or preferences, it consists of a large number of lower-level self concepts. The common elements and connections perceived in these lower-level self concepts are used by individuals in constructing higher-level self concepts; they

do this construction themselves, as when, for example, a person says: "I am the kind of person who should be a lawyer." In the case of an interest inventory, on the other hand, the ascertaining and combining of common elements and linkages which show that the subject has interests like those of lawyers is done by the item-weighting, scoring, and norming procedures. A score on an interest inventory is therefore not a measure of the self concept, as Bordin (1943, 1953) has suggested, but a conceptualization of a person by an outside agent (the scoring machine and scoring keys) based on his lower-level self concepts. The same criticism, it should be emphasized, applies to Q-sorts and to adjective checklists. In these, also, the lower-level self concepts (self-descriptions) are organized into higher-level concepts of the subject, not by himself, but by the scoring system. It is the "I am . . ." type statement that reveals the subject's own conceptualization of himself. To state this is not to deny the role of the self concept in answering an interest inventory or an adjective checklist, but rather to affirm it, for presumably the self concept system guides the self-descriptions as the individual answers the questions in the inventory or checklist; nor is it to deny the utility and importance of the data yielded by these instruments which are, after all, batteries of "I am . . ." statements from which such inferences as are made should be more parsimoniously made than they can be from motor behavior. The point is that an individual's self concept is *his* concept of himself, not the inferences concerning him made by an outside *other* — be that other man or machine.

Self concept theory was used by Carter and by Bordin to explain their findings with Strong's Vocational Interest Blank; it was used by Tyler (1951) to explain her findings on the relationships of aptitudes and interests in first-grade children. In the case of girls, there were no relationships, but positive results were found for boys. Her explanation is that presumably the role of the boy permits the development of interests in keeping with his abilities, whereas the role prescribed by society for girls permits less development of special interests in keeping with special aptitudes.

SELF CONCEPT AND OCCUPATIONAL CONCEPT. Nurses working in a New York hospital were asked by Brophy (1959) to complete an adjective checklist to describe themselves, their ideal selves, and kind of person their jobs required them to be. They also filled out a job satisfaction questionnaire. Brophy's relevant hypothesis was that similarity of the self concept and of the perceived occupational role requirements (occupational concept) is correlated with job satisfaction: the hypothesis was sustained.

Discrepancy between self concept and occupational role concept was studied also by Englander (1960), whose subjects were students in education and in other fields. She hypothesized that congruency of self concept and concept of the role of elementary school teacher would be greater in students preparing to work in this field than it would be in other students, and found differences significant at the .01 level. Occupation was therefore considered to be legitimately interpreted as a means of perpetuating the self.

A third study of agreement between self concept and occupational role concept is that of Tageson (1960). He used Q-sorts to obtain descriptions of the self, the ideal self, the ideal seminarian, and the average seminarian from 120 seminary students, together with faculty and peer ratings of realism in the vocational choice of each seminarian. He found positive and significant relationships between compatability of self and occupational role concepts, both actual and ideal, on the one hand and realism of vocational choice as rated by both peers and faculty (r = .30 to .39) on the other.

Blocher and Schutz (1961) hypothesized that the similarity of self and occupational concepts of adolescent boys is greater for occupations in which they express interest than for those in which they have little interest. They administered a 180-item check-list to 135 twelfth-grade boys; this was marked to describe the self, the ideal self, and the most and least liked of the 45 occupations for which the Strong Vocational Interest Blank is scored.

Mean similarity of self and liked occupation was greater than that of self and disliked occupation (.01 level). This was true also of ideal self and liked versus disliked occupations. A significant correlation (.01 level, size not reported) was also found between self-ideal agreement and the Strong Occupational Level score, interpreted as level of vocational aspiration.

Warren (1961) used a personality inventory to measure the self concept, a procedure which, as noted in connection with Carter's and Bordin's work, provides a measure of the self concept as organized by an external agent rather than by the individual into his own self system. For this reason there may be some doubt as to the justifiability of including Warren's inferred self concept results in a discussion of other studies using the reported self concept. Warren used also a measure of the expected occupational role, that is, of the occupational role concept, consisting of ratings of the sources of job satisfaction expected in the preferred occupation. Typical combinations of personality traits and expected job satisfactions were used as a measure of self-concept role-concept agreement, while atypical combinations of traits and values were treated as discrepancies between self and occupational role concepts. It was hypothesized that this self-role discrepancy measure would predict change of college major. The subjects were 525 high-scoring National Merit Scholarship competitors tested in high school and followed up through the sophomore year of college. When the criterion defined change of major as a minor change or as one change, the self-concept role-concept discrepant group was found not to have changed significantly more often than the self-concept role-concept compatible group; but when the criterion measure was made more sensitive at the upper end, and change was defined as a single major change, a double change, or a double major change, the expected differences were found. This seemed clearer when grade-point average and thinking introversion were controlled.

These five studies of the significance of agreement between the self concept and the occupational role concept agree in finding relationships between this variable and various internal and external criteria such as job satisfaction, occupational preference and goal, realism of vocational choice, and stability of occupational goal as defined by choice of college major. The relationships are not close, although they are consistent when sensitive criteria are used. But they are all subject to one criticism, a defect for several years unobserved in the use of adjective checklists and Q-sorts but recently pointed out by Wylie (1961) and Crowne and Stephen (1961): the social desirability of the items in such measures, now established, may produce, in some instances legitimately but in others spuriously, part of the correlation between self ratings and occupational ratings. The expectation that discrepancies between actual-self and ideal-self might in some instances control the social desirability of items has not been well supported, for self-ideal scores tend to be rather uniform, leaving the burden of individual differences to be borne by the actual-self ratings and by social desirability as well as self concept.

SELF CONCEPT AND OCCUPATIONAL ROLE REQUIREMENTS. Although the term occupational role requirements has been used in precisely this way by the authors presently under discussion, we have seen that Brophy, Englander, Tageson, and Warren studied occupational role concepts, that is, the perceptions of the subject. Two investigations have studied occupational role expectations, that is, the perceptions of others, organized as social expectations, societal demands, or job requirements. Nurses were the subjects in Kibrick and Tiedeman's (1961) study, which thus nicely supplements Brophy's. The independent variable was the actual-self or the ideal-self concept as measured by an adjective checklist treated in relation to supervisors' checking of occupational role expectations, and the relevant dependent variable was withdrawal from or continuation in nursing school. It is noteworthy that, with the partly phenomenological, partly external independent variable (self concept in agreement with social expectations) the hypothesis was not sustained, for in only one of the seven schools was the correlation between this measure of the compatibility of the self concept with the occupational role requirements significantly related to remaining in training, and there the point biserial correlation was only .20. Perhaps the criterion left something to be desired, for there is no indication whether the six-month period is the best for studying withdrawals; furthermore, all withdrawals for whatever reason were included in that group. Or perhaps the predictor is not the most appropriate for testing self-concept theory: it may be that self concept agreement with role concept, as in Brophy's study, is the psychologically significant variable, rather than self concept agreement with other-imposed role expectations, as in the Kibrick-Tiedeman study. And yet it is logical to derive, from self concept theory, the proposition that agreement of own and other's concepts is a behaviorally significant variable.

An external measure of role requirements was also used by Tageson (1960), who obtained peer and faculty concepts of the average and of the ideal seminarian as well as the other data described earlier. Compatibility of individual student and faculty concepts of the ideal member of the occupation was one predictor. The correlation between this predictor and the criterion variable was .27 when the criterion was faculty rating of vocational realism, statistically significant at the .01 level; but there was no relationship when the criterion was peer ratings of realism or when the predictor was compatibility of self concept and faculty concept of the average seminarian. The one instance in which there is disagreement with the largely negative findings of this aspect of the Kibrick-Tiedeman study, it should be noted, is when the predicator is deviation of the self concept from the faculty ideal and when the criterion is a faculty rating of the adequacy of the individual for the priesthood: this suggests criterion contamination, since both predictor and criterion are essentially comparisons of a person with faculty standards.

SELF CONCEPT AND INSIGHT.   Self concepts have been studied in relationship to insight into psychological characteristics of known occupational significance. O'Hara and Tiedeman (1959) tested the hypothesis (Super *et al.*, 1957) that "Self concepts begin to form prior to adolescence, become clearer in adolescence and are translated into occupational terms in adolescence," and Ginzberg's (1951) hypothesis that a "tentative choice period" is subdivided into four stages in which interest, capacity, value, and reality successively play major roles. O'Hara and Tiedeman collected appropriate test and self-rating data from 1,021 high school boys. They confirmed the hypothesis of increasing agreement between self-estimates and objective data such as test scores during the high school years, further demonstrating that there are differences in the ages at which the development of such insights is most rapid. Insight into vocational interests about reached its peak by grade 10, work values in grade 12; insight into general values changed little during the high school years, while insight into social status seemed, if anything, to decline somewhat; insight into aptitudes increased steadily during the four years of high school, but the correlations between self-estimates and test scores were still relatively low (.69 as compared to .83 and .84 for interests and work values) in grade 12. As Ginzberg's theory is based

on emphasis in talk and thought, and these data involve insight rather than emphasis, O'Hara and Tiedeman point out that they have perhaps not tested the Ginzberg hypothesis. The order in which insight develops does not, whatever the explanation may be, correspond to Ginzberg's, since insight into capacity develops late rather than early in adolescence.

The hypothesis developed and tested by Norrell and Grater (1960) was that self-awareness or insight into vocational interests as measured by agreement between self estimates and scores on Strong's Vocational Interest Blank is related negatively to needs which inhibit self awareness. These latter were measured by Edwards' Personal Preference Schedule, the scales of which were rated by psychologists for their effect on self insight. In the case of eight needs, the hypothesis was not sustained; in the case of four needs, it was supported. Those who had insight into their vocational interests tended to be higher on need for change and heterosexuality, lower on need for succorance and order. As the 10 per cent level of significance was accepted, the conclusions must be viewed with some caution, but the trend for all hypotheses was in the expected direction and lent some support to the theory.

SELF CONCEPT, PARENT IDENTIFICATION, AND VOCATIONAL INTERESTS.   Investigating the relationship between son-father identification and similarity of son's to father's vocational interests, Henderson (1958) developed an identification test which included measures of father-son shared activities, son's knowledge of father's job, son's perception of father's importance (a) in the community and (b) in the home, son's perception of his (a) physical and (b) psychological similarity to his father (adjective checklists), and son's affection for his father. He also devised a measure of the similarity of son's and father's scores on the Strong Vocational Interest Blank. The correlation of son's perceived physical similarity to father with psychological similarity was only .18 (nonsignificant) for 65 ninth-graders of the Career Pattern Study, but .515 (significant at the .01 level) for the 55 twelfth-graders in the same high school; perceived psychological similarity (self concept and father concept) and affection yielded intercorrelations of .48 and .53 (both significant at the .01 level) in the ninth and twelfth grades. The correlations between son's perceived psychological similarity to the father and total identification scores (similarity not included) were .64 and .84 at the ninth and twelfth grades, respectively, which suggests that similarity of the son's self concept and father concept constitutes a good measure of identification.

Henderson, having developed a self concept measure of identification, proceeded to ascertain the relationship between this measure and similarity of son's to father's scores on the Strong Vocational Interest Blank. The son's perceived similarity to his father and the similarity of son's to father's interests yielded a chi-square of 9.60, significant at the .01 level, at the ninth grade, but a nonsignificant chi-square at the twelfth. Henderson suggests that other role models may be more important in older adolescence than in early adolescence; it would be instructive to obtain data on the boys' perceived psychological similarity to other key figures (self concept and concept of role model), and correlate these scores with similarity of interest measures obtained from boys and these other key figures in the twelfth grade, for comparative purposes.

It was hypothesized by Stewart (1959) and then by White (1959) that the similarity of the child's to the parent's concepts of the actual child and ideal child is related to the nature of the child's vocational interests. Stewart's hypotheses dealt with the mother-son identification, and White followed up his work by formulating and testing hypotheses concerning both parents and daughters. Stewart found no relationships between any of his son-mother identification measures and agreement of measured interests with occupational preference, but did find that boys with no primary interest patterns and boys who rejected masculine interests tended to accept more fully than others the mother's picture of the ideal boy. Some of Stewart's other findings are somewhat contradictory and confusing; for this reason the subsequent study which White did under his sponsorship deserves more emphasis. White found that college freshman girls (N = 34) with stronger career motivation, as defined by high scores on Strong Vocational Interest Blank scales for occupations requiring extended or specialized training, tended to be less satisfied with themselves (to have greater actual-self ideal-self discrepancies), and to identify less with their parents (to have greater self-parent discrepancies), than do those whose interest is greater in stopgap and feminine occupations. White's findings show a consistent tendency for congruency of girls' and parents' concepts to be related to vocational interests.

CRYSTALLIZATION OF THE VOCATIONAL SELF CONCEPT   It has been suggested by Stephenson (1961) that persistence in the pursuit of an occupational goal (for example, medicine) despite obstacles (for example, failure to gain admittance to medical school) provided a good index of crystallization of the vocational self concept (vocational choice). He reasoned that the student who persists in seeking a medical or medically-related education after failure to enter medical school must have had a crystallized self concept when he first applied; the student who changes objectives may or may not have had a truly crystalized vocational self concept. Of 368 Minnesota premedical students who completed applications for medical school but were not admitted, 343 responded to a questionnaire concerning their status four to eight years later. Of these, 30 per cent were in medical occupations despite their first failure to gain entry, 32 per cent were in medically related occupations, and 38 per cent were in nonmedical occupations. The total group of premedical students numbered 783, of whom 402 were admitted on first application. Thus, 66 per cent of the total applicant group were eventually admitted to medical schools, and 80 per cent of the total group eventually entered medical or medically related occupations. Stephenson concludes that the vocational self concept of the student who attempts to enter the field of medicine has typically crystallized prior to making application for admission to medical school. The self concept has, apparently, been translated into vocational terms, and the translation has been confirmed, or crystallized, in the subject's own thinking before he has had significant experience in the field of work. This finding may be viewed as a substantiation of Carter's (1940) earlier finding that the inventoried interests or self percepts of adolescents are organized as are those of adults in various occupations even before they have had experience in those occupations.

VOCATIONAL SELF CONCEPT AND PROFESSIONAL STATUS The relationship between the vocational self concept (that is, one's concept of one's self as a member of an occupation) and the length of time and type of participation in that occupation has been of interest to occupational sociologists. Huntington (1957) obtained questionnaire data from medical students at different year levels, in order to throw light on these issues, and found that medical students' self images vary with awareness of the expectations of others, with the year-level attained in training, and with the status of the persons with whom they happen to be interacting. They may see themselves as students when with physicians and as physicians when with patients. The vocational self concept is thus a function of perception of the perceptions (role expectations) of others.

CONCLUSIONS FROM THE SELF CONCEPT STUDIES The studies just reviewed, on the relationships between self concept and

various criteria of vocational development, show that:

1. Agreement between the self concept and one's own occupational concept is related to occupational preferences and to both internal and external criteria of success and satisfaction.

2. Agreement between the self concept and the occupational role concepts of important persons has so far tended not to be related to external criteria of success.

3. Vocational self concepts are a function of perception of the occupational role expectations of important persons, and are related to level of attainment in an occupation.

4. Agreement between self concepts and other measures of the same characteristics, that is, self understanding, increases at varying rates with age in adolescence and is related to the strength of certain needs.

5. Adolescents' parent-identifications (agreement between self concept and concept of parent) are related to type of vocational interest. Identification with the like sexed parent tends, in boys, to be related to similarity of son's to father's vocational interests in the ninth-grade but not in the twelfth; in college girls it tends to be associated with having feminine and stopgap vocational interests. Identification with the opposite-sexed parent tends, in college girls, to be associated with occupational-career interests, and in boys, with rejection of masculine interests and lack of clear-cut vocational interests.

As more and better research is carried out on these topics the conclusions may perhaps be modified. When the individual's own concept of the occupation is the related variable, when objective measures of personal characteristics are related to self perceptions of the same traits, and when self and parent perceptions of the self and of the ideal are used as measures of identification, the results tend to support hypotheses derived from the theory. They suggest that the working counselor should devote some time to helping the student or client to explore his self concept, clarifying it and checking it against reality as represented by evaluated experience, test results, and the perceptions of others.

ELEMENTS OF A SELF-CONCEPT THEORY OF VOCATIONAL DEVELOPMENT What are the elements of a self-concept theory of vocational development, the processes by which the self concept affects vocational development? They have been described in scattered places (Super, 1957; Super *et al.*, 1957; Super and Bachrach, 1957). It may help to organize them somewhat more systematically here. They may be identified as the processes of formation, translation, and implementation of the self concept.

SELF CONCEPT FORMATION In infancy the individual begins the process of forming a concept of himself, developing a sense of identity as a person distinct from but at the same time resembling other persons. This is essentially an exploratory process which goes on throughout the entire course of life until selfhood ceases and identity is lost to the sight of man as we know him. How does this concept of self evolve?

Exploration appears to be the first phase and a continuing process so essential that Jordaan deals with it in his essay. Just as the infant plays with his toes, or holds his hand in front of his face to observe the movements of his fingers, so the adolescent tries his hand at writing poetry, or admires the skill revealed by the masterpiece which he has produced in shop. Similarly, the older worker who can no longer maintain the pace which he had set as a younger man tries himself out at new methods of work to which he may be better adapted in view of the physical and psychological changes which he senses in himself. The self is an object of exploration as it develops and changes; so, too, is the environment.

Self differentiation is a second phase in the development of the self concept. Moving his hand in front of his face, noting that it moves as he wills it to, whereas his mother's hand appears to move independently, the baby notes "This is I, that is someone else." He goes on to ask, "What am I like?" and thus begins the search for identity. The small boy, son of his father, is aware of the fact that he is smaller, weaker, a milk drinker but not a coffee drinker, and so forth. The adolescent, member of a teen-age group, may be aware of the fact that he does not dress as flashily or talk as much as most of his friends. Similarly, the recent graduate working at his first regular job notes differences in his approach to clients as contrasted with that which characterizes his fellow salesclerks, and is conscious of greater interest in the paper work associated with the job than they seem to manifest.

Identification is another process which goes on more or less simultaneously with differentiation. The man-child, aware of similarities between himself and his father and of differences between himself and his mother, aware and also envious of his father's strength and power, identifies with his father and strives in various ways to be like him. As Tyler has pointed out, the variety of male roles in our society, associated with the variety and prominence of occupations in men's lives, channels the boy's identifications importantly, although not solely, along occupational lines. The father, uncle, older brother, neighborhood men, all go to work, come home from work, talk about work (as well as baseball and politics which also are man-dominated), reinforcing the boy's impression that maleness and occupation are more or less synonymous. Men come to the house or apartment in connection with work which the boy has a chance to observe: meter readers, bill collectors, milkmen, mailmen, plumbers, and others. The boy, whose father was at first his only male object of identification, finds that he can resemble a number of other males and assume a variety of masculine roles, can choose his identification on the basis of what appeals to him most. This is less true of the girl-child, whose adult counterparts more often work at home or, if they go to work, tend to talk about it less than the man and seem less involved in their occupations. Tyler (1951) has shown that in line with these observations small boys' interests are more likely to agree with their measured aptitudes than those of little girls.

Role playing is a type of behavior which accompanies or follows identification. The small boy who identifies with his father seeks to emulate him: in his imagination or in his overt behavior the boy acts as he thinks his father does, later he bats left-handed because the baseball player with whom he now identifies is left-handed, and later still he aspires to be a physician and starts ninth-grade biology with zest because the man who did wonders for him when he was ill is a physician. Whether the role playing is largely imaginative or overtly participatory it gives some opportunity to try the role on for size, to see how valid the concept of oneself as a left-handed baseball player, or as a student of biology preparing to be a physician, actually is.

Reality testing stems as readily from role playing as role playing does from identification. Life offers many opportunities for reality testing, in the form of children's play (thus the raft a small boy built at age nine may have diverted him from a career as a ship builder by sinking with his weight on it), in school courses (how many men were convinced by high school algebra that they were not cut out to be engineers?), in extra-curricular activities (the girl who sang the lead role in the high school musical last year has gone on to a school of dramatic arts), and in part-time or temporary employment (as in the case of the draftee assigned to be a medical corpsman who unexpectedly discovered that the role of medic sat well upon him and went on to medical school). These reality testing experiences strengthen or modify self concepts, and confirm or contradict the way in which they have been tentatively translated into an occupational role.

TRANSLATION OF SELF CONCEPTS INTO OCCU-PATIONAL TERMS   The translation proceeds in several ways, although it should be noted that much of the theorizing on the subject is done by analogy from other aspects of developmental psychology and from every-day observation rather than inferentially from carefully collected and analyzed data. (1) Identification with an adult sometimes seems to lead to a desire to play his occupational role; this global vocational self concept, assumed as a whole, may be just as totally discarded when subjected to reality testing. (2) Experience in a role in which one is cast, perhaps more or less through chance, may lead to the discovery of a vocational translation of one's self concepts which is as congenial as it is unexpected. (3) Awareness of the fact that one has attributes which are said to be important in a certain field of work may lead one to look into that occupation; and the investigation may lead to confirmation of the idea that the role expectations of that occupation are such that one would do well in it and enjoy it. Here the translation may be made bit by bit, as when success in algebra leads to electing physics in the senior year of high school, and good work there leads to the belief that one's scientific as well as mathematical abilities and interests make engineering appropriate. Recognition of the importance of this process led to the development of a theoretical model, the subject of the essay by Starishevsky and Matlin.

IMPLEMENTATION OF THE SELF CONCEPTS   The implementation or actualizing of self concepts is the result of these processes as professional training is entered or as education is completed and the young man or woman moves from school or college into the world of work. In an early phase, the pre-medical student enters medical school, proud of his developing sense of professional identity. In a later phase, the young engineering graduate gets his first job as an engineer, and rejoices in his new title, symbol of his having converted a self concept into a reality; the young executive trainee who finishes his rotations through the planned sequence of training positions and settles at his own desk, with his own name-plate in front of him, feels that he has finally achieved success. At the other extreme, the high school drop-out who never did well in his studies, who was never accepted by his classmates, and who is fired from the job that he finally got only after a number of rejections, finds the occupational translation of his self concept as ne'er-do-well confirmed and implemented. After a series of negative experiences, it takes a great deal of reeducation to help him develop more positive self concepts, to find a suitable occupational translation of this favorable picture of himself, and to turn it into a reality. With the population explosion in the labor market which we shall now have every summer for years to come, the unfortunates who enter the market with poor self concepts and inadequate vocational translations of these self concepts will have all too many opportunities to confirm them.

These appear to be the elements of a self-concept theory of vocational development. They are still not formulated as testable hypotheses, but, judging by the research results so far, they do suggest and permit the formulation of hypotheses which tend to stand up when tested, and they can be helpful to counselors in dealing with the vocational decision making of students.

[1]Brophy, 1959; Stewart, 1959; White, 1959; O'Hara and Tiedeman, 1959; Tageson, 1960; Englander, 1960; Norrell and Grater, 1960; Kibrick and Tiedeman, 1961; Warren, 1961; Blocher and Schutz, 1961, Stephenson, 1961.

REFERENCES

Allport, G. W. "The Ego in Contemporary Psychology," 50 *Psychological Review* (1943), 451–478.

Blocher, D. H., and Schutz, R. A. "Relationships Among Self-Descriptions, Occupational Stereotypes, and Vocational Preferences," 8 *Journal of Counseling Psychology* (1961), 314–317.

Bordin, E. S. "A Theory of Interests as Dynamic Phenomena," 3 *Educational and Psychological Measurement* (1943), 49–66.

———, and Wilson, E. H. "Change of Interest as a Function of Shift in Curricular Orientation," 13 *Educational and Psychological Measurement* (1953), 297–307.

Borow, H., Pepinsky, H. B., and Dressel, P. L. "Frontiers in Personnel Research in Education," in Henry, N. B. (ed.) *Personnel Services in Education, 58th Yearbook, Part II* (Chicago: National Society for the Study of Education, 1959).

Brophy, A. L. "Self, Role, and Satisfaction," 59 *Genetic Psychological Monograph* (1959), 263–308.

Caplow, T. *The Sociology of Work* (Minneapolis: University of Minnesota Press, 1954).

Carter, H. D. "The Development of Vocational Attitudes," 4 *Journal of Counseling Psychology* (1940), 185–191.

Crowne, D. P., and Stephens, M. W. "Self-Acceptance and Self-Evaluative Behavior: A Critique of Methodology," 58 *Psychological Bulletin* (1961), 104–121.

Darley, J. G., and Hagenah, Theda. *Vocational Interest Measurement* (Minneapolis: University of Minnesota Press, 1955).

Englander, M. "A Psychological Analysis of Vocational Choice: Teaching," 7 *Journal of Counseling Psychology* (1960), 257–264.

Ginzberg, E., Ginsburg, S. W., Axelrad, S., and Herma, J. L. *Occupational Choice* (New York: Columbia University Press, 1951).

Henderson, H. L. *The Relationship Between Interests of Fathers and Sons and Sons' Identification with Fathers* (New York: unpublished doctoral dissertation, Teachers College, Columbia University, 1958.)

Holland, J. L. "A Theory of Vocational Choice," 6 *Journal of Counseling Psychology* (1959), 35–44.

Hughes, E. C. *Men and Their Work* (New York: Free Press of Glencoe, 1958).

Huntington, Mary-Jean. "The Development of a Professional Self-Image," in Merton, R. K. *et al.* (eds.) *The Student Physician* (Cambridge: Harvard University Press, 1959).

Kibrick, Anne, and Tiedeman, D. V. "Conception of Self and Perception of Role in Schools of Nursing," 8 *Journal of Counseling Psychology* (1961), 62–69.

Lecky, P. *Self-Consistency* (New York: Island Press, 1945), reprinted.

Mehenti, P. M. *Agreement Between Vocational Preference and Inventoried Interest in Relation to Some Presumed Indices of Vocational Maturity* (New York: unpublished doctoral dissertation, Teachers College, Columbia University, 1954).

Miller, D. C., and Form, W. H. *Industrial Sociology* (New York: Harper and Bros., 1951).

Norrell, Gwen, and Grater, H. "Interest Awareness as an Aspect of Self-Awareness," 7 *Journal of Counseling Psychology* (1960), 289–292.

O'Hara, R. P., and Tiedeman, D. V. "Vocational Self Concepts in Adolescence," 6 *Journal of Counseling Psychology* (1959), 292–301.

Roe, Anne. *The Psychology of Occupations* (New York: John Wiley and Sons, Inc., 1956).

———. "Early Determinants of Vocational Choice," 4 *Journal of Counseling Psychology* (1957), 212–217.

Stephenson, R. R. "Occupational Choice as a Crystallized Self Concept," 8 *Journal of Counseling Psychology* (1961), 211–216.

Stewart, L. H. "Mother-Son Identification and Vocational Interest," 60 *Genetic Psychological Monograph* (1959), 31–63.

Strong, D. J., and Feder, D. D. "Measurement of the Self-Concept," 8 *Journal of Counseling Psychology* (1961), 170–178.

Strong, E. K., Jr. *Vocational Interests of Men and Women* (Stanford, Calif.: Stanford University Press. 1943).

Super, D. E. "Vocational Adjustment: Implementing a Self Concept," 30 *Occupations* (1951), 88–92.

———. "A Theory of Vocational Development," 8 *American Psychologist* (1953), 185–190.

———. "Career Patterns as a Basis for Vocational Counseling," 1 *Journal of Counseling Psychology* (1954), 12–20.

———. *The Psychology of Careers* (New York: Harper and Bros., 1957).

———, and Bachrach, P. B. *Scientific Careers and Vocational Development Theory* (New York: Bureau of Publications, Teachers College, Columbia University, 1957).

———, Crites, J. O., Hummel, R. C., Moser, H. P., Overstreet, P. L., and Warnath, C. F. *Vocational Development: A Framework for Research* (New York: Bureau of Publications, Teachers College, Columbia University, 1957).

———, and Overstreet, P. L. *The Vocational Maturity of Ninth-Grade Boys* (New York: Bureau of Publications, Teachers College, Columbia University, 1960).

Tageson, C. F. *The Relationship of Self Perceptions to Realism of Vocational Preference* (Washington, D.C.: Catholic University of America Press, 1960).

Tiedeman, D. V., O'Hara, R. P., and Matthews, E. "Position Choices and Careers: Elements of a Theory," *Harvard Studies in Career Development, No. 8*, mimeo (Cambridge: Graduate School of Education, Harvard University, 1958).

Torrance, E. P. "Some Practical Uses of Knowledge of the Self Concept in Counseling and Guidance," 14 *Educational and Psychological Measurement* (1954), 120–127.

Tyler, L. E. "The Relationship of Interests to Abilities and Reputation Among First-Grade Children," 11 *Educational and Psychological Measurement* (1951), 255–264.

———. "The Development of 'Vocational Interests': The Organization of Likes and Dislikes in Ten-Year-Old Children," 86 *Journal of Genetic Psychology* (1955), 33–44.

Warren, J. R. "Self Concept, Occupational Role Expectation, and Change in College Major," 8 *Journal of Counseling Psychology* (1961), 164–169.

White, Becky J. "The Relationship of Self Concept and Parental Identification to Women's Vocational Interests," 6 *Journal of Counseling Psychology* (1959), 202–206.

Wrenn, C. G. "The Self Concept in Counseling," 5 *Journal of Counseling Psychology* (1958), 104–109.

———. "Vocational Choice Theory — An Editorial Comment," 6 *Journal of Counseling Psychology* (1959), 94.

Wylie, Ruth C. *The Self Concept* (Lincoln: University of Nebraska Press, 1961).

A Model for the Translation of Self Concepts into Vocational Terms

REUBEN STARISHEVSKY, *Columbia University*

NORMAN MATLIN

This essay attempts to formalize the relationships of translation and incorporation. The terms translation and incorporation have been used previously in this monograph. However, here incorporation, and a few other terms are developed differently.

Self-concept theory as used by the counseling psychologist is designed to predict the occupation ultimately chosen by the subject. The developing or maturing individual is constantly reacting to environmental stimuli in a manner characteristic of his own formulation of the nature of the environment and of himself. The way in which the person has reacted in the past, constructing his formulation of the world, determines his future and his choice of occupation as part of that future. One can, then, view vocational choice as an expression of self concepts

Reprinted with permission of the authors and publisher from *Career Development: Self Concept Theory.* New York: The College Entrance Examination Board, 1963, Pp. 33–41.

formulated and reformulated throughout the life stages. People differ both in their self concepts and in the ways in which they translate self concepts into occupational terms. Hence, people choose different occupations.

Implicit in the central idea of translation is a recognition, for purposes of analysis, of two realms or languages: an area of psychological statements and an area of occupational terms. Self concepts being expressable in psychological terms, are in the first area. They consist of all statements in psychological terms that the subject is willing to make about himself or others. A person's understanding of himself cannot develop without comparison and contrast with others. Furthermore, to understand a person's description of himself, we will need to know to whom else he applies this description. Suppose a person says: "I am intelligent." This statement will be quite different depending on whether he further says "everyone is intelligent" or "very few people are intelligent." In the first, since he shows no acknowledgement of non-intelligence, his statement may have little meaning, though it could be an index of confused thought. Alternatively, if he gives as the other example of intelligence a person whom he has described with a concatenation of feelings of annoyance and disgust, this data may be necessary to our understanding of what intelligence means to him. The position taken here is that a person's psychological pictures of others are an integral part of his self-concept system.

The self-concept system may be viewed as a person's psychological field, his formulation of the world. This definition departs in a measure from Sarbin's (1954) definition of the self concept as what a person believes himself to be, the combined self perceptions; the model's definition is more inclusive and self contained: what a person perceives himself and others to be.

Self concepts are verbalized in a series of statements in which the self or another person is the grammatical subject and a psychological variable the predicate, for example, "I am intelligent," "John is lethargic." All of these statements are statements that the person is willing to make. These statements represent, *ipso facto*, a choice. In making the statements in the example above, the person is denying the statements "I am stupid," "John is active." Both the statements asserted and the statements denied, being couched in terms meaningful to the speaker, are part of the language or psychological terminology called, for simplicity's sake, *psychtalk*. Since psychtalk is a sum of all statements whose predicates are dimensions a person habitually uses to differentiate people, the predicates may be aptitudes or interests or other variables in which the psychologist is interested, if these happen to be what the subject uses to differentiate people.

In the area of occupations a parallel situation exists. The statements that a person is willing to make of himself and others, the predicates this time being the names of occupations or their equivalents,

constitute his occupational self concept. Similarly, saying "I intend to be a physician" precludes saying "I am going to be a paleontologist."

All possible statements in this form constitute the realm of occupational terminology or *occtalk*. In the realm of occtalk, all statements need not be verbal. Applying to medical school is the equivalent of saying "I am going to be a physician." In the model no distinction is made between the manner of asserting a statement. At certain times one kind of assertion is more appropriate; nonetheless, they are treated as functionally equal.

RELATIONSHIPS OF STATEMENTS

The main assumption of this self-concept theory concerns the relationship between statements in these two realms. First, it is asserted that any statement in occtalk made by a particular person can be translated into a statement or series of statements in that person's psychtalk, just as a sentence in French can be translated into an equivalent sentence in English. For example, the statement "I want to be a lawyer" might mean "I am socially minded, I am aggressive, I am interested in upholding community values." Alternately, it might mean "I am theory oriented, I am introverted, and I am scholarly." In order to know, we must consult the person's "dictionary." A person's dictionary is a listing of predicates in psychtalk equivalent to predicates in occtalk. For the moment, let us assume that this book of equivalences can be obtained for each person.

The second assumption of this self-concept theory is that the occupational self concept, which is in effect defined as the occupational statements opted, is, at least in part, an incorporation of the self concept. In other words, any statement in occtalk that a subject is willing to make implies a translation of a psychtalk statement which is part of his psychological self concept. Of course the occupational self concept may include some parts which are not part of the psychological self concept, for example, a person may take a job which is not entirely satisfying. But the job must have some element in harmony with his self concept or he would not consider it.

Not all of a person's self concepts are necessarily incorporated in occtalk. People may differ in the level of incorporation, the degree to which a person's self concepts find expression in his occupational statements. The level is never zero, that is, a person never makes an occupational statement incompatible with his self concepts.

A simple version of the system might be represented as in Figure 1.

Let us assume that our subject has a psychtalk consisting of only three dichotomous dimensions: (1) intelligent — stupid, (2) healthy — sick, and (3) broad-minded — narrow-minded. Further, let us assume that there are only three people with whom the person is familiar enough to make statements: himself, John, and Bob. There would then be 18 possible statements in his psychtalk.

Self is	John is	Bob is
intelligent	intelligent	intelligent
Self is stupid	John is stupid	Bob is stupid
Self is healthy	John is healthy	Bob is healthy
Self is sick	John is sick	Bob is sick
Self is broad-	John is broad-	Bob is broad-
minded	minded	minded
Self is narrow-	John is narrow-	Bob is narrow-
minded	minded	minded

These statements come in pairs whose members are mutually exclusive, since dichotomies have been used in the example. If the dimensions had not been dichotomous, statements would come in sets whose members are mutually exclusive. If our subject says, "John is intelligent" he cannot completely assert "John is stupid." His self concept, therefore, will consist of nine statements. Let us further assume that our subject's self concept consists of the following nine statements:

PSYCHTALK

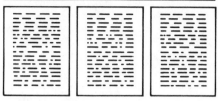

Statements subject
is willing to make = self-concept

OCC. TO PSYCH. DICTIONARY

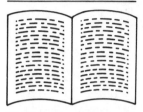

Dictionary is a collection of
assertions of the equivalence
of predicates

OCCTALK

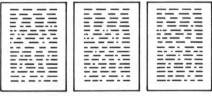

Statements subject is willing to make
= occupational self-concept

FIGURE 1.

Self is	John is	Bob is stupid
intelligent	intelligent	
Self is healthy	John is sick	Bob is healthy
Self is broad-	John is narrow-	Bob is narrow-
minded	minded	minded

Let us assume that our subject has four occupations in his occtalk: psychologist, physician, lawyer, and opium smuggler. Let us suppose further that his dictionary is as follows:

intelligent + healthy + broad minded
    = psychologist
intelligent + healthy + narrow-minded
    = physician
intelligent + sick + narrow-minded = lawyer
stupid + sick + narrow-minded
    = opium smuggler

It would then be possible to make such translations as the following from the above-listed dictionary and self concept:

Occtalk
I will be a psychologist
    = I am intelligent + healthy + broad-minded
I will be a physician
    = I am intelligent + healthy + narrow-minded
I will be a lawyer
    = I am intelligent + sick + narrow-minded
I will be an opium smuggler
    = I am stupid + sick + narrow-minded

Each of these statements in occtalk can be characterized as having a specific level of incorporation. The statement "I am a psychologist" since it means "I am intelligent, healthy, and broad-minded" agrees completely with the subject's self-concept, that is, has a level of incorporation of 100 per cent. The statement "I am a physician" on translation is found to agree with the subject's self concept on two of the three dimensions, that is, the statement has a level of incorporation of 67 per cent. Similarly the statement "I am a lawyer" has a level of 33 per cent, and "I am an opium smuggler" has a level of 0 per cent. The second postulate asserts that the subject, so long as he maintains his present self concept and dictionary, would not say "I would like to be an opium smuggler."

It can be seen from the formulation that numerous occupations are taken as compatible, in varying degrees, with a person's self concept. In fact, this picture would seem to fit the real world where many, if not most, people seem capable of entering many different occupations. While this has presented a problem of overlap to previous research, the present model seems to accommodate this perverse aspect of reality.

The level of incorporation shows promise of providing an important index. Several hypotheses can be made about statements on different levels of incorporation, for example, the hierarchy of a subject's statements rank-ordered by level of incorporation will correlate highly with his hierarchy of occupational preferences; the higher the level of incorporation the more likely it is the subject will choose that occupation; people leaving occupations will leave for an occupation on a higher level of incorporation; the lower the level of incorporation of one's occupation the more likely one is to pursue an avocation with a high level of incorporation of the self concept.

In a sense, the concept of level of incorporation is here being used in the way in which many researchers use the concept of motivation. Motivation in this model has been assimilated to the degree that the tendency toward greater incorporation is taken as the motivating force in vocational development.

POSTULATES

Two formal postulates constitute the model.

Postulate 1: Every statement in occtalk is translatable into psychtalk.
Definition:

1. *Statement:* a pairing of a specific person with a predicate. No distinction is made between verbal statements, for example, "I am broad-minded," "I am going to be a lawyer," action statements, for example, applying to law school, and mental statements, for example, daydreaming about being a lawyer.

2. *Occtalk:* the totality of all statements whose predicates are the names of occupations.

3. *Translatable into:* equivalent to. The equivalence of any two statements is asserted solely as an equivalence in the mind of a particular person. The translation of a particular statement requires a knowledge of the person's dictionary, that is, series of predicates equivalent in psychtalk and occtalk.

4. *Psychtalk:* the totality of all statements whose predicates are dimensions the person habitually uses to differentiate people.

Postulate 1, being unidirectional, makes no assertion about the translatability of any statement in psychtalk into occtalk, that is, there may be statements in psychtalk which differentiate people, but do not differentiate occupations. Nor does Postulate 1 imply any one-to-one correspondence between statements.

Postulate 2: Every statement in the occupational self concept is at least partly a translation of the self concept.

Definition:

1. *Occupational self concept:* the totality of statements in occtalk the person is willing to make. (Differs from Super's use of the term vocational self concept.)

2. *Self concept:* the totality of statements in psychtalk a person is willing to make.

The degree to which the self concept is translated by a statement in occtalk is the level of incorporation of that statement. Postulate 2 states that the level of incorporation of a statement in the occupational self concept is never zero.

PROCESSES OF INCORPORATION

Up to this point, level of incorporation, a measure of the degree of translation of the self concept occurring in specific occtalk statements, has been discussed without regard to the processes by which a high level occurs. It may be hypothesized that these processes, also called incorporation, will occur to achieve or maintain a high level of incorporation for the statements in the occupational self concept.

In certain cases deliberate incorporation takes place, that is, a person takes stock of some or all of his characteristics and considers various occupations in the light of the degree to which they allow him to exercise personality variables important to him. In general, this would be increasingly likely with greater maturity and sophistication. For example, a person just completing a doctorate in psychology might decide whether to be a therapist or a research person by so articulate a method.

At an earlier age a less deliberate process of incorporation, identification, may occur. The child perceives himself as similar to some important figure in his life. He creates the dictionary definition of the occupation of this figure on the bases of what he takes to be this figure's personality characteristics. Of necessity, the occtalk statement indicating desire to enter this occupation will have a high level of incorporation.

Following naturally from identification, role playing will serve to incorporate the self concept. A child playing a role may discover new aspects of an occupation which fit the picture he has of himself, that is, he may revise his dictionary to give the preferred occtalk statement a higher level of incorporation. He may discover new things about himself, adding to his self concept new statements which, being translated into the preferred occtalk statement, also raise the level of incorporation. Of course he may find the role uncongenial, causing him to seek another occupation to role play, hopefully productive of a higher level of incorporation.

The above processes sample, rather than exhaust, possible methods of incorporation. The model does seem amenable to hypotheses concerned with processes by which incorporation may occur.

METADIMENSIONS

Self-concept theory has been concerned with such dimensions as structure and congruence. These are characterizations by the theorist of the subject's self concept. To keep these distinct from the dimensions forming the predicates of psychtalk, these are referred to as metadimensions.

Of necessity, metadimensions are a nomothetic rather than an idiographic method of understanding; they rank order subjects according to some aspects of their self concept rather than attempt to understand the subject's interrelationships solely in terms of the subject's own system.

Complexity has been defined by Lundy and Berkowitz (1957) as that which distinguishes among a greater number of different aspects of people or situations, employing more functional concepts and showing more variety in the relationship between them.

The number of constructs in use determines the upward limit of the number of people or occupations that can be differentiated. A person whose psychtalk predicates are limited to two dichotomous dimensions can distinguish only four classes of people or occupations; three dichotomous dimensions permit recognition of eight groups. Obviously, the number of possible differentiated groups is X^n, when X is the number of choices along the dimension that are permitted and n the number of functioning dimensions. A subject with two dichotomous dimensions, asked to provide a dictionary of 10 occupations, is forced to make a minimum of six duplicates. He may, in fact, make more duplicates than this, and is likely to if the two dimensions are related in his mind.

Consideration of complexity in this fashion has several advantages. It enables prediction in the model; it identifies complexity with an operation which has shown adequate test-retest reliability on several occasions and which has been shown by Bieri and Blacker (1956) to correlate with behavior in the Rorschach Test; it is amenable to mathematical handling.

It will be noted that complexity can be a metadimension of the self concept or the dictionary, the maximum number of differentiations possible in the self concept serving as the upward limit of the dictionary. The occupational self concept is unidimensional and cannot be ordered by any metadimension which requires more than one dimension. Complexity cannot be applied to a language which contains all possible alternatives; a particular subject's psychtalk can be considered as allowing or not allowing for the possibility of complexity, although in itself it is neither complex nor simple.

Congruence is a measure of the incompatibility of statements, the sole criterion being the canons of logic. As a metadimension, it can be applied only to the self concept. It cannot apply to the languages, for a language being composed of all statements includes all possible contradictions. It cannot apply to the dictionary for no assertion about one occupation can contradict an assertion about another occupation. Nor can the occupational self concept show incongruences. The statements at their face value cannot be contradictory, for the model allows for the possibility that several occupations may be an implementation of the self concept, the assertion of acceptability of several occupations not being considered a contradiction. Nor can two occtalk statements in translation be considered incompatible, for we consider compatibility the compliance with the demand based on the laws of logic, while requiring compatibility in occupational self concept would demand compliance to both the laws of logic and the formulation of the model. Failure of the subject to agree with the model must be considered the theoretician's error, not the subject's. For example, a subject who describes himself as intelligent, healthy, broad-minded; describes physicians as stupid, sick, and narrow-minded; and maintains he wants to be a physician is a problem for the model. It may be that the instruments used were inadequate or the basic postulate may be false. In any event, our subject has not subscribed to the postulate, which purports to predict regularities in his behavior. Accusing the subject of inconsistency when the regularities fail to appear is frowned upon in certain circles. The metadimension is perforce restricted to the self concept.

However, congruence does have use, provided that it is kept in mind that the burden of proof is on the experimenter to demonstrate that the contradiction is existent in the thinking of the subject, and is not merely a paradox. Where incongruence is present to any marked degree, it suggests ambivalence and can be considered an indication of maladjustment.

Structuring, the amount of peakedness in the description of a particular person or occupation, is a metadimension that not only requires several dimensions, but requires the dimensions to be, if not continual, at least separable into several degrees. This formulation is quite compatible with the model and can generate useful hypotheses. The instrument for measuring the self concept will have to be geared to the use of finer breakdowns than dichotomies; but this may well repay the additional effort. Structure is applicable to the self concept and to the dictionary. The occupational self concept is unidimensional.

Realism as a metadimension differs in that it rank orders a subject on the basis of a comparison of the self concept, the dictionary, or the occupational self concept with some standard outside the subject's system; the previous metadimensions rank ordered subjects on the bases of characteristics internal to their systems.

The standard is reality. In practice, we would have to accept the psychologist's evaluation of reality, which, despite objective tests to answer specific questions, remains at this point a matter of judgment. Until we have an understanding of how the psychologist makes his judgment of reality, it will be difficult to know what to do with a ranking of subjects on this basis.

Stability is a metadimension applying to the self concept, the dictionary, and the occupational self concept. It can be opera-

tionally defined as a test-retest correlation for any period over a year, the long interval allowing the use of stability as a measurement of the subject rather than the test.

The metadimensions listed above are intended to sample rather than exhaust the universe of possible metadimensions.

OPERATIONS

Kelly's (1955) Role Construct Repertory Test may be used to generate statements in psychtalk. This test presents the subject with a series of role titles, three at a time, and asks him to state in what way two are alike and one is different. The dimensions set forth in the subject's answers may be taken as the dimensions of psychtalk. As part of the repertory test the subject is asked for each of the people named to indicate which end of each dimension is most appropriate. Each cell of this grid may be considered a statement in the subject's self concept.

Since it is basic to the model's understanding of the self concept that it must be mapped along dimensions that a subject himself chooses, it is necessary to forego the convenience of an inventory or adjective checklist. The latter would attempt to plot the subject's self concept in the dimensions of the inventor of the test, which are bound to differ to a greater or lesser degree from those of the subject. The dictionary may be built by asking subjects to rate each of a series of occupations on a seven-point scale for the constructs obtained on his repertory test.

The occupational self concept may be obtained in several ways, depending upon the hypotheses tested. For testing commonality hypotheses, working in a particular job can be taken as the statement of occupational self concept. In other cases the subject may be asked to rank order a series of occupations in terms of attractiveness. The ordering is assumed to represent the order of probability of a statement, the subject as grammatical subject, and the occupation as predicate being included in the occupational self concept.

SUMMARY

A model has been proposed based on a self-concept theory of vocational development. The model postulates that statements in the occupational field are translatable into statements in the psychological field, and that statements of the occupational self concept incorporate statements of the self concept. Some of the metadimensions of the self concept, some hypotheses, and the construct and index of the level of incorporation were discussed in terms of the proposed model.

REFERENCES

Bieri, J., and Blacker, E. "The Generality of Cognitive Complexity," 53 *Journal of Abnormal and Social Psychology* (1956), 112–117.

Kelly, G. A. *The Psychology of Personal Constructs* (New York: W. W. Norton & Co., Inc., 1955).

Lundy, R. M., and Berkowitz, L. "Cognitive-Complexity and Assimilative Projection," 55 *Journal of Abnormal and Social Psychology* (1957), 34–37.

Sarbin, T. R. "Role Theory," in Lindzey, G. (ed.) *Handbook of Social Psychology* (Cambridge: Addison-Wesley Publishing Co., Inc., 1954), Chap. 6.

Super, D. E. *The Psychology of Careers* (New York: Harper and Bros., 1957).

The Relationship between Certain Self Constructs and Occupational Preferences

ERNEST A. OPPENHEIMER, *Peace Corps*

Self-concept theory is one popular approach for explaining aspects of vocational development and choice. The extensive literature integrating aspects of self-concept theory with elements of vocational behavior was recently summarized by Super, Starishevsky, Matlin, Jordaan (1963).

Super uses self-concept theory as the organizing element in his efforts at refining a systematic theory of vocational development. A fundamental construct of Super's

Reprinted with the permission of author and publisher from the article of the same title, in *Journal of Counseling Psychology*, 1966, *13*, 191–197.

theory is that occupational preferences represent a translation of self concepts into vocational terms. The desire to find expression for self concepts is considered a motivating force in evaluating the attractiveness of an occupation.

Research has demonstrated that people prefer occupations perceived as congruent with their self concepts. Using Q sorts and adjective check lists to measure self and occupational concepts, studies by Englander (1960), Blocher and Schutz (1961) and Morrison (1962) found that students rated themselves more similar to an occupational preference than to a nonpreferred occupation. Two other investigations support the assumption of vocational self-concept theorists that helping people select occupations in which they can find expression for their self concepts is a suitable goal for vocational counselors. Brophy (1959) found that those nursing students who rated themselves more similar to their ratings of the role requirements of nurses reported greater satisfaction in their position as a student nurse. Tageson (1960) found that seminary students who rated their actual and ideal selves similar to their ratings of the average and ideal seminary student were rated by both faculty and students as having made a more realistic occupational choice.

THE PROBLEM

The need for systematic research on the linkage between self concepts and occupational preferences stimulated Starishevsky and Matlin (Super et al.,1963) to design a model of the translation process. The model suggests that one can predict a person's occupational preference hierarchy by examining the relationship between his self and occupational concepts. The higher the agreement between self concepts and concepts of a particular occupation, the higher the predicted position of that occupation on a person's expressed preference hierarchy.

The present investigation represents one of the initial tests of the potential of the model for examining the relationship between self concepts and occupational preferences. A self-concept instrument designed to meet the criteria for studying phenomenological theory (Super et al., 1963) was designed. The model's fundamental hypothesis, that there is a substantial correlation between the occupational hierarchy predicted from the agreement between self and occupational concepts and a person's expressed preference hierarchy, was examined. Effort was also directed at identifying variables related to individual differences in the level of agreement between self concepts

and occupational preferences. It was hypothesized that two metadimensions of the self concept, self-esteem and cognitive complexity, are positively related to this criterion.

Self-esteem and such terms as self-regard, self-acceptance, and satisfaction with self comprise a series of theoretical constructs that have been used interchangeably to denote the degree of satisfaction in self evaluation (Crowne and Stephens, 1961). The voluminous literature on self-esteem has been heavily focused in the areas of personal and social adjustment. Super has considered the implication of personal dissatisfaction for the process of formulating occupational preferences. He suggested that people need to reconcile aspects of their actual and ideal self concepts before they are ready to make satisfying vocational preferences (Super, 1951). It is therefore consistent with Super's theory to hypothesize that the degree of agreement between self concepts and occupational preferences is positively related to self-esteem.

The concept of cognitive complexity was developed by Bieri (1961) from Kelly's (1955) cognitive approach to explaining human behavior. Kelly conceptualizes man as a scientist, continually in the process of developing and organizing a system of personal constructs in man's efforts to improve his prediction of his social environment. The metadimension of cognitive complexity-simplicity has been used to explain differences in personal construct systems. The cognitively complex person has available a greater number of constructs to construe the behavior of others, while the cognitively simple person has relatively few personal constructs available. Bieri reasons that a larger number of constructs should improve a person's capacity to deal with his environment, allowing him to make finer discriminations and providing him with greater versatility in his responses.

Research indicates that cognitively complex people are more accurate in making social judgment (Bieri, 1955; Plotnick, 1961) and more moderate in their solutions to problems involving indeterminate probabilities (Higgins, 1959). One would therefore expect that cognitive complexity would be associated with more accurate and thoughtful judgments in formulating occupational preferences, which should be reflected in a higher level of agreement between self concepts and concepts of occupational preferences for cognitively complex people.

PROCEDURE

The sample consisted of 81 male liberal arts students at Rutgers University. The subjects were distributed relatively evenly among the first three undergraduate classes, the distribution including 30 sophomores, 27 juniors and 20 freshmen. The age range was from 18 to 24, but there were only two subjects older than 21.

The sample was selected from students who had registered for part-time employment at the Student Aid Office. These students were invited to earn three dollars for participating in a study designed to develop a new technique for vocational counseling. The first 90 students to apply were accepted.

INSTRUMENTS

Occupational Preference Ranking

This instrument was designed to elicit an expressed occupational hierarchy of seven occupations which represent a continuum from the occupation the subject would most like to enter to the occupation he would least like to work in.

Part A of the instrument contains a list of 50 occupations derived from the occupations included in the Strong Vocational Interest Blank (Strong, 1946) and the National Opinion Research Center's list (1947) of representative occupations. At least one occupation representing each of Roe's (1956) field and level categories was included. Subjects were asked to rank each of the 50 occupations on a scale from one to seven. In Part B subjects referred to their ratings of the 50 occupations in choosing one occupation to represent each of the seven ranks. The seven occupations designated were considered the expressed occupational preference hierarchy. A median Spearman rho of .93 was computed between the rank order on this instrument and the rank order obtained 48 hours later when the seven occupations were presented in random order.

Modified Repertory Test (MRT)

The MRT is a semi-structured test that allows the subject to use his own system of personal constructs to rate self and occupational concepts. This self concept instrument combines the first part of the Kelly Role Construct Repertory Test (KRCRT) with a modified semantic differential.

The KRCRT was used to elicit the dimensions the subject uses to differentiate people. Nineteen role titles describing figures in various spheres of a person's life, including the family, social, vocational and educational areas, were presented. The subject responded to each role title by supplying the name of the particular person in his life who best fulfills the specified role. The 19 role titles were then distributed into 22 triads. For each triad the subject was asked to describe in a word or phrase how two of the people are similar and different from the third. This word or phrase together with the word or phrase the subject considers to have the opposite meaning is referred to as a construct dimension. Twenty-two construct dimensions were elicited from the 22 triads of role titles.

The choice of specific role titles and their distribution into triads was governed by Kelly's (1955) suggestions for eliciting a representative sample of the dimensions a person customarily uses to evaluate himself and other people. Loosely, these construct dimensions may be considered the criteria for his choices. Kelly and his students have demonstrated that these dimensions differ from person to person and that they are reasonably stable in different situations.

On Part B of the MRT, the subject was asked to use his construct dimensions to rate nine titles along a seven interval semantic differential. The nine titles were "I am," "I would like to be," and the seven occupations he designated on the Occupational Ranking Measure as representative of his expressed preference hierarchy.

The initial step in scoring the MRT was to eliminate the dependent construct dimensions. The criteria for dependence were adopted from Bieri and Blacker (1956). A construct dimension was considered dependent if it duplicated a word that the subject used in either pole of a previous construct dimension. Two judges rated 20 protocols independently, obtaining a 96 per cent agreement on the number of construct dimensions considered independent.

The next step entailed obtaining a measure of the degree of agreement between subjects' ratings of "I am" with his ratings of each of the seven occupations. The intervals on the semantic differential were scaled from 1 to 7. A difference score was derived along each construct dimension by comparing the interval checked under "I am" with the interval checked under each occupation. The difference scores obtained for each construct dimension were added, yielding a summed difference score between ratings of "I am" and ratings of each of the occupations. The occupations were rank ordered from the smallest to the largest sum difference score. This rank order represents the predicted preference hierarchy.

The reliability of the predicted preference hierarchy was measured by comparing the hierarchy predicted on two administrations of the MRT. In studies using periods of two and three weeks between administrations of the MRT, median Spearman rho's of .80

(Starishevsky et al., 1961) and .79 (Shiner, 1963) were obtained.

RESULTS

The Spearman rho between the predicted and expressed preference hierarchies provided a measure of the accuracy of predicting the expressed preference hierarchy from the agreement between a subject's self and occupational concepts. This correlation coefficient will be referred to as r_1.

The distribution of r_1 coefficients ranged from 1.00 to $-.79$, with a median of .52. As the distribution was markedly skewed, it was advisable to use nonparametric statistics for operations using r_1 as the criterion.

HYPOTHESIS I People prefer occupations perceived as congruent with their self concepts.

The prediction was that subjects would show significantly more agreement between their self concepts and two preferred occupations, the occupations ranked one and two on their expressed hierarchy, than between their self concepts and two nonpreferred occupations, the occupations ranked six and seven on their expressed hierarchy. A summed difference score was computed between the subject's self ratings and his ratings of each of the four occupations. The summed difference score for each preferred occupation was compared to the summed difference score for each nonpreferred occupations. The analysis involved four sets of comparisons between preferred and nonpreferred occupations for each subject.

Sixty subjects rated themselves more similar to their preferred occupations, 9 subjects rated themselves more similar to their nonpreferred occupations and 12 subjects were tied. For the statistical analysis the latter 12 subjects were divided evenly between the two other groups. Incorporating a correction for continuity in the formula for the normal curve, the computation yielded a z score of 4.5, significant at the .001 level.

HYPOTHESIS II Self-esteem is positively related to the degree of agreement between self concepts and occupational preferences.

The measure of self-esteem was the actual-ideal self concept discrepancy. Agreement between self concepts and occupational preferences was measured by r_1. It was predicted that agreement between actual and ideal self concepts was positively related to r_1.

A subject's self ratings were compared with ratings of his ideal self on the MRT. A summed difference score was computed by adding the differences along each independent construct dimension. These summed difference scores were converted to percentages to control for interindividual differences in the number of independent construct dimensions. Subjects were rank ordered from the smallest to the largest per cent discrepancy and from the highest to the lowest r_1 scores. A Spearman rho of .33 was computed between these two rank orders. Application of the t test indicates this correlation coefficient is significant at the .01 level.

A secondary analysis involved an inter-quarter comparison of r_1 scores for subjects sorted into quarters based on their per cent discrepancy scores. The r_1 scores in each quarter were compared with the r_1 scores for every other quarter. For each comparison the r_1 scores were ranked on the basis of the 40 subjects in the two quarters. The r_1 ranks were then totaled for each quarter and a difference between the two sums of r_1 ranks was obtained. Application of the Mann-Whitney U test indicated that the r_1 scores in the quarters with the smallest and next to smallest discrepancy scores were each significantly higher than the r_1 scores for the third and fourth quarters at the .01 level. However, there was no appreciable gain in the accuracy of r_1 scores from the second quarter to the first quarter or from the fourth quarter to the third quarter.

The results indicate that self-esteem is positively related to the degree of similarity between self concepts and occupational preferences, but the relationship between self-esteem and r_1 is not a linear one.

HYPOTHESIS III Cognitive complexity is positively related to the degree of similarity between self concepts and occupational preferences.

The measure of cognitive complexity was the number of independent construct dimensions (NICD) produced on the MRT. Subjects in the quarter having the largest NICD were defined as cognitively complex and subjects in the quarter producing the smallest NICD were defined as cognitively simple.

The standard deviation of the NICD was 2.91 with a range from 6 to 22, but only one subject produced under 12 NICD. In order to circumvent the problem of resolving ties on the NICD, 21 subjects were included in each of the extreme quarters. The analysis involved a comparison of the r_1 scores similar to the procedure used in testing the previous hypothesis. Application of the Mann-Whitney U test failed to reveal a significant difference in r_1 scores between subjects in the extreme quarters on the NICD.

One possible explanation for the negative results is a limitation of the operational measure of cognitive complexity. The NICD measures the number of dimensions used to differentiate one's environment, but does not take into consideration the degree of discrimination with which these dimensions are used. Bieri (1961) has developed another measure of cognitive complexity which utilizes the versatility of responses within a given number of construct dimensions. Counting the number of different intervals checked on the first ten independent construct dimensions approximates Bieri's method of scoring for differentiation in check patterns on the Kelly grid. A comparison was made of the number of different intervals checked for the quarters with the highest and lowest r_1 scores. The results again fail to demonstrate a significant relationship between this measure of cognitive complexity and r_1.

DISCUSSION

The exploratory nature of the study, both in terms of the methodology and the theoretical constructs examined, suggests caution in interpreting the results. Systematic research on the MRT is needed to refine the instrument and assess its merits for testing phenomenological constructs. As this project represented the initial effort to relate self-esteem and cognitive complexity to the relationship between self concepts and occupational preferences, further research is needed to replicate the present findings. The size and characteristics of the sample indicate limitations in generalizing about the results.

Two novel aspects of the methodology deserve attention. The principal difference between the MRT and the adjective check lists and Q sorts used previously is that the MRT allows a subject to develop his own list of construct dimensions rather than relying on the dimensions chosen by the creator of the test. The present procedure also provided a measure of how accurately one can predict occupational preferences from a sample of the self and occupational concepts, whereas previous work has concentrated on establishing a relationship between these phenomenological variables.

The median r_1 of .52 suggests that there is a substantial relationship between self concepts and occupational preferences for the average college student. The broad range of r_1, from 1.00 to $-.72$, indicates wide individual differences in the degree with which students find expression for their self concepts in occupational preferences.

Confirmation of the first hypothesis demonstrated that people prefer occupations perceived as congruent with their self concepts. The results provide a cross-validation of previously cited research. By comparing self ratings with ratings of two preferred and two nonpreferred occupations, the present study used a broader sample of the subjects' behavior in order to develop a more reliable criterion measure than previous studies, which limited their comparisons to one preferred and one nonpreferred occupation. The fact that this relationship has been demonstrated with a sample of high school students (Blocher and Schutz, 1962), female college students (Englander, 1960; Morrison, 1962), and with the present sample of male liberal arts students suggests the results are applicable to the general population of adolescent and post-adolescent youth.

Results for the second hypothesis indicate that self-esteem is positively related to r_1. The discrepancy index accounted for 10 per cent of the variance in r_1 scores. Results of the interquarter comparison lead one to inquire why increments within the top and bottom halves on the discrepancy index are not associated with the expected changes in r_1.

The results are generally consistent with studies using a normal population to examine the relationship between the discrepancy index and criteria of personal adjustment and social acceptance. Researchers in these areas have tended to find support for their hypotheses, but the correlations tend to be low. Studies have demonstrated that subjects in the quarter with the least discrepancy tend to have a rigid, defensive orientation, but these subjects were generally not rated as better adjusted than subjects in the second quarter (Wylie, 1961). One explanation for the lack of more convincing results is that the discrepancy index does not provide a precise measure of self-esteem. Initial efforts to design a better measure of self-esteem by controlling for the social desirability factor with a procedure adopted from Edwards (1957) proved to be unsuccessful with the MRT.

A further analysis examined subjects in the quarter with the widest discrepancy. The accuracy of predicting the expressed hierarchy from self concepts was compared to the accuracy of predicting the expressed hierarchy from the ideal self concepts. For 14 of the 20 subjects the ideal self concepts provided a more accurate prediction of the expressed hierarchy. These findings suggest a tendency for people with low self-esteem to prefer occupations perceived as congruent with their ideal self concepts rather than occupations perceived as congruent with their self concepts.

The results are consistent with the thesis that people who are dissatisfied with themselves will also be dissatisfied with occupations that represent a translation of their self concepts. Further, there was some evidence to suggest that people with personal dissatisfaction are motivated to find expression for their ideal self concepts rather than their self concepts in formulating occupational preferences.

The lack of relationship between two measures of cognitive complexity and r_1 suggests that cognitive complexity is not a promising construct for identifying individual differences in r_1. One explanation for the failure to obtain the expected results is a limitation in the criterion measure. The r_1 coefficient fails to take account of the absolute number of dimensions along which a person finds expression for his self concepts. For example, the subject using 6 independent dimensions obtained as high an r_1 score as a subject using 20 independent dimensions, although it is presumed that the latter subject was considering many more aspects of himself and the occupations in formulating his preferences. One implication of the present results is that the cognitively complex person and the cognitively simple person have approximately the same relative accuracy in utilizing their self concept in formulating occupational preferences, but the cognitively complex person is considering more variables in evaluating himself and various occupations. Further research is needed to ascertain whether a consideration of more dimensions in arriving at one's choices is related to such indices of voca-

tional behavior as satisfaction with occupational choice or an objective measure of wisdom of choice.

REFERENCES

Bieri, J. Cognitive complexity-simplicity and predictive behavior. *J. abnorm. soc. Psychol.*, 1955, *51*, 263–268.

Bieri, J. Complexity-simplicity as a personality variable in cognitive and preferential behavior. In D. W. Fiske, and S. R. Maddi, (Eds.), *Functions of varied experience.* Homewood, Ill.: Dorsey Press, 1961, Pp. 355–379.

Bieri, J., and Blacker, E. The generality of cognitive complexity in the perception of people and inkblots. *J. abnorm. soc. Psychol.*, 1956, *53*, 112–117.

Blocher, D. H., and Schutz, R. A. Relationships among self-descriptions, occupational stereotypes, and vocational preferences. *J. counsel. Psychol.*, 1961, *8*, 314–317.

Brophy, A. L. Self, role, and satisfaction. *Genet. Psychol. Monogr.*, 1959, *59*, 263–308.

Crowne, D. P., and Stephens, M. W. Self-acceptance and self-evaluative behavior: a critique of methodology. *Psychol. Bull.*, 1961, *58*, 104–121.

Edwards, A. L. *The social desirability variable in personality assessment and research.* New York: Dryden Press, 1957.

Englander, M. A psychological analysis of vocational choice: teaching. *J. counsel. Psychol.*, 1960, *7*, 257–264.

Higgins, J. C. Cognitive complexity and probability preferences. Unpublished manuscript, Univer. Chicago, 1959.

Kelly, G. A. *The psychology of personal constructs.* Vol. I. New York: Norton, 1955.

Morrison, R. L. Self concept implementation in occupational choice. *J. counsel. Psychol.*, 1962, *9*, 255–260.

National Opinion Research Center. Final report of a special opinion survey among Americans 14 and over. Chicago: Univer. Chicago, 1947. (mimeographed)

Oppenheimer, E. A. A self-concept approach to predicting occupational preferences. Unpublished doctoral dissertation, Teachers Coll., Columbia Univer., 1964.

Plotnick, H. L. The relation between selected personality characteristics of social work students and accuracy in predicting the behavior of clients. Unpublished doctoral dissertation, Columbia Univer. School of Social Work, 1961.

Roe, Anne. *The psychology of occupations*. New York: John Wiley, 1956.

Shiner, E. V. Self concept and change of occupation. Unpublished doctoral project, Teachers Coll., Columbia Univer., 1963.

Siegal, S. *Nonparametric statistics for the behavioral sciences*. New York: McGraw-Hill, 1956.

Starishevsky, R., Matlin, N., and Oppenheimer, E. *The Modified Repertory Test.* New York: Teachers Coll., Columbia Univer., 1961. (mimeographed)

Strong, E. K. *The Strong Vocational Interest Blank*. Palo Alto, Calif.: Consulting Psychologists Press, 1946.

Super, D. E. Vocational adjustment: implementing a self concept. *Occupations*, 1951, *30*, 88–92.

Super, D. E., Starishevsky, R., Matlin, W., and Jordaan, J. P. *Career development: self-concept theory*. New York: College Entrance Examination Board, 1963.

Tageson, C. F. *The relationship of self perceptions to realism of vocational preference*. Washington, D.C.: Catholic Univer. of America Press, 1960.

Wylie, Ruth C. *The self concept*. Lincoln, Neb.: Univer. of Nebraska Press, 1961.

Self-Esteem Variable
in Vocational Choice

ABRAHAM K. KORMAN, *University of Oregon*

Current vocational choice theory has as its general framework the supposition that the choosing of an occupation should be viewed within context of the general personality development of the individual as he comes to view himself and the world around him (Holland, 1963; Siegelman and Peck, 1960; Super, 1953). More particularly, it postulates that the choosing of a certain set of social roles, such as that involved in vocational choice, and the rejecting of others is dependent on the characteristics which one

Reprinted with the permission of author and publisher from the article of the same title, in *Journal of Applied Psychology*, 1966, *50*, 479–486.

attributes to oneself, on either a conscious or unconscious level, and the characteristics which are attributed to performance in the various social roles. The choice is then made on the basis of the extent to which an individual "sees himself in the role" or the role as befitting himself.

Despite the support which has been provided this theory in a number of studies (Englander, 1960; Segal, 1961; Siegelman and Peck, 1960), many writers have pointed out that occupations are chosen on other bases besides that of implementation of a "self-concept," with these other factors quite often working against self-implementation. As Paterson (1962), among others, has said, both the level and direction of vocational aspiration may, to a great extent, be determined by the hopes and aspirations of parents, wives, and friends, with these perceptions and motives of others frequently at variance with those of the individual making the vocational choice.

The purpose of this paper is to report two studies designed to test several predictions relevant to the above question. These hypotheses are derived from a "balance-theoretical" framework, and are, in addition, relevant to the "moderator variable" concept discussed by Saunders (1956) and Ghiselli (1963a), among others. The theoretical approach proposed stems from the assumption that:

All other things being equal, individuals will engage in those behavioral roles which will maximize their sense of cognitive balance or consistency.

If we then define self-esteem, following Gelfand (1962), as:

A person's characteristic evaluation of himself and what he thinks of himself as an individual; low self-esteem is characterized by a sense of personal inadequacy and an inability to achieve need satisfaction in the past; high self-esteem is defined by a sense of personal adequacy and a sense of having achieved need satisfaction in the past;

Then the following general hypothesis seems to be a logical one:

Individuals high in self-esteem are likely to choose those occupations which they perceive to be most likely to fulfill their specific needs and to be in keeping with their self-perceived characteristics. Such a choice would be in balance with their cognition of themselves as need-satisfying individuals, and they are, thus more likely to reject those influences, social or otherwise, which might minimize the achievement of such balance.

Individuals low in self-esteem are less likely to choose those occupations which they perceive to be most likely to fulfill their specific needs and to be in keeping with their self-perceived

characteristics. Such a choice of a "nonself-appropriate" role would be more in keeping with their cognition of themselves as nonneed-satisfying individuals, and they would then be more likely to accept those influences, social or otherwise, which would maximize the probability of their entering an occupation which they would perceive as "nonself-appropriate."

In essence, these two hypotheses propose that an individual's self-esteem acts as a "moderator variable" on the extent to which his self-perceived needs are predictive of his occupational choice. For those high on self-esteem, the prediction is that such self-perceptions are highly predictive of eventual occupational choice, whereas, according to the hypothesis, such predictions break down for those low on this variable.

The research to be reported here derives from these considerations.

STUDY I

There is now clear evidence that occupations are perceived as calling for distinct behavioral and attitudinal patterns, and that such perceptions are invariant phenomena across different segments of some college-student populations (O'Dowd and Beardslee, 1960). As a result, from these studies of occupational stereotypes, one is provided with a very clear rationale for predicting that people with different self-perceived characteristics would be inclined to enter different occupations, as long as that occupation was being chosen on the basis of "self-implementation." To the extent, however, that choices were not being made on this basis, then there would be no reason to predict differences between people choosing different occupations from a knowledge of occupational stereotypes. Accordingly, the following specific predictions were made:

HYPOTHESIS 1   Since various occupations are thought of and perceived as differing in the extent to which they require interaction with other people and the extent to which social capability is required, those individuals choosing occupations which require a great deal of this behavior who have high self-esteem should have a greater degree of interaction-orientation than those low in self-esteem. The reverse relationship between self-esteem and interaction-orientation should occur for those choosing occupations which are perceived to require a small amount of interaction with others. These relationships, then, should result in the following:

HYPOTHESIS 1A For individuals high in self-esteem, those who have chosen a sales career should have a greater degree of "interaction-orientation" than those choosing an accounting career;

HYPOTHESIS 1B For individuals high in self-esteem, those who have chosen a sales career should have a greater degree of "interaction-orientation" than those choosing a career in production management;

HYPOTHESIS 1C For individuals low in self-esteem, there should be no difference in "interaction-orientation" between those choosing sales careers and those choosing accounting careers;

HYPOTHESIS 1D For individuals low in self-esteem, there should be no differences in "interaction-orientation" between those choosing sales careers and those choosing careers in production management.

HYPOTHESIS 2 It is quite clear that the salesman and the accountant play different roles in the world of work and are perceived as such (O'Dowd and Beardslee, 1960), with a major difference being in the degree of "structure" required in the work role. For example, the salesman can be conceived of as being in a dynamic ever-changing interaction with the customer where constraints are few and where a great premium is placed on being able to strike off in new directions and taking the initiative in such interchange. On the other hand, for the accountant, "regularity" and "structure" seem to be the keynote. He has a well-defined job with a given set of duties and responsibilities which are relatively routinized in nature. The "flux" of the sales situation is lacking.

Thus, the following predictions appear to be reasonable:

HYPOTHESIS 2A For individuals high in self-esteem, those choosing sales occupations will tend to perceive themselves in a manner which is descriptive of the individual with a high degree of "Initiative" while those entering the accounting field will tend to perceive themselves in a manner which is descriptive of the individual who is low on "Initiative";

HYPOTHESIS 2B For individuals low in self-esteem, there will be no differences between those choosing sales occupations and those choosing the accounting field insofar as their self-perceptions are descriptive of degree of "Initiative";

HYPOTHESIS 2C For individuals high in self-esteem, those choosing sales occupations will describe themselves as having a greater need for "Job Freedom" than those choosing the accounting area;

HYPOTHESIS 2D For individuals low in self-esteem, there will be no differences between those choosing sales occupations and those choosing accounting in terms of their self perceived need for "Job Freedom."

No hypotheses were offered for the production-manager samples in relation to "Job Freedom" and "Initiative" since these variables do not seem to be dominant parts of the production-manager stereotype.

METHOD

SUBJECTS Since the samples of each hypothesis varied, the subjects (*S*s) will be described separately below. In all cases, however, the samples consisted of male juniors and seniors taken from two upper-division schools of business administration in two large state universities in a far western state. Since there was no logical reason to separate the two, and since preliminary tests indicated no empirical basis, the data were combined from the two schools. Preliminary tests also indicated that there were no differences between any of the groups to be analyzed in grades or proportion of seniors as opposed to juniors.

By this type of sample limitation, several important variables could be controlled for and thus make the occupational choice measurement (to be described below) a highly meaningful one. The reason for this is that this type of sample limits the analysis to those individuals who have, for the most part, both the intellectual and financial resources to enable them to enter the occupation of their choice and who have also gone through the career and "major sampling" activities of the first 2 years of college life. On the other hand, the influence of occupational role performance is, of course, usually not present since they are still only college students. Finally, there is good evidence that choices at this state are highly predictive of later occupational membership (Schletzer, 1963).

The samples for the separate hypotheses are given in Table 1. In general, the procedure used for each hypothesis was to split each "occupational" group sample so that the "high self-esteem" group was defined by approximately the top one third of scores on "self-esteem" while the bottom two thirds defined the "low self-esteem group." In one sample, the pattern of scores seemed to justify a split somewhat closer to the median.

All measuring instruments were administered during the course of normal class-sessions, and there is no reason to think that full cooperation was not obtained.

MEASURING INSTRUMENTS   1. The occupational choice of the student was determined by means of a 3-part questionnaire. In the

TABLE 1

Samples for the Separate Hypotheses

Hypoth-esis	Size	Type	Occupational group
1A	10	High Self-Esteem	Sales
1A	15	High Self-Esteem	Accounting
1B	10	High Self-Esteem	Sales
1B	13	High Self-Esteem	Production managers
1C	23	Low Self-Esteem	Sales
1C	28	Low Self-Esteem	Accounting
1D	23	Low Self-Esteem	Sales
1D	15	Low Self-Esteem	Production managers
2A	20	High Self-Esteem	Sales
2A	19	High Self-Esteem	Accounting
2B	31	Low Self-Esteem	Sales
2B	31	Low Self-Esteem	Accounting
2C	9	High Self-Esteem	Sales
2C	13	High Self-Esteem	Accounting
2D	21	Low Self-Esteem	Sales
2D	20	Low Self-Esteem	Accounting

first two parts of the form, the student was asked first if he was interested in the business world as a career, and, second, if the answer was "Yes," whether he had also decided on a business specialty. The third part of the questionnaire asked if the individual had received any counseling in the vocational area from a university or college counseling center. This last part was used as a "control," and all individuals that had received such assistance were eliminated from the analysis.

The concurrent validity of the questionnaire was checked in two separate ways. Of 29 *S*s indicating a specific business specialty on their registration forms (they do not have to indicate any), 28 indicated the same area on the questionnaire. Second, a comparison between questionnaire response and stated departmental major indicated a similar degree of correspondence (44 of 45).

The test-retest reliability of the classification system was checked by administering the questionnaire to students twice over a

6-week period. Of the 47 respondents, 96% were classified in the same manner for the two administrations.

2. "Self-Esteem" was measured by the self-assurance scale of the Ghiselli Self-Description Inventory. This 31-item forced-choice adjective-pair scale is described by Ghiselli as measuring

the extent to which the individual perceives himself as being effective in dealing with the problems that confront him. There are those persons who see themselves being sound in judgment and able to cope with almost any situation, whereas others think of themselves as being slow to grasp things, making many mistakes, and being generally inept [p. 9].

"Initiative" was measured by the scale of the same name in the Ghiselli Self-Description Inventory. This scale consists of 17 forced-choice adjective pairs, with a high score indicating a person who is an inaugurator or originator who opens new fields and conceives of novel ways of doing things.

Evidence for the construct validity of these scales is available in Ghiselli (1963b)[1]

3. "Interaction-Orientation" was measured by the scale of the same name in the Bass Orientation Inventory (Bass, 1962). Evidence for the construct validity of this scale, which consists of 27 forced-choice triads, is provided in Bass.

4. "Need for Job-Freedom" was measured by the scale of the same name in the Crites Vocation Reaction Survey. Evidence for the construct validity of this scale, which consists of 10 Likert-type statements, is provided in Crites (1963).

RESULTS

HYPOTHESES 1A, 1B, 1C, 1D The results for these hypotheses are summarized in Table 2. Since all research hypotheses are specifically directional in nature, one-tail significance tests are utilized and so reported in both this and the following sections.

TABLE 2

Self-Perceived Interaction-Orientation as a Function of Occupational Choice and Self-Esteem

Group	N	M	SD	t
Hypothesis 1A				
High accountants	15	19.9	6.6	1.75*
High sales	10	24.7	7.2	
Hypothesis 1B				
High production managers	13	20.1	6.2	1.68*
High sales	10	24.7	7.2	
Hypothesis 1C				
Low accountants	28	21.8	7.6	.51
Low sales	23	22.7	4.1	
Hypothesis 1D				
Low production managers	15	23.7	4.8	.73
Low sales	23	22.7	4.1	

*$p < .05$.

These results indicate, in brief, that all hypotheses were supported in that differences in self-perceived personality characteristics occur only in the high self-esteem groups but do not occur for the low self-esteem groups.

HYPOTHESES 2A, 2B The results for these hypotheses are summarized in Table 3. They point to a similar conclusion to that of the previous, in that differences in self-perceived personality characteristics as a

TABLE 3

Self-Perceived Initiative as a Function of Self-Esteem and Occupational Choice

Group	N	M	SD	t
Hypothesis 2A				
High sales	20	35.7	5.4	2.41*
High accounting	19	31.6	5.1	
Hypothesis 2B				
Low sales	31	26.2	6.4	2.89
Low accounting	31	30.4	4.8	

*$p < .01$.

function of occupational choice predicted from occupational stereotypes occur only for high self-esteem individuals. On the other hand, such a prediction is poor for the low self-esteem individuals.

TABLE 4

Self-Perceived Need for Job Freedom as a Function of Self-Esteem and Occupational Choice

Group	N	M	SD	t
Hypothesis 2C				
High sales	9	11.78	3.45	2.34*
High accountants	13	8.0	4.04	
Hypothesis 2D				
Low sales	21	7.71	3.52	1.00
Low accountants	20	9.04	4.32	

*$p > .01$.

HYPOTHESES 2C, 2D The results for these hypotheses are given in Table 4 and similar conclusions are warranted. Occupational stereotypes and self-perceived personality characteristics of those individuals choosing the occupation are highly related, but only for high self-esteem individuals. Such relationships do not seem to occur for those low in self-esteem.

STUDY II

Although the results from the first study were highly consistent with the theoretical framework proposed, the possibility remains that the obtained results were due not to the hypothesized process but perhaps could be explained more parsimoniously by postulating different occupational perceptions by the individuals involved. That is, it could be proposed that low self-esteem people differ somewhat from high self-esteem people in their perceptions of occupations and this would explain the results obtained.

While such an explanation did not seem likely because of the high invariancy of occupational perceptions among college students, it was felt that such a possibility

should at least be explored, and controlled more directly rather than through the assumption of the invariancy of occupational stereotypes; thus, a second study was undertaken which would allow a more direct control of the match between occupational and self-perception. Hence, if the discrepancy between "desired" and "expected" continued to be greater for the low self-esteem than for the high self-esteem for relevant needs, the results of the first study will receive even more substantial support since the measure of "expected need satisfactions" is more unique to the individual in this case, and is not a common stereotype to which all may not subscribe.

The procedure that was followed, as a result, in this second study was to ask each individual who had made an occupational choice, using the same criterion as in the first study, to:

1. Rate the importance of each of several needs to himself;
2. Rate the probability of his chosen occupation being able to satisfy each of these same needs.

It was predicted that these ratings would show the following characteristics:

HYPOTHESIS 1 For highly important needs, the probability that the chosen occupation would satisfy these needs would be greater for those with high self-esteem than for those with low self-esteem.

HYPOTHESIS 2 For unimportant needs, the probability that the chosen occupation would satisfy these needs would be the same for those with high self-esteem and those with low self-esteem.

Hypothesis 1 is designed as a direct test of the extent to which self-expressed high needs are predictive of occupational choice for high self-esteem individuals, but not those of low self-esteem. Hypothesis 2 provides a control on the results of the first prediction in that, if upheld, it would indicate that the high self-esteem person sees the future role not just in terms of a "set" to see everything as more satisfying, but rather as more satisfying just in relation to oneself and one's own self-perceived needs.

METHOD

SUBJECTS Three separate samples, independent of those from the first study, and independent from each other, were utilized in this analysis. Sample 1 consisted of 37 students in a school of business administration at a far western state university. Sample 2 consisted of 39 lower-division students at a state college in a far western city. Sample 3 consisted of 26 upper-division students at a large mid-Atlantic state university. All students in Samples 1 and 3 were male, while 7 of the 39 in Sample 2 were female.

In addition to the occupational choice questionnaire previously discussed, and Ghiselli's Self-Description Inventory, each sample was measured as follows:

MEASURING INSTRUMENTS 1. Sample 1 was administered the Crites Vocation Reaction Survey twice, once under normal instructions of self-description and once when they were asked to describe the degree to which each characteristic was typical of their chosen occupation. This instrument provides a measure of seven vocational needs derived from factor-analytic research in this area (Crites, 1963), with these being Material Security, Job Freedom, Structure, System, Personal Status, Behavior Control, and Social Service.

The order of presentation, approximately 2 weeks apart, was reversed for one half of the group, but no order effect showed up on preliminary analysis.

2. Sample 2 was administered the Minnesota Importance Questionnaire (Weiss, Dawis, Englander, and Lofquist, 1964) twice under similar instructions and procedure to those of Sample 1.

The Minnesota Importance Questionnaire provides a rating of the importance of 20 vocationally relevant needs to an individ-

ual, and utilizes a Likert-type format. The 20 scales are Ability Utilization, Achievement, Activity, Advancement, Authority, Company Policies and Practices, Compensation, Co-Workers, Creativity, Independence, Moral Values, Recognition, Responsibility, Security, Social Service, Social Status, Supervision — Technical, Variety, and Working Conditions. It is a 100-item questionnaire, with 5 items devoted to each scale. The reliabilities, using the Hoyt analysis-of-variance procedure, of each scale are quite high, with only 2 below .80.

Evidence concerning the construct validity of this instrument is provided in Weiss et al. (1964).

3. Sample 3 was administered the Crites Vocation Reaction Survey under the same conditions and procedures as the first two samples.

METHOD OF ANALYSIS The following procedures were used in the data analysis:

1. For Samples 1 and 3, the two most important and least important needs were determined for each person on the Crites Vocation Survey. (In the few cases of ties, the three most/least important needs were used.) A total "high" and "low" need score was then computed for each individual. From this, the comparable score of satisfaction expectancy for these needs in the chosen occupation was compared, and discrepancy determined between "high needs and expectancy of satisfaction" and "low needs and expectancy of satisfaction" for each individual. This discrepancy score was computed as follows:

(*a*) For high needs:
Discrepancy = Need Score − Expected Satisfaction Score

(*b*) For low needs:
Discrepancy = Expected Satisfaction Score − Needs Score

Despite "ceiling" problems for the "high needs" analysis, there were two cases where expected satisfaction was greater than needs.

For the "low needs" analysis, there were two cases, despite the "basement effect," where the expected satisfaction was less than the need score. These were added in algebraically in the computations for the "low needs" group, but were treated as zero discrepancy for the "high needs" analysis, since any other treatment would lead to difficulties in interpretation.

2. For Sample 2, a similar procedure was followed as described above, except that the top four and bottom four needs were utilized from the more extensive Minnesota Importance Questionnaire. The few cases of ties were treated in a similar fashion.

RESULTS

The results of the investigation are summarized in Table 5. They indicate that all

TABLE 5

Discrepancies between Self-Perceived Needs and Expectancy of Need-Satisfaction as a Function of Self-Esteem

Sample	Important needs		Unimportant needs	
	High self-esteem	Low self-esteem	High self-esteem	Low self-esteem
1				
M	1.27	2.24	.72	.92
SD	1.3	1.6	.62	.94
N	13	24	13	24
t	1.82*	1.82*	.68	.68
2				
M	1.00	2.02	3.95	2.64
SD	1.2	1.7	3.4	2.4
N	14	25	14	25
t	1.96*	1.96*	1.41	1.41
3				
M	2.94	4.24	1.23	.79
SD	1.9	2.1	1.4	1.2
N	13	13	13	13
t	1.80*	1.80*	.80	.80

*$p < .05$, one-tailed.

hypotheses are supported as predicted for all samples. For important needs, the expectancy of satisfaction in the chosen occupation is significantly greater for those with high self-esteem than for those with low self-esteem. The difference does not appear for those needs which are self-perceived as unimportant.

DISCUSSION

The results of this investigation support quite strongly the prediction that "self-esteem" operates as a moderator variable in the process of vocational choice in that those who are high on this variable use their self-perceived needs differently from those who think relatively poorly of themselves. That is, for those high in self-esteem their self-perceived needs are those that have been satisfied in the past and it is, therefore, appropriate and consistent for the individual to seek out those roles where they will be satisfied in the future. On the other hand, for the individual low on self-esteem, such motivation may appear not to exist. His self-perceived needs have not been satisfied in the past and he has, more likely, become both more familiar with nonneed-satisfying situations and more accepting of them. To put it in our previous framework, such situations are more "consistent" for him than for the high self-esteem individual. This conclusion is solidified even further when we look at the significant results of Hypothesis 2B (Table 3) and the trends of Hypotheses 1D (Table 2) and 2D (Table 4). In these cases, the low self-esteem individuals are *opposite* to what would be predicted from the occupational stereotype, a situation which certainly provides negative evidence for a simple "match self to occupational stereotype" process in vocational choice. In essence, then, these results seem to support in a realistic, highly important life-choice situation, the findings of a number of laboratory investigations that individuals of low self-esteem are more likely to seek less reward for a similar task than individuals of high self-esteem (Pepitone, 1964, Ch. 2), and to rate information which confirms their low self-esteem more favorably than information which tells them they are better than low-esteem tells them they are (Wilson, 1965). Thus, while the results reported here are correlational in nature, they are supported by a number of experimental laboratory investigations of more circumscribed choice situations.

A number of implications for further research suggest themselves also. For example, since self-perception of abilities can also be measured and conceived of as part of the self-percept, would this mean that individuals of low self-esteem are more likely to accept those social roles (e.g., jobs, student roles, etc.) where they believe they do not have high abilities and less likely to wind up in those roles where they believe they do? If such self-perceived abilities are related to actual abilities, and at least a moderate relationship does exist (Arsenian, 1942), does this mean that such individuals guarantee themselves failures by the manner of their choice-making? In other words, does "self-esteem" operate as a moderator here also in that persons with a high sense of personal adequacy search for a situation where they will be adequate, that is, where they believe they have high abilities, whereas low self-esteem people are more likely to be accepting of a situation where they believe they are likely to be inadequate, that is, where they believe they do not have high abilities? Research is needed of both a correlational and experimental nature.

Finally, it also seems to be quite necessary that the generality of such choice-making patterns be determined. Do individuals of low self-esteem choose all roles in a similar manner, or are the concept and the postulated relationships too general in nature? Must we conceive of a "vocational self" choosing a "vocational role," a "marital self" choosing a "marital role," etc.? These questions are, of course, not new but their relevance remains.

[1]A minor problem which develops here is that the "Initiative" scale has an 8-item overlap with the Self-Assurance Scale (6 items scored in the same direction, and 2 opposite), thus tending to produce positive correlations between these scales. While these items could have been eliminated from the scoring key (and thus effectively partialed out), this would have resulted in the disadvantage of reducing the reliability of the scales. The use of the analysis of covariance as a method of correction was also rejected after an examination of the regression lines indicated the hypothesis of equality could not be accepted. Hence, the procedure that was followed was to score the data in a raw-score fashion, thus making it unlikely that there would be a negative correlation between Initiative and Self-Esteem for the Accountant group, such as was predicted for this group between (*a*) Interaction-Orientation and Self-Esteem and (*b*) Need for Job-Freedom and Self-Esteem. To the extent, however, that among the Accountant group there will be no difference on "Initiative" between those high and low in Self-Esteem, this will support the author's hypothesis since this will indicate that proportionately more low "initiative" people fall into the high Self-Esteem group than the low Self-Esteem group.

Analogous reasoning would hold in the case of those occupations where the correlation between initiative and self-esteem was predicted to be positive.

REFERENCES

Arsenian, S. Own estimate and objective achievement. *Journal of Educational Psychology*, 1942, *33*, 291–302.

Bass, B. *The Orientation Inventory*. Manual. Palo Alto: Consulting Psychologists Press, 1962.

Crites, J. O. Vocational interest in relation to vocational motivation. *Journal of Educational Psychology*, 1963, *54*, 277–285.

Englander, M. A psychological analysis of vocational choice: Teaching. *Journal of Counseling Psychology*, 1960, *7*, 257–2641

Gelfand, D. M. The influence of self-esteem on rate of verbal conditioning and social matching behavior. *Journal of Abnormal and Social Psychology*, 1962, *65*, 259–265.

Ghiselli, E. E. Moderating effect and differential reliability and validity. *Journal of Applied Psychology*, 1963, *47*, 81–86. (a)
———. The validity of management traits related to occupational level. *Personnel Psychology*, 1963 *16* 109–113. (b)

Holland, J. L. Explorations of a theory of vocational choice and achievement: II. A four-year prediction study. *Psychological Reports*, 1963, *12*, 547–594.

O'Dowd, D. O., and Beardslee, D. C. *College student images of a selected group of professions and occupations.* Cooperative Research Project No. 562 (8142), April 1960.

Paterson, D. G. Values and interests in vocational guidance. In *Industrial and Business Psychology*. Proceedings of the Fourteenth International Congress of Applied Psychology, 1962, Pp. 118–125.

Pepitone, A. *Attraction and hostility.* New York: Atherton, 1964.

Saunders, D. J. Moderator variables in prediction. *Educational and Psychological Measurement*, 1956, *16*, 209–222.

Schletzer, U. *A study of the predictive effectiveness of the Strong Vocational Interest Blank for job satisfaction.* Unpublished doctoral dissertation, University of Minnesota, 1963.

Segal, S. A psychoanalytic analysis of personality factors in vocational choice. *Journal of Counseling Psychology*, 1961, *8*, 202–210.

Siegelman, M., and Peck, R. F. Personality patterns related to occupation rates. *Genetic Psychology Monographs*, 1960, *61*, 291–349.

Super, D. E. A theory of vocational development. *American Psychologist*, 1953, *8*, 185–190.

Weiss, D. J., Dawis, R. V., Englander, G. W., and Lofquist, L. H. *The measurement of vocational needs.* Minnesota Studies in Vocational Rehabilitation, Bulletin 39, April 1964.

Wilson, D. Ability evaluation, post-decision dissonance and co-worker attractiveness. *Journal of Personality and Social Psychology*, 1965, *1*, 486–489.

OTHER RELEVANT ARTICLES

Other papers relevant to the self-concept or self-expression point of view include:

Bordin, E. S., A theory of vocational interests as dynamic phenomena. *Educational and Psychological Measurement*, 1943, *3*, 49–65.

Field, F. W., D. D. Kehas, and D. V. Tiedeman. The self-concept in career development: A construct in transition. *Personnel and Guidance Journal*, 1963, *41*, 767–771.

Galinsky, M. D. and Irene Fast. Vocational choice as a focus of the identity search. *Journal of Counseling Psychology*, 1966, *13*, 89–92.

Stefflre, B. Vocational development: Ten propositions in search of a theory. *Personnel and Guidance Journal*, 1966, *44*, 611–616.

A number of papers reporting tests of Super's proposition other than those included in this chapter have appeared. Some of them are:

Anderson, T. B. and L. C. Olsen. Congruence of self and ideal self and occupational choices. *Personnel and Guidance Journal*, 1965, *44*, 171–176.

Blocher, D. H., and R. A. Schutz. Relationships among self-descriptions, occupational stereotypes and vocational preferences. *Journal of Counseling Psychology*, 1961, *8*, 314–317.

Bordin, E. S. and E. H. Wilson. Change of interests as a function of shift in curricular orientation. *Educational and Psychological Measurement*. 1953, *13*, 297–308.

Brophy, A. L. Self, role and satisfaction. *Genetic Psychology Monographs*, 1959, *59*, 263–308.

Englander, M. E. A psychological anlaysis of voctional choice: teaching. *Journal of Counseling Psychology*, 1960, *7*, 257–264.

————. Q-Sort: A means to explore vocational choice. *Educational and Psychological Measurement*, 1961, *21*, 597–605.

Grigg, A. Occupational choice as crystallized self-concept. *Journal of Counseling Psychology*, 1961, *8*, 217–223.

Hay, J. E. Self-ideal congruence among engineering managers, *Personnel and Guidance Journal*, 1966, *44*, 1084–1088.

Hunt, R. A. Self and other semantic concepts in relation to choice of a vocation. *Journal of Applied Psychology*, 1967, *51*, 242–246.

James, F. Occupational choice and attitude change. *Journal of Counseling Psychology*, 1965, *12*, 311–315.

Kibrick, Anne, and D. V. Tiedeman. Conception of self and perception of role in schools of nursing. *Journal of Counseling Psychology*, 1961, *8*, 62–69.

Korman, A. K. Self-esteem as a moderator of the relationship between self-perception abilities and vocational choice. *Journal of Applied Psychology*, 1967, *51*, 65–67.

Morrison, R. Self-concept implementation in occupational choice. *Journal of Counseling Psychology*, 1962, *9*, 255–260.

Norrell, Gwen, and H. Grater. Interest awareness as an aspect of self-awareness. *Journal of Counseling Psychology*, 1960, *7*, 284–292.

Schutz, R. A., and D. H. Blocher. Self-concepts and stereotypes of vocational preferences. *Vocational Guidance Quarterly*, 1960, *9*, 241–244.

Stephenson, R. R. Occupational choice as crystallized self-concept. *Journal of Counseling Psychology*, 1961, *8*, 211–216.

Tageson, C. F. *The relationship of self-perceptions to the realism of vocational preference*. Washington, D.C.: Catholic University of America Press, 1960.

White, Becky. The relationship of self-concepts and parental identification in women's vocational interests. *Journal of Counseling Psychology*, 1959, *6*, 202–206.

Childhood Experiences
as Occupational Determinants

6

In this chapter, theory and evidence will be presented to point out that the factors which influence, even determine, occupations and careers are either the product of, or actually are early childhood experiences, especially with parental relationships.

The nucleus of the material is a theory developed by Anne Roe. It should be noted carefully that Roe has asserted in her theory that occupational interests are formed within the fabric of the interaction of child and parent, and that the kinds of interactions may be meaningfully categorized. But Roe is not the only theorist to enunciate this general concept. Several other investigators have examined the relationship of childhood experiences to later occupation without so highly developed a theoretical framework within which to work.

One theoretical school is confident of the determining role of early experiences, but chooses the mode of psychoanalytic thought to explain it. This frame of reference is presented separately in the next chapter. Assignment of an article to either chapter may seem arbitrary until the following distinction is understood: Roe's hypotheses concern personality patterns or needs which have been generated by the interaction between child and parents, while the psychoanalytic chapter is characterized by the central position given to sublimation and other defense mechanisms transforming infantile impulses, some instinctive, and some resulting from parental interaction, into vocational choices.

The reader of Roe's theory paper which introduces this chapter will note that she hypothesizes various climates of relationship between parent and child, which generate needs, attitudes and interests which will be given expression in adult life in many ways, including especially vocational choice.

The three articles which follow Roe's are reports of differing tests of this hypothesis. Powell examined data collected a number of years previously while the subjects were in college, and compared ratings of this data on Roe's constructs against their established occupations.

Switzer and his associates obtained students in only two contrasting majors, who stated that they had strong intentions of following through on their majors as occupations. Family atmosphere was assessed by the subjects' recall and perception of their parents in a specially designed questionnaire.

Green and Parker attempted to tap their subjects' perception of family interaction as it was occurring, by questioning seventh grade children. By this strategy, of course, the criterion was called into question, since the relationship of a choice expressed at this age is not perfectly equivalent with the occupation the chooser may attain.

In none of these studies was Roe's theoretical scheme substantially upheld. Partial support was obtained in all of them, but not so much that any synthesis of them could suppose that Roe has offered a fully valid theory.

Early Determinants
of Vocational Choice

ANNE ROE, *Vocational Consultant, Tucson, Arizona*

This paper suggests some hypotheses about the relationships between early experience and attitudes, abilities, interests, and other personality factors which affect the ultimate vocational selection of the individual. Although the writer has drawn heavily upon the general literature, as well as some of the psychoanalytical studies, upon studies of early interest patterns, of parent-child relations, and of personality differences related to parent attitudes and to birth order, data from individual studies are not quoted. This is a speculative paper, and there is little *direct* evidence for the hypotheses which are suggested. However, the writer does not know of any contradictory evidence and believes most of these

Reprinted with the permission of author and publisher from the article of the same title, in *Journal of Counseling Psychology*, 1957, 4, 212–217.

hypotheses would be relatively easy to check. In a paper of this length only an outline can be given.

These hypotheses have been developed with reference to the present United States culture, including the major variations due to gross socioeconomic subdivisions, but the author has not tried to consider alterations which might be introduced by minority positions of one sort or another. Differences between gross cultural subdivisions are primarily differences in percentages of incidence of types of behavior, rather than absolute differences in kind of behavior, and are analogous to the differences in incidence of different bloodgroups in different races. It is to be understood that these hypotheses are intended to indicate major trends, and that other variables not mentioned here can be expected to introduce modifications in specific instances.

Let us first consider some general hypotheses with regard to personality variables as these are expressed in behavior, and particularly in behavior of the sorts that psychologists concern themselves with, for example, intelligence, interests, and special abilities. Some of the individual variation in all of these is undoubtedly due to inheritance, to differences in genetic endowment, but of the extent and precise nature of these genetic differences we know almost nothing certainly. We not only know nothing about probable genetic differences in the strengths of basic needs or drives, but we have not even begun to consider this problem. Gross hereditary differences in such things as specific sensory capacities and the plasticity and complexity of the central nervous system must greatly affect behavior, but beyond these it is uncertain how far specifically genetic elements are primary factors.

In this connection the author offers five hypotheses.

HYPOTHESES ON RELATION OF EARLY EXPERIENCE TO VOCATIONAL CHOICE

1. *The hereditary bases for intelligence, special abilities, interests, attitudes, and other personality variables seem usually to be nonspecific.* There may be a genetic basis for some "factors" of intelligence or aptitudes, but on this there is no clear evidence. Sex, as genetically determined, also involves some differentiation of abilities. It is, nevertheless, probable that in most instances genetic elements limit the degree of development rather than directly determine the type of expression.

2. *The pattern of development of special abilities is primarily determined by the directions in which psychic energy comes to be expended involuntarily.* The statement applies also to interests, attitudes, and other personality variables. Please note the word *involuntarily*. It is intended to emphasize the fact that the things to which the individual gives auto-

matic attention are keys to his total behavior. The point will not be expanded here, but the relevance of these hypotheses to the relations between personality and perception is clear.

3. *These directions are determined in the first place by the patterning of early satisfactions and frustrations.* This is the developing pattern of need primacies or relative strengths. In the earliest years these are essentially unconscious, and they probably always retain a large unconscious element As noted before, we know nothing at all about genetic variability in basic needs, but it can be fairly assumed that it exists.

Maslow's hierarchical classification of needs is the most useful for focussing the present discussion (Table 1).

TABLE 1

Basic Needs (Maslow)

1. Physiological needs
2. Safety needs
3. Need for belongingness and love
4. Need for importance, respect, self-esteem, independence
5. Need for information
6. Need for understanding
7. Need for beauty
8. Need for self-actualization*

*The author would place this lower in the hierarchy or handle it as a more generalized need.

The hierarchical arrangement is important. Maslow's theory states that higher-order needs cannot appear until lower order needs are at least relatively well satisfied. It seems reasonable to assume that higher order needs are of later evolutionary development in man and some of them may not be well established in terms of species evolution. If this is so, it would follow that they would show greater variability within the species. Lower order needs, on the other hand, are essential for the maintenance of life, and this permits much less variability in their strength. Differences in the degree of variability of these needs are of significance for us, and it is particularly the higher needs with which we are concerned. It would also appear that there is some difference in the age at which these needs or drives may begin to function. By the time the healthy child is a few months old the first five are probably affecting his behavior, although in widely varying degree.

4. *The eventual pattern of psychic energies, in terms of attention directedness, is the major determinant of the field or fields to which the person will apply himself.* This is relevant not only to vocation, of course, but to the total life pattern of the individual. It determines what sort of special abilities and interests will be predominant.

5. *The intensity of these (primarily) unconscious needs, as well as their organization, is the major determinant of the degree of motivation as expressed in accomplishment.* This implies that all accomplishment is based on unconscious as well as on conscious needs, but it does not imply that these needs are necessarily neurotic. There is accomplishment which is a free expression of capacity, although this may be relatively rare. Accomplishment on this basis can generally be distinguished from accomplishment on other bases. The relevance of this hypothesis to eventual vocational performance is evident.

It may not be so evident how the patterns and intensities of these basic needs are affected in the first place by the early experiences of the child. The following three hypotheses are concerned with this problem.

6. *Needs satisfied routinely as they appear do not develop into unconscious motivators.* Intensity of the need is not a variable, since it is stated that the need is "satisfied." The fact that the satisfaction is gained routinely is important, and it implies the need to distinguish sharply between simple, direct, matter-of-fact need gratification and gratification with fuss and fanfare.

7. *Needs for which even minimum satisfaction is rarely achieved will, if higher order, become in* effect expunged, *or will, if lower order, prevent the appearance of higher order needs, and will become dominant and restricting motivators.* Lower order needs, of course, require some degree of satisfaction for the maintenance of life. The hypothesis would mean, e.g. that a child whose expressions of natural curiosity were thoroughly blocked, would cease to be curious. On the other hand, with less effective blocking, hypothesis 8 would apply.

8. *Needs, the satisfaction of which is delayed but eventually accomplished, will become unconscious motivators, depending largely upon the degree of satisfaction felt. This will depend, among other things, upon the strength of the basic need in the given individual, the length of time elapsing between arousal and satisfaction, and the values ascribed to the satisfaction of this need in the immediate environment.*

The last hypothesis is the most significant for this study. It must be understood that the forms in which need satisfaction will be ultimately sought, in adult life, may not be obviously related to the basic needs referred to in the hypothesis. All of the well-known mechanisms of displacement, projection, etc. may function here. The problem of tolerance of deferred gratification is linked to such experiences as are implied in this hypothesis.

PATTERNS OF EARLY EXPERIENCE WITH PARENTS

Let us turn now to variations in the early experiences of children, and in particular to differences in parental handling of children. We can consider only major variations here, and it must be understood that the classification used is an arbitrary one, intended to delimit, as usefully as possible, nodal areas in a series of essentially continuous distributions, Several levels of classification are suggested, overlapping variously. Major behavioral variations are presented in outline form below, and a figure shows these, together with their relation to basically warm and cold attitudes of parents, and their relation to the outcome in the child in terms of his orientation with regard to persons.

The specific behaviors of the parents are of less importance than their attitudes towards the child. It is impossible here to discuss the relative effect of maternal and paternal attitudes, of similarities or differences in them. The classification used here refers to the dominant pattern in the home. whether shown by one or both parents. The major subdivisions refer to the child's position in the family emotional structure: as the center of attention, as avoided, or as accepted.

A. Emotional Concentration on the Child

This ranges between the extreme of overprotection to that of overdemandingness. Perhaps a sort of mean between these two is the quite typical anxiety of parents over a first child, anxiety which, in the same parents, may be much alleviated for the second child, with resulting considerable differences in the personality pictures of the two children.

1. *Overprotection.* The parent babies the child, encourages its dependence and restricts exploratory behavior. There is often concentration upon physical characteristics and real or fancied "talents" of the child. The parents maintain primary emotional ties with the child.

2. *Overdemanding.* The parents make heavy demands upon the child in terms of perfection of performance and usually institute quite severe training. In later years they may push the child to high achievement in school and work. In somewhat milder forms we may have the sort of family status "noblesse oblige" pattern, in which development of skills is encouraged but the pattern of skills is a prescribed one. This is very typical of upper class families, with emphasis upon development of conceptual as opposed

to motor skills. Severer forms may blend into rejection or may be cover for this.

B. Avoidance of the Child

Here, too, two extremes are suggested — rejection and neglect. Care below the minimum adequate amount has well-documented effects, as studies of orphans have shown. Most other studies have few, if any, children in this group. Parents providing this sort of home do not cooperate in psychological studies. (The author would not suggest that non-cooperation is evidence of this type of care!) Minimal need gratification is provided.

1. *Emotional rejection of the child,* not necessarily accompanied by overt physical neglect. Lack of gratifications is intentional.

2. *Neglect of the child.* This may, in fact, be less harmful psychologically than emotional rejection accompanied by physical care. It shades into the next classification. Gratification lacks are generally not intentional.

C. Acceptance of the Child

Children in this group are full-fledged members of the family circle, neither concentrated upon, nor overlooked. Parents are noncoercive, nonrestrictive, and, actively or by default, encourage independence. The minimum amount of social interaction is supplied at one extreme (this may be very low) and at the other extreme the group approaches the overprotecting one. The major breakdown in this group is on the basis of the warmth or coldness of the family climate.

1. *Casual acceptance of the child.* Noninterference here is largely by default.

2. *Loving acceptance.* Noninterference and encouragement of the child's own resources and his independence may be intentional even planned, or a natural reflection of parental attitudes towards others generally.

RELATION OF PARENTAL ATTITUDES AND NEED SATISFACTION

Homes in which children are the center of attention provide pretty full satisfaction, of physiological and safety needs, and attention to needs for love and esteem, but gratification is usually not entirely routine. The overprotecting home places great emphasis upon gratification, and generally upon immediacy of gratification, which keeps lower level need satisfaction in the foreground. Belongingness, love, and esteem are often made conditional upon dependency and conformity, and genuine self-actualization may be discouraged. There is likely to be encouragement of any sort of any special or supposedly special capacities, however. The overdemanding parent may make satisfaction of needs for love and esteem conditional upon conformity and achievement, which is frequently oriented to status. Needs for information and understanding may be encouraged, but within prescribed areas, and the same is true for self-actualization needs.

By definition, the next group has major lacks in need gratification. Rejecting parents may provide adequate gratification of physiological and safety needs, but refrain from love and esteem gratification, and frequently seem deliberately to withhold the latter or even to denigrate the child. Neglect of physiological and safety needs, but not beyond necessary minimal gratification is much more tolerable than personal depreciation and deliberate withholding of love. If there is no contrast with attitudes towards others in the immediate group there will be stultification of the child's development in some respects but not distortion of it.

Accepting parents offer reasonable gratification of all needs. This is unlikely to be emphasized in the way in which the first group do it, although the extremes of the loving subgroup may tend in this direction. Gratifications will not be deliberately delayed, but neither will delay be made disturbing. The major difference in the subgroups is probably in the way in which gratifications are supplied, and in the degree of deliberate encouragement and gratification of needs.

PARENTAL HANDLING AND ADULT BEHAVIOR PATTERNS

It has been suggested before that perhaps the earliest subdivision of direction of attention, and one which has significance for the whole life pattern of the individual, is that referring to persons, and that this may be towards persons or towards nonpersons. The author does not say towards persons or away from persons, since away from persons may imply defensiveness; the term *object* is avoided since attention may go to animate or inanimate nonpersons, and because object, in psychoanalytic terminology usually comes out to mean other person. Perhaps primary attention to self should be a separate division, or a subdivision of attention to persons. (The exclusiveness with which one of these attitudes dominates the attention of any individual is, of course, another variable, not taken into account here.)

Possible relationships between these orientations and parent-child interaction are suggested in Figure 1. The next to the outer segment of the circle indicates the probable orientation of the child in terms of persons or nonpersons. The division is suggested by jagged lines, since it is uncertain. The other subdivisions were set arbitrarily.

This basic orientation with respect to persons later ramifies into patterns of special interests and abilities. The degree of social interests is clearly related, and it is likely that verbal abilities are associated with this, since personal interactions are so largely mediated through words. Scientific and mechanical interests reach their fullest development in those who are concerned with nonpersons.

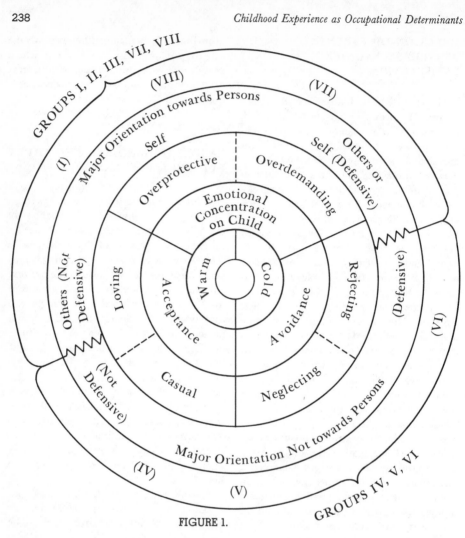

FIGURE 1.

REFLECTION OF EARLY EXPERIENCE IN VOCATIONAL CHOICE

Depending upon which of the above situations are experienced, there will be developed basic attitudes, interests and capacities which will be given expression in the general pattern of the adult's life, in his personal relations, in his emotional reactions, in his activities, and in his vocational choice. More than any other aspect of life, the occupation usually reflects most clearly the coalescence of the genetic and experiential variables discussed above.[1]

Persons from child-centered families who do not develop primary self-concentration will still be quite constantly aware of the opinions and attitudes of other persons towards themselves and of the need to maintain self-position in relation to others.

Persons brought up in rejecting homes may develop intense defensive awareness of others; if so they will probably have aggressive tendencies which may most readily find socially acceptable expression in occupational terms. On the other hand, they may strongly reject persons and turn defensively to nonpersons, or they may be unaware of other persons as different from objects in the environment, so far as their own relation to them goes.

Those from accepting homes may have primary interests in persons or in nonpersons; it will not be defensive in either case, and it will not carry the sort of uncertainty that many in the first group show.

It is possible to relate these attitudes quite directly to occupational choice (Roe, 1). The major occupational groups discussed below can, however, be thought of as indicating general patterns rather than specific occupational groups. This strengthens the general theory, but makes its relevance to this symposium less exact.

This classification has two dimensions: focus of activity and level at which the activity is pursued. The categories are shown in Table 2.

TABLE 2

Categories in Roe Classification of Occupations

Groups	Levels
I. Service	1. Professional and managerial 1.
II. Business Contact	
III. Organizations	2. Professional and managerial 2.
IV. Technology	
V. Outdoor	3. Semiprofessional, small business
VI. Science	
VII. General Cultural	4. Skilled
VIII. Arts and Entertainment	5. Semiskilled
	6. Unskilled

Relationships between group categorization and early experience are suggested in the outer section of Figure 1.

Although most of this discussion refers to Group rather than Level, Hypothesis 5 has relevance to the latter category. This concerns the degree of motivation. Need intensity may affect, within limits due chiefly to socioeconomic background and intelligence, the level at which the mature occupational life is set; it must definitely affect the relative position within that level which the individual attains, and even more specifically the position attained within his own occupational group. Most of those selecting occupations in Groups I, II, VII, and VIII have major orientation towards persons as do many, if not most, in Group III. Groups IV, V, and VI, are chiefly comprised of persons whose major orientation is towards nonpersons. More exact relations cannot be generally indicated. There are, however, some relations which are strongly suggested; these are shown in parentheses in the figure. Indeed, there is some indication that an ordered, counterclockwise arrangement of these groups is not untenable.

[1]There are clearly exceptions to the usual role of the occupation as a focus for attitudes, capacities, and interests. In these instances, an avocation, or some other aspect of life, serves the same purpose.

REFERENCE

Roe, Anne, *Psychology of occupations.* New York: Wiley and Sons, 1956.

Early Experiences
and Occupational Choice:
A Test of Roe's Hypothesis

DAVID K. SWITZER, *First Methodist Church, Pasadena, California*

AUSTIN E. GRIGG, *University of Richmond*

JEROME S. MILLER, *United States Public Health Service*

ROBERT K. YOUNG, *University of Texas*

One recent theory which seeks to deal with factors related to occupational choice is that of Roe (1956; 1957). Roe's theory evolved from the concept of the close relationship between an individual's interests and needs and his occupation, and the relationship between early life experiences and the development of these interests and needs. According to the theory the parents create a particular psychological climate by the manner in which they satisfy or frustrate the early needs of the child. As a result, a basic direction of attention is developed either toward persons or toward non-persons. This, in turn, results in predictable patterns of specific interests in the adult in terms of the field to which he will apply himself. His vocation is one of these. Roe's hypothesis was not supported in an investigation by Grigg (1959). The present study seeks to further the investigation of predictions based upon her theory.

The specific hypothesis derived from Roe and tested in the present investigation is that ministerial students will perceive their parents as having been more over-demand-

Reprinted with the permission of authors and publisher from the article of the same title, in *Journal of Counseling Psychology*, 1962, *9*, 45–48.

ing and less rejecting than will a group of chemistry majors. Roe does not devote much attention to the possible influence on occupational choice of differences between the attitudes of fathers and mothers. In this study, analysis is made to determine if there are differences between the perceived attitudes of the two parents and if the interaction of maternal and paternal attitudes is more predictive of occupational choice than the combined attitudes of the parents taken as a single unit.

METHOD

Design

Two groups of male Ss were employed in the study: ministerial students (M), and chemistry majors (C). Each group was given a questionnaire which was assumed to measure the S's perception of the parental attitudes characteristic of ministers and chemists according to Roe's theory, namely, overdemanding and rejecting, respectively. An additional group of male graduate theology students (T) was also included in the study to provide a gross approximation of the change, if any, occurring following an increase in age and additional training for the profession.

The questionnaire contained two scales (rejecting, overdemanding) designed to measure each parent separately. Thus, four scores were obtained from each *S*.

Subjects

Each group contained 40 *S*s. The undergraduate *S*s were selected from the student body at Southwestern University and the graduate theology students were from Perkins School of Theology, Southern Methodist University. All of the *S*s stated a strong certainty that they would go into the indicated occupation.

Questionnaire

A questionnaire was constructed to measure parental attitudes with reference to the dimensions of overdemanding and rejecting. Statements of the type used by Shoben (1949) and by the "Traditional Family Ideology Scale" (TFI) (Levinson and Huffman, 1958) were used. From these two sources, as well as additional statements designed by the senior author, two lists of statements were prepared. The statements were then scaled by the Method of Equal Appearing Intervals with 20 male undergraduate students serving as judges. Both scale value and *Q* score (semi-interquartile range) were used as criteria to select 20 statements from each list. These 40 statements were added to an additional 10 buffer statements to reduce the possibility of a response set and were randomly arranged to make a 50-item questionnaire.

For each parent, the *S*s were asked to respond to the statements on the questionnaire along a five-point scale. Each statement was given a score from 0 to 4 with the high score representing an overdemanding or a rejecting attitude on the part of the parent. The theoretical range of scores on each scale was from 0 to 80.

The mean reliability of the overdemanding scale, computed by the split-half technique and corrected by the Spearman-Brown prophecy formula, was found to be .91 and the mean reliability of the rejecting scale computed and corrected in the same way was .81. The correlation between the two scales was found to be .63 and presumably reflects such general factors as over-all attitude toward parents, attitude toward the testing situation, etc., as well as the possibility that the two scales are not independent.

RESULTS

The means of the perceived parental attitude scores as a function of scale, major, and sex of parent are presented in Table 1. The means indicate no consistent relationship between parental attitude and occupational choice and appear to be contrary to propositions based upon Roe's hypothesis. M and T parents tended to score lower than C parents on the overdemanding (O) scale and C parents tended to score lower on the rejecting (R) scale.

The major interest of the study was in the comparison of M and C groups. These data were analyzed by use of a Lindquist Type VI analysis of variance (Lindquist, 1953). Two other Type VI analyses were computed, one between the C and T groups and the other between the M and T groups. These analyses provide further tests of Roe's hypothesis by comparing the M and C groups with a group which is more committed to the ministry.

In the analysis of the M and C groups three *F*'s were found to be significant. The *F* between parents was found to equal 9.47 ($df = 1/234, p < .005$) with fathers tending to be both more overdemanding and rejecting than the mothers. The difference between the scales themselves was highly significant ($F = 120.35, p < .001$). Whether the obtained difference reflects a difference between degree to which parents are overdemanding or rejecting or merely that the two scales are not comparable is indeterminate. The third significant F was found to be the interaction between parent and major ($F = 7.35$, $df = 1/234$, $p < .05$) with the M fathers having higher scale scores on both scales than the C fathers and the M mothers having lower scale scores on both scales than the C mothers. Reference to Table 1 indicates that the magnitude of the parental differences was greater for the M group than for the C group. Roe's hypothesis predicts that the scale by major interaction should be significant with the M parents being more overdemanding and less rejecting than the C parents. The scale by major interaction was not found to be significant ($F < 1.00$).

The analysis comparing the M and T groups revealed no significant differences in scale scores *between* the groups. Three F's were significant. Parents differed ($F = 33.53$, $p < .001$), scales differed ($F = 136.76$, $p < .001$), and the interaction between parents and scale was also significant ($F = 6.27$, $p < .05$). It will be seen in Table 1 that both M and T parents tended to differ more on the R scale than on the O scale, and this is the apparent source of the parent by scale interaction.

The analysis comparing the C and T groups revealed one significant difference between the groups. The scale by major interaction was found to be significant ($F = 4.36$, $df = 1/234$, $p < .05$). Although this interaction would appear to support Roe's hypothesis, reference to Table 1 indicates that the interaction is exactly opposite what Roe would predict. The C parents tend to be more overdemanding while the T parents tend to be more rejecting, in contrast to Roe's prediction that the C parents should be more rejecting and less overdemanding than the T parents. Two other F's were significant in the C and T analysis. Parents differed ($F = 4.89$, $p < .05$) and scales differed ($F = 116.87$, $p < .001$).

DISCUSSION

The results of this study fail to support Roe's hypothesis.

The use of students as Ss may be questioned on the grounds that some of the Ss of this study actually may not enter their presently stated occupational preference. This criticism, however, tends to be negated by analysis of the M and T groups in which no differences were found between the two groups.

There is always the question of whether the questionnaire employed permits a sufficient and adequate test of Roe's hypothesis, a possibility which Grigg (1959) pointed out when discussing his failure to verify Roe's hypothesis. But the scale used in the present study is quite different from that employed in Grigg's study, so that negative results for both studies may represent more than poor construction of questionnaires.

TABLE 1

Means on Overdemanding and Rejecting Scales

| | Overdemanding | | | | Rejecting | | | |
| | Father | | Mother | | Father | | Mother | |
	Mean	SD	Mean	SD	Mean	SD	Mean	SD
Chemistry	35.53	12.28	36.15	11.99	27.28	11.43	26.18	11.10
Ministerial	37.38	10.96	35.00	9.85	31.10	9.07	25.18	6.88
Theology	35.25	10.21	33.63	8.19	30.35	9.36	26.20	6.78

In the present study, a significant finding is that there are differences between the perceived attitudes of fathers and of mothers. Roe's theory does not account adequately for any differences between attitudes of fathers and mothers and the influence that these differences have upon the child. From our results, it would appear that when one is speaking of "parental attitude," it often could mean the influence of the attitude of one parent as opposed to that of the other parent. When referring to "parental attitude" as a variable, the question may be *which parent* is being considered, and perhaps how that attitude is perceived by the child within the context of the attitude of the other parent.

It may be that greatly contrasting attitudes held by the parents, (which Roe mentions but does not use in her predictions) e.g., rejection by the father and acceptance by the mother, create conditions in which a child would be more likely to experience Roe's "emotional concentration" than he would in a situation where parents' reactions were similar. In a situation of radical differences in parental attitudes, needs may not be consistently and casually met, and the child presumably is sometimes frustrated, sometimes satisfied. Thus, this difference between the attitudes of the two parents would seem to make possible the kind of situation which Roe has described.

Roe has made a rather fine and perhaps confusing distinction between ministers and what she calls "religious workers," this latter group being categorized as Group I, Service, because they are "more interested in people than in theology" (Roe, 1956, p. 169). Predictions from Group I and from Group VII are quite different and the present study has been based on predictions from Group VII. A study of the concept of the ministry in Roe's system seems to be warranted.

It would appear that Roe's hypothesis should be modified to state that the *interaction* between the attitudes of the mother and the father is a significant variable. A possible significant interaction between recall of attitudes of fathers and of mothers toward vocational choice has been indicated.

SUMMARY

Two groups of 40 *S*s each were employed to test Roe's hypothesis that parental attitudes are a factor in occupational choice. They were ministerial students (M) and chemistry majors (C). An additional group, graduate theology students (T), was also included as a check for possible influence of drop-outs with age. Each group was given a 50-item questionnaire which was constructed to measure the parental attitudes of overdemanding (O) and rejecting (R), with scores obtained for each parent separately. The questionnaire was standardized on 20 male students.

On the basis of Roe's hypothesis the prediction was made the M group would perceive their parents as having been more overdemanding than the C group. In addition, separate scores for mothers and fathers were obtained and the interaction between the perceived attitudes of parents was studied as to its effect on later occupational choice.

The results of the study are not in agreement with the prediction. M scores are not higher on the O scale and C scores not higher on the R scale. However, significant differences were observed between recall of fathers' and of mothers' attitudes. It was found that magnitude of the difference *between* attitudes of parents was predictive of occupational choice.

REFERENCES

Grigg, A. E. Childhood experience with parental attitude: a test of Roe's hypothesis. *J. counsel. Psychol.*, 1959, *6*, 153–155.

Levinson, D. J., and Huffman, Phyllis E. Traditional family ideology and its relation to personality. In D. E. Dulaney, R. I. De Valois, D. C. Beardslee, and Marian R. Winterbottom (Eds.) *Contributions to modern psychology.* New York: Oxford University Press, 1958. Pp. 274–292.

Lindquist, E. F. *Design and analysis of experiments in psychology and education.* Boston Houghton Mifflin, 1953.

Roe, Anne. *The psychology of occupations.* New York: Wiley, 1956.

Roe, Anne. Early determinants of vocational choice. *J. counsel. Psychol.,* 1957, *4,* 212–217.

Shoben, E. J., Jr. The assessment of parental attitudes in relation to child adjustment. *Genet. psychol. Monogr.,* 1949, *39,* 103–145.

Careers and Family Atmospheres: An Empirical Test of Roe's Theory

DOUGLAS H. POWELL, *Harvard University*

From the numerous investigations of the life histories of scientists, Anne Roe recently has proposed a speculative theory which links occupational interests to experiences of childhood (1957). This represents the furthest theoretical advance in the study of childhood forces that influence the development of career interests to date.

Roe's scheme deals with one aspect of childhood, namely the family atmosphere in which the parent and child interact.

Roe predicts that certain kinds of family atmospheres orient the person to the career groups indicated in Figure 1. She predicts that a child from a *protecting* climate will select a Service occupation as an adult; a *demanding* climate disposes a person towards a career in either Business Contact or General Culture; a child from a *rejecting* childhood climate later chooses a Scientific vocation; a *neglecting* climate orients an individual toward an Outdoor occupation; and a person from a *casual* childhood atmo-

Reprinted with the permission of author and publisher from the article of the same title, in *Journal of Counseling Psychology,* 1960, 7, 251–256.

sphere pursues a career in Technology as an adult. It should also be noted that the specific hypotheses encompass the broader assumption that certain groups of home environments result in an orientation in the direction of careers which can be characterized as "toward-people" or "not-toward-people."

THE DATA

Longitudinal data with at least retrospective childhood material as well as current vocational information is needed to test Roe's hypotheses. Some of the data from the 245 participants of the Study of Adult Development meet such conditions.

Participants in the Study of Adult Development were first contacted as sophomores at Harvard College between 1938 and 1942. They are still being followed today. These men were admitted to the study because they showed no evidence of abnormality of any sort while in college. They were selected unsystematically from a list of "normals" submitted by physicians, psychiatrists, and deans. Although no strict sampling procedure was followed, the ranges of demographic characteristics of these men are similar to those in any college class, but the proportions are somewhat different.

Early in the study, extensive family histories were taken from the subject and his parents. The histories accumulated vocational, social, personal, and medical information for at least four generations. The parents, and sometimes other observers, provided retrospective information on the subject's childhood personality and on the training he received as an infant. Information about the way in which the subjects are rearing their children is available. In many cases this provides retrospective data about the childhood of the participants.

In postwar years, participants were contacted annually by questionnaires which included open-ended questions about their work experiences, attitudes, and adjustments. Complete occupational histories are available for every subject through the year 1953 and, for most, through 1956.

Because a mass of data was available for each individual, the investigator went through each case record and excerpted those remarks which were relevant to the childhood period. These excerpts were the basis for rating the family atmosphere in which the subject was reared during his childhood.[1]

Two judges independently rated each excerpt according to Roe's dimensions. The judges agreed in 70 per cent of the cases. They reviewed together each case on which they failed to agree and came to a mutual decision about it except for 34 cases which were eliminated because the evidence was insufficient to resolve disagreement.

The careers in which these subjects are currently engaged were classified according to Roe's system. The numbers were small in some occupational groups (cf. Table 1). Groups VIII, Arts and Entertainment, is not represented in this sample. Subjects who selected Organization occupations are not included in Table 1, as Roe did not suggest the family climate from which such men are reared.

Roe's hypothesis concerning the influence of a loving atmosphere upon later vocational choice is stated only generally, i.e.,

TABLE 1

The Observed Relationship Between Family Atmosphere and Selected Career Group†

	I: Service Careers	II: Business Contact VII: General Cultural	IV: Technology Careers	V: Outdoor Careers	VI: Science Careers	
Protecting Atmosphere	3*	8	3	0	6	20
Demanding Atmosphere	22	28*	10	1	23	64
Casual Atmosphere	2	1	6*	1	2	12
Neglecting Atmosphere	0	2	0	1*	1	4
Rejecting Atmosphere	0	8	2	0	3*	13
Totals	7	47	21	3	35	113

†Does not include members from Loving atmospheres or those who have selected careers among the Organization (III) group.

*Indicates predicted career group.

... Individuals with this background will develop interests closely in accord with their own special abilities and cultural backgrounds ... If situational pressures are minimal, inherited capacities should develop without interference or forcing (Roe and Siegelman, 1958).

Therefore careers had to be predicted from measured aptitudes in the case of this type of family atmosphere. These measured aptitudes were ascertained from test batteries given each subject as a sophomore. A distinction between greater verbal or quantitative ability was used. Service, Business Contact, Organization, and General Culture occupations were considered *verbal* occupations, while Technology, Outdoor, and Science occupations were considered primarily *quantitative* ones. All cases in which there were untoward situational problems in the family were eliminated from the sample (19 in all).

RESULTS

As Roe's theory is stated explicitly, the theoretical "hit" frequency, (i.e. the frequency with which the occupational group was successfully anticipated on the basis of family atmosphere) should be 100 per cent of any relevant instances. Table 1 indicates that the theory fails such a test. Careers are not solely dependent upon the atmosphere of the home in which a child is reared. The next question is whether career is at all dependent upon the atmosphere of the home. Are the observed hit rates greater than one could expect by chance or not?

To answer this question, the hit rate associated with a particular family atmosphere was contrasted with the aggregate hit rate of all remaining family atmospheres except for the loving category. The chi-square statistic was used in this evaluation in each instance. Yates' correction for continuity was employed when necessary. Appropriate attention was also given to the directed nature of Roe's hypotheses.

As noted in Table 2, only the casual family atmosphere has a hit rate beyond chance expectation. One other atmosphere, protecting, approaches but does not reach significance in its ability to predict the choice of a Service career.

Although only one category of family atmosphere had a hit rate significantly different from the hit rate of the aggregate except for that category, the significance of the hit rate for all categories was also evaluated. The exact proposition evaluated is that the number of hits represents only a chance coincidence of predicted and actual careers after allowance is made for the

TABLE 2

Correspondence of Actual and Predicted Vocational Choices

Home Atmosphere	Predicted Occupational Group	Hit	:	Miss	p^*
Protecting	Service (I)	3	:	17	.09
Demanding	Business Contact (II) General Cultural (VII)	28	:	36	.30
Rejecting	Science (VI)	3	:	10	.33
Neglecting	Outdoor (V)	1	:	3	insufficient N
Casual	Technology (IV)	6	:	6	.01
Loving	According to Dominant Aptitude	27	:	18	.95

*Probability of obtaining a value of chi beyond the computed one when null hypothesis is true.

observed variation in the proportions of the several kinds of careers. Tatsuoka, as reported by Kugris (1956), developed a chi-square test of this proposition which was used. The observed rate of 41 hits and 72 misses is exceeded by chance 9 times in 100. Therefore, it is concluded that the hit rate is only a chance occurrence.

It has already been noted that an intermediate postulate of Roe's theory is that family atmospheres in childhood lead to orientations either toward or not-toward-people. Children from *protecting* and *demanding* families will be predisposed towards the sphere of toward-people vocations, i.e.,

TABLE 3

Relationship between Specified Atmospheres and the Choice of Toward-Persons or Not Toward-Persons Careers*

	Choice of Toward-Persons Career	Choice of Not-Toward-Persons Career	Totals
Demanding and Protecting Atmospheres	69	43	112
Rejecting, Neglecting, and Casual Atmospheres	26	16	42
Totals	95	59	154

$$\chi^2 = .01 \qquad p\ .95$$

*Not including those from loving atmospheres.

Service, Business Contact, Organizations, and General Cultural; on the other hand, persons from *rejecting*, *neglecting*, and *casual* home environs will be oriented in the direction of not-toward-people vocations, i.e. Technology, Outdoor, and Science. The test of the validity of this supposition is presented in Table 3.

The p value of .95 indicates that there is essentially no difference in the proportional

incidence of toward-people and not-toward-people occupations in either category of family atmosphere. Roughly the same proportion of the subjects from rejecting, neglecting, and casual homes chose toward-people careers as did those from demanding and protecting climates.

DISCUSSION

The evidence seems quite clear that, with one possible exception, Roe's theoretical scheme in its literal translation and specific application lacks validity. Except in the case of a casual family atmosphere, the posited relationships between the specific family climates and a later career choice are not supported in these data.

Since results are based on rather small numbers, the fiducial limits for any hit rates induced from this sample are relatively large. In addition, induction of these hit rates is subject to any biases this special sample may contain, biases which are not presently understood fully. Roe does not restrict her theory, however, and there seems to be no reason why the theory should not apply to these men.

Before we discount Roe's theory as generally invalid it is well to consider two other explanations which may account for these findings. The first is that careers have generally been misclassified; the second is that family atmosphere may not have been revealed in our basic information and in its summation.

We are inclined to reject the proposition that Roe's theory failed because of our misclassification of the careers of the subjects. We had much better specification of career than is ordinarily available. In addition, rules for categorization are fairly explicit and were applied quite consistently by two investigators. Rather, we are inclined to think that failure occurred because sufficient differentiations among careers is not represented in Roe's theory.

Research on the personality determinants of careers ordinarily assumes that identifiable forces in the culture influence the development of need patterns in the personality of the individual and that the individual then expresses these need patterns in his work as well as in other aspects of his life. A further assumption is that various occupations allow for certain kinds of satisfactions and not others; hence, persons in a job will have certain personality patterns in common with others in the job.

The investigation of these propositions requires that the occupational spectrum be broken into manageable groups of vocations and that each group of careers must be homogeneous to the extent that similar personality needs may usually be expressed in its pursuit. Roe has attempted to categorize careers on this basis, but for at least two of her vocational groups, the range of vocational behavior, orientations to work or what she calls "factorizations of interest" which can be found among the occupations in each of these groups is extremely wide. This fact is most obvious in the occupations in the Scientific and General Culture classes but is apparent also in the Technology careers to a lesser degree.

For example, in a Scientific career one may teach, promote, administer, do research, or practice a specialty. The wide range of vocational orientations which can be followed within the limits of the group permit expression of many kinds of personalities or need patterns.

On the other hand, some of Roe's other vocational groups seem to be much more intrinsically homogeneous than the previously mentioned groups. The Service, Business Contact, and Outdoor careers each seem to have a relatively well defined "psychology," as it were. The range of vocational orientations which are available to them in their work is much smaller than in any of the other careers. It would be generally inconsistent for a person in a Service career to have found a not-toward-people orientation, or a person in sales (Business Contact) to have developed a deeply ingrained defensive reaction to

people and still find this career internally fulfilling and externally productive. True, there are psychological mechanisms that occasionally influence selection of careers, such as reaction formation and compensation, that might lead to such a paradoxical choice, but this is the exceptional case rather than the modal pattern.

The theory may also have failed because family atmosphere was inferred inadequately from the retrospective information which was available. Every caution was taken to infer family atmosphere from data of at least four generations, from data that were rich in opportunity for verification of inference, and from rules that could be applied consistently by two different people. It will be some time before any other data as complete as these can be assembled. Nevertheless, memories of childhood were used and not the events themselves. Certainly this fact lends an element of doubt to the validity of these findings.

These two possible difficulties — the criterion of vocational groups and the nature of the data of clinical abstracts — muddy the water somewhat. It is not certain that the source of error lies only with Roe's predicting atmospheres; however, it is considered likely that the trouble lies there, as the stated theory just appears too simple at this stage.

NEW DIRECTIONS

Roe's hypothesis about the influence of family atmospheres on occupational interests was projected into a vacuum in vocational theory. It is the first systematic set of predictions about the effect of childhood forces on occupational development.

Roe's theory is, of course, oversimplified; probabilities are not mentioned. This is perhaps why only one of her predictions approaches empirical significance.

It is not, however, the conclusion of this research that all but a small part of Roe's theory be discarded. It is possible, for example, that the total atmosphere of the home is not so much the important variable as the climate in which one or another parent and child interact. The mother-child relationship may be much more significant than the total atmosphere in the childhood period.

A second aspect that may be fruitful for later research is the child's response to the atmosphere in which he is raised rather than the atmosphere itself. A person may respond in terms of defensive or nondefensive reactions. Roe suggests that defensive reactions are more likely to occur in response to rejecting, neglecting, and some demanding homes, whereas the nondefensive reactions are said to be associated with loving, protecting, and casual families. It may be that defensive reactions also are associated with these latter atmospheres, and nondefensive responses with rejecting, neglecting home atmospheres. These defensive and nondefensive reactions may have altogether different vocational implications depending upon the atmosphere. A defensive reaction to a concentrating, overprotecting parent may have a somewhat different vocational influence than the same reaction to a cold, rejecting parent.

Roe's primary contribution to vocational research in the area of childhood has been to offer a series of hypotheses to be tested. The effect of this has been to stimulate and encourage research and speculation which may in time illuminate much more clearly the influence of childhood forces on careers. Herein, perhaps, is the real value and import of her work.

[1]The operational definitions of Roe's family atmospheres which were used are reported in Powell (Hagen, 1959, p. 175). Anne Roe kindly participated in the formulation and review of these operational definitions.

REFERENCES

Kugris, Violet. Allocation of differential aptitudes to various high school curricula in terms of pupil choices and counselor opinion. Unpublished doctoral dissertation, Harvard Univer., 1956.

Powell, D. Hagen. Family atmosphere and other childhood patterns as precursors of career interests. Unpublished doctoral dissertation, Harvard Univer., 1959.

Roe, Anne. Early determinants of vocational choice. *J. counsel. Psychol.*, 1957, 212–217.

———, and Siegelman, M. The origin of interests: a report on the California study. Duplicated, 1958.

Parental Influence upon Adolescents' Occupational Choice: A Test of an Aspect of Roe's Theory

LAURENCE B. GREEN, *University of Oklahoma*

HARRY J. PARKER, *University of Oklahoma*

The present study, using adolescents, represents a test of an aspect of Roe's (1957) theory of vocational choice. This aspect suggests that if a child experiences warm, loving parents he will orient towards occupations predominantly involving people; conversely, cold, rejecting parents will predispose the child to non-person occupations, i.e., occupations involving inanimate objects, other living things, or ideas. Five previous studies by Grigg (1959), Hagen (1960), Utton (1962), Switzer, et al. (1962), and Roe and Siegelman (1962) generally failed to support the theory. College or graduate students were subjects for each of these studies and all used the technique of retrospective recall to determine the early parent-child relationship. All but Switzer made comment about the weakness of the retrospective technique.

METHOD

Inasmuch as Roe's theory was predicated upon early parent-child relationship, an ongoing situation was selected for the present

Reprinted with the permission of authors and publisher from the article of the same title, in *Journal of Counseling Psychology*, 1965, *12*, 369–383.

study in order to elicit such information. Additionally, because the critical parent-child relationship is the one perceived and internalized *by the child*, and not the parents, children were used to report the relationship. Analysis of studies by Hall (1963), Ginzberg (1952), and O'Hara (1959) indicated that seventh graders (11–13 years) would provide subjects which best synthesized the following criteria:

1. Maximum reduction of retrospective recall.
2. An ability on the part of the subject to perceive and report experience reliably.
3. The subject to have contact with reality in regard to occupational choice.[1]

Further, it was felt that the parent-child relationship would be reported more accurately at an age before the influence of later adolescent peer group values tended to distort perception of, and thought patterns about parents.

The subjects used were seventh grade children living with their natural, cohabitating parents in the state of Oklahoma. Three-hundred fifty-five (205 boys, 150 girls) seventh graders who met the criteria were tested. Schools were selected that had a balance in urban, suburban and rural students. Subjects were administered a 260-item (130 for mother relationship, 130 for father) *Parent-Child Relations Questionnaire* (PCR) by Roe and Siegelman (1963). This questionnaire was adapted to more closely parallel seventh grade vocabulary and comprehension. Validity established by Roe and Siegelman (1963) was used for the present study. Reliability was computed by the Variance Form technique suggested by Tryon (1959) and ranged from .50 (Boys-Mothers Punishment Symbolic-Love scale) to .88 (Girls-Fathers Loving scale). All reliabilities compared favorably with those found by Roe and Siegelman (1963). Subjects also listed their primary occupational goal, which was then classified according to Roe's system (1956).

The PCR questionnaire was designed to elicit the child's on-going perception of parental behaviors of Protecting (Pro), Casual (Cas), Loving (Lov), Neglecting (Neg), Rejecting (Rej), Demanding (Dem), Reward Symbolic-Love (Rew SL), Reward Direct-Object (Rew DO), Punishment Symbolic-Love (Pun SL), and Punishment Direct-Object (Pun DO). These ten behaviors, plus six selected combinations of behaviors (Pro + Cas + Lov, Neg + Rej + Dem, Rew SL + Rew DO, Pun SL + Pun DO, Pro + Cas + Lov + Rew SL + Rew DO, and Neg + Rej + Dem + Pun SL + Pun DO) were used to test each of four parent-child relationships: Boys-Mothers, Boys-Fathers, Girls-Mothers, Girls-Fathers.

Within each of the four parent-child relationships, the subject's choice of occupa-

TABLE 1

Means and Standard Deviations of Each PCR Subtest in Each Configuration for Subjects Selecting Person Occupations and Subjects Selecting Non-Person Occupations

PCR Subtest	Towards Person or Non-Person Occupation	Boys[a]				Girls[b]			
		Mothers		Fathers		Mothers		Fathers	
		$\bar{X}$	S.D.	$\bar{X}$	S.D.	$\bar{X}$	S.D.	$\bar{X}$	S.D.
Pro	P	42.5	7.0	43.6	7.7	43.7	6.3	46.1	7.3
	NP	39.9	6.4	40.8	6.9	43.3	7.0	45.2	7.2
Pun SL	P	27.3	5.4	26.4	5.1	25.8	5.5	24.2	5.5
	NP	26.2	4.7	25.8	6.2	27.1	6.5	26.2	6.0
Rej	P	31.3	9.1	33.1	9.2	27.9	7.9	28.0	9.0
	NP	30.5	7.5	31.9	8.8	29.8	7.6	31.9	8.4
Cas	P	43.2	6.1	43.5	5.7	42.2	5.8	40.8	7.1
	NP	40.6	6.8	40.0	7.1	41.1	7.0	40.2	6.5
Rew SL	P	34.1	5.9	33.3	7.0	34.5	5.6	33.7	6.3
	NP	33.2	6.3	32.2	6.6	34.8	5.3	32.8	6.2
Dem	P	45.8	7.5	47.7	7.3	43.8	6.9	44.7	7.3
	NP	45.5	6.6	47.6	6.5	46.2	7.2	48.2	8.0
Pun DO	P	25.7	6.1	26.9	7.1	22.5	5.5	22.8	6.9
	NP	24.9	5.4	26.1	6.9	23.8	5.6	24.6	5.8
Lov	P	56.6	8.6	54.6	10.1	59.4	9.5	58.0	10.0
	NP	57.4	8.8	55.1	10.0	58.0	8.0	55.0	8.7
Neg	P	28.2	8.5	32.0	9.3	24.9	7.5	27.0	8.6
	NP	26.6	7.1	30.0	9.0	27.3	6.7	29.2	7.0
Rew DO	P	29.5	6.8	29.2	6.7	38.8	6.4	28.5	7.0
	NP	27.5	6.7	27.1	7.0	28.5	6.8	28.6	5.8

[a]Person n = 88; Non-Person n = 117.
[b]Person n = 113; Non-Person n = 37.

tion was categorized as person or non-person according to an adaptation of Roe's (1957) system. In the present study Dem was considered a cold, negative behavior, thus non-person oriented. Cas was considered more warm than cold, and categorized as person oriented. This dichotomy and the behavior scores[2] were analyzed with t tests for each of the four parent-child relationships for each of 16 hypotheses; one for each of 10 single behavior scales and one for each of 6 combinations of behavior scales. Table 1 and Table 2 contain means and standard deviations of the various scales and combinations. The six combinations of behavior scales were also tested by a Median Chi Square (χ^2) test in an attempt to determine the relative strength of the single scales.

RESULTS

Table 3 contains t tests which resulted in rejection of the statistical null hypothesis of no difference existing between the mean scores of the two groups under study, i.e., the person occupation group and the non-person occupation group. Table 3 also contains the results of those Median Chi Square (χ^2) tests, on the six PCR subtest combinations, which resulted in rejection of the statistical null hypothesis of no difference existing between the observed and the expected frequencies.

From Table 3, two generalizations may be made. For the boys, if the relationship with either mother or father is perceived as being warm, protecting and tangibly rewarding the sons gravitate towards person occupations. Cold, negative and punishing parents seem to have little effect upon their son's occupational orientation, when classified person, non-person. For the girls, it is a dynamically negative father and a more passively negative mother who affect the daughter's orientation towards non-person occupations. Warm, loving parents seem to have little effect upon the girls' occupational choice, when classified person, non-person.

TABLE 2

Means and Standard Deviations of Each Selected PCR Subtest Combination in Each Configuration for Subjects Selecting Person Occupations and Subjects Selecting Non-Person Occupations

PCR Subtest Combination	Towards Person or Non-Person Occupation	Boys[a]				Girls[b]			
		Mothers		Fathers		Mothers		Fathers	
		X̄	S.D.	X̄	S.D.	X̄	S.D.	X̄	S.D.
Pro+Cas+ Lov	P	142.3	14.3	141.7	17.5	145.2	13.8	144.8	18.1
	NP	137.8	14.5	135.7	17.3	142.3	13.4	140.1	15.2
Rej+Dem+ Neg	P	105.4	19.9	112.9	19.9	96.7	17.6	99.7	20.7
	NP	102.6	17.5	109.3	19.2	103.4	17.4	109.8	18.4
Rew SL + Rew DO	P	63.7	11.1	62.5	12.7	63.3	10.4	62.2	11.5
	NP	60.6	11.6	59.3	12.4	63.3	10.4	61.3	10.6
Pun SL + Pun DO	P	53.1	10.3	53.4	11.3	48.4	9.0	47.0	11.0
	NP	51.0	8.6	51.9	11.7	50.9	10.7	50.7	11.0
Pro+Cas+Lov+ Rew SL+DO	P	205.9	22.3	204.2	28.3	208.5	22.1	207.0	26.9
	NP	198.3	23.1	195.0	27.1	205.5	20.3	201.5	22.2
Rej+Dem+Neg+ Pun SL+DO	P	158.5	26.9	166.3	28.4	145.0	24.0	146.7	29.3
	NP	153.8	23.2	161.3	28.1	154.2	26.0	160.0	26.2

[a]Person $n = 88$; Non-Person $n = 117$.
[b]Person $n = 113$; Non-Person $n = 37$.

TABLE 3

PCR Subtests Supportive of Roe's Theory*

PCR Subtest	Parent-Child Relationship			
	Boys-Mothers	Boys-Fathers	Girls-Mothers	Girls-Fathers
Pro	*t*	*t*	—	—
Cas	*t*	*t*	—	—
Dem	—	—	—	*t*
Rej	—	—	—	*t*
Rew DO	*t*	*t*	—	—
Pro+Cas+Lov	*t*	*t*	—	—
Neg+Dem+Rej	—	—	$t\chi^2$	$t\chi^2$
Pro+Cas+Lov+ Rew DO+SL	*t*	*t*	—	—
Neg+Dem+Rej+ Pun SL+DO	—	—	*t*	$t\chi^2$

*All data presented significant at .05 level.

DISCUSSION

The present study partially supported the person, non-person aspect of Roe's general theory. Specific parent-child relationships appeared to affect boys and girls differently.

Boys tended to select a towards-person occupation when perceiving the positive parental behaviors of Pro, Cas, and Rew DO. This tendency was the same whether the relationship was with mother or father. These relationships were found to be statistically significant by the *t* test. When various PCR subtests were placed in combination there were no statistically significant χ^2 results. This suggests that either the PCR questionnaire is not sufficiently discriminating or that these parent-child relationships, as they affect occupational orientation, are not as strong as Roe hypothesized. There was no statistically significant tendency for boys to orient towards non-person occupations, as a result of any of the negative parent-child relationships (Neg, Rej, Dem, Pun SL, and Pun DO).

Girls tended to select a towards-non-person occupation when perceiving the father-daughter negative relationships of Dem, Rej, and Pun SL. These dynamic behaviors seem to be more powerful in influencing girls' occupational orientation than the passive behavior Neg. However, it appeared that maternal Neg was felt more deeply and seemed to be an influencing factor in the occupational choice of girls. Influence of fathers upon the occupational orientation of girls appeared to be much stronger than that of the mothers. An analysis of the effects of the two Pun scales (SL and DO) seemed to support this contention.

Considering the Girls-Fathers relationship, the "negative three" combination (Neg + Dem + Rej) showed statistical significance for both *t* and χ^2 at the .05 level of significance. Similar results were obtained with the "negative five" combination (Neg + Dem + Rej + Pun SL + Pun DO). However, the results of the Girls-Mothers relationship produced a slightly different pattern. Although the "negative three" was statistically significant for both *t* and χ^2 at the .05 level of significance, the "negative five" was statistically significant for the *t* test only. It might be concluded that the effect of the two Pun scales is to apparently mask an already weak relationship (Girls-Mothers). If the relationship is strong (Girls-Fathers), it can overcome the distortion which the two Pun scales might have contributed. There was no tendency for girls to select towards-person occupations as a result of Lov, Pro, Cas, Rew SL, or Rew DO parent-child relationship. Girls did not respond in a statistically significant manner to any of the eight tests made upon these positive dimensions of the parent-child relationship.

These data in general tend to be negative and likewise consistent with results of previous studies cited. The parent-child relationship and influence upon a subject's occupational choice, when dichotomized on a person, non-person basis, appears not to yield an effective means for exploring vocational development. It would appear that within any one job as well as occupational area, the range of inter-personal contact is too boundless to resort to a dichotomy. Accordingly, it might be concluded that the job as perceived includes important and unmeasured consequences which the individual interprets as person or non-person contact.

The extent to which the PCR device possesses sufficient validity and reliability requires further study. The matter of ten test items for scales Rew SL, Rew DO, Pun SL, and Pun DO, casts doubt upon the requisite sensitivity needed to measure complex behavior. The possibility of socially desirable responses is viewed as a variable coloring the results.

While these data do not positively support an aspect of Roe's theory, the issues of occupational classifications and PCR questionnaire remain as areas for further study. While a hint of support of the theory is noted, this optimism might be manifest if specific hypotheses were formulated around a modified PCR questionnaire and an expanded occupational classification scheme.

[1]Whether or not the subject knew the multitudinous job names in the world of work was not germane; nor was the individual's ultimate vocational choice as an adult. Major concern was if the child's choice of occupation, whatever it might be, was related to the parent-child relationship.

[2]Each questionnaire item received a score of one to five; one for "very untrue" to five for "very true." A low score for any one subtest indicated the subject did not perceive that particular relationship; a high score indicated a high perception of that relationship.

REFERENCES

Ginzberg, E. Toward a theory of occupational choice. *Occupations*, 1952, *30*, 492.

Grigg, A. E. Childhood experience with parental attitudes: a test of Roe's hypothesis. *J. counsel. Psychol.*, 1959, *6*, 153–155.

Hall, D. W. The vocational development inventory: a measure of vocational maturity in adolescence. *Personnel guid. J.*, 1963, *41*, 771–776.

O'Hara, R. P. Talk about self. *Harvard Studies in Career Development*, No. 14. Cambridge, Massachusetts: Harvard Graduate School of Education, Harvard Univer., October, 1959. (mimeographed)

Powell, Douglas H. Careers and family atmosphere: an empirical test of Roe's theory. *J. counsel. Psychol.*, 1960, *7*, 251–256.

Roe, Anne. *The psychology of occupations*. New York: John Wiley, 1956.

Roe, Anne. Early determinants of vocational choice. *J. counsel. Psychol.*, 1957, *4*, 212–217.

Roe, Anne, and Siegelman, M. *A Study of the Origin of Interests*. Cambridge, Massachusetts: Harvard Graduate School of Education, Harvard University, 1962. (mimeographed)

Roe, Anne, and Siegelman, M. A parent-child relations questionnaire. *Child Develpm.*, 1963, *34*, 357.

Switzer, D. K., Grigg, A. E., Miller, J. S., and Young, R. K. Early experiences and occupational choice: a test of Roe's hypothesis. *J. counsel. Psychol.*, 1962, *9*, 45–48.

Tryon, R. C. Reliability and behavior domain validity: reformulation and histori-

cal critique. *Psychol. Bull.*, 1959, *54*, 229–249.

Utton, A. C. Recalled parent-child relations as determinants of vocational choice. *J. counsel. Psychol.*, 1962, *9*, 49–53.

OTHER RELEVANT ARTICLES

An additional article related to the topic of this chapter:

Roe, A., and M. Siegelman. *The Origin of Interests*. Washington, D.C.: American Personnel and Guidance Association, 1964.

Roe and Siegelman have published in this monograph a carefully conceived and executed study of her theory, with similar limited positive results as the research reported in this chapter. They used as dependent variables recalled family atmospheres, as in the Green and Parker study, obtained from male and female subjects employed as engineers and social workers. They also included such measures as identification with the same or opposite sexed parent, early dissatisfactions, loss of a parent, stress or affection in the relationship, and the like. They found many more predicted relationships for men than women, and that for women engineers and male social workers there were likely to have been early pressures in their personal histories.

Other references relating early childhood experiences to vocational behavior include:

Brunkan, R. J. Perceived parental attitudes and parental identification in relation to field of vocational choice. *Journal of Counseling Psychology*, 1965, *12*, 39–47.

Grigg, A. E. Childhood experiences with parental attitudes: A test of Roe's hypothesis. *Journal of Counseling Psychology*, 1959, *6*, 153–155.

Holmes, D. S., and R. I. Watson. Early recollection and vocational choice. *Journal of Consulting Psychology*, 1965, *29*, 486–488.

McArthur, C. C. Career choice: It starts at home. *Think Magazine* (IBM Corporation), 1966, *32*, 15–18.

Norton, J. L. General motives and influences in vocational development. *Journal of Genetic Psychology*, 1953, *82*, 235–262.

Steimel, R., and Anastas Suziedeliz. Perceived parental influence and inventoried interests. *Journal of Counseling Psychology*, 1963, *10*, 289–295.

————. Childhood experiences and masculinity-feminity scores. *Journal of Counseling Psychology*, 1960, *7*, 212–217.

Stewart, L. Mother-son identification and vocational interests. *Genetic Psychology Monographs*, 1959, *60*, 31–63.

Utton, A. C. Recalled parent-child relations as determinants of vocational choice *Journal of Counseling Psychology*, 1962, *9*, 49–53.

A Psychoanalytic
Conception of
Occupational Determinants

7

This chapter represents yet another appearance of a subplot which was announced in the first chapter of this book: the psychoanalytic point of view. We have already seen the psychoanalyists' ideas on the meaning of work in general, and their conception of the distribution of work according to the kinds of gratifications it provides. Now we present a theoretical statement and some evidence concerning the possibility that different jobs with their different capacities to satisfy are linked mainly by the mechanism of sublimation to levels of psychosexual development, instinctual behavior, resolution of infantile conflicts and similar needs, as they are conceived by Freud and his interpreters.

Another contrast in theorizing which this chapter makes explicit is the careful analysis of occupations in terms of their capacity to satisfy certain needs, rather than a general lumping together and fitting of theory to the groups so obtained.

In addition, the theorists are careful to say that their ideas are only valid for persons who obtain the largest part of their gratifications from their work. This strategy increases the efficiency of their theory's predictiveness, at the expense of its generality.

The framework is laid out in the first paper, by Bordin, Nachmann and Segal. In it, a scheme of need-gratifying activities is proposed, and as illustration, their relevance to three contrasting occupations is noted.

The next paper is by Segal. He makes an exhaustive specification of the characteristics of creative writers and accountants which should differ within the framework of psychodynamic needs, from the same kind of analytic procedure in the previous paper. He then seeks verification of their existence from brief vocational autobiographies of the subjects and from Rorschach protocols and the administration of the Bender-Gestalt technique.

A few notes concerning the use of projective techniques in this kind of research might be appropriate here. Although the projective procedures were not administered by the experimenter, it is not clear who scored them. Since their scoring is not entirely an objective procedure, if the scorer(s) were aware of either the vocational identities or the hypotheses of the study, some bias could have intruded into data which are used to test the hypotheses. Further, although Segal employs frequencies of various characteristics of the responses, the basis for relating those indexes to their interpretation is not given. For instance, Segal accepts responsiveness to form on the Rorschach (F %) and number of popular (P) responses as two indicators of acceptance of social control. A reasonable question would concern how many other indexes of this or some other trait are available from the Rorschach protocols, and whether the negative findings would have outweighed the positive ones if all the indexes had been employed.

The degree to which Segal planned for these contingencies is not known. Nevertheless, his careful analysis of the two occupations and statements of the expectations of their characteristics must be admired, and the provocativeness of his results cannot be denied.

In the last paper, by Galinsky, one general trait, curiosity, is the focus of analysis for two contrasting occupations. It is interesting for its hypotheses concerning how this particular impulse may be handled — being kept alive in virtually its infantile form, displacement to other objects, or abandonment. It also has the same careful formulation of hypotheses evidenced in the other studies of this kind.

An Articulated Framework for Vocational Development

EDWARD S. BORDIN, *University of Michigan*

BARBARA NACHMANN, *University of Michigan*

STANLEY J. SEGAL, *Columbia University*

Over the past decade visible progress has been made toward a theory of vocational development which turns on early formative influences and links the adoption of occupational roles to personality organization. This

Reprinted with the permission of authors and publisher from the article of the same title, in *Journal of Counseling Psychology*, 1963, *10*, 107–117.

article aims to further that progress by: (a) presenting a scheme which identifies the gratifications that varieties of work can offer, (b) tracing these gratifications to the physiological functions necessary to their achievement, and emphasizing the importance of early experiences that lead to investments in particular modes of obtaining gratification. We shall start by surveying existing formulations to establish wherein we extend or depart from these conceptions and proceed to a detailed statement of our theory, closing with suggestions for further research in the hope that others will join us in the verification of our ideas.

CHOICE OR DEVELOPMENT?

Beginning with Super's presidential address to Division 17, APA (1953), there has been a seeming controversy over whether to concentrate on vocational choice or development. Super and Tiedeman and their coworkers emphasize vocational development and orient themselves to the prediction of successive choices, or patterns of choices. Roe and Holland emphasize vocational choice — that is, the prediction of the occupational role that the individual is fulfilling at a particular point in time. Our studies have been more in the tradition of Roe and Holland. It seems likely that the seeming differences in orientation are more apparent than real. It is clear that all contributors are unanimous in seeing vocational choice as a specific subgoal in a continuous process, and all agree that this particular choice is *not* synonymous with the end of the process. That point is probably only reached with the death of the individual.

The point at which differences appear seems, then, to be more a question of research strategy than of differences over whether development is continuous. Perhaps the central theoretical issue is that of the tenability of assuming that after certain maturation points have been reached the individual makes a vocational commitment which tends to be persevering. After such commitments, the individual's range of development is considerably restricted and will not change appreciably except in response to radical external forces or, perhaps, psychotherapy. Having gone through the energy, expenditures and trials of medical training and persisted after tastes of the gratifications to be obtained through the work of the physician, the young medical

doctor is unlikely to leave the practice of medicine, but may further refine and modify the nature of his development by choosing a medical specialty. Thus, we conclude that even though the full test of a theory of vocational development resides in its capacity to account for all of the major turnings in the individual's journey through the occupational world, expedient and meaningful studies can be conducted by concentrating on the theory's capacity to predict the individual's direction at the time that serious and encompassing commitments are made.

CURRENT THEORIES

All theories of occupational life take either one or both of two views of the individual, the structural and the developmental. The structural view analyzes occupations within some framework for conceiving personality organization, choosing its terms from that framework. The developmental view attempts to portray the kinds of shaping experiences that can account for personality organization and concomitant vocational pattern. Thus, Tiedeman and Super use the term "self" and speak of the process of acquiring self knowledge and of implementing it. From what is visible in his published work, Tiedeman appears to draw a version of self perception almost devoid of emotional and motivational influences. This is illustrated by the study in which he and O'Hara (O'Hara and Tiedeman, 1959) studied the accuracy with which boys in four different grades can estimate their own aptitudes, interests, social class and values. Similarly, on the assumption that curricular choices are implementations of self concepts, Cass and Tiedeman (1960) analyzed a wide variety of personal characteristics differentiating beginning freshmen in secondary schools, the assumption being that their self concepts will reflect their real characteristics. Though emphasizing unconscious elements in the formation of self perceptions, Super

(1953, 1956) gives us no explicitly formulated developmental theory. The self is a resultant of the individual's interpersonal experiences, experiences of reflected evaluations and awarenesses of reference groups in family and community. There is little treatment of the self as an active force with complex inner organization, although there is some suggestion in that direction when Super argues for the view of vocational development as a process of synthesis rather than compromise.

In the work of Ginsberg et al. (1951) we have a process formulation with virtually no structural assumptions. Although their perspective is developmental, their scheme, in which the individual is seen as passing through successive stages of fantasy, tentative and then crystalized choice in which fantasy has been tempered by reality, seems to be guided by an emphasis on a single decision point.

Both Holland and Roe strive for a more differentiated structural approach in which occupations are grouped according to personal characteristics or activities. Of the two, Holland (1959) offers a much more thoroughgoing attempt to map occupations in terms of personality characteristics. He defines six different personal orientations which seem to be roughly comprised of various combinations of masculinity-femininity, action vs. thinking, degrees and forms of expression of aggression, degree of need for achievement, and degree of orientation toward persons. It will be evident, when we present our own views that there are some similarities to Holland. One difference is that where Holland seems content to force occupations into particular classifications, we find it more meaningful to establish a series of pivotal personal dimensions, forming a matrix into which occupations can be mapped. This, we believe, permits more complete and more accurate description of the personality characteristics that are relevant to a given occupation. Although Holland makes explicit the goal of accounting for the development of these personal orientations, he does not move very far in this direction.

Roe's (1956) classification of occupations clings more nearly to those that have arisen out of factor analysis of interest inventories, stressing the activities of primary focus in the occupation. Her use of this classification in connection with her theory of the early determinants of vocational choice suggests that she has only one personal dimension in mind, namely the degree of orientation toward persons or nonpersons (Roe, 1957). Correspondingly, her developmental hypotheses are couched in terms of those formative experiences that might be thought to shape one's orientation toward persons, the warmth or coldness of parental attitudes. Although she acknowledges a debt to Maslow's hierarchical classification of needs, Roe makes little visible use of his stated needs in her classification system. She makes little use also of his principles about the appearance of needs in her basic developmental principle that the needs that will have relevance for vocational development are those for which there has been a delay in gratification, but for which subsequent gratification is achieved.

Thus far all attempts to verify Roe's theories have been directed toward her assumptions about the influences of parental attitudes on vocational choice, with negative results.[1] Though we remain convinced that Roe's basic direction is fruitful, we feel that it suffers from incompleteness in analyzing the basic personal dimensions relevant to occupations and requires much more specificity in stipulating formative experiences. Evidence that differences between the perceived attitudes of fathers and mothers with regard to warmth do exist and that the magnitudes of these differences are predictive of occupational choice (Switzer et al., 1962), point up the need for much greater specificity in examining parental attitudes or other formative experiences. Since we lean on a psychoanalytic orientation toward personality dynamics — we believe Roe does too —, the method of collecting verifying data is important. Evidence based on responses to direct questions will not always be satisfactory because of the presumed effects of repression. In such instances, indirect signs, e.g. spontaneous utterances, inflections, and fantasy materials, will be needed to provide satisfactory evidence.

FRAMEWORK FOR VOCATIONAL COMMITMENT

The theoretical formulation of work and vocational choice which we shall present had its original stimulus in three studies dealing with seven occupations. Each study applied psychoanalytic assumptions regarding personality development to the explanation of the behavior observed in detailed examination of the activities in an occupation. The pattern of the research in each instance was to make predictions on this basis regarding differences in the characteristics of members of differing occupations. The first (Segal, 1961) predicted differences between accountants and creative writers in their reactions to a variety of projective tests, important among them the Rorschach. The second (Nachmann, 1960) tested predictions regarding differences in childhood backgrounds of men in law, dentistry, and social work via biographical interviews. The third (Galinsky, 1962) used the same technique to compare the backgrounds of clinical psychologists and physicists. All of these studies were marked by a painstakingly thorough analysis of the occupation to identify what needs might be gratified and through what modes of expression through participation in it. With such analyses as a base, relevant personality measures reflecting these needs or childhood experiences which fix these needs were selected for study. Contrary to the failures to test Roe's developmental hypotheses, the latter two studies found strong evidences in childhood experiences.

Although each of these studies produced enough positive results to encourage the continuation of this general approach to occupational research, our understanding of the nature of the work and its relation to personality and early development shifted as we progressed. Though many of our predictions proved accurate they often seemed in retrospect to be not as important as others we could have made. There began to develop the need for a consistent framework which would apply to all occupations. We attempted then to set up a series of dimensions (needs, motivations, impulses, activities) which could account for all of the major gratifications which work can offer — which would make it possible to describe any occupation in terms of the relative strengths and the particular modifications of these component dimensions. The original studies only very partially fit into this theoretical framework to which they gave rise.

PRELIMINARY ASSUMPTIONS AND CONSIDERATIONS

We assume:

1. A continuity in development which links the earliest work of the organism in food getting and mastery of the body and coping with the stimulations of the environment to the most highly abstract and complex of intellectual and physical activities.

2. That the complex adult activities retain the same instinctual sources of gratification as the simple infantile ones.

3. That although the relative strengths and configurations of needs are subject to continual modification throughout the life span, their essential pattern is determined in the first six years of life. The seeking out of occupational outlets of increasingly precise appropriateness is the work of the school years, but the needs which will be the driving forces are largely set before that time.

We are concerned with the entire age span, from infancy, when the impulses common to all humanity begin to be molded toward the individualized parcels of varying strengths and varying outlets, through all the vicissitudes of the occupational history. We are concerned with all levels of skill and status and all areas of occupations though our research has thus far been confined to a few professions.

There is, however, one sharp limitation to our interests. Our theory does not deal with, and our research can relate only peripherally to, people who are motivated or constrained mainly by external forces. Certainly, economic, cultural, geographical and other external factors can exercise a severe limitation on freedom of choice and are outside the main structure of our theory. Perhaps however, even where there is little or no freedom of choice at the outset the relation between personal characteristics and job characteristics in terms of the dimensions we are considering may account for whether the job is intolerably unpleasant or not, and hence to productivity, success and failure, etc.

We are concerned with work as sublimation — but in the broad sense of all activity other than direct gratification, rather than in the narrower sense of pregenital impulses turned into artistic activities.

It is a theory of vocational commitment not only in the sense that a point of genuine commitment is a criterion against which our assumptions must be tested, but in the sense that it is only those activities to which the person has strongly committed his energies and his affections that we are discussing.

Consequently, we exclude from consideration those persons who have little capacity to get gratification from work. It may be that these tend to be found more in the simpler trades and the lower economic levels. There are some forces that would push in that direction — the greater pressure of external necessity and the fact that occupations requiring extensive training are not likely to be succeeded at by those lacking the capacity for sublimation, for example.

Knowledge of occupations is an external factor which curtails freedom of choice. The neurotic blocking off of knowledge of opportunities is an internal force and a part of the mechanisms with which we are concerned, but genuine nonmotivated ignorance we

TABLE 1

The Matrix Consisting of Basic Need Gratifying Activities and Their Further Defining Aspects into Which Three Occupations, Accounting (A), Social Work (S), and Plumbing (P), Have Been Mapped for Illustrative Purposes

I	II	III	IV	V	VI	VII
Dimension	*Occupation*	*Degree of Involvement*	*Instrumental Mode*	*Objects*	*Sexual Mode*	*Affect*
Nurturant	Aª	0				
Feeding	S	3	Material and Psychological Supplies	Needs of Clients	F	R
	P	0				
	A	1	Financial Advice and Safeguards	Client's Financial Affairs	M	A
Fostering	S	3	Encouragement and Protection	Client's Growth and	F	R-A
	P	0		Health		

ªDegree of involvement: 0 = no significant involvement; 1 = peripheral importance, 2 = secondary importance, 3 = primary importance. Sexual mode: M = masculine, F = feminine, O = not sex linked. Affect: A = affect experienced, R = reaction formation, I = isolation.

TABLE 1 (Cont.)

I	II	III	IV	V	VI	VII
Dimension	Occupation	Degree of Involvement	Instrumental Mode	Objects	Sexual Mode	Affect
Oral						
Aggressive	A	0				
Cutting	S	1	Words	Client's Resistance	F	I
	P	1	Lathes, Gouges, Clippers	Pipes	M	I
	A	0				
Biting	S	0				
Devouring	P	1	Wrenches, Pliers	Pipes	M	I
Manipulative	A	0				
Physical	S	0				
	P	2	Pipes, Valves	Steam, Water Pressure	M	A
	A	3	Advice, Recommendation	Business and Govt. Policy	M	A
Inter-						
personal	S	2	Provocation, Influence, Seduction	Feelings and Attitudes of Client	F	I
	P	0				
Sensual	A	0				
Sight	S	0				
	P	0				
	A	0				
Sound	S	0				
	P	0				
	A	0				
Touch	S	0				
	P	1	Hands-Smoothing-Sculpturing	Joints	M	A
Anal	A	2	Recommendations re Investment	Fortunes of Clients	O	A
Acquiring	S	1	Efforts to Equalize Distribution	Wealth of Society	F	R
	P	0				
Timing-						
Ordering	A	3	Sytems, Audits	Financial Policy	O	A
	S	1	Records, Budgets	Own Work, Lives of Clients	O	A
	P	0-1	Calculating Costs, Estimating	Materials	M	A
	A	2	Prevent Waste, Encourage Saving	Money of Client	O	I
Hoarding	S	0				
	P	2	Prevention of Blockage-Expulsion	Waste-Actual Anal Products	O	R
	A	2	Systems to Combat Disorder	Financial Affairs of Business	O	R
Smearing	S	0				
	P	2	Hands, Trowels	Pastes, Greases	O	A

TABLE 1 (Cont.)

I	II	III	IV	V	VI	VII
Dimension	*Occupation*	*Degree of Involvement*	*Instrumental Mode*	*Objects*	*Sexual Mode*	*Affect*
Genital	A	0				
Erection	S	0				
	P	0-1	Hands-Tools	Faucets-Fixtures	M	I
Penetra-tion	A	0				
	S	0				
	P	1	Reaming, Coupling	Pipes, Joints	M	I
	A	0				
Impregna-tion	S	1	Prevention or Encouragement	Family Planning, Marital Coun.	F	I-R
	P	0				
	A	0				
Producing	S	1	Giving or Withholding	Babies for Adoption	F	I
	P	0				
Exploratory	A	2	Audits to Detect Fraud	Financial Behavior of Others	O	A
Sight	S	2-1	Visual Investigation	Homes of Clients	O	A
	P	2	Detecting Leaks and Blockage	In Pipes and Water Systems	O	A
	A	0				
Touch	S	0				
	P	1	Hands-to Determine Shapes	Where Can't See	O	A
Sound	A	1	Questioning	Financial Statement of Clients	O	A
	S	2	Questioning	Private Life of Clients	O	I
	P	1	Detecting Leaks and Disturbances	Sound of Running Water	O	I
Flowing-Quenching	A	0				
	S	0				
	P	3	Arranging of Pipes, Valves	Flow of Fluids, Waste Products	M	I
Exhibiting	A	0				
	S	0				
	P	0				
Rhythmic Movement	A	0				
	S	0				
	P	1	Hands, Tools, Physical Movement	Pipes	O	I

assume can occur and limit a person's choice, or lead him into a field which does not in fact offer the satisfactions he anticipated.

THE DIMENSIONS

As has been mentioned, the elaboration and refinement of the structure of dimensions of work has to be carried out via a repeated weaving back and forth between job analysis, personality traits, and the assumptions regarding the childhood experiences which generate these traits. The list of dimensions presented here is not to be understood as final but rather an early, though by no means first, approximation. The nature of the dimensions is dictated by our theoretical assumptions. The level of breadth or specificity at which they are described is in part arbitrary. One may range from two: sex and aggression, to as many as there are activities listed in the *Dictionary of Occupational Titles*. Although our categories of work activity or of impulse expression may not at this stage be dimensions in a statistical sense, our aim is that they approach dimensionality. It is intended that they be independent at both ends of the developmental span — i.e., that each one stems in the beginning from a different physiological function, and that at the level of occupational expression one cannot be substituted for another but satisfies a different need.

In the accompanying table, Column I lists the dimensions. The remaining columns represent modifying characteristics which account for the varying forms of expression which the dimension may take in adult work activity.

1. By the first pair of dimensions, the nurturant ones, we mean those activities that involve the care of living things — feeding, protecting and promoting the growth of people, animals, plants, both literally with food and shelter and symbolically with words. We would see the interest in feeding activities as stemming from the infantile experiences of being fed. Special delight, pain, or anxiety about the taking in of nourishment develop into concerns that food be plentiful, that others not want and, more remotely, to interest in words. By fostering we mean those activities that involve either literally or figuratively shielding, comforting, protecting the young or the helpless — giving warmth and shelter as first one was warmed and sheltered. Their physical prototype is seen in the need to burrow into the warmth of mother, bed, home, and in the tactile and temperature sensitivity of the skin.

2. The second cluster of dimensions have to do with the teeth and the satisfactions to be had from biting, chewing and devouring. We would assume that these impulses are translated in the adult into the use of cutting and grinding and drilling tools — that these activities are delegated first from teeth to fingers then to knives and saws and drills, and finally to biting and cutting words and ideas.

3. The next two dimensions involve manipulation — power over people or physical objects. First with the bare hands over whatever comes within the infantile grasp — later on with all the machinery of technology that so enormously multiplies the power of the muscles. Secondly there is the power and manipulation which one exercises over people not physically but psychologically — influencing, persuading, threatening, seducing — first parents and siblings then a widening circle of other people.

4. Next are the dimensions that have to do with the use of the sense organs, not for gaining information, but for sensual pleasure — as the infant looks, touches and tastes because things are pretty and feel good, and are sensually gratifying apart from any other purposes they may serve. In the adult it finds expression perhaps most clearly in the artist whose senses are exquisitely sharpened and whose work is the giving of such pleasures to other people.

5. The group of occupational dimensions whose physical and genetic sources are

probably already most thoroughly explored and accepted as commonplace are those stemming from the anal impulses, to hold on to or let go of objects, to hoard, to order in time and space, and the impulses toward smearing or cleanliness. Their counterparts in all of the business detail occupations that require precision and order and economy in the handling of time and money and material are easily recognized.

6. Next are some activities relating to phallic and genital impulses, if indeed the latter can in some measure be sublimated. One may see some similarity between the child's interest in the phenomenon of physiological erection and the erection of skyscrapers and bridges and all kinds of structures, and even theoretical structures.

The dimension of penetration may seem similar to some of the orally attacking ones, but here the emphasis is upon intrusiveness rather than destruction, such as probing into the earth, the sea, and most currently, rocketing into space, as well as penetrations of a more abstract nature.

With the dimensions of impregnation and producing we are obviously dealing with impulses that are not present in children in a completed form but only in fantasy or in partial instinctual strivings. The most direct occupational translation of these impulses would seem to be in the agricultural occupations; a more displaced and abstracted one in the artist and writer who speaks so persistently of being impregnated with ideas and giving birth to artistic products.

7. The dimensions of curiosity have to do with the use of the sense organs for finding out about the world — investigating, exploring, knowing the facts. These dimensions are primary to every field of scientific investigation, the particular scientific area differing only in the object toward which the curiosity is directed and the degree to which it is displaced from the original objects of one's own body and one's parents.

8. The dimensions of flowing and quenching originate in urethral concerns and have their adult expression in such things as plumbing, fire fighting, hydraulic engineering, etc.

9. Next is the dimension relating to the impulse to exhibit the phallus or the body as a whole or later one's intellectual or artistic accomplishments. It is certainly easily seen in the child's "showing off" and in a host of adult occupations — acting, law, advertising, the ministry, etc.

10. Finally we have the dimension which has to do with rhythm — having its origin in the physiological rhythms of heartbeat and respiration or masturbatory rhythmic movement. Its occupational expression is seen in the musical occupations or in the industrial, craftsmanlike, and artistic occupations that involve bodily rhythm or its abstract equivalents.

The final list may differ somewhat, though not greatly from this one. For example, it is unclear whether the "sensuality" cluster should be separated as it is here from the exploratory uses of the sense organs on the one hand or from genital sensuality on the other. At present it seems necessary to do so. Similarly the relation of exhibitionism-voyeurism to exploratory "looking" as well as to genital concerns is questionable. Though some of the anal dimensions can be regarded as reaction formations against others their prominence as occupational motivations seemed to demand their treatment as separate dimensions.

Other Characteristics of the Dimensions

In Column III is indicated the amount, or importance, of the dimension in the particular occupation. That is, gradations in the degree of investment which a person has in finding expression for the impulse in question, or the degree to which a job requires this activity. Although we assume a continuous gradation we have as a matter of convenience rated the degree of involvement on a four-point scale.

In Column IV, Instrumental Mode indicates the tools and the activities through which the impulse is expressed. The range of possibilities is from physical actions of the body, the "bare hands," to tools, words, abstract concepts and symbols — a range from the physical and concrete to the abstract and symbolic.

In Column V, Object indicates the person(s) or thing(s) toward which the activity is directed. The range of possibilities is from human beings or body parts to animals, plants, inanimate objects, and abstractions. The differences here involve not only a range from concrete to abstract as in IV but degrees of displacement from the original objects of self and parents — displacement in space and time or restriction by defining a specific area to which the activity is limited.

Entries in Column VI indicate whether the activity appears to have been patterned after a masculine or a feminine model.

Column VII, headed Affect, indicates whether the affective component of the activity is accepted or repressed. In the actual investigation of an occupation it would be necessary to determine the particular mechanism of defense or mastery employed. For purposes of these illustrative examples we can only offer a rough estimation of whether it seems to be more a matter of reaction formation, of activity isolated from affect, or of at least partial acceptance of the affect.

Three Occupations

Entered in the cells of the chart for illustrative purposes are the occupations of *accounting*, *social work*, and *plumbing*, as one might view them in a highly abbreviated and schematic fashion. Accordingly social work would be seen as having feeding and fostering as its areas of primary investment, manipulation of people and a curiosity regarding their lives as secondary dimensions, and with several other peripheral concerns.

Accounting by contrast would have only a very peripheral involvement in the nurturant dimensions and its primary ones in the manipulation of people (albeit in an indirect form) and the timing and ordering dimension, with all of the other anal concerns as strong secondary investments. The accountant too enjoys a privileged curiosity into the lives of his clients but a much more circumscribed one than the social worker's.

The plumber contrasts with the accountant in another way. He too is unconcerned with nurturance; he manipulates physical objects and forces, not people, and though his investment in the anal dimensions is strong it is the converse of the accountant's. He has to be able to accept and even enjoy direct contact with dirt and disorder and to deal with anal products quite literally and directly whereas the accountant abhors messiness. The plumber's area of primary investment is that of flowing and quenching, in which the other two occupations have no interest at all, but he shares with them some of their peripheral dimensions — though consistently in a more direct and physical mode than they.

Every occupation can be described in terms of these dimensions. No occupation can be explained by a single dimension. On the contrary we would assume that most complex occupations (and most people) would include every dimension, at least in vestigial form; with one or two dimensions of primary importance in its spectrum and several others of secondary importance. Such a theoretical structure makes it possible to describe both jobs and people with the same set of terms. Therefore such issues as success, satisfaction, and productivity may be predicted on the basis of the degree of congruence between the patterning of dimensions in the two. With a relatively small number of basic activity dimensions a high level of specificity may be attained in describing a job by considering modifications of each component dimension in its displacement from its original infantile form and object. It thus becomes possible to deal not only with broad classes of occupations — social, biological, physical scientists, salesmen, administrators, etc. — but with particular jobs within these categories.

RESEARCH APPLICATIONS

We have referred to specific completed studies which have provided some measure of verification of the tenability of our approach to vocational choice and encourage our faith in its usefulness. Now we propose to offer a rough map of the areas of investigation that will be stimulated or nourished by our frame of reference and which are required to realize more fully the direct application of our concepts to the practical task of understanding and aiding vocational development.

Naturally, the core research issue is the verification of our ideas of how occupations can be charted in the space defined by our proposed dimensions. In so doing, we can expect to be jointly validating our theory of vocational development and theories of personality development. The occupations to be studied should be selected as centrally located on at least one of the dimensions until all of the dimensions have been sampled. Ideally, the designs of the Segal study of personality measures and the Nachmann study of childhood experiences should be incorporated within single investigations.

The analysis of occupations for the purpose of mapping them into our chart calls for a new conception of job analysts. For the most part, job analysis has in the past been focused on the identification of the general and special aptitudes and the levels of education or training that performance in specific jobs or groupings of jobs requires. Our view of the role of personality in vocational development points to the need for an entirely different purpose and style of job analysis. Direct observation of the worker on his job still remains an important procedure. In this instance, however, the observer aims to identify the modes of expressing and controlling one's impulses that the activities required or permitted affords the worker. In seeking insights into the gratifications that work affords, we look to the worker's experience of his work, his descriptions of his experiences, the psychological significance of the products of his work, and his fantasies. The diaries and autobiographies of literate and introspective men, usually in the profession, can be important sources of data.

One of the most difficult and yet most critical tasks in the confirmation of our scheme is the development of measures for the dimensions in terms of personality organization. Segal has demonstrated that this is possible, using our earlier version of the dimensions, but this was accomplished only after an extremely thorough sifting of Rorschach test theory and the available relevant data. We feel sure that a simple process of matching test names to dimension labels will not, in most instances, yield positive results. As research proceeds and the relevance of personality measures to the various dimensions is clarified by the accumulating data, this part of the research task will become progressively easier and, concomitantly, the diagnostic resources of the vocational counselor will have been enriched.

[1]See Grigg (1959), Utton (1962), Switzer et al. (1962), Hagen (1960).

REFERENCES

Cass, J. C., and Tiedeman, D. V. Vocational development and the election of a high school curriculum. *Personnel guid. J.*, 1960, *38*, 538–545.

Galinsky, M. D. Personality development and vocational choice. *J. counsel. Psychol.*, 1962, *9*, 299.

Ginzberg, E., Ginsburg, S. W., Axelrad, S., and Herma, J. L. *Occupational choice: An approach to a general theory.* New York: Columbia Univer. Press, 1951.

Grigg, A. E. Childhood experiences with parental attitudes: a test of Roe's hypothesis. *J. counsel. Psychol.*, 1959, *6*, 153–155.

Hagen, I. Careers and family atmosphere: a test of Roe's theory. *J. counsel. Psychol.*, 1960, *7*, 251–256.

Holland, J. L. A theory of vocational choice. *J. counsel. Psychol.*, 1959, *6*, 35–44.

Nachmann, Barbara. Childhood experience and vocational choice in law, dentistry, and social work. *J. counsel. Psychol.*, 1960, *7*, 243–250.

O'Hara, R. R., and Tiedeman, D. V. Vocational self concept in adolescence. *J. counsel. Psyhcol.*, 1959, *6*, 292–301.

Roe, Anne. *The psychology of occupations.* New York: Wiley, 1956.

Roe, Anne. Early determinants of vocational choice. *J. counsel. Psychol.*, 1957, *4*, 212–217.

Roe, Anne. Comment. *J. counsel. Psychol.*, 1959, *6*, 155–156.

Segal, S. J. A psychoanalytic analysis of personality factors in vocational choice. *J. counsel. Psychol.*, 1961, *8*, 202–210.

Super, D. E. A theory of vocational development. *Amer. Psychol.*, 1953, *8*, 185–190.

Super, D. E. Vocational development: the process of compromise or synthesis. *J. counsel. Psychol.*, 1956, *3*, 249–253.

Switzer, D. K., Grigg, A. E., Miller, J. S., and Young, R. K. Early experiences and occupational choices: a test of Roe's hypothesis. *J. counsel. Psychol.*, 1962, *9*, 45–48.

Utton, A. C. Recalled parent-child relations as determinants of vocational choice. *J. counsel. Psychol.*, 1962, *9*, 49–53.

A Psychoanalytic Analysis of Personality Factors in Vocational Choice

STANLEY J. SEGAL, *Columbia University*

The growth of vocational counseling has been marked by an increasing awareness, on the part of counseling psychologists, of the role personality plays in both vocational decisions and indecisions. Other than the extensive research into interests and their manifestations, however, there has been a rather clear neglect of research which attempts to relate other facets of adult

Reprinted with the permission of author and publisher from the article of the same title, in *Journal of Counseling Psychology*, 1961, *8*, 202–210.

personality and of personality development to the choice process. The research that has been reported is generally empirical and makes little or no use of personality theory (Segal, 1953).

This article is a report of a study of two occupational groups, creative writers and accountants, in which psychoanalytic theory has been utilized as a source of hypotheses related to differing personality characteristics of practitioners of each occupation. These hypotheses were then translated into specific testable predictions concerning the expected differences between the groups in their responses to a number of projective techniques.

GENERAL THEORETICAL APPROACH

If vocational choice is viewed, not as a peripheral decision of an individual, but as a concrete expression of personality development within the framework of the environmental pressures and opportunities with which the individual is confronted, then: the same theoretical factors that have been helpful in understanding personality development should be applicable to understanding vocational choice. Psychoanalytic concepts such as identification, the development of defense mechanisms and the theory of sublimation, can be used to gain insight into the personality characteristics of individuals who make a specific vocational choice.

Before such concepts are applied in this manner, careful evaluation of informational sources about the vocations to be studied is essential in order that an awareness of the behavioral demands of the practitioners be established. In addition to published occupational information (Shartle, 1946) such sources as the general cultural stereotype about an occupation, the objective occupational stereotype as defined by an instrument such as the Strong Vocational Interest Blank (Bordin, 1943) and other sociological and psychological research relevant to the specific occupations need to be consulted. Such a review gives, as a starting point, a view of the personality needs that a particular occupation can gratify.

This approach, using occupational information and stereotypes interpreted in the light of psychoanalytic theory to make predictions as to the common personality characteristics underlying a specific occupational choice, has been applied to the occupations of creative writing and accounting.

THEORETICAL BASIS FOR A STUDY OF CREATIVE WRITING AND ACCOUNTING

Creative writing and accounting were chosen as the occupations to be studied because they represent available choices having widely divergent occupational activities and social stereotypes.

Definitions of the field of private accounting place the individual accountant in the role of the financial detective and investigator for business.[1] The accountant has a definite, rather well-defined job with specific duties as well as obligations of a broad nature. His day-to-day activity involves the careful analysis of business records in order to determine the most economical method of business operation. These activities emphasize alertness, accuracy, methodicalness, honesty, perseverance, as well as a need for clear logical thinking. A talent for detailed work is part of the accountant's daily work but he needs to be able to integrate these details to obtain an accurate picture of the over-all situation so that his advice to management can be of a practical reality-testing variety.

While it is relatively easy to describe the day-to-day activities of the accountant, attempting to define the job of the creative writer is difficult. In contrast to the structured aspects of accounting, the writer is free to define his occupation according to his own inclinations. The major occupational activity of the writer is the translation of thoughts, feelings and experiences into words. This kind of activity does not impose a structure of office hours, accuracy and consistency, but rather allows the writer to see his world and all of his experience as his laboratory. The writer usually gambles on his unproven talents and abilities to express his thoughts so that they have general appeal and meaning. Because the writer does not have the financial security of the accountant, he must often supplement his income by a practical job, e.g., teaching (Colver, 1941).

The stereotypes of these two occupations seem to carry the ideas of conformity and lack of conformity that the descriptions of the occupations themselves demonstrate.

The general stereotype of an accountant is that of a respected, financially independent individual, who is capable of accepting social values, and does not deviate from society's demands for accuracy, preciseness and correctness. He is a clear thinker, not emotionally labile, who plans his own and other people's activities to minimize wastefulness. The accountant has a specific job with routine requirements and with constant deadlines to be met. Because the demands his work makes upon him are clearly outlined, he is not dependent on his own creativity but rather accepts a position in the dominant institution of a free enterprise society — business, wherein he is doing something for other people.

If one thinks of the occupational stereotype of the writer, associations of a Bohemian life, indifference to and rebellion against social norms, lack of conformity, free expression of feelings and emotions, and concern over creativity appear. Society views the writer as an "odd" person, in contrast to the view of the accountant as a follower of society's norms. The difference between these groups would relate to the conforming to social values of accountants as contrasted to rebellion against social values in creative writers.

To understand the meaning of this patterning of values in relationship to psychoanalytic theory, an analysis of the genetic development of conforming attitudes and rebellion against them is required. The hypothesized development of these two groups of people may give the impression that both groups are deviate in terms of adjustment. It seems important to realize that the developmental portraits emphasize extreme aspects of personality, and that they can exist within the framework of relatively normal individuals.

Conformity in early childhood seems to relate to the willingness to sacrifice individuality, to some extent, for guarantees of parental love and affection. Originally, conforming attitudes would appear to be the taking over of parental values, such as cleanliness, in order to avoid the loss of narcissistic gratification. To do those things demanded by parents is the best method of insuring continued love. If we ask at what point in development the child first becomes most clearly aware of parental approval as a response to conforming, we must consider the process of toilet training. This is usually the first experience in which the child must learn a specific control of important impulses, not for gratification of his own needs, but rather because of parental demands. Conformity, therefore, seems motivated to some extent by the fear that to indulge in one's own instinctual gratification will result in disapproval.

At this time in the development of the child the superego begins to form. If the child has learned that strict adherence to parental values leads to gratification, i.e., obtaining love, and that transgressions lead to punishment resulting in lowered self-esteem, then there will be a tendency to an unquestioning incorporation of parental attitudes and viewpoints and the repression of the instinctual drives that irritate them. Identification would be of a rigid non-questioning variety which would be fraught with overwhelming fears of loss of love should the child treasure or maintain any values other than the parental ones.

Isolation, reaction formation and intellectualization are the defenses which are usually associated with a compulsive complex and it is this compulsivity which becomes the means for maintaining the repression of unacceptable impulses.

As development proceeds, these basic attitudes of accepting the values of parents are transferred to all authority and particularly to culturally approved attitudes and institutions. The individual subordinates his own impulses and accepts socially dictated values in order to maintain his self-esteem and his feeling of being loved. When a vocational choice must be made by these individuals, the need to conform predominates. Accounting would seem to satisfy these needs in many respects.

The developmental background of the writer would be expected to be quite different since rebellion against social norms seems to be a major factor. The writer projects into his work his ability to mirror feelings to which large segments of people respond. Psychological events in the individual history can bring about this sensitivity. It appears to be an ability for multiple, fluid identifications which in many instances take the form of rebellion against social values.

This ability seems to arise from early reactions to parents — frustrations that make the child increasingly sensitive to his environment and that necessitate the constant searching in people about him for signs that they can be trusted. These feelings would seem to originate partially in the very early developmental stages of personality and to be reinforced later during the Oedipal period. Trust in the environment seems to originate from the satisfaction of expectations with regard to tension reduction. This would suggest that inconsistencies in parental behavior may be responsible if there is difficulty in development and acceptance of social norms and values.

These inconsistencies interfere with successful attempts to incorporate parental ideals and values and emphasize hostile feelings which develop as a result of the lack of assurance of continuing love and increased self-esteem. Identifications are neither complete nor stable and the Oedipal conflict is not adequately resolved. At the time when the individual's feelings of omnipotence are threatened and he tries to identify with parental figures, whom he would like to view as omnipotent, the early inconsistencies in parental attitudes seem to prevent the acceptance of parents in this role. This increases the difficulty in making adequate identifications and reinforces the need for omnipotence. This may be an explanation for the many poetic efforts which seem clearly to be attempts to gain such omnipotence.

Another resultant of the inability to solidify identifications is the creation of fluid ego boundaries and ill-defined self concepts. This lack of clarity of self may allow for the multiple identifications necessary in portraying various kinds of characters. The author may often be seeking a "self" in his own characters.

These factors result in an inability to maintain stable object relationships or to accept the ongoing social and cultural values. In attempting to regain omnipotence and to find stable identifications which did not adequately satisfy individual needs in their original form, parents, the individual seeks to change the present social milieu.

Because of these kinds of early developmental difficulties, such defenses as projection, repression, and denial, which are not necessarily related to compulsivity, would seem to be prevalent. The following is then a restatement of the foregoing theoretical considerations in the form of specific testable hypotheses.

1. Accounting students and creative writing students show no differences in their general adjustment level.

2. Accounting students show a greater acceptance of social norms than creative writing students.

3. Accounting students show greater attempts at emotional control than creative writing students, while creative writing students show greater awareness of feelings and emotions.

4. Compulsive defenses are seen with greater frequency in the accounting students as compared to the creative writing students.

5. Creative writing students show greater expressions of hostility than accounting students.

6. Creative writing students show greater tolerance for ambiguity and greater ability to deal with complex emotional situations.

7. Signs of a more rigid, fearful identification are seen in accounting students as compared to a seeking for the completion of multiple identifications in creative writing students.

METHODOLOGY

The subjects used in this study were 15 accounting students and 15 creative writing students at the University of Michigan. The accounting students were advanced students in the accounting curriculum of the School of Business Administration, who received a letter score of A or B+ on the accountant key of the Strong Vocational Interest Blank. The creative writing students were advanced students in the English Department of the College of Literature, Science, and Arts, having a score of B— or lower on the accountant key of the Strong,[2] whose names were included on a list of creative writing students prepared by a member of the faculty of the English Department. This group was, likewise, actively engaged in extracurricular literary activities while attending the university.[3]

The samples were compared with regard to age, rural-urban background, and intelligence since it was felt that significant differences between the two groups on any of these variables would have some effect on test performance. The obtained results were all statistically insignificant.[4]

The subjects were each administered the Rorschach, using Klopfer's instruction (Klopfer and Kelley, 1942) and Bender-Gestalt, using Hutt's instructions (Hutt, 1949). They were asked to write a brief, one-page vocational autobiography. Following are the instructions given for the autobiography:

In reaching your present vocational choice you probably went through many stages, from the first childhood ideas of becoming a police-man, fireman etc., up to your present choice. I would like you to trace the development of your vocational choice from your first memory of what you wanted to be or do up to your present decision. Be as complete as you are able to be. Write it down as it comes to you; don't be concerned with the structure of it or the grammar. I am interested in the things that first come to you when you think of the development of your vocational choice.

The battery was administered by ten psychology students who had completed at least one year of training in the use of the Rorschach technique. Subjects were assigned to examiners on the basis of common available time.

It is important to note several deviations from traditional Rorschach administration. The length of the test battery necessitated the administration of only seven of the ten cards, and thus Cards V, IX and X were not administered. Another change stemmed from the necessity to control the number of responses as a statistical control. Examiners were thus instructed to allow only a maximum of five responses to each card.

The rationale for this control stemmed from the obvious correlation between a wide range of determinants and the total number of responses. Cronbach (1949) suggests controlling the number of responses per card as a means of reducing such variation. Within these limitations, however, it was still possible that significant differences between the two groups might still be present. The finding of no difference indicates that the attempted control was successful.

Prior to the collection of the data, specific predictions with reference to each of the general hypotheses derived from psychoanalytic theory were made. These predictions were based on findings in the literature on the Rorschach and Bender, and on interpretations of the Vocational Autobiography in the light of the theoretical formulations.[5] The specific derivations of these predictions are outlined in Segal (1953).

RESULTS AND DISCUSSION

Hypothesis 1. There is no difference in general adjustment level of creative writing students and accounting students.

The findings based on the Davidson signs of adjustment (Davidson, 1950) indicate that, although there was a rather broad range with regard to the number of signs present, using the median of the entire distribution, there was no significant difference between the two groups. This therefore allows for the evaluation of subsequent findings without concern that what is reflected are different levels of adjustment.

Hypothesis 2. Accounting students show a greater conformity to social norms than creative writing students.

On the Rorschach, accounting students are more responsive to form (F) as a response determinant than are creative writing students. In addition to the higher $F\%$ they more frequently use form (F) as the determinant of their initial response to each of the Rorschach plates. The accounting students' Rorschach approach, the relationship of the various location categories, whole (W), detail (D), and small detail (Dd), show a greater emphasis on D than does that of the creative writing students, who in turn show a greater emphasis on W responses. Examination of the time of commitment to their present vocational choice, as given by the subjects in the Vocational Autobiography differentiates the two groups. The accountants appear to make their decision by the time of high school graduation while the creative writers do not commit themselves to writing as a career until college.

The two groups do not differ in the number of popular responses (P) given or the percentage of animal responses $(A\%)$ seen, on the Rorschach. There is also no difference in the placement of Figure A in the original Bender-Gestalt drawings.

These findings suggest that the accounting student more frequently reacts in a practical (D), formal $(F\%)$ manner restricting spontaneity for a responsiveness that is more in line with expected norms and values. The creative writers, on the other hand, seem more concerned with integrating and theorizing (W) and are less concerned with social expectation (lower $F\%$). Equally well, the accountants conform to the more usual societal expectation by having set their goal by the time they finish high school.

The lack of significant differences between the groups with regard to the number of popular responses (P), percentage of animal responses $(A\%)$, and placement of Figure A on the Bender do not confirm this hypothesis.

Hypothesis 3. Accounting students show greater attempts at emotional control than do creative writing students, while creative writing students show more awareness of feelings and emotions.

The Rorschach findings suggest that creative writing students are more able to respond to emotionally-toned situations with some form of response that shows their awareness of and responsiveness to the emotionally provoking situation than are the accounting students. This is seen in the higher *Sum C*, the dilated experience balance (*M* plus *Sum C*), the preponderance of shading responses (FY), and more frequent sexual and anatomical responses.

Color responses are generally interpreted as presenting evidence that an individual is sensitive to events seen as emotionally exciting to the healthy individual in his culture (Beck, 1945). However, the reduction of such responsiveness in healthy people does not indicate lack of reactivity to emotional stimuli, but more likely, a need to control their emotional reactions. The fact that accounting students give a larger percentage of responses to Card VIII would seem to reinforce the conclusion that they do experience emotional stimulation but suppress the direct expression of it. This increased responsiveness to the all-color card in combination with the lowered frequency of color responses and the greater use of form responses suggests a suppression of emotional responses that is similar to the defense of isolation.

The lack of a difference in the use of *FC* as compared to *CF* and *C* suggests that the obtained differences in *Sum C* do not reflect different types of emotional control, but rather a greater freedom of the writers to allow the expression of adequately controlled affective reactions.

On the Bender, changes in the angulation and curvature of the original drawings, usually interpreted as an indication of emotional lability (Hutt, 1949) are not different for the two groups studied. The Rorschach data, which suggest considerable differences between the groups, and the findings both here and for other hypotheses that the Bender predictions were not validated raises questions as to the appropriateness of the Bender for this type of study.

It should be noted that the two groups did differ in their verbal associations to their elaborations of the Bender figures. In this instance the creative writers did not draw concrete objects in elaborating the figures but rather reacted in a more abstract manner, verbalizing such ideas as stability, balance, relationship of elements of the figure, etc. These elaborations again seem to illustrate the writers' greater ease in reacting in a more affective way.

Hypothesis 4. Compulsive defenses are seen with greater frequency in the accountants as compared to the creative writers.

The results on both the Rorschach and the Bender do not differentiate the groups with regard to the presence or absence of compulsive defenses. These traditional measures of compulsive defenses: ambi-equal experience balance, greater emphasis on small details (*Dd*), and symmetry remarks on the Rorschach, the use of guide lines and the maintenance of the dots in elaborating Figure 5 on the Bender, do not differentiate the groups. The general clinical use of these variables is to diagnose more severe uses of compulsive defenses as neurotic mechanisms, so that these predictions violate the assumption that we are dealing with essentially

normal subjects. It is interesting to note that although no significant differences are found four of the five measures were in the direction predicted.

Hypothesis 5. Creative writing students show greater signs of hostility than accounting students.

Schneider (1953) derived scales which measure overt and latent hostility using various quantitative and qualitative aspects of the Rorschach test weighted as to their occurrence in a record. The groups were compared on each of these scales with the findings that the creative writers were significantly higher on the latent hostility scale. The findings on the overt hostility scale approach significance ($p = .06$) in the direction predicted.

It had been postulated that because the creative writers had suffered early deprivations which aroused feelings of distrust, they would be more prone to hostility. These findings would seem to bear out this hypothesis.

Hypothesis 6. Creative writers show greater tolerance for ambiguity and greater ability to deal with complex emotional situations than accountants.

The two Rorschach predictions relevant to this hypothesis were both validated.

Responses that involve the simultaneous use of more than one determinant are called blends. The psychological meaning relates to the complex psychic potential necessary for the adequate integration of a number of determinants in one percept (Beck, 1945). Another aspect of these responses is the ability of the individual to tolerate the multiple determination of percepts available in the ambiguous Rorschach plates and to sort them into meaningfully-integrated responses. It was found that the creative writing students did perceive greater numbers of such responses suggesting that they are better able to integrate complex data from an ambiguous source

Ambiguous situations often have a temporarily disorganizing effect on many individuals. This is particularly likely to happen if the individual is a well-controlled, somewhat compulsive person, and generally will last until the kinds of controls that the individual characteristically uses can be called into action. A subject is confronted by a new and ambiguous situation when the first card of the Rorschach test is presented to him (Cowan and Thompson, 1951). Although there may be a number of ways in which disorganization may show itself, it is likely that one of the most sensitive measures of this would be the appearance of a greater amount of inaccurately perceived responses (responses with a *F*-element). It was found, as predicted, that accounting students showed greater disorganization, in the form of minus percepts on Card I of the Rorschach than did creative writing students. In order to demonstrate that this was not a generalized reaction it was also shown, as predicted, that such differences did not appear in response to other cards of the Rorschach series.

These findings indicate that creative writers are more at ease with ambiguous situations and can react to them more productively than accountants.

Hypothesis 7. Signs of a more rigid, fearful identification are seen in accounting students as compared to a seeking for the completion of multiple identification in creative writing students.

Three of the four specific predictions with reference to this hypothesis significantly differentiated the two groups in the direction predicted. Since identification has been considered a rather crucial aspect of the vocational choice process, these results will be discussed in greater detail.

Writers are much more responsive to the movement (*M*) qualities of the Rorschach cards than are the accountants. Studies by Hertzman and Pearce (1947) and Cook (1942) are relevant to this finding. Cook administered Rorschach's to male Samoans and found that only a fifth of the group showed any *M* at all. The Samoans have as their ego-ideal the individual whose attitudes are in complete conformity with the social norm and who is never anxious in any situation. The culture is so arranged as to make possible the relative fulfillment of this ideal.

Hertzman and Pearce doubt the conception of *M* as an indicator of creative energy, but rather conclude that a large number of such responses may be produced by persons unable to maintain a direction because of failure of self-acceptance; the *M* in such cases is a symptom of the struggle for a self.

These studies accurately describe the expected finding that writers will show greater responsiveness to *M* and seem to be in accord with our theoretical framework. The accountant who is made to conform and to interiorize social norms as a prerequisite to parental acceptance accomplishes this identification with the parents. These ego-ideals then become constant models; and the business world, a dominant institution of our society becomes an appropriate means of fulfillment of the standards represented by the interiorized parental norms. On the other hand, the writer has been unable to find an acceptable self concept and is constantly seeking such identifications in his work. This would suggest that the writer has had greater difficulty in establishing an adequate identification. The differential occurrence of the Wheeler Signs (Wheeler, 1949) in the groups adds credence to the above finding.

A more superficial measure of the importance of identification in vocational choice is derived from the Vocational Autobiography. The testing of the hypothesis that accountants would refer to significant adults as important in the determination of a vocational goal more frequently than writers, was substantiated. This finding would seem to offer more direct evidence than the Rorschach findings in that fewer inferences need be made.

The prediction of a greater number of prevocational choices in writers was not validated. The work of Ginzberg et al. (1951) suggests the vacillation in the early period is so general that differences should not be expected.

SUMMARY

Summarizing all tests of hypothesis, 30 specific variables were tested, with 17 of them reaching at least the five per cent level of significance. In Table 1 the probability that such results could be obtained by chance is tested. The application of the exact text gives a probability value beyond the .001 level of significance.

TABLE 1

Comparison of Obtained Results
with Expected Results
Tabulated by Personality Techniques Used

Number of Specific Predictions

	Not Significant	Significant at or beyond p .05	Total
Rorschach	7	14	21
Bender-Gestalt	5	1	6
Vocational Autobiography	1	2	3
Total-Obtained	13	17	30
Expected	28.5	1.5	

$p < .001$.

Previous attempts to understand the role of personality factors as a determinant of occupational choice have proceeded without recourse to theory. In this study an attempt has been made to demonstrate that psychoanalytic theory can be utilized to predict personality differences in individuals choosing one of two vocational outlets, accounting or creative writing. These hypotheses were derived from information about the kinds of activities each of these professions required of an individual and the interaction of such activities with the satisfaction of the individual's needs. The testing of hypotheses was accomplished by comparing the performance of the groups on a number of projective techniques.

[1]In this study we will limit our discussion to private accounting. Private accountants handle the financial records of a single business firm and work on salary basis while public accountants provide accounting services to many businesses and the general public on a fee basis.

[2]The author-journalist key was not used as a means of selection since the total population used in standardizing this key consisted of creative writers and journalists (Strong, 1943, p. 695).

[3]Although not originally used as a criterion, at least 60 per cent of the subjects had won awards for literary achievement or had some of their writing published.

[4]The table summarizing this data, and tables indicating the specific findings for each of the three techniques used in the study can be obtained from the author.

[5]Predictions were not only made as to differences in Rorschach and other test variables, but also with regard to the definition of high-low on each variable. In many instances this could be determined from relevant statements in the literature. In all other cases it was decided that the median of the distribution for the entire sample would be used to distinguish high-low.

REFERENCES

Accounting. Washington, D.C.: Bureau of Placement, War Manpower Commission, 1946.

Beck, S. *Rorschach's test: Vol. 2, A variety of personality pictures.* New York: Grune & Stratton, 1945.

Beck, S. *Rorschach's test: Vol. 3, Advances in interpretation.* New York: Grune & Stratton, 1952.

Bordin, E. S. A theory of vocational interests as dynamic phenomena. *Educ. psychol. Measmt,* 1943, *3,* 49–65.

Colver, Alice R. *If you should want to write.* New York: Dodd, Mead, 1941.

Cook, P. H. The application of the Rorschach test to a Samoan group. *Rorschach Res. Exch.,* 1942, *6,* 51–60.

Cowan, E. L., and Thompson, G. C. Problem solving, rigidity and personality structure. *J. abnorm. soc. Psychol.*, 1951, *46*, 165–176.

Cronbach, L. J. Statistical methods applied to Rorschach scores: a review. *Psychol. Bull.*, 1949, *46*, 393–429.

Davidson, Helen H. A measure of adjustment obtained from Rorschach protocols. *J. proj. Tech.*, 1950, *14*, 31–38.

Ginzberg, E. et al. *Occupational choice.* New York: Columbia Univer. Press, 1951.

Hertzman, M., and Pearce, J. Personal meaning of the human figure in the Rorschach Test. *Psychiat.*, 1947, *10*, 413–422.

Hutt, M. Excerpt from clinical use of the revised Bender-Gestalt test. Univer. of Michigan, 1949. (Mimeographed)

Klopfer, B., and Kelley, D. M. *The Rorschach technique.* New York: World Book, 1942.

Schneider, S. F. The prediction of certain aspects of the psychotherapeutic relationship from Rorschach's test: An empirical and exploratory study. Unpublished doctoral dissertation, Univer. of Michigan, 1953.

Segal, S. J. The role of personality factors in vocational choice: A study of accountants and creative writers. Unpublished doctoral dissertation, Univer. of Michigan, 1953.

Shartle, C. *Occupational information: Its development and application.* Englewood Cliffs, N.J.: Prentice-Hall, 1946.

Strong, E. K. *Vocational interests of men and women.* Stanford: Stanford Univer. Press, 1943.

Wheeler, W. M. Rorschach indices of male homosexuality. *Rorschach Res. Exch.*, 1949, *13*, 97–126.

Personality Development and Vocational Choice of Clinical Psychologists and Physicists

M. DAVID GALINSKY, *University of North Carolina*

Studies by Segal (1961) and Nachmann (1960), utilizing psychoanalytic theory and job analyses, have shown that testable hypotheses about the relationship between personality and vocational choice can be generated, tested, and confirmed. In both of these studies hypotheses derived from psychoanalytic theory were tested. Segal studied creative writers' and accountants' current personality structure by means of projective

Reprinted with the permission of author and publisher from the article of the same title, in *Journal of Counseling Psychology*, 1962, 9, 299–305.

tests, while Nachmann compared the life histories of lawyers with those of social workers and dentists, employing biographical interviews. Roe (1957) has offered some provocative speculations about the relationship between early experience, personality and vocational choice.

The study is grounded in Nachmann's assumption that occupations provide a variety of opportunities for impulse expression, utilizing defenses, and for organizing one's dealings with the world, as well as the further hypothesis that developmental experiences play an important part in predisposing one to choose a particular occupation. One would, therefore, expect to find that individuals who choose one vocation would have had different developmental histories from those choosing a vocation with rather dissimilar characteristics.

Working within the framework of psychoanalytic theory, specific hypotheses about the relationship among life history, personality, and occupations were developed in the following manner. The first step in the process was to become familiar with the demands of various occupations as well as the gratifications provided by them. Next, thinking in terms of psychoanalytic theory one could map out the personality traits which would be compatible with particular job demands and gratifications. Lastly, it was possible to cast hypotheses about the probable development experiences of individuals who choose various occupations.

THEORETICAL DEVELOPMENT

The present study grew out of an attempt to understand the relationship between curiosity and occupational choice. According to psychoanalytic theory, early sexual curiosity is the prototype for all later curiosity. There appear to be two elements in what has been called sexual curiosity — (1) curiosity about the body, and (2) curiosity about interpersonal relations — e.g. what things do parents do that the child does not understand and has difficulty finding out about. This study is concerned with curiosity about interpersonal relations, which is said always to be aroused in the course of development. Three fates are possible for such curiosity. As the child develops he (1) may have experiences which keep alive and further focus his interest on the area of interpersonal relations, (2) may have his curiosity channeled into other areas (displacement), or (3) may have experiences which lead him to abandon all attempts at having his curiosity satisfied.

Clinical psychology is an occupation in which curiosity about interpersonal relations is an integral part; Physics is one in which curiosity about the structure of and relationships among elements of the physical world is a major focus of interest. People who hope to find job satisfaction as clinical psychologists would be expected to have had experiences which focused their curiosity on interpersonal relations and left that curiosity relatively undisplaced. On the other hand, the experiences of physicists served to channel their interest into another area via displacement. Therefore, in their childhoods, clinical psychologists must have had their curiosity treated with greater tolerance by their parents, and have been disciplined much less rigidly when they persisted in being curious beyond the limits of parental toleration. Physicists, on the other hand, must have had their curiosity about interpersonal relations rebuffed, but have had the displacement of their curiosity to another area facilitated by greater intellectual stimulation in the home.

In a similar way other job requirements of the two occupations — requirements such as the ability to tolerate emotional expression of others, the capacity for nurturance, the necessity for working with people or for working alone — were considered in terms of the possible developmental experiences which would lead to adult compatibility with such job expectations.

Out of this occupational analysis there were developed hypotheses to be tested about differing developmental experiences in the two groups. The actual hypotheses tested will be stated in the results section.

SUBJECTS AND PROCEDURE

The subjects (*S*s) for this study were 40 male graduate students in physics and clinical psychology at the University of Michigan. As was originally planned, one criterion for inclusion was that subjects must have completed their requirements for the Master of Arts or Science degree, but because there were not sufficient numbers available at that level, eight *S*s with lesser amounts of training were included. Again because of the limitation of possible *S*s, 12 *S*s who were less than maximally satisfied with their choice of vocation were included in the sample.

The two groups of *S*s were equated for social class of parents, which was measured by the method suggested by Allinsmith (1954), based on a weighted combination of father's occupation and education. Although it is not known whether equating for social class in the samples accurately reflects the distribution of social class in the population from which the samples were drawn, it was decided to equate the samples for social class lest the results be attributable to factors other than those which have been hypothesized. The groups were also equated for religious backgrounds of their parents, with the same numbers of Protestants, Jews, and Catholics in each group (listed in order of frequency). Here it is known that the sample does not accurately reflect the population distribution. In the population of physicists there is a much smaller percentage of Jews than in that of clinical psychologists. However, for the same reasons given for equating the samples for social class, it was decided to equate for religion.

The investigator was the interviewer in each case. The modal time of the interviews was about forty-five minutes. The interview was composed of a number of specific questions, each of which was asked in all cases. All of the interviews were tape recorded and verbatim written transcripts were prepared.

A coding system was devised from the predictions subordinate to each hypothesis in order to provide data in the form appropriate for the testing of those predictions. The coders worked from the transcripts of the interviews. In some instances the coder had only to attend to *S*'s answer to a particular question, while in other cases he was required to form an impression from a number of *S*'s replies. There were three coders employed in order to measure reliability. Coder 1 agreed with coder 2, 92 per cent of the time; coder 2 agreed with coder 3, 90 per cent; and coder 1 with coder 3, 90 per cent.

The chi-square test of independence was used for the analysis of the data. One-tailed tests of significance were used since the direction of differences was predicted in advance. Only differences at or beyond the .05 confidence level were considered significant.

RESULTS

HYPOTHESIS I As children, clinical psychologists had more opportunity to be curious about interpersonal relations than did physicists.

The specific predictions on the basis of which this hypothesis was tested are presented in Table I. It may be seen that each prediction touches a separate but related facet of the development of concern about interpersonal relationships. This hypothesis was supported by the confirmation of all of the predictions that relate to it. Both from the side of hearing about the behavior of people outside the family as well as from having the opportunity to observe emotional interaction within the family, clinical psychologists had greater opportunity to be curious about interpersonal relationships than physicists did.

The results pertaining to the remaining hypotheses will be summarized. The summaries are based on the outcomes of the testing of a number of specific predictions subordinate to each hypothesis as was illustrated in Table 1.

HYPOTHESIS II Fathers of physicists were more dominant and more clearly masculine figures than fathers of clinical psychologists.

The predictions dealt with the father's role as decision-maker, breadwinner, authoritative person. None of the predictions was confirmed, although all of the results were

TABLE 1

Distribution of Experimental Groups with Regard to Interpersonal Curiosity

Item and Prediction	Response	Occupational Group		Chi Square
		Clinical Psychology	Physics	
The behaviors of people (a) were or (b) were not discussed frequently in the home. Clinical Psychology higher on prediction (a).	a b	14 6	2 18	12.60**
Emotional expression (a) was or (b) was not characteristic in the family. Clinical Psychology higher on prediction (a).	a b	13 7	3 17	8.44*
Frank discussion of people's behavior (a) was or (b) was not characteristic of family conversation. Clinical Psychology higher on prediction (a).	a b	9 11	0 20	9.18*

*$p < .01$.
**$p < .001$.

in the predicted direction. However, the picture that emerges is of the fathers having been seen as masculine figures in both groups.

HYPOTHESIS III   Mothers of clinical psychologists will be described as the dominant parent more frequently than physicists' mothers.

This hypothesis may be viewed as the obverse of Hypothesis II. Therefore, it is not now surprising that the predictions relating to it were not confirmed either. In both groups, Ss viewed their mothers as being authoritative about as frequently as they saw them as passive. It would appear from these data that maternal dominance in the family is unrelated to the choice of occupation of physicists and clinical psychologists.

HYPOTHESIS IV   During childhood clinical psychologists had closer and warmer relationships with their mothers than did physicists.

The evidence was generally confirmatory of the fact that clinical psychologists had warmer relationships with their mothers than physicists did. However, it should be pointed out that the confirmation was based on inference. The data clearly indicated that mothers of clinical psychologists were the more expressive and demonstrative. Although it seems likely that demonstrative and emotionally expressive mothers have closer relationships to their sons than undemonstrative ones do, this hypothesis was confirmed only to the extent that the variables of demonstrativeness and close association between mother and child are related to one another.

HYPOTHESIS V   Physicists more than clinical psychologists took their fathers as identity models (role models).

Only one of three predictions was confirmed, although all of the results were in the predicted direction. Coding was difficult for the prediction that the physicist's choice of occupation was more frequently similar to his father's in part because virtually all of the subjects were working toward occupations which required a far greater amount of training than their father's work necessitated. From answers to a question related to the second prediction, one got the impression that the most frequent first response of clinical psychologists was that they saw themselves as being similar to neither parent, while physicists usually settled on one parent or pointed to characteristics of both parents that they saw as also being present in their own make-up. Although the specific prediction was not confirmed, it would seem that physicists see themselves as having some continuity with their parents, while psychologists do not. Coupling this with the confirmation of the last prediction that physicists more frequently describe their fathers as persons to emulate leads one to conclude that in some not clearly specified way the physicist sees himself as wanting to follow in his father's footsteps, while the clinical psychologist does not.

HYPOTHESIS VI   The home environments of clinical psychologists were less conventional than those of physicists.

None of the predictions which dealt with religious and political views was confirmed. While it was originally thought that conventionality was more of an issue for the clinical psychologist than for the physicist, it was also noted that anyone engaged in the enterprise of discovery must be free of rigid adherence to conventional ways of viewing the world. The physicist, then, was not seen as really being opposite to the clinical psychologist with regard to this hypothesis. Therefore, it is not surprising that this hypothesis was not confirmed.

HYPOTHESIS VII   Physicists received more intellectual stimulation from their families than did clinical psychologists.

Two of the three predictions relating to this hypothesis were confirmed. In describing their parents, physicists more frequently characterized them as having intellectual interests. Intellectual stimulation appears,

then, to have been provided the physicists by the behavior and example of their parents. In the second place, intellectuality was emphasized more directly in physicists' families in that family conversations turned more frequently to intellectual matters than in clinical psychologists' families. While such discussion had its positive features and stimulating aspects, it may also have served to avoid dealing with more personal matters which was the concern of Hypothesis I. A third prediction dealing with reading as a family custom was not confirmed.

HYPOTHESIS VIII   Discipline of physicists was rigid, stressed obedience, and was meted out by their fathers; while discipline of clinical psychologists was flexible, stressed appeal to feelings and was meted out by their mothers.

There are three separate issues involved in this hypothesis: (1) the focus of discipline, (2) the degree of consistency of discipline, and (3) the source of discipline. The predictions relating to the first two of these were confirmed. Appeal to feelings as a means of discipline was reported by a majority of the clinical psychologists, but was mentioned by virtually none of the physicists. On the other hand, knowing and following the rules was more frequently stressed in physicists' discipline. Secondly, the discipline of physicists tended to be consistent and predictable, while the clinical psychologists' was more frequently found to be unpredictable. With regard to the third issue, the prediction that physicists' fathers were more frequently chief disciplinarians in the family was not borne out, although the results were in the predicted direction.

HYPOTHESIS IX   Physicists had fewer but less stormy relationships with peers than did clinical psychologists.

Three of the four predictions stemming from this hypothesis were confirmed, supporting the original contention that physicists had few relationships with people throughout childhood and tended to spend much time by themselves, whereas clinical psychologists related to people a good deal, but more frequently had relationships that were conflictful. The prediction that physicists would have had more long illnesses than clinical psychologists was not confirmed. This fact does not detract from the support of the hypothesis, since the concern was not with the presence of illness *per se*, but the fact that long illnesses would have led to isolation from peers. The fact of physicists' greater isolation from peers was established by another prediction.

HYPOTHESIS X   In adolescence clinical psychologists manifested more interest in the opposite sex than did physicists.

The data were in support of the hypothesis of greater involvement with members of the opposite sex by clinical psychologists than by physicists. The latter had fewer dates and were older at the time of their first sexual experiences. One prediction — that clinical psychologists began dating earlier than physicists — was not confirmed, although results were in the predicted direction. The coding was set up in such a way that more than three-fourths of all subjects fell into one coding category, which may have obscured a difference which actually existed.

HYPOTHESIS XI   Clinical psychologists more frequently than physicists had strong but conflictual attachments to their families.

Two predictions relating to conflict with family members and emotional expression in the home were confirmed. The prediction relating to continued involvement between the subject and his family fell just short of significance. The latter prediction was a particularly difficult one to code, since it involved both the amount of present contact between the subject and his family as well as the degree to which the subject still had an emotional investment in his family, a factor which was rather difficult to assess. The hypothesis is supported to the extent that clinical psychologists gave evidence of having had in the past stronger, but more conflictual attachments to their families than did physicists.

An examination of how successfully all of the predictions taken together differentiate the groups serves to provide an overview. To give a general picture of how well the predictions taken as a whole discriminate between the groups, the coded response of each *S* to every item was given a score of one if it was in the direction predicted for physicists and a score of zero if in the direction predicted for clinical psychologists. It was possible for scores to range from zero (all items coded in the direction predicted for clinical psychologists) to 36 (all items coded in the direction predicted for physicists). Actually the scores ranged from 6 to 31. The distribution of scores appears in Table 2.

When the two groups are taken together, the median for the total distribution is 19.5. Only three of the twenty cases in each group fall on that side of the median on which the majority of cases of the other group appears. A median test applied to the data was significant beyond the .001 level of confidence.

DISCUSSION

The present study grew out of an interest in the vicissitudes of curiosity in the developmental process. The results point to several possible ways in which the socialization process may modify curiosity. Parental behaviors of various kinds can act as catalysts that intensify the interest of the child in certain areas of experience. At the same time, other parental attitudes can make clear to the child that there are certain things about which he is not permitted to be curious.

Discipline plays a part also. The more harsh it is and the more it emphasizes restrictions, the more likely the child is to avoid venturing into areas that parents consider taboo. The focus of the parent's discipline may re-emphasize to the child attitudes already expressed in another sphere. For

TABLE 2

Frequency Distribution of Total Scores on All Predictions

Scores	Psychologists	Physicists
6	1	
7		
8		
9	1	
10	1	
11	2	
12	1	
13	3	
14	1	
15	1	
16	1	
17	2	
18	1	1
19	2	2
20	1	
21		2
22	1	1
23	1	2
24		2
25		1
26		3
27		1
28		1
29		3
30		
31		1

example, in their everday life the parents of clinical psychologists showed concern about the behavior and feelings of other people. This concern was reiterated by their appealing to the child's feelings as means of disciplining him.

A natural question in connection with this study arises from the fact that the data represent verbal reports of past events rather than direct observations. The question that must be asked is whether the data, in fact, present evidence about developmental history, or whether they only provide indirect evidence about current personality traits. The rationale for taking the latter position is that the individual has a distorted view of his past based on his current personality make-up, present values, or group norms. An additional question in the same vein might emerge because of the expectation that social scientists have a greater inclination and willingness to talk about "bad" relations with parents and with others than physical scientists do.

It is, of course, not possible to say definitively whether or not the information gathered reflects actual childhood experience. However, there is some suggestion that the data do reflect actual happenings. It is expected that the likelihood of distortion would decrease as the specificity of material is increased, except for the placing of events at specific times, which seems very much subject to inaccuracies of memory. It seems more likely that current attitudes would influence one's impressions of the past than that they could contribute to the inaccuracy of reports about actual events. The predictions of the study were based on both specific facts and diffuse impressions in about equal numbers. About half of those predictions which were based on specific information, presumably not subject to great distortion, were confirmed, supporting the contention that the information gathered does describe actual developmental experiences. Furthermore, an examination of the unconfirmed hypotheses reveals that their subsidiary predictions deal equally often with specific as with diffuse material. The latter fact supports the idea that diffuse material was distorted no more than specific material.

The results of this study are also of practical significance to the vocational counselor. If he has information on the developmental histories of various occupational groups, a counselor is better able to help a client assess the likelihood of satisfaction with his choice of a vocation. These data alone might prove useful only in the rather unlikely situation of a person trying to decide between physics and clinical psychology. However, Nachmann has already provided similar data on three other occupations. Further research in the area will add to the list. Future investigation will be able not only to amass a body of data useful to the vocational counselor, but also to increase our understanding of personality development. Further work ought to focus on the isolation of other personality dimensions which seem to be closely related to various occupations. The final aim is to have the occupational spectrum analyzed in terms of important personality and developmental characteristics, and at the same time to add to the body of knowledge about the process of personality development.

SUMMARY

This study grew out of an attempt to understand the relationship between certain personality characteristics and vocational choice. Specifically, it was concerned with the relationship between the desire to satisfy curiosity and the varying opportunities which occupations afford for its satisfaction. An additional concern was to learn more about the vicissitudes of curiosity in the developmental process. The occupations of clinical psychology and physics were chosen to be studied because of the contrast they provide in terms of different objects of curiosity offered by each — curiosity about interpersonal relations in the first and curiosity about the nature of the physical world in the second. Hypotheses were developed about the probable developmental experiences which would account for each group's personality make-up and occupational choice. Each hypothesis was tested by means of a number of specific predictions about aspects of life history, predictions which were derived from that hypothesis.

The life histories of 40 male graduate students at the University of Michigan — 20 in physics and 20 in clinical psychology — were investigated by means of structured, tape-recorded interviews. The hypotheses were tested by comparison of groups on coded categories, derived from response to the interviews. Seven of the eleven hypotheses tested were in the main confirmed. All results were in the predicted direction. The effects of parental attitudes and styles of discipline on the development of curiosity in the child were discussed.

REFERENCES

Allinsmith, W. *The learning of moral standards.* Unpublished doctoral dissertation, University of Michigan, 1954.

Nachmann, Barbara. Childhood experience and vocational choice in law, dentistry, and social work. *J. counsel. Psychol.*, 1960, 7, 243–250.

Roe, Anne. Early determinants of vocational choice. *J. counsel. Psychol.*, 1957, 4, 212–217.

Segal, S. J. A psychoanalytic analysis of psychological factors in vocational choice. *J. counsel. Psychol.*, 1961, 8, 202–210.

OTHER RELEVANT ARTICLES

Nachmann, B. Childhood experience and vocational choice in law, dentistry, and social work. *Journal of Counseling Psychology*, 1960, 7, 243–250.

Nachmann pursues the hypothesis that different occupations afford differential opportunities for basic personality expression, and that these differences may be observed not only in adult personality, but in childhood experiences which might lead to the personality differences so expressed. She hypothesized the kinds of experiences which would lead to the central characteristics of the work of lawyers, dentists, and social workers, and checked for their presence by means of biographical interviews probing for specific information from twenty male students in each of the appropriate professional schools. Her results permitted retention of essentially the same pictures of the backgrounds of each occupational group as hypothesized.

Beall, L., and E. S. Bordin. The development and personality of engineers. *Personnel and Guidance Journal*, 1964, *43*, 23–32.

This article reports the extensive examination of biographies and other descriptive material of engineers, and the synthesis of their development and personality in terms of the modes of expressing and controlling impulses which the occupation affords. They conclude that the engineer is masculine and identifies with authority, is adventurous, curious, had parents with clearly differentiated sex roles, and experienced early demands for self-reliance and achievement.

Except for the two studies abstracted here, no additional tests of psychoanalytic framework for occupational determinants have appeared, and especially none undertaken in independent research programs. Additional tests or replications of the latter kind would seem appropriate to establish the validity of the theory.

A few other publications of related interest are:

Abeles, N., and J. F. Morse. A neo-Freudian look at occupational stereotypes. *American Psychologist*, 1960, *15*, 454–455 (Abstract).

Beall, Lynette. Vocational choice: The impossible fantasy and the improbable choice. *Journal of Counseling Psychology*, 1967, *14*, 86–92.

Cautela, J. R. The factor of psychological need in occupational choice. *Personnel and Guidance Journal*, 1959, *38*, 46–48.

Galinsky, M. D., and I. Fast, Vocational choice as a focus of the identity search. *Journal of Counseling Psychology*, 1966, *13*, 89–92.

Menninger, K. Psychological factors in the choice of medicine as a profession. *Bulletin of the Menninger Clinic*, 1957, *21*, 51–58, 99–106.

Need Reduction
as an Occupational
Determinant

8

It may be recalled that some theoretical views already presented propose intermediate constructs, such as needs, interests, manifest personality traits, or values, standing between more fundamental determinants and occupational behavior. This chapter focuses on theoretical formulations of how these intermediate determinants operate, and present some of the evidence from the broad distribution which is available.

The need reduction concept is in the direct lineage of the earlier chapter showing individual differences in occupations, expanded in the direction of showing that these differences may be perceived more or less accurately by the chooser of an occupation as indicative of the kind of satisfaction of which he may avail himself.

Variation in attractiveness is postulated to be the consequence of differing motivational states of the perceiver, organized in such concepts as interests, values or needs. Thus, the satisfaction of interests or values, or the reduction of needs by the choice of an occupation is the central operational statement of this theoretical view.

This position has developed without much in the way of any formal, explicit statements. One which has been carefully developed is that of Holland, presented as the first and only theoretical paper in this chapter. Note that he specifies a limited set of conditions seeking satisfaction, and an exactly corresponding set of satisfaction-providing environments. He adds that the level of the occupation chosen is a function of the chooser's evaluation of his ability, and that the individual's perception of both his needs and abilities is influenced by factors such as we would find in Roe's and similar formulations.

In the next paper, by Merwin and DiVesta, it is shown that a favorable disposition toward an occupation is the result of the perception that the occupation offers potential to facilitate the satisfaction of important needs. They chose one object to evaluate: teaching, which appears relatively diverse in perception of its potential or instrumentality for satisfaction. They found that it is attractive in proportion that it is perceived to provide satisfaction for the perceiver's needs. In an additional portion of the study, the authors report that perception of the instrumentality of teaching and the attitude toward it can be changed, variably, by a persuasive communication.

Burnstein, Moulton, and Liberty investigate the effect of achievement needs and values on the choice of occupations differing in the excellence they require relative to the prestige they confer. They demonstrate fairly conclusively that there exist some occupations which are discrepant in this way, and that the conscious valuing of achievement, accompanied by a deeper, perhaps more unconscious achievement motivation, move the individual to favor the occupations which demand more excellence in relation to the prestige they confer. The converse is true of low achievement oriented choosers.

The final article by Miller is notable in making a distinction between choice of occupational function and choice of setting in which the function is performed, as a result of personality factors and needs. Although undertaken partly to illustrate occupational differences, its careful exploration of the relationship between needs and chosen occupation marks it as another need reduction conception of occupational choice.

A Theory of Vocational Choice

JOHN L. HOLLAND, *American College Testing Program*

Previous theories of vocational choice appear to have two serious deficiencies: they are either too broad or too specialized. Some theories — for example, Ginzberg's theory and Super's theory of vocational development (1951, 1957) — are so general in statement that they are of negligible value for integrating present knowledge or stimulating further research. In contrast, other writers (Bordin, 1943; Hoppock, 1957; Roe,

Reprinted with the permission of author and publisher from the article of the same title, in *Journal of Counseling Psychology*, 1959, 6, 35–45.

1957) have concentrated on more limited aspects of vocational choice with more explicit theories, but these are incomplete in that they are self-concept-centered, need-centered, or etiologically-oriented, although there is an extensive literature implying that all of these divergent emphases are probably of importance in vocational choice. The need for more comprehensive theorizing is also indicated in previous papers by Bachrach (1957), Beilin (1955), and Blau, *et al.* (1956).

The present paper is an attempt to delineate a theory of vocational choice which is comprehensive enough to integrate existing knowledge and at the same time sufficiently close to observables to stimulate further research. Essentially, the present theory assumes that at the time of vocational choice the person is the product of the interaction of his particular heredity with a variety of cultural and personal forces including peers, parents and significant adults, his social class, American culture, and the physical environment. Out of this experience the person develops a hierarchy of habitual or preferred methods for dealing with environmental tasks. From an ecological standpoint, these habitual methods are associated with different kinds of physical and social environments, and with differential patterns of abilities. The person making a vocational choice in a sense "searches" for situations which satisfy his hierarchy of adjustive orientations. The following sections specify the theory in terms of the occupational environments, the person and his development, and the interactions of the person and the vocational environment.

THE OCCUPATIONAL ENVIRONMENTS

The following environments are the major classes of occupational environments useful in organizing knowledge about vocational choice. The classification, though not exhaustive, is assumed to include all the major kinds of American work environments. Ultimately the classification may include more subcategories; however, in view of the present state of evidence, it seems simpler and more desirable to predict for major occupational areas rather than for specific occupations. The major occupational environments are:

1. *The Motoric Environment.* Illustrative occupations are laborers, machine operators, aviators, farmers, truck drivers, and carpenters.

2. *The Intellectual Environment.* Illustrative occupations are physicists, anthropologists, chemists, mathematicians, and biologists.

3. *The Supportive Environment.* Illustrative occupations are social workers, teachers, interviewers, vocational counselors, and therapists.

4. *The Conforming Environment.* Illustrative occupations are bank tellers, secretaries, bookkeepers, and file clerks.

5. *The Persuasive Environment.* Illustrative occupations are salesmen, politicians, managers, promoters, and business executives.

6. *The Esthetic Environment.* Illustrative occupations are musicians, artists, poets, sculptors, and writers.

THE PERSON AND HIS DEVELOPMENT

The Development Hierarchy

At the time of vocational choice the person has a set of adjustive orientations. The adjustive orientations, corresponding to the six occupational environments, are designated as motoric, intellectual, supportive, conforming, persuasive, and esthetic methods or orientations. Each orientation represents a somewhat distinctive life style which is characterized by preferred methods of dealing with daily problems and includes such variables as values and "interests," preferences for playing various roles and avoiding others, interpersonal skills and other personal factors. For every person, the orientations may be ranked, according to their relative strengths, in a quasi-serial order or hierarchy. The life style heading the hierarchy determines the major direction of choice.

This intrapersonal hierarchy can be defined by coded "interest" inventories, though such inventories are incomplete estimates of the hierarchical ordering. "Interest inventories" are conceived here as personality inventories which reveal information such as the person's values, attitudes, needs, self-concept, preferred activities, and sources of threat and dissatisfaction.[1]

The Modal Personal Orientations

The following formulations are an attempt to integrate and conceptualize the extensive evidence about persons in the major occupational classes. In the main these formulations were derived by reviewing the Strong scoring keys, and a variety of major studies by Strong (1943), Gough (1955), Laurent (1951), Weinstein (1953), Forer (1951), and others. Although admittedly theoretical, these characterizations may help to integrate research and develop theory about occupational classes.

THE MOTORIC ORIENTATION   Persons with this orientation enjoy activities requiring physical strength, aggressive action, motor coordination and skill; and perhaps above all they wish to play masculine roles. They prefer dealing with concrete, well-defined problems as opposed to abstract, intangible ones. In a sense, they prefer to "act out," rather than to "think through," problems. They avoid situations which require verbal and interpersonal skills, because they lack such skills and are often threatened by close relationships with others. They conceive of themselves as aggressive, strong, masculine persons with conventional political and economic values. Persons of this orientation are typified by their masculinity, their physical strength and skills, their concrete, practical way of dealing with life problems, and their corresponding lack of social skills and sensitivities.

THE INTELLECTUAL ORIENTATION   Persons of this orientation appear to be task-oriented people who generally prefer to "think through," rather than to "act out," problems. They have marked needs to organize and understand the world. They enjoy ambiguous work tasks and intraceptive activi-

ties and possess somewhat unconventional values and attitudes. They avoid interpersonal problems which require interpersonal activity with groups of people or with new people from day to day.

In general this orientation is designated as intellectuality since the concept seems to subsume the following key variables represented in this classification: (a) Abstraction as opposed to concreteness; (b) Anality as opposed to orality; (c) Intraception as opposed to extraception; (d) Asociality as opposed to sociality. Weinstein's work suggests that this orientation represents the anal retentive character (1953). Stern's concept of the Rational type also resembles the major outline for this orientation (1956). Fromm's Hoarding orientation and Horney's Detached type appear to be similar types (Blum, 1953).

THE SUPPORTIVE ORIENTATION   Persons of this orientation prefer teaching or therapeutic roles, which may reflect a desire for attention and socialization in a structured, and therefore safe, setting. They possess verbal and interpersonal skills. They are also characterized as responsible, socially oriented and accepting of feminine impulses and roles. Their chief values are humanistic and religious. They are threatened by and avoid situations requiring intellectual problem-solving, physical skills or highly ordered activities, since they prefer to deal with problems through feeling and interpersonal manipulations of others.

Persons of this class are best typified as orally dependent in the sense of being verbal feminine, and dependent. This orientation corresponds to Fromm's Receptive orientation and Horney's Compliant type (Blum, 1953). Weinstein's study of social workers supports these hypotheses (1953).

THE CONFORMING ORIENTATION   Persons of this class prefer structured verbal and numerical activities, and subordinate roles. They achieve their goals through conformity. In this fashion, they obtain satisfaction and avoid the conflict and anxiety aroused by ambiguous situations or problems involving interpersonal relationships and physical skills. Their habitual subordination of personal needs appears to make them generally effective in well-structured tasks. Their values and attitudes represent strong identifications with power, externals, and status.

This orientation is perhaps best characterized as extraception: conformity, a whole-hearted acceptance of cultural values and attitudes, a living in the eyes of others with an emphasis on excessive self-control. The latter emphasis reveals a related pattern of adjustment which may develop almost necessarily from the need to conform — the obsessive concern with rules and regulations for living. The stereopathic type as conceptualized by Stern, *et al.* (1956) parallels this orientation.

THE PERSUASIVE ORIENTATION   Persons of this class prefer to use their verbal skills in situations which provide opportunities for dominating, selling, or leading others. They conceive of themselves as strong masculine leaders. They avoid well-defined language or work situations as well as situations requiring long periods of intellectual effort. Although they share a common orientation of extraception, they differ from persons of the Conforming orientation in their need for ambiguous verbal tasks and related skills; their sociality; and their greater concern with power, status, and leadership.

This class is best designated as having an "oral aggressive" orientation. Weinstein's study of lawyers supports this conceptualization (1933). Fromm's Marketing orientation and Horney's Aggressive type (Blum, 1953) correspond in general outline.

THE ESTHETIC ORIENTATION   In general, persons of this orientation prefer indirect relationships with others. They prefer dealing with environmental problems through self-expression in artistic media. They avoid problems requiring interpersonal interac-

tion, a high degree of structuring, or physical skills. They resemble persons with an intellectual orientation in their intraceptiveness and lack of sociability. They differ from the latter group in that they appear to have a greater need for individualistic expression, are more feminine, and perhaps have less ego strength; that is, they appear to have less self-control and a greater need for direct emotional expression, and they probably suffer more from emotional disturbance. Feather (1950), for example, has found that maladjusted students in MMPI terms tend to have high scores on the artistic, literary, and musical scales of the Kuder. The complex person on Barron's complexity-simplicity dimension (1953) reflects this orientation. Segal's findings (1954) for advanced accounting and creative writing students are also consonant with the summaries for the conformity and esthetic environments.

The Level Hierarchy

Within a given class of occupations the level of choice is a function of intelligence and self-evaluation, variables which can be defined by intelligence tests and status scales. Self-evaluation might best be defined by scales of occupational content, such as the OL scale of the Strong or Sim's occupational status scale (1952). The person's score for a status scale of the former type is assumed to represent an estimate of self-evaluation, a general concept which includes one's status needs, and perception of level of competence and potential competence, and the self-estimate of one's worth with respect to others. The most direct evidence for the existence of a self-evaluative disposition is furnished by the Q-sort analysis of high and low scores on an MMPI status scale employed by Block and Bailey (1955) in an assessment study of 100 Air Force Officers. The significant Q-sort statements for high and low scorers appear congruent with the "self-evaluation" hypothesis, especially since "low scorers" are described by raters as: ". . . lacks confidence in his own ability, is self-abasing; feels unworthy, guilty, humble; given to self-blame . . ." In contrast, the high scorers appear to reflect a very positive self-evaluation: ". . . is an effective leader, emphasizes success and productive achievement . . ." A study by Barnett is also consistent with the self-evaluation hypothesis. Barnett (1952) reports a correlation of −.73 between the OL score and an index of satisfaction with chronic unemployment. "As OL scores increased in magnitude expressed satisfaction with vagrancy declined."

Presumably self-evaluation is a function of the life history in which education, socio-economic origin, and family influences are major determinants. The importance of these factors for determining level of choice is exemplified by Hollingshead's study (1949) of adolescents in a midwestern community, in which level of choice was closely related to student socio-economic status.

The factors of self-evaluation and intelligence are assumed to summate and determine level of choice. Their relative degree of influence is presently unclear, although this theory assumes their equal importance. The following formula indicates the relationship between the more significant factors affecting level of occupational choice.

Occupational Level = (Intelligence + Self-evaluation), where self-evaluation is a function of socio-economic origin, need for status, education, and self-concept.

By categorizing these factors in terms of their implication for approximate level of choice, it may be possible to manipulate them for prediction and exploratory purposes. For example, the intelligence levels developed by Miner (1957) or others could be used in conjunction with status scales categorized for similar levels to make predictions about occupational level. It appears possible to make predictions by averaging the ranks for these variables. The resultant of these variables is designated as the occupational level; the ordering of levels is the level hierarchy. For example, if four intelligence and self-evaluation levels are assumed, then the averaging of levels yields the series of predictions shown below. Presumably the empirical study of these variables should yield an analogous formula for predicting level of choice.

Person	Intelligence Level +	Self-evaluation Level =	Occupational Level
A	1	1	1.0
B	1	2	1.5
C	1	3	2.0
D	1	4	2.5
E	2	3	2.5
F	2	4	3.0
G	3	4	3.5
H	4	4	4.0

THE INTERACTION OF THE PERSON AND THE VOCATIONAL ENVIRONMENTS

Schematically, the vocational choice process may be outlined as follows:

1. The person directs himself toward the major occupational class for which his development has impelled him by selecting the occupational class at the head of his particular hierarchy of classes. This dimension of choice is designated as the range of choice, or the variety of relatively different major choices.

2. Within a major class of occupations, the person's selection of an occupation is a function of his self-evaluation and his ability (intelligence) to perform adequately in his chosen environment.

3. Both of the above processes are mediated by a series of personal factors, including self-knowledge and evaluation, knowledge of occupational classes (range of information and the degree of differentiation between and within occupational environments), the orderliness of the developmental hierarchy; and a series of environmental

factors including the range of potential environments, social pressures from family and peers, evaluations of employers and potential employers, and limitations — arbitrary in terms of the theory — imposed by socio-economic resources and the physical environment.

The Role of the Developmental Hierarchy

In the development of the person, a quasi-serial order is established so that the person has an ordering of preferences for the six major environments. In analytic terms, this ordering appears analogous to the effects of the psycho-sexual history. The orientation heading the hierarchy may represent the highest level of fixation, and the ordering of subsequent orientations may represent the traces of other levels of development in order of their influence in the adult personality. The nature of this ordering affects the person's range of vocational choice in a variety of ways:

1. A well-defined hierarchy (one developmental pattern dominating all others) results in directional choice with minimal conflict or vacillation.

2. An ambiguous hierarchy (two or more competing developmental patterns) results in vacillation in direction of choice, or no choice.

3. Blocking of the hierarchical choice by economic factors, employer evaluation (rejection), or any other factor in a well-defined hierarchy results in the selection of the second developmental pattern if the second pattern dominates the third pattern. If the second and third patterns are of equal strength, then vacillation in direction of choice occurs.

4a. Although persons with the same dominant adjustive pattern may head in the same direction, differences in the ordering of the remaining patterns will result in

differences in stability of choice; that is, modal patterns will be associated with stability and atypical patterns with instability. The work of Hoyt, Smith, and Levy (1957) is relevant to the latter hypothesis. They hypothesized that "the greater the integration of an individual's interest pattern, the greater the stability of his SVIB profile." Their re-testing of a sample of 121 students over a four-year period confirmed this hypothesis.

More convincing evidence of the relation of profile patterns and stability of choice has been obtained by Strong (1943, pp. 388–411), and Strong and Tucker (1952). The latter study of military physicians appears to illustrate "drifting" in terms of "range of choice." Strong finds that physicians who have become Army Command and Staff medical officers differ from other service physicians in that they have higher average scores on the SVIB for the following occupational keys: public administrator, office worker, personnel manager, math-science teacher, life insurance salesman. These results suggest that physicians with secondary business and leadership motivation are more apt to "drift" into administrative roles than are physicians with more typical or modal patterns for physicians.

4b. Modal patterning for a particular class of occupations makes for optimal functioning. A useful index of modal patterning can be obtained from the Strong literature. A sample of modal Kuder patterns has been classified by Holland, *et al.* (1953) and appears to be more amenable to research than are the Strong patterns. The latter study in which Barnette's data (1951) were re-examined by the use of modal Kuder patterns suggests that veterans with modal patterns for a particular occupational class are more apt to be judged "successful" than are veterans with more atypical patterns. Similarly, Terman reports that his "C" group, or the low achievers of his gifted group, were characterized by a "considerable number of men . . . whose employment records indicated they were drifters"

(1947, p. 325). They were characterized further by having more C's and fewer A's on the SVIB as well as having lower OL scores. His findings suggest that his C group had many individuals without well-defined hierarchies, with negative self-evaluations (low OL), and with a history of vocational indecision, which seems loosely consistent with the present theory.

4c. Patterning may affect the intensity of a particular direction or the resistance to external forces. Persons with a particular adjustive orientation and modal pattern for that particular direction may be expected to have more resistance to external pressures than will persons with the same dominant direction but with an atypical pattern for that direction. Modal patterns as opposed to atypical patterns probably should be regarded as integrated patterns — integrated in the sense that they represent a set of values, attitudes, and adjustive skills consistent with modal profiles found among many people, so that related classes of occupations occur at the top of the hierarchy and unrelated classes occur at the bottom. The examination of Strong's scale matrices and patterns (1943; Darley and Hagenah, 1955), and the classification codes developed by Holland, *et al.* for the Kuder (1953), demonstrate the clustering of similar occupations not only in terms of positive values and desired situations, but also in terms of values, problems, and environments which are devaluated or avoided.

Personal and Occupational Knowledge

Self-knowledge operates to increase or decrease the accuracy with which the person makes a choice. Self-knowledge is defined as a person's ability to make discriminations among potential environments in terms of his own attributes. Self-knowledge may or may not be expressed in verbal statements of "insight." Self-evaluation as distinguished from self-knowledge is the worth the person attributes to himself. Self-knowledge refers

to the amount of information the person possesses about himself. Over-evaluation leads to the selection of environments beyond the person's adaptive skills (unrealistic aspirations) and under-evaluation leads to the selection of environments below the persons's skills.

HYPOTHESES This formulation suggests the following hypotheses:

1. Persons with inaccurate self-knowledge make inadequate choices more frequently than do persons with more accurate self-appraisals.
2. Persons with limited self-knowledge, including self-evaluation, may make inadequate choices with respect to both range and level of choice.
3. Persons whose self-knowledge is limited in both range (direction) and level (relative level of intelligence) will represent the extremes of inadequate vocational choice. In contrast, persons with relatively accurate self-knowledge will make more adequate choices.

A person's knowledge of occupational classes sets loose limits on his range of choice. A person's differentiation of the major classes and the specific occupations within classes also affects the accuracy with which he can make adequate and stable choices. If, for example, he thinks only of "laboring jobs" versus "clerical jobs," he can make only crude choices with a relatively low probability of being adequate. The person who can differentiate kinds of clerical and laboring jobs is apt to make choices with a higher probability of adequacy. Since it is assumed that the person learns about occupational environments, it is assumed further that a "selective perception" of environments takes place which results in learning more about some environments than about others, especially of the environments potentially meaningful for the person's developmental hierarchy.

HYPOTHESES This formulation suggests hypotheses such as the following:

1. Persons with more information about occupational environments make more adequate choices than do persons with less information.

2. Adequacy of choice is in part a function of age, since time alone provides more learning opportunities for the accumulation of information.

3. Persons with more adequate choices will exhibit greater differentiation and organization of occupational knowledge than will persons with less adequate choices.

4. The amount of occupational knowledge will be positively correlated with the person's developmental hierarchy; that is, the person will know more about the occupations heading his hierarchy than he will about occupations at the bottom of the hierarchy.

The validity of the first hypothesis is suggested by Stone's study of the effects of occupational courses and vocational counseling (1948). In clinical practice, much vocational counseling rests on this assumption, since it is the basis for providing occupational information to clients.

External Influences

A variety of obvious external influences also affects the operation of the developmental hierarchy. Vocational opportunities, for example, limit the range of possible choices; likewise, the social pressures created by significant persons affect both the level and direction of choice. Persons who have a well-ordered hierarchy with a modal pattern for a given class of occupations will be least affected by such forces, while persons with ambiguous hierarchies will be most affected.

The time at which social influence occurs is crucial in affecting choice. In early adolescence, prior to a well-integrated hierarchy, social pressures probably have marked effect. Similarly, the childhood relationships outlined by Roe (1957) undoubtedly are of considerable importance in establishing a particular hierarchy, although parental relationships are only one set of many important environmental influences.[2] In contrast, social pressures in late adolescence or early adulthood would be less influential.

In Figure 1 the interactions are diagrammed for a person with a typical Motoric orientation at the second level of choice. The basic dimensions of the occupational classification shown in this figure are, of course, similar to Roe's (1956). The major differences lie in the rationale for level of choice and the number and definition of the major occupational classes. This classification scheme will be treated more extensively in a separate paper.

The dotted lines from peer, parents, and sibling to the person indicate the social influences exerted for particular occupational environments (E) and the level (L) within a particular environment. The numbers accompanying these symbols refer to the numbered environments and levels. Similarly, the dotted lines from the environments to the person symbolize knowledge (K), including knowledge of barriers, that the person has about the various environments. The magnitude of the accompanying number is an index of the amount of information that the person possesses about each environment. In conjunction with occupational knowledge, self-knowledge operates to facilitate or inhibit the operation of the hierarchies by acting as a screen among these various forces and hierarchies.

SOME POTENTIAL RESEARCH

The present theory suggests a number of research problems. Admittedly in order to execute these studies more explicit definitions and additional clarification of some concepts are required in most instances; however, these difficulties do not appear insurmountable. The following paragraphs summarize some research directions.

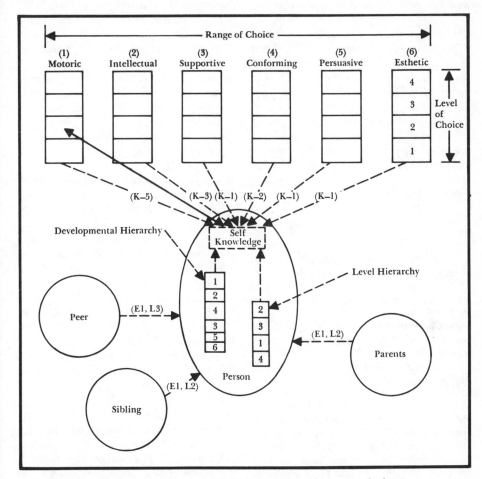

FIGURE 1. Constructs and dimensions for the prediction of vocational choice.

1. The value of the concept of a developmental hierarchy appears amenable to study and extension through the use of coded interest inventories. Recent work by Hoyt, *et al.* (1957) also provides a method and some evidence for the value of this concept.

2. The determination of level of choice might be explored through the use of intelligence, status, and self-concept measures, in order to define the relationships among these variables and the integrative value of the concept, self-evaluation.

3. Simple occupational knowledge tests might be devised to explore the relationships

hypothesized in the theory concerning the amount and selective perception of occupational information as well as the correlations between developmental and level hierarchies, and occupational information.

4. The proposed occupational environment classification might be examined and clarified rationally by reviewing the evidence for a sample of typical occupations for each orientation and at each level, and by the administration of appropriate assessment devices. A systematic review of the evidence relating to major occupations, and an examination of the extent to which the present theory adequately integrates the

available data, are the next steps in checking the theory. The present classifications are, of course, only a set of preliminary sketches. What is needed is a set of well-integrated portraits obtained by reviewing the evidence, classifying it, and interpreting it in terms of meaningful patterns and variables.

5. More complex studies of the interaction of the key variables in the theory might be attempted by using the available definitions. Such studies even if done without precise definition may serve to highlight neglected variables and relationships.

[1]Blau, *et al.* (1956) have also indicated the need for a "preference hierarchy." Their conceptualization and definition of this concept are, however, quite dissimilar from the one proposed here.

[2]The inherited physical, temperamental, and psychological abilities are probably of equal significance. Likewise, sibling and peer relationships, as well as childhood and adolescent social, educational, and prevocational experiences, are assumed to make significant contributions to the formation of the personal hierarchy. In the present theory it is assumed that vocational interest inventories reflect the end product of this developmental process. This is especially plausible when the individual Strong keys are reviewed clinically. For example, the parental atmospheres suggested by Roe's theorizing may be obtained by inference from the Strong keys. Such inferences, however, are not necessary to implement the present theory and appear of lesser *immediate* value in studying the vocational choice process, although the effects of childhood training practices are required to provide a more complete analysis of vocational choice in an ultimate sense.

REFERENCES

Bachrach, P. B. Research notes from here and there. *J. counsel. Psychol.*, 1957, *4*, 71–74.

Barnett, G. J., Handelsman, I., Stewart, L. H., & Super, D. E. The occupational level scale as a measure of drive. *Psychol. Monogr.*, 1952, *66*, No. 10 (Whole No. 342).

Barnette, W. L., Jr. Occupational aptitude patterns of selected groups of veterans. *Psychol. Monogr.*, 1951, *65*, No. 5 (Whole No. 322).

Barron, F. Complexity-simplicity as a personality dimension. *J. abnorm. soc. Psychol.*, 1953, *48*, 163–172.

Beilin, H. The application of general developmental principles to the vocational area. *J. counsel. Psychol.*, 1955, *2*, 53–57.

Blau, P. M., Gustad, J. W., Jessor, R., Parnes, H. S., and Wilcock, R. C. Occupational choice: a conceptual framework. *Industr. Labor Relat. Rev.*, 1956, *9*, 531–543.

Block, J. and Bailey, D. Q-sort item analysis of a number of MMPI scales. *Tech. Memo.* OERL-TM-55-7, AFPTRC, 1955.

Blum, G. S. *Psychoanalytic theories of personality.* New York: McGraw-Hill, 1953.

Bordin, E. S. A theory of vocational interests as dynamic phenomena. *Educ. psychol. Measmt*, 1943, *3*, 49–65.

Darley, J. G. and Hagenah, Theda. *Vocational interest measurement.* Minneapolis: Univer. of Minnesota Press, 1955.

Feather, D. B. The relation of personality maladjustments of 503 University of Michigan students to their occupational interest. *J. soc. Psychol.*, 1950, *32*, 71–78.

Forer, B. R. Personality dynamics and occupational choice. Paper read at APA convention, 1951.

Ginsberg, E., Ginzburg, S. W., Axelrad, S., and Herma, J. L. *Occupational choice: An approach to a general theory.* New York: Columbia Univer. Press, 1951.

Gough, H. G., McKee, M. G., and Yandel, R. J. Adjective check lists analyses of a number of selected psychometric and assessment variables. Berkeley: The Institute of Personality Assessment and Research, University of Calif., 1955, Mimeo.

Holland, J. L., Krause, A. H., Nixon, M. Eloise, and Trembath, Mary F. The classification of occupations by means of Kuder interest profiles: I. The development of interest groups. *J. appl. Psychol.*, 1953, *37*, 263–269.

Hollingshead, A. B. *Elmtown's youth.* New York: Wiley, 1949.

Hoppock, R. *Occupational Information.* New York: McGraw-Hill, 1957.

Hoyt, D. P., Smith, J. L. Jr., and Levy, S. A further study in the prediction of interest stability. *J. counsel. Psychol.*, 1957, *4*, 228–233.

Laurent, H., Jr. A study of the developmental backgrounds of men to determine by means of the biographical information blank the relationship between factors in their early backgrounds and their choice of professions. Unpublished doctoral dissertation, Western Reserve Univer., 1951.

Miner, J. B. *Intelligence in the United States.* New York: Springer, 1957.

Roe, Anne. *The pyschology of occupations.* New York: Wiley, 1956.

Roe, Anne. Early determinants of vocational choice. *J. counsel. Psychol.*, 1957, *4*, 212–217.

Segal, S. J. The role of personality factors in vocational choice: A study of accountants and creative writers. Unpublished doctoral dissertation, Univer. of Michigan, 1954.

Sims, V. M. *Sims SCI Occupational Rating Scale.* New York: World Book, 1952.

Stern, G. G., Stein, M. I., and Bloom, B. S. *Methods in personality assessment.* New York: The Free Press, 1956.

Stone, C. H. Are vocational orientation courses worth their salt? *Educ. pyschol. Measmt*, 1948, *8*, 161–181.

Strong, E. K., Jr. *Vocational interests of men and women.* Stanford: Stanford Univer. Press, 1943.

Strong, E. K., Jr., and Tucker, L. R. The use of vocational interest scales in planning a medical career. *Psychol. Monogr.*, 1952, *66*, No. 9 (Whole No. 341).

Super, D. E. *The psychology of careers.* New York: Harper, 1957.

Terman, L. M. *Genetic studies of genius IV: The gifted child grows up.* Stanford: Stanford Univer. Press, 1947.

Weinstein, M. S. Personality and vocational choice. Unpublished doctoral dissertation, Western Reserve Univer., 1953.

A Study of Need Theory and Career Choice

JACK C. MERWIN, *University of Minnesota*

FRANCIS J. DiVESTA[1], *Syracuse University*

In recent years a number of investigations have demonstrated that students undergo a change in attitudes as a result of college

Reprinted with the permission of authors and publisher from the article of the same title, in *Journal of Counseling Psychology*, 1959,6, 302–308.

experience. Typical of such studies are those by Webster (1958), Lagey (1956) and Sandgren and Schmidt (1955). In the main, these studies have been concerned with changes in attitudes toward issues treated in course content rather than with the more informal pressures of the over-all college environment. Little, if any, attention has been given to the general effects on attitudes toward careers, particularly toward teaching as a career. This, together with a comparison of changes resulting from experimental communications is the subject of the present paper. Such information would appear to be of particular interest in a day when educators, and the public in general, are concerned about the supply of teachers. Certainly, the question is of no small importance for liberal arts colleges whose graduates, in increasing numbers, are going on to prepare to teach through an additional year of study at schools of education or teachers colleges.

The theoretical orientation of this study was based on the attitude-concept view (Rhine, 1958; Woodruff, 1942) of attitude structure. Briefly, it states that attitudes are a function of the individual's belief-value matrix. Favorable attitudes are said to result from perceptions that the attitude-object facilitates need-satisfaction, while unfavorable attitudes result from perceptions that attitude-objects block or hinder need-satisfaction. Under this formulation the strength of an attitude will be dependent not only upon the individual's perceptions about the attitude object but also the dominant need(s) engaged by the attitude object. This theory can be applied to career choice by a simple substitution of terms. Thus, the degree of acceptance (or rejection) of a career is dependent upon the individual's perceptions that the career facilitates (or hinders) the satisfaction of his important needs — a formulation somewhat similar to that used by Decker (1955) in a study of job satisfaction.

In accordance with this rationale three different measures were obtained for a group of freshmen who indicated preference for teaching as a career and for a second group of freshmen who indicated a preference for other occupations. One measure was that of a general expression of the individual's feeling of acceptance or rejection of teaching as a career (*attitude*); a second measure was that of the strength of each of

four *needs* selected on an *a priori* basis as related to teaching; and, a third was a measure of the individual's concept of the extent to which teaching facilitated or hindered the satisfaction of each of the four needs (*perceived instrumentality*).

METHOD

Subjects

The *S*s taking part in this experiment were 218 freshmen enrolled in the College of Liberal Arts at Syracuse University. Of this group 67 indicated a preference for teaching as a career and 151 indicated a preference for other occupations. Additional students from this same freshman class and a group of high school upperclassmen were used in reliability studies.

Procedure

Since the experimental procedure used in this study has been described in detail elsewhere (DiVesta and Merwin, 1958) only a brief description of the design will be presented here.

In September, 1957 (*Pre-test₁*), as part of the freshman testing program, the *S*s responded to (a) the *Activities Index* (Stern, 1956), a measure of need strength; (b) a perceived instrumentality instrument, a measure of the extent to which *S* perceived teaching as instrumental to the satisfaction of each of four needs; and, (c) an "Attitude toward Teaching" scale, a measure of the *S*'s feelings of acceptance or rejection of teaching as a career.

In February, mid-way through the freshman year, the *S*s were assigned at random to one of three groups. They were told that their assistance had been solicited to aid in the evaluation of an educational radio program for the university radio station and that they would be asked to respond to questionnaires both before and after the playing of the program. The Ss then responded (*Pre-test₂*) to two scales of the four needs under study and the attitude scale. Each of the three groups then listened to a 14-minute tape recorded communication. One experimental group heard a communication organized around the implied assertion that, "teaching is a good career because it satisfies the achievement need" (*positive* communication). A second experimental group heard a communication implying that, "teaching is a good career because it does not involve satisfaction of the achievement need" (*negative* communication). The third group listened to a nonrelevant communication on "Going to College" (*control* communication). At the conclusion of the program Ss were administered (*Post-test*) the perceived instrumentality instrument and the attitude scale.

Measures

1. Two Likert-type needs scales (each 40 items in length and composed of 10 items for each need under study) were developed for this study. These scales permitted a check on the reliability of comparable measures of need strength and facilitated experimental procedure by attacking only the needs relevant to the study. The equivalence of these two scales, as indicated by the correlation between corresponding subscales, is .62 for achievement (nAch), .57 for affiliation (nAff), .70 for dominance (nDom), and .68 for exhibition (nExh). One of these scales had statements similar to those used on the *Activities Index*, though a six-point scale was used rather than the original two-point scale. Thus some evidence of stability is provided by the correlation between the corresponding submeasures from these two instruments over a four-month period (September to February). The coefficients obtained were .53 for nAch. .53 for nAff, .64 for nDom, and .60 for nExh,

2. The perceived instrumentality (*PI*) instrument was composed of 56 items to measure S's concept of the potential that teaching has for satisfying the four needs. The 14 items of the subscales were intermixed at random. The coefficients of stability for a four-month period were .59 for *PI*ach, .55 for *PI*aff, .70 for *PI*dom, and .65 for *PI*exh.

3. An 11-item, six-point, Likert-type scale was used to measure attitude toward career teaching. The corrected split-half coefficient of equivalence was .71. The coefficient of stability of the scale obtained over a four-month period was .79.

On the basis of the rationale, it was necessary that the perceived instrumentality instrument and the attitude scale probe different aspects of S's views of career teaching. Evidence of this was obtained by correlating attitude scores with each of the subscales of the perceived instrumentality instrument. The obtained coefficients with attitude were .24 for *PI*ach, .29 for *PI*aff, .14 for *PI*dom, and .26 for *PI*exh. These figures indicate that the two types of measures are sufficiently independent.

RESULTS

1. The strength of each of four needs for the teaching and nonteaching groups were compared using the t test of significance of difference in means. These comparisons on each of the needs scales are presented in Table 1. The direction of difference in means for each need was consistent across all three scales. For two of the needs the difference was significant on all scales; the teaching group had a significantly higher mean score on need for affiliation and the nonteaching group had a significantly higher mean score on need for dominance. On only one of the three scales was a significant difference found for either the achievement need or the exhibition need, the "nonteaching" group being higher on both.

TABLE 1

Comparison of Need Scores of Teaching and Nonteaching Groups

Needs	Teaching (N = 67) Mean	S.D.	Nonteaching (N = 151) Mean	S.D.	t
Pre-test₁ᵃ					
Achievement	4.91	2.14	5.34	2.02	−1.37
Affiliation	7.36	1.58	6.85	1.81	2.08*
Dominance	4.54	2.15	5.59	2.21	−3.30**
Exhibition	3.85	2.10	4.41	2.38	−1.73
Pre-test₂ — Scale Aᵇ					
Achievement	21.94	5.45	19.10	5.17	3.60**
Affiliation	16.16	4.38	17.79	5.46	−2.33*
Dominance	28.46	7.64	26.12	7.40	2.11*
Exhibition	32.36	7.08	30.24	7.66	2.00*
Pre-test₂ — Scale Bᵇ					
Achievement	29.69	7.28	28.48	7.59	1.11
Affiliation	21.61	7.73	24.87	8.95	−2.74**
Dominance	37.79	6.41	34.74	7.16	3.12**
Exhibition	32.91	7.70	32.07	6.98	0.77

ᵃThe higher score represents the stronger need strength.
ᵇThe lower score represents the stronger need strength.
*$p < .05$.
**$p < .01$.

TABLE 2

Comparison of Teaching and Nonteaching Groups on Pre-test Measures

Score	Teaching (N = 67) Mean	S.D.	Nonteaching (N = 151) Mean	S.D.	t
Perceived Instrumentality					
Achievement	44.54	8.57	48.98	9.07	3.57**
Affiliation	45.22	8.22	48.14	7.62	2.46*
Dominance	42.48	7.72	43.19	8.59	0.60
Exhibition	44.82	9.78	45.82	5.45	0.78
Attitude					
Pre-test₁	26.57	8.74	41.85	9.77	11.48**
Pre-test₂	26.30	6.00	40.49	9.87	13.01**

ᵃHigher scores indicate less favorable attitude or PI.
*$p < .05$.
**$p < .01$.

2. The means and the *t* values of the differences between means on the pretest measures of attitudes and perceived instrumentality for the two groups are presented in Table 2. The teaching group perceived teaching as having more potential for satisfying each of the four needs than did the nonteaching group. However, only the difference in mean scores of perceived instrumentality of teaching for satisfying the needs of achievement and of affiliation were significant at the .05 level. On both pretest measures the "teaching" group had a significantly (p<.01) more favorable attitude toward teaching. This is as would be expected if the attitude scale is measuring attitudes toward teaching(considering the basis for forming groups.

3. The changes in attitude scores for the two groups over a four-month period are presented in Table 3. The nonteaching group changed significantly (p<.05) in a positive direction during this period. The mean change in the attitude scores for teaching group was not significant. The difference in the mean changes for the two groups was not significant.

4. In Tables 4 and 5 are presented the data with respect to the effects of the experimental communications on the two groups of *S*s.

In Table 4 are shown the results with the positive communication. The mean change in score on perceived instrumentality of teaching for satisfying the achievement need was significant for both groups; at the

TABLE 3

Change in Attitude toward Teaching over a Four-Month Period

Vocational Choice	*N*	*Mean*	*t* (H:$\mu = 0$)[a]	*t* (H:$\mu_1 = \mu_2$)[b]
Teaching	67	0.27	0.31	
				1.06
Nonteaching	151	1.36	2.24*	

[a]Mean tested against a hypothesized population mean of zero.
[b]Difference in means of teaching and nonteaching groups tested against the hypothesized equality of the means in the populations.
  p<.05.

TABLE 4

Changes in Attitude and *PI*ach for *S*s Receiving the Positive Communication

Vocational choice	*N*		Change in PI*ach*			Change in Attitude (*Pre-test₂ — Post-test*)		
		Mean	*t* (H:$\mu = 0$)	*t* (H:$\mu_1 = \mu_2$)	*Mean*	*t* (H:$\mu = 0$)	*t* (H:$\mu_1 = \mu_2$)
Teaching	28	4.36	2.98**		0.07	0.12	
				0.86			0.54
Nonteaching	48	2.73	2.33*		1.62	2.35*	

  p<.05.
  **p*<.01.

.01 level of significance for the teaching group and at the .05 level of significance for the nonteaching group. The difference in the mean changes was not significant.

The mean of the changes in the attitude scores for the nonteaching group over the experimental session (Pre-test$_2$ — Post-test) was significant at the .05 level. The mean of of the changes in attitude scores for the teaching group over this period was negligible and not statistically significant. The difference in the mean changes in attitude scores for the two groups was not significant.

In Table 5 are presented the results with the negative communication. This communication had a generally negative effect on both attitude toward teaching and perceived instrumentality of teaching for

satisfying the achievement need. The change in instrumentality scores for the nonteaching group was significant at the .01 level, while the change for the teaching group was not significant at the .05 level. The difference in the mean changes for the two groups was significant at the .05 level.

The mean change in the attitude scores was in the negative direction for both groups. The change for the teaching group was significant at the .05 level and the change for the nonteaching group was not significant. The difference in the means of the changes for the two groups was not significant

In Table 6 are presented the results with the control communication. As shown, the changes in attitude and perceived instrumentality for both groups were negligible.

TABLE 5

Changes in Attitude and *PI*ach for Subjects Receiving the Negative Communication

Vocational Choice	N	Change in PIach			Change in Attitude (Pre-test$_2$ — Post-test)		
		Mean	t (H:μ = O)	t (H:μ_1 = μ_2)	Mean	t (H:μ = O)	t (H:μ_1 = μ_2)
Teaching	19	−3.32	−1.72		−1.84	−2.22*	
				2.16*			0.76
Nonteaching	50	−8.54	−5.89**		−1.08	−1.92	

*p < .05.
**p < .01.

TABLE 6

Changes in Attitude and *PI*ach for Ss Receiving the Control Communication

Vocational Choice	N	Change in PIach			Change in Attitude (Pre-test$_2$ — Post-test)		
		Mean	t (H:μ = O)	t (H:μ_1 = μ_2)	Mean	t (H:μ = O)	t (H:μ_1 = μ_2)
Teaching	20	−0.15	−0.02		−0.60	−0.80	
				0.20			0.32
Nonteaching	53	0.91	0.82		−0.89	−1.65	

DISCUSSION

1. A first question asked was, "How does the 'nonteaching' group differ, initially, from the 'teaching' group on each of the three measures?" The group selecting occupations other than teaching had greater measured needs for achievement, dominance and exhibition than the group selecting teaching. The latter group, on the other hand, indicated a higher need for affiliation. It is not our intent to imply that these are the only needs that would differentiate between the two groups. Had a greater variety of needs been measured other distinctions between the two groups may have been noted.

On all measures of perceived instrumentality the teaching group viewed a career of teaching as being more beneficial to the satisfaction of the four needs than did the nonteaching group. The perceptions of the two groups differed most widely on the perceived instrumentality of teaching for satisfying the achievement need and the affiliation need, the teaching group taking the more favorable view in each case.

If these results are viewed in combination it may be seen that the teaching group had a relatively higher need for affiliation, coupled with the concept that teaching satisfies the need for affiliation. On the other hand, the nonteaching group had a higher need for achievement coupled with the concept that teaching *does not* satisfy the need for achievement. In view of these combinations of two important facets, need strength and perceived instrumentality, of attitude structure it is not surprising to see the wide difference in attitude of the two groups. Thus, the teaching group has generally favorable feelings of acceptance about teaching as a career; while the nonteaching group feels that teaching would be undesirable as a career. These results are consistent with the rationale presented earlier and indicate the validity of the attitude scale.

2. A second question of concern in our analysis was, "What effect does one semester of attendance in a liberal arts college have on attitudes toward teaching?" Here the findings indicate that those who selected teaching as a career retain their initial position with no change. Those *Ss* who feel that other vocations were more suitable as careers do change significantly toward a more favorable attitude, although their general position remains one of rejection. These results, of course, do not signify what factors were influential in effecting this change. Presumably, any one or more of such variables as courses taken, experiences of success and failure, interaction with peers, and the like may have had their effect on attitude structure.

The results indicate a general positive effect, however slight, of the environment in which the study was conducted on attitude toward teaching as a career. However, it may be that this is the effect of a "press" peculiar to the institution or to a type of institution it represents (Pace and Stern, 1958). Whether similar studies conducted in other colleges would result in the same effect or reflect pressures unique to those environments is a question for further investigation.

3. A third question in the interpretation of the results is, "Do the two groups differ in receptivity to two persuasive communications in which the instrumentality of teaching for satisfying the need for achievement is differentially engaged?" From the theoretical point of view this is an important question since the results indicate that attitudes may be changed by manipulating cognitive structure, *i.e.* by proving information about the consequences of an activity with respect to satisfaction of needs. From a practical viewpoint it suggests a means of developing communications for persuasive appeals.

The analyses indicate that the perceived instrumentality of both the teaching and nonteaching groups changed in a positive direction to a significant degree as a result of the positive communication. The nonteaching group, however, was the only group that showed a significant change in attitude.

The negative communication had an opposite effect on these two groups. The teaching group became slightly more negative in perceived instrumentality, although not significantly so, while the non-teaching group became significantly more confirmed in its convictions that teaching lacked instrumentality for satisfying the need for achievement. The attitudes of both groups changed toward a more negative position as a result of the negative communication, although only the change for the teaching group was significant.

In view of the negligible changes in the control group, the significant changes in the experimental groups may be attributed to the effects of the communications. Thus, it would appear that appeals based on the rationale underlying the communications used in this study can be used effectively to change concepts and attitudes in desired directions.

4. The changes in perceived instrumentality provide a demonstration of the Levine and Murphy (1943) effect, *i.e.* that subjects accept information more readily when the information coincides with their existing, or initial, convictions. The changes in attitudes indicate that communications are more effective for those whose initial positions are farther removed from that of the communication than for subjects close to the position advocated in the communication.

5. This study has demonstrated that a change in attitude toward a career field can be altered by manipulating cognitive structure. In addition, a means is suggested by which persuasive appeals may be used to enlist the interest of potential candidates in a particular career field.

[1]This research was supported in part by the United States Air Force under Contract No. AF 41(657)-73 monitored by the Office for Social Science Programs, Air Force Personnel and Training Research Center, Lackland Air Force Base, Texas, F. J. Di Vesta, principal investigator. Permission is granted for reproduction, translation, publication and disposal in whole and in part by or for the United States Government. This is not an official publication under the contract. Views or opinions expressed or implied herein are not to be construed as necessarily reflecting the views or endorsement of the Department of the Air Force or of the Air Research and Development Command.

REFERENCES

Decker, R. L. A study of three specific problems in the measurement and interpretation of employee attitudes. *Psychol. Monogr.*, 1955, *69*, No. 16 (Whole No. 401.)

DiVesta, F. J., and Merwin, J. C. *The effects of need-oriented communications on attitude structure and change.* WADC-TR-58-93. ASTIA Document No. AD-151-044. Lackland Air Force Base, Texas: Personnel Laboratory, Wright Air Development Center, 1958.

Lagey, J. C. Does teaching change students' attitudes? *J. educ. Res.*, 1956, *50*, 307–311.

Levine, J. M., and Murphy, G. The learning and forgetting of controversial material. *J. abnorm. soc. Psychol.*, 1943, *38*, 507–515.

Pace, C. R., and Stern, G. G. An approach to the measurement of psychological characteristics of college environments. *J. educ. Psychol.*, 1958, *49*, 269–277.

Rhine, R. J. A concept-formation approach to attitude acquisition. *Psychol. Rev.*, 1958, *65*, 362–370.

Sandgren, D., and Schmidt, L. G. Does practice teaching change attitudes toward teaching? *J. educ. Res.*, 1955, *49*, 673–680.

Stern, G. G. *Activities index.* Syracuse, N. Y.: Psychological Research Center, Syracuse Univer., 1956.

Webster, H. Changes in attitudes during college. *J. educ. Psychol.*, 1958, *49*, 109–117.

Woodruff, A. D. Personal values and the direction of behavior. *Sch. Rev.*, 1942, *50*, 32–42.

Prestige versus Excellence
as Determinants of Role Attractiveness

EUGENE BURNSTEIN, *University of Michigan*

ROBERT MOULTON, *University of Michigan*

PAUL LIBERTY, JR., *Southwestern Cooperative Educational Laboratory, Inc.*

An occupational role requires a certain level of excellence, and the role incumbent who meets that level accrues a certain amount of prestige. According to Davis and Moore,[1] when the amount of prestige conferred is incommensurate with excellence required, marked variations must occur in role attractiveness. Their theory would predict that the direction of variation will depend on whether prestige is high or low relative to the labor, skill or talent demanded by the activity. When prestige is high relative to the demands of the role, attraction to the role should be strong; when role prestige is low relative to demands, attraction should be weak. But, we will here argue, the validity of this hypothesis for any given role system depends on the motivational structure of the members. Just as motives other than prestige may determine performance once one occupies a role,[2] motives other than prestige may also determine the attractiveness and, thus, the choice of a role. The key question is: Are there motives which make prestige unnecessary or relatively unimportant in attracting a sufficient number of individuals toward arduous but functionally important roles?

Reprinted with the permission of authors and publisher from the article of the same title, in *American Sociological Review*, 1963, *28*, 212–219.

McClelland, Atkinson, French, Strodtbeck, and Rosen[3] have investigated the motivation (need for achievement) and value orientations (achievement values) energizing and directing performance in a wide range of activities where the person competes with some standard of excellence. Here we will be concerned with the effects of achievement motivation and achievement values on the attractiveness of occupational roles which vary in the prestige they confer and in the excellence they demand.

Laboratory studies with relatively simple activities such as games and puzzles indicate that high need achievers anticipate an increase in positive affect via successful task performance when the task indicates personal excellence.[4] They are more concerned than low need achievers with doing the task well. Such concerns are reflected in superior performance. When, however, performance does not reflect personal competence — that is, when the reward for productivity is extrinsic (e.g., getting out of work early, and where standards for gauging improvement are absent) — subjects high in achievement motivation do not perform better than those low in achievement motivation.

Individuals high in need-achievement have a strong internal push to excel. When an activity permits the demonstration of excellence, they are likely to be more attracted to it and out-perform low need achievers. If the activity is irrelevant to personal competence, the differences as a function of need-achievement tend to disappear. In fact under the latter conditions, when high productivity leads to an early escape from work, performance seems to be negatively related to achievement motivation.[5] This suggests that getting out of work has more appeal as achievement motivation decreases. Thus, individuals high in need-achievement desire activities which provide an unambiguous test of competence, while those low in need-achievement seem to avoid such a test. These latter individuals may be forced into striving for a "successful" situation in life, but at the same time they hesitate to approach positions which afford a clear, realistic assessment of their competence. Under these conditions individuals low in need-achievement may be attracted to activities which do not require excellence but do give the external appearance of "success," e.g., occupations which confer high prestige but demand relatively little competence. As a first approximation, low achievement motivation may imply an other-directed person, highly impressed by the positive evaluations of others, who tends to avoid tests of his capacities.[6]

This relation between need-achievement and striving has been noted outside the laboratory as well as in it. Thus, achievement motivation has been shown to be positively associated with social status,[7] mobility,[8] entrepreneurial activity,[9] and role aspirations.[10] For example, individuals high in achievement motivation are less likely to be defensive about their occupational future; they tend to have a higher level of aspiration and are less willing to settle for relatively unsatisfying occupational roles if the struggle for success could be foregone.

Nevertheless, achievement motivation, in and of itself, may not be sufficient to produce a stable and widespread predilection for difficult occupational roles. It is unlikely to provide adequate direction for achievement motivated performance (e.g., need-achievement may be expressed through such nonvocational activities as sports and hobbies) nor is it likely to support the onerous choices which accompany occupational striving (e.g., deciding that familial ties are secondary concerns). In considering the consequences of achievement motivation for social mobility, Rosen[11] has noted that the need-achievement can be expressed through a wide range of behavior, some of which may not facilitate social mobility. Even when expressed through vocational activity, the achievement motive may be directed into deviant occupations (e.g., the criminal) or into low status vocations (e.g., the individual whose achievement motivation is expressed and satisfied through his desire to be the best welder among his peers). Whether the individual will decide to seek success in situations which facilitate mobility in our society will, in part, be determined by his *values*. In a factor analysis of value-achievement items,[12] Strodtbeck found that beliefs which (a) stress the possibility of rational mastery of the situation, and (b) sanction independence of, or separation from the family are postively related to indices of achievement striving, e.g., academic success, socio-economic status. Since similar relationships exist between such indices and need-achievement, it is likely that achievement values and achievement motivation also act jointly as determinants of achievement striving in the selection of role activities.

Prestige is rewarding to most individuals independent of need-achievement and value-achievement. Yet in a society containing a sufficient number of members with high achievement motivation and strong achievement values, prestige may be a *relatively unimportant* incentive for choosing certain occupational activities. For these individuals the correlation between the amount of competence required by an occupational role and its attractiveness should be markedly greater than the correlation between occupational prestige and attractiveness. On the other hand, the correlation between prestige and attractiveness among individuals low in need-achievement and value-achievement should be appreciably greater than that between required competence and attractiveness. Thus, at any level of prestige, occupational roles requiring a relatively high level of competence will be more attractive to individuals high in achievement motivation and achievement values than roles requiring a relatively low level of competence. Furthermore, the attractiveness of occupations which require a high level of competence should be greater for these individuals than those low in achievement motivation and achievement values, who are not differentially attracted as a function of excellence. However, in order to test these hypotheses a representative sample of occupations is needed in which prestige is unrelated, or at least only weakly related to required competence. As the correlation between prestige and excellence increases, it becomes more difficult to separate their independent effects on role attractiveness. But, given a sample of occupations covering a broad range of prestige values, it is highly unrealistic to expect prestige and required competence to be independent of each other.

However, a small subset of occupations is likely to be present in which prestige is not commensurate with the degree of excellence required. When an appreciable discrepancy obtains between prestige and required competence, activities demanding a high degree of excellence relative to their prestige are likely to be more attractive to individuals high in achievement motivation and achievement values than activities which award a good deal of prestige relative to the excellence demanded. The reverse should be true for those weak in need-achievement and value-achievement.

RESEARCH PROCEDURE

The sample consisted of 116 undergraduate males in different sections of an introductory psychology course at the University of Texas. To measure achievement motivation, responses to four Thematic Apperception Test type pictures were scored by a procedure that Atkinson and his associates have standardized,[13] in which the strength of achievement motivation is measured by the frequency of achievement imagery in the stories. Subjects with scores above the median were considered high in achievement motivation; those below the median were considered low. A month later a second experimenter administered a "Student Questionnaire." Subjects evaluated 17 occupations (see Table 1) and answered items relevant to achievement values.

The evaluations of occupations were made along three dimensions — occupational prestige, competence required by the occupation, and the attractiveness of the occupation. These evaluations were made in terms of the following questions: 1. "How pleased or disappointed would you be if you had the following occupations as an adult?" Six alternatives ranging from "highly pleased" to "highly disappointed" were given. 2. "All jobs have a certain amount of social standing or social prestige associated with them. Encircle the statement next to each job that indicates your own opinion of its social standing or prestige." Besides each occupation in this second listing, six alternatives were given ranging from "A job of the highest social standing" to "A job of poor social standing." 3. "All jobs differ in the amount of competence, i.e., specialized training, ability, knowledge, and skill, they require. Encircle the statement that indicates your own opinion of the amount of competence required by the particular job." Next to each occupation in this third listing were six alternatives ranging from "A job requiring an extremely high degree of competence" to "A job requiring almost no competence." In all three questions a score of "one" was given for the first alternative a score of "six" for the last. No neutral categories were presented.

Two sets of items have been used in the past to assess achievement values. One set developed by deCharms[14] consists of nine items which must all be answered positively in order to be high in value-achievement. A second set used by Strodtbeck[15] consists of eight items, all but one of which must be answered negatively to be high in achievement values. A large body of research[16] has clearly shown that there is a general tendency based on stimulus properties of the item and on personality characteristics of the respondent to answer affirmatively or negatively *independent of the content of the item.*

This fact most likely accounts for the positive correlation deCharms, et al.,[17] obtained between their measure and the F-scale. It was decided to combine both the deCharms and the Strodtbeck items to form an approximately balanced scale of achievement values — ten items which must be answered positively and seven items requiring negative answers to be high in achievement values. Only those who were high (above the median) on *both* the deCharms and the Strodtbeck items were used as high value-achievement subjects while only those who scored low (below the median) on *both* sets of items were included as low value-achievement subjects, This provided a sample of 82 subjects who completed the occupational ratings and for whom adequate need-achievement and achievement value scores were available. For the purposes of analysis two subjects were discarded at random, so that the four subgroups, high achievement motivation-high achievement values, high achievement motivation-low achievement values, low achievement motivation-high achievement values, low achievement motivation-low achievement values each contained 20 subjects.

RESULTS AND DISCUSSION

The representativeness of our sample may in part be determined by comparing their ratings of prestige with that made by a national sample. A rank order correlation of .96 obtains between our prestige ranking and that found by the National Opinion Research Center[18] during the mid-1940's (see Table 1). In terms of their evaluation of occupational prestige our sample is in no sense deviant. The discrepancies that occur, e.g., college professor, may be due to the sample's special familiarity with the occupation or to shifts in normative evaluations over time.

The rank order correlations between prestige and competence, .90 and between prestige and attractiveness, .92, suggest that (a) prestige inequalities correspond to differences in the level of excellence required by the roles, and (b) such inequalities may induce individuals to strive for the more prestigeful roles, i.e., they increase the attractiveness of the more prestigeful roles. Given the strong association between prestige and competence, it is not possible to separate the independent effects of these factors on role attractiveness for the total sample of occupations. However, an examination can be made of the two sets of rankings to select a subset of occupations whose positions in regard to prestige are not commensurate with their positions in regard to competence. In selecting such occupations the following criteria were used: An occupation with high prestige relative to its required competence is one whose prestige rank is 2.5 or more positions higher than its competence rank *in all four conditions.* An occupation with high required competence relative to its prestige is one whose competence rank is at least 2.5 positions higher than its prestige rank *in all four conditions.* Three occupations fall within each of these categories. Member of the board of directors of a large corporation (mean prestige rank of 2.1, and a mean competence rank of 4.9, across all four conditions), banker (mean prestige rank of 3.5 and mean competence rank of 7.9), and clergyman (mean prestige rank of 4.0 and mean competence rank of 7.6) were per-

TABLE 1

Ranking of Occupations in Terms of Their Required Competence (C) and Their Prestige (P) by Individuals Differing in Their Motivational Structure (Achievement Motivation and Achievement Values) and by a National Sample (N.O.R.C.)

		Rank								
		High Achievement Motivation				Low Achievement Motivation				
		High Achievement Values		Low Achievement Values		High Achievement Values		Low Achievement Values		
Occupation	N.O.R.C. P	P	C	P	C	P	C	P	C	
Physician	1	1	1	1	1	1	1	1.5	2	
College professor	2	5.5	3	7.5	4	7	4	7	3	
Banker	3	3	7	2.5	8.5	2.5	6	6	10	
Minister	4	4	8.5	5	8.5	4	7.5	3	6	
Chemist	6	7	4	6	3	6	3	8	4	
Member of board of directors of large corporation	6	2	5	2.5	6	2.5	5	1.5	5	
Nuclear physicist	6	5.5	2	5	2	5	2	5	1	
Accountant	8	8	6	9	6	9	7.5	7	7	
Novelist	9	9	10	7.5	6	8	9	9	8	
Public school teacher	10	10	8.5	10	10	10	10	10	9	
Undertaker	11	11	12	12	12	11	11.5	11	12	
Mail carrier	12	14	13.5	14	16	13	14	14	14.5	
Auto mechanic	13	13	11	13	11	14	11.5	13	11	
Clerk	14	12	13.5	11	13	12	13	12	13	
Taxi driver	15	16	15	16	15	15	15	15.5	16	
Night watchman	16	15	16	15	14	16	16	15.5	14.5	
Janitor	17	17	17	17	17	17	17	17	17	

ceived in all four conditions as occupations with high prestige relative to the competence required. Nuclear physicist (mean prestige rank of 5.1 and mean competence rank of 1.8) chemist (mean prestige rank of 6.8 and mean competence rank of 3.5), and college professor (mean prestige rank of 6.8 and mean competence rank of 3.5) were perceived in all four conditions as requiring a good deal of competence relative to the prestige they confer.

The mean attractiveness ratings of these two sets of three occupations are presented in Table 2. It was hypothesized that individuals high in achievement motivation and achievement values are more attracted by the low prestige-high competence occupations than by the high prestige-low competence occupations while individuals low in need-achievement and value-achievement are more attracted by the latter than by the former. In terms of the scoring of attraction, i.e., the higher the attraction, the lower the numerical value assigned, the difference in attractiveness between the sets of occupations (low prestige-high competence minus high prestige-low competence), should tend to be some negative value for individuals high in achievement motivation and achievement values and some positive value for individuals low in achievement motivation and achievement values (the mean differences are presented at the bottom of Table 2). An analysis of variance of the difference scores in the four conditions confirm this prediction. A summary of the analysis is presented in Table 3. The difference in attraction to the two sets of occupations is significant as a function of both achievement motivation and achievement values. In addition, *t*-tests of the attractiveness rating given to the low prestige-high competence set versus that given to the high prestige-low competence set within each condition indicates that high need achievers-high value achievers are more attracted to the low prestige-high competence occupations ($t = 2.56$, $p < .05$) while low need achievers-low value achievers are more attracted to the high prestige-low competence occupations ($t = 2.73$, $p < .05$). The differences within the other two subgroups did not approach significance. The shift in attraction as a function of our motivational antecedents can be easily seen if the

TABLE 2

Mean Attractiveness of Occupations Low in Prestige Relative to Required Competence and High in Prestige Relative to Required Competence for Individuals with Different Motivational Structures

Motivational Structure of the Individual	Low Prestige-High Competence Occupations	High Prestige-Low Competence Occupations
High achievement motivation High achievement values	1.82* (a)	3.46 (b)
High achievement motivation Low achievement values	2.98 (c)	3.10 (d)
Low achievement motivation High achievement values	3.03 (e)	2.87 (f)
Low achievement motivation Low achievement values	3.68 (g)	2.03 (h)
Differences in attractiveness	(a) − (b) = −1.64 (c) − (d) = −0.12 (e) − (f) = 0.16 (g) − (h) = 1.65	

*1 = a job of the highest attractiveness.
6 = a job of the lowest attractiveness.

proportions of individuals within each condition who rate the low prestige-high competence set as more attractive, equally attractive, or less attractive than the high prestige-low competence set are examined. Table 4 demonstrates that as achievement motivation and achievement values increase in strength, the preference for occupations demanding a high level of excellence increases.

The findings, thus, indicate that *both* the excellence demanded by a role and the prestige conferred by a role may act to increase role attractiveness and presumably, the striv-

TABLE 3

Analysis of Variance of Differences in Attractiveness of High Prestige-Low Competence and Low Prestige-High Competence Occupations

Source of Variation	df	Mean Square	F
Achievement values (V)	1	110.59	16.12*
Achievement motivation (M)	1	27.83	4.06**
V × M	1	1.39	—
Within groups	76	6.86	—
Total	79		

*Significant at the .01 level of confidence.
**Significant at the .05 level of confidence.

TABLE 4

Per Cent of Individuals with Different Motivational Structures Who are More Attracted by a Role's Required Competence than by Its Prestige (C > P), Equally Attracted by Both (C = P), and More Attracted by Its Prestige than by Its Required Competence (C < P)

Motivational Structure of the Individual	Attractiveness of Competence vs. Attractiveness of Prestige		
	C > P	C = P	C < P
High achievement motivation / High achievement values	55%	25%	20%
High achievement motivation / Low achievement values	30%	15%	55%
Low achievement motivation / High achievement values	35%	30%	35%
Low achievement motivation / Low achievement values	20%	5%	75%

ing for role attainment. However, the relative strength of these incentives depends on the motivational structure of the members of the role system. A system containing a sufficient number with high achievement motivation and strong achievement values may not have to rely on prestige inequalities to promote and guide role striving. The challenge of the role will in part perform these functions.

Of course, there are certain dysfunctional potentials. Roles that demand a high level of excellence tend to increase in importance and may also increase in prestige. They thereby become attractive both to individuals

high in their need for achievement and those high in their need for prestige. Over time, as importance and prestige increases, concomitant innovations in technology and social organization may reduce the level of excellence required. The outcome of such a process would be a decrease in the attractiveness of important and formerly desirable roles for individuals with high achievement motivation and strong achievement values. Such a state of affairs could be quite disruptive for a social system containing a large number of such members. Nevertheless, in terms of the present analysis, whether or not prestige differences are necessary for an adequate allocation of members to roles depends on the prevalence of individuals who are high in achievement motivation and achievement values. With a sufficient number of such people, prestige distinctions become an unnecessary inequality.

reasoned, therefore, that conformity to the judgments and suggestions of others will decrease as achievement motivation increases. Their analysis of stories written by subjects in Asch's classic conformity experiment substantiated this hypothesis. However, more recent findings suggest that the relationship between conformity and achievement motivation depends on whether or not the person perceives the former as instrumental to achievement. See Franz Samuelson, "The Relation of Achievement and Affiliation Motives to Conforming Behavior in Two Conditions of Conflict with a Majority," in J. W. Atkinson, editor, *op. cit.*, pp. 421–433; Robert B. Zajonc and N. Kishor Wahi, "Conformity and Need-Achievement under Cross-Cultural Norm Conflict," *Human Relations*, 14 (August, 1961) pp. 241–250.

[1]Kingsley Davis and Wilbert E. Moore, "Some Principles of Stratification," *American Sociological Review*, 10 (April, 1945), pp. 242–249.

[2]Melvin M. Tumin, "Some Principles of Stratification: A Critical Analysis," *American Sociological Review*, 18 (August, 1953), p. 390; Dennis H. Wrong, "The Functional Theory of Stratification: Some Neglected Considerations," *American Sociological Review*, 24 (December, 1959), pp. 772–782.

[3]For example, see David C. McClelland, John W. Atkinson, Russell A. Clark and Edgar L. Lowell, *The Achievement Motive*, New York: Appleton-Century-Crofts, 1953; David C. McClelland, "Risk Taking in Children with High and Low Need for Achievement," in John W. Atkinson, editor, *Motives in Fantasy, Action and Society*, Princeton, N.J.: Van Nostrand, 1958; John W. Atkinson, "Motivational Determinants of Risk-Taking Behavior," *Psychological Review*, 64, (November, 1957), pp. 359–372; Elizabeth G. French, "Some Characteristics of Achievement Motivation," *Journal of Experimental Psychology*, 50, (October, 1955), pp. 232–236; Fred L. Strodtbeck, "Family Interaction, Values, and Achievement," in David C. McClelland, Alfred L. Baldwin, Urie Bronfenbrenner and Fred L. Strodtbeck, *Talent and Society*, Princeton, N.J.: Van Nostrand, 1958; B. C. Rosen, "The Achievement Syndrome: A Psychocultural Dimension of Social Stratification," *American Sociological Review*, 21, (April, 1956), pp. 203–211.

[4]David C. McClelland, John W. Atkinson, Russell A. Clark, and Edgar L. Lowell, *op. cit.*

[5]Elizabeth G. French, *op. cit.*

[6]David C. McClelland, John W. Atkinson, Russell A. Clark, and Edgar L. Lowell, *op. cit.*, hold that the high need achiever has strongly internalized standards of excellence and is comparable to Riesman's inner-directed type. They

[7]Bernard C. Rosen, *op. cit.*

[8]Harry J. Crockett, Jr. "The Achievement Motive and Differential Occupational Mobility in the United States," *American Sociological Review*, 27 (April, 1962), 191–204.

[9]David C. McClelland, "Some Social Consequences of Achievement Motivation," in Marshal R. Jones, *Nebraska Symposium on Motivation*, 1955, Lincoln: University of Nebraska Press, 1955; D. C. McClelland, *The Achieving Society*, Princeton, N.J.: Van Nostrand, 1961.

[10]Charles H. Mahone, "Fear of Failure and Unrealistic Vocational Aspirations," *Journal of Abnormal and Social Psychology*, 60 (March, 1960), pp. 253–261; Eugene Burnstein, "Fear of Failure, Achievement Motivation and Aspiring to Prestigeful Occupations," *Journal of Abnormal and Social Psychology* (in press).

[11]Bernard C. Rosen, *op. cit.*

[12]Fred L. Strodtbeck, *op. cit.*

[13]See "Appendix I," in J. W. Atkinson, editor, *op. cit.*, pp. 685–734. The two independent scorers used in the present study had inter-judge reliability of .92 (product-moment correlation).

[14]Richard C. deCharms, H. William Morrison, Walter R. Reitman and David C. McClelland, "Behavioral Correlates of Directly and Indirectly Measured Achievement Motivation," in David C. McClelland, editor, *Studies in Motivation*, New York: Appleton-Century-Crofts, 1955.

[15]Fred L. Strodtbeck, *op. cit.*

[16]For example, see Charles Hanley, "Response to the Wording of Personality Test Items," *Journal of Counsuling Psychology*, 23

(July, 1959), pp. 261–265; Arthur Couch and Kenneth Keniston, "Yeasayers and Naysayers: Agreeing Response Set as a Personality Variable," *Journal of Abnormal and Social Psychology*, 60 (March, 1960), pp.151–174; Dean Peabody, "Attitude Content and Agreement Set in Scales of Authoritarianism, Dogmatism, Anti-Semitism, and Economic Conservatism," *Journal of Abnormal and Social Psychology*, 63 (July, 1961), pp. 1–11.

[17]Richard C. deCharms, H. William Morrison, Walter R. Reitman and David C. McClelland in David C. McClelland, editor, *op. cit.*

[18]National Opinion Research Center, "Jobs and Occupations: A popular Evaluation," in Reinhard Bendix and Seymour M. Lipset, editors, *Class, Status and Power: A Reader in Social Stratification*, Glencoe, Ill.: The Free Press, 1953.

Relationship of Personality to Occupation, Setting, and Function

SUTHERLAND MILLER, JR., *Columbia University*

Today's adult male spends most of his waking hours working to provide a livelihood. More specifically, he works at a particular job which can be grouped with other similar jobs into an occupation. What is the relationship of the individual man, with his own peculiar personality, to his occupation? Do men within an occupational group have common personality traits that distinguish them from members of other occupational groups?

Because an occupation means more than a grouping of similar tasks and includes such factors as implicit and explicit values and purposes, it is important to study the relationship of such variables to personality differences. The purpose of the present study was to determine, after having examined the nature of certain specific occupational groups, (1) whether personality differences between groups can be found and predicted,

Reprinted with the permission of author and publisher from the article of the same title, in *Journal of Counseling Psychology*, 1962, 9, 115–121.

(2) whether the differences are more related to the job tasks than to the job setting, and (3) what effects time spent in the occupation has on personality patterns.

BACKGROUND

By "setting" is meant the value orientations of the occupation as seen in the general goals of the occupation and as communicated by the members of the occupational group. For example, the broad goal of social service occupations is to serve people, whereas the goal of commercial occupations is to secure financial gain. "Function" refers to the tasks that the worker performs and the activities in which he engages. Although the definition of personality is not a completely settled issue, Shaffer and Shoben offer a workable definition when they state, "The personality of an individual may be defined as his persistent tendencies to make certain kinds and qualities of adjustment" (1956). For them, personality is a product of social learning, acquired through experiences with other human beings.

Hypotheses

Implied in Shaffer and Shoben's definition are two principles of learning — that learned behavior is motivated and that the probability of behavioral occurrences is increased through reinforcement, one form of which may be need gratification. It was therefore hypothesized that there are personality differences between occupational groups because occupations provide differential reinforcements for different behavior and provide differential satisfactions for different needs.

But from these formulations it also seems that similarities within occupational families are a function of (1) shared traits and perceptions of need fulfillments leading to occupational choice, and (2) shared traits developed through reinforcement and involvement in the occupation. It is therefore expected that differences in personality traits are greater as a function of time spent in the occupation.

Within the framework of learning theory, it is possible to define a personal goal as being the end activity or consummatory response that terminates a sequence of motivated behavior. Further, some goals may be intermediary and instrumental to the realization of more distant goals. Given this base, further relationships between personality and the elements of occupation (setting and function) are hypothesized. Functions, as defined here, are necessary sequential elements or subgoals for goal realization which become satisfying in themselves because of their relationships to the over-all goal. By the definition of setting, occupational and individual goals are fused to constitute the value orientations of the occupation. An institution, then, has certain values which direct the activities of the workers and which are reflected and communicated not only through the institutional structure but also through the selection of

workers employed there. If this interpretation holds, then values govern the application of rewards and provide a greater range of satisfactions than do functions. Consequently, it is hypothesized that the work setting is more closely related to personality than are sheer tasks or operations.

These three general hypotheses were stated as follows:

1. People in different occupations differ in personality characteristics relevant to the specific occupation.
2. Differences in these particular personality characteristics are greater in relation to work setting than in relation to work functions.
3. Differences in these characteristics are greater as a function of time spent in the occupations.

PROCEDURE

Sample

Fifty YMCA boys workers, 50 YMCA business secretaries, and 50 controllers (comptrollers) in business were selected from the same cities of the U.S. Controllers were drawn from firms with an annual dollar volume of sixty million or less. Since job analyses indicated that the Y business secretaries and the controllers performed the same job functions, there were two groups (Y Boys and Y Business) with the same settings (social service) and different functions (planning and leading youth activities as against maintaining a business), and there were two groups (Y Business and Controllers) with the same functions (maintaining a business) and different settings (social service as against commercial or seeking financial gain). There was no evidence to suggest that the three groups differed in educational background, religious background, marital status, occupational level of fathers, educational level of parents, birth order, or family size. There was, however, a significant difference in age and length of service; Y business secretaries and controllers were higher in both areas than Y boys workers. The reason that there were fewer boys workers with longer lengths of service seemed to be due to the fact that boys workers earned lower incomes than the business secretaries and occasionally moved to other YMCA positions, but less than two per cent changed to the Y business secretaryship. As the Y business men are less well paid than the controllers in business, it would seem that the more service oriented the task, the less well paid the worker is.

Variables

As the YMCA is "person-directed," with a service and religious orientation, and the controllers in business are "thing-directed," with an emphasis on details and monetary reward, the variables were selected to reflect these differences. To investigate the general hypotheses, the variables have been stated in a way consistent with the expectancy that YMCA workers score higher on all variables with the differences between the Y groups being less than those between either of them and the controllers.

The variables were as follows: 1. preference for a way of life characterized by receptivity and sympathetic concern; 2. friendly tolerance for a greater number of traits of people; 3. considering oneself religious; 4. coming from a religious home; 5. preferring to work with people rather than things; 6. preferring to work with others rather than alone; 7. preferring to work with few details; 8. socially extraverted; 9. nonprejudicial; 10. having a need to be understanding; 11. having a need to help others; 12. having a need for close fellowship; 13. having little need for order.

Measures

As variables one through seven are expressions of the S's personal preferences, the most logical and direct way to collect such data was to use a biographical questionnaire. The questionnaire was based on Roe's biographical inquiry (1951, 1953), also incorporating items from Part V and Part VII of the Strong Vocational Interest Blank. Part V of the Strong deals with traits of people, and Part VII of the Strong explores preferences between two opposing activities in a work setting. Ideas from the work on "paths of life" by Charles Morris (1942, 1956) provided the basis for the section on ways of life.

On variables 1, 3, and 4, S rated himself on a five-point scale. On variables 5, 6, and 7, he had three choices, either of the two opposites (people or things) or "equal preference." On variable 2, there were 47 traits of people or kinds of persons; S was asked to indicate whether he liked, was indifferent to, or disliked each of them.

Social extraversion (variable 8) and non-prejudicial attitude (variable 9) were measured by the Social Introversion and Prejudice scales, respectively, of the MMPI.

Various scales on the Edwards Personal Preference Schedule were used to measure the remaining variables: having a need for close fellowship — the Affiliation scale; having a need to help others — the Nurturance scale; having a need to be understanding — the Intraception scale; and having little need for order — the Order scale.

Cooperation was requested by letter, and, after a respondent agreed to cooperate, he was sent an envelope containing the questionnaire, the MMPI, and the PPS. His instructions were to complete all of the tests, answering each item, at his own convenience but to return them within about a month. As 50 seemed a reasonable sample size for each group, no further attempt was made to obtain Ss when that number was reached. Of the men originally contacted, 53 per cent of the boys workers, 70 per cent of the Y business secretaries, and 22 per cent of the controllers returned and completed the material. The difference in response can be accounted for, in part, on the basis of the YMCA's endorsement of the study and the author's personal contacts with the YMCA.

RESULTS

Occupational Differences

To test the hypothesis that there are significant differences among the three groups on the 13 variables, an analysis of variance was applied to the data on the continuous variables and a chi-square test was applied to the data on the discrete variables.

Tables 1 and 2 indicate nine significant differences on the 13 personality characteristics: *considering oneself religious; coming from a religious home; liking traits of persons; social extraversion; having a need for order; having a need for affiliation; having a need to help others; having a need to be understanding; preferring few details.* There is no evidence of difference on variables 1 (ways of life), 9 (non-prejudicial), 5 (their preference for

working with people as opposed to things), and 6 (their preference for working with others as opposed to alone).

It can therefore be concluded that occupational groups differ on personality variables that appear to be relevant to the characteristics of the occupations.

Setting and Function

To investigate whether the differences were more related to setting than to function, it was necessary to determine between which groups the differences actually occurred. Tukey's formula for comparing pairs was applied to the significant results in Table 1, and Table 2 was inspected for the locus of the relevant variance. The results

TABLE 1

Analysis of Variance for Comparing YMCA Boys Workers, YMCA
Business Secretaries, and Controllers on Ten Personality Variables

Variable	Degrees of Freedom	Source of Variation	Mean Square	F
Way of Life	2	S_b	1.58	
	147	S_w	1.10	1.43
Liking Traits	2	S_b	240.73	
	147	S_w	36.25	6.64**
Considering Self Religious	2	S_b	3.23	
	147	S_w	.78	4.13*
Religious Home	2	S_b	2.58	
	147	S_w	.84	3.06*
Social Extraversion	2	S_b	292.65	
	147	S_w	56.13	5.21**
Nonprejudicial	2	S_b	73.39	
	147	S_w	38.52	1.91
Intraception	2	S_b	203.89	
	147	S_w	11.50	17.73**
Nurturance	2	S_b	389.66	
	147	S_w	9.29	41.93**
Affiliation	2	S_b	1,079.57	
	147	S_w	108.36	9.96**
Order	2	S_b	490.30	
	147	S_w	85.66	5.72**

*Significant at the .05 level.
**Significant at the .01 level.

TABLE 2

Chi-Square Comparisons of YMCA Boys Work Secretaries (Bo), YMCA Business Secretaries (Bu), and Controllers (Co) on Three Variables

Category	Bo	Bu	Co	Chi Square	p
Things	1	2	8		
Equal	19	22	16		
People	30	26	26	9.08	>.05
Alone	2	3	5		
Equal	14	18	23		
Others	34	29	22	6.20	>.05
Few Details	12	4	16		
Equal	28	25	17		
Many Details	10	21	17	13.64	<.01

TABLE 3

Tukey's Test for Significances Between Differences As Applied to the Variables on Which There Were Significant Differences Between YMCA Boys Workers (Bo), YMCA Business Secretaries (Bu), and Controllers (Co)

Variable	Significant Means				Level of Significance
Liking Traits	Bo	13.10	> Co	10.00	.05
	Bu	14.24	> Co	10.00	.01
Considering	Co	1.96	> Bu	1.52	.05
Self Religious[1]	Co	1.96	> Bo	1.52	.05
Religious Home	no significant differences				
Social Extroversion[2]	Co	24.88	> Bo	20.10	.01
Intraception	Bo	57.44	> Bu	53.30	.01
	Bo	57.44	> Co	54.70	.01
Affiliation	Bu	57.24	> Co	48.54	.01
	Bo	55.72	> Co	48.54	.01
Order[3]	Co	50.92	> Bo	45.88	.05
	Bu	51.62	> Bo	45.88	.01
Nurturance	Bo	50.72	> Co	45.76	.01
	Bu	50.46	> Co	45.76	.01

[1]The higher the score the less religious one considers himself to be.
[2]The higher the score the less extroverted.
[3]The higher the score the more in need of order.

indicate that setting was more important than function in the case of *considering oneself religious, liking traits of persons, nurturance,* and *affiliation,* but function had the greater influence with respect to having a need to be understanding and having little need for order. Both function and setting had to be different on social extraversion in order for differences to be significant. Even though in the analysis of variance there were significant differences between the three groups on the variable of coming from a religious home, Tukey's test revealed no stable difference between pairs of groups.

Inspection of Table 2 reveals that the Y boys workers and the controllers preferred *fewer details* than the Y business secretaries, and that the Y business secretaries and the controllers preferred working with *many details* more than did the Y boys workers. On the variable of preferring few details to many details, much of the variance was taken up in the "equal preference" category, and the fact that the controllers were fairly evenly distributed in the three categories may also explain the rather confusing results here.

Thus, the results on four of the variables indicated that setting was more important than function, whereas in two cases function seemed to be the deciding factor. In one instance, both setting and function had to be different for there to be a significant difference, and in two cases, the results did not seem susceptible to any persuasive interpretation.

Length of Service

Because the distributions of the three groups were dissimilar on length of service, and because some of the variables were discrete rather than continuous, the most feasible way to analyze the data was to apply an analysis of covariance to the continuous variables and test the hypothesis of common slope. As the third hypothesis predicted that the differences between the groups would increase with time spent in the occupation, a test of common slope would indicate whether the rates of change were the same, and the regression coefficients would attest to the relationship between the variables and length of service. The relationship between the discrete variables and length of service was investigated by dividing each occupational group into two groups — 1 to 15 years of service, and 15 years and more — and by obtaining a *phi* coefficient

between these length-of-service groups on their scores on the variables.

The hypothesis of common slope had to be accepted in all cases, and there was *no evidence to indicate a relationship between length of service and any of the variables.*

Obviously, the limitations imposed on this aspect of the study make any conclusions highly tentative, but the general direction of the data seemed to imply that the amount of time spent in the occupation had little relationship to personality variables in this research.

DISCUSSION

The finding of differences among the three groups on personality variables suggests that it may be possible to order occupations on continua of personality variables. The knowledge that men in a particular occupation are generally higher in a certain number of personality traits than men in other occupations would provide information about what traits are compatible with the over-all occupational pattern and what traits are rewarded in that occupation, as well as what needs are fulfilled. Knowing the personality demands of an occupation would add another factor on which more reliable predictions could be made, thus providing an invaluable aid in vocational and personal guidance and in making better use of manpower.

On four variables in the present study there was no evidence of discriminating differences. Rather than choosing a way of life characterized by receptivity and sympathetic concern, a fairly evenly distributed majority in each group *selected a way of life stressing progress and over-coming obstacles.* It is suggested that this latter way of life most adequately reflects the general social climate of our times, and this more dominant value seemed to exert a stronger influence than the values of any of the particular groups studied here. The fact that the groups were not significantly different on being nonprejudicial may be explained on the basis that though there is reason to predict that the Y groups are more nonprejudicial, there is no reason to infer that the controllers are particularly prejudiced. No differences were found between the groups on preferring people over things and preferring working with others rather than alone. It may be that the social desirability of preferring working with people masks any differences that actually characterize the groups.

Setting and Function

At first examination of the data related to the hypothesis exploring the importance of setting versus function, it would appear that there is no clear cut evidence to favor one factor over the other, but the results suggest that the issue is far more complex. In the precent study, the occupation was considered in terms of setting and function, but there was no attempt to classify personality characteristics along these lines. It seems probable that personality variables related to work can be divided into two categories (perhaps even more): the "value-oriented" and the "function-oriented." Value-oriented personality characteristics are associated with goals, ends, values, and beliefs. Function-oriented personality characteristics are related to means, processes, and objective procedures.

These two categories need not be in conflict. For example, a man may well be dedicated to a life of service, having high needs to be nurturant and desirous of the company of others, and may still have a high need for order which could easily coexist with these other needs and traits. To understand the way in which an individual's personality is related to his occupation, value and functional traits would have to be examined in terms of the possible conflicts between them, their place in hierarchies within each orbit, and the interaction between the occupation's demands and the individual's personality structure.

Perhaps dimensions besides level, interest, and enterprise could profitably be added to occupational classification. Such dimensions might include personality characteristics subdivided on the basis of value and function.

Length of Service

The relationship between length of participation in an occupation and personality variables important to the occupation was not adequately investigated here because the groups differed from each other in length of service. Nevertheless, the data suggest that length of service has little effect within the population sampled in this study. It is possible that by the time these Ss were tested (the mean age of the youngest group was 35.98 years), their personality traits were fairly set. An interesting research project might be attempted to find the age at which personality traits relevant to occupations have stabilized enough to permit meaningful predictions.

SUMMARY

The purpose of this study was to investigate the relationship of personality to occupation, setting, and function. Fifty YMCA boys workers, 50 YMCA business secretaries, and 50 controllers were selected, representing two groups with similar settings and different functions and two groups with similar functions and different settings.

On 13 personality characteristics reflecting value differences between the settings, there were nine significant differences; four supported setting and two function. One required both setting and function differences, and two were not open to interpretation. Though there were procedural limitations, the results indicated little relationship between the variables studied here and length of service. It was suggested that occupational differences on relevant personality characteristics may usefully be classified as value- or function-oriented.

REFERENCES

Morris, C. W. *Paths of life*. New York: Harper, 1942.

Morris, C. W. *Varieties of human value*. Chicago: Univer. of Chicago Press, 1956.

Roe, Anne. A psychological study of eminent biologists. *Psychol. Monogr.*, 1951, *65*, No. 14 (Whole No. 331).

Roe, Anne. A psychological study of eminent psychologists and anthropologists and a comparison with biological and physical scientists. *Psychol. Monogr.*, 1953, *67*, No. 2 (Whole No. 352).

Roe, Anne. A psychological study of physical scientists. *Genet. Psychol. Monogr.*, 1951, *43*, 121–239.

Shaffer, L. F., and Shoben, E. J., Jr. *The psychology of adjustment*. Boston: Houghton Mifflin, 1956.

OTHER RELEVANT ARTICLES

Holland has published the latest version of his theoretical views and a summary of his research to date in his book, *The Psychology of Vocational Choice*, Waltham, Mass: Blaisdell Press, 1966.

Similarly, a number of tests of aspects of Holland's theory have been conducted either by him, or under his direction. They include:

Holland, J. L. A personality inventory employing occupational titles. *Journal of Applied Psychology*, 1958, *42*, 336–342.

———. A theory of vocational choice. *Journal of Counseling Psychology*, 1959, *6*, 35–45.

———. Some explorations of a theory of vocational choice: I. One- and two-year longitudinal studies. *Psychological Monographs*, 1962, *76*, 26 (Whole No. 545).

———. Some explorations of a theory of vocational choice and achievement: II. A four-year prediction study. *Psychological Reports*, 1963, *12*, 545–594.

———. Explorations of a theory of vocational choice: IV. Vocational preferences and their relation to occupational images, daydreams, and personality. *Vocational Guidance Quarterly*, published in four parts in Summer, Autumn, and Winter issues. 1963–1964.

———, and R. C. Nichols. Explorations of a theory of vocational choice: III. A longitudinal study of change in major field of study. *Personnel and Guidance Journal*, 1964, *45*, 235–242.

———, and ———. The development and validation of an indecision scale: The natural history of a problem in basic research. *Journal of Counseling Psychology*, 1964, *11*, 27–34.

For additional study:

Centers, R. Motivational aspects of occupational stratification. *Journal of Social Psychology*, 1948, *28*, 187–217.

Decker, R. L. A study of three specific problems in the measurement and interpretation of employee attitudes. *Psychological Monographs*, 1955, *69*, 16 (Whole No. 401).

Gunderson, E. K., and P. D. Nelson. Personality differences among Navy occupational groups. *Personnel and Guidance Journal*, 1966, *44*, 956–961.

Kassarjian, H. H. and W. M. Kassarjian. Occupational interests, social values, and social character. *Journal of Counseling Psychology*, 1965, *12*, 48–54.

Levin, M. M. Status anxiety and occupational choice. *Educational and Psychological Measurement*, 1949, *9*, 29–37.

Levine, S. Occupation and personality: Relationship between the social factors of job and human orientation. *Personnel and Guidance Journal*, 1963, *41*, 602–605.

Norton, J. L. General motives and influences in vocational development. *Journal of Genetic Psychology*, 1953, *82*, 263–278.

Small, L. Personality determinants of vocational choice. *Psychological Monographs*, 1953, *67*, (Whole No. 351).

Suziedelis, Antanas, and R. Steimel. The relationship of need hierarchies to inventoried interests. *Personnel and Guidance Journal*, 1963, *42*, 393–396.

Thompson, O. E. Occupational values of high school students. *Personnel and Guidance Journal*, 1966, *44*, 850–853.

Wagman, M. Interests and values of career and homemaking oriented women. *Personnel and Guidance Journal*, 1966, *44*, 791–801.

Walsh, R. P. The effect of needs on responses to job duties. *Journal of Counseling Psychology*, 1959, *6*, 194–198.

The Decision-Making
Concept of Occupational
Determinants

9

Of all the chapters in Part V, this one, presenting the decision theory point of view, offers the least consistently developed position. It is not unrelated to the preceding chapter — decision theory supposes that individuals value the rewards of varied kinds of behavior differently, which is another way of stating the need reduction theory. But from economic decision theory two additional factors in the decision matrix are accounted for: (1) the likelihood of attaining any given outcome, and (2) the cost of attaining each. These factors are easily imagined: the relationship between deciding to become a physician and actually becoming one is accepted as uncertain. The prospects of being a very successful salesman after entering the occupation is regarded as a matter of probability. In one formulation of reward and expectancy, developed by Vroom (1964) from concepts of Lewin and others, the factors are combined multiplicatively to predict the "valence" or net attractiveness of an alternative. This conception is similar to the expectancy X value theory of achievement motivation advanced by Atkinson (1964). The paper by Morris included in this chapter is conceived in terms of Atkinson's framework. Evidence for Vroom's similar formulation is provided from an unpublished study reported by Rosen (1961). High school students were given falsified information concerning their abilities relevant to certain occupations which they had previously rated for their attractiveness, effectively manipulating their expectancy of success or payoff. Not only was their perception of the valence of occupations altered, but also their willingness to undergo further testing to determine whether they might qualify for special training in one of their preferred occupations was reduced, proportionately to decreasing expectancy.

The factor of cost entering into the decision process can be imagined, but little formal inclusion of it in any theory of vocational choice has appeared. If the most attractive aspect of becoming a physician is its high income, it is logically reduced by the expense of attending school for more years than the norm, and by the lost income in the years of training, compared to other occupations. Other costs are more psychological than economic. The anticipated value of being a professional baseball player must be weighed against its potential for injury, its required absence from home and family for part of the year, the period expended in the minor leagues without certainty that the payoff will be getting in the line-up of a major league team. A theoretical formulation accounting for the cost of choice among job alternatives is found in an unpublished paper by Kaldor (1967). He postulates that the choice of an occupation is determined by the *net* reward of each of the considered alternatives. That is, the amount of need gratification which an occupation is perceived to afford, reduced by the cost of attaining the gratification, comprises the net value of that occupational alternative to an individual.

Likely too, is the possibility that the satisfaction gained from the performance (as contrasted with the anticipation) of an occupation is reduced by the cost of performing it. This prospect is hinted at by some of the studies noted in Chapter 10 under equity theory, and the brief selection on occupational difficulty in Chapter 3 is also relevant.

Other decision-theory formulations concentrate not on the factors which determine choice, but on the process of the choice, particularly the handling of information relevant to assessing the factors which determine valence, and of the handling of the rejected alternatives once the choice has been made. Hilton (1962) has produced one formulation of this kind, drawing from the dissonance-reduction theory of Festinger (1957) for concepts. Evidence that dissonance-reduction enters into the act of choice is offered in the Vroom paper summarized at the end of this chapter.

In the first paper in this chapter, Hershenson and Roth draw up a similar formulation, treating not only the determinants of individual decisions, but also the process of sequential decisions which amount to vocational development. It is not dissimilar from the Tiedeman statement in Chapter 4, except that it focuses on the two trends of narrowing the range of alternatives and the strengthening of the valence of remaining alternatives.

In Ziller's paper, next, a more complete account is made of the utility elements in choice, and a new construct, utility for risk, is introduced in the strategy of decision making. The concept refers to the additional value or preference for differing degrees of probability of attainment which enters the matrix of factors along with values associated with the alternatives themselves.

While Ziller shows that preference for differing degrees of risk determine the occupation chosen to some extent, Morris' research elaborates on it to show that utility for risk is the result of two components, approach for success and avoidance of failure. In addition, Morris finds that persons high on achievement motivation tend to choose moderate risk occupations for themselves, while those low in achievement tend to avoid moderate risks. Similarly, Mahone (1960) has found that persons whose motivation is strongly founded on the avoidance of failure tend to make unrealistic choices.

Economic decision theory also concerns itself with strategies used to arrive at a choice with varying reward, cost, and probability levels. In the Sherlock and Cohen report, one occupation is examined for the way in which probability of attainment and prestige reward is combined to arrive at a choice of dentistry. It should be remembered that prestige and probability of success or attainment are strongly inversely correlated, so that such a consideration is possible. In addition, the authors show how another factor, father's occupational status, influences recruitment to an occupation. This finding should be recalled when reading the following chapter, on social influences on choice.

REFERENCES

Atkinson, J. W. *An Introduction to Motivation*. Princeton, N. J.: Van Nostrand, 1964.

Festinger, L. *A Theory of Cognitive Dissonance*. New York: Harper & Row, 1957.

Hilton, T. L. Career decision making. *Journal of Counseling Psychology*, 1962, 9, 291–298.

Kaldor, D. R. A theory of occupational choice. Paper presented at NC-86 Conference. Iowa State University, 1967.

Mahone, C. H. Fear of failure and unrealistic vocational aspiration. *Journal of Abnormal and Social Psychology*, 1960, 60, 253–261.

Rosen, M. Valence, expectancy, and dissonance reduction in the prediction of achievement striving. Paper read at the annual meeting of the Eastern Psychological Association, 1961.

Vroom, V. H. *Work and Motivation*. New York: Wiley, 1964.

A Decisional Process Model of Vocational Development

DAVID B. HERSHENSON, *Illinois Institute of Technology*

ROBERT M. ROTH, *Illinois Institute of Technology*

Recognition of the fact that vocational development involves the making and implementing of decisions is not new. Ziller

Reprinted with the permission of authors and publisher from the article of the same title, in *Journal of Counseling Psychology*, 1966, *13*, 368–370.

(1957), using concepts derived from game theory, suggested that vocational choices could be studied in terms of their utility for risk for the individual. Tyler (1959, 1961) explored the nature of decisional patterns in individuals, especially relating them to the vocational choice process. Tiedeman (1961) utilized a decision-making model in his conceptualization of the vocational exploration and implementation process. Gelatt (1962) suggested a "sequential decision-making" conception of vocational development could provide counselors with a consistent, workable frame of reference. Hilton (1962) reviewed five decision-making models (attribute-matching need-reduction, probable gain, social structure, and complex information processing) and offered a model of career decision-making which utilized mainly the last of these, as triggered by a variant of cognitive dissonance (see Comment by James, 1963).

All of these models or part-models have much to contribute to the conceptualization of vocational decision-making. However, they all focus, to greater or lesser degree, on the antecedents, concomitants and sequelae of single decisions in the course of vocational development. It is the thesis of this paper that the value of the decisional model for vocational development lies as much in its implications for the over-all process of vocational development as in its contribution to the understanding of individual decisions within that process. Hence, this paper undertakes to suggest several implications of the decisional process for vocational development theory and for counseling practice.

It it here posited that, in general, through the decisional process, two basic trends are brought about in an individual's vocational development. First, the range of possibilities available to him is narrowed. Second, those possibilities which remain are strengthened. Eventually, through the process of successively narrowing alternatives and strengthening the remaining ones, the individual arrives at his career choice. These two trends may be conceived of as coming about through the following process:

1. Each vocationally-relevant decision limits the range of possible subsequent experiences for the individual.

2. As the range of experiences becomes narrower, the range of alternatives open to him becomes narrower.

3. As the range of alternatives becomes narrower, the individual becomes more focused on a given course through one or more of the following causes:
a. positive choice
b. adaptation to existing conditions
c. ignorance of other possibilities
d. inability to shift to other alternatives

4. The more focused on a given course the individual becomes, the more likely it is that he will perceive or structure future events as consistent with that course, thus reinforcing it.

The first two steps in this sequence relate mainly to the trend of narrowing the range of possibilities. The third step relates to both trends, and the fourth step relates mainly to the trend of strengthening the remaining possibilities.

It is necessary to expand somewhat on several of the points in the sequence posited above. As to the first step, the "vocationally-relevant decision" may either be made by the individual himself or be made for him by someone else, such as a parent, teacher, counselor, admission officer, scholarship committee, employment office interviewer, personnel manager or work supervisor. Even such factors as the socioeconomic class, geographical region and particular family occupational history into which one "chooses" to be born may be thought of as "vocationally-relevant decisions."

To illustrate the first two steps, an individual, upon completion of elementary school, may have to decide between a vocational high school, a general high school and a college preparatory school. Should he choose the first of these, he would thereby rule out for himself experiences with general courses, commercial courses and college preparatory courses. The decision to choose the vocational school would thus confront him with the options of, let us say, automotive, sheet metal and refrigeration courses, while at the same time excluding him from experiences with accounting, Latin and calculus courses. As possibilities become excluded, the chance for successful experiences in them is lost, and so these areas become even further removed from consideration. Similarly, as the individual goes on to select courses in the automotive field, the possibilities of his going into refrigeration diminish.

As the individual's sequence of decisions channel him toward a given goal, that goal becomes more and more inevitable. This process is facilitated by the causes listed in the third step. The first of these, "positive choice," may be realistic or unrealistic, conscious or unconscious. As an example of the fourth cause, the individual in the vocational-automotive course would encounter almost insurmountable difficulties in trying to implement a decision to shift into a liberal arts college-preparatory course after his third year of high school. The other two causes are self-explanatory.

The fourth step in the sequence may be conceived of in terms of the principles of perceptual defense, conflict resolution, or dissonance reduction. Insofar as the individual has committed himself to a goal, experiences tend to be seen or interpreted as consistent with that goal, if at all possible. One may go a step further and posit that if the experiences are interpreted as consistent with the goal, they serve to reinforce the individual's belief in the correctness of his choice. It may be hypothesized that the interpretation made of an experience is a function of how far along toward a career goal the individual is in his decisional process. For example, a first semester freshman in a college engineering program may, in his physics course, hook up some apparatus incorrectly and blow a fuse. As a result, he may earn a reprimand from his lab instructor. The student may place any of a number of constructions on this reprimand, each of which has different implications for his subsequent decisional process with regard to the goal of engineering. For example, he may see the reprimand as appropriate and decide to "shape up." He may see the reprimand as stemming from the lab instructor's personal animosity and so shrug it

off. He may see lab technique as irrelevant to his goal of engineering and so not be affected by it. Alternatively, he may see the reprimand as reflecting on his potential to become an engineer, thus leading him to explore alternative career goals or to invest more energy in his non-engineering subjects. Which interpretation of the experience he will make is largely a function of how committed he is to the goal of engineering. The final alternative would doubtless be more likely in the case of someone for whom engineering was a recent, tentative decision than in the case of someone who had been directing his actions toward this goal for a protracted period.

Taking the processes of career selection as postulated above, one may arrive at the graphical representation shown in Figure 1.

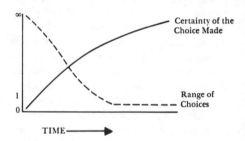

FIGURE 1. General trends produced by the decisional process.

Thus, over time, through successive decisions, the range of alternatives asymptotically approaches unity and the certainty of that choice asymptotically approaches infinity. As with all asymptotic functions, neither curve actually touches the base line toward which it is tending. It may further be suggested that the psychological magnitude of a disconfirmatory experience must exceed the area under the "certainty" curve at the time it occurs for it to be significant enough to throw the choice into question. Thus, earlier in the decisional process, a less significant event may have a greater impact on an individual's career decisional process, The illustration of the engineering freshman cited above may serve as an example of this; for the tentatively decided, a minor incident may have more far-reaching consequences. It may further be pointed out that the shape of the curves represents a generalization, and may be steeper, sharper or shallower for any individual.

Thus, the pattern of an individual who arrives at a sudden, defensive career choice of the "I-have-to-have-something-to-tell-people-when-they-ask" variety, may be graphed as shown in Figure 2.

It may be observed that the continued low level of certainty of this choice leaves it open to alteration through the vicissitudes of even minor events. The phenomena of individual differences also account for the lack of specific values along the time dimension. Different individuals begin their career decisional processes at different ages and move through them at different rates. Finally, it should be pointed out that the correlation between the two curves need not be unity. An individual may have limited himself to a single career choice but yet remain quite uncertain of it, as in Figure 2.

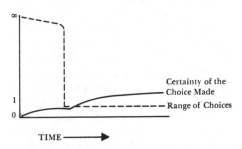

FIGURE 2. Trends produced by a defensive decisional process.

This conceptualization of career development has a number of implications for both research and counseling practice. As to the former, it is necessary to spell out what factors promote or impede the decisional process One obvious possibility is information, both about oneself and about occupations. All decisions are, to at least some extent, based on information or misinformation. However,

the exact role of information in the course of vocational decision-making remains to be spelled out. Another factor which suggests itself for investigation is capacity for commitment to one's decisions. Decisions, no matter how in tune they are with logical or cosmic progression, are only functional to the extent that the individual is able to involve himself in them. It may also be suggested that the elements of interpretation and impact of experiences would be amenable to study by the critical incident technique.

In terms of counseling practice, awareness of the implications of the decisional process behooves the counselor to explore with the client exactly where in the course of his decisional process he stands, how he arrived at his current status, and in what directions subsequent decisions will channel him. Past decisions which have excluded appropriate areas from consideration or have cast a stilted interpretation on experiences should be reviewed. The limiting consequences of the decisional possibilities with which the client is currently faced could be explored with him. As has been suggested by others (especially Gelatt, 1962), the client's process of decision-making and implementation should be examined with him, to facilitate future activities of these sorts in the vocational and in other life spheres. Finally, it should be pointed out to the client that awareness of the inevitable consequences of decisional processes should constitute a maturing and liberating influence, rather than a constricting or fatalistic one.

REFERENCES

Gelatt, H. Decision-making: a conceptual frame of reference for counseling. *J. counsel. Psychol.*, 1962, *9*, 240–245.

Hilton, T. L. Career decision-making. *J. counsel. Psychol.*, 1962, *9*, 291–298.

James, F., III. Comment on Hilton's model of career decision-making. *J. counsel. Psychol.*, 1963, *10*, 303–304.

Tiedeman, D. V. Decision and vocational development: a paradigm and its implications. *Personnel guid. J.*, 1961, *40*, 15–21.

Tyler, Leona. Distinctive patterns of likes and dislikes over a twenty-two year period. *J. counsel. Psychol.*, 1959, *6*, 234–237.

Tyler, Leona. Research explorations in the realm of choice. *J. counsel. Psychol.*, 1961, *8*, 195–201.

Ziller, R. C. Vocational choice and utility for risk. *J. counsel. Psychol.*, 1957, *4*, 61–64.

Vocational Choice and Utility for Risk

ROBERT C. ZILLER, *University of Delaware*

Since vocational selection is a critical individual decision-making situation, the stochastic models of human decision-making behavior developed in recent years should be helpful in the current efforts to formulate a theory of vocational choice (Meadow 4, Super 6). In the present report a theory of vocational choice based on a model of individual decision-making behavior under conditions of uncertainty and risk is sketched, and an experiment is described within this framework. Briefly, it is proposed that vocational choice is a decision-making situation in which risk plays a major role, and therefore, individual *risk-taking* tendencies determine, in part, occupational choice.

THEORETICAL BACKGROUND

An idea similar to the hypothesis just presented was first suggested by Friedman and Savage (3). However, in their discussion the economic aspects of vocational choice were emphasized almost to the

exclusion of the psychological aspects of the problem. Yet, their decision-making model may be adapted to accommodate psychological variables.

On the other hand, psychologists have long felt that personality characteristics are related to vocational choice. The classic examples relative to the theory presented here are the flights of individuals into rarely chosen occupations in order to insure success. However, no clear-cut theory has embraced these aspects of vocational choice. Thus, it is suggested that a stochastic model of individual decision-making behavior in a vocational choice situation be developed to admit both economic and psychological variables.

In the process of selecting a vocation,[1] the vast array of alternatives is reduced enormously as a consequence of individual interests, abilities, economic limitations, and lack of information. The remaining possibilities form the individual's scale of judgment. These alternatives under consideration by the subject vary with regard to prize, price, and possibility of success; it is these factors along with *utility for risk* which determine the final decision.

The *prize* is the object which an individual stands to gain in the event of success. The *price* or *stake* is the object which an individual stands to lose in the event of failure. The probability of success is the ratio of the number of persons who succeed and the number of persons who enter the field. These three variables are regarded as psychological variables and are not necessarily related to *real* properties such as *dollar* values or *objective* probability. Thus, the prize may be a perceived gain in wealth or prestige or an expanded and more acceptable self-concept.

In the decision-making process, the price is compared with the prize under the condition of probability of success. However, the decision is not made on a purely probability basis (Coombs and Beardslee, 1). Liking to gamble or willingness to take a risk (utility for risk) may also be a parameter of decision-making under uncertainty. Actually, the latter variable, utility for risk, may be the more fruitful area of inquiry for psychologists and is, in fact, the variable selected for study in the experiment reported here.

Thus, an individual in the process of selecting a vocation may be compared to a gambler who must decide what he is prepared to wager for a given prize under certain expectations of success. However, the variables involved in vocational choice are of a more subjective nature. Furthermore, the value of the prize and price and the probability of success are subject to continuous changes over time with reference to a given vocation, as a result of the decisions of others and a multitude of economic, psychological, and sociological factors.

Continuing with the gambling model, it is proposed that vocations vary with regard to the degree to which the prize is commensurate with the price under the given probability of success (fair-risk). Compare the vocational choices of engineering and engineering sales. The latter in comparison with the former offers a chance of greater gain or income, but the income is also more variable due to the usual commission arrangements. Thus, the choice of engineering sales entails a greater degree of risk, and individual choice may be predicted from a measure of individual utility for risk.

METHOD

Subjects

The subjects for the experiment were 182 Sophomores from the University of Delaware Army ROTC program.

Procedure

During the last period of a three-hour final-testing session for ROTC Sophomores, the measure of utility for risk was administered ostensibly as an achievement test to determine, in part, the course grade for the semester. Following this, the subjects completed a questionnaire supposedly distributed by the Army to gauge the expected flow of Army inductees with various skills, abilities, and interests.

Utility for Risk

The development of the instrument measuring utility for risk is described in detail elsewhere (Torrance and Ziller, 8; Ziller, 9). Essentially, the device is patently a short true-false achievement test. In the present study, the instrument was composed of twenty items pertaining to military terms most of which were at least vaguely familiar to the subjects either from newspaper reports or through ROTC course work. For example:

1. Defilade is the delivery of fire so as to sweep the length of a line of troops.
2. Texas Towers has reference to the radar system of the Air Defense Command.
3. The Army is responsible for NIKE operations.

A valid item in this instrument is that for which the subjects have insufficient information and thus are unable to respond with any great assurance of success. The directions to the test were as follows:

Knowledge of military terms is an important objective of the military training program. Familiarity with the following terms also indicates an interest in military affairs in general. In the items below, indicate whether the statement is True or False by circling the appropriate symbol. Your score will be determined by subtracting two times the number wrong from the number correct; that is, you will be penalized if you guess incorrectly.

Theoretically, the measure of utility for risk is the ratio of the number of items on which the subject hazards a guess to the number of items not known by the subject. The risk score is derived from the formula:

$$R = \frac{2\ W}{2\ WU}$$

where W refers to the number of incorrect responses and U refers to the number of items omitted. In an earlier study (Swineford, 8), the reliability of a similar device was estimated as .796. In the present study, no relation was found between the risk index and intelligence as measured by the total score of the ACE ($r = .02$).

In general, the device appears to measure the ability to sustain a loss in a decision-making situation under conditions of uncertainty and risk (Ziller, 9).

Vocational Choice

When the vocational questionnaire data were analyzed, eighteen categories developed. However, due to the small number of subjects in accounting, art, general engineering, law, medicine, ministry, armed services, physics, and physical education, these categories were excluded from the

analysis. Moreover, the agriculture group was eliminated because of the diversity of positions necessarily included in this category (dairy farmer, plant pathologist, creamery manager, poultry nutritionist, etc.). A separate category labeled *Unknown* was indicated by the responses of nine subjects who wrote that they "did not know" for what vocation they were preparing. In general, these latter students were enrolled in the College of Arts and Sciences and may be referred to as liberal arts students.

RESULTS

The arcsine transformation was applied to the risk scores and the resulting indexes tabulated according to vocational choice. Subsequently, an analysis of variance test was calculated (see Table 1). The results are statistically significant at about the 5 per cent level of confidence. Students selecting sales as a vocation are found to have the highest index of risk preference, and the undecided students tend to show the lowest risk proclivity.

TABLE 1

Analysis of Variance of the Utility for Risk among Vocations

Vocation	N	Mean Utility for Risk
Sales	19	65.5
Mechanical Engineering	14	60.7
Education	12	60.3
Business Administration	15	59.9
Chemical Engineering	33	53.1
Electrical Engineering	8	43.8
Civil Engineering	14	43.6
Undecided	9	40.6

	Mean Variance	d.f.	$F.*$
Between	1154.54	7	2.16
Within	535.56	116	

*F required at .05 level 2.08.

DISCUSSION OF RESULTS

The study was designed to test the validity of a theory of vocational choice based upon a model of individual decision-making behavior under conditions of uncertainty and risk. The results lend support to the proposal and encourage further testing of various aspects of the theory as it applies to vocational choice.

It is tempting to speculate as to the job characteristics which lead high risk-takers to select the various vocations. For example, what explanation can be offered for the wide differences in the utility for risk between mechanical engineers on the one hand and electrical and civil engineers on the other? Personnel from the University of Delaware's School of Engineering and the Placement Bureau suggest that a greater variety of positions are open to mechanical engineers in comparison to other engineering fields. Thus a college degree in mechanical engineering may not insure success on a specific job to the same extent as a degree in other fields of engineering.

The results with regard to the students who are undecided as to vocational objectives at the end of their sophomore year are also intriguing. These undecided students tend to score low on the risk measure. Abstracting somewhat, it may be hypothesized that indecision and utility for risk are negatively correlated. Now, if this line of reasoning is extended, the measure of utility for risk may be useful in predicting the effectiveness of potential business executives who are continually faced with the necessity of making decisions on the basis of inadequate and incomplete information.

The results with regard to salesmen are in accord with the stereotype of this group. It would be interesting to determine the relation of utility for risk and success within a sales group of a particular organization.

Finally, it is worth noting the risk-taking tendencies of the three individuals considering a military career. While these data were not included in the statistical analysis due to the small sample involved, it was observed that this group scored higher than the sales group with reference to risk taking. On the other hand, the directions to the test may have encouraged those interested in a military career to guess.

In general, the results are supporting and provocative. However, the study should be cross-validated. Moreover, a larger scale project including both men and women and a larger number of vocational areas will provide additional information upon which a theory of vocational choice based upon an individual decision-making model may be developed in greater detail.

SUMMARY

Recent theoretical developments in the area of individual decision-making behavior were adapted for conditions of vocational choice. A test of the resulting theory was described. The results supported the theory and suggested further investigations relating utility for risk and specific occupational choices,

[1]In general, the terminology used throughout the theoretical presentation follows Preston and Baratta (5) and Coombs and Beardslee (1).

REFERENCES

1. Coombs, C. H., and Beardslee, D. On decision-making under uncertainty. In R. M. Thrall, C. H. Coombs, and R. L. Davis, *Decision Processes*. New York: John Wiley, 1954. Pp. 255–282.

2. Friedman, M., and Savage, L. J. The utility analysis of choices involving risk. *J. political Econ.*, 1948. *56*, 279–304.

3. Ginzberg, E., Ginsburg, J. W., Axelrad, S., and Herma, J. L. *Occupational Choice*.

New York: Columbia University Press, 1951.

4. Meadow, L. Toward a theory of vocational choice. *J. counsel. Psychol.*, 1955, *2*, 108–112.

5. Preston, M. G., and Baratta, O. An experimental study of the auction-value of an uncertain outcome. *Amer. J. Psychol.*, 1955, *61*, 183–193.

6. Super, D. E. A theory of vocational development. *Amer. Psychologist*, 1953, *8*, 185–190.

7. Swineford, Francis. The measurement of a personality trait. *J. educ. Psychol.*, 1938, *29*, 295–300.

8. Torrance, E. P., and Ziller, R. C. Risk and life experience. *Research Bulletin*, Air Force Personnel and Training Research Center, Lackland Air Force Base, San Antonio, Texas, in press.

9. Ziller, R. C. A measure of the gambling response set in achievement examinations (submitted to *Educ. psychol. Measmt*).

Propensity for Risk Taking as a Determinant of Vocational Choice:

An Extension of the Theory of Achievement Motivation

JOHN L. MORRIS, *University of California, Berkeley*

The purpose of this study is to extend a theoretical model of motivation and risk taking (Atkinson, 1957, 1958; McClelland, Atkinson, Clark, and Lowell, 1953). The model stipulates that an individual's preference for an intermediate degree of risk — probability of success $(P_s = .5)$ — varies directly as the strength of his achievement motivation and inversely as the strength of his avoidance motivation.

Previous studies have tended to look at vocational choice either from the viewpoint of interest inventories or from the viewpoint of level of aspiration. This study is exploratory inasmuch as vocational choice is seen as

Reprinted with the permission of author and publisher from the article of the same title, in *Journal of Personality and Social Psychology*, 1966, *3*, 328–335.

the result of the interaction of the two. The intention is to show that the risk-taking propensity of an individual is related to his estimate of his P_s in a chosen occupation. This probability estimate is considered to have two components: One pertaining to the level of difficulty of the occupation and the other pertaining to the field of choice. In this study an index of resultant achievement motivation was used. Atkinson and Litwin (1960) suggest that when measures of achievement motivation (approach tendency) and fear of failure (avoidance tendency) are used conjointly then the resultant index is more closely related to certain outcome measures than either of the variables used independently.

There are series of studies which have demonstrated that the two motives have relevance for vocational choice. McClelland

(1956) has shown that the person who is highly motivated to achieve is disposed to take moderate or calculated risks in preference to very speculative or very safe undertakings. Minor and Neel (1958) have demonstrated a significant positive relationship between an individual's achievement motivation and the prestige rank of his occupational preference. Mahone (1960) showed that persons who are high in achievement motivation and low in fear of failure tend to be realistic in their vocational choice with respect to both ability and interest. Persons low in achievement motivation and high in fear of failure tend to be unrealistic. Atkinson and O'Connor[1] supported Mahone's findings and also demonstrated that intelligence, as conventionally measured by a single score omnibus test, is an important factor associated with the realism of vocational choice: individuals low in intelligence tending to make unrealistic choices irrespective of their motivation. Burnstein (1963) showed that, as fear of failure increases, the prestige of the aspired-to occupation decreases and the willingness to settle for less satisfying and less prestigeful occupations increases. Burnstein, Moulton, and Liberty (1963) found that when a discrepancy obtains between prestige and required competence, activities demanding a high degree of excellence relative to prestige conferred are likely to be more attractive to individuals high in achievement motivation and achievement values.

The four pictures used in this study were those recommended by Atkinson. The source of each picture and detailed instructions for administration are given in Appendix III (Atkinson, 1958). The pictures were shown in a group setting under neutral conditions; that is, a condition in which no experimental attempt is made to either arouse the motive or create an especially relaxed state prior to the writing of the stories (Atkinson and Reitman, 1956). A measure of test anxiety, first developed by Mandler and Sarason (1952), provides an assessment of the tendency to be anxious about failure in achievement situations. This anxiety tends to interfere with efficient performance of complex intellectual tasks when there is external pressure to achieve. The self-report questionnaire for use with high school students, developed by Judith Cowen (Mandler and Cowen, 1958), was used in this study.

Hypotheses

Let us assume that an individual estimates his P_s in general as very high in mechanical jobs, as moderate in persuasive, and very low in artistic. Assume further that he is presented with a list of jobs in each of these fields and that each list is composed of jobs ranging from very easy (high P_s) to very difficult (low P_s). It has been demonstrated that senior-high-school and college students are able to rank occupations reliably in order of difficulty and that the order corresponds very closely to the order of occupations on the National Opinion Research Center Prestige Scale (Atkinson and O'Connor[2]; Mahone, 1960). As would be expected, students perceive that high-level or difficult jobs have a lower probability of success than easy or low-level jobs.

It is envisaged that where an individual sees himself as competent or as having a high P_s in the field (high P_{sf}), he would bias the P_s of all the occupations in the field upward so that even the most difficult job is not far removed from the intermediate degree of risk ($P_s = .5$). Where he sees himself as incompetent and as having a low P_s in the field, he would bias the P_s of all occupations downward so that the easiest is not remote from the intermediate degree of risk. This situation is illustrated in Figure 1.

The risk-taking model stipulates that individuals high in resultant motivation will prefer occupations having an intermediate degree of risk. It is deducted from Figure 1 that this requirement would be met by the selection of relatively difficult jobs in a field of high P_s and relatively easy jobs in a field of low P_s. These possibilities will be termed the typical bias. The model also stipulates that

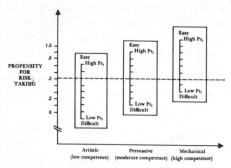

PERCEPTIONS OF COMPETENCE IN VARIOUS OCCUPATIONAL CATEGORIES

FIGURE 1. A concept of the effect of an individual's expectancy of success in various occupational fields upon his expectancy of success in specific occupations typically equated in level of difficulty in conventional occupational scales.

individuals low in achievement-related motivation will prefer a degree of risk which is divergent from the intermediate level. Referring again to Figure 1, it is seen that such an individual should prefer relatively easy jobs in a field of high P_s and relatively difficult jobs in a field of low P_s, These possibilities are called the atypical bias. This brings us to the research hypotheses.

1. The probability that individuals who are high in resultant motivation make typical choices is greater than the probability that individuals who are low in resultant motivation make typical occupational choices.

If this prediction is supported, it should then be possible to compare the absolute rather than the relative levels of difficulty of choices made by persons differing in achievement-related motivation.

2. In making choices within occupational fields perceived as having a high P_s, the probability that individuals who are high in resultant motivation choose difficult jobs is greater than the probability that individuals low in resultant motivation choose difficult jobs.

3. In making choices within occupational fields perceived as having a low P_s, the probability that individuals who are high in resultant motivation choose easy jobs is greater than the probability that individuals low in resultant motivation choose easy jobs.

It is proposed that this first set of hypotheses should be tested by asking the respondents to choose jobs from prepared lists representing a variety of fields of interest or job activity. If the hypotheses are adequately demonstrated, then it should be possible to make predictions about expressions of vocational choices which individuals make on leaving school. That is to say, an individual's freely expressed job choice obtained from a questionnaire (called "career choice") should represent a convergence of the risk-taking potential and his perceived P_s. It is anticipated that few individuals will make a choice in a field of low P_s and so a parallel hypothesis for this contingency has not been given.

4. If a career choice is made in a field in which an individual estimates his P_s as high, the level of difficulty of the choice is positively related to his resultant motivation.

METHOD

The experimental sample consisted of 108 senior-high-school boys drawn from a suburban high school in the San Francisco Bay Area. The sample was not chosen at random because of administrative difficulties within the school. The boys were enrolled in physical education classes which drew from all sections of the curriculum, and a comparison of measures of their ability, occupational interests, and socio-economic status showed them to be typical of the total enrollment of seniors. Twelve boys were absent on the first day of testing and the test protocols of two more were incomplete.

The group was divided on the basis of the strength of their approach and avoidance motivation. Atkinson and O'Connor's technique was used whereby the scores of each individual on the measures of Achievement and Test Anxiety were first standardized and the difference between these two standardized scores was determined. The resulting distribution of "resultant motivation" was then split at the median score.

A specially designed "Level of Difficulty Scale" was then administered to elicit the level of difficulty of choice within various occupational interest areas. Each subject was required to state a preference of occupation from each of 10 lists of occupations each comprising nine jobs. Each list contained jobs homogeneous with respect to the dominant interest (Kuder, 1956) required of an individual undertaking that kind of work. The ordering of difficulty of items in each of the 10 lists was randomized from list to list. Scores were assigned to each of the occupations; the most difficult being assigned a score of 9 and the least difficult a score of 1. The lists were compiled using the Haller Occupational Aspiration Scale (Haller and Miller, 1963) and the National Opinion Research Center (1953) Survey's Occupational Prestige Scale as referents. The test-retest reliability of the instrument was established using a sample of 25 boys drawn at random from the same group as the main experimental sample. They were asked to rank the jobs in each list in order of difficulty on two occasions 2 weeks apart. The median rank assigned on the first occasion was used as the index of difficulty with which a particular occupation is perceived by the senior-high-school boys used in the main experimental sample.

Estimates of probabilities of success in various occupational fields were obtained from a second specially designed "Probability of Success Scale." The subject was simply asked to make an estimate of his chance of success in each of 10 fields (Kuder, 1956) of work. He responded to definitions of these fields by checking a line representing various degrees of probability of success. The test-retest reliability of this scale was established in the manner reported above. The level of difficulty of jobs chosen within fields perceived as having the highest and lowest P_s was then examined for two groups of subjects: those high and those low in resultant motivation.

Hypothesis 4 was based on the premise that freely expressed occupational preferences in response to a questionnaire item, "What occupation do you desire to enter when you have finished your schooling?" would follow the same pattern as preferences for jobs included in the prepared lists. The preference of each subject was classified according to its relevant occupational field using the Kuder manual as a referent; and the difficulty level of the choice was obtained using the Level of Difficulty scales as a referent. The subject's perceived P_s in the field was ascertained from the Probability of Success scales. It was originally intended

TABLE 1

Frequency of Occurrence of the Typical and Atypical Bias for the Group as a Whole and for Subjects above and below the Median IQ

Group and Bias	Resultant Motivation		Total
	High	Low	
Total			
Typical	33	22	55
Atypical	6	22	28
Total[a]	39	44	83[b]**
High IQ			
Typical	21	10	31
Atypical	1	9	10
Total[c]	22	19	41**
Low IQ			
Typical	12	12	24
Atypical	5	13	18
Total[d]	17	22	42*

[a]$\chi^2 = 11.05$, $df = 1$.

[b]Eight high resultant-motivated and 3 low resultant-motivated individuals did not bias at all (zero bias) and results for 11 subjects do not appear in this analysis.

[c]$\chi^2 = 7.90$, $df = 1$, Yates' correction.

[d]$\chi^2 = 1.90$, $df = 1$, Yates' correction.

*$p > .10$.

**$p < .05$, one-tailed test.

that all analyses would be replicated for subjects high and low in socio-economic status using the Hollingshead and Redlich (1958) index. However, the obtained range of SES scores was considered too small and the variable was deleted. For reasons already given, IQ was introduced as an experimental variable. The Henmon-Nelson omnibus, single score measure of general ability was used.

For Hypotheses 1–4, the one-tailed test of significance was used in analyses for the group as a whole and for high IQ subjects. However, the way in which low IQ would affect the results was not predicted and a two-tailed test of significance was used.

RESULTS

According to Hypothesis 1, the probability that individuals who are high in resultant motivation make typical choices is greater than the probability that individuals who are low in resultant motivation make typical choices. The frequency of occurrence of the typical and atypical choices or bias among subjects differing in resultant motivation appears in Table 1. This table includes the results for the group as a whole and for subjects above and below the group median in intelligence. A statistically significant difference is found in the frequency of the typical bias between subjects high and low in resultant motivation ($\chi^2 = 11.05$, $df = 1$, $p < .05$). Thus, Hypothesis 1 is clearly supported. When the results for high intelligent individuals are examined, it is seen that those who are also high in resultant motivation choose strongly in the predicted direction ($\chi^2 = 7.90$, $df = 1$, $p < .05$). The results for low intelligent individuals are in the predicted direction but fail to meet the required level of significance.

Hypotheses 2 and 3 are more demanding tests of the biasing model. The earlier test required only that the choice would be in a certain direction; having established this we may now examine the data to see if the bias

is strong enough to cause individuals differing in resultant motivation to choose at one end or the other of distributions of jobs varying in level of difficulty. It was necessary to set criteria for high and low levels of difficulty. The four jobs ranked as easiest by students in each of the 10 occupational fields were termed low level of difficulty; the four jobs ranked as hardest by the same students were termed high level of difficulty. The job ranked fifth among the nine alternatives in each case was termed intermediate.

Hypothesis 2 states that in making choices within an occupational field perceived as having a *high P_s*, the probability that indi-

TABLE 2

Frequency of Selection of Difficult and Easy Occupations in Fields Perceived as Having a High Probability of Success

Group and Level of Difficulty	Resultant Motivation		Total
	High	Low	
Total			
High	27	17	44
Low	11	21	32
Total[a]	38	38	76[b,c]**
High IQ			
High	17	7	24
Low	5	9	14
Total[d]	22	16	38[c]*
Low IQ			
High	10	10	20
Low	6	12	18
Total[e]	16	22	38*

Note. — Based on forced choices from prepared lists.

[a]$\chi^2 = 5.40$, $df = 1$.

[b]Eighteen individuals chose occupations defined as "intermediates." Results for these subjects do not appear in Table 2.

[c]One-tailed test.

[d]$\chi^2 = 1.62$, $df = 1$.

[e]$\chi^2 = .52$, $df = 1$.

*$p > .10$, Yates' correction.

**$p < .05$.

TABLE 3

Frequency of Selection of Difficult and Easy Occupations in Fields Perceived as Having a Low Probability of Success

Group and Level of Difficulty	Resultant Motivation		Total
	High	Low	
Total			
High	13	22	35
Low	29	22	51
Total[a]	42	44	86[b,c]**
High IQ			
High	8	9	17
Low	19	11	30
Total[d]	27	20	47[c]*
Low IQ			
High	5	13	18
Low	10	11	21
Total[e]	15	24	39*

Note. — Based on forced choices from prepared lists.

[a] $\chi^2 = 3.23$, $df = 1$.

[b] Eight subjects chose occupations defined as "intermediate" level of difficulty. Results for these individuals do not appear in Table 3.

[c] One-tailed test.

[d] $\chi^2 = .60$, $df = 1$.

[e] $\chi^2 = .88$, $df = 1$.

*$p > .10$, Yates' correction.

**$p < .05$.

viduals who are high in resultant motivation choose difficult jobs is greater than the probability that individuals low in resultant motivation choose difficult jobs. The estimated P_s of each individual, in each of the 10 fields, was examined. The area in which the estimated P_s was highest was used for further analysis. Table 2 shows the frequency with which easy and difficult jobs are chosen by individuals differing in resultant motivation when the choices are made within fields of high P_s. The results are statistically significant in the predicted direction and the hypothesis is supported ($\chi^2 = 5.40$, $df = 1$, $p < .05$). The results for high and low IQ individuals are in the predicted direction in

both cases but they fail to reach the required level of significance.

According to Hypothesis 3, in making choices within occupational fields perceived as having a *low* P_s, the probability that individuals who are high in resultant motivation will choose easy jobs is greater than the probability that individuals low in resultant motivation will choose easy jobs. As before, the estimated P_s of each individual in each of the 10 fields was examined. That area in which the estimated P_s was lowest was used for further analysis. Results for the group as a whole and for subjects differing in intelligence appear in Table 3 which shows the frequency with which easy and difficult occupations are chosen when the choices are made within fields of low P_s. A statistically significant difference is found in the predicted direction in the frequency of selection of easy jobs among subjects high and low in resultant motivation ($\chi^2 = 3.23$, $df = 1$, $p < .05$). Hypothesis 3 is therefore supported. The results for high and low intelligent individuals are in the predicted direction in both cases but fail to meet the required level of significance.

Hypothesis 4 is a more stringent test again of the model. The criterion variable shifts from the laboratory-oriented, forced-choice decisions from prepared lists to expression of actual future intention concerning vocational choice. According to this hypothesis, if a career choice is made in a field in which an individual estimates his P_s as very high, the level of difficulty of choice is positively related to his resultant motivation. Each job choice was classified according to the dominant interest category involved in that line of work. This was done by locating the occupation in Table 2 in the Kuder (1956) examiners manual, "Percentile Ranks of the Mean Scores of Men in Various Occupational Groups." If the specific occupation was not listed then the most similar listed occupation was used. By reading across the table the percentiles attained in each of the 10 Kuder categories were located. The dominant interest area was that category

TABLE 4

Frequency of Selection of Difficult and Easy Occupations in Fields Perceived as Having a High Probability of Success

Group and Level of Difficulty	Resultant Motivation		Total
	High	Low	
Total			
High	21	10	31
Low	10	14	24
Total[a]	31	24	55[b]**
High IQ			
High	15	6	21
Low	4	4	8
Total[c]	19	10	29[b]*
Low IQ			
High	6	4	10
Low	6	10	16
Total[d]	12	14	26*

Note. — Based on expressions of career choice per questionnaire.

[a] $\chi^2 = 4.31$, $df = 1$.
[b] One-tailed test.
[c] $\chi^2 = .03$, $df = 1$.
[d] $\chi^2 = .51$, $df = 1$.
* $p > .10$, Yates' correction.
** $p < .05$.

TABLE 5

Level of Difficulty of Job Choices within Fields Perceived as Having a High and a Low Probability of Success

Perceived P_s in Vocational Fields and Level of Difficulty of Choice	Resultant Motivation					
	High IQ			Low IQ		
	High	Low	Total	High	Low	Total
High	*N =*					
High	15	6	21	6	4	10
Intermediate	2	4	6	4	1	5
Low	4	6	10	4	10	14
Total	21	16	37	14	15	29
Intermediate						
High	1	0	1	1	0	1
Intermediate	2	0	2	1	1	2
Low	0	1	1	0	4	4
Total	3	1	4	2	5	7
Low						
High	0	1	1	0	3	3
Intermediate	0	0	0	0	1	1
Low	1	1	2	0	2	2
Total	1	2	3	0	6	6

Note. — Based on expression of career choice per questionnaire.

TABLE 6

Estimated Probability of Success and Realism of Career Choices by Individuals Differing in Achievement-Related Motivation

Realism of Choice	Resultant Motivation					
	High IQ			Low IQ		
	High	Low	Total	High	Low	Total
Career choices made in areas of high P_s (realistic)	21	16	37	14	15	29
Career choices made in areas of low P_s (unrealistic)	4	3	7	2	11	13
Total	25	19	44	16	26	42

which showed the highest percentile rank for that occupation. The individual's estimate of P_s in that dominant field was ascertained from the Probability of Success scales. Estimated P_s's of 8, 9, and 10 were classified high and those of 1, 2, and 3 were termed low. The remainder were termed intermediate. The level of difficulty of an occupation was found by comparing the chosen occupation with the list of nine jobs in the Level of Difficulty scale for the appropriate field. The results for the group as a whole are analyzed in Table 4 and a statistically significant positive relationship is found between resultant motivation and difficulty of choice ($\chi^2 = 4.31$, $df = 1$, $p < .05$) when the choices are made in a field of high P_s. The chi-square one sample test was used to test the significance of the relationship (Dixon and Massey, 1957). The degree of relationship was measured using the phi coefficient (Hays, 1963). The obtained coefficient of .28 deviates significantly from 0 at the .05 level. Hypothesis 4 was therefore supported. High-resultant-motivated individuals who are high in intelligence choose as anticipated, as do low-resultant-motivated individuals who are low in intelligence. However, the results fail to meet the required level of significance.

Specific hypotheses were not formulated for choice made in areas of low P_s, since it was considered that the cell frequencies would be too low to permit meaningful analyses. Table 5 contains additional data

TABLE 7

Kuder Interest Inventory Scores and the Realism of Career Choice of Individuals Differing in Achievement-Related Motivation

Realism of Choice	Resultant Motivation					
	High IQ			Low IQ		
	High	Low	Total	High	Low	Total
Career choices congruent with high Kuder scores (realistic)	18	15	13	10	5	15
Career choices not congruent with high Kuder scores (unrealistic)	4	2	4	4	11	15
Total	22	17	39	14	16	30

for us to examine certain questions which are suggested by earlier research; for example, Do high-resultant-motivated individuals tend to choose within areas of high P_s or high inventoried interest, and can we expect the reverse for individuals low in resultant motivation? Two methods of presenting the relationship between achievement motivation, IQ, and realism of choice are shown in

Tables 6 and 7. Implications are drawn in the discussion.

DISCUSSION

The significant contribution of this study concerns the effects of self-perceptions of competence in vocational fields (interest areas) on the subjective probability of success in specific occupations. An individual is believed to accept an occupation having a certain probability of success for him because of his predilection to approach or avoid risky situations. In the light of the results it would seem illogical to assume that the perceived level of difficulty of a job is always analogous to an objectively defined level of difficulty such as its position on a scale which is heterogeneous with respect to the interest content of the jobs contained in it. It has been amply demonstrated herein that individuals choose jobs differing more widely in level of difficulty when the choices are made in a field of high P_s than when they are made in a field of low P_s. An examination of this kind of variance in level of aspiration behavior has not been reported previously in the literature.

This study may have contributed to an understanding of the dynamics of vocational choice behavior. There is a close similarity between the difficulty and interest area dimensions used in this research and the level and field dimensions of the Roe (1956) occupational classification. One of the implications of the Roe system is that the occupational psychologist may be able to predict choice by measuring an individual's level of vocational aspiration thus locating him at a point on the level of difficulty dimension. The subject would then be located on the field dimension through the use of an interest inventory. The point of intersection should be, theoretically, the optimal job choice for the individual. It is suggested that this two independent factors theory is insufficient to account for the choices which individuals actually make. One of the reasons, advanced here, is that individuals are concerned with the degree of risk involved in a situation and the test of their competence which they are prepared to undergo is related to another set of motivational variables. The variables considered here were achievement motivation and fear of failure, or avoidance motivation. Generalizing from the results we may say that the counsellor should be cautious in applying measures of the client's interest and level of aspiration unless he knows something of the motivational system of the client.

Previous research (Burstein et al., 1963) suggests that prestige and excellence would be valued differently by each of the two motivational groups. Although there is some evidence that high-resultant-motivated individuals are more concerned with choosing in a field of high P_s, prestige (the choice of a difficult occupation) did not appear to be as much a concern of the low-resultant-motivated individuals as anticipated. The results do show that some individuals choose jobs in an area in which they perceive their P_s as low and this phenomenon was explored further.

Mahone (1960) and Atkinson and O'Connor[3] suggest that realism of choice is positively related to intelligence and to achievement motivation. If we consider the level of perceived P_s in the chosen field of work another index of realism, we might anticipate the same findings as Mahone and others. A career choice made in an area of high perceived P_s ($P_s > 80\%$) was termed realistic and a choice made in an area of low perceived P_s ($P_s < 80\%$) was termed unrealistic. Table 6 illustrates the fact that 84% of the sample of individuals high in intelligence made choices in a field of high P_s and that only 70% of individuals low in intelligence made choices in a field of high P_s. Those high in resultant motivation tended to make realistic choices irrespective of their intelligence whereas those low in resultant motivation *and* low in intelligence made a relatively greater number of unrealistic choices (42%).

There are also data available to make a more direct comparison between these results and the Mahone and others' findings.

The job choices of all subjects were already classified according to the dominant interest field. The Kuder Preference Record scores of the majority of subjects were also available. Where the Kuder score was above the 75 percentile the choice was termed realistic and if below this level it was termed unrealistic. The realism of career choices of individuals differing in achievement-related motivation is illustrated in Table 7. The findings are in close agreement with the analysis based on estimated P_s. A high proportion (70%) of the low-intelligent, low-resultant-motivated individuals make unrealistic choices.

[1]"The Effects of Ability Grouping in Schools," report to the Department of Health, Education, and Welfare, 1963.
[2]*Ibid.*

REFERENCES

Atkinson, J. W. Motivational determinants of risk-taking behavior. *Psychological Review*, 1957, *64*, 359–372.

Atkinson, J. W. (Ed.) *Motives in fantasy, action, and society.* Princeton, N.J.: Van Nostrand, 1958.

Atkinson, J. W., and Litwin, G. H. Achievement motive and test anxiety conceived as motive to approach success and motive to avoid failure. *Journal of Abnormal and Social Psychology*, 1960, *60*, 52–63.

Atkinson, J. W., and Reitman, W. R. Performance as a function of motive strength and expectancy of goal-attainment. *Journal of Abnormal and Social Psychology*, 1956, *53*, 361–366.

Burnstein, E. Fear of failure, achievement motivation, and aspiring to prestigeful occupations. *Journal of Abnormal and Social Psychology*, 1963, *67*, 189–193.

Burnstein, E., Moulton, R., and Liberty, P. Prestige vs. excellence as determinants of role attractiveness. *American Sociological Review*, 1963, *28*, 212–219.

Dixon, W. J., and Massey, F. J. *Introduction to statistical analysis*. New York: McGraw-Hill, 1957.

Haller, A. O., and Miller, I. W. The Occupational Aspiration Scale. *Michigan State University, Technical Bulletin*, 1963, No. 288.

Hays, W. L. *Statistics for psychologists*. New York: Holt, 1963.

Hollingshead, A. B., and Redlich, F. C. *Social class and mental illness*. New York: Wiley, 1958.

Kuder, G. F. *Kuder Preference Record Vocational Form — CH: Examiners manual*. (6th ed.) Chicago, Ill.: Science Research Associates, 1956.

Mahone, C. H. Fear of failure and unrealistic vocational aspiration. *Journal of Abnormal and Social Psychology*, 1960, *60*, 253–261.

Mandler, G., and Cowen, Judith. Test anxiety questionnaires. *Journal of Consulting Psychology*, 1958, *22*, 228–229.

Mandler, G., and Sarason, S. B. A study of anxiety and learning. *Journal of Abnormal and Social Psychology*, 1952, *47*, 166–173.

McClelland, D. C. Interest in risky occupations among subjects with high achievement motivation. Unpublished manuscript, Harvard University, 1956.

McClelland, D. C., Atkinson, J. W., Clark, R. A., and Lowell, E. L. *The achievement motive*. New York: Appleton-Century-Crofts, 1953.

Minor, C. A., and Neel, R. C. The relationship between the achievement motive and occupational preference. *Journal of Counseling Psychology*, 1958, *1*, 39–43.

Morris, J. L. The relation between the perceived probability of success in chosen occupations and achievement related motivation. Unpublished doctoral dissertation, University of California, Berkeley, 1964.

National Opinion Research Center. Jobs and occupations: A popular evaluation. In R. Bendix and S. M. Lipset (Eds.), *Class, status and pwer: A reader in social stratification*. New York: Free Press, 1953. Pp. 411–426.

Roe, Anne. *The psychology of occupations*. New York: Wiley, 1956.

The Strategy of Occupational Choice: Recruitment to Dentistry

BASIL SHERLOCK, *University of California at Los Angeles*

ALAN COHEN, *University of California at Los Angeles*

The investigation described here developed from a longitudinal study of the evolution of the professional in dentistry which is concerned with the recruitment, socializa-

Reprinted with the permission of authors and publisher from the article of the same title, in *Social Forces*, 1966, *44*, 303–313.

tion and initial careers of dental students. As a first phase of this research, the process of self-recruitment or the development of a commitment to study dentistry was studied with a sample of predental students. The present paper describes the development of an occupational choice; i.e., the decision to study dentistry.[1]

In this study two opposing approaches to occupational choice were considered. As an example of the first approach, Katz and Martin conceive of occupational choice as essentially *adventitious* in nature.[2] This approach characterizes occupational choice as nonrational, spontaneous and based upon situational pressures. Contingencies and influences external to the occupational world are seen as bringing about a fortuitous choice of one's life work. In their study of career choice among student nurses, Katz and Martin advance the thesis that ". . . the decisions which underlie embarkation on a nursing career *for at least some persons* revolve around limited, situational contingencies — in which the matter of nursing-as-career enters only tangentially or not at all. Thus, rational considerations play a minor or absent role. Examples of these contingencies are also given by Caplow:

The bases for decision are often trivial. A student decides to study law because he has gotten his highest grade in history courses, dislikes the idea of teaching and knows that courses in history are required for entrance to law school . . . A high school sophomore transfers from the academic sequence to the clerical course to be with her best friend.[3]

The essence of the adventitious approach is that career choice is made without due regard to employment opportunities or long range rewards. In the adventitious approach, the process of negotiating between aspirations and opportunities is only minimally present. This is expressed in the "getting by" orientation described by Kahl:

. . . the boys who were not aiming toward college occasionally had a specific common man job as their goal, but more often had no firm goal at all; they would take "anything that comes along."[4]

and further:

. . . many boys looked forward to a job in romantic terms. It symbolized to them an escape from childhood, an end to the school routine, a freedom from dependency on father's pocketbook, a chance to get money for cars and girls.[5]

The study of Ginzberg *et al.*, and that of Blau *et al.*, represent a second approach which stresses the *purposive* nature of occupational choice; conceiving of the final choice as contingent upon a sequence of previous choices.[6] Each realistic choice is a compromise between an individual's desires and the occupational opportunities available to him. According to Ginzberg, there are three periods in the process. Briefly, the first period is one dominated by the pleasure principle in which mainly fantasy choices are considered. The child wishes to have an exciting occupation such as policeman, cowboy, railroad engineer or physician. Following the fantasy period, a period of tentativeness occurs wherein choices are made, but no attempt to realize or implement them is made. Finally, the process terminates in a third or realistic period in which the individual explores alternatives and gradually becomes committed to a given occupation. In this phase, which is generally coterminous with late adolescence, difficult compromises between wishes and aspirations on the one hand and opportunities and objective conditions on the other hand have to be made. Thus, occupational choice involves a compromise between reward preferences and opportunities for access to specific occupations. These two factors, reward and access, serve as a basis for a conceptual framework developed by Blau and his co-workers. They specify and define the factors that are involved in reward preference and access. Also, they attempt to describe typical strategies used in compromising between the individual's wishes and the realities of the occupational world.

Both of these approaches have some degree of empirical validity. The adventitious approach, as we have called it, perhaps best describes recruitment to unskilled or semiskilled occupations. The purposive approach seems to fit the case of the skilled occupations, including the professions. Since we are dealing with professional recruitment, the second approach was used; and a hypothesis based upon it will be presented.

HYPOTHESIS AND METHOD

A model of the choice of dentistry as a career was developed to serve as our basic hypothesis.

1. Father has relatively high income and is able to provide the son with a professional education. Thus, the father's position serves as a financial springboard for the son.[7]
2. Son's occupational choice is dictated by two strategies: (a) attain a higher status than the father; and (b) select an occupation with a perceived minimal difficulty of access and perceived maximal rewards. This "minimax" strategy involves choosing an occupation that combines the advantages of relative ease of entry and the rewards of high income, prestige and autonomy.
3. These strategies dictate a choice of one of the professions and usually narrows the choice down to a high-status entrepreneurial profession such as medicine, law, or dentistry, rather than college teaching, engineering or social work.
4. As a group, predental students will perceive dentistry as offering a better combination of access and reward than other professions. Although some professions will offer greater reward, e.g., medicine *or* easier access, e.g., pharmacy; dentistry will be perceived as offering the best combination.
5. In summary, choice of dentistry is an outcome of two strategies; a status-aggrandizing strategy and a minimax strategy which balances access against reward preference.

Having described the concepts and the model which we used, we now turn to a brief description of the procedure for collecting data. The research sample comprised all students enrolled in the predental curriculum during the academic year of 1963 at the University of California at Los Angeles. Questionnaires were administered to these students at an orientation program. Ninety-six percent, or 154 students, participated in our study by completing a questionnaire dealing with occupational origins, career perspectives and a variety of background matters such as age, marital status, academic record, political preference, etc. Forty percent of the respondents were freshmen, 34 percent were sophomores, 20 percent were juniors and only five percent were seniors. The majority (63%) were born in the West and raised in a metropolitan environment by families of better than average income and education.

Occupational information such as the name of the occupation, a brief description of its duties and the source of income regarding their maternal and paternal grandfathers, maternal and paternal uncles and parents was obtained from respondents. An attempt was made to elicit as much information about his relatives' occupations as could be remembered and to assemble this data into an occupational genealogy. For each adult male relative the status, situs and setting of his occupation were determined by coding procedures. Occupational status, the prestige associated with an occupation, was determined by an occupational status index, the SES, developed by Bogue.[8] The objective status of any occupation can be specified by a formula using the educational attainment and yearly income data provided in the national Census. Bogue's index is constructed so that the average status score of all occupations is 100; scores above or below 100 represent the percentage deviation with respect to the national average.

Occupational situs is a classification of occupations according to their social function; i.e., the services they perform for society. Where status classification separates occupations into vertical groups representing a prestige hierarchy, the situs classification separates occupations into horizontal groups of theoretically equal status ranges which form occupational families in terms of primary work functions. Ten situs categories which were developed by Morris and Murphy are: Legal Authority, Finance and Records, Manufacturing, Transportation, Extraction, Building and Maintenance, Commerce, Arts and Entertainment, Education and Research, and Health and Welfare.[9]

Occupational setting connotes the setting in which one works, especially with regard to whether one is self-employed or works for others; it provides the structural conditions which permit one to conceive of himself as an entrepreneur or an employee, autonomous or as part of a bureaucracy. Occupational setting, therefore, was assessed by determining whether the source of income was from self-employment or a salary or wage.

EXPECTANCY OF ACCESS: ASSESSMENT OF OPPORTUNITIES

To the extent that career choice involves a rational process, there is an attempt to assess the opportunities present in the occupational market place. Only the most committed or foolhardy individuals would attempt to enter into an already overcrowded occupation or profession; the rational individual is concerned about the

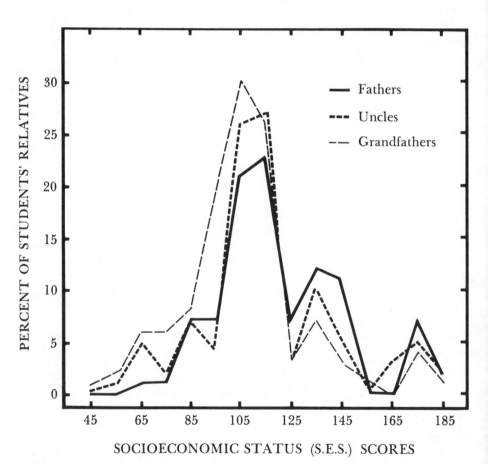

FIGURE 1. Occupational status of students' relatives.

degree of access available to him. *Expectancy of access* may be defined as the individual's assessment of the recruitment structure of that occupation; i.e., his perception of the amount of difficulty that would be encountered in becoming a member of a specific occupational group. It was measured by asking the student if he felt it was "very," "somewhat" or "not at all" difficult for him to be admitted to several specified careers.

The assessment of opportunities by the students was considerably influenced by their occupational origins. Therefore, it is necessary to discuss the occupational backgrounds of their families at this point. The status distribution of father, grandfathers and combined maternal and paternal uncles is depicted in Figure 1. In general, their grandfathers' average was 105; uncles were 111; and fathers were 120. The fathers' status score was significantly higher than the grandfathers' and the uncles' scores. These data confirm the findings of other studies that dental students are generally recruited from white-collar, rather than blue-collar backgrounds. The average SES of the fathers indicates their status level is approximately that of managers, officials and proprietors. A crucial finding is that the fathers are highly mobile, indicating that the father is generally the most successful relative known by the student. It appears that the father's mobility may provide both the motivation as well as the actual opportunity for the son to pursue professional training. Having achieved a secure middle-class occupation, the financial success of the father could be readily translated into a pursuit of professional prestige by the son. Apparently, a cumulative increase in a family's status over generations is the basis for the choice of a career in dentistry, rather than a sizeable leap in the socioeconomic hierarchy. Contrary to the belief that dentistry is an "open-door profession" for ambitious young men regardless of their background, our data suggest that dentistry today recruits the majority of its aspirants from the middle class. Perhaps dentistry previously offered a

more readily accessible avenue of mobility to young men from blue-collar families, but present-day dental education is expensive and the majority of students will receive a good deal of their economic support from their parents. The preceding interpretation, however, should not be taken to imply that becoming a dentist does not represent substantial upward mobility, since the majority of predental students do not come from professional backgrounds. A career in dentistry will, in most cases, mean a substantial increase in occupational prestige with respect to family background.

The proportion of fathers, combined maternal and paternal uncles and combined maternal and paternal grandfathers in the ten occupational situses is presented in Table 1. There were heavy concentrations in certain situses such as Commerce, and surprisingly light concentrations in others such as Health and Welfare or Education and Research, casting doubt on the existence of situs inheritance in our sample. For the fathers of the predental students, the ordering of major situses was Commerce, Building and Maintenance, and Manufacturing. Over 40 percent of the fathers were in different situses than the grandfathers, as compared to 30 percent of the uncles. The higher situs mobility of the fathers was also revealed by correlating the ranking of the situs distribution of fathers and grandfathers (Rho = .65); the rank order correlation between uncles and grandfathers was much higher (Rho = .85). The fathers, therefore, not only exhibited greater status mobility, but also greater situs mobility than other males in the extended family; and were concentrated in situses which permit entrepreneurial activity.

Regarding the occupational setting of the respondent's relatives, the results show that approximately 54 percent of the grandfathers were self-employed as compared to 52 percent of the uncles and 38 percent of the fathers. Again, the father differs not only from the grandfather but also from his own generation of relatives. An interesting

TABLE 1

Occupational Situs of Students' Relatives*

Situs	Grandfathers		Uncles		Fathers	
	Percent	Ranks	Percent	Ranks	Percent	Ranks
Health and Welfare	6	5	7	6	9	4
Legal Authority	2	9	3	9	4	7
Finance and Records	4	6	8	5	7	5.5
Manufacturing	18	3	15	2.5	10	3
Transportation	2	7.5	4	8	3	8.5
Extraction	25	2	12	4	3	8.5
Building and Maintenance	17	4	15	2.5	20	2
Commerce	27	1	27	1	32	1
Arts and Entertainment	3	7.5	1	10	7	5.5
Education and Research	1	10	4	7	1	10

*Spearman rank order correlations were calculated: Grandfathers' and uncles' situs distributions correlate .85 (P < .01); grandfathers' and fathers' situs distributions correlate .65 (P < .05); uncles' and fathers' situs distributions correlate .65 (P < .05).

paradox is that the respondents aspire to be self-employed professionals; i.e., dentists, although the majority of their fathers, 62 percent, are not self-employed. Autonomy or the freedom to decide hours of work, type of client and other working conditions was a major reason for choosing a career in dentistry. If dentistry were not an independent, "fee-for-service" profession, but rather a salaried profession, 49 percent of the respondents would renounce their aspirations to be a dentist. The disavowal of salaried occupations by the respondents seems to be a rejection of bureaucratic life style and a desire for an autonomous life style characteristic of the "fee-for-service" professions.

To summarize, there is considerable evidence that the father's occupational position represents not only upward status mobility but also situs mobility. The fathers tended to be concentrated in higher status managerial or proprietorship positions in the Commerce and Building and Maintenance situses. They were also predominantly salaried as regards their source of income. Although they were higher than average in occupational status, in income and in educa-

tion, the majority were not professionals. If realized, the desire of the respondents to become professionals represents a large stride forward. Thus, the favored occupational positions of the fathers may serve as a basis for launching the son into a professional career. To an important degree, the choice of a professional occupation may be a function of status ambitions created by the upward mobility of a middle-class family.

It was hypothesized that the position of the predental student's family in the socio-economic hierarchy would partially determine his perception of the difficulty of access into a dental career. The higher the position of his family in terms of occupation, income and education, the greater would be his expectancy of easy access into dentistry; because there would be greater resources and facilities available to him. The data give a partial confirmation of this hypothesis. While there is not the expected continuous decrease in perceived difficulty of access with increasing status, there is a sharp demarcation between those of very high status and the rest of the sample. Below a score of 160 on the Bogue scale for father's occupation, approximately 70 percent say that it is "very" difficult for them to become a dentist, whereas above this score, 90 percent say it is only "somewhat" or "not at all" difficult for them to become a dentist. Since there are relatively few respondents in this category, however, about ten percent of the sample, the difference is merely suggestive. In spite of its tenuousness, it is interesting that this relationship appears to be independent of whether or not the father is in the same occupational situs as dentistry. Sons of non-health situs, but high-ranking occupations expect access to dentistry to be as easy as those sons whose fathers are both high-ranking occupationally and in the health situs. Similarly, those whose fathers are in the lower status group, but in the health situs, perceive access to be as difficult as those whose fathers are in the lower status group and not in the health situs.

In addition to the effect of status on *perceived* difficulty of access, the more direct effect of status on the *actual* difficulty of access should be considered. Comparing our sample with the population of Los Angeles, one finds that the median income for Los Angeles is $7,046; while for the sample, it is $10,000 annually; thus, about 83 percent of the sample are above the median income of Los Angeles families. In Los Angeles, only eight percent of the families earn over $15,000 a year; while in the sample, the corresponding figure is 25 percent. Other indicators of status also show a high status distribution for the sample. The average status score of fathers in the sample of predental students is 120, whereas the average for the nation is 100. Regarding the father's education, one finds that in Los Angeles 24.5 percent of the population have one or more years of college, while in our sample the number is 56 percent; in Los Angeles the median number of years of education is 12.1, while in our sample the median number of year is 12.9.[10]

Another occupational variable that was considered in terms of its effect on expectancy of access was the *status mobility* of

the father; i.e., his movement or lack thereof within the occupational status hierarchy in relation to an origin point defined by the occupational status of the grandfather. Those in the sample whose fathers were upwardly mobile felt that becoming a dentist was relatively easy; 60 percent said it was only "somewhat" or "not at all" difficult to become a dentist. Those whose fathers were downwardly mobile were in the middle, since 40 percent found it only "somewhat" or "not at all" difficult. Finally, those whose fathers were non-mobile found it the most difficult; only 20 percent said access to dentistry was "somewhat" or "not at all" difficult. It appears that a father who has been mobile imparts his mobility aspirations to his son. Within the mobile group, those whose fathers were upwardly mobile perceive access as easier than those whose fathers moved downward in occupational status. This appears to be a result of two factors. The upwardly mobile father is aware of mobility in the social system and apprehends the value of aiming for high status. Thus, he would probably be quite effective in imparting these aspirations to his son. Also, the son has a father who is an example of possible success and whom he can emulate.

All of the other background factors, religious background, political beliefs, father's job setting, and exposure to dentistry, with which the study was concerned had no effect on the student's expectancy of access, with one exception — the birth order of the respondents. The first or only child had a higher expectancy of easy access than those who had younger siblings. Perhaps, this may be due to greater financial support available to the first or only child. This support can increase the actual ease of access and, in turn, raise the student's expectancy of easy access. Our data indicate that 78 percent of the sample meet their college expenses by parental support or parental support supplemented by income from a part-time or summer job; furthermore, 76 percent of our sample expect to use these same means of support while in dental school. Clearly, financial assistance from one's family is a common characteristic of our sample of predental students.

A high desire for specialization was correlated with a greater expectancy of access, as shown in Table 2. There is a similar, although not significant, relationship between expectancy of specialization and expectancy of access which appears to be due to a high correlation ($\phi = .77$) between these two attitudes toward specialization. When each is controlled for the other, only desire for specialization shows a relationship with the expectancy of access. This suggests that there is an underlying distinction between the two attitudes toward specialization; and corroborates Quarantelli's finding that the intention to specialize is related to a realistic appraisal of the possibilities of becoming a specialist, whereas the desire to specialize is a function of other social-psychological attitudes.[11] Also, this study, like Quaran-

TABLE 2

Expectancy of Access and Desire for Specialization

	Easy Access	Difficult Access
Low Desire	35%	53%
High Desire	65%	47%

$$\chi^2 = 4.0 \quad p < .05$$

telli's found that the degree of specialization desired is much greater than the degree of specialization expected.

A relationship was found between commitment in terms of earliness of decision to choose dentistry and the expectancy of access; i.e., those who decided before high school had a somewhat higher expectancy of easy access ($\phi = .24$, p < .05). However, when controlled for status, the early decider was found to be from a higher status back-

ground. Expectancy of access, as the findings strongly suggest, was dependent upon an awareness of the socio-economic position of one's family. Children from families of above average financial position can aspire realistically to a professional career. Expectancy of easy access to dentistry seems to be a function of a high parental status score, upward mobility of the father, and being the only or oldest male child in the family. All of these conditions combined to generate a boy's ambition to seek professional training. Thus, expectancy of access was based not only upon an actual existence of opportunities for entering an occupation, but also to a considerable extent upon a subjective assessment of the total resources at one's disposal.

REWARD VALUE: THE ASSESSMENT OF PREFERENCES

In making an occupational choice, an individual not only considers the chances of gaining entry, but perhaps more important, the rewards he desires. In this section, we discuss the factors which influence those desires.[12] *Reward value* of a career was measured in terms of (1) the perceived relative satisfaction to be derived from one career as opposed to other possible career choices; and (2) in terms of the individual's preference for extrinsic or intrinsic rewards derivable from the career he has chosen. Perceived relative satisfaction with choice of dentistry was operationally measured by asking the predental students which of the following statements best described the way he felt about a career in dentistry: "Only career for me"; "Other careers are equally satisfying"; "Other careers are more satisfying"; "Dentistry is not too satisfying a career." Those who said dentistry was the only career for them, 45 per cent of our sample, were classified high in relative satisfaction; those who said that there were other careers which were equally or more satisfying (55%) were classified low in relative satisfaction. There were no respondents who felt that dentistry was not too satisfying a career. Intrinsic rewards are rewards derived specifically from the nature of the tasks which are directly and inherently involved in the practice of the occupation such as creativity, use of certain mental and/ or physical abilities, etc. Extrinsic rewards are those such as money, prestige, or power, which are not inherent in the nature of the tasks of the occupational role.[13]

TABLE 3

Career Commitment and Relative Satisfaction

A. *Strength of Commitment*

	Low Satisfaction	High Satisfaction
Firm Commitment	27%	88%
Weak Commitment	73%	12%

$$\chi^2 = 52 \text{ p} < .001 \; \phi = .61$$

B. *Time of Commitment*

	Low Satisfaction	High Satisfaction
Early Commitment	40%	72%
Late Commitment	60%	28%

$$\chi^2 = 9.3 \text{ p} < .01 \; \phi = .32$$

Relative satisfaction was correlated with the strength and the earliness of the commitment to become a dentist. Strength of commitment was measured along a five-point scale on which the response of "definitely planning to be a dentist" represented the firmest commitment. Regarding time of decision, an "early decision" was considered as one made before coming to college, and a "late decision" was made after coming to college. Tables 3A and B show that the earlier and the firmer the decision to become a dentist, the higher the satisfaction with their choice. Once this important choice was made, it was usually perceived as the best possible choice, unless future events gave rise to doubts about the wisdom of the choice. In any event, those who developed an unwavering commitment to dentistry tended to evaluate dentistry very favorably.

Health-situs orientation is a measure of the predental student's desire for a career within the health situs as opposed to a desire for a high status occupation regardless of situs. Those students who were health-situs oriented were higher in relative satisfaction than those who were status oriented. Situs orientation, which measures concern for a type of work, and status orientation, which measures concern for the rewards of high income and prestige, were rather closely related to intrinsic and extrinsic reward orientation, respectively. Because of the parallel between these two sets of variables, the above findings suggest that intrinsically oriented students were more satisfied with the choice of dentistry than extrinsically oriented students. This was indicated by a relationship ($\phi = .19$, $p = .02$) between reward-type orientation and relative satisfaction. Those who have an intrinsic orientation tend to be higher in relative satisfaction than the extrinsically oriented.

It was also found that if the respondent had a strong self-image as a dentist, placing himself on the high end of a ten-point scale ranging from layman to dentist, then he had a high satisfaction with his choice of dentistry. The lowest degree of satisfaction was not associated with a self-image as a layman, but with a self-image which was intermediate between layman and dentist. This suggests that self-image was an important predictor of relative satisfaction.

Type of reward, the relative emphasis on the extrinsic or intrinsic benefits derived from a dental career is a final measure to be considered. In a study of occupational choice, Rosenberg found a direct relationship between the level of parental income and the desire for money and status in deciding upon a career; the higher the parental income, the more the student valued these extrinsic rewards.[14] However, Table 4 suggests a different relationship; both those from our high income and low income families emphasize extrinsic rewards; it is those from our middle income families who are intrinsically oriented. This

TABLE 4

Type of Reward Orientation and Parental Income

	Over $15,000	$7,000–$14,999	Under $7,000
Extrinsic	65%	42%	68%
Intrinsic	35%	58%	32%

$$\chi^2 = 8.25 \; p < .02$$

same relationship holds true using Bogue's status scores in place of income. The emphasis upon intrinsic or work-related rewards in the middle income range may be due to an inculcation of the work ethic and an emphasis upon the importance of a career or life's work during the formative years. The finding suggests that intrinsic rewards appeal to those students who come from neither deprived nor high income backgrounds, but have been raised in moderate circumstances.

ACCESS AND REWARD: THE STRATEGY OF COMPROMISE

Earlier in the paper, expectancy of access and reward value were described as separate elements of a career choice. At this point, the manner in which access and reward are combined in the actual decision-making process is described. There are conflicting views of this process. One view suggests that a high expectancy of easy access is correlated

with a high satisfaction with the career choice. An opposite view of the relationship between reward and access holds that an occupation with difficult access is considered more challenging and produces a higher satisfaction. Our data support the latter hypothesis; an expectancy of difficult access tends to be associated with high relative satisfaction, while an expectancy of easy access is strongly associated with low relative satisfaction as shown in Table 5. However, when reward type orientation is used as a control in Table 6, there are important differences between intrinsically and extrinsically oriented students. Two-thirds of the easy access group are low in relative satisfaction, regardless of whether they are intrinsically or extrinsically oriented. On the other hand, the intrinsic-extrinsic dimension does show a marked effect on relative

TABLE 5

Expectancy of Access and Relative Satisfaction

	Difficult Access	Easy Access
High Satisfaction	52%	33%
Low Satisfaction	48%	67%

$$\chi^2 = 3.8 \; p = .05 \; \phi = .66$$

TABLE 6

Expectancy of Access, Relative Satisfaction and Type of Reward Orientation

	Intrinsic[a]		Extrinsic[b]	
	Difficult Access	Easy Access	Difficult Access	Easy Access
High Satisfaction	64%	33%	42%	32%
Low Satisfaction	36%	67%	58%	68%

$$^a\chi^2 = 12.7 \; p < .001 \quad ^b\chi^2 = .7 \; p > .05$$

satisfaction of those who expect difficult access. There is a greater percentage (64%) of high satisfaction among the intrinsically oriented; there is a lesser percentage (42%) among the extrinsically oriented. These findings suggest that the student who values dentistry on intrinsic grounds because he expects to enjoy the duties and professional relationships, rather than the income or autonomy, will be satisfied with his choice.

One can establish two strategies of occupational choice using expectancy of access and relative satisfaction. The first, a minimax strategy, predicts that an individual will choose that occupation which minimizes the difficulty of access and maximizes the rewards which may be obtained. Although high reward is associated with high expectancy of difficult access, this simply means that the individual must carefully weigh these factors to produce the best combination of reward and access. Under the second strategy, the individual chooses his occupation by selecting that one which maximizes both the reward and the difficulty of access. The individual using this strategy is likely to find his occupational career more rewarding, but he will have a more difficult time entering it. However, the challenge created by difficulty access may itself be a positive inducement for some and may explain why those who expect difficult access to dentistry are more satisfied with their choice. For the first strategy, the ranking was produced by multiplying the percentage of our sample who felt the occupation was very rewarding by the percentage who felt access was relatively easy. For the second strategy, the ranking was formed by multiplying the percentage who felt that the occupation was very rewarding by the percentage who felt access was difficult. The products of these multiplications were used to produce a rank ordering of each occupation in terms of each of the two models. For the minimax strategy, the ranking was *Dentistry*, Law, Medicine, University Teaching, Business and Accounting. Under the second strategy, maximizing both reward and difficulty of access, the ranking was Medicine, *Dentistry*, Law, University Teaching, Accounting and Business.

The data suggest the view that both strategies were used during the different stages of the process of occupational choice. In an early stage, the individual seeks an occupation which maximizes both reward and difficulty of access. As indicated above, medicine was the first choice for the students using this strategy. However, for many, the difficulty of access to medicine proved to be too challenging and formed an insurmountable obstacle to that profession. At this point, the individual will enter the realistic stage in the process and switch to a minimax strategy which will lead to an occupation that is not quite as high in reward but more accessible. In this case, the above ranking indicates that the most suitable career, for this strategy and the type of individual in our sample, was dentistry. If this line of reasoning is correct, it suggests that many of our sample of predental students may have chosen dentistry as a second choice after medicine because of the perceived difficulty of being admitted to medical school. To the extent that this is true, there is an apparent contradiction in the data that must be explained; 65 percent of the sample say that access to dentistry is very difficult, which should not be the case if they had used the minimax strategy in choosing dentistry. It appears that once dentistry as been decided upon in the realistic stage by the minimax strategy, the individual will then claim that access to this choice is difficult in order not to feel that the challenge of medicine was too great for him. It indicates that the student has arrived at a realistic aspiration and has adjusted his career perspectives to be consistent with his final decision. The final decision is then regarded as a reasonable choice in the light of interests, aptitudes and resources of the student.

CONCLUSIONS

The first phase in the process of entering a professional occupation is to arrive at a choice based upon rewards and opportunities for access to given occupations. Whereas Katz and Martin describe the process of career choice as essentially dictated by considerations extraneous to these factors, there is considerable evidence that the factors of reward and access indeed are important determinants. Thus, our findings tend to support the approach of Ginzberg *et al.*, and Blau *et al.*, which describes career choice as a rational compromise between desired rewards and the realities of access. This approach seems particularly relevant in understanding the choice of dentistry wherein a sizeable proportion aspired to medicine at an earlier phase in choosing a career.

Although career choice is a function of reward and access, these variables, in turn, seem to be influenced by the occupational history of the individual's family. Thus, considerable attention was devoted to describing the occupational origins of the student's family. Our data indicate that career perspectives were developed with reference to the occupational statuses, situses, and sources of income of one's extended family. Prospective dentists tend to come from families where the father is upwardly mobile with respect to his father and is more successful than his brothers or his wife's brothers. The achievements of the father may not only serve to motivate the respondent, but provide financial opportunities for a professional education, permitting a realistic expectation of becoming a professional. These and other findings relating career perspectives to their structural antecedents in the student's background strongly suggest that the roots of a career choice extend back into the occupational history of one's family.

Some may argue that we have not shown how predental students differ from other male college students. This was not our intent; rather we intended to show the interrelationships of factors entering into a specific occupational choice. Certainly, predental students are similar in many respects to other male college students who also may come from upwardly mobile families. However, it is reasonable to contend that our sample students have different career perspectives and indeed utilize these perceptions in the manner described in the model of occupational choice.

Regarding the interaction of reward and access, it was found that dentistry was usually a minimax choice because it combined high rewards with an easier access than medicine. It is noteworthy that the aspiration to medicine was an earlier one, considerably diminished by the time the student entered college. Although medicine was the first choice in terms of rewards, the difficulty of gaining entry — especially the higher grade-point average required for medical school admission, as well as the greater responsibilities of a medical career — combined to present considerable access problems.

These two career perspectives, reward and access, appeared to be major factors in the choice of dentistry as a career. In addition, certain structural antecedents were important either as determinants of these career perspectives or as independent influences on the process of career choice. Primary among these were the status and status mobility of the respondent's father. Finally, exposure to dentistry, in terms of having a dentist or other health-situs professional among the relatives or friends of the student's family was, surprisingly, very unimportant both in the choice of dentistry and in the commitment to that choice. Dentistry, like other professions, receives some who lowered their original aspirations, some who originally aimed lower but elevated their aspirations, and finally, some who developed an early and unwavering commitment.

[1]The following studies are pertinent: William R. Mann, "Dental Education," in *The Survey of Dentistry*, (ed.), Byron S. Hollinshead (Washington, D.C.: American Council on Education, 1961); Douglas M. More, "The

Dental Student," *Journal of the American College of Dentists* (March 1961); Ronald M. Pavalko, "The Predental Student: A Study of Occupational Choice and Professional Recruitment," unpublished Ph.D. dissertation, University of California at Los Angeles, 1963: Enrico L. Quarantelli, "The Dental Student; A Social Psychological Study," unpublished Ph.D. dissertation, University of Chicago, 1959; and Walter I. Wardell, "Limited, Marginal and Quasi-Practitioners," in *Handbook of Medical Sociology*, (eds.), Howard E. Freeman et al. (Englewood Cliffs, New Jersey: Prentice-Hall, 1963).

[2]Fred E. Katz, and Harry W. Martin, "Career Choice Processes," *Social Forces*, 41 (December 1962), pp. 149–154.

[3]Theodore Caplow, *The Sociology of Work* (New York: McGraw-Hill Book Co., 1954), p. 218.

[4]Joseph A. Kahl, "Common Man Boys," in *Education, Economy and Society*, (eds.), A. H. Halsey, Jean Floud and C. Arnold Anderson (Glencoe, Illinois: The Free Press, 1963), p. 357.

[5]*Ibid.*, p. 359.

[6]Eli Ginzberg *et al.*, *Occupational Choice: An Approach to a General Theory* (New York: Columbia University Press, 1951); and Peter M. Blau *et al.*, "Occupational Choice: A Conceptual Framework," *Industrial and Labor Relations Review*, 9 (1956), pp. 531–543. The following statement succinctly expresses this approach: ". . . there seems to be an element of flexibility in occupational desires which bends to the toughness of reality. If entry into the occupation is considered easy then the aspirations hold sway, but if it is perceived as difficult, then the individual tends to modify his aspirations in terms of what he believes the external situation will enable him to get." Morris Rosenberg, *Occupations and Values* (Glencoe, Illinois: The Free Press, 1957), p. 76. See also Donald Super, *The Psychology of Careers* (New York: Harper & Row, 1957), pp. 286–289.

[8]Donald J. Bogue, *Skid Row in American Cities* (Chicago: Community and Family Study Center, University of Chicago, 1963), pp. 315–320.

[9]Richard T. Morris and Raymond J. Murphy, "The Situs Dimension in Occupational Structure," *American Sociological Review*, 24 (April 1959), pp. 231–239.

[10]Marcia Meeker, *Background for Planning,* 1963 (Los Angeles: Los Angeles Welfare Planning Council, 1964), pp. 64–67.

[11]Enrico L. Quarantelli, "Attitudes of Dental Students Toward Specialization and Research," *Journal of American College of Dentists* (1960), pp. 101–107.

[12]The perceived reward value of dentistry, in terms of both relative satisfaction and reward type, was unrelated to most of the variables in the student's background. A relationship was found between relative satisfaction and the status mobility of the student's father. Students whose fathers were mobile, either upward or downward, were less satisfied with dentistry as a career than the students whose fathers were non-mobile. Possibly the reason for this may lie in a greater range of experiences, a higher level of aspiration, and a greater awareness of possible careers to be found among students from mobile backgrounds.

[13]Intrinsic rewards are those rewards which result from the activity as an end-in-itself rather than as an instrument to the achievement of other ends. If an activity is engaged in purely for its own sake and not because of any by-products, it has intrinsic rewards. Further, if this activity incurs nonreinforcement or even punishment from others and is still engaged in — it may be considered to have intrinsic rewards. An operational definition of intrinsic rewards would then be that ego would engage in that activity regardless of alter's response. Extrinsic rewards are correlated with alter's response; intrinsic rewards are independent. It appears that the existence of alter's response to the "product" or outcome of the activity is the crucial factor in designating a reward as extrinsic.

An important characteristic of the professions seems to be the primacy of intrinsic rewards. If extrinsic rewards are more important and dominate the professional's work, then the requirement of a disinterested stance is violated. One purpose of professional ethics is to specify what is legitimately an intrinsic reward and what is an extrinsic reward in a given profession. Further, professional ethics seem to discourage the professional practitioner from seeking only the latter or allowing these extrinsic rewards to distort or undermine his performance. Effective socialization for a profession is also designed to instill a sense of the relative priority of these two types of rewards.

[14]Rosenberg, *op. cit.*, p. 58.

OTHER RELEVANT ARTICLES

The following articles are relevant to the topic of this chapter:

Alexander, I. E., L. B. Macht, and B. P. Karon. The level-of-aspiration model applied to occupational preference. *Human Relations*, 1959, *12*, 163–170.

This is a little-known report (neither Vroom nor Atkinson refer to it) of a study of the choice of occupational goals conceived in the terms of Lewin's level-of-aspiration model. It was found that a person's stated intentions concerning entering a number of broad occupational fields were most closely predicted by his estimate of probability of success in that field, and that the prediction was improved only slightly by the addition of the valence of success factor. The investigators were surprised to find that in their experimental population of bright college undergraduates that the valence of failure of an occupational goal is strongly associated with the attractiveness of the goal; that failure would be as painful as success would be satisfying.

Vroom, V. H. Organizational choice: A study of pre- and post-decision processes. *Organizational Behavior and Human Performance*, 1966, *1*, 212–255.

Vroom employed the model described briefly in the introduction to this chapter predict relative attractiveness of various employers to graduate students of business about to finish their studies. As suggested by Hershenson and Roth, the mean attractiveness of the chosen employer increased after the decision to join them was made, as did perceptions of the employers' potency for goal attainment. The same features of the unchosen employers decreased.

A few additional references are available on the decision-making frame of reference:

Dilley, J. S. Decision-making ability and vocational maturity. *Personnel and Guidance Journal*, 1965, *44*, 423–427.

Gelatt, J. Decision-making: A conceptual frame of reference for counseling. *Journal of Counseling Psychology*, 1962, *9*, 240–245.

Harmon, L. On decision-making in high school. *Bulletin of the National Association of Secondary School Principals*, 1962, *46*, 71–81.

Harren, V. A. The vocational decision-making process among college males. *Journal of Counseling Psychology*, 1966, *13*, 271–277.

Katz, F. E., and H. W. Martin. Career choice process. *Social Forces*, 1962, *41*, 149–154.

Montesano, N., and H. Geist. Differences in occupational choice between ninth and twelfth grade boys. *Personnel and Guidance Journal*, 1964, *43*, 150–154.

Tyler, Leona, Distinction patterns of likes and dislikes over a twenty-two year period. *Journal of Counseling Psychology*, 1959, *6*, 234–237.

Additional studies stemming from investigations of McClelland's *Theory of Achievement Motivation*, drawn in terms of vocational choice are:

Burnstein, E. Fear of failure, achievement motivation, and aspiring to prestigeful occupations. *Journal of Abnormal and Social Psychology*, 1963, *67*, 189–193.

Bernstein, E., R. Moulton, and P. Liberty. Prestige vs. excellence as determinants of role attractiveness. *American Sociological Review*, 1963, *28*, 212–219.

Mahone, C. H. Fear of failure and unrealistic vocational aspiration. *Journal of Abnormal and Social Psychology*, 1960, *60*, 253–261.

Minor, C. A., and R. C. Neel. The relationship between the achievement motive and occupational choice. *Journal of Counseling Psychology*, 1958, *1*, 39–43.

Some discussion growing out of the Sherlock and Cohen study is as follows:

Katz, F. E. A comment on the strategy of occupational recruitment. *Social Forces*, 1966, *45*, 120–124.

Sherlock, B., and A. Cohen. A reply to Katz. *Social Forces*, 1966, *45*, 282.

Social Determinants
of Occupations

10

So far, the factors which have been explored as determining the kind of occupation a person has or attains have been mainly resident within the person. This is consistent with the manner in which the psychologist prefers to examine behavior. But the sociologist, with his consciousness of how the social group affects individual behavior reminds us that there are more factors to account for. One observer of this kind is Caplow (1954). Among other things, he points out that certain occupations are more typically "inherited" by sons from their fathers than they are chosen in response to internal personal characteristics.

A variety of modes of this transmission can be imagined; imitation or identification with a parent and his occupation; the reduction or heightening of opportunity by economic factors as in obtaining a seat on the stock exchange; geographic factors such as in sons of fishermen becoming fishermen because of the dominance of that industry on the seacoast; or the forced transmission of the father's occupation, as in bell and cymbal casting spanning a number of generations, or liqueur or perfume blending formulas retained from generation to generation.

The converse of this invariance in fathers' and sons' occupations, as determined by social factors, is differences in generations. This is the sociologist's "intergenerational mobility," referring to differences in social status of the occupations of father and son. Generally its direction is upward, but not always.

This term is distinct from "intragenerational mobility," which denotes change in level of occupation within the career pattern of an individual, and it is distinct from occupational migration, which denotes geographical movement in the pursuit of career without reference to change in status. Some of the classic studies of these phenomena are listed among the references at the end of this chapter.

Still other social factors appear to be influential in the attainment of an occupation. They can be seen in the finding of fewer scientists among Catholic as compared to liberal Protestant and Jewish faiths, or observations of the lack of women symphony conductors, Italian and Negro dominance in the heavyweight class of professional boxing, Greeks in the food distribution business, Irish policemen in urban centers, and a host of occupational stereotypes.

Finally, the health of the economy, or change in its composition may affect which occupations may be attained; these may be understood as influences in the reduction of manual workers owing to automation in farming and factory work, or the increasing need for technically skilled persons to support the automated production of goods and services. Lipsett (1962) has documented these and some additional social factors in vocational development.

This chapter is presented for the purpose of ordering these factors and integrating their operation into the determinants of occupational behavior. Evidence is scattered and uneven in quality, but a sample of studies is presented to support the assumption of their instrumentality.

Blau and his coauthors name few of the distinct determinants, but organize them into groups by similarities and formulate a scheme to show just how and where external factors interact with internal determinants. This scheme could well have been presented in the previous chapter relating decision theory to occupational choice because of its use of concepts of preference and expectancy. It is located here, though, because it is the only formulation which explicitly encompasses social determinants of careers. There is no theoretical formulation which links *only* social factors to vocational behavior, in the sense that Caplow presents it, paralleling the psychological theories which link *only* internal, personological determinants to choice, entry and career.

Blau, et al., raise the question of whether some occupations are not chosen, but that a selection process accounts for a person being in one occupation rather than another. The paper by Katz and Martin expands on this possibility. Although authors concede that the central concept of distinguishing purposive versus adventitious choice — definiteness of decision — is crude, as are some of the other distinctions which are made, the general concept is appropriate to a consideration of social factor influences on occupations.

The papers which follow attempt to demonstrate the effect of one or another external, social determinant or influence on the occupation chosen or attained.

In Duncan's paper, the effects of the socioeconomic status of the family are shown to affect the kind of occupational role attained at one status level, the professional. This is only one of several papers on intergenerational mobility published at about the same time. Its advantage over the others is to demonstrate fairly graphically the different circumstances surrounding the attainment of self-employment and salaried status at a high level. In addition, it shows how these two categories occur relative to the first employment, reflecting on intragenerational mobility also.

Finally, Sewell and Orenstein show how occupational choice is influenced by the size of the town or city in which the chooser lives. Because of some uncertainties about how variables affect this relationship, they control for the chooser's socioeconomic status, sex, and intelligence. Their findings suggest that boys, but not girls, from rural areas and smaller towns have lower occupational aspirations than those from larger towns and cities, irrespective of status of family or intelligence. Their data also allow them to refute Lipsett's and Bendix's argument that lower class status is the more powerful determinant of reduced occupational status aspirations.

It should be pointed out that most of the research in this chapter has concerned itself with social influences on the level or status of choices. What is needed now is similar studies of their relationship to the occupational field or situs.

REFERENCES

Caplow, T. *The Sociology of Work*. Minneapolis, Minn.: University of Minnesota Press, 1954.

Lipsett, L. Social factors in vocational development. *Personnel and Guidance Journal*, 1962, *40*, 432–437.

Occupational Choice: A Conceptual Framework

PETER M. BLAU, *University of Chicago*

HERBERT S. PARNES

JOHN W. GUSTAD, *Ohio State University*

RICHARD JESSOR, *University of Colorado*

RICHARD C. WILCOCK

Why do people enter different occupations? The problem of explaining this can be approached from various perspectives. One may investigate, for example, the psychological characteristics of individuals and the processes of motivation that govern their vocational choices and, for this pur-

Reprinted with the permission of authors and publisher from the article of the same title, in *Industrial and Labor Relations Review*, 1956, *9*, No. 4, 531–543. Copyright © 1956 by Cornell University. All rights reserved.

pose, consider the social and economic structure as given conditions which merely impose limits within which these psychological processes operate. It is also possible to examine the ways in which changes in the wage structure and other economic factors channel the flow of the labor force into different occupations, in which case the psychological motives through which these socioeconomic forces become effective are usually treated as given. Still another approach would focus upon the stratified social structure, rather than upon either the psychological makeup of individuals or the organization of the economy, and would analyze the effects of parental social status upon the occupational opportunities of children. Each of these perspectives, by the very nature of the discipline from which it derives, excludes from consideration some imporatant variables which may affect occupational choice and selection. For this reason, representatives from the three disciplines — psychology, economics, and sociology — have collaborated in the development of a more inclusive conceptual framework, which is presented in this paper.[1]

CONCEPTUAL SCHEME

It should be stressed that we are proposing a conceptual framework, not a theory of occupational choice and selection. A scientific theory must, in our opinion, be derived from systematic empirical research. To be sure, many empirical studies have been carried out in this area, and a variety of antecedents have been found to be associated with occupational position, such as intelligence,[2] interests,[3] and job-market conditions,[4] to name but a few. The identification of isolated determinants, however, cannot explain occupational choice; indeed, it may be highly misleading. While it is true that Negroes are less likely to become surgeons than whites, this finding does not mean what it seems to imply (namely, that race determines the capacity to develop surgical skills). To understand this correlation, it is necessary to examine the intervening processes through which skin color affects occupational position, notably the patterns of discrimination in our society and their implications for personality development. In general, theory is concerned with the order among various determinants, that is, the interconnections between direct and more remote ones. The function of a conceptual scheme of occupational choice and selection is to call attention to different kinds of antecedent factors, the exact relationships between which have to be determined by empirical research before a systematic theory can be developed.[5]

Occupational choice is a developmental process that extends over many years, as several students of the subject have pointed out.[6] There is no single time at which young people decide upon one out of all possible careers, but there are many crossroads at which their lives take decisive turns which narrow the range of future alternatives and thus influence the ultimate choice of an occupation. Throughout, social experiences — interactions with other people — are an essential part of the individual's development. The occupational preferences that finally crystallize do not, however, directly determine occupational entry.[7] Whether they can be realized, or must be modified or even set aside, depends on the decisions of the selectors, that is, all persons whose actions affect the candidate's chances of obtaining a position at any stage of the selection process (which includes, for instance, acceptance in a teachers college as well as employment as a teacher). Of course, the candidate's qualifications and other characteristics influence the decisions of selectors, but so do other factors which are beyond his control and which may even be unknown to him, such as economic conditions and employment policies. Hence, the process of selection, as well as the process of choice, must be taken into account in order to explain why people end up in different occupations. Moreover, clarification of the selection process requires analysis of historical changes in the social and economic conditions of selection, just as study of the choice process involves analysis of personality developments.

The social structure — the more or less institutionalized patterns of activities, interactions, and ideas among various groups — has a dual significance for occupational choice. On the one hand, it influences the personality development of the choosers; on the other, it defines the socioeconomic condi-

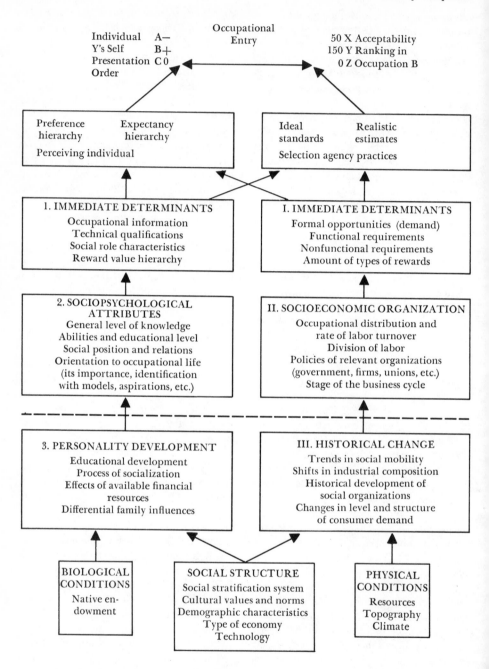

FIGURE 1.

tions in which selection takes place. These two effects, however, do not occur simultaneously. At any choice point in their careers, the interests and skills in terms of which individuals make their decisions have been affected by the past social structure, whereas occupational opportunities and requirements for entry are determined by the present structure. The values that orient a person's efforts and aspirations may have developed in a period of prosperity, but he has to find a way to make a living in a depression.

This twofold effect of the social structure is schematically presented in Figure 1. The left side suggests that the molding of biological potentialities by the differentiated social structure (Box 3) results in diverse characteristics of individuals (Box 2), some of which directly determine occupational choice (Box 1), At the same time, as indicated on the right side, the social structure changes (Box III), resulting in a socioeconomic organization at any point in time (Box II), some aspects of which directly determine occupational selection (Box I).[8] These two developments, separated only for analytical purposes, must be joined to explain entry into occupations. The explication of the schema may well start with the process of entry, presented at the top of the chart.[9]

PROCESSES OF CHOICE AND SELECTION

A choice between various possible courses of action can be conceptualized as motivated by two interrelated sets of factors: the individual's valuation of the rewards offered by different alternatives and his appraisal of his chances of being able to realize each of the alternatives.[10]

These valuations and appraisals of chances are acquired through and modified by social experience, and both are conceived to be roughly ordered in hierarchical fashion for each person — a hierarchy of preferences (valuations) and a hierarchy of expectancies (appraisals). The course of action upon which an individual decides will reflect a compromise between his preferences and his expectations (an attempt to maximize expected value). Thus, his actual choice will

probably not be identical with his first preference if his expectation of reaching the preferred goal is very low.

Before applying this formulation to the study of occupational choice, some possible objections must be met. Katona's distinction between habitual action, which is not preceded by *deliberate* decisions, and problem-solving behavior, which is governed by explicit choices,[11] raises the question whether some people do not simply drift into jobs without ever having made explicit choices between alternative occupations. Indeed, Reynolds' findings suggest that this is the case for many workers, since they do not have sufficient information about the range of alternative opportunities to make deliberate rational choices in their careers.[12] This calls attention to the importance of taking labor market information into account in the study of occupational choice, because a person can obviously choose only among the alternatives known to him. Within the limits of their information, however, potential workers do take action by seeking jobs in one occupation rather than another, and prior to any action, as Parsons and Shils have noted, "a decision must always be made (explicitly or implicitly, consciously or unconsciously)."[13]

Even if an individual has not made a deliberate occupational choice and is not aware of the factors that induced him to look for one kind of job instead of others, these factors are subject to scientific inquiry, and the conception of a compromise between values and expectations suggests one method by which such inquiry can proceed. (The utility of this conception depends on the possibility of actually obtaining empirical data on the compromise process, a research problem which is discussed below.) To be sure, if it is a matter of *complete* indifference to a worker which of several occupations he enters, we cannot analyze the choice he made between them, but neither could he possibly have made such a choice. To the extent to which complete indifference prevails, it can only be the selection process (or fortuitous circumstances) which accounts for workers being in one occupation rather than another.

In sum, occupational choice is restricted by lack of knowledge about existing opportunities; it does not necessarily involve conscious deliberation and weighing of alternatives; and in the polar case of complete indifference, no choice between occupations does in fact take place. Variations in knowledge, in rationality, and in discrimination between alternatives constitute, therefore, the limiting conditions within which individuals choose occupations by arriving at a compromise between their preferences and expectancies. This compromise is continually modified up to the time of actual entry, since each experience in the labor market affects the individual's expectations, and recurrent experiences may also affect his preferences.

Let us examine, as a simplified illustration of this compromise process, a graduate of the Fashion Institute whose training as a designer included learning the various skills needed for making dresses. His first preference would be to become a fashion designer, but his expectation of getting a job in this most desirable occupation in the garment industry is so low that he does not even apply for one. The first occupational position for which he presents himself as a candidate is that of sample maker, which ranks lower on his preference hierarchy but where his expectation of success is somewhat greater. Unable to get such a position (A on top of the chart), he tries to find work as a finisher, another skilled trade that may lead to a career as a designer. Since he obtains employment as a finisher (B), what position he would have looked for next (C) is irrelevant; indeed, this third alternative may not have crystallized in his own mind.

This account of why an individual chooses a given occupation must be supplemented by an explanation of why he is selected for it. Let us assume that the employment practices in the industry have the result, whether achieved by deliberate effort or inadvertently, that persons with certain characteris-

tics, including considerable practical experience, have the greatest chance of being hired as finishers. Since only fifty candidates of this type present themselves for two hundred openings (X), employers also accept 150 applicants whom they consider not quite as suitable for the job, such as individuals with more than adequate training but without experience (Y). Having found a sufficient number of workers, employers are not forced to lower their requirements further and hire persons who are not properly trained (Z). There is probably a floor below which employers would not be willing to drop their requirements. The closer the qualifications of applicants approach this floor, the greater is the likelihood that employers will redefine the entry situation by increasing rewards in order to attract better qualified workers.

Occupational choice, then, can be conceptualized as a process involving a series of decisions to present oneself to employers or other selectors as a candidate for a number of more or less related occupations. Each decision is governed by the way in which the individual compromises his ideal preference and his actual expectations of being able to enter a given occupation, the latter being conditioned by previous rejections and other experiences. Occupational selection, on the other hand, consists of successive decisions of employers (or other selectors) about applicants for jobs. The decision concerning each candidate is guided by the employer's ideal standards and by his estimate of the chances that a better qualified candidate than the one under consideration will present himself in the near future. The process of occupational selection involves a regression from ideal standards (or an increase of rewards), the limits of which are defined by the occupational choices of potential workers. Correspondingly, the process of occupational choice involves a descent in a hierarchy of preferences (or the acquisition of new qualifications), which comes to an end, at least temporarily, by being selected for an occupation.

DETERMINANTS
OF OCCUPATIONAL ENTRY

Eight factors, four pertaining to occupations (Box I) and four characterizing individuals (Box 1), determine occupational entry. First, the demand for new members in an occupation is indicated by the number of vacancies that exist at any one time, which can be more easily ascertained, of course, for the employed than for the self-employed. The size of the occupational group, its tendency to expand, and its turnover rate will influence the demand for new members. The second factor, functional requirements, refers to the technical qualifications needed for optimum performance of occupational tasks. The third one, non-functional requirements, refers to those criteria affecting selection that are not relevant to actual performance, such as veteran status, good looks, or the "proper" religion. Fourth, rewards include not only income, prestige, and power, but also opportunities for advancement, congenial fellow workers, emotional gratifications, and indeed, all employment conditions that are defined as desirable.

Turning now from the attributes of occupations to those of potential workers, a fifth factor that influences occupational entry is the information people have about an occupation — their knowledge about the requirements for entry, the rewards offered, and the opportunities for employment and advancement. Two characteristics of individuals are complementary to the two types of occupational requirements, namely, their technical skills to perform various occupational duties and their other social characteristics that influence hiring decisions, such as a Harvard accent or skin color.[14] Finally, people's value orientations determine the relative significance of different kinds of rewards and thus the attractive force exerted by them.[15]

To be sure, many other characteristics of individuals influence their careers — their level of knowledge, ability, and education,

their social position and relationships, and their orientation toward occupational life, to cite only the most general ones (Box 2). It may be hypothesized, however, that the effects of all other factors can be traced through the immediate determinants of occupational entry. In other words, unless a social experience or attribute affects the information individuals have about occupations, their technical or social qualifications for entry, or their evaluation of occupations, it is not expected to influence their careers. Similarly, whereas many aspects of the socioeconomic organization (exemplified in Box II) must be examined to explain the four characteristics of occupations outlined in Box I, it is these four (plus the four directly relevant characteristics of individuals) that directly account for occupational entry, according to the hypothesis advanced here.

PROBLEMS FOR RESEARCH

It is evident that the significance of such a conceptual scheme depends entirely on whether the empty categories it supplies can be "filled" through empirical research and, if so, whether theoretical propositions that explain occupational choice and selection can be derived from the data. The conceptual framework merely suggests the variables to be taken into account, but the crucial theoretical question concerning the relative influence of these various determinants of occupational entry cannot be answered by conceptual analysis but only on the basis of empirical research. The type of research needed for this purpose may be briefly illustrated.

As a starting point, one could select a town in which most of the labor force is employed by a few large companies. Interviews with a sample of high-school students would be designed to determine the four factors in Box 1; that is, the information they have about working conditions and opportunities in different occupations, their occupational skills and qualifications, their other social characteristics that may influence employment chances, and the value they place upon different kinds of rewards. Since reward is defined as any employment condition that contributes to satisfaction, an important function of the interview would be to identify the various conditions that constitute rewards for different individuals. Three of the four items called for in Box I could be obtained from personnel officers in the various companies: the number and types of vacancies to be filled, the qualifications required to fill each type, and the rewards offered by each position (including under rewards again all working conditions that may contribute to satisfaction). The remaining factor, nonfunctional requirements, would be determined in a follow-up interview with the student respondents after they entered the labor market. By comparing applicants who were rejected with those who were accepted for a given position, it would be possible to discern the social characteristics that do, in fact, govern hiring practices, whether the selectors are aware of it or not. The occupational positions of the respondents, also ascertained in the follow-up survey, would constitute the criterion for constructing a theoretical model that makes it possible to predict occupational entry on the basis of a knowledge of the eight determinants. To validate this model, the predictions made with it in *other* studies *prior* to obtaining data on occupational entry would have to be confirmed by these data.[16]

The research outlined does not take into account the social and psychological processes through which the determinants affect occupational entry. An empirical investigation of the process of choice as here conceptualized would have to inquire, first, whether individuals actually rank occupations in a hierarchy of preferences and a hierarchy of expectancies, and, second, what the nature of these hierarchies is. One method for doing this is to administer questionnaires employing paired comparisons of occupations to young people prior to entry into the labor market. The instructions, which would be designed to control

one of the two variables while measuring the other, might read, respectively: "If you had an opportunity to get either of these two kinds of jobs, which one would you prefer?" and "Without considering which job you like better, which one of these two would you have the best chance of getting?" Respondents would be permitted to state that they are indifferent to the two alternatives.

Answers to such questions raise problems of validity as well as reliability. Repeating the same procedure after a month or so could furnish a check on its reliability, that is, on whether the answers are meaningful or sheer guesswork. Validation would consist of determining whether the data on preference and expectancies, properly weighted, make it possible to predict the occupational positions for which respondents later actually present themselves as candidates. If this is now possible, improved instruments for measuring preferences and expectancies might be devised. For example, short descriptions of different kinds of work could be substituted for occupational labels, which often have little meaning, particularly for less educated respondents. As a matter of fact, a comparative analysis of the rankings obtained by using occupational labels and different descriptive statements would itself help to clarify the character of preferences and expectancies.

Of course, not all people end up in the first occupation for which they present themselves. Many are not accepted; others quit or are fired after a brief trial period.[17] The individual's second choice, however, is not likely to be governed by the same preferences and expectancies as his first one, since his experiences in the labor market, and possibly elsewhere, have probably given rise to changes in his expectations and even his preferences.

These socially induced changes in the two hierarchies constitute the core of the compromise process.[18] To study this process, repeated intensive interviews with entrants into the labor market would have to discern how modifications in occupational expectations and values are produced by various social experiences, such as inability to get a job, expulsion from professional or vocational school, being repelled by unanticipated aspects of the work, and many others. Also of interest would be an analysis of the contingency factors that influence the compromise process. For instance, what is the significance of differences in the tenacity with which an individual adheres to his first choice despite continuing inability to realize it? What difference does it make whether initial expectations are more or less realistic, as indicated by a comparison between an individual's expectations and the actual occupational chances of persons with his qualifications and social characteristics?

Inasmuch as the compromise process is conceived as an intervening variable between various determinants and occupational entry, its relationships to these antecedents raise a host of additional problems for research. What are, for example, the effects of differences in knowledge of employment and working conditions on preferences and expectancies? How does the importance his career assumes in the thinking of an individual influence the compromise process? What differences are there between socioeconomic classes with respect to evaluation of various rewards, preferential ranking of occupations, and discrimination made in these rankings? Do members of the working class generally discriminate less in their occupational preferences, or do they make finer discriminations than middle-class people between different working-class occupations? What is the relative significance of income and education in producing these differences between socioeconomic classes? How is the process of occupational choice affected by other social characteristics, such as ethnic background, rural-urban residence, religious affiliation, and frequency of church attendance?

Empirical investigation of the processes of occupational selection is, perhaps, even more complicated than that of choice processes. At this point, a few illustrations to indicate the range of research problems in this area must suffice. How are selection practices changed in response to a shortage of skilled workers? Specifically, under what conditions does such a shortage result not in increased rewards, but in a reorganization of the production process that makes it possible to employ workers with lesser qualifications? (The answer to this question has far-reaching implications for economic theory as well as for social welfare.) If nonfunctional barriers to occupational entry (such as sex, age, or skin color) are withdrawn during a temporary labor shortage, what determines whether these nonfunctional requirements are reintroduced once the labor shortage subsides? Are the differences in nonfunctional requirements between occupations greater than those between employers within each occupation? (Only if analysis of variance gives an affirmative answer to this question is it permissible to speak of differences in nonfunctional requirements between occupations.)

Research might also test the hypothesis that the greater the rewards offered by an occupation, the more pronounced are the barriers to entry that are unrelated to technical qualifications. Cases of persisting shortages in essential occupations, such as nursing and teaching, could be investigated to determine the political and social factors that prevent the so-called law of supply and demand from increasing rewards sufficiently to overcome the shortages. The impact of bureaucratization on the selection process might be studied by comparing hiring procedures, say, for typists in the federal government, in a large private concern, and in a sample of small firms. Corresponding comparisons could be made to examine the influence of labor unions on occupational selection.

THE HISTORICAL DIMENSION

We must now turn our attention to the developments that precede the period of occupational entry, to which only occasional references have been made so far. On the chart, the time dimension is presented as cut between the second and third boxes. The upper part indicates the social and psychological conditions of choice and selection; the lower part, the developments that produce these conditions. Thus, the family's position in the stratified social structure determines the financial resources available for preparing children for their careers. It is also reflected in the parents' value orientations, their child-rearing practices, the number of children, and the likelihood that the family is organized along authoritarian rather than egalitarian lines. These elements of family structure affect the process of socialization, in which biological potentialities are transformed into personality traits. Of course, the process of socialization is not confined to the home; associations with peers and teachers constitute other important socializing experiences for an individual, but these are not independent of the neighborhood in which his family lives, the attitudes toward people it has instilled in him, and the behavior patterns that it has cultivated and which encourage one kind of person instead of another to befriend him. With advancing specialization, the individual's educational development in school assumes increasing significance as a ladder for occupational mobility or as a barrier against it.[19] The internal conditions that govern occupational entry are the result of these different processes of personality development (Box 3), and the external conditions that govern entry have their roots in historical changes in the social structure (Box III).[20]

It is an oversimplification, however, to conceive of occupational choice and selection as occurring at one point in time, even if this is defined as a limited time interval rather than an instant, and even if the effects of earlier developments are taken into consideration. To think of the transition from graduation from medical school to the establishment of a medical practice as the time of occupational choice, and of entry into medical school as merely one of the

factors that influenced it, is hardly realistic; but to treat entry into medical school as the point of choice is not a satisfactory procedure either, since not all students become physicians. A series of successive choice periods must be systematically analyzed to show how earlier decisions limit or extend the range of future choices.

This requires the repeated application of the conceptual scheme at crucial stages in the individual's development. Thus, choice of high-school curriculum could be investigated (see Box 1) by examining the information pupils have about each curriculum and its vocational significance, their grades, their role characteristics and relationships with other pupils and teachers in different programs, their value orientation toward education and occupational life, and the social experiences that gave rise to these characteristics, as well as the direct influence parents exerted on choice of curriculum. Of equal relevance would be (see Box I) an analysis of the existing opportunities for entering various high-school programs, the grades needed for acceptance, the other criteria that govern selection, the rewards offered by different programs (including parental resources or scholarships that permit a pupil to anticipate going to college), and the historical trends that produced these conditions in the educational system.[21] Once the curriculum has been decided upon, the consequent diverse experiences at high school become part of the developments of individuals that affect immediate determinants of subsequent choices.

The study of the process of occupational entry itself often involves more than one application of the schema. An individual who is not accepted in the first occupation for which he presents himself may have to retrace his steps before he can choose another, by reorienting his thinking or acquiring new skills. Hence, a new choice situation, influenced by the earlier rejection and the actions it stimulated, must be investigated the next time he presents himself as a candidate for an occupation. Indeed, there is no reason to discontinue the analysis with the first full-time job. The schema can be applied again to explain how shifts to new occupations result from the modifications of immediate determinants produced by the experiences during previous employment and the contemporaneous changes in social conditions.[22] The comparison of choice patterns at successive stages in the life history of individuals will indicate the way in which the relative significance of each determinant changes, and the contrast of patterns under varying socioeconomic conditions will suggest how such conditions affect the relative significance of the determinants. Technical qualifications, for example, may be of decisive importance at one stage or under certain conditions, but relatively unimportant at another stage or under different conditions.[23]

The study of historical trends in occupational selection also involves analysis of the processes through which the patterns of selection at an earlier period influence those at a later one. For example, interviews with high-school teachers and students could be designed to determine how differences in personality and conduct between natural science and social science instructors — differences which are expressions of earlier selection processes — affect occupational selection in the next generation by attracting different types of youngsters to work in the two fields. Another project might be concerned with the effects that the contrasting social characteristics of the members of various occupations have upon the public image of these occupations and with the implications of differences in public image for occupational entry. A related question is that of the significance of upward mobility into an occupation for subsequent selection. If two professions are compared, one with many members who originated in lower socioeconomic strata and one with only few such members, is there any distinction between the criteria that govern the selection of future colleagues in the two groups? (A

parallel problem is posed by the impact of upward mobility on occupational *choice*, which could be examined by contrasting the occupational choices of children whose fathers, although holding similar occupational positions now, had different socioeconomic origins.) As a final illustration of research in this area, a hypothesis may be suggested for investigation: the influence of parental social class on occupational selection is partly due to the fact that the common interests of individuals reared in the same social class affect their chances of being accepted in an occupational group.[24] Interviews with students in professional schools, repeated at successive stages in their training, could furnish data to test this hypothesis. Confirming evidence would consist of finding that there is a relationship between parental social class and failure to complete professional training, but that this relationship disappears if either degree of acceptance by fellow students or extent of common interests with them is controlled.

SUMMARY AND CONCLUSION

The main points of this paper can be briefly outlined:

1. The conceptual scheme presented is not a substitute for a theory of occupational choice and selection, but merely a framework for systematic research which, in due course, will provide the material needed for constructing such a theory.

2. The social structure affects occupational choice in two analytically distinct respects: as the matrix of social experiences which channel the personality development of potential workers, and as the conditions of occupational opportunity which limit the realization of their choices.

3. Although four characteristics of individuals and four of occupations have been specified as determinants of occupational entry, the two crucial questions are: what developments in the lives of potential work-

ers and in the history of the socioeconomic organization determine these characteristics, and what are the processes of choice and selection through which they affect occupational entry?

4. Occupational choice is conceived as a process of compromise between preferences for and expectations of being able to get into various occupations. This compromise is continually modified, since the experiences of individuals in the course of searching for suitable careers affect their expectations and often also their preferences.

5. Lest the complicated and extended developmental process that culminates in occupational choice be oversimplified, it is necessary to consider it as a series of interrelated decisions rather than as a single choice. The repeated application of the suggested framework for analysis at crucial turning points in the lives of individuals makes it possible to trace this development and to show how earlier decisions, by narrowing the range of future possibilities, influence the final choices of occupations.

6. The analysis of the processes by which individuals choose one occupation in preference to others must be complemented by an analysis of the processes by which some individuals, and not others, are selected for a certain occupation. To be sure, it is legitimate scientific procedure to treat the actions of selectors as given conditions in the investigation of occupational choice, and it is equally legitimate to treat the actions of choosers as given conditions in the investigation of occupational selection, but only the combination of both procedures makes it possible to explain why people end up in different occupations.

Although this article is concerned with the determinants of occupational entry, not its consequences, the distinction between the latter and the former breaks down once historical developments are taken into account, since the consequences of earlier occupational choices and selections become determinants of later ones. A labor shortage may result in changes in the wage structure or in technological reorganizations that permit the employment of less skilled workers — new conditions which help determine future occupational entry. When it becomes generally known that dissatisfaction with their career is less prevalent among the members of one occupation than of another, these psychological consequences of occupational entry become one of the rewards the anticipation of which influences the occupational choices of the next generation. Whether a person experiences upward mobility or finds his aspirations frustrated in his career will also find expression in the orientation toward occupational life that he transmits to his children and thus in their occupational choices. At these points where consequences turn into determinants, the study of occupational choice and selection merges into the economic study of labor markets, the psychological study of personality adjustment, and the sociological study of social mobility.

[1]We gratefully acknowledge the assistance of the Social Science Research Council, which sponsored the interuniversity summer research seminar (1954) that provided the opportunity for our collaboration. Although one member of this seminar, Leonard Reissman, has not joined the rest of us in the authorship of this article, we are indebted to him for his help in formulating many of the ideas in it.

[2]Naomi Stewart, "A.G.C.T. Scores of Army Personnel Grouped by Occupation," *Occupations*, Vol. 26, 1947, pp. 5–41; Carroll D. Clark and Noel P. Gist, "Intelligence as a Factor in Occupational Choice," *American Sociological Review*, Vol. 3, 1938, pp. 683–694.

[3]Edward K. Strong, "Predictive Value of the Vocational Interest Test," *Journal of Educational Psychology*, Vol. 26. 1935, pp. 331–349.

[4]Donald E. Super and R. Wright, "From School to Work in the Depression Years," *School Review*, Vol. 49, 1940, pp. 123–130.

[5]For a discussion of the distinction between conceptual scheme and systematic theory, see

Robert K. Merton, *Social Theory and Social Structure* (New York: Free Press of Glencoe, 1949), pp. 83–96.

[6]See especially Eli Ginzberg, *et al.*, *Occupational Choice* (New York: Columbia University Press, 1951); and Donald E. Super, "A Theory of Vocational Development," *American Psychologist*, Vol. 8, 1953, pp. 185–190.

[7]Several studies have shown that occupational preferences are "unrealistic," that is, fewer students become professionals than had aspired to do so; for instance, Earl D. Sisson, "Vocational Choices of College Students," *School and Society*, Vol. 46, 1937, pp. 763–768. This disproportionate attractiveness of some occupations is, of course, the expected result of the fact that they offer much higher rewards than others. Occupational expectations, on the other hand, are much more realistic than aspirations; see, for example, E. S. Jones, "Relation of Ability to Preferred and Probable Occupation," *Educational Admininstration and Supervision*, Vol. 26, 1940, pp. 220–226.

[8]The lists of factors in the second and third boxes are illustrative rather than exhaustive.

[9]The oversimplification involved in treating occupational entry as occuring at a single point in time will be dealt with presently.

[10]This conceptualization constitutes a point of covergence between recent economic and psychological formulations concerning the conduct of individuals in choice situations that involve some risk. See Samuel P. Hayes, "Some Psychological Problems of Economics," *Psychological Bulletin*, Vol. 47, 1950, pp. 289–330; John von Neumann and Oskar Morgenstern, *Theory of Games and Economic Behavior* (Princeton: Princeton University Press, 1944); Kurt Lewin, *et al.*, "Level of Aspiration," in J. McV. Hunt, *Personality and the Behavior Disorders* (New York: Ronald Press, 1944); Julian B. Rotter, *Social Learning and Clinical Psychology* (Englewood Cliffs, N.J.: Prentice-Hall, 1954); and Egon Brunswik, *The Conceptual Framework of Psychology* (Chicago: University of Chicago Press, 1952).

[11]George Katona, "Rational Behavior and Economic Behavior," *Psychological Review*, Vol. 60, 1953, pp. 307–318.

[12]Lloyd G. Reynolds, *The Structure of Labor Markets* (New York: Harper & Row, 1951).

[13]Talcott Parsons and Edward A. Shils, eds., *Toward a General Theory of Action* (Cambridge: Harvard University Press, 1951), p. 89.

[14]Discrimination and nepotism illustrate how the relationship between nonfunctional requirements and role characteristics — being a Jew or a nephew, respectively — influences chances of entry.

[15]Indeed, these values determine which employment conditions constitute rewards; for instance, whether working in a group is more rewarding than working alone.

[16]To demonstrate that the model contains all immediate determinants of occupational entry, it would be necessary to show that the correlation between occupational position and any other antecedent factor (not included in the model) disappears if the variables included in the model are controlled.

[17]In any research on occupational choice, it has to be decided how long an individual must have remained in an occupation before he is considered to have entered it rather than merely to have tried it out or to have been tried out for it in the process of choice and selection. Various studies have shown that first jobs are not indicative of future careers. See, for example, Reynolds, *op. cit.*, pp. 113–114, 127–133; and Gladys L. Palmer, *Labor Mobility in Six Cities* (New York: Social Science Research Council, 1954), pp. 135–136.

[18]Super, *loc. cit.*, p. 187, emphasizes the importance of investigating the compromise process and criticizes Ginzberg, *et al.*, *op. cit.*, for failing to do so. We are here suggesting some conceptual tools with which the empirical investigation of the compromise process could be carried out.

[19]The growing significance of specialized formal education first reduces the family's influence on careers but later enhances it again. At an early stage, it means that the school has become the substitute for parents as the provider of vocational skills. Once this is an accomplished fact, further specialization in the educational system has the consequence that educational decisions made before the child can act independently have crucial implications for his subsequent occupational life.

[20]Changes in the social structure also affect the course of personality development, as previously mentioned, and basic historical change, in turn, may well be contingent on the emergence of new personality patterns. See on this point Erich Fromm, *Escape from Freedom* (New York: Holt, Rinehart & Winston, Inc., 1941).

[21]For two studies of the significance of social class for the selection process in high school, see B. Hollingshead, *Elmtown's Youth* (New York: Wiley, 1949), and W. Lloyd Warner, *et al.*, *Who Shall be Educated?* (New York: Harper & Row, 1944).

[22]The Experience can be "negative," such as the absence of expected promotions.

[23]In addition, variations in the relative significance of determinants exist among occupational groups. Thus, technical qualifications are not equally important for entry into all occupations, and discrimination against ethnic minorities is more prevalent in some than in others.

[24]On the relationship between occupational entry and having interests in common with the successful members of an occupation, see Edward K. Strong, *Vocational Interests of Men and Women* (Stanford: Stanford University Press, 1943).

Career Choice Processes

FRED E. KATZ, *University of Missouri*

HENRY W. MARTIN, *University of Texas Medical Center*

This paper investigates career choices among student nurses. It explores the possibility that entry upon an occupational career, such as nursing, may be predicated less upon a deliberate choice of nursing than upon a series of limited decisions focused upon immediate problems encountered at the stage of the life cycle in which the adolescent girl finds herself. The view which is here adopted is that the process of entry into an occupation may be looked upon as the cumulative product of a series of specific acts, which may or may not be directly focused upon a deliberate career choice. In the present paper the emphasis is primarily upon non-career oriented acts. It is not suggested that such acts characterize all types of career choice.

Eli Ginzberg has done pioneering work in the study of decision-making processes involved in career choice. In his *Occupational Choice*[1] he took as his point of departure Lazarsfeld's admonition to seek a genetic approach to the topic.[2] Ginzberg and his colleagues build a theory based on an evolution of increasing self-determination as well as increasingly realistic attunement of the individual to his environment as he matures. The individual is thought to go through a period of fantasy (when he cannot assess his capacities), a tentative period (when he weighs various satisfactions), and finally, a realistic period (when he makes compromises between his individual wants and the actual opportunities which exist for him). We are in broad agreement with Ginzberg's basic thesis that "occupational choice is a process," that "the process is largely irreversible" (that is, decisions once made cannot be "unmade," and that they affect the subsequent career life), and that the process "ends in a compromise." Our main divergence from Ginzberg is one of emphasis. Whereas his focus is upon career choices as seen in the context of the individual's maturation, we suggest conceiving career choices as courses of action which are composites of adaptations — by individuals, to be sure — to meet the exigencies of particular, immediate situations.

Our study deals with students at the School of Nursing of a southern university.

Reprinted with the permission of authors and publisher from the article of the same title, in *Social Forces*, 1962, *41*, 149–154.

The study spanned a four-year period. It was possible, therefore, to obtain data on one class from the time of admission to the time of graduation. The questionnaires on which the present paper is largely based included some questions which Columbia University researchers asked medical students;[3] this provides an opportunity of comparing career choice behavior of student nurses with that of student physicians.

The thesis of this paper is as follows: The decisions which underlie embarkation on a nursing career *for at least some persons* revolve around limited, situational contingencies — in which the matter of nursing-as-career enters only tangentially or not at all. Such "situationally delimited" decisions, we are suggesting, do not involve definite career decisions in terms of a subjective career commitment,[4] but nonetheless these decisions constitute the active steps toward entry upon a career.

We first began to formulate the thesis when a perusal of answers to open-ended questions suggested that the student nurses exhibited much vagueness as to the time and occasion when they first began to consider becoming nurses. In response to the open-ended question "In your own words, what were the main reasons that let you to choose nursing for your career?" We received such answers as: "I really don't know exactly, but for a long time I wanted to be a nurse. . . ."[5] and, "As do many little girls, I had an early childhood ambition of becoming a nurse — I never became disinterested (sic) in this field although I had no specific reasons for entering nursing. . . ." It is conceivable, of course, that the events which are crucial in the "decisions" have been forgotten or repressed. This is the customary explanation of answers of this kind. It is supported by the fact that when we posed the question "When did you definitely decide on nursing?"[6] over 99 percent of the nurses did indicate that they had made a "definite decision." Unfortunately this type of question assumes that there was a "definite decision" — that it is only a question of finding out when it occurred. The real question, we suggest, is to what extent were there *actually* definite decisions or, conversely, to what extent are the *"decisions"* artifacts of the research procedure?[7] Do we not have to reckon with the likelihood that a student — or any individual, for that matter — is inclined to give a reply within the scope of the framework provided for him? And, more pointedly, we are inclined to ask to what extent and in what manner are the "decisions" related to a desire for a career of nursing, or are they merely decisions relating to the solutions of problems which may be quite removed from the notion of a career of nursing?

Support for the thesis comes from statements by girls concerning uncertainty and vagueness as to when they first thought of nursing as a career for themselves. We combined answers to the two open-ended questions: "Which occupations or professions did you consider (before deciding on nursing), and why did you decide against them?" and "In your own words, what were the main reasons that led you to choose nursing for your career?" from a class of freshman students. Twenty-six percent (17 out of 65) made statements to the effect that they did not know when they began to be interested in nursing, or that they "had always" wanted to do the sort of work which they felt nursing entailed (helping the sick, alleviating suffering, being around hospitals, etc.). We were persuaded to think that students' statements to the effect that they could not recall specific occasions on which they first entertained the idea of becoming nurses might point to an absence of specific career decisions. We asked ourselves whether it is not likely that for some of the students, the expressions of vagueness about career decisions constitute *relatively accurate descriptions of a series of unplanned, situation-bound acts* — acts which were not specifically and explicitly tied to a conception of a career of nursing but which, in their totality, added up to the girl's entering a nursing training program.

This is amplified by responses to the question: "At what age did you *definitely* decide to study nursing?" The following results emerged:

Group 1	Number	Percent
Before 14	7	10.6
At 14 or 15	8	12.1
At 16 or 17	41	62.1
Between 18 and 20	10	15.2
Since 21	—	——
Total	66	100.0

Group 2	Number	Percent
Before 14	17	13.0
At 14 or 15	27	20.6
At 16 or 17	72	54.9
Between 18 and 20	14	10.7
Since 21	1	.8
Total	131	100.0

The first group is comprised of a freshman class. The second is made up of a freshman, a sophomore, and a junior class. (The members of the first freshman class are not included in the second group.) It is apparent that in both groups the responses concentrate heavily in the period immediately preceding entrance to college and during the early years in college. On the basis of our conceptualization, we propose that persons who have made only situationally-delimited decisions will be more likely to place themselves in the "16 or 17 years of age" or "18 to 20 years of age" categories of the above question than any other category. Our thinking is based on the notion that even though they have not definitely decided that they wish to become nurses, they must, at this stage of their life, make decisions about their occupational future (including the type of course they wish to follow in college). We are suggesting that what many of these persons reported as "definite" career decisions were really decisions revolving around such things as the choice of college education — rather than a definite desire to be a nurses (The corollary to this postulate is that per. sons who have made definite career decision- are no more likely to place themselves in the "16 to 17" and "18 to 20" age categories

than in any other category of the above question.) We would then expect a greater proportion of the persons with definite commitment to nursing to fall in the "under 16" age category. If we can take successful completion of nursing school as an index of "commitment" to nursing,[8] we would expect that a greater proportion of the persons stating that they made a definite career decision before the age of 16 will complete the nursing program than persons placing themselves in the "16 and over" categories. This is, indeed, borne out by the data in Table 1.[9]

The question regarding age of definite decisions was asked of medical students by the Columbia researchers.[10] The findings were quite similar to ours: 67 percent of the

TABLE 1

Relation Between Graduating from Nursing School and Age When Definitely Decided to Study Nursing*

	Age at Time of "Definite Decision"		
	Under 16	16 or Over	Total
Graduated	12	24	36†
	80%	47%	
Not Graduated	3	27	30
	20%	53%	
Total	15	51	66

$x^2 = 3.8352$, corrected for continuity; significant at the .025 level for a one-tail test; 1 d.f.
*We have graduation data only for the first group.
†We do not know what proportion of the 36 graduates are persons who have made definite subjective career commitments. The practical importance of discovering the proportion of subjectively committed graduates need hardly be elaborated.

students reported that they made their definite decisions between the ages of 16 and 20.[11] However, the explanation offered by the Columbia researchers differs markedly from ours. They state:

For the modal student—the definite career choice is keyed to the institutional requirements of the educational system. He does not prolong his choice much *beyond* the point when he must select courses appropriate to medical school prerequisites, nor does he arrive at the decision before the socially prescribed time.[12]

We may ask, to what extent do the requirements of the institutional system make it *seem* (to the medical student himself as well as to the behavioral researcher) that there have been definite career decisions? As far as the institutional system goes, signing up for premedical course work at a time when the medical school program requires it means that the individual has empirically demonstrated compliance with the system. He has, indeed, made a decision. But is it *necessarily* a decision involving a definite desire for a medical career?[13] To what extent can one accept the responses of "definite decisions" at face value? We are not suggesting that the students are deliberately making false statements. But we are suggesting that those students who have not made definite career commitments are likely to place themselves in the 16 to 20 year age group because, at this period, our system of education dictates taking certain definite steps in the direction of a career. These steps may be perceived, in the absence of other commitments, as definite career choices. Rogoff's explanation of the clustering of responses in the 16 to 20 age category is that the time of "definite career choice is geared to the institutional requirements of the educational system."[14] While *some* students may make their definite decisions at this time — and may be encouraged to do so by the character of the system — we would voice an element of caution as to the adequacy of this explanation in view of our previous considerations.

It might seem that persons who have given longest consideration to a nurse career are most likely to graduate. This gains some support from our finding that early "definite deciders" are more likely to graduate than late "definite deciders."[15] In order to ex-

amine this further we considered responses to the question "At what age did you first think of becoming a nurse?" This yielded the following results:

Before 10	35	53.0
Between 10 and 13	12	18.2
At 14 or 15	10	15.2
At 16 or 17	8	12.1
Since 18	1	1.5
Total	66	100.00

A large proportion of the answers fall into the "before 10" age category. This led us to investigate whether a preponderant proportion of these "before 10" persons are "committed" to nursing. We shall again use graduation from nursing school as an index of commitment. The present question, it must be emphasized, does not purport to deal with *definite decisions* — but merely with "thinking about" studying nursing. It is our contention that this difference is crucial in career commitments. The latter, we suspect, may frequently connote little more than cultural exposure to "playing nurse" — a childhood experience to which almost

TABLE 2

Relation between Graduation from Nursing School and Age When First Thought of Becoming a Nurse

	Age at Time of First Thinking of Becoming a Nurse		
	Under 10	10 and Over	Total
Graduated	20	16	36
	57.1%	50%	
Not Graduated	15	16	31
	42.9%	50%	
Total	35	32	67

$\chi^2 = .167$, corrected for continuity; not significant at 0.05 level; 1 d.f.

When using the same age breakdown as in Table 1 — "under 16" and "16 and over" — the χ^2 is .087.

every girl in our society is exposed. On the basis of this consideration we would expect no significant difference in the proportion of graduates from those who first state they thought of nursing before the age of 10 and those who first thought of nursing at 10 or later. The results are in line with this expectation.

We may carry this a step further. It seemed to us that many of the persons who claimed they thought of becoming nurses before the age of 10 were quite vague and unclear about the occasion when they first thought of becoming nurses. To check whether such "vagueness" might also connote an absence of definite commitment to a nursing career we investigated whether persons placing themselves in the "under 10" category of the question concerning first thinking about nursing also placed themselves in the "16 and over" category on the question dealing with definite decision about nursing.

TABLE 3

Relation between Early Consideration of Nursing and Definite Decision to Study Nursing

Definite Decisions to Study Nursing

	Under 16	16 or Over	Total
First thought of becoming a nurse before age 10	11 31.4%	24 68.6%	35

$\chi^2 = 4.114$; corrected for continuity; significant at .05 level; 1 d.f.

A significantly high proportion of those who first thought of nursing before age 10 regard their definite decisions as having been made at age 16 or later. The latter age category has been postulated to have a high proportion of non-committed persons (in com-

parison with the "under 16" age category). On this basis it would seem that the "vagueness" regarding the occasion of initial interest in nursing bespeaks an absence of commitment. But the evidence cannot be claimed to be conclusive.

An inspection of the distribution of students by age of "definite decisions" and "first thinking" about nursing yields further insights.

TABLE 4

Distribution of Age of Definite Decision To Study Nursing by Age of First Thinking about Nursing

Age at Time of First Thinking of Becoming a Nurse	Age at Time of Definite Decision			
	Before Age 14	At 14 or 15	At 16 or 17	Between 18–20
Before age of 10	7	4	19	5
Between 10–13	—	3	7	2
At 14 or 15	—	1	9	—
At 16 or 17	—	—	6	2
Since 18	—	—	—	1

Those who report that they first thought of nursing before the age of 10 tend to fall into a bimodal pattern: One cluster of "definite decisions" comes before the age of 14, and another at 16 or 17 years of age. On the basis of our thesis and data already presented we hold that early "definite decisions" are positively related to definite commitment, as indicated by graduation from the nursing program. We found that five of the seven persons who "first thought" of nursing before the age of 10 and "definitely decided" before 14, graduated (71 percent). Only nine of 19 (47 percent) persons who "first thought" of nursing before 10 and "definitely decided" at 16 or 17, graduated from nursing school. We suggest that one cluster of the bimodal distribution consists of persons who made primarily "situationally-delimited" decisions, whereas the other cluster consists of persons who made relatively explicit "career" decisions.

In summary, data has been presented in support of the thesis that it is possible to demonstrate the existence of a type of career choice process which does not involve subjective career-oriented decisions. This formulation involved the postulation of being able to distinguish between subjective career commitment and compliance with the institutionalized process leading to embarkation upon a career.[16] It also involved postulation of a form of sequential process, where embarkation on a course of action — in the present case, entry upon a particular occupational career — may be the end result of a series of steps which, individually, are not teleologically oriented to that course of action. (Thus, for a particular young woman, the decision to enter a nursing school and, subsequently, to be a nurse may rest primarily upon following her immediate desire to be in the proximity of young, eligible physicians, or to remain close to a friend of her own sex who has chosen nursing training.) Such "situationally delimited" actions are deemed to be basic ingredients in this process. It is felt that this conceptualization might fruitfully be applied to areas other than career choice.

The data for our formulations are based on a small sample — one professional school. Hence, it is probable that refinements in the thesis will need to be made as data from broader samples become available. In practical terms, understanding career commitments[17] has obvious importance. Ultimately, one would wish to be able to correlate patterns of commitment which develop in the course of actual career choice behavior with patterns of performance by occupational practitioners. Also, a clear understanding of occupational commitments might enable streamlining of career training procedures.

[1] Eli Ginzberg and Associates, *Occupational Choice: An Approach to a General Theory* (New York: Columbia University Press, 1951).

[2] Paul Lazarsfeld, *Jugend und Beruf* (Jena: G. Fischer, 1931). Cited in R. K. Merton, G. G. Reader, P. L. Kendall, Editors, *The Student Physician* (Cambridge: Harvard University Press, 1957), p. 110.

[3] R. K. Merton, G. G. Reader, P. L. Kendall, Editors. *The Student Physician.*, *op. cit.* We are particularly referring to N. Rogoff's article entitled, "The Decision to Study Medicine."

[4] By "subjective commitment to a career" we refer to an individual's incorporating conceptions about practicing the career into himself; we do not know, at this stage, what conceptions are involved, and we do not wish to make statements about the degree of "depth" of personality and emotional involvement.

Although there may be no subjective *career* commitment, the situationally-delimited decisions are likely to involve action commitments for the individual. For example, enrolling in nursing school carries a degree of commitment to complete nursing education — the third year student may feel that she has "invested" in nursing education and, if lacking other motivations, she may continue in nursing because of this investment alone. In Ginzberg's terms we might say that the situationally-delimited decisions are not "realistic" in terms of a career.

[5] This is the type of response which is often discarded in the analysis of data.

[6] This question is a replica of the question asked by the Columbia researchers (Merton, et. al., *op. cit.*, p. 14 ff). The question is worded thus:

"At what age did you definitely decide to study nursing?

——Before the age of 14
——At 14 or 15 years of age
——At 16 or 17 years of age
——Between 18 or 20 years of age
——Since the age of 21"

[7] The senior author's present thinking was affected by another study on which he has been engaged. This involves case studies of practicing physicians. One of the subjects of that study stated that it was only in his second year of medical school that he discovered that he *really* wanted to become a physician. We would venture the opinion that if the above question concerning a definite career decision had been asked of this man in his *first* year in medical

school, he would probably have indicated a "definite decision" in his past. One must of course reckon with retrospective bias here. The older man may feel that his basic decision was made after he entered medical school — on the basis of his current perspective. To the young man, however, an earlier decision may have appeared crucial and definitive (rationalization may or may not have been involved). But another explanation, the one we are here exploring, is that there was no definite career decision before the person entered professional school, and that this can be objectively demonstrated.

[8] This is an admittedly crude yardstick.

[9] We would also expect drop-out rates during the school program to reflect this differential rate of graduation. The questionnaire was administered to the first group at the beginning of their freshman year when no students had yet dropped out of the program. When the second group took the questionnaire there had been a drop-out of 27.5 percent — based on the initial freshman enrollment of the respective classes. As we compare the responses of the two groups we note that in the second group the "under 16" age categories make up 33.6 percent of the responses (as against 22.7 percent of the first group) and the "16 and over" categories account for the remaining 66.4 percent of the responses of that group (as against 77.3 percent in the first group). This would seem to suggest that more of the "under 16" persons are remaining in the program — that is, "drop-outs" of the second group seem to follow the same pattern as the "non-graduates" in the first group. Our conclusions must be tentative, however, since we do not have the distribution of responses from the second group at an earlier period of time.

[10] *The Student Physician, op. cit.* See N. Rogoff's "The Decision to Study Medicine."

[11] *Ibid.*, p. 115.

[12] *Ibid.*

[13] We are making a distinction between a subjective commitment and an overt compliance with a system. The two may proceed with varying degree of interdependence; but we postulate that they need not be identical.

[14] Rogoff, *loc. cit.*

[15] We might add, parenthetically, that psychoanalytic theory leads us to expect that *definite* career decisions are quite likely to occur in the early part of life, and that definite commitments may have occured even when there is no explicit recollection of the occasion when they came into being.

[16] In this study, completion of professional training has been used as an index of subjective commitment — and non-completion as an index of absence of such commitment. Yet it must be pointed out that it is by no means claimed that all persons who lack subjective commitment are likely to fail to complete their professional training, and thus be excluded from the ranks of professional practitioners. What is claimed — and used in the present study — is that there is a greater likelihood, statistically, that those who lack a subjective commitment will not complete their professional training.

[17] We hope that our paper, an essentially theoretical discussion, will not lead to exaggerated notions as to the actual proportion of non-committed persons in occupations. We make no claim to have assessed what this proportion is in the nursing profession. There is also indication that some nursing students may lose commitment in the course of the experience in nursing school. See Ida Harper Simpson, "The Development of Professional Self-Images among Student Nurses" (Unpublished doctoral dissertation, University of North Carolina, 1956).

Social Origins of Salaried and Self-Employed Professional Workers

OTIS DUDLEY DUNCAN, *University of Michigan*

In studies of social mobility and the correlates of socioeconomic stratification, attention is often focused on professional workers, because of their presumed location at the top of the occupational status structure. Investigators are nevertheless aware of considerable differentiation within the "professional" category. In most conventional classifications, specifically those based on census codes, this category includes not only the classic professions, but also a variety of semi- and quasi-professional occupations, technical specialties, and the like. In most cross-sectional sample studies, it is not feasible to work with fine subdivisions of the professional category. This paper suggests that a useful intermediate level of disaggregation is afforded by the simple dichotomy of self-employed vs. salaried (private or government employed) professional, technical, and kindred workers.

Some self-employed persons are to be found in most professional and allied occupations. There are, however, only three large professions a majority of whose male practitioners are self-employed. Of the 683,000 self-employed male professionals in 1960, 252,000 were physicians and surgeons, lawyers and judges, and dentists. Another 39,000 were chiropractors, optometrists, osteopaths, and veterinarians, the only other

Reprinted with the permission of author and publisher from the article of the same title, in *Social Forces*, 1965, *44*, 186–189.

professional occupations in which a majority were self-employed.[1]

These occupations are clearly selective of the higher socioeconomic levels within the professional bracket. Thus annual data on incomes since 1950[2] typically show the median income of self-employed professional males to be about half again as large as that of salaried professionals, although the income of both groups has risen markedly during this period.

Another clear distinction between the two groups is the much more rapid increase of the salaried over the past decade. From 1951 to 1964, according to Current Population Survey data, the number of self-employed professional males was augmented by no more than two-fifths, while the number of salaried more than doubled.[3] No doubt related to the differential growth rate, but also to genuine distinctions between career patterns, is the fact that the salaried professionals are considerably younger. Certain of the salaried professional jobs are entered by very young men, while at the higher ages full retirement is more common for salaried than for self-employed professionals The percentages of self-employed by age, as of March 1962, are as follows (unpublished Current Population Survey data):

20–24	1
25–34	6
35–44	15
45–54	16
55–64	19

To some extent, the age difference should probably be taken to discount the socioeconomic differential, though it is by no means a major source of the latter.

The foregoing facts suffice to establish the wisdom of subdividing the so-called "professional" category in any precise analysis of the correlates of socioeconomic status. They also suggest that the two subgroups, the self-employed and the salaried, may well differ appreciably in the patterns of recruitment to professional pursuits. The remainder of the paper summarizes some evidence pertinent to this hypothesis.

In connection with the March 1962 Current Population Survey[4] of the Bureau of the Census, some 25,000 males 20 to 64 years old were requested to complete a supplementary questionnaire, "Occupational Changes in a Generation," comprising a few items concerning the socioeconomic background of the respondent and his wife, if any. The present report concerns only two

of these items: the occupation of the father (or head of the family if it was not the father) at the time the respondent was "about 16 years old"; and the first full-time job of the respondent after he left school. The current (March 1962) occupation of the respondent was ascertained as part of the regular Current Population Survey interview. Response to the questionnaire was about 84 percent complete. A subsample of the initial non-response group was followed up, so that with appropriate weighting an essentially unbiased set of estimates could be prepared. The reader may refer to a summary report on this survey for details on procedures and definitions and for information on sampling variation.[5]

In the first and third columns of Table 1, self-employed and salaried professionals are compared with regard to their respective distributions by occupation of the father. We may first note the coincidence that the proportions of the two groups with farm origins

TABLE 1

Percent Distribution of Self-employed and Salaried Professional, Technical, and Kindred Workers, by Father's Occupation and by First Job, for Males 25 to 64 Years Old in the Experienced Civilian Labor Force of the United States: March 1962

Father's Occupation or First Job	Self-employed		Salaried	
	By father's occupation	By first job	By father's occupation	By first job
Professional, technical, and kindred workers				
Self-employed	14.5	25.7	3.9	1.7
Salaried	7.0	32.8	9.5	39.0
Managers, officials, and proprietors, except farm				
Salaried	8.7	1.0	7.9	2.4
Self-employed	18.5	0.3	9.6	0.4
Sales, clerical and kindred workers	11.4	19.2	13.0	19.3
Manual and service workers	22.1	14.8	39.1	31.4
Farm workers	11.5	2.6	11.3	3.1
Occupation not reported	6.3	3.5	5.7	2.6
Total, percent	100.0	100.0	100.0	100.0
(Number, in thousands)	(573)	(573)	(4,065)	(4,065)

Source: Unpublished tabulations by the Bureau of the Census from March 1962 Current Population Survey and supplementary questionnaire "Occupational Changes in a Generation" (see footnote 5).

are virtually the same. If there is any propensity of farm youth, upon entering the nonfarm work force, to select occupations of a distinctively entrepreneurial type, it is not evidenced in these data. This finding, happenstance or otherwise, simplifies the subsequent analysis.

In studying the origins of professionals with nonfarm backgrounds, we must assume that the occupations listed in the stub of the table comprise at best a partially-ordered scale of socioeconomic status. There is distinct overlap between the salaried professionals and the salaried managers and officials. The latter, on the whole, clearly outrank the self-employed proprietors who, in turn, overlap the sales and clerical workers.[6] If, as is done in this table, all manual occupations are combined, then the manual group as a whole clearly ranks below any of the white-collar categories, though some specific craft occupations have distinctly higher incomes than the less favored sales and clerical jobs.

On this interpretation, it is apparent that self-employed professionals are drawn from higher levels of parental status than are the salaried professionals. About three-fifths of the self-employed, but little more than two-fifths of the salaried professionals come from a family whose head was engaged in white collar work during the respondents' adolescence. Not only do the self-employed originate at somewhat higher levels than the salaried, but also the two categories of professionals manifest an appreciable differential in degree of self-recruitment. Thus the proportion of self-employed professionals whose fathers had the same classification is half again as large as the proportion of salaried professionals whose fathers were likewise salaried professionals. This difference may reflect in part the time trend mentioned earlier. In any event, it suggests that the incidence of direct occupational transmission or inheritance, though not large for either group, is appreciably greater for the occupations concentrated in the self-employed category.

While these findings are not inconsistent with expectations based on the assumption of a moderate positive correlation between sons' and fathers' occupational socioeconomic status, there is one deviation from the pattern that may merit attention, to wit, the strikingly high proportion of self-employed professionals whose fathers were self-employed managers, officials, and proprietors (i.e., proprietors primarily). This proportion is twice as large as the corresponding figure for salaried professionals. If we recall the clear evidence that the proprietor occupations as a group rank lower than the salaried managerial occupations, then the differential is quite suggestive of a specific orientation toward self-employment on the part of men whose fathers were entrepreneurs. Some caution in interpreting the finding is advisable, since there is some suggestion of overreporting of self-employed proprietor as a father's occupation. There is no known reason, however, why this should be more characteristic of the self-employed than of the salaried professionals.

The other pair of columns (two and four) in the table is equally productive of contrasts. Note that fully one-quarter of the self-employed professionals and two-fifths of the salaried professionals began their occupational careers in jobs in the same category as their current jobs. Among those undergoing mobility to the current job, however, the self-employed began with occupations at considerably higher levels. Thus 33 percent of the self-employed began as salaried professionals, but only two percent of the salaried commenced work as self-employed professionals. Managerial and farm occupations were quite infrequent entry jobs for both groups, while lower white-collar jobs were important for both, and about equally so for the two groups. Nearly one-third of the salaried professionals began as manual workers, but less than one-sixth of the self-employed started at that level. In this respect there is a distinct parallel between occupational origins as indexed by the father's occupation and as suggested by the classification of the first job. Taking either as the base line, pronounced upward mobility is rather more characteristic of the salaried than of the self-employed professionals.

Substantive issues in the analysis of social structure often appear in the guise of methodological dilemmas. The revision of classifications and the specification of their meaning are not merely technical problems. Our conceptions of occupational structure and career patterns probably are of necessity obsolescent in a changing society. If our image of the "professional" is one derived from the patterns of just a few decades ago, it will require considerable revision with the absolute and relative expansion of the salaried sector of what we now call "professional" work. This shift, among other things, implies an increase in the proportion of upwardly mobile men found at or near the "top" of the occupational structure as we now conceive of it.

[1] U.S. Bureau of the Census, *U.S. Census of Population: 1960*, "Occupational Characteristics, Final Report PC(2)-7A (Washington, D.C.: U.S. Government Printing Office, 1963), Table 21.

[2] U.S. Bureau of the Census, *Current Population Reports*, "Consumer Income," Series P-60, (Washington, D.C.: U.S. Government Printing Office, 1948).

[3] *Ibid.*, Nos. 9 (March 1952) and 43 (September 1964).

[4] Daniel B. Levine and Charles B. Nam, "The Current Population Survey: Methods, Content, and Sociological Uses," *American Sociological Review*, 27 (August 1962), pp. 585–590.

[5] U.S. Bureau of the Census, "Lifetime Occupational Mobility of Adult Males: March 1962," *Current Population Reports*, Series P-23, No. 11 (Washington, D.C.: U.S. Government Printing Office, May 1964).

[6] See "Consumer Income" reports, *op. cit.*, and Albert J. Reiss, Jr. *et al.*, *Occupations and Social Status* (New York: The Free Press of Glencoe, 1961), Appendix B.

Community of Residence and Occupational Choice[1]

WILLIAM H. SEWELL, *University of Wisconsin*

A. M. ORENSTEIN, *Tufts University*

Studies in Europe and the United States show that rural and small-town migrants to cities hold lower-status occupational positions than the urban-born residents with whom they compete.[2] Lipset explains these differences in occupational achievement, at least in part, by assuming that there are differences in the occupational aspirations of those raised in rural and urban com-

Reprinted with the permission of authors and publisher from the article of the same title, in *American Journal of Sociology*, 1965, 70, 551–563.

munities. He argues that urban-reared youth have greater acquaintance with the broad spectrum of occupational possibilities that exist in the cities than do rural youth. It is the knowledge of these opportunities which stimulates urban youth to aspire to and work toward high-status occupations.[3]

Lazarsfeld's finding that German and Austrian school youth planned to enter an occupation in direct proportion to the number of persons in their community engaged in that occupation supports Lipset's formulation.[4] Research recently conducted in this country also supports Lipset's claim that there are rural-urban differences in the occupational aspirations of youth. Studies in Florida,[5] Iowa,[6] Kentucky,[7] Washington,[8] Michigan,[9] and Utah[10] all show that youth reared on farms, in rural non-farm areas, or in smaller cities aspire to lower prestige and less well-paid occupations than those reared in larger communities.[11]

The present paper provides no direct evidence to test Lipset's supposition that occupational aspirations are the product of familiarity with the occupational structure of the community — nor did Lipset, for that matter. However, we do have quite adequate data to test the relationship between community structure as reflected by size, and the occupational choices of youth. Our data also make it possible to control for sex, intelligence, and socioeconomic status, all of which have been shown to be related to occupational choice and differentially distributed by residence.[12] Thus, control of one or a combination of these variables might account for the association between occupational aspirations and community size without reference to community structure.

Only one study has simultaneously controlled these variables. Grigg and Middleton[13] found in their Florida study that the relation between residence and occupational aspiration held for boys when intelligence and socioeconomic status were controlled, but not for girls when either was controlled. This study, however, was based on ninth-grade students, so the lack of realism characteristic of the occupational choices of younger students may have affected their findings. There is some evidence that this may have been the case because their results indicated that the effect of controlling intelligence differed for ninth- and twelfth-grade boys. Among ninth-grade boys, residence differences in occupational choice held within each intelligence group. Among high-school seniors, no statistically significant differences were found except for boys of low intelligence, though differences in the other intelligence groups were in the pre-

dicted direction.[14] Thus, the further control of socioeconomic status might eliminate the remaining differences among high-school seniors. This would limit any assumed effect of community structure to young boys with relatively unrealistic occupational choices.

The present research tests the hypothesis that among Wisconsin high-school seniors there is no relation between size of community of residence and occupational choice when sex, intelligence, and socioeconomic status are controlled. The analysis proceeds by the following steps: (1) the relation between community of residence (the independent variable) and occupational choice (the dependent variable) is established; (2) the relation between sex, intelligence, and socioeconomic status (the control variables) and both community of residence and occupational choice is determined; (3) because the three control variables are related to the independent and dependent variables, sex, intelligence, and socioeconomic status are simultaneously controlled.[15] The tables generated by these operations also provide data for testing empirical findings of Lipset and Bendix that rural-urban differences in occupational choice are greatest for boys from low-status families[16] and of Middleton and Grigg that these differences are greatest for less intelligent boys.[17]

THE DATA

The present study is based on a 1957 survey of graduating seniors in all public, private, and parochial schools in Wisconsin.[18] Information was obtained from the respondents and school authorities on the student's educational and occupational plans, measured intelligence, attitudes toward college, and socioeconomic status. The analysis employs a one-third random sample of all cases having the requisite data.[19] Because the major hypothesis of this study is based on Lipset's explanation for differential achievement in the urban làbor market in terms of differences in occupational aspiration, students planning to farm were eliminated from the sample. This reduced the number of cases available for analysis from 10,321 to 9,986.

The independent variable, community of residence, is based on the size of the community in which the student attended high school, except that all students residing on farms, regardless of where they attended high school, are classified as farm residents. Data are presented for the following categories: farm, village (places under 2,500), small city (2,500 to 25,000), medium city 25,000 to 100,000), and large city (100,000 and over). A second set of categories is used in which the farm and village students are combined into a rural category, the small and medium cities into a smaller urban category, with the large-city category left as it is, but for the sake of symmetry, now called larger urban.

The dependent variable, occupational choice, is based on a series of questions about the type of occupation the respondent eventually plans to enter and the type of schooling or work he will be involved in during the following year.[20] The answers to these questions, obtained late in the senior year after the students had given considerable thought to the matter, may be taken as fairly realistic occupational choices. These choices were coded according to major occupational groupings as specified in the 1950 detailed classification of the Bureau of the Census. "Professional, Technical and Kindred Workers," and "Managers, Officials, and Proprietors" are considered high-status occupational choices. Plans falling within the other major occupational groupings are considered low-status choices. Those choosing to be "Farmers" or "Farm Managers" are of course eliminated from the sample.

The control variables in the analysis are sex, intelligence, and socioeconomic status. The intelligence variable is based on scores on the Henmon-Nelson Test of Mental Maturity which is administered annually to all high-school seniors in Wisconsin.[21] Students were divided into approximately equal thirds in measured intelligence: high (I.Q.: 116 and above), middle (I.Q.: 105–115), and low (I.Q.: below 105). The socioeconomic status classification is based on a factor-weighted combination of father's educational level, mother's educational level, an estimation of the funds the family could provide if the student were to attend college, the degree of sacrifice this would entail for the family, and the approximate wealth and income status of the student's family.[22] The sample was divided into three roughly equal-sized categories labeled high, middle, and low in socioeconomic status.

RESULTS AND ANALYSIS

The first data presented in the analysis demonstrate the association between the independent and dependent variables of the study. The "total" column of Table 1 indicates a monotonic relation between size of community and occupational choice. Rural students rank considerably below those from small- and medium-size cities, who in turn are less likely to choose professional and managerial positions than those from large cities; the range between the farm and large-city categories is from 29.8 per cent to 48.6 per cent.[23]

The next step is to examine the relation between the control variables and occupational choice and between the control variables and community size. From data presented in Tables 1 and 2 it is evident that each of the control variables is associated with occupational choice since boys, students with high intelligence, and those from high socioeconomic status backgrounds are more likely to choose high-status occupations than are girls, students of lower intelligence, and those of lower socioeconomic status.[24]

The data on the relation between the control variables and community size have been published elsewhere and need not be

TABLE 1

Percentage with High Occupational Choices, by Place of Residence, for Male and Female High-School Seniors*

Place of Residence	Males	Females	Total
(1) Farm	32.9 (678)†	27.6 (935)	29.8 (1,613)
(2) Village (under 2,500)	35.7 (905)	31.1 (930)	33.3 (1,835)
(3) Small city (2,500–25,000)	45.4 (1,217)	38.1 (1,219)	41.7 (2,436)
(4) Medium city (25,000–100,000)	45.7 (1,085)	40.8 (1,226)	43.1 (2,311)
(5) Large city (100,000 and more)‡	57.2 (802)	41.7 (989)	48.6 (1,791)
Rural (1 and 2)	34.5 (1,583)	29.3 (1,865)	31.7 (3,448)
Smaller urban (3 and 4)	45.5 (2,302)	39.4 (2,445)	42.4 (4,747)
Larger urban (5)	57.2 (802)	41.7 (989)	48.6 (1,791)
Total (1–5)	43.8 (4,687)	36.3 (5,299)	39.9 (9,986)

*All χ^2's for each column and any set of residence categories in this table are significant beyond the 0.05 level.

†In this and all other tables the number in parentheses is the denominator on which the percentage preceding it is based.

‡Only two cities are included in this category — Madison (population 126,706) and Milwaukee (population 741,324).

TABLE 2

Percentage with High Occupational Choices, by Intelligence and Socioeconomic Status, for Male and Female High-School Seniors*

	Males	Females	Total
Intelligence:			
Low	20.8 (1,510)	17.0 (1,795)	18.7 (3,305)
Middle	42.5 (1,549)	35.8 (1,790)	38.9 (3,339)
High	66.4 (1,628)	57.1 (1,714)	61.6 (3,342)
Total	43.8 (4,687)	36.3 (5,299)	39.8 (9,986)
Socioeconomic status:			
Low	23.9 (1,521)	14.7 (1,848)	18.8 (3,369)
Middle	41.9 (1,540)	34.8 (1,724)	38.1 (3,264)
High	64.3 (1,626)	60.9 (1,727)	62.5 (3,353)
Total	43.8 (4,687)	36.3 (5,299)	39.8 (9,986)

*All χ^2's for each column in this table are significant beyond the 0.05 level.

presented here, but they indicate a significant positive association between community size and intelligence and community size and socioeconomic status.[25] The association between community size and sex is less regular in that the proportion of males is lower in the farm and larger urban categories than in other categories.

Since the control variables are each related to occupational choice and differentially distributed by community size, the next step is to partial out sex, then sex and intelligence, then sex and socioeconomic status, and finally sex, intelligence, and socioeconomic status simultaneously to see if any of these operations will cause community of residence differences in occupational choice to vanish.

Table 1 gives the results of controlling by sex. The monotonic relation between community of residence and occupational choice remains for both sexes, but partialling increases the residential differences for boys and reduces them for girls. When both sex and intelligence are controlled, as in Table 3, the community of residence differences in

occupational choice (compared with the distribution shown in the "total" column) is reduced but not eliminated. For boys the association remains for each intelligence third. Though there are two reversals in ordering in the high-intelligence third, clear community size differences are evident. For girls, residence differences in occupational choice are practically eliminated in the low-intelligence third, reduced in the middle third, but increased in the high-intelligence third.[26]

The results of controlling socioeconomic status for male and female students are shown in Table 4. For boys, there are clear residence differences at each status level —

TABLE 3

Percentage with High Occupational Choices, by Place of Residence and Intelligence, for Male and Female High-School Seniors*

Place of Residence	Intelligence			
	Low Third	Middle Third	High Third	Total
Males:				
Farm	12.6 (247)	32.5 (234)	58.9 (197)	32.9 (678)
Village	18.2 (351)	38.5 (283)	55.4 (271)	35.7 (905)
Small city	20.7 (376)	41.6 (401)	69.8 (440)	45.4 (1,217)
Medium city	21.7 (350)	46.2 (351)	67.2 (384)	45.7 (1,085)
Large city	34.9 (186)	51.4 (280)	74.4 (336)	57.2 (802)
Rural	15.9 (598)	35.8 (517)	56.8 (468)	34.5 (1,583)
Smaller urban	21.2 (726)	43.8 (752)	68.6 (824)	45.5 (2,302)
Larger urban	34.9 (186)	51.4 (280)	74.4 (336)	57.2 (802)
Total	20.8 (1,510)	42.5 (1,549)	66.4 (1,628)	43.8 (4,687)
Females:				
Farm	15.6 (333)	27.2 (345)	43.6 (257)	27.6 (935)
Village	15.0 (353)	35.8 (307)	46.7 (270)	31.1 (930)
Small city	19.6 (424)	36.5 (411)	60.2 (384)	38.1 (1,219)
Medium city	16.5 (387)	40.7 (386)	61.6 (453)	40.8 (1,226)
Large city	17.8 (298)	37.8 (341)	65.7 (350)	41.7 (989)
Rural	15.3 (686)	31.3 (652)	45.2 (527)	29.3 (1,865)
Smaller urban	18.1 (811)	38.5 (797)	60.9 (837)	39.4 (2,445)
Larger urban	17.8 (298)	37.8 (341)	65.7 (350)	41.7 (989)
Total	17.0 (1,795)	35.7 (1,790)	57.1 (1,714)	36.3 (5,299)

*All χ^2's for each column in this table for any set of five and three residence categories, except for females in the low-intelligence third (N.S.), are significant beyond the 0.05 level.

TABLE 4

Percentage with High Occupational Choices, by Place of Residence and Socioeconomic Status, for Male and Female High-School Seniors*

Place of Residence	Socioeconomic Status			
	Low	Middle	High	Total
Males:				
Farm	22.0 (305)	37.4 (238)	49.6 (135)	32.9 (678)
Village	19.2 (338)	37.5 (315)	55.6 (252)	35.7 (905)
Small city	24.3 (374)	42.4 (363)	64.0 (480)	45.4 (1,217)
Medium city	23.8 (311)	40.3 (360)	66.9 (414)	45.7 (1,085)
Large city	34.2 (193)	52.7 (264)	73.6 (345)	57.2 (802)
Rural	20.5 (643)	37.4 (553)	53.5 (387)	34.5 (1,583)
Smaller urban	24.1 (685)	41.4 (723)	65.3 (894)	45.5 (2,302)
Larger urban	34.2 (193)	52.7 (264)	73.6 (345)	57.2 (802)
Total	23.9 (1,521)	41.9 (1,540)	64.3 (1,626)	43.8 (4,687)
Females:				
Farm	17.1 (439)	30.7 (313)	47.5 (183)	27.6 (935)
Village	14.5 (359)	33.1 (296)	50.5 (275)	31.1 (930)
Small city	11.2 (402)	34.7 (400)	67.1 (417)	38.1 (1,219)
Medium city	16.8 (375)	36.7 (390)	63.8 (461)	40.8 (1,226)
Large city	13.5 (273)	38.1 (325)	64.2 (391)	41.7 (989)
Rural	15.9 (793)	31.8 (609)	49.3 (458)	29.3 (1,865)
Smaller urban	13.9 (777)	35.7 (790)	65.4 (878)	39.4 (2,445)
Larger urban	13.5 (273)	38.1 (325)	64.2 (391)	41.7 (989)
Total	14.7 (1,848)	34.8 (1,724)	60.9 (1,727)	36.3 (5,299)

*All χ^2's for each column in this table for any set of five residence categories, except for females in the low- and middle-intelligence third (N.S.), are significant beyond the 0.05 level.

the differences being greatest among the high-status boys and least among the low-status boys.[27] In two instances there are reversals in ordering in the low-status group and in one instance in the middle-status category, whereas there are no exceptions to the monotonic ordering in the high-status group. For girls, controlling on socioeconomic status eliminates residence differences for the low-status group, reduces differences in the middle-status group to a non-significant level, and increases the differences in the high-status category.

The above analysis indicates that control of sex and intelligence or sex and socioeconomic status does not eliminate community-of-residence differences in occupational choice. For boys, significant differences are found for each subpopulation examined. For girls, statistically significant differences are eliminated for the low-intelligence third and for those in the low- and middle-socioeconomic status categories. Within the other subpopulations, however, the originally observed differences are maintained or increased as a result of partialling.

Partialling on all three variables produces nine tables for each sex in which each of the three socioeconomic status categories is combined with each of the three intelligence categories (see Table 5). For example, the first column of the table shows that 12.4

per cent of farm boys in the lowest socioeconomic third who are also in the lowest
intelligence third choose a high-status occupation, while 9.2 per cent of the village,
10.4 per cent of the small-city, 11.9 per cent
of the medium-city, and 18.8 per cent of the
large-city boys with the same characteristics
choose high-status occupations. These differences are small and not statistically significant. For the low-status-middle-intelligence
boys and the low-status-high-intelligence
boys the differences, in comparison with the
original differences (shown in the "total"
column at the far right of the table), are also
reduced and not statistically significant.

Among boys in the middle-socioeconomic
status third, residence differences are considerably altered for all but the low-intelligence third, where high-status choices may
be unrealistic in any case.

Among boys from high-socioeconomic-
status families the community-of-residence
differences in occupational choice remain
for each intelligence third. The greatest
differences, however, are now found among
the high-status boys of low intelligence.
There are still fairly large differences between the farm, village, and city boys in
the high-status-middle-intelligence third,
whereas the differences in the high-status-
high-intelligence group are greatly reduced
but still favor the city boys.

If only the three-level residence categories are considered, the monotonic relationship between size of community and
occupational choice of boys is never altered
by the control of socioeconomic status and
intelligence: the percentage of rural boys
choosing high-status occupations is always
lower than for those from the smaller urban
places, and they in turn are always less
likely to choose high-status occupations
than are boys from larger urban places.[28]

Data for girls are presented in the bottom
half of Table 5. There is no significant
association between residential background
and occupational choice for girls in any of
the subpopulations shown in the first seven
columns of the table. In each of these groups

the differences between communities are
small and the ordering is irregular. For the
two remaining subpopulations, high-status-
middle-intelligence and high-status-high-
intelligence groups, the association is significant, but the ordering is irregular and the
differences are not great. Consequently, we
conclude that the control of socioeconomic
status and intelligence largely eliminates the
relation of residence and occupational choice
for the girls but not for the boys in our
sample.

To obtain a more precise test of our conclusions, direct standardization was applied
to the original data. This demographic
technique provides a summary measure of
what population rates would be if specified
population characteristics were held constant. In this application, standardization
provides a simple and precise summary
measure of the effect on size of community
differences in occupational choice of controlling sex, intelligence, and socioeconomic
status for the sample as a whole and of
controlling intelligence and socioeconomic
status for each sex.[29] The results are shown
in Table 6 along with the original or un-
standardized data.

Again, controlling on sex, intelligence,
and socioeconomic status is shown to reduce
the relation between residential background
and occupational choice for the sample as a
whole, but the combined effect of these
variables does not eliminate the original
association. The original 18.6 percentage-
point difference between the two extreme
categories, farm and large city, is reduced
by more than one-half. For females, standardization on intelligence and socioeconomic status largely eliminates the community-of-residence differences in occupational choice. For males the differences are
reduced in magnitude but the pattern remains. These findings constitute the most
impressive evidence yet available in support
of Lipset's hypothesis that the occupational
structure of a community, to the extent that
it is inferable from community size, is
related to the occupational aspirations of

TABLE 5

Percentage with High Occupational Aspirations; by Place of Residence, Socioeconomic Status, and Intelligence, for Male and Female High-School Seniors

Place of Residence	Low Socioeconomic Status			Middle Socioeconomic Status			High Socioeconomic Status			Total†
	Low Intelligence	Middle Intelligence	High Intelligence*	Low Intelligence*	Middle Intelligence	High Intelligence	Low Intelligence*	Middle Intelligence†	High Intelligence†	
Males:										
Farm	12.4 (129)	20.0 (100)	40.8 (76)	9.4 (85)	40.9 (88)	69.2 (65)	21.2 (33)	43.5 (46)	71.4 (56)	32.9 (678)
Village	9.2 (164)	24.8 (109)	35.4 (65)	23.9 (113)	39.4 (104)	51.0 (98)	29.7 (74)	58.6 (70)	71.3 (108)	35.7 (905)
Small city	10.4 (163)	27.1 (129)	47.6 (82)	23.3 (116)	40.3 (134)	64.6 (113)	35.1 (97)	56.5 (138)	79.6 (245)	45.4 (1,217)
Medium city	11.9 (135)	26.2 (103)	42.5 (73)	19.0 (121)	44.3 (113)	57.1 (126)	39.4 (94)	63.0 (135)	83.8 (185)	45.7 (1,085)
Large city	18.8 (64)	34.2 (79)	54.0 (50)	35.4 (65)	46.3 (95)	69.2 (104)	52.6 (57)	68.9 (106)	83.0 (182)	57.2 (802)
Rural	10.6 (293)	22.5 (209)	38.3 (141)	11.7 (198)	40.1 (192)	58.3 (163)	27.1 (107)	52.6 (116)	71.3 (164)	34.5 (1,583)
Smaller urban	11.1 (298)	26.7 (232)	45.2 (155)	21.1 (237)	42.1 (247)	60.7 (239)	37.2 (191)	59.7 (273)	81.4 (430)	45.5 (2,302)
Larger urban	18.8 (64)	34.2 (79)	54.0 (50)	35.4 (65)	46.3 (95)	69.2 (104)	52.6 (57)	68.9 (106)	83.0 (182)	57.2 (802)
Total	11.6 (655)	26.2 (520)	43.7 (346)	21.6 (500)	42.1 (534)	61.7 (506)	36.6 (355)	60.0 (495)	79.6 (776)	43.8 (4,687)
Females:										
Farm	8.9 (190)	19.0 (142)	29.0 (107)	23.5 (98)	28.1 (121)	41.5 (94)	26.7 (45)	40.2 (82)	75.0 (56)	27.6 (935)
Village	5.9 (187)	18.5 (108)	32.8 (64)	20.7 (106)	31.3 (99)	49.4 (91)	33.3 (60)	59.0 (100)	52.0 (115)	31.1 (930)
Small city	4.8 (187)	12.8 (141)	24.3 (74)	21.1 (142)	37.2 (137)	47.9 (121)	46.3 (95)	60.9 (133)	82.0 (189)	38.1 (1,219)
Medium city	7.3 (179)	18.9 (127)	37.7 (69)	15.8 (120)	41.2 (131)	50.4 (139)	36.4 (88)	61.7 (128)	74.7 (245)	40.8 (1,226)
Large city	4.9 (122)	14.7 (95)	30.4 (56)	24.1 (108)	31.3 (106)	58.6 (111)	30.9 (68)	58.6 (140)	80.9 (183)	41.7 (989)
Rural	7.4 (377)	18.8 (250)	30.4 (171)	22.0 (204)	29.5 (220)	45.4 (185)	30.5 (105)	50.5 (182)	59.6 (171)	29.3 (1,865)
Smaller urban	6.0 (366)	15.7 (268)	30.8 (143)	18.7 (262)	39.2 (268)	49.2 (260)	41.5 (183)	61.3 (261)	77.9 (434)	39.4 (2,445)
Larger urban	4.9 (122)	14.7 (95)	30.4 (56)	24.1 (108)	31.3 (106)	58.6 (111)	30.9 (68)	58.6 (140)	80.9 (183)	41.7 (989)
Total	6.5 (865)	16.8 (613)	30.5 (370)	20.9 (574)	34.2 (594)	49.9 (556)	36.2 (356)	57.3 (583)	74.6 (788)	36.3 (5,299)

*χ² significant beyond 0.05 level for males only.   †χ² significant beyond 0.05 level for males and females.

TABLE 6

Original and Standardized Relations between Place of Residence
and High Occupational Choice

Place of Residence	Males		Females		Total	
	Original	Standard-ized*	Original	Standard-ized*	Original	Standard-ized†
Farm	32.9	38.1	27.6	33.1	30.0	35.5
Village	35.7	39.4	31.1	32.8	33.3	35.9
Small city	45.4	43.8	38.1	37.5	41.7	40.5
Medium city	45.7	44.4	40.8	37.9	43.1	40.0
Large city	57.2	51.9	41.7	35.7	48.6	44.2
Rural	34.5	39.3	29.3	32.4	31.7	34.1
Smaller urban	45.5	44.0	39.4	36.5	42.6	39.7
Larger urban	57.2	51.9	41.7	37.4	48.6	44.2

*Direct standardization of intelligence and socioeconomic status.
†Direct standardization of sex, intelligence, and socioeconomic status.

youth. The evidence, however, is still far from complete. There are doubtless other factors associated with community size and occupational choice which would help to account for the association. This possibility should be explored in future research.

DISCUSSION

The foregoing analysis shows that boys, but not girls, from rural areas and smaller communities have lower occupational aspirations than those from larger urban places — independent of intelligence and socioeconomic differences. This finding agrees with the general conclusion of Grigg and Middleton for Florida boys at the ninth-grade level, but is more conclusive because it is based on more extensive community-of-residence breakdowns and is for high-school seniors whose occupational aspirations are likely to be realistic and meaningful.[30] Our findings are also of particular interest because the only past study failing to demonstrate a relation between residence and occupational plans used a sample of Wis-

consin students. In an earlier study, Haller and Sewell found no differences in the occupational plans of farm boys who did not plan to enter farming and other non-farm high-school seniors.[31] At that time, however, the high schools of Wisconsin were retaining a much smaller proportion of farm youth than at present. Thus differential dropout rates probably affected the earlier findings in that many farm youth with relatively low occupational aspirations dropped out of school. By the time the present data were gathered, changes in Wisconsin compulsory school laws had resulted in retention in high school of many more low-aspiring farm youth with the consequence that rural-urban differences in occupational choice may now appear greater.[32]

Whatever may account for the differences between the two Wisconsin studies, clearly other factors than those tested are currently operating to produce the residence differences in the present study. Much literature suggests that certain aspects of community structure may be influential. One of these is the limited educational opportunities found in most rural communities. In Wisconsin all publicly supported colleges and most private colleges are in urban communities. Thus, the greater cost and difficulty of attending college away from home may prevent youth in rural places from continuing their education beyond high school. This limits the range of occupational positions available to them and might result in their aspiring to lower-status positions. If this were a major factor, however, we would expect the greatest residence differences among boys from low-status families, those families least able to send their children away to college. In fact we find that community-of-residence differences in occupational choice are least among lower-status youth.

As previously noted, Lipset argues that the occupational structure of the community influences occupational aspirations. Lipset and Bendix further suggest that residence differences should be greatest for youths from lower-status families: "Middle-class youth, even those living in smaller communities, will receive the stimulus to obtain a high-status occupation from their families and from other aspects of their environment which are related to middle-class status. It is among the working class youth that size of community makes a major difference. Those living in smaller communities will not be as stimulated by their environment to aspire to higher goals."[33] Our results contradict this point. Size-of-community differences in occupational plans are greatest for high-socio-economic-status youth whether status is controlled separately or controlled with intelligence, while there are only small differences among low-status youth.

This finding calls for further specification of the type of information derived from the local occupational structure which could influence occupational plans. Certainly high-school seniors in the smaller community are not completely ignorant of the major professional, managerial, and technical positions available in larger urban communities. Nor do we assume a marked deficiency in their knowledge of the entrance

requirements of most of these positions. We doubt that such differences as exist are sufficient to explain the residence differences in occupational choice. More likely, there are differences in the direct personal knowledge youth have about high-status positions, and these differences are related to both residence and status.

This paper deals with fairly realistic occupational choices, based in part on the youth's belief that he will be able to achieve his goals. A youth in immediate contact with persons holding high-status positions, or receiving a more or less continuous flow of information concerning their daily activities, will perceive these persons as occupational role models and will feel that their occupational positions are reasonable personal goals. This belief will be reinforced when parents, teachers, and friends encourage high goals. All of this is less likely to be the experience of youth from smaller communities.

Higher-status youth in small communities are exposed to a more restricted range of occupations than are higher-status youth in larger places. They personally know fewer of the occupants of high-status positions and hear little about their activities from adult acquaintances. Moreover, the relevant adults in their lives probably recommend lower-prestige occupations than would urban adults of similar status who have better acquaintance with a complex occupational structure.

Also working against the higher-status youth in the small community is the restricted interactional situation in the school and community in which he lives. This forces him to associate with many low-aspiring peers who may have a depressing influence on his aspirations.[34] On the other hand, the higher-status youth in the larger community is likely to interact mainly with high-status peers who reinforce his high occupational aspirations.

The case of the lower-status boy, whether rural or urban, is of course quite different. His intimate adult contacts are restricted to those in lower-status occupational positions. Lower-status adults lack intimate and detailed knowledge of the activities of high-status persons to pass on to the lower-status youth. They also have lower economic aspirations for themselves and recommend lower-status occupations to others.[35] Thus, the lower-status boy tends to aspire to low-status positions regardless of the occupational structure of his community.

Another, perhaps more crass, interpretation of our findings is that higher-status urban families manage through friends, relatives and acquaintances to give their children advantages in the urban labor market. Higher-status rural parents whose knowledge and influence are limited to the local community can provide only limited assistance in obtaining high-status urban positions. Higher-status rural youth, knowing this, may direct their aspirations toward the more limited opportunity structure of the local community or toward the less prestigeful positions they perceive as open to them in the larger communities.

Our findings regarding the influence of controlling intelligence generally fail to support the finding of Middleton and Grigg that the rural-urban differences are primarily for boys of low intelligence. We find significant differences in each intelligence third, and even though they are somewhat greater for the lower third, the differences are still quite sizable in the highest intelligence group. It may be, as they reason, that the boys of lower intelligence are most influenced by firsthand impressions of the local labor market, while the highly intelligent rural boys become aware of the variety of opportunities beyond the local community as a result of reading, counseling, and other secondary sources of information.[36] But if this is true, it has not produced any very marked effect on the boys in our sample.

A more sociologically significant finding is that when both intelligence and socioeconomic status are controlled, community-of-residence differences in occupational

choice are greatest among those of low intelligence and high socioeconomic status and are minimal among those of low intelligence and low socioeconomic status. Perhaps direct contact with a highly differentiated occupational structure overcomes the tendency to low occupational aspiration of those of low intelligence if their status makes them optimistic about their life chances. Also, the proportion of high-status openings for those of limited ability may be greater in urban than rural communities. These "sinecure" positions are entered primarily through family influence and financial aid. If this type of family inheritance is more common in urban society, it may help to account for the particularly marked rural-urban differences in the occupational plans of the high-status-low-intelligence boys in our sample.

Finally, our finding that the original association between community of residence and occupational choices of girls can be largely accounted for by intelligence and socioeconomic status differences agrees with previous studies. The occupational alternatives for girls in rural communities are so severely limited that those who wish to work, and most of the girls in our sample plan on some period of employment before marriage, must look to the urban labor market for desirable employment. There the job restrictions generally encountered by women force them to consider essentially the same limited set of occupational alternatives, as urban girls — mainly teaching school, nursing, social work, and a few other lower-status professions and white-collar jobs. These occupations are widely known, and rural girls, lacking satisfactory rural occupational opportunities, are as likely to aspire to them as urban girls of similar intelligence and socioeconomic status.[37]

[1]This research program is currently financed by a grant (M-6275) from the National Institutes of Health, U.S. Public Health Service. The basic data were obtained by J. Kenneth

Little in a survey conducted in 1957 under a contract with the U.S. Office of Education (J. Kenneth Little, *A Statewide Inquiry into Decisions of Youth about Education beyond High School* [Madison, Wis.: School of Education, University of Wisconsin, 1958]). For this paper, a new sample was drawn, data recoded, and new indexes constructed. The writers wish to acknowledge the assistance of J. Michael Armer, Vimal P. Shah, and Herschel S. Shosteck, the critical suggestions of Russell Middleton, Archie O. Haller, and Murray A. Straus, and the computational services of the Numerical Analysis Laboratory of the University of Wisconsin.

[2]Gunnar Boalt, "Social Mobility in Stockholm," *Transactions of the Second World Congress of Sociology* (London: International Sociological Association, 1954), pp. 67–73; G. Beijer, *Rural Migrants in Urban Areas* (The Hague: Martinus Nijhoff, 1963); Howard W. Beers and Catherine Heflin, *Rural People in the City* (Kentucky Agricultural Experiment Station Bull. 478 [Lexington, Ky., 1946]); Ronald Freedman and Deborah Freedman, "Farm-reared Elements in the Non-farm Population," *Rural Sociology*, XXII (March, 1956), 50–61; and Seymour M. Lipset and Reinhard Bendix, *Social Mobility in Industrial Society* (Berkeley: University of California Press, 1962), pp. 203–26.

[3]Seymour M. Lipset, "Social Mobility and Urbanization," *Rural Sociology*, XX (September–December, 1955), 220–28.

[4]Paul F. Lazarsfeld, *Jugend und Beruf* (Jena: C. Fisher, 1931), p. 13, cited in Lipset and Bendix, *op. cit.*, p. 221.

[5]Russell Middleton and Charles M. Grigg, "Rural-Urban Differences in Aspirations," *Rural Socology*, XXIV (December, 1959), 347–54, and Charles M. Grigg and Russell Middleton, "Community of Orientation and Occupational Aspirations of Ninth Grade Students," *Social Forces*, XXXVIII (May, 1960), 303–8.

[6]Lee G. Burchinal, "Differences in Educational and Occupational Aspirations of Farm, Small-Town and City Boys," *Rural Sociology*, XXVI (June, 1961), 107–21; and Donald R. Kaldor, Eber Eldridge, Lee G. Burchinal, and I. W. Arthur, *Occupational Plans of Iowa Farm Boys* (Iowa Agricultural Experiment Station Research Bull. 508 [Ames, Iowa, 1962]).

[7]Harry K. Schwarzweller, *Socio-cultural Factors and the Career Aspirations and Plans of Rural Kentucky High School Seniors* (Kentucky Agricultural Experiment Stations Progress Report, No. 94 [Lexington, Ky., 1960]).

[8]Walter L. Slocum, *Occupational and Educational Plans of High School Seniors from Farm and Nonfarm Homes* (Washington Agricultural Experiment Station Bull. 564 [Pullman, Wash., 1956]); John B. Edlefsen and Martin J. Crowe, *Teen-agers' Occupational Aspirations* (Washington Agricultural Experiment Station Bull. 618 [Pullman, Wash., 1960]).

[9]E. Grant Youmans, "Occupational Expectations of Twelfth Grade Michigan Boys," *Journal of Experimental Education*, XXIV (June, 1956), 259–71; James D. Cowhig, Jay Artis, J. Allen Beegle, and Harold Goldsmith, *Orientations toward Occupation and Residence: A Study of High School Seniors in Four Rural Counties of Michigan* (Michigan Agricultural Experiment Station Spec. Bull. [428 East Lansing, Mich., 1960]).

[10]John R. Christiansen, James D. Cowhig, and John W. Payne, *Educational and Occupational Aspirations of High School Seniors in Three Central Utah Counties* (Social Science Bull. No. 1 [Provo, Utah: Brigham Young University, 1962]).

[11]An exception to this general finding comes from a Wisconsin study (Archie O. Haller and William H. Sewell, "Farm Residence and Levels of Educational and Occupational Aspiration," *American Journal of Sociology*, LXII [January, 1957], 407–11).

[12]For residential distribution by sex, intelligence, and socioeconomic status see William H. Sewell, "Residential Background and College Plans," *American Sociological Review*, XXIX (February, 1964), 24–38; and for relation of these variables to occupational plans see William H. Sewell, Archie O. Haller, and Murray A. Straus, "Social Status and Educational and Occupational Aspirations," *American Sociological Review*, XXII (February, 1957), 67–73. Both papers contain numerous references to the revelant literature.

[13]*Op. cit.*

[14]Middleton and Grigg, *op. cit.* Other possible reasons for the apparent differences in the Florida ninth- and twelfth-grade studies are that the latter had a much smaller sample than the former, and the ninth-grade study reported aspirations to professional occupations while the twelfth-grade study was concerned with aspirations to white-collar occupations.

[15]This technique is called "elaboration" or "elaboration by partials" and is fully described in Herbert Hyman, *Survey Designs and Analysis* (Glencoe, Ill.: Free Press, 1955), chaps. vi and vii.

[16]*Op. cit.*, p. 222.

[17]*Op. cit.*, p. 352.

[18]For further details about how the original survey was conducted, see Little, *op. cit.*, pp. 2–6. The information upon which Little's report was based was derived from a one-sixth sample of all cases, while for the present analysis a new sample consisting of one-third of the cases was drawn.

[19]This requirement resulted in the loss of 426 cases. Practically all of the losses were due to failure to obtain intelligence-test scores. A comparison of those omitted by sex, residence, father's occupation, rank in high-school class, and college plans showed that they did not differ significantly from those included in the sample.

[20]The student's occupational choice was evoked by the following item: "I hope eventually to enter the type of occupation checked below." This was followed by a series of pre-coded socioeconomic categories, such as professional, executive, small business ownership or management, salesman, office worker, etc., and a blank in which unlisted occupations were to be entered. Students were also asked to specify their field or training program if they planned to enter a trade or vocational school, or their field of interest if they planned to enter a college or university. The primary information in determining occupational choice was obtained from answers to the first item. No one was classified as having a professional or executive choice unless he planned to continue with some kind of formal education beyond high school — with a few exceptions, such as entertainers, dancers, and musicians. Respondents who planned on college but whose occupational plans were not indicated were coded as having high-status occupational choices. For 7.3 per cent of the sample no information on occupational choice could be obtained from the responses. There were no large differences by community of residence or sex. An additional 1.1 per cent of the girls gave no information on occupational plans other than that they planned to marry after graduation, and 9.0 per cent of the male respondents indicated only that they planned to enter military service after gradua-

tion. Since none of these youths indicated that they planned to go to college at some later time, it was inferred that they were not choosing high-status occupations as defined in this study. There were no significant differences among the residence groups in the proportion of girls planning to marry or of boys planning to enter military service.

[21]V. A. C. Henmon and M. J. Nelson, *The Henmon-Nelson Test of Mental Ability* (Boston: Houghton Mifflin Co., 1942).

[22]The five indicators were factor-analyzed using the principal-components method, and were orthogonally rotated according to the verimax criterion. This produced a two-factor structure composed of a factor on which the three economic items were most heavily loaded, and a factor on which the two educational items were most heavily loaded. The composite socioeconomic status index was developed by squaring the loadings of the principal items of each factor as weights, then multiplying student scores on the items by the respective weights, and finally summing the weighted scores of the principal items on each factor. The two factors were combined into a composite socioeconomic status score after multiplying the factor scores of all students by certain constants which would produce approximately equal variances for both status dimensions. The resulting sum of the weighted scores was then multiplied by a constant to produce a theoretical range of scores between 0 and 99.

[23]If the cutting point between high- and low-status choices had been white-collar occupations rather than professional and executive positions, the percentages in Table 1 would have been as follows: *For Males:* farm, 47.3, village, 50.3; small city, 59.6; medium city, 60.5; large city, 70.0; rural, 49.0; smaller urban, 60.0; larger urban, 70.0. *For females:* farm, 79.5; village, 76.7; small city, 81.0; medium city, 83.4; large city, 87.9; rural, 78.0; smaller urban, 82.2; larger urban, 87.9. *For the total sample:* farm, 65.9; village, 64.6; small city, 70.3; medium city, 72.6; large city, 79.9; rural, 64.7; smaller urban, 71.4; larger urban, 79.9. Thus, no important change in the pattern of occupational choice by residence occurs when all white-collar positions are included as high-status occupational choices.

[24]Both intelligence and socioeconomic status appear to contribute more to differences in occupational choice than does community of

residence. Rough evidence is that the three-category break for residence shows a percentage difference in high occupational choice between the rural and larger urban categories of only 16.9 for the whole sample (Table 1), while the percentage difference between the low- and high-intelligence thirds is 42.9; and the percentage difference between the low- and high-socioeconomic status thirds is 43.7 (Table 2).

[25]Sewell, *op. cit.*, Table 3, p. 29. The data presented in this table are based on the total sample, while the present study excludes 335 farm boys who planned to farm. Consequently, the sex distribution in the farm category is much more unbalanced for the present sample (males 42 per cent, females 58 per cent) than is shown in the above-mentioned table. Otherwise, the distributions are closely similar.

[26]Middleton and Grigg, *op. cit.*, p. 351, and Grigg and Middleton, *op. cit.*, p. 306, find no differences between rural and urban girls when they control for intelligence or socioeconomic status.

[27]This is opposite to the findings of Lipset and Bendix, *op. cit.*, p. 213.

[28]This confirms Grigg and Middleton's general conclusion for ninth-grade Florida boys (*op. cit.*, pp. 307–8).

[29]See Morris Rosenberg, "Test Factor Standardization as a Method of Interpretation," *Social Forces*, XL (October, 1962), 53–61.

[31]*Op. cit.*, p. 410.

[32]In 1950 the proportions of sixteen- and seventeen-year-old Wisconsin farm, rural non-farm, and urban youth attending school were 70, 82, and 91 per cent, respectively, while in 1960 the corresponding figures were 88, 87, and 89 per cent (see Douglas G. Marshall, *Wisconsin's Population, Changes and Prospects, 1900–1963* (Wisconsin Agricultural Experiment Station Research Bull. 241 [Madison, Wis., 1963], p. 29).

[33]*Op. cit.*, p. 222.

[34]James S. Coleman, *The Adolescent Society* (New York: Free Press of Glencoe, 1961); Coleman, "The Adolescent Subculture and Academic Achievement," *American Journal of Sociology*, LXV (January, 1960), 337–47; and Archie O. Haller and C. E. Butterworth, "Peer Influences on Levels of Occupational and Educational Aspiration," *Social Forces*, XXXVIII (May, 1960), 289–95.

[35]Genevieve Knupfer, "Portrait of the Underdog," in Reinhard Bendix and Seymour M. Lipset (eds.) *Class, Status and Power* (Glencoe, Ill.: Free Press, 1953), pp. 255–63; and Herbert Hyman, "The Values Systems of Different Classes: A Social Psychological Contribution to the Analysis of Stratification," in Bendix and Lipset, *ibid.*, pp. 426–42.

[36]*Op. cit.*, p. 352.

[37]Many non-occupational features of the urban community are also attractive to rural girls, including the wider range of marital opportunities, more varied social life, and higher standard of living.

OTHER RELEVANT ARTICLES

The following articles are relevant to the topic of this chapter:

Rossi, A. S. Women in science: Why so few? *Science*, 1965, *148*, 1196–1202.

Rossi asks why there are so few women maintaining themselves in scientific careers, and brings various kinds of data to light in seeking the answer. She notes that women employed in science and engineering fields are less likely to have advanced degrees than men, and that they are less likely to be married and work in industry, and that they are paid less and work fewer hours. She shows that women physicians have lower withdrawal rates to home and child rearing responsibilities, and that the rate of withdrawal for women engineers is similar to the rate for women secondary school teachers. Her explanation for these contrasts is couched partly in terms of the differential in cultural expectations for boys and girls, but also in terms of sex differences in cognitive development.

Astin, A. W. Effect of different college environments on the vocational choices of high aptitude students. *Journal of Counseling Psychology*, 1966, *12*, 28–34.

In this article, Astin studies the influence of the college environment on the type of choice which the person expresses at the end of four years of school, compared to the type of choice he had when he entered. Specifically, he finds that the student's career choice comes to conform more and more to the dominant or model career choice in his college environment if it did not conform at first. Equally interesting is the finding that some choices are more susceptible than others to this kind of influence: realistic (engineering) choices were significantly tied to a number of college types, while a social, such as teaching, choice appeared to be uninfluenced by college environment.

Additional references relating to the topic of this chapter are as follows:

Books:

Caplow, T. *The Sociology of Work.* Minneapolis, Minn.: University of Minnesota Press, 1954 (Chapter 9).

Davis, J. A. *Undergraduate Career Decisions.* Chicago: Aldine, 1965.

Gross, E. *Work and Society*, New York: Crowell, 1958.

Harris, I. *The Promised Seed: A Comparative Study of First and Later Sons.* New York: Free Press, 1964.

Nosow, S., and W. H. Form. (Eds.) *Man, Work and Society.* New York: Basic Books, 1962 (Chapter 10).

Rosenberg, M. *Occupations and Values.* New York: Free Press, 1957.

Slocum, W. L. *Occupational Careers.* Chicago: Aldine, 1966. (Ch. 10)

Super, D. E. *The Psychology of Careers.* New York: Harper & Row, 1957 (Chapters 17 and 18).

Articles:

Blau, P. M. The flow of occupational supply and recruitment. *American Sociology Review*, 1965, *30*, 475–490.

Boynton, P. L., and R. D. Woolwine. The relationship between the economic status of high school girls and their vocational wishes and expectations. *Journal of Applied Psychology*, 1942, *26*, 399–415.

Chalmers, W. E., and M. W. Dorsey. Research on Negro job status. *Journal of Intergroup Relations*, 1962, *3*, 344–359.

Galle, O. Occupational composition and the metropolitan hierarchy: The inter- and intra-metropolitan division of labor. *American Journal of Sociology*, 1963, *68*, 260–269.

Hershenson, D. B. Some personal and social determinants of occupational role taking in college students. *Journal of Counseling Psychology*, 1965, *12*, 206–208.

Hyman, B. The relationship of social status and vocational interests. *Journal of Counseling Psychology*, 1956, *3*, 12–16.

Jenson, P. G., and W. K. Kirchner. A national answer to the question: Do sons follow their father's occupation. *Journal of Applied Psychology*, 1955, *39*, 419–421.

Kinnane, J. F., and M. Pable. Family background and work value orientation. *Journal of Counseling Psychology*, 1962, *9*, 320–325.

————, and Margaret Bannon. Perceived parental influence and work value orientation. *Personnel and Guidance Journal*, 1964, *43*, 273–279.

Moser, W. B. The influence of certain cultural factors upon the selection of vocational preferences by high school students. *Journal of Educational Research*, 1952, *45*, 523–526.

Pavalko, R. M. Aspirants to teaching: Some differences between high school senior boys and girls planning on a career of teaching. *Sociology and Social Research*, 1965, *50*, 47–62.

Sampson, Ruth, and B. F. Stefflre. Like father . . . like son? *Personnel and Guidance Journal*, 1952, *31*, 35–39.

Sewell, W. H., A. O. Haller, and M. A. Strauss. Social status and educational and occupational aspiration. *American Sociological Review*, 1957, *22*, 67–73.

Smith, R. J., C. E. Ramsey, and Gelia Castillo. Parental authority and job choice: Sex differences in three cultures. *American Journal of Sociology*, 1963, *69*, 143–149.

Strauss, M. A. Societal needs and personal characteristics in the choice of farm, blue collar and white collar occupations by farmers' sons. *Rural Sociology*, 1964, *29*, 408–425.

Tausky, C., and R. Dubin. Career anchorage: Managerial mobility motivations. *American Sociological Review*, 1965, *30*, 725–735.

Wilson, J. Q. Generational and ethnic differences among career police officers. *American Journal of Sociology*, 1963, *69*, 522–528.

Youmans, E. G. Social factors in the work attitudes and interests of twelfth grade Michigan boys. *Journal of Educational Sociology*, 1954, *28*, 35–48.

Some of the major works and recent publications on occupational intergenerational mobility are:

Chinoy, E. Social mobility trends in the United States. *American Sociological Review*, 1955, *20*, 180–186.

Crockett, H. J. The achievement motive and differential occupational mobility in the United States *American Sociological Review*, 1962, *27*, 191–204.

Duncan, O. D., and R. W. Hodge. Education and Occupational mobility. *American Journal of Sociology*, 1963, *68*, 624–644.

————. Social origins of salaried and self-employed professional workers. *Social Forces*, 1965, *44*, 186–189.

Gunderson, E. K. E. and P. D. Nelson, Socioeconomic status and Navy occupation. *Personnel and Guidance Journal*, 1965, *44*, 263–266.

PART V

After Choice: Occupational Satisfaction, Performance and Adjustment

BUTCHER

Job Satisfaction

11

If an occupation is chosen, it must be that it is chosen in the expectation of achieving a satisfying state of affairs. This is stated explicitly in the decision-making formulation of occupational determination. It may also be observed in each of the other formulations: to implement a self-concept must be satisfying; to find a work environment which complements one's personality must also be to find gratification, however sublimated, of some fundamental need or drive, and so on.

After an occupational role is attained with some degree of permanency, can the amount of satisfaction it provides be elicited? In general, the answer is yes. Most persons, if asked, can estimate the degree to which their job generates positive feelings. This essentially describes the beginnings of this kind of measurement in Hoppock's first monograph (1935).

Since that beginning, though, much additional information has been gathered on job satisfaction. One thrust of this research has been to identify the sources of satisfaction from elements within the job. These include such varied factors as the quality of supervision, the setting in which the work is performed, salary, intrinsic satisfactions in the performance of the work, associations the job provides, and the like. Another thrust has been to seek recombinations of these elements by factor analysis in order to reduce them to a parsimonious number. An exhaustive review of these kinds of studies may be found in Vroom's *Work and Motivation* (1964).

Besides studies of the components of job satisfaction, several points of view on the structural qualities of job satisfaction have become apparent in the periodical literature. One is most similar to the need reduction outlook of vocational determinants, stating simply that job satisfaction is proportionate to the degree that the elements of the job satisfy the particular needs which the person feels most strongly. This approach is exemplified by the first article in this chapter by Kuhlen. He found, like most other investigators, that his subjects, teachers, reported a high degree of satisfaction with their work, even when he made a distinction between occupation and present position or job. He further had the occupation of teaching rated for its potential to satisfy various needs, finding variation among the fourteen needs from potentially very satisfying to very frustrating. He finds that for men, at least, job satisfaction does vary with the degree to which the person's constellation of needs is satisfied from the occupation. Several other studies similar to Kuhlen's have been performed, obtaining similar results, of which one notable example is Schaffer (1953).

In contrast to the straight need-reduction concept is the formulation of Herzberg, Mausner, and Snyderman (1959) which posits that certain factors relating to the work itself or "job centered," tend to associate with the expression of satisfaction, but when lacking do not so strongly stimulate dissatisfaction. Conversely, a second set of factors relating to the context in which the job is performed, if absent stimulate dissatisfaction, but when present do not enhance satisfaction. This position is also known as the motivation-hygeine theory of job satisfaction.

The Schwartz, Jenusaitis, and Stark article presents data on the Herzberg motivation-hygiene hypothesis. It is chosen partly because it was not performed by Herzberg himself. This might reduce any effects of experimenter bias, should they be present. The authors also introduce the same needs which Kuhlen used, but find that none of them correlate significantly with the job satisfaction factors. Their results are similar to those of Herzberg, finding a stronger association of job-related factors with positive response to work, and context-related factors with negative feelings.

The Herzberg motivation-hygiene hypothesis, while naturally appealing, has met with a fairly vocal and substantial body of criticism, supported and not supported by data. Ewen's article provides a review of the Herzberg study which generated the motivation-hygiene hypothesis, noting some of its shortcomings, and suggesting that there is no justification to generalize from it.

A third point of view does not specify which factors relate in what ways to satisfaction and dissatisfaction, but rather speculates on the possibility that satisfaction is strictly a relativistic phenomenon; that persons develop different personal standards for evaluating the amount of whatever kinds of satisfactions the work offers. This outlook is only now in its beginning stages of development, and experimenters in the field are using several different models for their investigations. One which most perfectly expresses the relativistic concept is the equity model, in which outcomes of the work are evaluated against the input it demands. Thus, a reward of work, such as pay, may be satisfactory or not, compared against the amount of physical exertion a job requires, or the level of acquired skill it calls for, or similar factors.

While no direct test of the equity hypothesis employing job satisfaction as its dependent variable has yet been published, the article by Hulin may provide some indirect evidence. In essence, it shows that the worker may assess his present status by referring to the alternative opportunities which are available to him. Since attractive alternatives are fewer in poorer socioeconomic conditions, the worker's job is seen as relatively better, compared with the worker surfeited by attractive surroundings.

SATISFACTION AND SATISFACTORINESS

While the worker's goal for his work is some kind of satisfaction, the employer's goal is for him to be satisfactory, which usually means productive. Management lore holds that the happy worker is the productive worker.

A great many studies of the relationship between job satisfaction and job satisfactoriness or performance have been done. Usually, job satisfaction is measured with only little difficulty; enough work on the concept has been done to produce reliable and valid measurements. But job performance is another matter: what is to be measured to reflect the satisfactoriness of an employee's work? Depending on whether the job output is a tangible good or a service, on whether it emanates from a line or a staff position, on the competition in the market and the costs of materials or training, or a host of other possible factors, vastly different indexes of satisfactory performance may be appropriate. The character of this situation is reflected in a term in current use among industrial psychologists: "the criterion problem."

In their review of the satisfaction and performance literature, Brayfield and Crockett (1955) make a distinction in the conceptualization of performance in terms of absenteeism and turnover compared against performance on the job. They also outline the intuitive relationship between satisfaction and production in more precise terms. They suggest that the dissatisfied worker may use low productivity as a form of aggression or reprisal against management, which of course has goals of high productivity. They also assert that productivity should increase in proportion to the amount of added satisfaction management can induce in employees by various means. Their review of the literature relating to this hypothesis is disappointingly negative, finding no certain association between the two factors.

On the other hand, Brayfield and Crockett judge from the knowledge that the organism tends to remove itself from unpleasant or aversive conditions, that employees whose morale or attitude toward work is poor would tend to be absent more frequently or quit work more regularly. And they find the literature of empirical data essentially in support of this idea.

The relationship between job satisfaction and performance is explored in the next article presented in this chapter, by Heron. It produces positive results, even in the face of Brayfield's and Crockett's conclusions. It is not presented, though, to argue for the existence of a link between the two constructs, but as an example of the kind of research, and also as the conceptual forerunner of the concept of occupational adjustment which is taken up in the next paper.

Curiously, Heron finds after extracting a general factor from his job satisfaction indexes a second factor which contains positively loaded items concerned with the intrinsic aspect of work, and a third factor of negative items relating to the job in a wider context. This should remind the reader not only of Herzberg, but of positive and negative reasons for working discussed in some of the articles comprising the first chapter.

Some investigators have hypothesized that moderating factors exist between satisfaction and productivity. A few of these are listed in the references at the end of this chapter.

The authors of the next article, Betz, et al, used Heron's dual criteria to develop a concept of work adjustment. Their report is a summary of some twenty monographs on work adjustment issued by the Industrial Relations Center at the University of Minnesota. Their definition of work adjustment is essentially psychological — the process by which the individual interacts and comes to terms with his work environment.

Surely this is the pre-eminent task of the period identified by Super as the establishment and maintenance stages, by Havighurst as becoming and maintaining productiveness, and by Miller and Form as trial and stable.

However, another concept of the developmental task occurring after choice has been formulated: the ability to adapt to the contingencies which career progression or development presents. This is the concept of the sociologist, which believes that the stage after choice consists of "occupational socialization," or of meeting "career contingencies." The former term depends upon a conception of work as a social activity, and supposes that an important task of work is to learn what the group's standards of occupational behavior are, and to adopt them as one's own. The latter term recognizes that occupational progression is not fully predictable and that events occur which require new behaviors, or revisions of self-concepts and ideologies. Some of these come with the progression to higher status, while some come with disappointments, failures, or events which cannot be averted or controlled.

Becker and Strauss describe career development in terms of a flow from lesser to greater status positions. They recapitulate in some detail the factors in occupational attainment entertained in Chapter 10, and go on to delineate the factors, called contingencies, which operate as the individual progresses further in his career. Their formulation of the adult identity which is "never gained nor maintained once and for all" is reminiscent of Super's self-concept which continues to seek implementation throughout occupational life.

Some evidence on the manner in which adjustments are made — by change of attitude to accompany change of position — is presented in the final article, by Lieberman. It brings to mind a remark by Mark Twain in *More Tramps Abroad:* "A man cannot be expected to fit a square hole right away. He must have time to modify his shape."

Lieberman found that workers who were forced unexpectedly into new work roles adopted attitudes consonant with the dominant ideology of their new reference groups. It is remarkable to find also that when some of these same workers had to return to their former jobs, owing to a downturn in business, their attitudes changed once again in the direction of those they had formerly held.

REFERENCES

Brayfield, A. H., and W. H. Crockett. Employee attitudes and employee performance. *Psychological Bulletin*, 1955, *52*, 396–424.

Herzberg, F., B. Mausner, and B. Snyderman. *The Motivation to Work*. New York: Wiley, 1959.

Hoppock, R. *Job Satisfaction*. New York: Harper & Row, 1935.

Schaffer, R. H. Job satisfaction as related to need satisfaction in work. *Psychological Monographs*, 1953, *67*, No. 14 (Whole No. 364).

Vroom, V. H. *Work and Motivation*. New York: Wiley, 1964.

Needs, Perceived Need Satisfaction Opportunities, and Satisfaction with Occupation[1]

RAYMOND G. KUHLEN

It may be hypothesized that satisfaction or dissatisfaction *with* an area of life is a function of the degree to which one finds satisfaction for major needs *in* that area of living. This presumably will hold true especially among those for whom a given area of living (e.g., occupation) represents a major source of life satisfaction, and may not obtain at all in a sphere of life with which a person is little concerned, even though he is participating. Schaffer (1953) has advanced a similar hypothesis with respect to work (though without the latter restriction) and has presented supporting evidence. In the area of marriage, Ort (1950) has reported a correlation of −.83 between happiness and frequency with which role expectations (needs) were not satisfied.

From: Kuhlen, R. G., Needs, perceived need satisfaction opportunities, and satisfaction with occupation, *Journal of Applied Psychology*, *47*, 1963, 56–64. Copyright 1963 by the American Psychological Association, and reproduced by permission.

In the present investigation, a first hypothesis was that those individuals whose measured needs are relatively stronger than the potential of the occupation for satisfying those needs (as they perceived this potential) will tend to be frustrated and hence to be less well satisfied with their occupation. Where needs and the perceived need-satisfaction potential of the occupation are more in harmony, it was anticipated that satisfaction with occupation would be rated higher. However, since a career role tends to be primary for males and relatively secondary for females, a second hypothesis was that these relationships will hold to a greater degree among men than among women. Relevant to this hypothesis is the finding of Brayfield, Wells, and Strate (1957) that job adjustment is correlated with general adjustment to a higher degree among men than among women, a finding which they attributed to the greater importance of work in the life scheme of men.

The general hypothesis of this phase of the study relates to the degree of overall satisfaction or frustration of needs experienced in the occupation. The specific needs involved are, for this hypothesis, unimportant, as long as they are vocationally relevant. One man, with high achievement needs, is frustrated because he sees no future. Another, with strong dominance needs, is irked by the sub-missiveness required of him. Both are in the same occupation; both are frustrated and dissatisfied. It is recognized that certain needs may not be perceived as being satisfi-able in the occupational context whereas others are. Thus the satisfaction or frustra-tion of the need for achievement would presumably bear a relationship to satisfac-tion with career whereas sex needs typically would not. In fact, it may be assumed that career is a major source of satisfaction for the achievement need and thus it was predicted (a third hypothesis) that satisfaction of this need would be particularly important for (i.e., more highly related to) occupational satisfaction.

METHOD

Subjects

Students in certain of the writer's graduate classes, enrolling mainly teachers-in-service, were tested in the present phase of the investigation. Of some 323 tested, complete data were available for 203 (108 men and 95 women) who were engaged in junior and/ or senior high school teaching. These 203 people constituted the major sample, though numbers varied slightly from analysis to analysis (in some instances more, others less than 203) since it was desired to capitalize all the data available. The subjects were mainly in their 20s and 30s.

Procedure

The subjects were asked to respond to three instruments, administered in the following order: the Edwards Personal Preference Schedule (a measure of needs);

a questionnaire which asked for ratings of satisfaction with present job and occupation, and for other information relating to job satisfaction and plans; and an instrument entitled "Personality Types and Occupa-tions" which was designed to obtain esti-mates of the perceptions the respondents had of the need-satisfaction potential of their occupation. In some instances these in-struments were administered in the same sitting, but mainly the data were collected in two separate sessions with the Edwards scale constituting the first session.

Rating of satisfaction with occupation was on an 11-point scale, with instructions to "think of your occupation in general, not your particular job." Similar ratings were obtained with respect to satisfaction with present position. Previous research (Johnson, 1955) has shown that ratings so obtained correlate .64 with job satisfaction scores obtained from an extensive questionnaire, and .61 with pooled ratings of teachers by colleagues as to their job satisfaction, the latter sample, however, being quite small ($N = 18$). Test-retest reliability over 3 weeks was .89. The questionnaire also con-tained questions inquiring as to whether or not the occupation was something they truly wanted to do or in which they planned to continue. Strong (1955, pp. 98–117) had found answers to these questions related to other evidences of satisfaction (see Table 1).

Personality Types and Occupations was the same instrument employed in a previous study (Kuhlen and Dipboye, 1959) with slight modification of directions to make it appropriate for people already employed. "Personality types," which were actually the descriptions (or slight modifications thereof) of various needs from Edwards' (1954) test manual, were presented with instructions for the subject to rate the degree to which a person of this type would likely be satisfied or frustrated in the teaching profession.[1] In assigning such ratings he was instructed to ignore whether the type being considered would make a "good" member of this profession, to ignore his own attitude toward this type of person, and to think of the occupation in general, not a particular school or system. An example, relating to achievement need, will illustrate this device.

Type 1. This person has a high need to achieve. He likes to do his best to accomplish tasks requiring skill and effort, to be a recognized authority, to accomplish something of a great significance, to do a difficult job well, to solve difficult problems, to be able to do things better than others, to get ahead, to be a big success.

Will this occupation offer him opportunity for satisfying experiences or will it pose frustrations? And to what degree? Circle one number to indicate your judgment.

−5 −4 −3 −2 −1 0 +1 +2 +3 +4 +5

This occupation will pose exceedingly high frustration	No special satisfactions of frustrations	This occupation will offer exceedingly high satisfactions

One focus of the present study is upon the degree to which satisfaction with occupation (in this instance, teaching) is related to the discrepancy between strength of one's basic needs and the perceived potential of the occupation for satisfying those needs. Discrepancies were determined in the following fashion: First, index values of 1 through 5 were assigned to indicate on the same scale (*a*) strength of needs and (*b*) perceived potential of occupation for satisfying those needs. Edwards raw scores were converted into standard scores (based on norms) before index values were assigned. The index values had the following meanings:

Index Value	Edwards Score	Need-Satisfaction Potential
1	−34	−5, −4
2	35–44	−3, −2
3	45–54	−1, 0, +1
4	55–64	+2, +3
5	65+	+4, +5

Discrepancies were computed by subtracting the index assigned to need strength from the index assigned to the perceived need-satisfaction potential of the occupation. Thus a person with need-strength of 4 (between .5 and 1.5 SDs above the mean on Edwards norms) on achievement need who perceived need-satisfaction potential of the occupation as being at an index value of 2 (i.e., rated it −2 or −3 on the scale) would have a "need-need satisfaction discrepancy" of −2. Negative discrepancies thus identify instances of presumed probable frustration, whereas zero or positive discrepancies imply adequate or more than adequate opportunities for satisfaction in the occupation, as perceived by the particular individual.

It was predicted that negative discrepancies would be associated with low satisfaction with occupation, particularly in the instance of needs (e.g., need for achievement) which are commonly satisfied through occupation and career. In general, it was anticipated that positive discrepancies (implying ample opportunity for need satisfaction) would be associated with high satisfaction in occupation. However, it is conceivable that an occupation that offers considerable opportunity for the satisfaction of a particular need may actually be frustrating to a person low in this need, if, along with the opportunity, colleagues or superiors expect or demand a high level of motivation of the particular type. It was not anticipated that the occupation of public school teaching would be "demanding" with respect to the type of needs here studied and analyses were not designed to reveal curvilinear relations between satisfaction with occupation and the need-need satisfaction discrepancies.

SATISFACTION WITH OCCUPATION

Generally speaking, this group of subjects was quite satisfied with their careers. Their occupational satisfaction ratings ranged from 1 to 11 for 108 males and from 3 to 11 for 95 females, with the respective medians being 8.9 and 8.8. About three-fourths of the ratings of each sex fell in the categories of 8, 9, and 10. A rating of 6 represented "average satisfaction."

Table 1 presents the distributions of answers to questions which might also be expected to reflect job satisfaction. It will be noted that the vast majority of both sexes (*a*) felt that teaching was something they truly wanted to do, or approximately so, and (*b*) wanted to continue in or at least had no plan to leave.[2] (However, in this sample the majority of men indicated they were contemplating changing or making an effort to change their particular *positions*.) The mean occupational satisfaction-ratings of those selecting various alternatives in this table suggest that the questions and ratings are measuring the same variable, to a degree at least.

It is to be noted, in line with the hypothesis that relationships will be less pronounced in a group for whom career has lower saliency, that there is a reliable relationship between satisfaction with *current* position and statements reflecting attitude toward career choice and expected permanency of career in the case of men, but not in the case of women. The correlation between *ratings* of satisfaction with current position and with occupation were also higher in the case of men than women, the respective *r*'s being .62 and .36.

NEEDS, PERCEPTIONS, AND OCCUPATIONAL SATISFACTION

Table 2 contains the means and *SD*s for the two sexes for each of the 15 needs and for ratings as to the potential of the occupation

TABLE 1
Occupational Satisfaction of the Teacher Sample

		Men			Women	
	N	Mean Occupational Satisfaction	Mean Job Satisfaction		Mean Occupational Satisfaction	Mean Job Satisfaction
Attitude toward career						
Truly wanted to do	39	9.59	9.28	25	9.40	8.80
Approximately what wanted	49	8.47	7.90	47	8.74	7.96
Came to accept	9			5		
Would not have chosen	10	7.50	6.75	14	6.84	7.79
Dislike	1			0		
F		13.69***	11.46***		25.29***	1.93
Permanence of career						
Want to continue	53	9.17	8.85	40	9.08	8.60
No plan to change	38	8.66	8.13	34	8.47	7.68
Contemplate change	7			9		
Making effort to change	3	7.29	6.24	2	7.44	8.12
Will definitely change	7			5		
F		9.45***	11.38***		7.61***	1.40

***$p < .01$.

TABLE 2

Mean Scores of the Teacher Sample

Edwards PPS Need Subscales	Edwards Score				Ratings of Perception of Need-Satisfaction Potential[a]			
	Males		Females		Males		Females	
	M	SD	M	SD	M	SD	M	SD
Ach	50.1	9.9	50.5	10.5	0.5	3.3	0.2	3.5
Def	52.9	9.3	53.1	11.0	0.7	2.8	0.5	3.2
Ord	51.1	11.8	52.1	11.7	1.8	2.8	1.2	3.2
Exh	49.3	10.4	49.7	11.3	−0.1	3.4	0.3	3.4
Aut	49.8	9.6	47.6	9.3	−2.9	2.4	−3.2	2.4
Aff	49.1	9.9	48.0	10.6	2.5	2.0	2.2	2.2
Int	49.6	10.4	51.6	9.8	3.4	1.8	2.9	2.2
Suc	48.0	9.9	46.8	10.6	−2.7	2.1	−2.6	2.4
Dom	48.5	9.8	47.6	9.3	1.7	2.8	1.0	3.0
Aba	50.0	10.0	48.8	9.9	−2.4	2.6	−3.1	2.3
Nur	50.5	9.5	49.4	10.2	3.0	1.9	3.6	1.9
Cha	49.0	11.2	50.7	10.5	−0.1	3.5	0.2	3.3
End	52.9	10.5	52.6	11.1	2.6	2.3	2.3	2.7
Het	47.6	10.5	51.4	10.8	—	—	—	—
Agg	51.7	9.3	51.0	9.7	−2.7	2.6	−3.3	2.5
N	107		91		107		91	

[a]On this rating, +5 means this occupation will be extremely satisfying to a person high in this need; −5 indicates the likelihood of extreme frustration of such a person.

for satisfying those needs. The Edwards raw scores were translated into standard scores according to the published norms, which have a mean of 50 and an *SD* of 10. Thus one can make certain comparisons of teachers with Edwards norms, if he so desires, though age and probably marital status differences make such comparisons tenuous. Compared to the norms, teachers are at about the mean in achievement need, are high in deference, low in succorance (women), high in endurance, to select examples.

The instrument devised to obtain ratings of the perceived potential of the occupation for satisfying various needs yielded especially pertinent information. Table 2 presents mean values (ratings were on an 11-point scale, −5 to +5) for each of 14 needs. Both

sexes agreed that needs for affiliation, intraception, dominance, nurturance, and endurance might be readily satisfied in the teaching profession, but that the individuals with strong needs for autonomy, succorance, abasement, and aggression would likely be extremely frustrated. These findings would be anticipated through even a casual evaluation of the teacher's role and activities. In fact, the latter needs might be expected to be frustrated in most work situations.

However, an unanticipated finding was the marked differences in perception of the need-satisfaction potential of teaching with respect to certain needs. The overall distributions of ratings are presented in Table 3 for the three needs (achievement, exhibition, and change) having the largest *SD*s.

TABLE 3

Distribution of Ratings of Perceived Need Satisfaction of Teaching

Need-Satisfaction Potential Ratings	Type of Person Rated					
	High Achievement Need		High Exhibition Need		High Change Need	
	Male	Female	Male	Female	Male	Female
Highly frustrating						
−5	11	14	13	12	17	12
−4	8	5	8	6	10	6
−3	13	13	14	10	14	6
−2	9	5	10	6	3	10
−1	9	3	6	3	3	4
0	0	6	6	12	7	9
+1	6	6	12	6	10	8
+2	14	9	8	9	13	8
+3	17	18	11	13	15	16
+4	17	6	10	9	12	11
+5	9	13	14	12	9	6
Highly satisfying						
Number of ratings[a]	113	98	112	98	113	96

[a]These Ns differ slightly from those reported in the preceding table. All of the data was used here, whereas the previous table is based on cases with complete data.

The facts for achievement need are especially interesting. It had been anticipated that teachers would view teaching as being somewhat frustrating to individuals with strong achievement needs. But the *mean* rating suggested only that the profession would be neither especially frustrating nor satisfying. Actually the distribution of ratings is sharply bimodal. Many view teaching as extremely satisfying to the high achievement need person; many others view teaching as highly frustrating to such a person. Relatively few view it as in between. And this is true for both sexes. One can only speculate regarding the reasons for sharply divergent views. Is one group perceptive as to avenues for advancement in public education, the other not? Is one group from low socioeconomic and occupational background, and thus views the teaching profession as evidence of marked achievement,

whereas the other group represents offspring of high socioeconomic or occupational level parents?

A similar tendency toward bimodality is evident in the case of "exhibition." Perhaps one group perceives the opportunities for the satisfaction of need exhibition before students, and the other is more aware of the unacceptability of such behavior on the part of a teacher in the community. In the instance of the need for change, it may be that the teachers who see opportunities for satisfaction of this need are in progressive schools while those who view teaching as frustrating to the need for change are in static schools. To be sure, though, certain kinds of people may perceive a static profession as frustrating to the need for change whereas others perceive it as offering unusual opportunities for change precisely *because* of its long-term static character.

In any event, these findings illustrate that perceptions of an occupation may vary greatly from one person to another. The need for further study of the variables that produce these contrasting perceptions is apparent.

The next analysis involved the computation of correlations between measured needs and the ratings of the need-satisfaction potential of the occupation, and between these two variables and rated occupational satisfaction. Table 4 contains the results. It will be noted that, in the data for men, reliable correlations existed between the measured need and rated need-satisfaction potential of the occupation for about half the needs, the highest r being .27 in the instance of dominance. Throughout the table, one notes fewer reliable correlations for women.

Although Table 2 suggested that teachers *as a group* were average in achievement need and saw no special frustration of this need in the teaching profession, the facts in Table 4 which involve rated satisfaction as related to the raters' needs are in line with the prediction. In the case of men, those with high achievement needs tend to be dissatisfied, but those who *perceive* teaching as being potentially satisfying to the high achievement need person tend to be satisfied. In the case of women, only the latter was true. Among men, again, the data suggest that high

TABLE 4

Correlations among Measured Needs and Ratings

| | Correlations Between: | | | | | |
| | Need and Perception | | Satisfaction and Need | | Satisfaction and Perception | |
Need	Male	Female	Male	Female	Male	Female
Ach	.03	.10	−.19*	−.02	.21**	.32***
Def	.11	.14	.07	.11	−.12	−.05
Ord	.00	.16	.04	.01	−.06	−.10
Exh	.19*	.14	−.01	.08	.08	−.19
Aut	.25***	.09	−.28***	−.19	.04	.06
Aff	.15	.22*	.04	.00	−.03	.16
Int	.20*	.05	.05	.03	.03	.14
Suc	.21*	.20	−.07	−.03	−.05	.01
Dom	.27***	.06	.20*	−.12	.22*	−.05
Aba	.23*	.08	.15	−.03	−.10	−.20
Nur	.12	.10	.14	−.01	.12	−.16
Cha	.24*	−.01	−.12	.05	.16	.03
End	.05	.27**	−.11	.19	.20*	.03
Het	—	—	−.04	−.01	—	—
Agg	.11	.13	.14	−.10	.17	−.11
N	107	91	107	91	107	91

Note — All levels of confidence represent two-tailed tests, except in the case of achievement need where a one-tailed test was justified by a specific directional prediction.

*$p \leq .05$.
**$p \leq .025$.
***$p \leq .01$.

autonomy need individuals are likely to be frustrated, and that those with high dominance needs are likely to be satisfied. Those who perceive the teaching as potentially satisfying to the high endurance need person tended to be more satisfied. Among women, only one of the 29 correlations was reliable, suggesting that for them satisfaction with occupation is not so dependent upon need satisfaction as is true of men. This finding is in line with the hypothesis that such relationships will be lower among those for whom occupation has low saliency.

It will be recalled that other measures of occupational satisfaction were available in addition to the overall rating. Two questions asked that the subjects categorize themselves with respect to their attitudes toward their career and their judgments as to their permanence in the profession (see Table 1). Three groups were set up with respect to each question: those who checked Response

Number 1 constituted one group; Response Number 2, the second group; and those who checked either Response Numbers 3, 4, or 5 constituted the third group. The three groups presumably varied in degree of satisfaction with the third group being least satisfied. Separate analyses of variance (simple one-way classification) were computed for each need and for each rating as to need-satisfaction potential, with the sexes separate.

This analysis was not particularly informative. Only 9 of 116 comparisons yielded reliable differences. The three that occurred (out of 58) in the case of women is the number expected by chance. These included *achievement* need in the instance of attitude toward career and perception of occupation with respect to *abasement* and *aggression* in the instance of expected permanence of career. Six were reliable among the 58 comparisons involving men. But again need for achieve-

TABLE 5

Analysis of Variance Showing Relationship between Need for Achievement and Perception of the Occupations Potential for Satisfying Achievement Needs versus Attitude toward Career and Expected Permanence of Career

	Grouped by Attitude Toward Career				Grouped by Expected Permanence of Occupation			
	1 High	2 Medium	3 Low	F	1 High	2 Medium	3 Low	F
Need[a]								
Men	48.8	51.6	48.9	0.82	49.5	49.4	53.5	1.65
Women	52.0	48.1	55.3	3.19*	51.6	49.7	49.9	1
Perception[a]								
Men	6.3	7.1	4.0	3.50*	6.8	6.5	5.1	2.16
Women	7.3	5.9	5.2	2.34	6.1	6.5	5.9	1
Number of subjects								
Men	39	49	20		53	38	17	
Women	25	47	19		40	34	16	

Note. — For meaning of the groups see Table 1.
[a]Achievement.
*$p < .05$.

ment seemed to be a significant variable in work satisfaction. These included need for *change* in the instance of attitude toward career and in the same classifications perception of occupation with respect to *achievement, affiliation,* and *dominance,* and in the classifications related to attitude toward career, perception with respect to *autonomy* and *change.* As Table 5 shows, in the four comparisons involving need achievement and attitude toward career (the two sexes, need and perception), two were characterized by significant *F*s. The women who were dissatisfied had highest achievement needs, and those (both sexes, though only one reliably) who were most satisfied tended to *perceive* the occupation as potentially satisfying to the high achievement need person. No significant difference with respect to achievement need appeared when the subjects were classified according to attitude toward career.

DISCREPANCIES BETWEEN NEEDS AND NEED-SATISFACTION POTENTIAL

Although several tables of findings have already been presented the main focus of the study was the relationship between occupational satisfaction and the *discrepancy* between strength of one's needs and the perceived potential of the occupation for satisfying the particular needs.

An overall index of the degree to which the array of needs studied was viewed as being satisfiable or susceptible to frustration in the occupational context of public school teaching was computed *for each individual* by summing algebraically the discrepancies for the 14 needs (see above for description of the discrepancy score). This total index was then correlated with satisfaction-with-occupation ratings. The obtained correlations for the teacher sample of 108 men and 95 women were .25 and .02, respectively. The value for men is significantly different from zero at the .01 level of confidence (one-tailed test) while

that for women obviously is not. The two correlations differ reliably at the .01 level of confidence.

This finding may be interpreted as supporting in the case of men the general hypothesis that satisfaction with occupation is a function of the degree to which one's array of needs can be satisfied in that occupation. It should be noted that the procedure employed did not ask directly the degree to which it was expected that particular needs would be satisfied or were actually satisfied *in the occupation.* One would expect higher correlations between such an index, if it could be obtained, and satisfaction with occupation than were obtained with the present index, the obtained correlation probably being somewhat attenuated by lumping together occupationally relevant and irrelevant needs. As anticipated the correlation for women was smaller than that for men, though it had been expected that this correlation also would be reliably positive. The low correlations, even for the men, may also be attributed to the probability (suggested in a previous study by Kuhlen and Dipboye, 1959) that teachers as a group are *not* career-minded, i.e., are not the type of people who look to career as a major source of satisfaction.

To test the relationship of discrepancies between a specific need and the perceived potential of the occupation for satisfying that need, the data were dichotomized so that those individuals whose need strength equaled or was less than the potential for satisfying that need were in one group (0 or + discrepancies) and the remainder (− discrepancies) were in the second group. Occupational satisfaction ratings were dichotomized roughly at the median, with those with ratings of 9 and above falling in the top groups, numbering 71 men and 56 women. The dissatisfied had ratings of 8 or below and numbered 37 men and 39 women. The data were then classified in 2×2 tables and the null hypothesis tested by chi square. Table 6 shows the findings for those three needs where significant differ-

TABLE 6

Percentage of High and Low Occupational Satisfaction Groups with Favorable "Discrepancy" Scores

Need	Low Satisfaction (%)	High Satisfaction (%)	Chi Square	*p*
Ach				
Men	49	68	2.92	<.10 > .05
Women	48	73	4.92	<.05 > .02
Exh				
Men	57	60	.013	ns
Women	77	50	5.92	<.02 > .01
End				
Men	68	89	5.89	<.02 > .01
Women	72	88	2.74	<.10 > .05
N				
Men	37	71		
Women	39	56		

Note. — This table may be read as follows: 49% of the men who fell in the low satisfaction group had, in the case of achievement need, discrepancy scores indicating that their rating of the need-satisfaction potential of the occupation was equal to or greater than their need strength (discrepancy scores of 0 or +).

ences occurred for at least one of the sexes. It will be noted that the prediction with respect to the achievement need is supported at the .05 level in the case of women, but not in the case of men (*p* in this instance, <.10 > .05). Thus the finding gives only tenuous support to the hypothesis, though the differences were in the same direction for both sexes. It had been anticipated that the stronger relationship would hold for men.

Though no specific hypotheses were formulated with respect to endurance and exhibition, the finding is reasonable in the former. But the excess of zero or positive discrepancy scores in the *low satisfaction* group of women in the instance of the need for exhibition is hard to explain. A possible explanation is that those who see the job as a place for gaining satisfaction of this need run into other difficulties that lower their satisfactions. But it should be noted that only 5

of 58 analyses yielded significant *F*s, and thus focusing upon these differences runs considerable risk of capitalizing chance. This would not be the case in the instance of achievement need, however, since a specific prediction was made in this instance.

DISCUSSION

The findings tend to support the general hypotheses of the study in the case of men, with respect to the array of needs, and with particular reference to the achievement need regarding which a specific prediction was made. While those correlations which were significantly different from zero were low in the case of men, correlations were generally lower for women, with only an occasional *r* reaching significance. Both the low correlations for men and the less positive findings for women are reasonable in view of the fact that as already noted, a major restriction must be placed on the hypothesis that occupational satisfaction is a function of the degree to which needs are satisfied in the occupation. This hypothesis would be expected to hold only for the people, and for occupations which attract the kind of people, who view occupation and career as a major source of need gratification; i.e., people for whom career and occupation have high "saliency." Other evidence (Kuhlen and Dipboye, 1959) suggests that career is less salient for teachers than for other occupational groups. Also occupation appears to be clearly a secondary role for women (i.e., not a primary source of need gratification), especially for *young* single teachers and for married teachers (Kuhlen and Johnson, 1952).

Although the present study was conducted with subjects homogeneous with respect to occupation, it would be expected that the major hypothesis relating to the array of needs would also be supported, and probably more clearly, in an occupationally heterogeneous sample. The major hypothesis does not, and need not, specify particular needs; but only that occupationally relevant "needs" in general must be satisfied in the occupation if satisfaction is to be found. Findings which relate to the relationship of frustration or satisfaction of *particular* needs might be expected to be relatively specific to the occupation, and presumably would be suggestive of potential tension areas, worthy of attention of workers, of those selecting personnel, of supervisors in that occupation, or of those concerned with assisting young people to sound vocational decisions. In certain situations, for example, it is probably undesirable to employ people with particular need patterns. For many jobs, the ambitious man, the aggressive, dominant go-getter, may be an extremely poor choice. And not infrequently there is a conflict between the type of person needed to do a particular job and the potential of the position for satisfying fundamental career needs of the person who can do that job.

[1]Heterosexual needs, though included in Edwards scale, was not included in the present scale because of the disruptive influence occasioned by the humorous reaction generated by a trial form.

[2]In this connection, it is of interest that only nine men and five women rated their positions as less satisfactory than the typical teaching position.

REFERENCES

Brayfield, A. H., Wells, R. V., and Strate, M. W. Interrelationships among measures of job satisfaction and general satisfaction. *J. appl. Psychol.*, 1957, *41*, 201–208.

Edwards, A. L. *Edwards Personal Preference Schedule (manual).* New York: Psychological Corporation, 1954.

Johnson, G. H. An instrument for the measurement of job satisfaction. *Personnel Psychol.*, 1955, *8*, 27–38.

Kuhlen, R. G., and Dipboye, W. J. Motivational and personality factors in the selection of elementary and secondary school teaching as a career. Technical report, 1959, United States Office of Education Cooperative Research Program, Washington, D.C.

Kuhlen, R. G., and Johnson, G. H. Changes in goals with increasing adult age. *J. consult. Psychol.*, 1952, *16*, 1–4.

Ort, R. S. A study of role-conflicts as related to happiness in marriage. *J. abnorm. soc. Psychol.*, 1950, *45*, 691–699.

Schaffer, R. H. Job satisfaction as related to need satisfaction in work. *Psychol. Monogr.*, 1953, *67* (14, Whole No. 364).

Strong, E. K., Jr. *Vocational interests 18 years after college.* Minneapolis: Univer. Minnesota Press, 1955.

Motivational Factors among
Supervisors in the Utility Industry

MILTON M. SCHWARTZ, *Rutgers, The State University*

EDMUND JENUSAITIS, *Rutgers, The State University*

HARRY STARK, *Rutgers, The State University*

The rapid growth of interest in social and psychological variables such as attitudes, values and needs among all levels of industrial personnel is reflected in an extensive literature which describes a variety of investigative techniques. These devices, frequently of a psychometric nature, seem to be more useful and effective in attitude and morale surveys than in disclosing motivational factors in the work environment.

The present study is an extension of a major portion of *Motivation to Work* by Herzberg, *et al.*, 1959, and is more directly concerned with motivational factors in the work situation. Herzberg, *et al.*, utilized a somewhat impure but emergent and promising investigative procedure that appears to extend the meaning of motivational variables pertinent to the work situation. It focuses specifically on the motivation of accountants and engineers and utilizes a semi-standardized interview method similar to Flanagan's "critical-incident" technique (Flanagan, 1954, pp. 327–358). Essentially the interviewee must recall two experiences, one pleasant and the other unpleasant, from his employment tenure. A logical scoring system was developed by the authors consisting of 16 "first-level" and 12 "second-level" motivational "factors" (Herzberg, *et*

Reprinted with the permission of authors and publisher from the article of the same title, in *Personnel Psychology*, 1963, *16*, 45–53.

al., 1959, p. 37). The first five factors listed in the first column of Table 1 were identified by the authors as appearing most frequently and as related to the job itself. The authors concluded that the remaining eleven factors were more related to "the characteristics of the context in which the job is done" (Herzberg, *et al.*, 1959, p. 63). The separately reported job experiences, pleasant and unpleasant, were designated as "high" or "low" job attitude sequences and each was scored as some combination of the 16 first-level factors.

The two groups of factors, job-centered and context-centered, related differentially to expressed experiences. Context-centered factors tended to be associated more frequently with attitudes of job dissatisfaction whereas feelings of satisfaction were closely related to job-centered factors. The implication of particular significance in their findings is that conditions of work become important when poor or inadequate, but such context factors when high do not contribute significantly to satisfaction. Work satisfaction, however, is related to the job itself. These findings go beyond the enumeration of needs and need strength. A recent review of *Motivation to Work* stated that it was a promising book both methodologically and substantively. Of more direct pertinence was the reviewer's statement that "perhaps the single most important finding from this work is that satisfaction and dissatisfaction

TABLE 1

Scoring Categories for Total Study Including First-Level Factors, Edwards Personal Preference Schedule, and Non-Test Items

First-Level Job-Attitude Factors	Personal Preference Test Categories	Non-Test Items
†1. Achievement	1. Achievement	1. Union Membership
†2. Recognition	2. Deference	2. Age
†3. Work itself	3. Order	3. Length of Supervisory Experience
†4. Responsibility	4. Exhibition	4. Supervisory Level
†5. Advancement	5. Autonomy	5. Department
6. Salary	6. Affiliation	6. Education
7. Possibility of Growth	7. Intraception	
8. Interpersonal Relations — subordinate	8. Succorance	
9. Status	9. Dominance	
10. Interpersonal Relations — superior	10. Abasement	
11. Interpersonal Relations — peers	11. Nurturance	
12. Supervision — technical	12. Change	
13. Company policy and administration	13. Endurance	
14. Working conditions	14. Heterosexuality	
15. Personal life	15. Aggression	
16. Job security		

†Job-related factors. Others in this column are context-related.

on the job are caused by different factors rather than by varying amounts of the same factors" (Kahn, 1961).

PROCEDURE

Because of the apparent potential of this method of inquiry coupled with the highly suggestive finding, it was felt that the major aspect of this research should be the subject of further study incorporating certain changes. Accordingly, men with a supervisory responsibility in different and largely non-professional occupational groups were selected. The Herzberg subjects were primarily non-supervisory professionals, but the question of supervisory status apparently did not enter into their study design.

Another change required that the respondents write their two experiences rather than state them orally as in an interview. A final modification of the original method involved restriction of scoring to the 16 first-level factors, omitting the other twelve second-level factors. No serious loss was felt to derive from these changes, as our intent was to keep the method as direct and objective as possible without fundamentally altering the original experimental procedure. Other omissions were deliberately made since they were beyond the particular focus of our interest. These included such aspects of the job-attitude sequence analyses as "duration" and "effects" of each sequence. On the other hand, two sets of independent variables which did not appear in Herzberg's book were introduced in a further effort to explore and possibly clarify the meaning of the factors. The first set of variables was based on the utilization of the Edwards Personal Preference Schedule and consisted of its 15 scoring categories (Edwards, 1959). The rationale for the selection of this instrument stems from the desire for an objective outside measure of "need," permitting direct comparison of the two sets of motivational constructs. The second set of variables which were compared with the factors of this study consisted of six non-test items describing the background and status of the subject.

Table 1 lists the materials of the study. The first column is based upon the open-end job-attitude sequences and contains the 16 logical scoring categories originally contrived by Herzberg for scoring the interviews. The second column names the 15 Edwards scoring categories, and the last column lists the six non-test items selected on the basis of their pertinence to the present design.

The subjects consisted of 111 male supervisors, all of whom were employees of 21 public utility (electric and/or gas) companies from the Middle Atlantic and New England states. These men were enrolled in a management training program conducted by the management services section of the Rutgers University Extension Division during the academic year 1960–1961. They were distributed among ten one-week training units, each of which had an enrollment of between 20–30 supervisors. The age range was 27–62 years with a mean of 40. Half the group had some college education, but only a few had not finished high school. Of those with some college, 31 were graduates. The men were drawn from basic supervisory and lower middle management levels — that is, from line foreman to assistant district superintendent.

The men represented a comprehensive range of utility work operations, including generation, distribution, construction, commercial, and engineering activities. The typical supervisor was a long-service employee in an industry noted for low personnel turnover and a high security and stability emphasis. These characteristics were uniformly present in all participating firms, which significantly share the same basic and applied technology, market situation, and legal restrictions. These and other common features provide a remarkable degree of situational homogeneity which the authors believe to be of great importance. With "all other things" being reasonably equal due to a highly uniform economic and technical environment, critical examination of organizational variables and human response is more likely to be valid.

The tests were administered in a group setting after the first day of classes, the job-attitude sequence on the second day and the preference schedule the third day. No test resistance was encountered. In fact, the supervisors generally maintained an enthusiastic interest. Anonymity was guaranteed by the investigator who assured the subjects that the data would remain under his control, that individual results would under no circumstances be released to their employees, and that the research focus was on group results. Scoring of the job attitude sequences and the preference schedule was based directly on the standard methods prescribed by the authors.

Instructions for the "high" job-attitude sequence were: "Please think of a time when you felt exceptionally good about your job. Tell what happened during this period. Tell something about what made you begin to feel so good, about what happened to end this feeling (if it has ended). If your feelings affected the way you worked, try to give as detailed an example as possible." Instructions for the "low" sequences were identical with the above except that the word "bad" was substituted wherever the word "good" appeared. A separate page was given for the subjects to write each experience.

Of the 111 subjects who completed the job-attitude sequence, 75 completed the preference schedule as well. The 111 job-attitude protocols were subjected to a chi-square analysis as shown in Table 2.

The purpose was to determine whether job-related or context-related factors were associated with high or low-job-attitude sequences. To further check on this relationship, the results of this study were compared with those of the Herzberg study in which the frequency of occurrence of each of the first-level factors was tabulated independently (cf. Herzberg, *et al.*, 1959, p. 72) for the high and for the low job-attitude sequences. The results are shown in Table 3.

TABLE 2

Chi Square for Job-Related and Context Related Factors and High and Low Job-Attitude Sequences ($N = 111$)

	Job-Attitude Sequences	
	Low	High
Job-Related Factors	29	59
Context-Related Factors	41	8
Mixed (Job and Context)	32	41

$df = 2$, chi square $= 35.42$, $p < .01$.

TABLE 3

Percentage Comparison of Each First-Level Factor Appearing in High and Low Job Attitude Sequences in Herzberg's Study with this Study[1] ($N = 111$)

	High		Low	
First-Level Factors	Herzberg	Present Study	Herzberg	Present Study
†1. Achievement	41**	55**	7	19
†2. Recognition	33**	44**	18	22
†3. Work itself	26**	12	14	13
†4. Responsibility	23**	23**	6	5
†5. Advancement	20**	20**	11	8
6. Salary	15	8	17	5
7. Possibility of Growth	6	9**	8	1
8. Interpersonal Relations — subordinate	6	23**	3	15
9. Status	4	1	4	4
10. Interpersonal Relations — superior	4	14	15**	16
11. Interpersonal Relations — peers	3	4	8**	3
12. Supervision — technical	3	1	20**	14**
13. Company policy and administration	3	7	31**	25**
14. Working conditions	1	0	11**	12**
15. Personal life	1	1	6**	3
16. Job security	1	0	1	5**

[1]The percentages total more than 100 per cent since more than one factor can appear in any single sequence of events.

†Job-related factors. Others are context-related.

**Differences between high and low statistically significant at .01 level of confidence.

Finally, intercorrelations were computed between both the high and low first-level factors and each of the remaining variables, namely the 15 preference schedule categories and the six non-test items. Thus, 21 variables were compared to each of the 16 high first-level factors and 16 low first-level factors, making 21×32 comparisons or

672 correlations. Only the 75 subjects who had completed all tests were included in the analysis. The processing of these data was carried out at the Rutgers University Computation Center utilizing the 650 IBM Data Processing Machine.

RESULTS

The results of the comparison of the job attitude factors with the "criterion" variables were essentially negative. There were fewer significant intercorrelations than might be expected by chance. The authors felt that, had certain patterns of relationship emerged between the test and non-test variables and the job-attitude factors, they would have served to clarify and validate the meaningfulness of the logically-derived job-attitude factors of the original study. The absence of relationship of the open-end free recall type "test" to empirically-assembled forced-choice multiple-choice scoring categories of a standardized test is not altogether surprising in light of somewhat similar reported researches, as for example when projective and objective test scoring categories are statistically compared.

Although such observations are speculative, it may be that the shared environmental context not only adds to the soundness of the primary conclusions, but also is sufficiently dominant to overcome and mask effects expected from the preference schedule and non-test variables. Thus the high degree of homogeneity may logically account for the absence of correlation. It may also be that broader and fewer factor groupings than the sixteen used in both the Herzberg and the present studies would reveal some correlation, especially with a larger number of respondents.

Examination of Tables 2 and 3 generally substantiates the findings of the Herzberg study. The highly significant chi-square in Table 2 supports the conclusion that job- and context-related factors are differentially associated with good and bad job experiences. Most pleasant (i.e., high) experiences were related to conditions of the job itself and, conversely, unpleasant (i.e., low) experiences went together with factors in the work environment. This is also seen in Table 3 which compares the major findings of the two studies. The trend of agreement of this and Herzberg's findings is all the more meaningful in view of the differences in the two samples as well as the modified method of gathering the data in the present study.

Results of the Herzberg study (Table 3) show that percentages in all five job-related factors are significantly greater in high than in low sequences. In the present study, four of the five job-related factors show the same results. The similarity, though not as great, is also seen for the context cluster. Here the Herzberg study shows six context-related factors having significantly higher percentages in the low sequences whereas the present study shows only four factors, of which three correspond with those of Herzberg.

There is one intriguing difference, evident from Table 3, between the findings of the Herzberg study and the present inquiry. For the Herzberg group of accountants and engineers, interpersonal relations with superiors and peers were significant factors in the low sequences, while for utility supervisors in the present study interpersonal relationships with subordinates was a significant factor in the high sequences. We do not now have sufficient evidence to explain this variation, but it seems logical that the leadership component of the utility positions was rather clearly evident in contrast to the upward orientation of more professionally conscious non-supervisory technicians in the Herzberg sample. The utility supervisors most frequently came up "through the ranks" and had a common background and close identity with their subordinates. Homogeneity may also be an influence here since utility supervisors share with both superiors and subordinates the public service consciousness and pride in uninterrupted work flow apparently typical in the industry.

These speculations also bear on the contrast between the Herzberg findings and the present study with respect to "the work itself" and the "possibility of growth." The utility group showed growth as a significant factor in the high sequences, with the work itself not significant, a reversal of the Herzberg results. This also defies interpretation on the evidence, and the situation is further confused by some lack of specificity in the Herzberg book (Herzberg, *et al.*, 1959) concerning the definition of job-related and contextual elements. However, it is quite likely that the identification of non-supervisory professionals with their disciplines accounts, in part at least, for the differential findings of the two studies with respect to the "work itself" factor.

SUMMARY

The present study is an extension of a major portion of the technique reported in Herzberg, *et al.* (1959), utilizing supervisors as subjects from separate but substantially homogeneous environments and involving two additional sets of independent variables. The current findings strongly support the conclusions of the previous study, identifying job-related factors with positive work experiences and contextual factors with negative experiences. Further, no variation was found in terms of subjects' age, job classification, education, personality characteristics, etc. The study also demonstrates that a simplified methodology produces effective results and suggests that less refined "factor" definitions may be more useful.

The validation of basic findings indicates the value of future research to test the effects of supervisory status and environmental homogeneity. The possibility of controlled experiments by manipulation of contextual factors within such an environment also warrants investigation. Such research can be directed toward both organizational analysis and administrative practice through identifying causal relationships between motivational response and intrinsic and situational determinants.

REFERENCES

Edwards, A. L. *Manual for the Edwards Personal Preference Schedule* (Revised). New York: Psychological Corporation, 1959.

Flanagan, J. C. "The Critical Incidents Technique." *Psychological Bulletin*, LI (1954), 327–358.

Herzberg, F., Mausner, B., and Snyderman, P. D. *The Motivation to Work*. New York: John Wiley & Sons, 1959.

Kahn, R. L. Review of *Motivation to Work*. *Contemporary Psychology*, January, 1961.

Some Determinants
of Job Satisfaction:
A Study of the Generality
of Herzberg's Theory[1]

ROBERT B. EWEN, *University of Illinois*

A recent study by Herzberg, Mausner, and Snyderman (1959) found that the determinants of job satisfaction ("satisfiers") were qualitatively different from the determinants of job dissatisfaction ("dissatisfiers"). It was stated that:

the three factors of work itself, responsibility, and advancement stand out strongly as the major factors involved in producing high job attitudes. Their role in producing poor job attitudes is by contrast extremely small. Contrariwise, company policy and administration, supervision (both technical and interpersonal relationships), and working conditions represent the major job dissatisfiers with little potency to affect job attitudes in a positive direction. . . . Poor working conditions, bad company policies and administration, and bad supervision will lead to job dissatisfaction. Good company policies, good administration, good supervision, and good working conditions will not lead to positive job attitudes. In opposition to this . . . recognition, achievement, interesting work, responsibility, and advancement all lead to positive job attitudes. Their absence will much less frequently lead to job dissatisfaction [pp. 81–82].

From: Ewen, R. B., Some determinants of job satisfaction: A study of the generality of Herzberg's theory, *Journal of Applied Psychology*, *48*, 1964, 161–163. Copyright 1964 by the American Psychological Association, and reproduced by permission.

It was also stated that:

It would seem that as an affector of job attitudes salary has more potency as a job dissatisfier than as a job satisfier [p. 82].

These findings are in direct opposition to the traditional idea that a given variable in the work situation can cause both job satisfaction and job dissatisfaction.

It is in general difficult to compare the results of other research to the findings of Herzberg et al. (1959). For example, supervision is a dissatisfier in the Herzberg schema. However, the supervisor may be a source of recognition, which is satisfying. Similarly, salary is a dissatisfier, but it may represent achievement and recognition, which are satisfiers. Such distinctions have usually not been made in other studies. Therefore, this discussion will concentrate primarily on the Herzberg study.

Various procedures of questionable merit were used in the Herzberg study. Some of these may have been responsible for the singular results that were obtained.

NARROW RANGE OF JOBS INVESTIGATED
The Herzberg study investigated only engineers and accountants, which represents only a small sample of the jobs which might have been studied. Data obtained from nine different locations were combined into one

analysis, and consequently the effect of different situations could not be ascertained. Herzberg et al. (1959) attempted to demonstrate the generality of their findings by tracing the history of human work and showing that they could account for various historical phenomena in terms of their theory. This does not constitute an adequate test of the generality of the theory. It is necessary to replicate the findings with different workers in different job situations, but the authors did not do this. Instead, suggestions and prescriptions were made for industry on the basis of the one study (Herzberg et al., 1959, pp. 120 ff.).

USE OF ONLY ONE MEASURE OF JOB ATTITUDES The Herzberg study used only a semistructured interview to measure job attitudes. This would be acceptable if the study were only of an exploratory nature. In view of the high generality ascribed by the authors to the results, however, the single method of measurement raises questions as to the generality and validity of the findings. The problems of attitude measurement have not as yet been completely resolved and no one method has been shown to be adequate. The need for more than one method of measurement has been effectively argued by Campbell and Fiske (1959).

It is possible that some or all of the Herzberg results were due to the method of measurement that was used. The method was a critical incidents technique; subjects (*S*s) told of times when they were particularly happy (or unhappy) and described the cause of their feelings. This procedure could have led to biased results. For example, achievement and advancement were found to be satisfiers. It is likely that when these variables are causes of satisfaction, a critical incident will occur (the employee finishes a difficult job or he is promoted). However, it is difficult to see what incidents would accompany no achievement, or not being promoted. Hence, the critical incidents technique would make it appear as if these variables caused only satisfaction,

since only then would a critical incident occur. This is of course only speculation, but the possibility of bias due to the method of measurement employed cannot be discounted when only one method is used.

NO VALIDITY AND RELIABILITY DATA Herzberg et al. (1959) presented no evidence for the validity of the semistructured interview used in their study. No parallel-form or test-retest reliability coefficients were reported.

NO MEASURE OF OVERALL SATISFACTION Inasmuch as the Herzberg study claimed that satisfiers caused job satisfaction and dissatisfiers caused job dissatisfaction, it would seem desirable to have included measures of overall job satisfaction in the study, but this was not done. Thus, there is no basis for assuming that the factors described in the critical incidents caused overall job satisfaction (or dissatisfaction). Smith and Kendall (1963) have shown that a worker may dislike some aspects of his job yet still think that it is acceptable overall because "as jobs go, this isn't bad." Similarly, workers may dislike the job despite many desirable characteristics. Likert (1961), questioning the merit of rank-order studies of the determinants of job satisfaction, made a similar point:

if employees say that the thing they like best about their job situation is the clean, well-lighted space in which to work, it does not follow that this factor is most important in producing favorable over-all attitudes. It is even possible that those who give this as their first choice have the least favorable over-all attitudes toward the company. Similarly, the items which are reacted to least favorably cannot be interpreted as the variables which are most important in producing the unfavorable over-all attitudes. . . . It is not the level of favorableness or unfavorableness of response to an item which shows the importance of that item in influencing the over-all job attitudes. Its importance is revealed by the extent to which it is correlated with the total or over-all job attitude score [p. 195].

It is evident, then, that Herzberg, et al. have made statements about the causes of overall job satisfaction and dissatisfaction without having any data relevant to overall job satisfaction and dissatisfaction on which to base the conclusions.

The recommendations and generalizations made by Herzberg and associates are unjustified in view of the limitations described above. In fact, the authors have disregarded their own statement about the need for further research in new situations (Herzberg et al., 1959, p. 102).

The Herzberg procedure may be contrasted with that of the Cornell Studies of Job Satisfaction. In this investigation, the researchers used the multitrait-multimethod technique of Campbell and Fiske (1959), and took the trouble to determine the convergent and discriminant validity of their four measures of five aspects of job satisfaction (Macaulay, Smith, Locke, Kendall, and Hulin, 1963) as well as obtaining other estimates of validity (Kendall, Smith, Hulin, and Locke, 1963). In the introduction to the Cornell studies, Smith (1963) stated that

Since generality across a wide range of situations was of primary importance, each step in the construction and validation of the scales was undertaken in a new situation, as different as possible from those used in preceding steps. Thus . . . mean annual earnings for men in the different plants ranged from $3,080 to $8,300, locations ranged from Massachusetts to Tennessee, size of plant varied from 79 to 4,000 employees, and percentage of female employees was from 0 to 50%, with some non-union plants and some closed shops. Individual levels of education ranged from 0 to 20 years, and jobs from janitor to top management [p. 12].

The present writer conducted an exploratory study in an attempt to determine the generality of the Herzberg theory. Responses of 1,021 full-time life insurance agents to a 58-item four-point anonymous attitude scale were obtained. The Ss were divided into two groups, one of 541 Ss who answered in 1962 and one of 480 Ss who answered in 1960. The 1960 group served as a cross-validation sample. For the 1962 sample, the data were factor analyzed by the method of principal components (unities in the diagonal) and rotated by the varimax method (cf. Harman, 1960). Six clearly interpretable factors emerged: Manager Interest in Agents, Company Training Policies, and Salary (dissatisfiers); The Work Itself and Prestige or Recognition (satisfiers); and General Morale and Satisfaction.

The following analysis was conducted for each satisfier and dissatisfier. The Ss were divided into subgroups which were satisfied, neutral, or dissatisfied with respect to the satisfier or dissatisfier in question. The neutral group consisted of those Ss who checked either of the two middle points of the four-point scale. The general satisfaction of the satisfied and dissatisfied groups was compared to the general satisfaction of the neutral group by using t tests of significance. The attribute not tested was held constant; e.g., if the effect of a satisfier was being investigated, only Ss who were neutral on the dissatisfiers were used.

The results indicated that Manager Interest in Agents and Training, supposedly dissatisfiers, actually acted like satisfiers in both groups. Salary also acted like a satisfier in the 1960 group; in the 1962 group, salary caused both job satisfaction and job dissatisfaction. In both samples, the Work Itself was a satisfier as the Herzberg theory predicted; but Prestige or Recognition caused both satisfaction and dissatisfaction. This study, however, has some of the same deficiencies as the Herzberg study, and is hardly conclusive. The same is true for a recent study by Schwartz, Jenusaitis, and Stark (1963), who used essentially the same methods that were used in the Herzberg study and obtained results which supported most of the Herzberg results.

A more extensive research design is necessary in order to adequately test the Herzberg theory. For the present, however, it must be concluded that the nature of satisfiers and dissatisfiers (if such variables do in fact exist) is as yet far from clear, and may be different in different jobs. Further research is necessary in different occupational situations before any definite statements about the problem are made. There is as yet no justification for generalizing the Herzberg results beyond the situation in which they were obtained.

REFERENCES

Campbell, D. T., and Fiske, D. W. Convergent and discriminant validation by the multitrait-multimethod matrix. *Psychol. Bull.*, 1959, *56*, 81–105.

Harman, H. H. *Modern factor analysis.* Chicago: Univer. Chicago Press, 1960.

Herzberg, F., Mausner, B., and Snyderman, Barabara B. *The motivation to work.* New York: Wiley, 1959.

Kendall, L. M., Smith, Patricia C., Hulin, C. L., and Locke, E. A. Cornell studies of job satisfaction: IV. The relative validity of the job descriptive index and other

methods of measurement of job satisfaction. Ithaca: Cornell University, 1963. (Mimeo)

Likert, R. *New patterns of management.* New York: McGraw-Hill, 1961.

Macaulay, D. Anne, Smith, Patricia C., Locke, E. A., Kendall, L. M., and Hulin, C. L. Cornell studies of job satisfaction: III. Convergent and discriminant validity for measures of job satisfaction by rating scales. Ithaca: Cornell University, 1963. (Mimeo)

Schwartz, M. M., Jenusaitis, E., and Stark, H. Motivational factors among supervisors in the utility industry. *Personnel Psychol.*, 1963, *16*, 45–53.

Smith, Patricia C. Cornell studies of job satisfaction: I. Strategy for the development of a general theory of job satisfaction. Ithaca: Cornell University, 1963. (Mimeo)

Smith, Patricia C., and Kendall, L. M. Cornell studies of job satisfaction: VI. Implications for the future. Ithaca: Cornell University, 1963. (Mimeo)

Effects of Community Characteristics on Measures of Job Satisfaction

CHARLES L. HULIN, *University of Illinois*

The influence of community characteristics on job satisfaction and job performance has been documented empirically by Cure-

From: Hulin, C. L., Effects of community characteristics on measures of job satisfaction, *Journal of Applied Psychology, 50*, 1966, 185–192. Copyright 1966 by the American Psychological Association, and reproduced by permission.

ton and Katzell (1962), Katzell, Barrett, and Parker (1961), and Kendall (1963), and has been discussed by Hulin (1963b) and Worthy (1950) in somewhat more speculative papers. Katzell et al. (1961) and Cureton and Katzell were interested in the possible use of community characteristics as moderator variables. That is, variables which would serve to moderate the direction and strength of the relationship between job satisfaction and certain behavioral variables such as job performance, absences, and turnover. Katzell et al. (1961) found, for example, that the average group satisfaction scores and the group productivity of warehouse workers were positively related to each other. They regarded this positive correlation as dependent on the relationship of the two variables to certain situational characteristics. In their sample of warehouses both satisfaction and productivity were negatively related to size of work force, city size, and degree of unionization. These complex relationships appeared more clearly in an oblique re-rotation of the two centroid factors which they had extracted originally from their set of situational measures. Cureton and Katzell (1962) concluded that the nonurban culture pattern which had originally been discussed by Katzell et al. may be best thought of as being made up of two positively correlated aspects, one reflecting a small plant and small community syndrome and the other reflecting a female employee syndrome. Both of these factors were related to the job satisfaction and job performance of the work groups. Their explanation for this finding was that in small-town cultures the needs and expectations of the workers are such that the workers view high productivity as a means to the desirable end of high rewards. Katzell et al. also state that the nature of the retailing industry affords conditions for positively correlated performance and satisfaction varying with employee motivations. It is of interest to note that job performance (behavior in the job situation) was unrelated to turnover (behavior directed toward leaving the situation).

Kendall (1963), however, was concerned with using community characteristics to index frames of reference of the workers and the alternatives available to them in the community. With this as his theoretical framework, Kendall used canonical regression to analyze the data obtained from a nation-wide study of job and retirement satisfcation. His data were gathered from an initial sample of 1,008 male workers drawn from 21 different plants, a replication sample of 1,002 male workers and a generalization sample of 642 female workers from the same sample of 21 plants. He found that measures of satisfaction with various aspects of the job bear *no* relationship to measures of performance and absences even under conditions designed to maximize such relationships (canonical correlations). He found, however, that "satisfactoriness" (high performance and low absence rates) was related to personal background variables; high absence rates were related to unattractive community features; and high performance was related to personal background and unattractive community features. More importantly (for the purposes of this study) he found that high general job satisfaction, high satisfaction with the pay received, and high satisfaction with the work done on the job were related to unattractive community features.[1]

Worthy (1950) discussed in a speculative and qualitative paper many of the relationships which Katzell et al. obtained in their sample of warehouse work groups. He was mainly concerned with the interrelationships between morale, performance, and situational characteristics for employees of a large retailing establishment. Still along the same lines, Hulin (1963b) presented a model which utilized both plant variables (i.e., size, union management relationships, wage rate, etc.) and community characteristics (urban-rural dimensions, unemployment, etc.) as moderator variables which should serve to moderate the relationship between job satisfaction and job performance. In this model it was hypothesized that community characteristics and the personal characteristics of the workers would exert their strongest affect on the relationship between satisfaction and behavior directed toward leaving the situation (turnover, absences, lateness) while plant characteristics would exert their strongest affect on the relationship between satisfaction and behavior in the situation (job performance).

It has been stressed on numerous occasions that job satisfaction must be considered as a feeling which has arisen in the worker as a response to the total job situation. In addition to being related to the present job situation, this feeling is associated with perceived differences between what the worker expects for his services and what he actually experiences *in relation to the alternatives available to him*. The Cornell Studies of Job Satisfaction, begun in 1959, represent one intensive program of research developed within this framework (See Hulin and Smith, 1965; Smith, Kendall, and Hulin, in press). These investigators have utilized variables such as age or tenure, and education to index changing expectation-experience discrepancies and community variables to index the alternatives open to the worker and to index the frame of reference established by the community. The results of these studies have generally been in the expected direction if the problem of nonequivalence of measures is considered. If these formulations of job satisfaction are correct, and if the results obtained have generality to other jobs, other workers, and other situations, then two predictions could be made regarding satisfaction and community characteristics.

1. Measures of job satisfaction should be associated with community variables which reflect the prosperity, the extent of the slums, the amount of productive farming, and the amount of unemployment in the area. The direction of this association should be that more attractive community features lead to lower satisfaction values. This prediction stems directly from the conviction that a worker's feelings of satisfaction do not arise out of context. Rather, the worker evaluates his present position in the context of the alternatives open to him. If he lives in a slum, in a poor community, or in a community in which there is a great deal of unemployment, even if he has a relatively poor job, he is probably better off than any of his neighbors. Essentially, in a slum there are no alternatives that offer a better life. This same worker in a prosperous community would be relatively less well off. We would expect his satisfaction to be lower also. This is not to say that the *residents* of a slum or a poor community are more satisfied than they would be if they lived in a prosperous community. We are concerned only with workers who live in slums in comparison to residents of prosperous communities who have similar jobs.

2. Measures of a worker's satisfaction with his pay should be more strongly associated with community characteristics than are the other aspects of job satisfaction. In a prosperous community a worker's pay level is made very clear to him by the goods and services purchased by other members of the community as compared to what he is able to purchase. Feelings toward this aspect of a worker's job should be affected more strongly by the community characteristics since his pay level and his identification as "an employee of Company X" are the only aspects of the job that the worker *must* take with him when he leaves the plant gate.

The present research was designed to assess the validity of these two predictions when applied to groups of white collar (sales) personnel employed by a large retail sales organization. This research design is similar to the Katzell et al. study in that only employees from one company are studied and group satisfaction and performance measures were used. The present research has the added advantage of controlling to a great extent the urban-rural dimension whose affects were discussed by Katzell et al. This research should then be considered as a replication and extension of the work first reported by Kendall (1963) and represents a more detailed exploration of specific relations suggested only tentatively by the previous work. Both of the hypotheses as well as the methods of indexing community characteristics can be traced to his dissertation. Thus, while there are differences in approach, this research fits into the framework of the Cornell Studies on Job Satisfaction.

METHOD

Research Setting

This study was conducted in a large merchandising and retail company. This company establishes a regular retail outlet store in communities which are large enough to support such an enterprise. The company has a large number of catalog order establishments (COEs) in addition to these retail stores. These COEs are located in small communities which are not large enough to support the operation of a regular retail outlet store. The function of these offices is to provide outlets for the store's merchandise through sales catalogs and the employees are mainly to provide assistance in completing catalog orders and to perform the usual routine duties of sales personnel. The personnel of these COEs consists of a supervisor and a number of female sales persons, the size of the staff varying with the demand in the area. The average number of employees at these offices is about 6.5 with a standard deviation of about 3.8.

The data to be reported in this study were gathered from 300 of these COEs. This sample of 300 COEs represented a geographically stratified random sample of the population of the COEs operated by the company. The COEs were stratified on the basis of the home store to which they were attached and 30% of the COEs from each area were drawn. Within the company structure many of the day-to-day decisions are left to the discretion of the local managers. Thus, while the company policies under which the employees work are constant throughout the sample, the store level practices may be somewhat different depending on the store manager.

Community Characteristics

The number of community variables which could reasonably be measured in a study of this type is too large to be handled efficiently by any model relating satisfaction to productivity and/or situational variables. A taxonomy of community variables developed by Kendall (1963) from a principal component analysis of the intercorrelations of 55 per capita census variables from 370 countries originally presented by Johnson (1958) was employed. As far as possible the variables suggested by Kendall to index the community dimensions were used. No claim is made that this taxonomy is *the* way to describe population units. These variates were chosen because, for the purposes of this study, they seemed to be measuring those aspects to the community which would be most salient to the workers living in the area. Although there are always problems involved in using the results of an analysis not designed to answer the questions must crucial to your problem, the savings in clerical labor, money, and time are sufficient to enable one to make the compromise. The first three variates described below are intended to index the general economic situation of the community. The third variable, unemployment, was included to index job opportunities in the community. The last two variates were included for general interest value.

Values for each of the community characteristics to be described below were taken from the publications of the United States Bureau of the Census (1962) or United States Department of Commerce (1963). In the case of "degree days" the value for the adjacent county was taken if there was no weather station established in the county in question.

SLUMS This variate is indexed by "per cent non-white" and "per cent owner occupied housing" (reversed scoring).

PROSPERITY The general prosperity of the community is indexed by "median income per family," "per cent earning over $10,000," "per cent sound housing," and "per capita retail sales."

PRODUCTIVE FARMING This aspect of the community's economic condition is indexed by "median rural income per family."

UNEMPLOYMENT The amount of unemployment in the community is measured by the percentage of the population over 14 who were not "at work" but were looking for work (in 1960).

DECREPITUDE This variate is indexed by "per cent sixty-five and over" and "per capita heart deaths." Decrepitude was included in this analysis in an attempt to obtain a variable which would be likely to make a community a relatively unpleasant place in which to live and which should be independent of economic variables.

NORTHERN MALE WORK FORCE This aspect of the community is measured by "per cent male workers" and "degree days." This variate was included to give some indication of the industrially oriented northern communities as opposed to the southern communities with their more pastorale orientation.

Office Variables

Several variables related to the immediate work environment in the COE were obtained. These variables, which are described below, were included in order to assess the amount of business handled, the efficiency of the office, and the number of employees working at the office. In all cases the measures of these variables were taken from the company records.

GROSS DEMAND (1962) The gross demand made on any office is obtained by assessing the worth of the orders handled by the COE during 1962 (the year during which

the morale survey was made). While this quantity is an accurate reflection of the volume of business done by the office, it is not a reflection of the efficiency of the work force.

PERCENTAGE OF INCREASE IN GROSS DEMAND 1961–1962 Payroll and social security taxes/gross demand. Payroll and social security taxes divided by gross demand was included as an assessment of the relative efficiency of the staff of the COE (group productivity). Only by handling a greater volume of orders with the same staff or reducing the staff for a given volume of orders could the manager of the office change the value of this ratio. A low value of this index represents an efficient staff.

RETURNS/GROSS DEMAND The dollar value of the returned merchandise as a function of gross demand would be a reflection in a COE setting of the quality of work turned out by the employees. Low values indicate high quality work. Since there are many variables affecting returns, this is likely a crude estimate at best.

Satisfaction Measures

The satisfaction measures to be reported in this study are taken from a survey made by the company during 1962. These surveys are made periodically by the company and the employees have come to accept them as a matter of course. The questionnaires are treated anonymously by the company and are intended purely as aids to better working relationships between management and the workers.

The specific job satisfaction questionnaire employed was developed by the company for its own needs. The questions in this inventory are directed toward nine different content areas. These content areas (supervision, kind of work, amount of work, coworkers, working conditions, pay, career and security, company identification, and organizational effectiveness) are measured in two different ways. One set of questions is descriptively worded and asks the worker to describe different aspects of his work. A second set of questions over the content areas is evaluatively worded and asks for evaluations of these same aspects (see Yuzuk, 1961). The questionnaire generally displays adequate convergent validity but the discriminant validity tends to be less impressive. Nonetheless, it was felt that this instrument would yield a reasonable estimate of the overall job satisfaction of these work groups. The discrimination between the areas of satisfaction might not be as clear cut.

These variables were intercorrelated using Pearson product-moment correlations in all cases.

RESULTS

A 34×34 intercorrelation matrix was the result of this analysis. The correlations in this matrix represent the relationships between the average values of variables associated with each of the offices and not the individual employees of the offices.[3] A general inspection of this matrix revealed several relationships of general interest. The variables chosen to index the extent of slums, prosperity, and productive farming of the community are more closely related than one would like under ideal conditions. The present sample of COEs *does not* represent a random sample of communities. *None* of the large metropolitan centers of the United States is represented in these data. This deliberate over-sampling of the rural areas and small towns is because the COEs are located in these areas. This amount of bias may well have affected these relationships.

A second point of general interest is the submatrix of intercorrelations between the measures of job satisfaction. For the most part these different measures indicate adequate convergent validity. The average heteromethod-monotrait (Campbell and Fiske, 1959) correlation is .58 ($p < .001$). This would indicate that the two different "methods" of assessing the workers' reaction to their jobs are tapping somewhat the same variables. However, the heterotrait-monomethod and heterotrait-heteromethod correlations are larger than the Campbell-Fiske model indicates they should be. Several instances of low discriminant validity are evident.

A third point of general interest is the generally near-zero correlations between the group-satisfaction measures and the group-productivity measure ($\bar{r} = .04$). This would seem to indicate that, contrary to Katzell's et al. prediction, the retailing industry does not *necessarily* provide the type of situation conducive to positive correlations between job satisfaction and productivity which they obtained in a study of a group of warehouses.

A final point of general interest is indicated in the near-zero ($r = -.03$) correlations between group size and satisfaction measures. This is also contrary to expectations in this area. Previously reported findings would suggest a negative correlation between group size and satisfaction.

The correlations relevant to the two predictions made above are presented in Table 1. In this table the content area of the satisfaction questions is indicated on the left and the community variables are indicated at the top. If we look first at the correlations between the satisfaction variables and the variables used to index slums (percentage of nonwhite and percentage of owner occupied housing), prosperity (median income, percentage earning over $10,000, percentage of sound housing, per capita retail sales), and productive farming (median rural income per family) we find Prediction 1 strikingly confirmed. Sixty-two of the 63 correlations are in the predicted direction and 44 of these 63 correlations are significant at the .05 level or better. Thus, it appears that the less attractive the community, in terms of slums, prosperity, and productive farming, the more satisfied are the workers

TABLE 1

Average Correlations between Community Characteristics and Satisfaction Variables

	Community Characteristics							
	Slums		Prosperity				Productive Farming	Unemployment
	1[a]	2[b]	3	4	5	6	7	8
Supervision	01	−08	−03	01	−02	−06	−04	05
Kind of work	14*	−11	−18**	−15*	−20**	−14*	−19**	02
Amount of work	12*	−11	−16**	−12*	−16**	−12**	−20**	00
Co-Workers	08	−06	−05	−01	−07	−13*	−04	−04
Working conditions	20**	−08	−24**	−21**	−26**	−20**	−26**	06
Pay	26**	−15*	−44**	−38**	−45**	−24**	−45**	10
Career and security	10	−06	−16**	−12*	−16**	−14*	−15*	02
Company identification	19**	−06	−34**	−30**	−30**	−26**	−31**	11
Organizational effectiveness	31**	−19**	−36**	−28**	−34**	−23**	−38**	03

[a]Variables in following order: (*a*) percentage of nonwhite, (*b*) percentage of owner occupied housing, (*c*) median income, (*d*) percentage earning over $10,000, (*e*) percent sound housing, (*f*) per capita retail sales, (*g*) median rural income per family, (*h*) percentage of unemployed workers.
[b]Reverse scoring to obtain same direction as Variable 1.
$*p < .05.$
$**p < .01.$

with their jobs. It is of some interest to note that of the 19 correlations that failed to reach significance at the .05 level, 13 were contributed by two satisfaction areas — supervision and co-workers. It appears that while satisfaction with most aspects of a worker's job is affected by the community, reactions to other people on the job are relatively unaffected.

The data testing the validity of Prediction 2 are more equivocal. Pay satisfaction has the highest correlation with the slum, prosperity, and productive farming variables only four times. Three times it has the second highest correlation. The other variable displaying strong relationships with the economic community variables — organizational effectiveness — has the strongest correlation twice, is second three times, and third twice. While, on the average, pay satisfaction was the satisfaction variable most strongly affected by community variables,

Prediction 2 must be regarded as only partially confirmed. (Average correlation between pay satisfaction and the economic variables listed in Table 1 is .31. The average for the other aspects of satisfaction is .14.)

Further examination of Table 1 reveals that not only are most of the correlations significant and in the expected direction, but that the rank order of the correlations between the nine satisfaction variables and the seven community items within the three economic variates appears to be consistent. A test of concordance on these results indicates a significant degree of consistency of the relative magnitudes of the correlations ($W = .81, p < .01$).

The fourth variable which was used to assess the job opportunities of the community did not yield this degree of confirmation of the predictions. Eight of the nine correlations between satisfaction and "percentage of unemployed workers" were positive as predicted but none reached the .05 level of significance. Thus, this aspect of the community does not appear to be related to job satisfaction to a significant degree.

The remainder of the community variables for which no predictions had been made indicated no consistent and significant relationships.

DISCUSSION

The results of this study indicate generally significant and often sizable correlations between job satisfaction and economic community characteristics. Further, pay satisfaction appears to be somewhat more affected by these characteristics than are the other areas of job satisfaction. These predicted results appear to be more evidence indicating the validity of the conception of job satisfaction which stresses that job satisfaction is a product of the discrepancies between expectations and experience, of the actual experience on the job, of the frame of reference of the worker, and of the alternatives open to the worker.

The major question is why these results should occur. Assuming the conception of job satisfaction presented above is correct, the explanation for these results can be derived from it with a minimum of difficulty. Let us consider the general economic condition of the community as serving two major purposes. First, would be the function of establishing a frame of reference against which the workers evaluate their present position. If this is indeed the case, then in a poor community a low-level white-collar worker ($1.25/hour–$1.70/hour) is relatively better off than he would be if he lived in a wealthy community. In a poor community he may well be one of the "middle class." The same worker in a wealthy community would be considered, and probably would consider himself, somewhat less well off. The relationship of this explanation to Helson's adaptation level theory (1948)

is obvious. It should be noted that these results were obtained on a sample of relatively low level clerical workers but if our conception of job satisfaction is correct these same relationships should be obtained regardless of the occupational level of the worker. Five dollars or 1 dollar per hour should make you a richer person in Yazoo City, Mississippi, than the same wage does in Shaker Heights, Ohio, Thus even though these results were obtained on relatively low-level workers, they should hold true for workers from all strata. If the function of these community characteristics is indeed to provide the workers with a frame of reference, then we should expect these results.

An alternative explanation for the function of the community variables would be that these variables are serving to index the alternatives open to the worker (see Smith, 1963; Kendall, 1963). In communities with a great many slums and which have a low level of prosperity, the worker may already have the best of the available alternatives. Any change he makes will likely be for the worse. In a wealthy community there may be several alternatives open to him which are more attractive. We would expect that the worker in the poor community who sees no alternatives which are more attractive should be more satisfied with his job than his counterpart in a wealthy community who is surrounded by more attractive alternatives.

If this latter explanation is correct, we would expect that satisfaction measures would also be related to the amount of unemployment in the area since this variable is a very direct reflection of the alternatives open to "workers in general." The present data do not indicate the presence of such a relationship. There are, however, many problems connected with the rejection of this latter hypothesis on the basis of these data. Our measure of the percentage of unemployed workers in the area was the least satisfactory of the community characteristics studied. We were forced to rely on the 1960 census figures regarding this measure and the amount of unemployment may well have changed considerably during the 2-year span until the job satisfaction measures were obtained. Also, employed workers may not be aware of the amount of unemployment in their area. We would have to regard both explanations of the findings as tenable until more evidence is available regarding the relationship between satisfaction and unemployment.

Equally intriguing are the satisfaction variables which appear to be *unaffected* by community characteristics. Nineteen of the 63 correlations between satisfaction variables and community characteristics were nonsignificant. Thirteen of these 19 nonsignificant correlations were contributed by satisfaction with supervision and satisfaction with co-workers. These two variables are the only two satisfaction variables that are directly related to satisfaction with interpersonal relations. Previously Hulin (1963a). Hulin and Smith (1965), and Kendall (1963) determined that these two areas of satisfaction did not behave in the same manner as the satisfaction variables related to other aspects of the job. Hulin and Smith found that while work, pay, and promotions satisfactions were related to a worker's age, tenure, salary, and job level; supervision and co-worker satisfaction were not affected by this set of independent variables. Kendall found that these two areas of satisfaction were less frequently associated with the community characteristics than one would expect. The reasons for this apparent lack of correspondence between interpersonal satisfactions and satisfactions with other aspects of the job may simply be because there is very likely more agreement on what constitutes a good promotion policy or what constitutes an acceptable rate of pay than there is on what constitutes a good supervisor or work group. To be sure there will be a certain amount of agreement of acceptable standards but these agreements will probably be outnumbered by the disagreements. When we attempt to study these aspects of job satisfaction we will be forced to include variables which will predict a worker's reaction to another person. We may be forced to widen the class of independent variables to include personality, personal background, or other similar types of measures. Kendall (1963) has demonstrated that the addition of such measures produces more general and replicable results in the investigation of satisfaction and behavior in industry. This will undoubtedly lead us to a program of personality research applied to job satisfaction.

The results of this study would seem to indicate that a conceptualization of job satisfaction which does not include recognition of the part played by frames of reference or alternatives available to the worker is going to be inadequate. At the same time, investigations of job satisfaction should include the community and plant or office characteristics if these are allowed to vary. These results also raise serious questions concerning the validity of the suggestion by Herzberg (Herzberg, Mausner, and Snyderman, 1959) that the determinants of how a man reacts to his job are to be found in the intrinsic characteristics of the job, and not in the environmental characteristics surrounding the job. It is no longer enough to consider community and situational variables as moderator variables or nuisance variables. The direct effect of these variables on satisfaction must be considered. These considerations may complicate the life of the researcher in this area but greater understanding would seem to be the inevitable result.

---

[1]Only those relationships which were significant in all three samples are discussed.

REFERENCES

Campbell, D. T., and Fiske, D. W. Convergent and discriminant validation by the multitrait-multimethod matrix. *Psychological Bulletin*, 1959, *56*, 81–105.

Cureton, E. E., and Katzell, R. A. A further analysis of the relations among job performance and situational variables. *Journal of Applied Psychology*, 1962, *46*, 230.

Helson, H. Adaptation level as a basis for a quantitative theory of frames of reference. *Psychological Review*, 1948, *55*, 297–313.

Herzberg, F., Mausner, B., and Snyderman, B. B. *The motivation to work.* New York: Wiley, 1959.

Hulin, C. L. A linear model of job satisfaction. Unpublished doctoral dissertation, Cornell University, 1963. (a)

Hulin, C. L. Research implications of attitude surveys in large organizations. Paper presented to the Illinois Psychological Association annual meeting, Springfield, Illinois, 1963. (b)

Hulin, C. L. and Smith, Patricia C. Sex differences in job satisfaction. *Journal of Applied Psychology*, 1964, *48*, 88–92.

Hulin, C. L., and Smith, Patricia C. A linear model of job satisfaction. *Journal of Applied Psychology*, 1965, *49*, 209–216.

Johnson, G. H. A search for functional unities: An analysis of United States county data. Unpublished doctoral dissertation, New York University, 1958.

Katzell, R. A., Barrett, R. S., and Parker, T. C. Job satisfaction, job performance, and situational characteristics. *Journal of Applied Psychology*, 1961, *45*, 65–72.

Kendall, L. M. Canonical analysis of job satisfaction and behavioral, personal background, and situational data. Unpublished doctoral dissertation, Cornell University, 1963.

Smith, Patricia C. Cornell studies of job satisfaction: I. Strategy for the development of a general theory of job staisfaction. Ithaca: Cornell University, 1963. (Mimeo)

Smith, Patricia C., Kendall, L. M., and Hulin, C. L. *Measurement of satisfaction in work and retirement.* New York: Rand-McNally, in press.

Decennial Census of United States Climate-Heating Degree Day Normals. Climatology of the United States, United States Department of Commerce, Washington, D.C., 1963, No. 83.

United States Bureau of Census, County and City Book, 1962. (A statistical abstract supplement), United States Government Printing Office, Washington, D.C., 1962.

Worthy, J. C. Organizational structure and employee morale. *American Sociological Review*, 1950, *15*, 169–179.

Yuzuk, R. P. The assessment of employee morale. Columbus, Ohio: Ohio State Univer. Press, 1961.

Satisfaction and Satisfactoriness: Complementary Aspects of Occupational Adjustment

ALASTAIR HERON, *University of Zambia*

INTRODUCTION

In a previous paper (Heron, 1952) a report was made on the development of two criteria; one was of individual productivity, the other measured the extent to which an employee was a source of concern to his supervisors. Both these criteria were therefore of 'satisfactoriness,' *i.e.*, of that aspect of occupational success which represents the viewpoint of the employer.

The objective of the later work here reported was threefold: first, to effect if possible some methodological improvement in the evaluation of satisfaction; second, to ascertain the way in which the previous measure of 'supervisory concern' is related to other measures of satisfactoriness; and, third, to provide a little further evidence concerning the relationship between the two complementary aspects (Rodger, 1937) of occupational success. The whole enterprise formed part of a long-term follow-up of new entrants as bus conductors (without previous experience), concerning whom a large quantity of psychological data had been obtained in their first fortnight of employment.

Reprinted with the permission of author and publisher from the article of the same title, in *Occupational Psychology* (1954, *28*, 140–153), the quarterly journal of the National Institute of Industrial Psychology, 14 Welbeck Street, London, W. 1.

THE SAMPLE

Of the 210 men originally studied, 147 completed 26 weeks of service at their respective garages. Of these, 3 resigned or were discharged almost immediately afterwards. The remaining 144 men were interviewed within a fortnight of the date on which they reached the 26-week 'target.' It will be evident that the range of any measures of satisfaction or satisfactoriness is restricted by the loss of the non-stayers, and that the results to be presented are based upon a group of relatively stable and successful men so far as this particular occupation is concerned. The age range was 19–45.

SATISFACTION

Content of Interview

Each man was seen individually for thirty minutes in a private room near the central training school, at a time convenient to himself. The interview was expected by the man, insofar as at a preliminary ten-minute talk four months before, the writer had mentioned his desire to see everybody after 26 weeks of service in order to get their views about the job. The interview session was structured except for the last section, and adhered to a pattern which is here set out in full to make clear the context in which the assessment of job satisfaction was attempted:

1. Explanation of the purposes behind the whole research of which this formed the final stage.

2. Appeal for complete frankness about the demands of the job, with reminder of confidential basis.

3. Clarification of man's attitude towards becoming a driver.

4. Rank-ordering or relative importance to him of 12 aspects of "any job — ignoring this job altogether."

5. Procedure to assess job satisfaction.

6. Rank-ordering of 10 aspects of the bus-conductor job from most liked to most disliked.

7. Standard questions leading to choice.

8. Open-ended section concerned with stresses and causes of grievance.

Assessment of Job Satisfaction

Items were gathered from the unpublished work of Kristy (1952) and of Carlsson (1951) of the Survey Research Center to form a job satisfaction inventory. A few were altered sufficiently to make them more relevant to the bus conductor job, and one, relating to hours and shifts, was specially prepared in view of the general opinion that this aspect was one of the least-liked about the job. The inventory contained 15 items, which are listed in Appendix 1 with annotations to indicate source. Two administrative procedures were used with each man. The first, to be referred to as Form A, involved the presentation to the subject of each item in straight question form on a card 12 inches long by 5 inches wide. Below the question was a strip of plain paper, octavo length (8 inches), through which was visible a black horizontal line. One end of the line was always "FULL MARKS" and the other end styled appropriately to the question, *e.g.*, "DON'T LIKE," or "VERY POOR." Each card was reversible, so that a single

sheet of octavo paper, folded lengthwise, and held by paper-clips, served two questions. This simplified scoring and preparation for re-use.

A demonstration item (unrelated to work) was worked through with the subject, in order to ensure that he understood clearly what to do. He was told: "One end of the line that you can see through the paper represents perfection — couldn't possibly be better — so it's called FULL MARKS. The other end is the opposite extreme — couldn't possibly be worse. Where you make your pencil mark on the paper will be a way of saying how you feel about the matter raised by the question. If you think there is *no* room for improvement, then of course you'll put your mark right up at the FULL MARKS end. If you think there is *some* room for improvement, then your mark will have to be back a bit from the end. The idea would be the same at the other end, of course. You can use this way of saying how you feel so as to grade your answer as finely as you want. Is that clear? (*Pause.*) (*Answer questions.*) Now use this one as an example and put your mark across the line at the point which indicates how you feel on this matter." His mark was then interpreted to him in words, and further explanation and practice used if necessary. Great emphasis was laid upon the desirability of making use of the whole line and of avoiding extreme judgments unless they were what he really felt about the particular question. No attempt was made to suggest normality of distribution.

On completing the 15 items by this method, of a general type described by Viteles as 'linear rating scales' (1932, p, 211), a start was made immediately with Form B, introduced by explaining that "we are now going to do the same thing in a different way, because what suits one man doesn't always suit another."

The second method, using the same items (in the same order) as questions or incomplete statements (Form B) followed by five descriptive phrases, is familiar from merit-rating procedures. Each item was on a separate card, and the subject was asked to "say which of the five descriptions *comes nearest* to expressing how you feel. Just say 'a' or 'b' or 'c' or 'd' or 'e' and I'll make a note of it here." A warning was added: "By the way, the five descriptions are NEVER in any order of merit or goodness; I've purposely mixed them up."

While recording the answers to each item using this descriptive method, the answer given to the corresponding item in Form A was inspected. Any items involving contradictions were put to one side, and at the end of Form B administration the writer said, "Now let's have a look at some of the questions where perhaps you didn't find it equally easy to say how you felt by both methods." This comparison led to discussion of contradictions, clarification of meanings, and to the subject being asked to "alter either or both of your answers so that you feel they both represent your opinion fairly."

Statistical Treatment

The linear method was scored by the simple expedient of laying a ruler along the record paper and making a note of the distance in centimetres which the subject's pencil mark was from the 'unfavorable' end. The distribution of these Form A scores for each item was then split as close to the median as possible and tetrachoric correlation coefficients calculated between Form A and Form B, the latter responses being split in such a way as to conform as nearly as possible to the Form A split. Wherever feasible, two Form B splits were tried out and the average coefficient taken. These coefficients provide a rough estimate of internal consistency for each of the 15 items in the inventory, and are listed in Table 1; it should be noted that the consistency referred to is of the item *after* discussion and alteration.

For the purpose of examining the inter-correlations between the 15 items, the linear (Form A) scores were used, divided for each item into 'Satisfied,' 'Middle,' and 'Dissatisfied' groups by splits at the 30th and 70th percentiles. Product-moment correlations were calculated* and the resulting matrix factor-analysed by the centroid method. Three factors were extracted which together accounted for 37.2% of the variance. Examination of bi-variate plots of the loadings on each pair of factors before rotation suggested the possibility of two main group factors, each consisting of two sub-groups. This suggestion was strengthened after rotation, and a group-factor analysis was therefore carried out, following Burt (1950); the impression was, with some imperfections, confirmed. Table 1 lists the 15 items in their four groups, showing the loadings of each item on the general factor obtained in the first stage of the group-factor analysis; the group-factor loading; and the estimate of internal consistency.

It seems obvious that the general factor represents "overall extent of satisfaction." The two main components may perhaps be described as the 'positive' and 'negative' aspects of satisfaction. The positive section seems to fall fairly clearly into one group of items (5, 10 and 13) concerned with what has been called "an intrinsic liking for the actual nature of the work itself"; and a second, contrasting, group of items (1, 2 and 8) representing a more general satisfaction with the job in a wider context. The negative section falls into one group (Nos. 3, 7 and 14), which may (with less confidence) be styled "aspirations and adjustments," and another (Nos. 4, 6, 9, 11 and 12) which seems to involve the acceptance of pressures — physical, financial and disciplinary.

Pooling squares (Thomson, 1948) were used to estimate the contribution made by each item to a unit-weight multiple correlation with the appropriate group factor, and ten items were selected by this means to form a composite Job Satisfaction Score which would adequately represent all the four components revealed by the factor analyses. These ten items are marked with

TABLE 1

Structure of the Satisfaction Criterion

A — Positive Elements	Rotated Loading on General Factor	Loading on G.F.A. General Factor	Loading on Relevant Group Factor	Consistency Estimate
A-1. *Intrinsic Liking for the Work Itself*				
*5. How do you like the *kind of work* that you do?..	67	59	46	65
*10. How *interesting* is this job?	69	64	41	70
*13. How do you *like* your job?	81	74	39	70
A-2. *Satisfaction with Present Employment*				
*1. How do you feel you have *got on* since coming here?	49	37	49	55
*2. How does........compare as a *place to work*?..	56	49	42	65
8. As an *employer*.......... is.........	52	47	11	55
15. How *satisfied* are you with your job?	79	66	17	75
B — Negative Elements				
B-1. *Aspirations and Adjustments*				
*3. How much does your job give you a chance to *do the things you are best at?*	30	40	37	90
*7. The *hours* on this job......... ..	31	48	46	50
14. How do you feel about your prospects of *advancement* here?	36	47	22	80
B-2. *Acceptance of Pressures (Physical, Financial, Disciplinary).*				
*4. How *tired* are you at the end of the day?	09	23	55	65
*6. My *mates* think this job is	06	19	31	75
9. My *average earnings are*	29	38	10	70
*11. *During peak hours* a guard has to work	00	17	50	80
12. How well is the .... *run?* ..	17	31	32	85

an asterisk in Table 1. The four group factors are represented to the extent of unit weight R's of .50, .55, .50 and .65 respectively; the general factor to the extent of an R of .80. The average internal consistency of the ten items is .70; this means, of course, that the consistency of the 10-item composite score is considerably higher. All the subjects were, of course, equated for experience at this kind of work; there is a slight but significant linear correlation with age ($+.178$, $P < .01$). There is no suggestion in this sample of the cyclical relationship with age mentioned by Hoppock and Super (1950, p. 130).

VALUE TO THE EMPLOYER ("SATISFACTORINESS")

Variables Obtainable from Records

These were five in number, all in totals for the first 26 weeks of garage service:

(a) Gross earnings;

(b) 'Shorts' on cash handed in for tickets sold;

(c) Number of periods of absence, irrespective of cause or duration;

(d) Divisional disciplinary actions;

(e) Number of times late for duty.

Some comment is necessary in respect of this group as a whole and also in reference to individual items. The 144 men were drawn from four garages, and it was therefore essential, for each variable, to compute separate means and variances, to test for significant differences between garages, and to apply simple systems of weighting where necessary. This was the case with items (d) and (e).

'Gross earnings' can be regarded as a valid measure of 'value to the employer' in this instance, insofar as it is a direct measure of the extent to which individuals varied in their availability for overtime duty in a system which is dependent for its smooth operation upon a large measure of such 'additional' work. 'Divisional Disciplinary Actions' are in respect of reports made by the uniformed traffic inspectors, and arise from 'offences' such as failure to collect fares, or to alter route indicators at the termini.

Normalised 5-Point Rating —
"Source of Concern to Supervisors"

This was obtained within each garage by the method described in a previous paper (Heron, 1952), with a slight modification made desirable by the circumstances. After each of the three supervisors within each garage concerned had completed his set of normalised ratings, the writer arranged a meeting at which the supervisors were asked to discuss first all the men who had received a grade 5 (poor) from any of them, and to decide which were the men whom they could agree to be the worst. (The maximum sought was of course the number equivalent to the required proportion [11%] of grade 5's in the total number of men at that garage involved in the rating procedure.) When the supervisors had done this, all the remaining 5's automatically became grade 4's, and the procedure was then applied to grade 4, grade 1 and grade 2, in that order. This method avoided the difficulty of combining dissimilar gradings without adequate

statistical evaluation, and also satisfied the supervisors that the method was designed to be fair to the men and to themselves as judges.

It is probably reasonable to assume that the re-test reliability of this normalised 5-point rating is of the same order as that obtained in the previous study, viz., about .8.

Statistical Treatment

All but one of the 5 variables obtained from records were converted to normalised percentile scores: Earnings and Shorts in 5 groups, Lates and Disciplinary Actions in 3 groups. It should be noted that it was not possible to normalise Absences, in view of the acute J– distribution usual with such data. A 3-group score was used, which divided the 144 men into 57 with no periods of absence, 37 with 1 period only, and 50 with 2 or more.

These 5 variables and the rating were then intercorrelated and the resulting matrix of product-moment coefficients factor-analysed by the centroid method. Two factors were extracted, accounting respectively for 32.4% and 8.3% of the variance. The intercorrelation matrix and the factor loadings and communalities appear in Table 2.

That Divisional Disciplinary Actions is less closely related to the other five variables is explicable mainly by the fact that administratively there had been little or no liaison between the supervisory staff in the garage and on the road so far as the conduct of individual men is concerned. For theoretical purposes this is fortunate, as it enables us to take note of the correlations between this administratively independent variable, shortages (.230), and lateness (.274), which though small do suggest a significant pattern of individual differences. To some extent there may be a tendency for these three criteria to reflect a form of behaviour which might be called 'irresponsibility' or 'lack of attention to details' — the opposite of 'meticulous' or 'obsessional.' Some support for this conjecture may be found in the fact

TABLE 2

**Intercorrelation Matrix, Factor Loadings and Communalities,
"Value to the Employer"**

	Scoring Direction	Correlation Matrix					Factor Loadings		
		2	3	4	5	6	I	II	h2
1. Superv. Rating	Poor	.304	.505	.382	.127	.483	.70	.03	.493
2. Gross Earnings	Low	—	.095	.414	.057	.241	.44	−.42	.372
3. Cash Shorts	High		—	.272	.230	.447	.61	.32	.473
4. Periods of Absence	Many			—	.018	.369	.56	−.33	.426
5. Divl. Disc. Actions	Many				—	.274	.28	.27	.148
6. Lates	Many					—	.70	.14	.513

Variance accounted for: 40.7%.

that among the men regarded by a psychiatrist colleague as 'below average in obsessionality or meticulousness,' a disproportionately large number were found to be 'high' in shortages, lates and disciplinary actions. (Of these associations, the two former were statistically significant, and the last, while obtaining a P of .3, was in the same direction.)

The general factor, Value to the Employer, has a multiple correlation of .86 with variables 1, 2, 3 and 6, using unit weights, after omitting variable 5 because of its independence and variable 4 because of its statistical shortcoming referred to earlier. The composite score was found to be correlated significantly and linearly with age (+.522). The four components of the composite score exhibit a similar association with age, as follows: Supervisors' Rating, +.403; Earnings (Availability), +.418; Shortages, +.282; Lates, +.445. In summary, younger men tend to be more often late, to be less available for overtime duties, and to be more 'out' in their cash. However, although the Supervisors' Ratings are to some extent influenced by the age of the men, largely no doubt as a result of the tendencies just summarised, they are still based in fair degree upon impressions derived from actual

behaviour, as can be found by holding age constant when examining the correlations between Supervisors' Ratings and the other criteria: with Earnings (Availability), +.163; with Shortages, +.445; with Lates, +.370. This may justifiably be regarded as providing evidence of the validity of the Supervisors' Rating, while making it clear that for the purposes of raising the reliability (and probably the validity) of the Satisfactoriness criterion it is desirable to add the objective records to the rating, thus in effect giving additional weight to the former by reason of the overlap. When using the composite criterion score in connection with independent variables, it is of course essential to hold age constant by partial correlation.

The data and remarks above should be compared with the finding in an earlier study (of factory workers) that although the Supervisory Rating was correlated +.425 with age, this shrank to +.015 when the effects of length of service were held constant. No such problem arises in the present study, as all the men had equal service. This comparison emphasises the imperative need for obtaining and using all possible collateral data when establishing and evaluating criteria of occupational success.

Relation between Job Satisfaction and Value to the Employer

These two criteria of the complementary aspects of occupational success of new entrants as bus conductors were found to be correlated +.353. The regression is linear and when age is held constant by partial correlation, the correlation between the criteria becomes +.308. Further reference to this finding appears in the Discussion.

DISCUSSION

Method of Eliciting Satisfaction Responses

The evaluation of job satisfaction usually seems to be attempted by one of two means: the questionnaire or the interview, *cf.* Ghiselli and Brown (1948); Lawshe (1953). There seems to be no good reason why the two methods should not be combined in order to maximise the advantages and minimise the drawbacks of them both, though no suggestion to this effect is made by Blum (1949) or by Hoppock and Super (1950) in their respective reviews of this topic. This is not likely to be achieved simply by bringing a man to an interview room in order to let him fill out a questionnaire, but rather by re-designing the questionnaire procedure in such a way as to make it an integral part of the interview, which has, for example, been done by Marriott (1953) and his collaborators. Doing this by treating each item separately is in any event likely to reduce halo effect by separating in time items similar in content, and by focussing the subject's attention on each item in visual isolation from all others. This, however, is still not enough of a marriage between the two methods; and the technique reported in this paper — of ensuring discussion about item meaning through the use of two ways of item-presentation and scoring, within the context of an interview situation — is suggested as the next step.

One consequence of using this double-presentation approach was to convince the writer afresh of the dangers and difficulties implicit in the descriptive-phrase type of multiple response when used on its own — and especially when in the form of a printed questionnaire uncontrolled by interview. The majority of the discussion on contradictory responses arose directly from individual differences in perception of the values implicit in the five choices of response. There is no doubt that the wording of many of them could now be greatly improved; an attempt could be made to get them into scale form by recognized methods: but the problem would remain. This is not to say that the graphical method as used is perfect: far from it; but the experience with these 144 men was clearly that, once explained and worked through by example, the graphical method gave rise to less difficulty. However, it seemed to need the check provided by the verbal-description method, especially for those men who tended to hug the extreme position and waste the flexibility afforded by the length of the line. The writer feels justified in hoping that other workers will try out the double-presentation technique and report their experience. In this way, something may be done towards meeting the practical challenge thrown out by Rodger (1952): "The main task of the psychologist in this field . . . is not to disparage the interview but to improve it."

A word may here be in order concerning the choice of statistical methods for the treatment of these data. The first principle employed was that of avoiding a spurious appearance of precision; the second, of maximising independence from the judgments of the interviewer. The choice of tetrachoric correlation coefficients for estimating the degree of association between the responses obtained to alternative methods of presentation adheres to the first principle; the use of factor analysis, by avoiding impressionistic grouping of the satisfaction and satisfactoriness variables, is loyal to the second principle. It should be noted in passing that the sub-scores of the satisfaction criterion, based on the group-factor analysis, were employed in the follow-up study, as separate variables additional to the total score; and that 'satisfaction with earnings' was also used as an independent single-item criterion.

The Analysis of Occupational Success

It is not proposed to review here the literature in this field, especially as valuable summaries exist (Blum, 1949; Ghiselli and Brown, 1948; Hoppock and Super, 1950; Viteles, 1932); attention should however be drawn to the useful service rendered regularly for some years by Hoppock, with various collaborators, in summarising job satisfaction researches. Verbal discussion of the whole problem reached a high level in the series of articles by Davies (1950), Stott (1950) and Reeves (1950), but it is probably safe to assume that none of these authors would feel they had provided an adequate, factually-based answer to the question, "What is Occupational Success?"

A 'dimensional' analysis seemed to be the next step. To be useful, it had to cover both the 'satisfaction' and the 'satisfactoriness' aspects of success simultaneously. Beginnings were made independently and roughly simultaneously by Kristy (1952) in a doctoral research under the direction of Rodger; by Carlsson (1951) and others in the Human Relations Project of the Survey Research Center; and by the writer. Through the courtesy of Rodger and Kristy and of the Director of the Survey Research Center, the writer was enabled for the present study to use items drawn from barely completed and still unpublished researches in the construction of his job-satisfaction inventory.

The situation in the bus conductor project was such as to preclude the use of a long and detailed satisfaction inventory, such as that employed by the Survey Research Center. Accordingly, the items were chosen as representative of the main areas of satisfaction reported by Kristy and by Carlsson, with the exception of supervision. This was omitted because there is a very real sense in which it is true to say that 'supervision' as ordinarily understood has no meaning for the bus conductor. He has no chargehand or foreman constantly nearby, as is the case in a factory, and it is very doubtful whether one can legitimately assume that he perceives the occasional inspector or the garage superintendent as supervisors in an analogous way.

Coverage of several possible areas of satisfaction was either not attempted or was inadequate; an example of the latter is 'earnings.' The 15 items used were expected to provide a rather broader-based evaluation than could be achieved simply by asking each man how satisfied he was with the job, and thus to enable some further examination of overall satisfaction.

Both Kristy and Carlsson used factor analysis to classify their satisfaction items, the former also including proficiency criteria in his combined matrices. Both workers obtained group factors, Kristy by Burt's method, Carlsson by "somewhat unorthodox orthogonal rotational methods" from a Thurstone multiple group analysis. Starting from grossly differing populations (261 post office counter clerks; 1,709 industrial workers, all grades, in a single factory), using dissimilar questionnaires and means of administration, and approaching the statistical analysis with contrasting theoretical considerations in mind, one would not expect anything resembling close agreement. One does not find it, but both workers demonstrated that job satisfaction was not uni-dimensional in their respective studies. Kristy also showed — he considers it himself to be his main finding — that satisfaction and satisfactoriness are almost wholly uncorrelated in his sample. In a later report (1951), based on Carlsson's work so far as job satisfaction is concerned, the Survey Research Center stated (p. 49) that more high than low producing employees say "(1) they prefer their present job rather than another job;

(2) they like the actual kind of work they do." The writers of the report continue (p. 51): "It is difficult to interpret the positive relationship between productivity and overall job satisfaction. The relationship shows no causal direction. . . . Perhaps dislike of the job is what leads to low productivity. It is also possible that failure to meet productivity standards, with its concomitant effects of increased pressure, etc., leads to dislike of the job."

Some comparison is possible between the results obtained in the present study and those of Kristy and Carlsson. Of the 15 items used in the writer's job satisfaction inventory, seven came from Kristy's 18-item questionnaire and seven from the 117-item booklet used by the Survey Research Center at the Caterpillar Tractor Company. Of the former seven, two, and of the latter seven, three, were modified slightly to make them useable in the bus conductor study. Both sets of seven were found to be represented in all four group factors obtained in the present analysis.

Of the four items used in the Caterpillar report (1951) to form an index of satisfaction 'with the job' based on Carlsson's factor analysis, two were used in the present study (Nos. 3 and 5). It will be seen that on this occasion they did not come in the same group factor; as their intercorrelation was .18,[1] compared with .71 in the Caterpillar study, this is not surprising. Item 12 in the writer's inventory ("How well is the Transport Department run?") obtained a loading of .75 in Carlsson's analysis on what he called the 'halo' factor; if this may reasonably be regarded as comparable to the writer's 'general' factor, the equivalent loading is .39 (unrotated) or .17 (rotated). In brief, there is little resemblance between the two studies so far as the degree of association between these few common items is concerned.

By contrast, two (Nos. 10 and 13) of the three items defining group factor A-1 in the present analysis are also items with high loadings in Kristy's comparable group factor and have commensurate loadings on the general factor in both studies. Other items in common also have similar loadings on the general factor, but the greatest difference is found in respect of the 'blanket' item, No. 15. In Kristy's analysis it has a relatively low loading on the rotated general factor (.54) compared with figures of .66 (unrotated) and .79 (rotated) in the present analysis, and the highest loading (.77) in his group factor 'D' (Satisfaction with Job Conditions) compared with a loading of .17 on group factor A-2 (Satisfaction with Present Employment). This strongly suggests that the major determinants of response to an overall or 'blanket' item are in fact located in areas differing from one job to another. While new bus conductors vary in their overall satisfaction mainly in terms of *positive* aspects of the job, post office counter clerks may well be more uniform in these aspects, and tend to vary more in consequence of their dissatisfaction with the *negative* aspects.

Finally, the present study does not in general repeat Kristy's finding that in an occupationally homogeneous sample there was no relationship between satisfaction and satisfactoriness; as previously mentioned, the two criteria were found to intercorrelate +.308 with age held constant. In connection with earnings treated in isolation, however, it was found that actual earnings (effectively a measure of voluntary overtime) only correlated +.160 (barely significant at $P = .05$ level) with answers to the question "How well do your average earnings (including overtime) supply a decent standard of living?"

The method of presentation employed by the Survey Research Center report (1951), while appropriate for an audience of industrial managers, does not provide enough detail for the present purpose. Without additional data concerning the interrelationships of satisfaction and productivity with other potentially relevant variables, it is impossible to evaluate the reported association between the two criteria of occupational success. As the writer has pointed out elsewhere (1954), we are evidently still a long way from understanding the composition of 'morale,' and one stage on that journey would seem to be a clearer delineation of the relationship between productivity, satisfactoriness in other respects, and the various aspects of satisfaction. Blum (1949, pp. 76–77) was probably right when he insisted that job satisfaction is not morale, but only one of its components.

SUMMARY

1. This paper reports the development of criterion measures for satisfaction and satisfactoriness in respect of new omnibus conductors.

2. The method of assessing satisfaction is in some respects novel, and is put forward for consideration and further trial by other investigators.

3. Results obtained from the statistical evaluation of these criteria are compared with those obtained previously by the writer and by others.

4. Discussion is focussed on the continuing inadequacy of our knowledge about the structure of occupational success.

[1]It will be remembered that this coefficient is shrunk by coarse grouping, but so is the Survey Research Center figure.

REFERENCES

Blum, M. L. (1949): *Industrial Psychology and Its Social Foundations*. New York, Harper.

Burt, Cyril (1950): Group factor analysis. *Brit. J. Statist. Psychol., 3*, 40–75.

Carlsson, G. (1951): *An analysis of morale dimensions — preliminary report*. Unpublished.

Davie, J. G. W. (1950): What is occupational success? *Occ. Psychol., 24*, 7–17.

Ghiselli, E. E. and Brown, C. W. (1948): *Personnel and Industrial Psychology*. New York, McGraw-Hill.

Heron, Alastair (1952): The establishment for research purposes of two criteria of occupational adjustment. *Occ. Psychol., 26*, 78–85.

Heron, Alastair (1954): Industrial Psychology, in Stone, C. P., *Annual Review of Psychology*, Vol. V. Stanford, Annual Reviews Inc.

Hoppock, R., and Super, D. E. (1950): Vocational and Educational Satisfaction, in Fryer, D. H., and Henry, E. R., *Handbook of Applied Psychology*. New York, Rinehart.

Kristy, N. F. (1952): *Criteria of occupational success among post-office counter clerks*. Unpublished thesis, Univeristy of London.

Lawshe, C. H. (1953): *The Psychology of Industrial Relations*. New York, McGraw-Hill.

Marriott, R. (1953): Some problems in attitude survey methodology. *Occ. Psychol., 27*, 117–127.

Reeves, J. W. (1950): What is Occupational Success? *Occ. Psychol., 24*, 153–159.

Rodger, Alec (1937): *A Borstal Experiment in Vocational Guidance*. Industrial Health Research Board Report 78. London, H.M.S.O.

Rodger, Alec (1952): The worthwhileness of the interview. *Occ. Psychol., 26*, 101–106.

Stott, M. B. (1950): What is occupational success? *Occ. Psychol., 24*, 105–112.

Survey Research Center (1951): *The Caterpillar Tractor Co. Study, Report VI*. Ann Arbor, University of Michigan.

Thomson, Godfrey H. (1948): *The Factorial Analysis of Human Ability*. 3rd Edition. London, University of London Press.

Viteles, M. S. (1932): *Industrial Psychology*. New York, Norton.

The Concept
of Work Adjustment

E. BETZ, *Iowa State University*

D. J. WEISS, *University of Minnesota*

R. DAWIS, *University of Minnesota*

C. W. ENGLAND, *University of Minnesota*

L. H. LOFQUIST, *University of Minnesota*

In 1959 the then Office of Vocational Rehabilitation awarded a five-year grant to the investigators in support of research to develop criterion measures for, and a methodology for the evaluation of, vocational rehabilitation outcomes. One of the first projects undertaken was a survey of the pertinent research literature in psychology, sociology, and industrial relations, as well as in rehabilitation.[1]

After thorough review and evaluation of the research literature, the concept of "work adjustment" was developed to designate the general area encompassing evaluative criteria. The appropriateness of the concept of work adjustment to the evaluation of vocational rehabilitation outcomes was strongly suggested by research findings from a variety of sources, such as job satisfaction studies, employee attitude studies, studies of industrial conflict and industrial morale, studies utilizing counseling interviews and exit interviews, studies of productivity and efficiency, job tenure studies, and studies of work history patterns.

Reprinted with the permission of authors and publisher from the article of the same title, in *Minnesota Studies in Vocational Rehabilitation*, XX. Minneapolis, Minnesota: The Industrial Relations Center, University of Minnesota, 1966, pp. 1–13.

The investigators' concept of work adjustment was first formally described in 1960 in the monograph, *A Definition of Work Adjustment*.[2] Following Rodger's suggestion in an early article,[3] the variables of satisfaction and satisfactoriness were selected as the indicators of work adjustment. "Satisfaction" was defined as work adjustment viewed from the vantage point of the individual, while "satisfactoriness" designated work adjustment viewed from the employer's standpoint.

Satisfaction, according to the 1960 monograph, included overall job satisfaction, and satisfaction with various specific aspects of the individual's work environment, such as his supervisor, his co-workers, his working conditions, hours of work, pay, and type of work. It included the satisfaction of his needs and the fulfillment of his aspirations and expectations, and the similarity of his interests to those of successful persons working in his chosen occupation.

Satisfactoriness, as the other index of work adjustment, included such components as the worker's productivity and efficiency, the congruence of his abilities with job requirements, his ability to get along with his supervisor and his co-workers, and to follow company policies.

Work adjustment was described as a process that occurred throughout the individual's working years. Cycles of satisfaction and dissatisfaction, and of satisfactoriness and unsatisfactoriness, might occur in the individual's work history. Work adjustment patterns might vary for individuals in different occupations, and were likely to be affected by such factors as age, sex, education, training, disability, and adjustment outside the work setting. The study of the interrelationships among work adjustment variables was essential.

The definition of work adjustment in the 1960 monograph provided a useful framework for the Work Adjustment Project. Studies were carried out to develop measures of the work adjustment variables and to enlarge the understanding of work adjustment, especially as it related to the disabled.[4] Research was undertaken to obtain and validate work histories of employees,[5] to measure attitudes of employers,[6] and to develop criterion measures of satisfaction and satisfactoriness.[7]

Increasingly, the explanation and prediction of work adjustment became the major concern of the project. Although the definition of work adjustment had included some useful principles, a more elaborate and integrated theoretical statement concerning work adjustment was needed. As a result, a theory of work adjustment was published in January, 1964.[8]

THE THEORY OF
WORK ADJUSTMENT

The Theory of Work Adjustment is based on the premise that the proper subject matter for vocational psychology is the individual as a responding organism. As such, he is assumed to have a set of response potentials, the upper limits of which are presumably determined by heredity. The individual will respond when his response potentials make responding possible, and when the environment permits and/or stimulates responding. As he responds, his responding becomes associated with rein-

forcers — environmental conditions which maintain responding.

Over a period of time, responses that are utilized most frequently by the individual become identifiable as a primitive set of "abilities." At the same time, the reinforcers in the environment which occur most frequently in the reinforcement of the individual's responding become identified with a primitive set of "needs." Together, these abilities and needs constitute the beginnings of the individual's work personality.

As he grows and develops, the individual's sets of abilities and needs undergo change. Some abilities and needs are strengthened. Others disappear. New abilities and needs are added. The strengths of abilities and needs become more stable as the individual develops an increasingly fixed style of life. Eventually they crystallize, at which point successive measurements of ability and need strength will show no significant change. The individual can then be said to have a stable work personality. The theory of work adjustment is premised on a stable work personality.

Work adjustment is defined as the process by which the individual interacts and comes to terms with his work environment. The outcome of the process is measured by two indicators: satisfactoriness and satisfaction. The significant aspect of the individual in this process is his work personality, that is, his sets of abilities and needs. The significant aspects of the work environment include the abilities required for successful performance of the job and the reinforcers available to the individual. Work adjustment is determined both by the correspondence between abilities and ability requirements, and by the correspondence between reinforcer system and needs.

The theory of work adjustment is stated in the following nine propositions:

Proposition I. An individual's work adjustment at any point in time is defined by his concurrent levels of satisfactoriness and satisfaction.

Proposition II. Satisfactoriness is a function of the correspondence between an individual's set of abilities and the ability requirements of the work environment, provided that the individual's needs correspond with the reinforcer system of the work environment.

Proposition III. Satisfaction is a function of the correspondence between the reinforcer system of the work environment and the individual's set of needs, provided that the individual's abilities correspond with the ability requirements of the work environment.

Proposition IV. Satisfaction moderates the functional relationship between satisfactoriness and the correspondence of the individual's ability set with the ability requirements of the work environment.

Proposition V. Satisfactoriness moderates the functional relationship between satisfaction and the correspondence of the reinforcer system of the work environment with the individual's set of needs.

Proposition VI. The probability of an individual's being forced out of the work environment is inversely related to his measured satisfactoriness.

Proposition VII. The probability of an individual's voluntarily leaving the work environment is inversely related to his measured satisfaction.

Proposition VIII. Tenure is a function of satisfactoriness and satisfaction.

Proposition IX. The correspondence between the individual (abilities and needs) and the work environment (ability requirements and reinforcer system) increases as a function of tenure.

INSTRUMENTATION FOR THE THEORY OF WORK ADJUSTMENT

A formal test of the Theory of Work Adjustment requires the translation of its concepts into operational terms. The main concept, "correspondence," requires that both the individual and the environment be described using the same or comparable sets of measurement dimensions. These dimensions, according to the theory, are of two kinds: abilities and needs. The theory also requires the measurement of two intervening variables:[9] satisfactoriness and satisfaction. These variables "intervene" between individual-environment correspondence on the one hand, and tenure outcomes (stay-leave) on the other. Several Work Adjustment Project studies were concerned with the measurement of these variables (abilities, needs, satisfactoriness, and satisfaction). The report on these studies given below follows the historical sequence.

Measurement of Satisfaction

The first work adjustment instrumentation studies were directed toward the development of criterion measures of job satisfaction.[10] The initial study involved Hoppock's Job Satisfaction Blank (a 4-item general satisfaction measure) and the Industrial Relations Center's 54-item Employee Attitude Scale. The latter instrument measured seven aspects of job satisfaction: satisfaction with company, supervision, co-workers, working conditions, hours and pay, type of work and communication. To these two instruments were added 22 experimental job-attitude items, making a total of 80 items for the study.

These instruments were administered to a sample of 638 disabled (physically handicapped) persons and 530 "control" persons (non-handicapped co-workers of the disabled persons). The sample was cross-classified into four occupational groups: nonskilled blue-collar, skilled blue-collar, nonskilled white-collar, and skilled white-collar, making a total of eight groups for the study. Scales were developed to measure different components of satisfaction for each group. These scales were found, for the most part, to be highly reliable and relatively independent of each other.

In general, satisfaction was found to be "organized" in a similar fashion for each of the eight groups. Five components of satisfaction were found in common for all groups: general job satisfaction, satisfaction with working conditions, with supervision, with compensation and with co-workers. In addition, some significant differences in satisfaction components were observed among the groups. For example, a "satisfaction-with-type-of-work" scale appeared only for the disabled, skilled blue-collar group; a "satisfaction-with-company" scale appeared only for skilled blue-collar workers, both disabled and control.

For the most part, differences in scale content were observed more frequently among the occupational groups than between the disabled and the control (non-disabled) groups. However, presence or absence of disability did tend to be more important than occupation in determining the level of satisfaction expressed by workers. *For all components of satisfaction, the level of satisfaction expressed by the disabled groups was invariably lower than that of their control counterparts.*

This study was the basis for the later development of the Minnesota Satisfaction Questionnaire (MSQ), a 100-item, 20-scale instrument to measure satisfaction along the following dimensions: ability utilization, achievement, activity, advancement, authority, company policies and practices, compensation, co-workers, creativity, independence, moral values, recognition, responsibility, security, social service, social status, supervision — human relations, supervision — technical, variety, and working conditions.[11] The MSQ was developed on 1,793 employees in jobs ranging from unskilled blue-collar to managerial. The scales were found to have high reliabilities (median reliability coefficient was .88) and to be relatively independent (median interscale correlation was .45). A factor-analysis of scale intercorrelations resulted in two factors identified as "satisfaction with the 'intrinsic' aspects of reinforcement at work" and a

"supervision factor, relating to aspects 'extrinsic' to the work itself."[12] Scale means and scale variabilities indicated adequate discrimination potential for the instrument.

A 20-item short form of the MSQ has also developed. The short form consists of the one item from each scale which correlated the highest with the total scale score for the development group (N = 1,793).

Measurement of Satisfactoriness

The development of a satisfactoriness measure was undertaken with a sample of 483 disabled persons and 496 "control" individuals grouped into the same four occupational categories used in the first satisfaction study.[13] Three instruments were used to define employment satisfactoriness: 1) an alternation ranking form on which the supervisor ranked all the persons in the work group on overall job performance; 2) a supervisor evaluation form, consisting of nine questions answered on a 5-point scale with regard to absences, lateness, accident record, need for disciplinary action, general quality of work, promotability, probability of pay raise recommendation, transferability, and a general adjustment item indicating how much of the time the individual was a matter of concern to his supervisor; and 3) a personnel records questionnaire, not used in the final analysis of the data because of insufficient variability in the information which it elicited. There were other serious limitations to the use of this latter form due to the fact that too many companies did not keep the kind and quality of records adequate for the evaluation of work habits, productivity and efficiency variables.

For all groups, two factors appeared to underlie these satisfactoriness measures: a performance factor, which included such considerations as promotability, general adjustment, and quality of work; and a conformance factor, which consisted of such items as absences, lateness, accidents. *On* measures of both performance and conformance, the disabled workers were evaluated as equal to the matched "control" workers.

The relationship between the measures of satisfactoriness and the measures of satisfaction was investigated for each occupational group separately. For all groups in this study, the general finding was that the satisfactoriness and satisfaction components of work adjustment were virtually unrelated. Little statistical relationship was found between how well people did their work and how well they liked their work.[14]

Measurement of Needs

The first measure of vocational needs developed in the Work Adjustment Project was the N-Factors Questionnaire (NFQ),[15] an instrument based largely on R. H. Schaffer's work.[16] This instrument consisted of 12 four-item scales measuring the following dimensions: achievement, authority, co-workers, creativity and challenge, dependence, independence, moral values, recognition, security, self-expression, social service, and social status. The questionnaire was developed on 1,014 persons. Analysis of the development data indicated that, while the NFQ scales were relatively independent and had adequate discrimination potential, only five of the twelve scales had acceptable reliabilities.

Based on the NFQ, a second questionnaire was constructed to improve scale reliabilities and the variability of scale scores, and to increase the number of need dimensions measured. This instrument, called the Minnesota Importance Questionnaire (MIQ),[17] consisted of 20 scales, each measured by 5 items. The 20 scales were as follows: (The illustrative item following each scale title is the item which correlated most highly with total scale score in a development sample of 2,308 employed individuals.)

1. *Ability Utilization*. I could do something that makes use of my abilities.

2. *Achievement*. The job could give me a feeling of accomplishment.

3. *Activity*. I could be busy all the time.

4. *Advancement*. The job would provide an opportunity for advancement.

5. *Authority*. I could tell people what to do.

6. *Company Policies and Practices*. The company would administer its policies fairly.

7. *Compensation*. My pay would compare well with that of other workers.

8. *Co-workers*. My co-workers would be easy to make friends with.

9. *Creativity*. I could try out some of my own ideas.

10. *Independence*. I could work alone on the job.

11. *Moral Values*. I could do the work without feeling that it is morally wrong.

12. *Recognition*. I could get recognition for the work I do.

13. *Responsibility*. I could make decisions on my own.

14. *Security*. The job would provide for steady employment.

15. *Social Service*. I could do things for other people.

16. *Social Status*. I could be "somebody" in the community.

17. *Supervision — Human Relations*. My boss would back up his men (with top management).

18. *Supervision — Technical*. My boss would train his men well.

19. *Variety*. I could do something different every day.

20. *Working Conditions*. The job would have good working conditions.

Analysis of the development data indicated that most persons responded to many of the items as being "important," or "very important," with few responses of "very unimportant," "not important," or "neither." However, there was enough scale score variation to allow reliable measurement, and most of the scales were relatively independent of the other scales. Subsequent studies showed the MIQ to be capable of discriminating between various groups of individuals, such as disabled vs. non-disabled groups, different occupational groups, and employed vs. pre-employment groups.

In the study of disabled vs. non-disabled groups, analysis of the data showed that *response to the MIQ was apparently related to the presence or absence of disability. Significant differences in response to the MIQ were also observed among four occupational groups.* These differences were consistent with "common-sense" expectations concerning the vocational needs of these occupational groups. Furthermore, *response to the MIQ was found to be affected by presence or absence of employment experience,* a finding anticipated by the Theory of Work Adjustment. These studies, therefore, provided evidence of construct validity for the MIQ as a measure of vocational needs.

Since both the MIQ and MSQ were similar in format and items, a study was conducted to compare response to the two instruments administered at the same time. Both the MIQ and MSQ were completed at the same time by 1,793 employees. It was found that on 11 scales the MIQ item which correlated most highly with MIQ scale score was the "need" counterpart of the "satisfaction" item which had, in turn, correlated most highly with its MSQ scale score. Further, analysis of the data showed that the scores on the MIQ and the MSQ were relatively independent of each other. Parallel scales (measuring need and satisfaction on the same reinforcement dimension) had a median correlation of .19, while the highest correlation between nonparallel scales was .31. Factor analysis resulted in two "need" factors and two "satisfaction" factors. It was concluded, then, that the two instruments, the MIQ and the MSQ, measure two different sets of variables.[18]

Research is currently being conducted on a paired-comparisons revision of the MIQ. Preliminary analyses suggest that the paired-comparisons format yields better scale score variabilities, better factor structure of scale

scores, and better intra-individual variability of scores, than the rating-scale format of the original MIQ. However, the administration time for the revised MIQ is considerably longer, and respondents require more motivation to complete the questionnaire.

Measurement of Abilities

With the availability of several carefully constructed measures of abilities, one of these was selected for use in the research program. The United States Employment Service's General Aptitude Test Battery (GATB)[19] was an obvious choice, primarily because of the psychometric qualities of the battery and the wealth of data available concerning the GATB, and also because of the vocational rehabilitation orientation of the research program. It was felt that, of all available multifactor ability tests, the GATB was the most frequently used in public rehabilitation agencies, and probably in private agencies as well.

Recently, work aimed at supplementing the GATB was started in two directions. First, measures of ability dimensions not covered by the GATB are being studied. Data on several of these are now being collected. Second, development work is proceeding on an experimental type of aptitude test which makes use of a gain score (from pre-test to post-test) resulting from the interposition of a standard practice sequence between pre- and post-tests.

SUMMARY

With the preceding developments, the Work Adjustment Project is "tooled up" for a first major test of some of the propositions of the Theory of Work Adjustment. Initially, the test requires the administration of GATB, MIQ and MSQ to large occupational samples, and the collection of satisfactoriness data on these individuals. Each occupational sample must be large enough to permit division into a "development" group, to be used in determining ability requirements and reinforcers for the occupation, and a "validation" group on which to test the theory. Such a study is currently being carried out.

In addition, findings from several studies conducted during the past two years support the validity and utility of the Theory of Work Adjustment. The most important of these studies are discussed in the next chapter.

[1]*Minnesota studies in vocational rehabilitiation*, X.
[2]Ibid.
[3]The initial source was Heron, A. Satisfaction and satisfactoriness: complementary aspects of occupational adjustment. *Occupational Psychology.* 1954, *28*, 140–153. Professor Alec Rodger, University of London, in a personal communication, May 1965, pointed out that he originated the terms "satisfaction and satisfactoriness" in an early article.
[4]*Minnesota studies in vocational rehabilitation*, XIII, XIV, XVI, XVII.
[5]*Minnesota studies vocational rehabilitation*, XII.

[6]*Minnesota studies in vocational rehabilitation*, XI.
[7]*Minnesota studies in vocational rehabilitation*, XIII, XIV.
[8]*Minnesota studies in vocational rehabilitation*, XV.
[9]In the sense defined by Meehl, P.E., and MacCorquodale, K. On a distinction between hypothetical constructs and intervening variables. *Psychological Review*, 1948, 55, 95–107.
[10]*Minnesota studies in vocational rehabilitation*, XIII.
[11]A copy of the MSQ appears in *Minnesota studies in vocational rehabilitation*, XVIII, pp. 65–71.
[12]Ibid. p. 14.
[13]*Minnesota studies in vocational rehabilitation*, XIV.
[14]Ibid, pp. 31 ff.
[15]A copy of the NFQ appears in *Minnesota studies in vocational rehabilitation*, XVI, pp. 79–81.
[16]Schaffer, R. H. Job satisfaction as related to need satisfaction in work. *Psychological Monographs*, 1953, No. 364.
[17]A copy of the MIQ appears in *Minnesota studies in vocational rehabilitation*, XVI, pp. 83–89.
[18]*Minnesota studies in vocational rehabilitation*, XVIII, pp. 16–21.
[19]United States Department of Labor, Bureau of Employment Security.

Careers, Personality, and Adult Socialization[1]

HOWARD S. BECKER, *Stanford University*

ANSELM L. STRAUSS, *University of California Medical Center*

In contradistinction to other disciplines, the sociological approach to the study of personality and personality change views the person as a member of a social structure.

Reprinted with the permission of authors and publisher from the article of the same title, in *American Journal of Sociology*, 1956, *62*, 253-263.

Usually the emphasis is upon some cross-section in his life: on the way he fills his status, on the consequent conflicts in role and his dilemmas. When the focus is more developmental, then concepts like career carry the import of movement through structures. Much writing on career, of course, pertains more to patterned sequences of passage than to the persons. A fairly comprehensive statement about careers as related both to institutions and to persons would be useful in furthering research. We shall restrict our discussion to careers in work organizations and occupations, for purposes of economy.

CAREER FLOW

Organizations built around some particular kind of work or situation at work tend to be characterized by recurring patterns of tension and of problems. Thus in occupations whose central feature is performance of a service for outside clients, one chronic source of tension is the effort of members to control their work life themselves while in contact with outsiders. In production organizations somewhat similar tensions arise from the workers' efforts to maintain relative autonomy over job conditions.

Whatever the typical problems of an occupation, the pattern of associated problems will vary with one's position. Some positions will be easier, some more difficult; some will afford more prestige, some less; some will pay better than others. In general, the personnel move from less to more desirable positions, and the flow is usually, but not necessarily, related to age. The pure case is the bureaucracy as described by Mannheim, in which seniority and an age-related increase in skill and responsibility automatically push men in the desired direction and within a single organization.[2]

An ideally simple model of flow up through an organization is something like the following: recruits enter at the bottom in positions of least prestige and move up through the ranks as they gain in age, skill, and experience. Allowing for some attrition due to death, sickness, and dismissal or resignation, all remain in the organization until retirement. Most would advance to top ranks. A few reach the summit of administration. Yet even in bureaucracies, which perhaps come closest to this model, the very highest posts often go not to those

who have come up through the ranks but to "irregulars" — people with certain kinds of experiences or qualifications not necessarily acquired by long years of official service. In other ways, too, the model is oversimple: posts at any rank may be filled from the outside; people get "frozen" at various levels and do not rise. Moreover, career movements may be not only up but down or sideways, as in moving from one department to another at approximately the same rank.

The flow of personnel through an organization should be seen, also, as a number of streams; that is, there may be several routes to the posts of high prestige and responsibility. These may be thought of as escalators. An institution invests time, money, and energy in the training of its recruits and members which it cannot afford to let go to waste. Hence just being on the spot often means that one is bound to advance. In some careers, even a small gain in experience gives one a great advantage over the beginner. The mere fact of advancing age or of having been through certain kinds of situations or training saves many an employee from languishing in lower positions. This is what the phrase "seasoning" refers to — the acquiring of requisite knowledge and skills, skills that cannot always be clearly specified even by those who have them. However, the escalator will carry one from opportunities as well as to them. After a certain amount of time and money have been spent upon one's education for the job, it is not always easy to get off one escalator and on another. Immediate superiors will block transfer. Sponsors will reproach one for disloyalty. Sometimes a man's special training and experience will be thought to have spoiled him for a particular post.

RECRUITMENT AND REPLACEMENT

Recruitment is typically regarded as occurring only at the beginning of a career, where the occupationally uncommitted are bid for, or as something which happens only when there is deliberate effort to get people to commit themselves. But establishments must recruit for all positions; whenever personnel are needed, they must be found and often trained. Many higher positions, as in bureaucracies, appear to recruit automatically from aspirants at next lower levels. This is only appearance: the recruitment mechanisms are standardized and work well. Professors, for example, are drawn regularly from lower ranks, and the system works passably in most academic fields. But in schools of engineering young instructors are likely to be drained off into industry and not be on hand for promotion. Recruitment is never really automatic but depends upon developing in the recruit certain occupational or organizational commitments which correspond to regularized career routes.

Positions in organizations are being vacated continually through death and retirement, promotion and demotion. Replacements may be drawn from the outside ("an outside man") or from within the organization. Most often positions are filled by someone promoted from below or shifted from another department without gaining in prestige. When career routes are well laid out, higher positions are routinely filled from aspirants at the next lower level. However, in most organizations many career routes are not so rigidly laid out: a man may jump from one career over to another to fill the organization's need. When this happens, the "insider-outsider" may be envied by those who have come up by the more orthodox routes; and his associates on his original route may regard him as a turncoat. This may be true even if he is not the first to have made the change, as in the jump from scholar to dean or doctor to hospital administrator. Even when replacement from outside the organization is routine for certain positions, friction may result if the newcomer has come up by an irregular route — as when a college president is chosen from outside the usual circle of feeding occupations. A candidate whose background is too irregular is likely to be eliminated unless just this irregularity makes

him particularly valuable. The advantage of "new blood" versus "inbreeding" may be the justification. A good sponsor can widen the limits within which the new kind of candidate is judged, by asking that certain of his qualities be weighed against others; as Hall says, "the question is not whether the applicant possesses a specific trait . . . but whether these traits can be assimilated by the specific institutions."[3]

Even when fairly regular routes are followed, the speed of advancement may not be rigidly prescribed. Irregularity may be due in part to unexpected needs for replacement because a number of older men retire in quick succession or because an older man leaves and a younger one happens to be conveniently present. On the other hand, in some career lines there may be room for a certain amount of manipulation of "the system." One such method is to remain physically mobile, especially early in the career, thus taking advantage of several institutions' vacancies.

THE LIMITS OF REPLACEMENT AND RECRUITMENT

Not all positions within an organization recruit from an equally wide range. Aside from the fact that different occupations may be represented in one establishment, some positions require training so specific that recruits can be drawn only from particular schools or firms. Certain positions are merely way stations and recruit only from aspirants directly below. Some may draw only from the outside, and the orbit is always relevant to both careers and organization. One important question, then, about any organization is the limits within which positions recruit incumbents. Another is the limits of the recruitment in relation to certain variables — age of the organization, its relations with clients, type of generalized work functions, and the like.

One can also identify crucial contingencies for careers in preoccupational life by noting the general or probable limits within which recruiting is carried on and the forces by which they are maintained. For example, it is clear that a position can be filled, at least at first, only from among those who know of it. Thus physiologists cannot be recruited during high school, for scarcely any youngster then knows what a physiologist is or does. By the same token, however, there are at least generally formulated notions of the "artist," so that recruitment into the world of art often begins in high school.[4] This is paradoxical, since the steps and paths later in the artist's career are less definite than in the physiologist's. The range and diffusion of a public stereotype are crucial in determining the number and variety of young people from whom a particular occupation can recruit, and the unequal distribution of information about careers limits occupations possibilities.

There are problems attending the systematic restriction of recruiting. Some kinds of persons, for occupationally irrelevant reasons (formally, anyway), may not be considered for some positions at all. Medical schools restrict recruiting in this way: openly, on grounds of "personality assessments," and covertly on ethnicity. Italians, Jews, and Negroes who do become doctors face differential recruitment into the formal and informal hierarchies of influence, power, and prestige in the medical world. Similar mechanisms operate at the top and bottom of industrial organizations.[5]

Another problem is that of "waste." Some recruits in institutions which recruit pretty widely do not remain. Public caseworkers in cities are recruited from holders of Bachelor's degrees, but most do not remain caseworkers. From the welfare agency's point of view this is waste. From other perspectives this is not waste, for they may exploit the job and its opportunities for private ends. Many who attend school while supposedly visiting clients may be able to transfer to new escalators because of the acquisition, for instance, of a Master's degree. Others actually build up small businesses during this "free time." The only permanent recruits, those who do not constitute waste, are those who fail at such endeavors.[6] Unless an organization actually finds useful a constant turnover of some sector of its personnel, it is faced with the problem of creating organizational loyalties and — at higher levels anyhow — satisfactory careers or the illusion of them, within the organization.

TRAINING AND SCHOOLS

Schooling occurs most conspicuously during the early stages of a career and is an essential part of getting people committed to careers and prepared to fill positions. Both processes may, or may not, be going on simultaneously. However, movement from one kind of job or position or another virtually always necessitates some sort of learning — sometimes before and sometimes on the job, sometimes through informal channels and sometimes at school. This means that schools may exist within the framework of an organization. In-service training is not only for jobs on lower levels but also for higher positions. Universities and special schools are attended by students who are not merely preparing for careers but getting degrees or taking special courses in order to move faster and higher. In some routes there is virtual blockage of mobility because the top of the ladder is not very high; in order to rise higher, one must return to school to prepare for ascending by another route. Thus the registered nurse may have to return to school to become a nursing educator, administrator, or even supervisor. Sometimes the aspirant may study on his own, and this may be effective unless he must present a diploma to prove he deserves promotion.

The more subtle connections are between promotion and informal training. Certain positions preclude the acquiring of certain skills or information, but others foster it. It is possible to freeze a man at given levels or to move him faster, unbeknownst to him.

Thus a sponsor, anticipating a need for certain requirements in his candidate, may arrange for critical experiences to come his way. Medical students are aware that if they obtain internships in certain kinds of hospitals they will be exposed to certain kinds of learning: the proper internship is crucial to many kinds of medical careers. But learning may depend upon circumstances which the candidate cannot control and of which he may not even be aware. Thus Goldstein has pointed out that nurses learn more from doctors at hospitals not attached to a medical school; elsewhere the medical students become the beneficiaries of the doctors' teaching.[7] Quite often who teaches whom and what is connected with matters of convenience as well as with prestige. It is said, for instance, that registered nurses are jealous of their prerogatives and will not transmit certain skills to practical nurses. Nevertheless, the nurse is often happy to allow her aides to relieve her of certain other jobs and will pass along the necessary skills; and the doctor in his turn may do the same with his nurses.

The connection between informal learning and group allegiance should not be minimized. Until a newcomer has been accepted, he will not be taught crucial trade secrets. Conversely, such learning may block mobility, since to be mobile is to abandon standards, violate friendships, and even injure one's self-regard. Within some training institutions students are exposed to different and sometimes antithetical work ideologies — as with commercial and fine artists — which results in sharp and sometimes lasting internal conflicts of loyalty.

Roy's work on industrial organization furnishes a subtle instance of secrecy and loyalty in training.[8] The workers in Roy's machine shop refused to enlighten him concerning ways of making money on difficult piecework jobs until given evidence that he could be trusted in undercover skirmishes with management. Such systematic withholding of training may mean that an individual can qualify for promotion by perfor-

mance only by shifting group loyalties, and that disqualifies him in some other sense. Training hinders as well as helps. It may incapacitate one for certain duties as well as train him for them. Roy's discussion of the managerial "logic of efficiency" makes this clear: workers, not trained in this logic, tend to see short cuts to higher production more quickly than managers, who think in terms of sentimental dogmas of efficiency.[9]

Certain transmittible skills, information, and qualities facilitate movement, and it behooves the candidate to discover and distinguish what is genuinely relevant in his training. The student of careers must also be sensitized to discover what training is essential or highly important to the passage from one status to another.

RECRUITING FOR UNDESIRABLE POSITIONS

A most difficult kind of recruiting is for positions which no one wants. Ordinary incentives do not work, for these are positions without prestige, without future, without financial reward. Yet they are filled. How, and by whom? Most obviously, they are filled by failures (the crews of gandy dancers who repair railroad tracks are made up of skid-row bums), to whom they are almost the only means of survival. Most positions filled by failures are not openly regarded as such; special rhetorics deal with misfortune and make their ignominious fate more palatable for the failures themselves and those around them.[10]

Of course, failure is a matter of perspective. Many positions represent failure to some but not to others. For the middle-class white, becoming a caseworker in a public welfare agency may mean failure; but for the Negro from the lower-middle class the job may be a real prize. The permanent positions in such agencies tend to be occupied by whites who have failed to reach anything better and, in larger numbers, by Negroes who have succeeded in arriving this far.[11] Likewise, some recruitment into generally undesirable jobs is from the ranks of the disaffected who care little for generally accepted values. The jazz musicians who play in Chicago's Clark Street dives make little money, endure bad working conditions, but desire the freedom to play as they could not in better-paying places.[12]

Recruits to undesirable positions also come from the ranks of the transients, who, because they feel that they are on their way to something different and better, can afford temporarily to do something *infra dig*. Many organizations rely primarily on transients — such are the taxi companies and some of the mail-order houses. Among the permanent incumbents of undesirable positions are those, also, who came in temporarily but whose brighter prospects did not materialize, they thus fall into the "failure" group.

Still another group is typified by the taxi dancer, whose career Cressey has described. The taxi dancer starts at the top, from which the only movement possible is down or out. She enters the profession young and good-looking and draws the best customers in the house, but, as age and hard work take their toll, she ends with the worst clients or becomes a streetwalker.[13] Here the worst positions are filled by individuals who start high and so are committed to a career that ends badly — a more common pattern of life, probably, than is generally recognized.

Within business and industrial organizations, not everyone who attempts to move upward succeeds. Men are assigned to positions prematurely, sponsors drop protégés, and miscalculations are made about the abilities of promising persons. Problems for the organization arise from those contingencies. Incompetent persons must be moved into positions where they cannot do serious damage, others of limited ability can still be useful if wisely placed. Aside from outright firing, various methods of "cooling out" the failures can be adopted, among them honorific promotion, banishment "to the sticks," shunting to other departments, frank demotion, bribing out of the organization, and down-grading through departmental mergers. The use of particular methods is related to the structure of the organization; and these, in turn, have consequences both for the failure and for the organization.[14]

ATTACHMENT AND SERVERANCE

Leaders of organizations sometimes complain that their personnel will not take responsibility or that some men (the wrong ones) are too ambitious. This complaint reflects a dual problem which confronts every organization. Since all positions must be filled, some men must be properly motivated to take certain positions and stay in them for a period, while others must be motivated to move onward and generally upward. The American emphasis on mobility should not lead us to assume that everyone wants to rise to the highest levels or to rise quickly. Aside from this, both formal mechanisms and informal influences bind incumbents, at least temporarily, to certain positions. Even the ambitious may be willing to remain in a given post, provided that it offers important contacts or the chance to learn certain skills and undergo certain experiences. Part of the bargain in staying in given positions is the promise that they lead somewhere. When career lines are fairly regularly laid out, positions lead definitely somewhere and at a regulated pace. One of the less obvious functions of the sponsor is to alert his favorites to the sequence and its timing, rendering them more ready to accept undesirable assignments and to refrain from champing at the bit when it might be awkward for the organization.

To certain jobs, in the course of time, come such honor and glory that the incumbents will be satisfied to remain there permanently, giving up aspirations to move upward. This is particularly true when allegiance to colleagues, built on informal relations and conflict with other ranks, is intense and runs counter to allegiance to the institution. But individuals are also attached to positions by virtue of having done particularly well at them; they often take great satisfaction in their competence at certain techniques and develop self-conceptions around them.

All this makes the world of organizations go around, but it also poses certain problems both institutional and personal. The stability of institutions is predicated upon the proper preparation of aspirants for the next steps and upon institutional aid in transmuting motives and allegiances. While it is convenient to have some personnel relatively immobile, others must be induced to cut previous ties, to balance rewards in favor of moving, and even to take risks for long-run gains. If we do not treat mobility as normal, and thus regard attachment to a position as abnormal, we are then free to ask how individuals are induced to move along. It is done by devices such as sponsorship, by planned sequences of positions and skills, sometimes tied to age; by rewards, monetary and otherwise, and, negatively, by ridicule and the denial of responsibility to the lower ranks. There is, of course, many a slip in the inducing of mobility. Chicago public school teachers illustrate this point. They move from schools in the slums to middle-class neighborhoods. The few who prefer to remain in the tougher slum schools have settled in too snugly to feel capable of facing the risks of moving to "better" schools.[15] Their deviant course illuminates the more usual patterns of the Chicago teacher's career.

TIMING IN STATUS PASSAGE

Even when paths in a career are regular and smooth, there always arise problems of pacing and timing. While, ideally, successors and predecessors should move in and out of offices at equal speeds, they do not and cannot. Those asked to move on or along or upward may be willing but must make actual and symbolic preparations; mean-

while, the successor waits impatiently. Transition periods are a necessity, for a man often invests heavily of himself in a position, comes to possess it as it possesses him, and suffers in leaving it. If the full ritual of leave-taking is not allowed, the man may not pass fully into his new status. On the other hand, the institution has devices to make him forget, to plunge him into the new office, to woo and win him with the new gratifications, and, at the same time, to force him to abandon the old. When each status is conceived as the logical and temporal extension of the one previous, then severance is not so disturbing, Nevertheless, if a man must face his old associates in unaccoustomed roles, problems of loyalty arise. Hence a period of tolerance after formal admission to the new status is almost a necessity. It is rationalized in phrases like "it takes time" and "we all make mistakes when starting, until . . . ."

But, on the other hand, those new to office may be too zealous. They often commit the indelicate error of taking too literally their formal promotion or certification, when actually intervening steps must be traversed before the attainment of full prerogatives. The passage may involve trials and tests of loyalty, as well as the simple accumulation of information and skill. The overeager are kept in line by various controlling devices: a new assistant professor discovers that it will be "just a little while" before the curriculum can be rearranged so that he can teach his favorite courses. Even a new superior has to face the resentment or the cautiousness of established personnel and may, if sensitive, pace his "moving in on them" until he has passed unspoken tests.

When subordinates are raised to the ranks of their superiors, an especially delicate situation is created. Equality is neither created by that official act, nor, even if it were, can it come about without a certain awkwardness. Patterns of response must be rearranged by both parties, and strong self-control must be exerted so that acts are appropriate. Slips are inevitable, for, although the new status may be full granted, the proper identities may at times be forgotten, to everyone's embarrassment. Eventually, the former subordinate may come to command or take precedence over someone to whom he once looked for advice and guidance. When colleagues who were formerly sponsors and sponsored disagree over some important issue, recrimination may become overt and betrayal explicit. It is understandable why those who have been promoted often prefer, or are advised, to take office in another organization, however much they may wish to remain at home.

MULTIPLE ROUTES AND SWITCHING

Theoretically, a man may leave one escalator and board another, instead of following the regular route. Such switching is most visible during the schooling, or preoccupational, phases of careers. Frequently students change their line of endeavor but remain roughly within the same field; this is one way for less desirable and less well-known specialities to obtain recruits. Certain kinds of training, such as the legal, provide bases for moving early and easily into a wide variety of careers. In all careers, there doubtless are some points at which switching to another career is relatively easy. In general, while commitment to a given career automatically closes paths, the skills and information thereby acquired open up other routes and new goals. One may not, of course, perceive the alternatives or may dismiss them as risky or otherwise undesirable.

When a number of persons have changed escalators at about the same stage in their careers, then there is the beginning of a new career. This is one way by which career lines become instituted. Sometimes the innovation occurs at the top ranks of older careers; when all honors are exhausted, the incumbent himself may look for new worlds to conquer. Or he may seem like a good risk to

an organization looking for personnel with interestingly different qualifications. Such new phases of career are much more than honorific and may indeed be an essential inducement to what becomes pioneering.

Excitement and dangers are intimately tied up with switching careers. For example, some careers are fairly specific in goal but diffuse in operational means: the "fine artist" may be committed to artistic ideals but seize upon whatever jobs are at hand to help him toward creative goals. When he takes a job in order to live, he thereby risks committing himself to an alternative occupational career; and artists and writers do, indeed, get weaned away from the exercise of their art in just this way. Some people never set foot on a work escalator but move from low job to low job. Often they seek better conditions of work or a little more money rather than chances to climb insitutional or occupational ladders. Many offers of opportunities to rise are spurned by part-time or slightly committed recruits, often because the latter are engaged in pursuing alternative routes while holding the job, perhaps a full-time one providing means of livelihood. This has important and, no doubt, subtle effects upon institutional functioning. When careers are in danger of being brought to an abrupt end — as with airplane pilots — then, before retirement, other kinds of careers may be prepared for or entered. This precaution is very necessary. When generalized mobility is an aim, specific routes may be chosen for convenience' sake. One is careful not to develop the usual motivation and allegiances. This enables one to get off an escalator and to move over to another with a minimum of psychological strain.

Considerable switching takes place within a single institution or a single occupational world and is rationalized in institutional and occupational terms, both by the candidates and by their colleagues. A significant consequence of this, undoubtedly, is subtle psychological strain, since the new positions and those preceding are both somewhat alike and different.

CLIMACTIC PERIODS

Even well-worn routes have stretches of maximum opportunity and danger. The critical passage in some careers lies near the beginning. This is especially so when the occupation or institution strongly controls recruitment; once chosen, prestige and deference automatically accrue. In another kind of career the critical time comes at the end and sometimes very abruptly. In occupations which depend upon great physical skill, the later phases of a career are especially hazardous. It is also requisite in some careers that one choose the proper successor to carry on, lest one's own work be partly in vain. The symbolic last step of moving out may be quite as important as any that preceded it.

Appropriate or strategic timing is called for, to meet opportunity and danger, but the timing becomes vital at different periods in different kinds of careers. A few, such as the careers of virtuoso musical performers, begin so early in life that the opportunity to engage in music may have passed long before they learn of it. Some of the more subtle judgments of timing are required when a person wishes to shift from one escalator to another. Richard Wohl, of the University of Chicago, in an unpublished paper has suggested that modeling is a step which women may take in preparation for upward mobility through marriage; but models may marry before they know the ropes, and so marry too low; or they may marry too long after their prime, and so marry less well than they might. Doubtless organizations and occupations profit from mistakes of stragetic timing, both to recruit and then to retain their members.

During the most crucial periods of any career, a man suffers greater psychological stress than during other periods. This is perhaps less so if he is not aware of his opportunities and dangers — for then the contingencies are over before they can be grasped or coped with: but probably it is more usual to be aware, or to be made so by colleagues and seniors, of the nature of imminent or current crises. Fortunately, together with such definitions there exist rationales to guide action. The character of the critical junctures and the ways in which they are handled may irrevocably decide a man's fate.

INTERDEPENDENCE OF CAREERS

Institutions, at any given moment, contain people at different stages in their careers. Some have already "arrived," others are still on their way up, still others just entering. Movements and changes at each level are in various ways dependent on those occurring at other levels.

Such interdependence is to be found in the phenomenon of sponsorship, where individuals move up in a work organization through the activities of older and more well-established men. Hall[16] has given a classic description of sponsorship in medicine. The younger doctor of the proper class and acceptable ethnic origin is absorbed, on the recommendation of a member, into the informal "inner fraternity" which controls hospital appointments and which is influential in the formation and maintenance of a clientele. The perpetuation of this coterie depends on a steady flow of suitable recruits. As the members age, retire, or die off, those who remain face a problem of recruiting younger men to do the less honorific and remunerative work, such as clinical work, that their group performs. Otherwise they themselves must do work inappropriate to their position or give place to others who covet their power and influence.

To the individual in the inner fraternity, a protégé eases the transition into retirement. The younger man gradually assumes the load which the sponsor can no longer comfortably carry, allowing the older man to retire gracefully, without that sudden cutting-down of work which frightens away patients, who leap to the conclusion that he is too old to perform capably.

In general, this is the problem of retiring with honor, of leaving a life's work with a sense that one will be missed. The demand may arise that a great man's work be carried on, although it may no longer be considered important or desirable by his successors. If the old man's prestige is great enough, the men below may have to orient themselves and their work as he suggests, for fear of offending him or of profaning his heritage. The identities of the younger man are thus shaped by the older man's passage from the pinnacle to retirement.

This interdependence of career may cross occupational lines within organizations, as in the case of the young physician who receives a significant part of his training from the older and more experienced nurses in the hospital; and those at the same level in an institution are equally involved in one another's identities. Sometimes budding careers within work worlds are interdependent in quite unsuspected ways. Consider the young painter or craftsman who must make his initial successes in enterprises founded by equally young art dealers, who, because they run their galleries on a shoestring, can afford the frivolity of exhibiting the works of an unknown. The very ability to take such risk provides the dealer a possible opportunity to discover a genius.

One way of uncovering the interdependence of careers is to ask: Who are the important *others* at various stages of the career, the persons significantly involved in the formation of one's own identity? These will vary with stages; at one point one's agemates are crucial, perhaps as competitors, while at another the actions of superiors are the most important. The interlocking of careers results in influential images of similarity and contrariety. In so far as the significant others shift and vary by the phases of a career, identities change in patterned and not altogether unpredictable ways.

THE CHANGING WORK WORLD

The occupations and organizations within which careers are made change in structure and direction of activity, expand or contract, transform purposes. Old functions and positions disappear, and new ones arise. These constitute potential locations for a new and sometimes wide range of people, for they are not incrusted with traditions and customs concerning their incumbents. They open up new kinds of careers to persons making their work lives within the institution and thus the possibility of variation in long-established types of career. An individual once clearly destined for a particular position suddenly finds himself confronted with an option; what was once a settled matter has split into a set of alternatives between which he must now choose. Different identities emerge as people in the organization take cognizance of this novel set of facts. The positions turn into recognized social entities, and some persons begin to reorient their ambitions. The gradual emergence of a new speciality typically creates this kind of situation within occupations.

Such occupational and institutional changes, of course, present opportunity for both success and failure. The enterprising grasp eagerly at new openings, making the most of them or attempting to; while others sit tight as long as they can. During such times the complexities of one's career are further compounded by what is happening to others with whom he is significantly involved. The ordinary lines of sponsorship in institutions are weakened or broken because those in positions to sponsor are occupied with matters more immediately germane to their own careers. Lower ranks feel the consequences of unusual pressures generated in the ranks above. People become peculiarly vulnerable to unaccustomed demands for loyalty and alliance which spring from the unforeseen changes in the organization. Paths to mobility become indistinct and less fixed, which has an effect on personal commitments and identities. Less able to tie themselves tightly to any one career, because such careers do not present themselves as clearly, men become more experimental and open-minded or more worried and apprehensive.

CAREERS AND PERSONAL IDENTITY

A frame of reference for studying careers is, at the same time, a frame for studying personal identities. Freudian and other psychiatric formulations of personality development probably overstress childhood experiences. Their systematic accounts end more or less with adolescence, later events being regarded as the elaboration of, or variations on, earlier occurrences. Yet central to any account of adult identity is the relation of change in identity to change in social position; for it is characteristic of adult life to afford and force frequent and momentous passages from status to status. Hence members of structures that change, riders on escalators that carry them up, along, and down, to unexpected places and to novel experiences even when in some sense foreseen, must gain, maintain, and regain a sense of personal identity. Identity "is never gained nor maintained once and for all."[17] Stabilities in the organization of behavior and of self-regard are inextricably dependent upon stabilities of social structure. Likewise, change ("development") is shaped by those patterned transactions which accompany career movement. The crises and turning points of life are not entirely institutionalized, but their occurrence and the terms which define and help to solve them are illuminated when seen in the context of career lines. In so far as some populations do not have careers in the sense that professional and business people have them, then the focus of attention ought still to be positional passage, but with domestic, age, and other escalators to the forefront. This done, it may turn out that the model sketched here must undergo revision.

[1]Everett C. Hughes, of the University of Chicago, has undoubtedly done more than any other sociologist in this country to focus attention and research on occupational careers. Several of our illustrations will be drawn from work done under his direction, and our own thinking owes much to his writing and conversation.

[2]Karl Mannheim, *Essays on the Sociology of Knowledge*, ed. Paul Kecskemeti (New York: Oxford University Press, 1953), pp. 247–49.

[3]Oswald Hall, "The Stages in a Medical Career," *American Journal of Sociology*, LIII (March, 1948), 332.

[4]Cf. Strauss's unpublished studies of careers in art and Howard S. Becker and James Carper, "The Development of Identification with an Occupation," *American Journal of Sociology*, LXI (January, 1956), 289–98.

[5]Cf. Hall, *op. cit.;* David Solomon, "Career Contingencies of Chicago Physicians" (unpublished Ph.D. thesis, University of Chicago, 1952); Everett C. Hughes, *French Canada in Transition* (Chicago: University of Chicago Press, 1943), pp. 52–53; Melville Dalton, "Informal Factors in Career Achievement," *American Journal of Sociology*, LVI (March, 1951), 407–15; and Orvis Collins, "Ethnic Behavior in Industry: Sponsorship and Rejection in a New England Factory," *American Journal of Sociology*, LI (January, 1946), 293–98.

[6]Cf. unpublished M.A. report of Earl Bogdanoff and Arnold Glass, "The Sociology of the Public Case Worker in an Urban Area" (University of Chicago, 1954).

[7]Rhoda Goldstein, "The Professional Nurse in the Hospital Bureaucracy" (unpublished Ph.D. thesis, University of Chicago, 1954).

[8]Donald Roy, "Quota Restriction and Goldbricking in a Machine Shop," *American Journal of Sociology*, LVII (March, 1952), 427–42.

[9]Donald Roy, "Efficiency and the 'Fix': Informal Intergroup Relations in a Piecework Machine Shop," *American Journal of Sociology*, LX (November, 1954), 255–66.

[10]Cf. Erving Goffman, "On Cooling the Mark Out: Some Aspects of Adaptation to Failure," *Psychiatry*, XV (November, 1952), 451–63.

[11]Bogdanoff and Glass, *op. cit.*

[12]Howard S. Becker, "The Professional Dance Musician and His Audience," *American Journal of Sociology*, LVII (September, 1951), 136–44.

[13]Paul G. Cressey, *The Taxi-Dance Hall* (Chicago; University of Chicago Press, 1932), pp. 84–106.

[14]Norman Martin and Anselm Strauss, "Patterns of Mobility within Industrial Organizations," *Journal of Business*, XXIX (April, 1956), 101–10.

[15]Howard S. Becker, "The Career of the Chicago Public Schoolteacher," *American Journal of Sociology*, LVII (March, 1952), 470–77.

[16]Hall, *op. cit.*

[17]Erik H. Erikson, *Childhood and Society* (New York: W. W. Norton & Co., 1950), p. 57.

The Effects of Changes in Roles on the Attitudes of Role Occupants[1]

SEYMOUR LIEBERMAN, *Kenyon and Eckhardt, Inc., New York*

PROBLEM

One of the fundamental postulates of role theory, as expounded by Newcomb (1952), Parsons (1951), and other role theorists, is that a persons' attitudes will be influenced by the role that he occupies in a social system. Although this proposition appears to be a plausible one, surprisingly little evidence is available that bears directly on it. One source of evidence is found in common folklore. "Johnny is a changed boy since he was made a monitor in school." "She is a different woman since she got married." "You would never recognize him since he became foreman." As much as these expressions smack of the truth, they offer little in the way of systematic or scientific support for the proposition that a person's attitudes are influenced by his role.

Somewhat more scientific, but still not definitive, is the common finding, in many social-psychological studies, that relationships exist between attitudes and roles. In other words, different attitudes are held by people who occupy different roles. For

Reprinted with the permission of author and publisher from the article of the same title, in *Human Relations*, 1956, *9*, 383–402.

example, Stouffer *et al.* (1949) found that commissioned officers are more favorable toward the Army than are enlisted men. The problem here is that the mere existence of a relationship between attitudes and roles does not reveal the cause and effect nature of the relationship found. One interpretation of Stouffer's finding might be that being made a commissioned officer tends to result in a person's becoming pro-Army — i.e. the role a person occupies influences his attitudes. But an equally plausible interpretation might be that being pro-Army tends to result in a person's being made a commissioned officer — i.e. a person's attitudes influence the likelihood of his being selected for a given role. In the absence of longitudinal data, the relationship offers no clear evidence that roles were the "cause" and attitudes the "effect."

The present study was designed to examine the effects of roles on attitudes in a particular field situation. The study is based on longitudinal data obtained in a role-differentiated, hierarchical organization. By taking advantage of natural role changes among personnel in the organization, it was possible to examine people's attitudes both before and after they underwent changes in roles. Therefore, the extent to which changes in roles were followed by changes in attitudes could be determined, and the cause and effect nature of any relationships found would be clear.

METHOD: PHASE 1

The study was part of a larger project carried out in a medium-sized Midwestern company engaged in the production of home appliance equipment. Let us call the company the Rockwell Corporation. At the time that the study was done. Rockwell employed about 4,000 people. This total included about 2,500 factory workers and about 150 first-level foremen. The company was unionized and most of the factory workers belonged to the union local, which was an affiliate of the U.A.W., C.I.O. About 150 factory workers served as stewards in the union, or roughly one steward for every foreman.

The study consisted of a "natural field experiment." The experimental variable was a change in roles, and the experimental period was the period of exposure to the experimental variable. The experimental groups were those employees who underwent changes in roles during this period; the control groups were those employees who did not change roles during this period The design may be described in terms of a three-step process: "before measurement," "experimental period," and "after measurement."

BEFORE MEASUREMENT   In September and October 1951, attitude questionnaires were filled out by virtually all factory personnel at Rockwell — 2,354 workers, 145 stewards, and 151 foremen. The questions dealt for the most part with employees' attitudes and perceptions about the company, the union, and various aspects of the job situation. The The respondents were told that the questionnaire was part of an overall survey to determine how employees felt about working conditions at Rockwell.

EXPERIMENTAL PERIOD   Between October 1951 and July 1952, twenty-three workers were made foremen and thirty-five workers became stewards. Most of the workers who became stewards during that period were elected during the annual steward elections held in May 1952. They replaced stewards who did not choose to run again or who were not re-elected by their constituents. In addition, a few workers replaced stewards who left the steward role for one reason or another throughout the year.

The workers who became foremen were not made foreman at any particular time. Promotions occurred as openings arose in supervisory positions. Some workers replaced foremen who retired or who left the company for other reasons; some replaced foremen who were shifted to other supervisory positions; and some filled newly created supervisory positions.

AFTER MEASUREMENT   In December 1952, the same forms that had been filled out by the rank-and-file workers in 1951 were readministered to:

1. The workers who became foremen during the experimental period (N = 23).

2. A control group of workers who did not become foremen during the experimental period (N = 46).

3. The workers who became stewards during the experimental period (N = 35).

4. A control group of workers who did not become stewards during the experimental period (N = 35).

Each control group was matched with its parallel experimental group on a number of demographic, attitudinal, and motivational variables. Therefore, any changes in attitudes that occurred in the experimental groups but did not occur in the control groups could not be attributed to initial differences between them.

The employees in these groups were told that the purpose of the follow-up questionnaire was to get up-to-date measures of their attitudes in 1952 and to compare how employees felt that year with the way that they felt the previous year. The groups were told that, instead of studying the entire universe of employees as was the case in 1951, only a sample was being studied this time. They were informed that the sample was chosen in such a way as to represent all kinds of employees at Rockwell — men and women, young and old, etc. The groups gave no indication that they understood the real bases on which they were chosen for the "after" measurement or that the effects of changes in roles were the critical factors being examined.[2]

Statistical significance of the results was obtained by the use of chi square.[3] The probability levels that are differentiated in the tables are: less than .01, between .01 and .05, between .05 and .10, and N.S. (not significant — p is greater than .10).

RESULTS: PHASE 1

The major hypothesis tested in this study was that people who are placed in a role will tend to take on or develop attitudes that are congruent with the expectations associated with that role. Since the foreman role entails being a representative of management, it might be expected that workers who are chosen as foremen will tend to become more favorable toward management. Similarly, since the steward role entails being a representative of the union, it might be expected that workers who are elected as stewards will tend to become more favorable toward the union. Moreover, in so far as the values of management and of the union are in conflict with each other, it might also be expected that workers who are made foremen will become less favorable toward the union and workers who are made stewards will become less favorable toward management.

Four attitudinal areas were examined: 1. attitudes toward management and officials of management; 2. attitudes toward the union and officials of the union; 3. attitudes toward the management-sponsored incentive system; and 4. attitudes toward the union-sponsored seniority system. The incentive system (whereby workers are paid according to the number of pieces they turn out) and the seniority system (whereby workers are promoted according to the seniority principle) are two areas in which conflicts between management and the union at Rockwell have been particularly intense. Furthermore, first-level foremen and stewards both play a part in the administration of these systems, and relevant groups hold expectations about foreman and steward behaviors with respect to these systems. Therefore, we examined the experimental and control groups' attitudes toward these two systems as well as their overall attitudes toward management and the union.

The data tend to support the hypothesis that being placed in the foreman and steward roles will have an impact on the attitudes of the role occupants. As shown in Tables 1 through 4, both experimental groups undergo systematic changes in attitudes, in the predicted directions, from the "before" situation to the "after" situation. In the control groups, either no attitude changes occur, or less marked changes occur, from the "before" situation to the "after" situation.

Although a number of the differences are not statistically significant, those which are significant are all in the expected directions, and most of the non-significant differences are also in the expected directions. New foremen, among other things, come to see Rockwell as a better place to work compared with other companies, develop more positive perceptions of top management officers, and become more favorably disposed toward the principle and operation of the incentive system. New stewards come to look upon labor unions in general in a more favorable light, develop more positive perceptions of the top union officers at Rockwell, and come to prefer seniority to

TABLE 1

Effects of Foreman and Steward Roles on Attitudes toward Management

	Kind of Change					
	More Favorable to Management	No Change	More Critical of Management	*Total*	*N*	*p*
	%	%	%	%		
1. *How is Rockwell as a place to work?*						
New foremen	70	26	4	100	23	N.S.
Control group*	47	33	20	100	46	
New stewards	46	31	23	100	35	N.S.
Control group**	46	43	11	100	35	
2. *How does Rockwell compare with others?*						
New foremen	52	48	0	100	23	.01–.05
Control group	24	59	17	100	47	
New stewards	55	34	11	100	35	N.S.
Control group	43	46	11	100	35	
3. *If things went bad for Rockwell, should the workers try to help out?*						
New foremen	17	66	17	100	23	N.S.
Control group	17	66	17	100	46	
New stewards	26	74	0	100	35	N.S.
Control group	14	69	17	100	35	
4. *How much do management officers care about the workers at Rockwell?*						
New foremen	48	52	0	100	23	<.01
Control group	15	76	9	100	46	
New stewards	29	62	9	100	35	N.S.
Control group	20	80	0	100	35	

*Workers who did not change roles, matched with future foremen on demographic and attitudinal variables in the "before" situation.

**Workers who did not change roles, matched with future stewards on demographic and attitudinal variables in the "before" situation.

TABLE 2

Effects of Foreman and Steward Roles on Attitudes
toward the Union

	Kind of Change					
	More Favorable to the Union	No Change	More Critical to the Union	Total	N	p
	%	%	%	%		
5. How do you feel about labor unions in general?						
New foremen	30	48	22	100	23	N.S.
Control group*	37	48	15	100	46	
New stewards	54	37	9	100	35	.01–.05
Control group**	29	65	6	100	35	
6. How much say should the union have in setting standards?						
New foremen	0	26	74	100	23	<.10
Control group	22	54	24	100	46	
New stewards	31	66	3	100	35	N.S.
Control group	20	60	20	100	35	
7. How would things be if there were no union at Rockwell?						
New foremen	9	39	52	100	23	.01–.05
Control group	20	58	22	100	46	
New stewards	14	86	0	100	35	N.S.
Control group	11	72	17	100	35	
8. How much do union officers care about the workers at Rockwell?						
New foremen	22	69	9	100	23	N.S.
Control group	15	78	7	100	46	
New stewards	57	37	6	100	35	.01–.05
Control group	26	68	6	100	35	

*Workers who did not change roles, matched with future foremen on demographic and attitudinal variables in the "before" situation.

**Workers who did not change roles, matched with future stewards on demographic and attitudinal variables in the "before" situation.

TABLE 3

Effects of Foreman and Steward Roles on Attitudes toward the Incentive System

	Kind of Change					
	More Favorable to Incentive System	No Change	More Critical of Incentive System	*Total*	*N*	*p*
	%	%	%	%		
9. *How do you feel about the principle of an incentive system?*						
New foremen	57	26	17	100	23	.01
Control group*	15	52	33	100	46	
New stewards	17	54	29	100	35	N.S.
Control group**	31	40	29	100	55	
10. *How do you feel the incentive system works out at Rockwell?*						
New foremen	65	22	13	100	23	.05–.10
Control group	37	41	22	100	46	
New stewards	43	34	23	100	35	N.S.
Control group	40	34	26	100	35	
11. *Should the incentive system be changed?*						
New foremen	39	48	13	100	23	.01
Control group	11	69	20	100	46	
New stewards	14	63	23	100	35	N.S.
Control group	20	60	20	100	35	
12. *Is a labor standard ever changed just because a worker is a high producer?*						
New foremen	48	43	9	100	23	.01
Control group	11	74	15	100	46	
New stewards	29	57	14	100	35	N.S.
Control group	26	65	9	100	35	

*Workers who did not change roles, matched with future foremen on demographic and attitudinal variables in the "before" situation.

**Workers who did not change roles, matched with future stewards on demographic and attitudinal variables in the "before" situation.

TABLE 4

Effects of Foreman and Steward Roles on Attitudes
toward the Seniority System

| | Kind of Change | | | | | |
	More Favorable to Seniority System	No Change	More Critical of Seniority System	*Total*	*N*	*p*
	%	%	%	%		
13. *How do you feel about the way the seniority system works out here?*						
New foremen	0	65	35	100	23	.01–.05
Control group*	20	63	17	100	46	
New stewards	23	48	29	100	35	N.S.
Control group**	9	71	20	200	35	
14. *How much should seniority count during lay-offs?*						
New foremen	9	52	39	100	23	.05–.10
Control group	24	59	17	100	46	
New stewards	29	48	23	100	35	N.S.
Control group	29	40	31	100	35	
15. *How much should seniority count in moving to better jobs?*						
New foremen	17	44	39	100	23	N.S.
Control group	20	54	26	100	46	
New stewards	34	46	20	100	35	.01–.05
Control group	17	34	49	100	35	
16. *How much should seniority count in promotion to foreman?*						
New foremen	17	70	13	100	23	N.S.
Control group	15	52	33	100	46	
New stewards	31	35	34	100	35	N.S.
Control group	17	43	40	100	35	

*Workers who did not change roles, matched with future foremen on demographic and attitudinal variables in the "before" situation.

**Workers who did not change roles, matched with future stewards on demographic and attitudinal variables in the "before" situation.

ability as a criterion of what should count in moving workers to better jobs. In general, the attitudes of workers who become foremen tend to gravitate in a pro-management direction and the attitudes of workers who become stewards tend to move in a pro-union direction.

A second kind of finding has to do with the relative *amount* of attitude change that takes place among new foremen in contrast to the amount that takes place among new stewards. On the whole, more pronounced and more widespread attitude changes occur among those who are made foremen than among those who are made stewards. Using a *p*-level of .10 as a criterion for statistical significance, the workers who are made foremen undergo significant attitude changes, relative to the workers who are not made foremen, on ten of the sixteen attitudinal items presented in Tables 1 through 4. By contrast, the workers who are made stewards undergo significant attitude changes, relative to the workers who are not made stewards, on only three of the sixteen items. However, for the steward role as well as for the foreman role, most of the differences found between the experimental and control groups still tend to be in the expected directions.

The more pronounced and more widespread attitude changes that occur among new foremen than among new stewards can probably be accounted for in large measure by the kinds of differences that exist between the foreman and steward roles. For one thing, the foreman role represents a relatively permanent position, while many stewards take the steward role as a "one-shot" job and even if they want to run again their constituents may not re-elect them. Secondly, the foreman role is a full-time job, while most stewards spend just a few hours a week in the performance of their steward functions and spend the rest of the time carrying out their regular rank-and-file jobs. Thirdly, a worker who is made a foreman must give up his membership in the union and become a surrogate of management,

while a worker who is made a steward retains the union as a reference group and simply takes on new functions and responsibilities as a representative of it. All of these differences suggest that the change from worker to foreman is a more fundamental change in roles than the change from worker to steward. This, in turn, might account to a large extent for the finding that, although attitude changes accompany both changes in roles, they occur more sharply among new foremen than among new stewards.

A third finding has to do with the *kinds* of attitude changes which occur among workers who change roles. As expected, new foremen become more pro-management and new stewards become more pro-union. Somewhat less expected is the finding that new foremen become more anti-union but new stewards do not become more anti-management. Among workers who are made foremen, statistically significant shifts in an anti-union direction occur on four of the eight items dealing with the union and the union-sponsored seniority system. Among workers who are made stewards, there are no statistically significant shifts in either direction on any of the eight items having to do with management and the management-sponsored incentive system.

The finding that new foremen become anti-union but that new stewards do not become anti-management may be related to the fact that workers who become foremen must relinquish their membership of the union, while workers who become stewards retain their status as employees of management. New foremen, subject to one main set of loyalties and called on to carry out a markedly new set of functions, tend to develop negative attitudes toward the union as well as positive attitudes toward management. New stewards, subject to overlapping group membership and still dependent on management for their livelihoods, tend to become more favorable toward the union but they do not turn against management, at least not within the relatively limited time period covered by the present research project. Over time, stewards might come to develop somewhat hostile attitudes toward management, but, under the conditions prevailing at Rockwell, there is apparently no tendency for such attitudes to be developed as soon as workers enter the steward role.

METHOD: PHASE 2

One of the questions that may be raised about the results that have been presented up to this point concerns the extent to which the changed attitudes displayed by new foremen and new stewards are internalized by the role occupants. Are the changed attitudes expressed by new foremen and new stewards relatively stable, or are they ephemeral phenomena to be held only as long as they occupy the foreman and steward roles? An unusual set of circumstances at Rockwell enabled the researchers to glean some data on this question.

A short time after the 1952 re-survey, the nation suffered an economic recession. In order to meet the lessening demand for its products, Rockwell, like many other firms, had to cut its work force. This resulted in many rank-and-file workers being laid off and a number of the foremen being returned to non-supervisory jobs. By June 1954, eight of the twenty-three workers who had been promoted to foreman had returned to the worker role and only twelve were still foremen. (The remaining three respondents had voluntarily left Rockwell by this time.)

Over the same period, a number of role changes had also been experienced by the thirty-five workers who had become stewards. Fourteen had returned to the worker role, either because they had not sought re-election by their work groups or because they had failed to win re-election, and only six were still stewards. (The other fifteen respondents, who composed almost half of this group, had either voluntarily left Rockwell or had been laid off as part of the general reduction in force.)

Once again, in June 1954, the researchers returned to Rockwell to re-administer the questionnaires that the workers had filled out in 1951 and 1952. The instructions to the respondents were substantially the same as those given in 1952 — i.e. a sample of employees had been chosen to get up-to-date measures of employees' attitudes toward working conditions at Rockwell and the same groups were selected this time as had been selected last time in order to lend greater stability to the results.

In this phase of the study, the numbers of cases with which we were dealing in the various groups were so small that the data could only be viewed as suggestive, and systematic statistical analysis of the data did not seem to be too meaningful. However, the unusual opportunity to throw some light on an important question suggests that a reporting of these results may be worthwhile.

RESULTS: PHASE 2

The principal question examined here was: on those items where a change in roles resulted in a change in attitudes between 1951 and 1952, how are these attitudes influenced by a reverse change in roles between 1952 and 1954?

The most consistent and widespread attitude changes noted between 1951 and 1952 were those that resulted when workers moved into the foreman role. What are the effects of moving out of the foreman role between 1952 and 1954? The data indicate that, in general, most of the "gains" that were observed when workers became foremen are "lost" when they become workers again. The results on six of the items, showing the proportions who take pro-management positions at various points in time, are presented in Table 5. On almost all of the items, the foremen who remain foremen either retain their favorable attitudes toward management or become even more favorable toward management between 1952 and

TABLE 5

Effects of Entering and Leaving the Foreman Role on Attitudes toward Management and the Union

	Workers Who Became Foremen and Stayed Foremen (N = 12)			Workers Who Became Foremen and Were Later Demoted (N = 8)		
	(W) 1951	(F) 1952	(F) 1954	(W) 1951	(F) 1952	(W) 1954
% who feel Rockwell is a good place to work	33	92	100	25	75	50
% who feel management officers really care about the workers at Rockwell	8	33	67	0	25	0
% who feel the union should not have more say in setting labor standards	33	100	100	13	63	13
% who are satisfied with the way the incentive system works out at Rockwell	17	75	75	25	50	13
% who believe a worker's standard will not be changed just because he is a high producer	42	83	100	25	63	75
% who feel ability should count more than seniority in promotions	33	58	75	25	50	38

1954, while the demoted foremen show fairly consistent drops in the direction of re-adopting the attitudes they held when they had been in the worker role. On the whole, the attitudes held by demoted foremen in 1954, after they had left the foreman role, fall roughly to the same levels as they had been in 1951, before they had ever moved into the foreman role.

The results on the effects of moving out of the steward role are less clear-cut. As shown in Table 6, there is no marked tendency for ex-stewards to revert to earlier-held attitudes when they go from the steward role to the worker role. At the same time, it should be recalled that there had not been particularly marked changes in their attitudes when they initially changed from the worker role to the steward role. These findings, then, are consistent with the interpretation offered earlier that the change in roles between worker and steward is less significant than the change in roles between worker and foreman.

A question might be raised about what is represented in the reversal of attitudes found among ex-foremen. Does it represent a positive taking-on of attitudes appropriate for respondents who are re-entering the worker role, or does it constitute a negative, perhaps embittered reaction away from the attitudes they held before being demoted from the foreman role? A definitive answer to this question cannot be arrived at, but it might be suggested that if we were dealing with a situation where a reversion in roles did not constitute such a strong psychological blow to the role occupants (as was probably the case among demoted foremen), then such a marked reversion in attitudes might not have occurred.[4]

One final table is of interest here. Table 7 compares the attitudes of two groups of respondents: 1. the twelve employees who were rank-and-file workers in 1951, had been selected as foremen by 1952, and were still foremen in 1954; and 2. the six employees who were rank-and-file workers in

TABLE 6

Effects of Entering and Leaving the Steward Role on Attitudes toward Management and the Union

	Workers Who Were Elected Stewards and Were Later Re-elected (N = 6)			Workers Who Were Elected Stewards But Were Not Later Re-elected (N = 14)		
	(W) 1951	(S) 1952	(S) 1954	(W) 1951	(S) 1952	(W) 1954
% who feel Rockwell is a good place to work	50	0	0	29	79	36
% who feel management officers really care about the workers at Rockwell	0	0	0	14	14	0
% who feel the union should not have more say in setting labor standards	0	17	0	14	14	14
% who are satisfied with the way the incentive system works out at Rockwell	17	17	0	43	43	21
% who believe a worker's standard will not be changed just because he is a high producer	50	50	17	21	43	36
% who feel ability should count more than seniority in promotions	67	17	17	36	36	21

1951, had been elected as stewards by 1952, and were still stewards in 1954. At each time period, for each of the sixteen questions examined earlier in Tables 1 through 4, the table shows: 1. the proportion of foremen or future foremen who took a pro-management position on these questions; 2. the proportion of stewards or future stewards who took a pro-management position on these questions; and 3. the difference between these proportions. The following are the mean differences in proportions for the three time periods:

1. In 1951, while both future foremen and future stewards still occupied the rank-and-file worker role, the mean difference was only −.1 per cent, which means that practically no difference in attitudes existed between these two groups at this time. (The minus sign means that a slightly, but far from significantly, larger proportion of future stewards than future foremen ex-

pressed a pro-management position on these items.)

2. In 1952, after the groups had been in the foreman and steward roles for about one year, the mean difference had jumped to +47.8 per cent, which means that a sharp wedge had been driven between them. Both groups had tended to become polarized in opposite directions, as foremen took on attitudes consistent with being a representative of management and stewards took on attitudes appropriate for a representative of the union.

3. In 1954, after the groups had been in the foreman and steward roles for two to three years, the mean difference was +62.4 per cent, which means that a still larger gap had opened up between them. Although the gap had widened, it is interesting to note that the changes that occurred during this later and longer 1952 to 1954 period are not as sharp or as dramatic as the changes

TABLE 7

Effects of Foreman and Steward Roles over a Three-Year Period: Before Change in Roles, after One Year in New Roles, and after Two-Three Years in New Roles

% Who Take a Pro-Management Position on the Following Questions:**	Before Change in Roles (1951)			After 1 Year in New Roles (1952)			After 2–3 Years in New Roles (1954)		
	Workers Who Became Foremen	Workers Who Became Stewards	D%*	Workers Who Became Foremen	Workers Who Became Stewards	D%*	Workers Who Became Foremen	Workers Who Became Stewards	D%*
Question 1.	33	50	−17	92	0	+92	100	0	+100
Question 2.	33	33	0	75	33	+42	67	17	+50
Question 3.	92	83	+9	100	100	0	100	50	+50
Question 4.	8	0	+8	33	0	+33	67	0	+67
Question 5.	67	100	−33	67	17	+50	33	17	+16
Question 6.	33	0	+33	100	17	+83	100	0	+100
Question 7.	8	0	+8	50	0	+50	58	0	+58
Question 8.	75	67	+8	75	50	+25	58	17	+41
Question 9.	33	83	−50	83	17	+66	83	0	+83
Question 10.	17	17	0	75	17	+58	75	0	+75
Question 11.	17	17	0	25	0	+25	67	0	+67
Question 12.	42	50	−8	83	50	+33	100	17	+83
Question 13.	58	50	+8	100	17	+83	100	17	+83
Question 14.	33	67	−34	50	17	+33	75	17	+58
Question 15.	33	0	+33	58	0	+58	67	0	+67
Question 16.	67	33	+34	67	33	+34	67	67	0
No. of Cases	12	6		12	6		12	6	
Mean D%			−0.1			+47.8			+62.4

*Percentage of workers who became foremen who take a pro-management position minus percentage of workers who became stewards who take a pro-management position.

**Question numbers refer to the question numbers of the attitudinal items in *Tables 1* through *4*.

that occurred during the initial and shorter 1951 to 1952 period.

These findings offer further support for the proposition that roles can influence attitudes. The data indicate that changes in attitudes occurred soon after changes in roles took place. And inside a period of three years those who had remained in their new roles had developed almost diametrically opposed sets of attitudinal positions.

DISCUSSION

A role may be defined as a set of behaviors that are expected of people who occupy a certain position in a social system. These expectations consist of shared attitudes or beliefs, held by relevant populations, about what role occupants should and should not do. The theoretical basis for hypothesizing that a role will have effects on role occupants lies in the nature of these expectations. If a role occupant meets these expectations, the "rights" or "rewards" associated with the role will be accorded to him. If he fails to meet these expectations, the "rights" or "rewards" will be withheld from him and "punishments" may be meted out.[5]

A distinction should be made between the effects of roles on people's attitudes and the effects of roles on their actions. How roles affect actions can probably be explained in a fairly direct fashion. Actions are overt and readily enforceable. If a person fails to behave in ways appropriate to his role, this can immediately be seen, and steps may be taken to bring the deviant or non-conformist into line. Role deviants may be evicted from their roles, placed in less rewarding roles, isolated from other members of the group, or banished entirely from the social system.

But attitudes are not as overt as actions. A person may behave in such a way as to reveal his attitudes, but he can — and often does — do much to cover them up. Why, then, should a change in roles lead to a change in actions? A number of explanatory factors might be suggested here. The present

discussion will be confined to two factors that are probably generic to a wide variety of situations. One pertains to the influence of reference groups; the other is based on an assumption about people's need to have attitudes internally consistent with their actions.

A change in roles almost invariably involves a change in reference groups. Old reference groups may continue to influence the role occupant, but new ones also come into play. The change in reference groups may involve moving into a completely new group (as when a person gives up membership in one organization and joins another one) or it may simply involve taking on new functions in the same group (as when a person is promoted to a higher position in a hierarchical organization). In both situations, new reference groups will tend to bring about new frames of reference, new self-percepts, and new vested interests, and these in turn will tend to produce new attitudinal orientations.

In addition to a change in reference groups, a change in roles also involves a change in functions and a change in the kinds of behaviors and actions that the role occupant must display if he is to fulfil these functions. A change in actions, let us assume, comes about because these actions are immediately required, clearly visible, and hence socially enforceable. If we further assume a need for people to have attitudes that are internally consistent with their actions, then at least one aspect of the functional significance of a change in attitudes becomes clear. A change in attitudes enables a new role occupant to justify, to make rational, or perhaps simply to rationalize his change in actions. Having attitudes that are consistent with actions helps the role occupant to be "at one" with himself and facilitates his effective performance of the functions he is expected to carry out.

The reference-group principle and the self-consistency principle postulate somewhat different chains of events in accounting for the effects of roles on attitudes and actions. In abbreviated versions, the different chains may be spelled out in the following ways:

1. Reference-group principle: A change in roles involves a change in reference groups . . . which leads to a change in attitudes . . . which leads to a change in actions.

2. Self-consistency principle: A change in roles involves a change in functions . . . which leads to a change in actions . . . which leads to a change in attitudes.

In the former chain, a person's attitudes influence his actions; in the latter chain, a person's actions influence his attitudes. Both chains might plausibly account for the results obtained, but whether either chain, both chains, or other chains is or are valid cannot be determined from the data available. A more direct investigation of the underlying mechanisms responsible for the impact of roles on attitudes would appear to be a fruitful area for further research.

But apart from the question of underlying mechanisms, the results lend support to the proposition that a persons' attitudes will be influenced by his role. Relatively consistent changes in attitudes were found both among workers who were made foremen and among workers who were made stewards, although these changes were more clear-cut for foremen than for stewards. The more interesting set of results — as far as role theory in general is concerned — would seem to be the data on the effects of entering and leaving the foreman role. It was pointed out earlier that the foreman role, unlike the steward role, is a full-time, relatively permanent position, and moving into this position entails taking on a very new and different set of functions. When workers are made foremen, their attitudes change in a more pro-management and anti-union direction. When they are demoted and move back into the worker role, their attitudes change once again, this time in a more pro-union and anti-management direction. In both in-

stances, the respondents' attitudes seem to be molded by the roles which they occupy at a given time.

The readiness with which the respondents in this study shed one set of attitudes and took on another set of attitudes might suggest either that 1. the attitudes studied do not tap very basic or deep-rooted facets of the respondents' psyches, or 2. the character structures of the respondents are such as not to include very deeply ingrained sets of value orientations. Riesman (1950) deals with this problem in his discussion of "other directedness" vs. "inner-directedness." How much the rapid shifts in attitudes observed here reflect the particular kinds of respondents who underwent changes in roles in the present situation, and how much these shifts reflect the national character of the American population, can only be speculated on at the present time.

SUMMARY

This study was designed to test the proposition that a person's attitudes will be influenced by the role he occupies in a social system. This is a commonly accepted postulate in role theory but there appears to be little in the way of definitive empirical evidence to support it. Earlier studies have generally made inferences about the effects of roles on attitudes on the basis of correlational data gathered at a single point in time. The present study attempted to measure the effects of roles on attitudes through data gathered at three different points in time.

In September and October 1951, 2,354 rank-and-file workers in a factory situation were asked to fill out attitude questionnaires dealing with management and the union. During the next twelve months, twenty-three of these workers were promoted to foreman and thirty-five were elected by their work groups as union stewards. In December 1952, the questionnaires were re-administered to the two groups of workers who had changed roles and to two matched control groups of workers who had not changed roles. By comparing the attitude changes that occurred in the experimental groups with the attitude changes that occurred in their respective control groups, the effects of moving into the foreman and steward roles could be determined.

The results on this phase of the study showed that the experimental groups underwent systematic changes in attitudes after they were placed in their new roles, while the control groups underwent no changes or less marked changes from the "before" situation to the "after" situation. The workers who were made foremen tended to become more favorable toward management, and the workers who were made stewards tended to become more favorable toward the union. The changes were more marked among new foremen than among new stewards, which can be probably accounted for by the fact that the change from worker to foreman seems to be a more significant and more meaningful change in roles than the change from worker to steward.

In the months following the second administration of the questionnaire, a number of the workers who had become foremen and stewards reverted to the rank-and-file worker role. Some of the foremen were cut back to non-supervisory positions during a period of economic recession, and some of the stewards either did not run again or failed to be re-elected during the annual steward elections. In June 1954, the questionnaires were once again administered to the same groups of respondents. By comparing the attitude changes that occurred among foremen and stewards who left these roles with the attitude changes that occurred among foremen and stewards who remained in these roles, the effects of moving out of these roles could be assessed.

The results of this phase of the study showed that foremen who were demoted tended to revert to the attitudes they had previously held while they were in the worker role, while foremen who remained in the foreman role either maintained the attitudes they had developed when they first became foremen or moved even further in that direction. The results among stewards who left the steward role were less consistent and less clear-cut, which parallels the smaller and less clear-cut attitude changes that took place when they first became stewards.

The findings support the proposition that a person's role will have an impact on his attitudes, but they still leave unanswered the question of what underlying mechanisms are operating here. A more direct investigation of these underlying mechanisms might comprise a fruitful area for further research.

[1] This study was one of a series conducted by the Human Relations Program of the Survey Research Center, Institute for Social Research, at the University of Michigan. The author wishes to express a special debt of gratitude to Dr. Gerald M. Mahoney and Mr. Gerald Gurin, his associates on the larger study of which the present one was a part, and to Dr. Daniel Katz, Dr. Theodore M. Newcomb, and Dr. Eugene Jacobson for their many useful suggestions and contributions.

[2] Some of the top officials of management and all of the top officers of the union at Rockwell knew about the nature of the follow-up study and the bases on which the experimental and control groups were selected.

[3] In those instances where there was a theoretical frequency of less than five in one or more cells, the following procedures, which are an adaptation of the rules of thumb suggested by Walker and Lev (1953), were used:

a. If only one theoretical frequency was less than five but it was not less than two, and there were two or more degrees of freedom, then the chi-square test was used without combining any classes or applying any corrections.

b. If more than one theoretical frequency was less than five or if any theoretical frequency was less than two, then classes were combined to increase cell expectations before the chi-square test was applied.

c. If, after combining classes, the theoretical frequency was still less than five and there was only one degree of freedom, then Fisher's exact test was used.

⁴There were a number of reactions to demotion among the eight ex-foremen, as obtained from informal interviews with these respondents. Some reacted impunitively (i.e. they blamed uncontrollable situational determinants) and did not seem to be bothered by demotion. Others reacted extrapunitively (i.e. they blamed management) or intrapunitively (i.e. they blamed themselves) and appeared to be more disturbed by demotion. One way of testing the hypothesis that attitude reversion is a function of embitterment would be to see if sharper reversion occurs among extrapunitive and intrapunitive respondents. However, the small number of cases does not permit an analysis of this kind to be carried out in the present situation.

⁵An earlier discussion of the role concept, with particular reference to its application to the study of complex organizations, is found in Jacobson, Charters, and Lieberman (1951).

REFERENCES

Jacobson, E., Charters, W. W., Jr., and Lieberman, S. "The use of the Role Concept in the Study of Complex Organizations." *J. Soc. Issues*, Vol. 7, No. 3, pp. 18–27, 1951.

Newcomb, T. M. *Social Psychology*. New York: The Dryden Press, 1950; London: Tavistock Publications Ltd., 1952.

Parsons, T. *The Social System*. New York: The Free Press, 1951; London: Tavistock Publications Ltd., 1951.

Riesman, D. *The Lonely Crowd*. New Haven: Yale Univ. Press, 1950.

Stouffer, S. A., Suchman, E. A., DeVinney, L. C., Star, S. A., and Williams, R. M., Jr. *The American Soldier: Adjustment During Army Life* (Vol. 1). Princeton: Princeton University Press, 1949.

Walker, H. M., and Lev, J. *Statistical Inference*. New York: Henry Holt and Co., Inc., 1953.

OTHER RELEVANT ARTICLES

The number of studies of job satisfaction which have been published in the periodical literature is of such magnitude that it would be foolhardy to attempt any compilation or evaluation of them here. Fortunately, Hoppock and his associates have published periodic reviews of job satisfaction research in the *Personnel and Guidance Journal*. The last one, by H. A. Robinson, R. P. Connors, and Ann Robinson, Job satisfaction researches of 1963, *Personnel and Guidance Journal*, 1964, *43*, 360–366, includes the month and year of all previous summaries.

Another more recent important source of experiments in the measurement of job satisfaction is under the direction of Patricia C. Smith, published at Cornell University in 1963. Some of this material has also appeared in the *Journal of Applied Psychology* with co-authorship of C. L. Hulin, E. A. Locke, or L. M. Kendall. Smith, Kendall, and Hulin are the authors of the book, *Measurement of Saatisfaction in Work and Retirement*, to be published by Rand McNally.

See also:

Katzell, R. A. Personal values, job satisfaction and job behavior. In H. Borow (Ed.) *Man in a World at Work*. Boston: Houghton Mifflin, 1964.

The controversy relating to the Herzberg two-factor formulation of job satisfaction merits a separate presentation of references for the ease of the student who wishes to review it. Herzberg's basic publications, which develop and validate the theory are:

Herzberg, F., B. Mausner, R. Peterson, and Dora Capwell. *Job Attitudes:* Research and Opionion. Pittsburgh: Psychological Service of Pittsburgh, 1957.
————, et al. *Motivation to Work.* New York: Wiley, 1959.
————. *Work and the Nature of Man.* Cleveland: World Publishing, 1966.

Some confirmatory findings for the Herzberg theory from independent research are:

Myers, M. S. Who are your motivated workers? *Harvard Business Review*, 1964, 73–88.
Schwartz, N. M., E. Jenusatis, and H. Stark. Motivational factors among supervisors in the utility industry. *Personnel Psychology*, 1963, *16*, 45–53.

Some critical and disconfirmatory articles on the Herzberg two-factor theory include:

Burke, R. J. Are Herzberg's motivators and hygienes unidimensional? *Journal of Applied Psychology*, 1966, *50*, 317–321.
Dunnette, M. D., J. P. Campbell, and M. D. Hakel. Factors contributing to job satisfaction and job dissatisfaction in six occupational groups. *Organizational Behavior and Human Performance*, 1967, *2*, 143–174.
Ewen, R. B., Patricia Smith, C. L. Hulin, and E. A. Locke. An empirical test of the Herzberg two-factor theory. *Journal of Applied Psychology*, 1966, *50*, 544–550.
Graen, G. B. Addendum to "An empirical test of the Herzberg two-factor theory. *Journal of Applied Psychology*, 1966, *50*, 551–555.
Hinrichs, J. R., and L. A. Mischkind. Empirical and theoretical limitations of the two factor hypothesis of job satisfaction. *Journal of Applied Psychology*, 1967, *51*, 191–200.
Triandis, H. Review of Herzberg's *Work and the Nature of Man. Industrial and Labor Relations Review*, 1967, *20*, 529–531.
Wernimont, P. F. Intrinsic and exterinsic factors in job satisfaction. *Journal of Applied Psychology*, 1966, *50*, 41–50.

References relating to the equity point of view in satisfaction include:

Adams, J. S. Toward an understanding of inequity. *Journal of Abnormal and Social Psychology*. 1963, *67*, 422–436.
————, and W. B. Rosenbaum. The relationship of worker productivity to cognitive dissonance about wage inequitites. *Journal of Applied Psychology*, 1962, *46*, 161–164.
Andrews, I. R. Wage inequity and job performance: An experimental study. *Journal of Applied Psychology*, 1967, *51*, 39–45.

Homans, G. C. *Social Behavior: Its Elementary Forms.* New York: Harcourt, 1961.

Jaques, E. *Measurement of responsibility: A study of work, payment and individual capacity.* Cambridge, Mass.: Harvard University Press, 1956.

Jaques, E. *Equitable Payment.* New York: Wiley, 1961.

Lawler, E. E., III, and P. W. O'Gara. Effects of inequity produced by underpayment on work output, work quality, and attitude toward work. *Journal of Applied Psychology,* 1967, *51*, 403–410.

Mann, F. C. A study of work satisfactions as a function of the discrepancy between inferred aspirations and achievement. *Dissertation Abstracts,* 1953, *13*, 902.

Patchen, M. *The Choice of Wage Comparisons.* Englewood Cliffs, N. J.: Prentice-Hall, 1961.

Zaleznick, A., C. R. Christensen, and F. J. Roethlisberger. *The Motivation, Productivity, and Satisfaction of Workers: A Prediction Study.* Boston: Harvard University Graduate School of Business, 1958.

References concerning the relationship between satisfaction and job performance are organized into two parts: review of studies of the relationship, and some recent or important studies since these reviews which might modify their conclusions. There are four major review papers:

Brayfield, A. H., and W. H. Crockett. Employee attitudes and employee performance. *Psychological Bulletin,* 1955, *52*, 396–424.

Herzberg, F. *et al., Job Attitudes: Review of Research and Opinions.* Pittsburgh: Psychological Service of Pittsburgh, 1957.

Katzell, R. Industrial Psychology. *Annual Review of Psychology,* 1957, *8*, 237–268.

Vroom, V. H. *Work and Motivation.* New York: Wiley, 1964.

Articles of interest are:

Charters, W. W., Jr., The relation of morale to turnover among teachers. *American Educational Research Journal,* 1965, *2*, 163–173.

Cureton, E. E., and R. A. Katzell. A further analysis of the relations among job performance and situational variables. *Journal of Applied Psychology,* 1962, *46*, 230.

Hulin, C. H. Job satisfaction and turnover in a female clerical population. *Journal of Applied Psychology,* 1966, *50*, 280–285.

Kahn, R. L. Productivity and job satisfaction. *Personnel Psychology,* 1960, *13*, 275–287.

Katz, P., N. MacCoby, and Nancy Morse. *Productivity, Supervision and Morale in an Office Situation.* Ann Arbor: Survey Research Center, University of Michigan, 1950.

Meltzer, L., and J. Salter. Organizational structure and the performance and job satisfaction of physiologists. *American Sociology Review,* 1962, *27*, 351–362.

Strauss, P. Job satisfaction and productivity of engineers and scientists. *Perceptual and Motor Skills,* 1966, *23*, 471–476.

————. Psychology of the Scientist: XXI. Growth and belongingness perceptions as factors in the behavior of engineers and scientists. *Perceptual and Motor Skills* 1966, *23*, 883–894.

References on the topic of occupational adjustment are essentially divisible into the psychological and the sociological. A few from the former category are:

Gellman, W. Components of vocational adjustment. *Personnel and Guidance Journal*, 1953, *31*, 536–539.

————, H. Gendel, N. M. Glaser, S. D. Friedman, and W. S. Neff. *Adjusting People to Work.* Chicago: Jewish Vocational Service, 1957.

Scott, T. B., R. V. Dawis, G. W. England, and L. H. Lofquist. *A Definition of Work Adjustment,* Minnesota Studies in Vocational Adjustment, X, Minneapolis: Industrial Relations Center, 1958.

Super, D. E. *The Dynamics of Vocational Adjustment.* New York: Harper & Row, 1942.

————. Vocational adjustment: Implementing a self-concept. *Occupations*, 1951, *30*, 88–92.

Sociology references either describe some of the contingencies which are common to upward career mobility, or peculiar to certain kinds of careers. A number of the latter studies are referred to in the Becker and Strauss article, Becker having either done them himself or supervised them. They will not be listed here. A few more sociology references relating to adjustment to career contingencies are:

Cohen, A. Sociological studies of occupations as "a way of life." *Personnel and Guidance Journal*, 1964, *42*, 267–272.

Corwin, R. The professional employee: A study of conflict in the nursing role. *American Journal of Sociology*, 1961, *61*, 604–615.

Golden, F. H. Demotion in industrial management. *American Sociological Review*, 1965, *29*, 714–724.

Hughes, E. C. *Men and Their Work.* New York: Free Press, 1958.

Nosow, S., and W. H. Form. (Eds.) *Man, Work and Society.* New York: Basic Books. 1962 (Chapters 13 and 14).

Palmer, Gladys. *The Reluctant Job Changer: Studies in Work Attachments and Aspirations.* Philadelphia: University of Pennsylvania Press, 1962.

Sheppard, H. L., and A. H. Belitsky. *The Job Hunt: Job-Seeking Behavior of Unemployed Workers in a Local Economy.* Baltimore: Johns Hopkins University Press, 1966.

Wilensky, H. L., and H. Edwards. The skidder: Ideological adjustment of downward mobile workers. *American Sociological Review*, 1959, *24*, 215–230.

Index

Index